Foundations of Marketing

PRIDE·FERRELL

FOUNDATIONS

of Marketing

SECOND EDITION

William M. Pride

Texas A&M University

O. C. Ferrell

University of Wyoming

Houghton Mifflin Company   **Boston   New York**

To Nancy, Michael, and Allen Pride

To Kathlene Ferrell

Publisher: George T. Hoffman
Associate Development Editor: Suzanna Smith
Editorial Assistant: Amy Galvin
Senior Project Editor: Rachel D'Angelo Wimberly
Editorial Assistant: Anthony D'Aries
Art and Design Coordinator: Jill Haber
Photo Editor: Jennifer Meyer Dare
Composition Buyer: Chuck Dutton
Manufacturing Coordinator: Florence Cadran
Marketing Manager: Mike Schenk
Marketing Coordinator: Lisa E. Boden
Production Technology Coordinator: Rich Brewer

Cover Image: © Michael Doret

Microsoft® Internet Explorer reprinted by permission from Microsoft® Corporation.

Printed in the U.S.A.

Library of Congress Control Number: 2005935213

Instructor's Exam Copy —
ISBN 13: 978-0-618-73227-2
ISBN 10: 0-618-73227-6

For orders, use student text ISBNs —
ISBN 13: 978-0-618-70500-9
ISBN 10: 0-618-70500-7

2 3 4 5 6 7 8 9 — WC — 10 09 08 07 06

Brief Contents

PART ONE   **Strategic Marketing and Its Environment** 1

  1 Marketing's Role in Business and Society 2
  2 Planning Marketing Strategies 25
  3 The Marketing Environment, Social Responsibility, and Ethics 51

PART TWO   **Using Technology for Customer Relationships in a Global Environment** 77

  4 E-Marketing and Customer Relationship Management 78
  5 Global Markets and International Marketing 101

PART THREE   **Target Market Selection and Research** 123

  6 Marketing Research and Information Systems 124
  7 Target Markets: Segmentation and Evaluation 149

PART FOUR   **Customer Behavior** 175

  8 Consumer Buying Behavior 176
  9 Business Markets and Buying Behavior 201

PART FIVE   **Product Decisions** 223

  10 Product, Branding, and Packaging Concepts 224
  11 Developing and Managing Goods and Services 255

PART SIX   **Pricing Decisions** 285

  12 Pricing Fundamentals 286
  13 Pricing Management 311

PART SEVEN   **Distribution Decisions** 333

  14 Marketing Channels and Supply-Chain Management 334
  15 Retailing, Direct Marketing, and Wholesaling 361

PART EIGHT   **Promotion Decisions** 389

  16 Integrated Marketing Communications 390
  17 Advertising and Public Relations 415
  18 Personal Selling and Sales Promotion 441

Appendix: Careers in Marketing 465

Contents

Note: Each chapter concludes with a Chapter Review, Key Concepts, Issues for Discussion and Review, and Marketing Applications.

Preface xv

PART ONE Strategic Marketing and Its Environment 1

 Marketing's Role in Business and Society 2

Corvette Honored as Best Sports Car 2

● **Marketing Defined** 3
Customers Are the Focus 3
Marketing Deals with Products, Price, Distribution, and Promotion 4
Marketing Builds Satisfying Exchange Relationships 8
Marketing Occurs in a Dynamic Environment 8

● **Understanding the Marketing Concept** 9
  ▶ MARKETING ENTREPRENEURS: **Norman Ray Lambert & Family** 10
Evolution of the Marketing Concept 11
Implementing the Marketing Concept 12

● **Managing Customer Relationships** 12

● **Value-Driven Marketing** 13

● **Marketing Management** 15

● **The Importance of Marketing in Our Global Economy** 16
Marketing Costs Consume a Sizable Portion of Buyers' Dollars 16
Marketing Is Used in Nonprofit Organizations 16
Marketing Is Important to Businesses 16
Marketing Fuels Our Global Economy 17
Marketing Knowledge Enhances Consumer Awareness 17
Marketing Connects People Through Technology 18
Socially Responsible Marketing Can Promote the Welfare of Customers and Stakeholders 18
Marketing Offers Many Exciting Career Prospects 19
  ▶ MARKETING AROUND THE WORLD: **Procter & Gamble Products are Number 1 Around the World** 6
  ▶ ETHICS AND SOCIAL ISSUES: **A Greener Ford?** 19
  ▢ VIDEO CASE: Finagle A Bagel 22

 Planning Marketing Strategies 25

Sears and Kmart Join Forces to Compete 25

● **Understanding the Strategic Planning Process** 26

● **Assessing Organizational Resources and Opportunities** 27
SWOT Analysis 29
  ▶ MARKETING ENTREPRENEURS: **Ryan Garman** 29

● **Establishing an Organizational Mission and Goals** 30

● **Developing Corporate, Business-Unit, and Marketing Strategies** 32
Corporate Strategy 32
Business-Unit Strategy 32
Marketing Strategy 34

● **Creating the Marketing Plan** 38

● **Implementing Marketing Strategies** 38
Approaches to Marketing Implementation 39
Organizing Marketing Activities 41
Controlling Marketing Activities 43
  ▶ MARKETING AROUND THE WORLD: **Digital Revolution Forces Kodak to Refocus its Strategy** 35
  ▶ MARKETING LEADERS: **Cereal-ity** 37
  ▢ VIDEO CASE: The Global Expansion of Subway Sandwich Shops 48

The Marketing Environment, Social Responsibility, and Ethics   51

Model Train Companies Collide   51

● **The Marketing Environment**   52

Responding to the Marketing Environment   53
Competitive Forces   53
Economic Forces   54
Political Forces   57
Legal and Regulatory Forces   57
Technological Forces   60

▶ **MARKETING ENTREPRENEURS: Jo Waldron**   61
Sociocultural Forces   62

● **Social Responsibility and Ethics in Marketing**   64

Economic Dimension   64
Legal Dimension   65
Ethical Dimension   67
Philanthropic Dimension   69
Incorporating Social Responsibility and Ethics into Strategic Planning   71

▶ **ETHICS AND SOCIAL ISSUES: Has Wal-Mart Become Too Powerful?**   66

▶ **ETHICS AND SOCIAL ISSUES: Will the Martha Stewart Brand Survive a Legal Scandal?**   67

▣ VIDEO CASE: Social Responsibility at New Belgium Brewing Company   74

PART TWO   Using Technology for Customer Relationships in a Global Environment   77

E-Marketing and Customer Relationship Management   78

Amazon.com Finds Success with Technology and Positive Relationships   78

● **Marketing on the Internet**   79

Basic Characteristics of Electronic Marketing   81

▶ **MARKETING ENTREPRENEURS: Matt Drudge**   83
E-Marketing Strategies   84

● **Customer Relationship Management**   90

Technology Drives CRM   91
Customer Satisfaction Is the End Result of CRM   92

● **Legal and Ethical Issues in E-Marketing**   93

▶ **MARKETING AROUND THE WORLD: Internet Banking at ING**   87

▶ **E-MARKETING AND TECHNOLOGY: Yellow Freight Manages Customer Relationships with Technology**   94

▣ VIDEO CASE: 4SURE.com Targets Business Customers   100

Global Markets and International Marketing   101

Foreign Brands Challenge Cola Giants   101

▶ **MARKETING ENTREPRENEURS: Tom Monaghan**   103

● **Environmental Forces in International Markets**   103

Cultural and Social Forces   103
Economic Forces   105
Political, Legal, and Ethical Forces   106
Technological Forces   108

● **Regional Trade Alliances, Markets, and Agreements**   108

The North American Free Trade Agreement (NAFTA)   109
The European Union (EU)   109
The Common Market of the Southern Cone (MERCOSUR)   110
Asia-Pacific Economic Cooperation (APEC)   110

General Agreement on Tariffs and Trade (GATT) and World Trade Organization (WTO)   111

● **International Involvement**   113

Importing and Exporting   113
Licensing and Franchising   115
Contract Manufacturing   116
Joint Ventures   116
Direct Ownership   116

● **Customization Versus Globalization of International Marketing Strategies**   118

▶ **MARKETING AROUND THE WORLD: China—The New Economic Powerhouse**   112

▶ **MARKETING LEADERS: Aristocrat Angus**   114

▣ VIDEO CASE: BMW International   121

PART THREE Target Market Selection and Research 123

6 Marketing Research and Information Systems 124

McDonald's Responds to Changing Customer Desires 124

● The Importance of Marketing Research 125

● The Marketing Research Process 126
Locating and Defining Research Issues or Problems 126
Designing the Research Project 127
Collecting Data 129
▶ MARKETING ENTREPRENEURS: **Marc Ecko** 136
Interpreting Research Findings 138
Reporting Research Findings 139

● Using Technology to Improve Marketing Information Gathering and Analysis 139

Marketing Information Systems 139
Databases 140
Marketing Decision Support Systems 142
The World Wide Web 142

● Issues in Marketing Research 143
The Importance of Ethical Marketing Research 143
International Issues in Marketing Research 143
▶ E-MARKETING AND TECHNOLOGY: **Taking a Look-Look at Youth Trends** 131
▶ E-MARKETING AND TECHNOLOGY: **Wal-Mart's Data Warehouse Brings Efficiency and Profits** 141
▯ VIDEO CASE: IRI Provides Marketing Research Data from Multiple Sources 147

7 Target Markets: Segmentation and Evaluation 149
Nickelodeon Targets Tots, Tweens, and Teens 149

● What Is a Market? 150

● Target Market Selection Process 151
Step 1: Identify the Appropriate Targeting Strategy 152
Step 2: Determine Which Segmentation Variables to Use 155
Step 3: Develop Market Segment Profiles 164
Step 4: Evaluate Relevant Market Segments 165
Step 5: Select Specific Target Markets 167

● Developing Sales Forecasts 167
Executive Judgment 168
Surveys 168

▶ MARKETING ENTREPRENEURS: **Tim Keck and Chris Johnson** 169
Time Series Analysis 169
Regression Analysis 170
Market Tests 170
Multiple Forecasting Methods 170
▶ MARKETING LEADERS: **LittleMissMatched Pairs Socks** 155
▶ CUSTOMER RELATIONSHIP MANAGEMENT: **Targeting Mature Customers** 159
▯ VIDEO CASE: BuyandHold.com Targets Smaller Investors 173

PART FOUR Customer Behavior 175

8 Consumer Buying Behavior 176
Buying Cars with a Click at AutoTrader.com 176

● Level of Involvement and Consumer Problem-Solving Processes 177

● Consumer Buying Decision Process 179
Problem Recognition 180
Information Search 180
Evaluation of Alternatives 181

Purchase 181
Postpurchase Evaluation 182

● Situational Influences on the Buying Decision Process 182

● Psychological Influences on the Buying Decision Process 183
Perception 183

Motives   185
Learning   186
▶ MARKETING ENTREPRENEURS: Melissa and Mallory
   Gollick   186
Attitudes   187
Personality and Self-Concept   188
Lifestyles   189

● Social Influences on the Buying Decision
Process   189
Roles   189
Family Influences   190

Reference Groups and Opinion Leaders   191
Social Classes   192
Culture and Subcultures   194

▶ E-MARKETING AND TECHNOLOGY: Marketing "Cool"
Before the Frenzy Fizzles   192

▶ CUSTOMER RELATIONSHIP MANAGEMENT: Celebrate the
Similarities and Differences of Subcultures   196

VIDEO CASE: Build-A-Bear Builds Memorable
   Customer Experiences   199

⑨ Business Markets and Buying Behavior   201

Using the 3Rs to Drive Product Innovation
   at 3M   201

● Business Markets   202
Producer Markets   203
Reseller Markets   204
Government Markets   204
Institutional Markets   206

● Dimensions of Marketing to Business
Customers   206
Characteristics of Transactions with Business
   Customers   206
Attributes of Business Customers   207
Primary Concerns of Business Customers   207
Methods of Business Buying   208
Types of Business Purchases   209
Demand for Business Products   210

▶ MARKETING ENTREPRENEURS: Shazad Mohamed   211

● Business Buying Decisions   212
The Buying Center   212
Stages of the Business Buying Decision Process   213
Influences on the Business Buying Decision
   Process   215

● Industrial Classification Systems   216

▶ MARKETING LEADERS: Brighton Supports Special
Marketing for Specialty Retailers   205

▶ E-MARKETING AND TECHNOLOGY: The Business of
Online Auctions   209

VIDEO CASE: VIPdesk.com Serves Business
   Customers   221

PART FIVE   Product Decisions   223

⑩ Product, Branding, and Packaging Concepts   224

Dell Mixes It Up with Customers, Electronics, and
   More   224

● What Is a Product?   226

● Classifying Products   227
Consumer Products   227
Business Products   228

● Product Line and Product Mix   230

● Product Life Cycles and Marketing
Strategies   232
Introduction   233
Growth   233

Maturity   234
Decline   235

● Production Adoption Process   236

● Branding   238
Value of Branding   239
Brand Equity   239
Types of Brands   241
Selecting a Brand Name   242
Protecting a Brand   242

▶ MARKETING ENTREPRENEURS: Elise and
Evan MacMillan   243
Branding Policies   243

Branding Extensions   244
Co-Branding   244
Brand Licensing   245

● Packaging   245
Packaging Functions   245
Major Packaging Considerations   246
Packaging and Marketing Strategy   247

● Labeling   249

▶ MARKETING AROUND THE WORLD: **Nokia Is Calling All Game Players**   234

▶ CUSTOMER RELATIONSHIP MANAGEMENT: **Harley-Davidson Revs Up Brand Equity**   240

🖵 VIDEO CASE: Sony's PlayStation Gets Personal   253

⑪ Developing and Managing Goods and Services   255

XM Satellite Radio Tunes in Extra-Special Features   255

● Managing Existing Products   256
Line Extensions   256
Product Modifications   257

● Developing New Products   258
Idea Generation   260
Screening   260
Concept Testing   261
Business Analysis   261
Product Development   262
Test Marketing   262
Commercialization   263

● Product Differentiation Through Quality, Design, and Support Services   265
Product Quality   265
Product Design and Features   266
Product Support Services   267

● Product Positioning and Repositioning   267
Perceptual Mapping   267

Bases for Positioning   268
Repositioning   269

● Product Deletion   270

● Managing Services as Products   272
Nature and Importance of Services   272
Characteristics of Services   272
Creating Marketing Mixes for Services   275

▶ MARKETING ENTREPRENEURS: **Ercan Tutal**   278

● Organizing to Develop and Manage Products   279

▶ MARKETING LEADERS: **Demeter Makes Scents of New Products**   259

▶ CUSTOMER RELATIONSHIP MANAGEMENT: **General Motors Takes Slow-Selling Products Off the Road**   271

🖵 VIDEO CASE: Cali Cosmetics Offer the Benefits of Olive Oil   283

PART SIX   Pricing Decisions   285

⑫ Pricing Fundamentals   286

The New Napster Dances to a Different Tune   286

● The Role of Price   287

● Price and Nonprice Competition   288
Price Competition   288
Nonprice Competition   289

● Analysis of Demand   290
The Demand Curve   290
Demand Fluctuations   291
Assessing Price Elasticity of Demand   291

▶ MARKETING ENTREPRENEURS: **Pankaj Arora**   292

● Demand, Cost, and Profit Relationships   292
Marginal Analysis   293
Breakeven Analysis   296

● Factors Affecting Pricing Decisions   297
Organizational and Marketing Objectives   297
Types of Pricing Objectives   297
Costs   298
Other Marketing Mix Variables   298
Channel Member Expectations   299
Customer Interpretation and Response   299
Competition   301
Legal and Regulatory Issues   302

● **Pricing for Business Markets**   303

Price Discounting   303
Geographic Pricing   305
Transfer Pricing   306

▶ **E-Marketing and Technology:**   **Will the PC Price War Continue?**   289

▶ **Customer Relationship Management:**   **Universal Fine-Tunes CD Prices**   303

▶ VIDEO CASE: Low-Fare JetBlue Competes on More Than Price   309

⑬ Pricing Management   311

Can General Motors Keep Riding on Rebates?   311

● **Development of Pricing Objectives**   312

Survival   312
Profit   313
Return on Investment   313
Market Share   314
Cash Flow   314
Status Quo   314
Product Quality   314

● **Assessment of the Target Market's Evaluation of Price**   315

● **Evaluation of Competitors' Prices**   316

● **Selection of a Basis for Pricing**   316

Cost-Based Pricing   317
Demand-Based Pricing   318
Competition-Based Pricing   318

● **Selection of a Pricing Strategy**   318

Differential Pricing   319
New-Product Pricing   321
Product-Line Pricing   322
Psychological Pricing   323

▶ **Marketing Entrepreneurs:**   **Rich Stachowski**   323
Professional Pricing   326
Promotional Pricing   326

● **Determination of a Specific Price**   328

▶ **Marketing Leaders:**   **Pricing New Music for Profit**   313

▶ **Customer Relationship Management:**   **Wireless Companies Call Up Competitive Pricing Strategies**   319

▶ VIDEO CASE: How New Balance Runs Its Pricing Strategy   331

PART SEVEN   Distribution Decisions   333

⑭ Marketing Channels and Supply-Chain Management   334

Grainger Wires the Business Supply Chain   334

● **Marketing Channels and Supply-Chain Management**   335

The Importance of Marketing Channels   337
Types of Marketing Channels   338
Channel Leadership, Cooperation, and Conflict   342
Channel Integration   344

▶ **Marketing Entrepreneurs:**   **Dineh Mohajer**   345
Intensity of Market Coverage   345

● **Physical Distribution in Supply-Chain Management**   347

Order Processing   349
Inventory Management   350
Materials Handling   351
Warehousing   351
Transportation   353

▶ **E-Marketing and Technology:**   **Technology Keeps the Hard Rock Café Rocking**   348

▶ **Marketing Around the World:**   **Oshkosh B'Gosh Changes Course on Transportation**   354

▶ VIDEO CASE: SmarterKids Uses Smarter Channel Management   359

⑮ Retailing, Direct Marketing, and Wholesaling 361

Mercantile Stores Serve Small-Town USA 361

● Retailing 362

Major Types of Retail Stores 363
Strategic Issues in Retailing 370

▶ MARKETING ENTREPRENEURS: **Joseph Tantillo** 371

● Direct Marketing and Direct Selling 374

Direct Marketing 374
Direct Selling 378

● Wholesaling 378

Services Provided by Wholesalers 379
Types of Wholesalers 380

▶ MARKETING AROUND THE WORLD: **Gas, Coffee, and Convenience in Thailand** 372

▶ CUSTOMER RELATIONSHIP MANAGEMENT: **Direct Marketing Keeps Profits Flowing for Dell** 377

🖥 VIDEO CASE: Adventures in Retailing at REI 387

PART EIGHT   Promotion Decisions 389

⑯ Integrated Marketing Communications 390

Apple's iPOD Shines with Promotion 390

● What Is Integrated Marketing Communications? 391

● The Role of Promotion 392

● Promotion and the Communication Process 393

● Objectives of Promotion 395

Create Awareness 395
Stimulate Demand 396
Encourage Product Trial 397
Identify Prospects 397
Retain Loyal Customers 398
Facilitate Reseller Support 398
Combat Competitive Promotional Efforts 398
Reduce Sales Fluctuations 399

● The Promotion Mix 399

Advertising 399
Personal Selling 400

Public Relations 401
Sales Promotion 402

● Selecting Promotion Mix Elements 404

Customer Involvement 404

▶ MARKETING ENTREPRENEURS: **Mike Gellman** 404
Promotional Resources, Objectives, and Policies 405
Characteristics of the Target Market 406
Characteristics of the Product 406
Costs and Availability of Promotional Materials 407
Push and Pull Channel Policies 408

● Criticisms and Defenses of Promotion 408

▶ CUSTOMER RELATIONSHIP MANAGEMENT: **The Perils of Celebrity Advertising** 401

▶ MARKETING LEADERS: **Jones Soda Benefits from Publicity** 403

🖥 VIDEO CASE: Jordan's Furniture 413

---

⑰ Advertising and Public Relations 415

"Livestrong" Wristbands Raise Funds for Cancer Survivors 415

● The Nature and Types of Advertising 416

● Developing an Advertising Campaign 417

Identifying and Analyzing the Target Audience 417
Defining the Advertising Objectives 418
Creating the Advertising Platform 418
Determining the Advertising Appropriation 420

Developing the Media Plan 421
Creating the Advertising Message 423
Executing the Campaign 427
Evaluating Advertising Effectiveness 428

● Who Develops the Advertising Campaign? 430

▶ MARKETING ENTREPRENEURS: **Cathey Finlon** 431

● Public Relations 431

Public Relations Tools   432
Evaluating Public Relations Effectiveness   434
Dealing with Unfavorable Public Relations   434

▸ E-MARKETING AND TECHNOLOGY: **Think Technology
Lets You Avoid All Those Commercials?**   428

▸ MARKETING LEADERS: **UNC's Monfort College Excels
at Public Relations as Malcolm Baldrige Winner**   433

▣ VIDEO CASE: Vail Resorts Uses Public Relations to
Put Out a Fire   438

⑱ **Personal Selling and Sales Promotion**   441

Frequent-Flyer Programs Encourage Customer
Loyalty   441

● **What Is Personal Selling?**   442

▸ MARKETING ENTREPRENEURS: **Lara Merriken**   443
The Personal Selling Process   443
Types of Salespeople   446
Managing the Sales Force   447

● **What Is Sales Promotion?**   455

Consumer Sales Promotion Methods   456
Trade Sales Promotion Methods   459

▸ ETHICS AND SOCIAL ISSUES: **Responsible Selling
Improves Customer Relationships**   448

▸ MARKETING LEADERS: **The Pampered Chef**   450

▣ VIDEO CASE: Selling Bicycles and More at
Wheelworks   463

◉ **Appendix: Careers in Marketing**   465

● **Changes in the Workplace**   465

● **Career Choices Are Major Life Choices**   465
Personal Factors Influencing Career Choices   465

● **Job Search Activities**   466

● **Planning and Preparation**   468

● **The Résumé**   469
The Job Interview   470
After the Interview   472
After the Hire   472

● **Types of Marketing Careers**   473
Marketing Research   473
Sales   474
Industrial Buying   475
Public Relations   476
Distribution Management   477

Product Management   477
Advertising   478
Retail Management   479
Direct Marketing   480
E-Marketing and Customer Relationship
Management   480

Glossary   482
Notes   495
Photo Credits   512
Name Index   515
Organization Index   520
Subject Index   527

Preface

Not everyone wants a super-sized introductory marketing textbook. *Foundations of Marketing* provides instructors and students of introductory marketing a concise, direct approach to understanding the basic concepts and decisions of marketing. The Second Edition of this highly successful textbook remains true to our goal of providing a teaching package that allows the professor more flexibility in bringing in his or her own personal involvement in the classroom. This book will not weigh you down; it will free you up to bring in the dynamic and exciting world of marketing.

We continue to conduct extensive market research to determine the current needs of professors and students. Check the endnotes to see how the latest research in marketing has been used to make the content the most accurate and up-to-date introductory text available. Also based on our research, there has been increased emphasis on entrepreneurship, new forms of promotion, and a broadened view of the interface between marketing and its stakeholders in the development of marketing strategies. We identified content areas that professors indicated that they might want more detail on specific topics. Therefore, we have developed supplemental **custom modules** on marketing ethics, customer relationship management, sports marketing, electronic word-of-mouth marketing, the Super Bowl as a marketing event, and marketing history.

This book presents marketing issues and concepts in enough depth and detail to both challenge students and ensure a general knowledge of marketing. To stimulate students' interests, this text is written in an accessible style and includes numerous real-life, contemporary examples throughout. A new feature placed within every chapter, ***Marketing Entrepreneurs,*** highlights individuals who have used innovative marketing to launch a new business, whereas our use of familiar illustrations continues to make *Foundations of Marketing* compelling, relevant, and application oriented.

> ### Custom Content Modules
> Readily available to view at:
> college.hmco.com/pic/prideferrellfom2e
>
> Custom Content Modules allow instructors to customize their textbooks with more in-depth coverage of hot marketing topics found in the traditional text. For customization details, please contact your sales representative.

> **MARKETING ENTREPRENEURS**
>
> **Norman Ray Lambert & Family**
>
> THE BUSINESS: Lambert's Café: The only home of "Throwed Rolls"
>
> FOUNDED: 1942
>
> SUCCESS: Serves more than 226 tons of vegetables a year

With a logical organization, precise definitions, and the marketing vocabulary that students need to know, our thorough coverage permits students to efficiently form an integrated and balanced overview of the marketing discipline. This concise and straightforward approach gives the professor enough freedom to expand activities and materials beyond the textbook and yet ensures that students will be well grounded in marketing. Fly through this course in your own style and pace with the book providing the necessary support for effective teaching. Free yourself from the extra content that can drag a course down and lose student interest in the process.

Organization of This Text

We have organized the eight parts of *Foundations of Marketing* to give students a conceptual and practical understanding of marketing decisionmaking. **Part One** presents an overview of marketing and examines strategic market planning, marketing environment forces, and social responsibility and ethics. **Part Two** focuses on e-marketing, customer relationship management, and global marketing. **Part Three** considers information systems, marketing research, and target market analysis. In **Part Four,** we examine consumer and business buying behavior. **Part Five** focuses on the conceptualization, development, and management of goods and services. **Part Six** is devoted to pricing decisions. **Part Seven** deals with marketing channels and supply-chain management, retailing, wholesaling, and direct marketing. **Part Eight** covers integrated marketing communications and promotion methods including advertising, personal selling, sales promotion, and public relations.

◉ Pedagogical Features that Facilitate Learning

In *Foundations of Marketing*, we provide a comprehensive and practical introduction to marketing that is both easy to teach and to learn. The entire text is structured to excite students about the subject and to help them learn completely and efficiently.

Organizational model

- An **organizational model** at the beginning of each part provides a road map of the text and a visual tool for understanding the connection between concepts.

- **Learning Objectives** at the start of each chapter present concrete expectations about what students are to learn as they read the chapter.

- An **opening vignette** about a particular organization, brand, or marketing practice introduces the topic for each chapter. These vignettes include interesting anecdotes about the marketing issues surrounding a variety of goods and services from diverse organizations such as Corvette, Nickelodeon, XM Satellite Radio, and the Lance Armstrong Foundation. Through these vignettes, students are exposed to contemporary marketing realities and are better prepared to understand and apply the concepts that they will explore.

- **Key term definitions** appear in the margin to help students build their marketing vocabulary.

- Numerous figures, tables, photographs, **advertisements,** and Marketing Entrepreneurs and E-Site features increase comprehension and stimulate interest.

igation system, XM satellite radio, and other options. This Corvette C6 has push buttons instead of door handles, like General Motors' Cadillac XLR roadster, which is also built in the Corvette factory at Bowling Green, Kentucky.

When *Road and Track* magazine compared the Corvette C6 with the new Porsche 911, it gave the Corvette high praise. In testing, *Road and Track* compared a $54,000 Corvette with an $89,000 Porsche 911, a considerable price difference, but concluded that the two cars gave a "remarkably similar racetrack performance." In most of the comparisons, including speed, ability to maintain agility, and grip on the road, the cars are quite similar. The big difference is in terms of styling and design, and of course, brand name is very important to the consumer. *Road and Track* later named the Corvette C6 the best all-round sports car over tough competitors from Porsche, Dodge, BMW, Honda, Mercedes, and Nissan.

To promote the launch of the new car, which was unveiled at the Detroit Auto Show, Mattel released a large-scale (1:18) Hot Wheels model of the muscle car. Mattel and Chevrolet have had a marketing partnership for 36 years. GM also inked a deal with premium guitar maker Paul Reed Smith Guitars—favored by celebrities such as Carlos Santana and Melissa Ethridge—to put the Corvette logo on some custom-designed guitars and the PRS name on a C6 race car during the 2005 racing season.

GM predicts that the typical Corvette buyer is a male between the ages of 35 and 50, probably a college graduate with a $121,000 median household income. There will be only about 31,000 sold per year, and Chevrolet will use the Corvette as its flagship sports car to gain visibility and attention to its complete product line.[1]

Opening vignette

company expects the j
year during product d
e-mail, groupware (so
ent locations to access
ument over the Inte
coordinate activities a
Because such technolo
communications, the
cantly to any industry.
net as a communicat
positively influence bu

Telecommunicatic
benefits to marketers, i
customer service capat
week, or 24/7), decrea
geographic barriers. D
and decision times and
tomers more efficientl
ability to shop for boo
at midnight, when trad
benefit for both buyer
comScore Networks fo
ping occurs between 9
even small firms to re
their operations. For (
small power tool and s
erated sales from aroun

Despite these bene
make the Internet the (
often called "dot-coms"—failed to earn profits
remain in business. Many dot-coms failed becau:
mattered was brand awareness. In reality, howeve
to traditional markets than they are different.[7] Tl
gies, like traditional marketing ones, depend on

Electronic Marketing Through Expedia.com buyers and sellers can learn about travel services, destinations, and prices.

Advertisements

• Five types of **boxed features** reinforce students' awareness of particular issues affecting marketing and the types of choices and decisions marketers must make.

• **Marketing Leaders** boxes explore interesting, young companies operating at the cutting edge of marketing. Companies and products highlighted include Cereality, Jones Soda, and the Pampered Chef.

MARKETING LEADERS

JONES SODA BENEFITS FROM PUBLICITY

Seattle-based Jones Soda Company markets premium soft drinks known for creative flavors, labels, and promotions that clearly differentiate them from mass-market offerings by Coca-Cola and PepsiCo. The 55-person company continuously promotes its premium brand and regularly changes flavors and labels, which may include photos sent in by customers. Customers can even suggest new flavors to Jones on the company's website or customize their own soda labels.

Despite its reputation for curious flavors, Jones's management was surprised by the deluge of publicity generated by the release of a turkey-and-gravy-flavored soft drink around Thanksgiving. The company produced just a few thousand bottles of the seasonal flavor to draw attention to its 15 other soft drinks. Turkey & Gravy Soda sold out in a matter of hours, perhaps because it seemed fun, unique, and timely. Although product developers at Jones characterized the product as a sipping soda rather than a thirst-satisfying

Van Stolk, was contacted more th... media, resulting in nearly 100 ra... *Business Week* acknowledged the... particularly pleased by Turkey & Gr... company's target market is teenage... be devoted radio listeners. Van Sto... the public relations impact by men... interview that the company planned... from Turkey & Gravy Soda to the Toy... doubtful that paid advertising co... nearly as much interest in the c... drink as this buzz marketing a... Turkey & Gravy Soda ha... successful promotio... the impact of... associated with... and Fish-Tac... Such... beneficial... does ver... Much of... budget i... ships of...

Marketing Leaders feature box

• **Customer Relationship Management** boxes consider how organizations try to build long-term relationships with their customers. Examples include Harley-Davidson, General Motors, and Universal Music Group.

• **E-Marketing and Technology** boxes include discussions about the impact of technological advances on products and how they are marketed. Examples of topics are data mining, online auctions, and cell phones.

• **Ethics and Social Issues** boxes raise students' awareness of social responsibility and ethical issues, and the types of choices that marketers face every day. Some of the organizations on which we focus are Ford, Wal-Mart, and Martha Stewart.

• **Marketing Around the World** boxes examine the challenges of marketing in widely diverse cultures for companies such as Kodak, ING, and OshKosh B'Gosh.

CHAPTER REVIEW

① **Understand the nature of global markets and international marketing.**
International marketing involves developing and performing marketing activities across national boundaries. International markets can provide tremendous opportunities for growth.

② **Analyze the environmental forces affecting international marketing efforts.**
Environmental aspects of special importance include cultural, social, economic, political, legal, ethical, and technological forces. Because marketing activities are primarily social in purpose, they are influenced by beliefs and values regarding family, religion, education, health, and recreation. Cultural differences may affect decision-making behavior, product adoption, and product use. Gross domestic product (GDP) and GDP per capita are common measures of a nation's economic standing. Political and legal forces include a nation's political and ethics systems, laws, regulatory bodies, special-interest groups, and courts. Significant trade barriers include import tariffs, quotas, embargoes, and exchange controls. Advances in technology have greatly facilitated international marketing.

③ **Identify several important regional trade alliances, markets, and agreements.**
Various regional trade alliances and specific markets, such as the North American Free Trade Agreement,

the European Union, the Common Market of the Southern Cone, Asia-Pacific Economic Cooperation, the General Agreement on Tariffs and Trade, and the World Trade Organization, create both opportunities and constraints for companies engaged in international marketing.

④ **Examine methods of involvement in international marketing activities.**
Importing (the purchase of products from a foreign source) and exporting (the sale of products to foreign markets) are the easiest and most flexible methods of entering international markets. Licensing and franchising are arrangements whereby one firm pays fees to another for the use of its name, expertise, and supplies. Contract manufacturing occurs when a company hires a foreign firm to produce a designated volume of the firm's product to specification and the final product carries the domestic firm's name. Joint ventures are partnerships between a domestic firm and a foreign firm or a government; strategic alliances are partnerships formed to create competitive advantage on a worldwide basis. A firm can also establish its own marketing or production facilities overseas. When companies have direct ownership of facilities in many countries, they may be considered multinational enterprises.

Chapter Review

• A **Chapter Review**, organized by learning objectives, summarizes the major topics discussed, and the list of key concepts provides another end-of-chapter study aid to expand students' marketing vocabulary.

• **Issues for Discussion and Review** at the end of each chapter encourages further study and exploration of chapter content.

• **Marketing Applications** ask students to engage in an activity or consider a situation. An Online Exercise at the end of the application questions asks students to examine a web site and assess one or more strategic issues associated with the site.

ISSUES FOR DISCUSSION AND REVIEW

1. How does international marketing differ from domestic marketing?

2. What factors must marketers consider as they decide whether to become involved in international marketing?

3. Why do you think this chapter focuses on an analysis of the international marketing environment?

4. A manufacturer recently exported peanut butter with a green label to a nation in the Far East. The product failed because it was associated with jungle sickness. How could this mistake have been avoided?

5. If you were asked to provide a small tip (or bribe) to have a document approved in a foreign nation where this practice is customary, what would you do?

6. How will NAFTA affect marketing opportunities for U.S. products in North America (the United States, Mexico, and Canada)?

7. In marketing dog food to Latin America, what aspects of the marketing mix would a U.S. firm need to alter?

8. What should marketers consider as they decide whether to license or enter into a joint venture in a foreign nation?

Issues for Discussion and Review

MARKETING APPLICATIONS

1. Which environmental forces (sociocultural, economic, political/legal, or technological) might a marketer need to consider when marketing the following products in the international marketplace, and why?
   a. Barbie dolls
   b. Beer
   c. Financial services
   d. Televisions

2. Which would be the best organizational approach to international marketing of the following products, and why?
   a. Construction equipment manufacturing
   b. Cosmetics
   c. Automobiles

3. Describe how a shoe manufacturer would go from

ONLINE EXERCISE

4. Founded in 1910 as "Florists' Telegraph Deliv... FTD was the first company to offer a "flowers wire" service. FTD does not itself deliver flow... depends on local florists to provide this servi... 1994, FTD expanded its toll-free telephone-o... service by establishing a website. Visit the sit... www.ftd.com.
   a. Click on International Deliveries. Select... country to which you would like to sen... flowers. Summarize the delivery and pri... information that would apply to that co...
   b. Determine the cost of sending fresh-cut... seasonal flowers to Germany.
   c. What are the benefits of this global dist... system for sending flowers worldwide?... other consumer products could be disti...

Marketing Applications

• A **Video Case** at the end of each chapter helps students understand the application of chapter concepts. Some examples of companies highlighted in the cases are Finagle A Bagle, BMW, JetBlue, New Balance, and REI.

• A **Careers in Marketing** appendix introduces students to issues they will face when they are ready to enter the work force. Coverage includes types of marketing careers, changes in the workplace, career/life choices, job search activities, résumé writing, and interviewing skills. A comprehensive **Glossary** defines more than 600 important marketing terms.

Video Case

Resources for Instructors

Foundations of Marketing includes a comprehensive package of teaching materials.

Instructor's Web Site

• **Online Teaching Center Instructor's Web Site.** This continually updated, password-protected site includes valuable tools to help design and teach the course. The website has been redesigned to enhance the ease of use, so that you can spend your time preparing for class rather than clicking links. Website contents include sample syllabi, downloadable text files from the *Instructor's Resource Manual,* role-play exercises, PowerPoint® slides, *CRS (Classroom Response System) Clicker Content,* and suggested answers to questions posed on the student web site. Also, we provide a downloadable game, *Who Wants to Be an 'A' Student?,* by John Drea, Western Illinois University. This easy-to-use game makes in-class review challenging and fun, and has been proven to increase students' test scores.

In addition to these password-protected support items, you will also be able to preview the custom content modules on expanded marketing topics (no password required). From here, you can determine which modules would enhance your instruction and your students' learning. To include modules in your text, contact your Houghton Mifflin sales representative.

• **HMClassPrep® with HMTesting CD.**

HMClassPrep provides a variety of teaching resources in electronic format allowing for easy customization to meet specific instructional needs. Resources on HMClassPrep include Word files from the *Instructor's Resource Manual,* Word files from the *Test Bank,* PowerPoint® presentations, and the *Who Wants to Be an 'A' Student?* game.

HMTesting is the computerized version of the *Test Bank* that allows instructors to select, edit, and add questions or generate randomly selected questions to produce a test master for easy duplication. Online Testing and Gradebook functions allow instructors to administer tests via their local area network or the World Wide Web, set up new classes, record grades from tests or assignments, analyze grades, and produce class and individual statistics. This program can be used on both PCs and Macintosh computers.

- **Online *Instructor's Resource Manual* and *Test Bank*.** Written by the text's authors, the *Instructor's Resource Manual* includes a complete set of teaching tools. For each text chapter, there is (1) a teaching resources quick reference guide, (2) a purpose and perspective statement, (3) a guide for using the transparencies, (4) a comprehensive lecture outline, (5) special class exercises, (6) a debate issue, (7) a chapter quiz, (8) answers to discussion and review questions, (9) comments on the end-of-chapter cases, and (10) video information.

  The *Test Bank* provides over 2,300 test items including true/false, multiple-choice, and essay questions. Each objective test item is accompanied by the correct answer, a main text page reference, and a key to whether the question tests knowledge, comprehension, or application. The *Test Bank* also provides difficulty and discrimination ratings derived from actual class testing for most of the multiple-choice questions. Lists of author-selected questions that facilitate quick construction of tests or quizzes appear in an appendix. These author-selected lists of multiple-choice questions are representative of chapter content.

- **PowerPoint slide presentations.** For each chapter, over 25 slides related to the learning objectives have been specially developed for this book. The slides contain outlines suitable for use in class lectures and discussions as well as selected figures and tables from the text. In addition, there are some illustrations not directly from the text compiled to create Premium PowerPoint slides. The Premium PowerPoint slides include additional material such as advertisements, surveys and graphs, and important terms. These slides, along with a PowerPoint reader, are available on the instructor's website and on the *HMClassPrep CD.*

- **Blackboard/WebCT CD-ROM.** Instructors can create and customize online course materials to use in distance learning, distributed learning, or as a supplement to traditional classes. Blackboard and WebCT systems include a variety of study aids for students as well as course management tools for instructors. Included are the IRM, *Test Bank,* PPTs, class exercises, and quizzes, ACE practice tests, video questions and quizzes, sample marketing plan, marketing plan worksheets, flashcards, glossary, chapter outlines, chapter summaries, and role-play exercises.

- **EduSpace powered by Blackboard.** The *EduSpace* course management tool includes chapter outlines, detailed lecture outlines, chapter objectives, chapter summaries, PowerPoint slides, Premium PowerPoint Slides, Classroom Response System questions (clicker questions), all questions from the textbook with suggested answers, Interactive Annotations with author's notes, auto-graded quizzes (different from quizzes that appear on student website and BB/WebCT), links to content on the websites, video activities, downloadable Microsoft Word files for every chapter or the entire PDF version of the *Instructor's Resource Manual,* and *Test Bank* content.

- **CRS (Classroom Response System) Clicker Content.** Using state-of-the-art wireless technology and text-specific Pride/Ferrell content, a Classroom Response System (CRS) provides a convenient and inexpensive way to gauge student comprehension, deliver quizzes or exams, and provide "on-the-spot" assessment. Ideal for any classroom, a CRS is a customizable handheld response system that will complement any teaching style. Various answering modes, question types, and display options mean that a CRS is as functional as you want it to be. As a testing platform, as an assessment tool, or simply as a way to increase interactivity in the classroom, a CRS provides the technology you need to transform a lecture into a dynamic learning environment. Content is available on the Instructor Web Site.

Marketing Video Clip

• **Marketing videos.** This series contains videos for use with the end-of-chapter video cases. The *Instructor's Resource Manual* provides specific information about each video segment.

• **Online color transparencies.** A set of over 200 color transparencies, available on the text-specific instructor web site, offers the instructor visual teaching assistance. About half of these are illustrations from the text. The rest are figures, tables, and diagrams that can be used as additional instructional aids.

• **Call-in test service.** This service lets instructors select items from the *Test Bank* and call our toll-free number to order printed tests.

• **Role-play exercises.** Three role-play exercises that allow students to assume various roles within an organization are available in the *Instructor's Resource Manual* and on the instructor's web site. The exercises are designed to help students understand the real-world challenges of decision making in marketing. Decisions require a strategic response from groups or teams. These exercises simulate a real-world experience, and give students an opportunity to apply the marketing concepts covered in the text. Accompanying the exercises is in-depth information concerning their implementation and evaluation.

Student Supplements Facilitate Learning

The complete package available with *Foundations of Marketing* includes numerous support materials that facilitate student learning.

• **Pride/Ferrell Marketing Study Center.** Our student web site at **www.pride-ferrell.com** contains the following:

Marketing Study Center

Audio Chapter Review MP3 downloadable files. The MP3 files provide unique audio chapter summaries and test-preppers for the on-the-go student. Available with the *"Guide to an 'A'" Media Passkey.*

ACE online self-tests. Written by the text authors, these questions allow students to practice taking tests and get immediate scoring results. Available with the *"Guide to an 'A'" Media Passkey.*

Online Flash Study Tutorials. Written by the text's authors, this supplement helps students review and integrate key marketing concepts. The Study Tutorials contain questions different from those in the online study aids and include chapter outlines as well as matching, true/false, multiple-choice, and mini-case sample tests with answers. Available with the *"Guide to an 'A'" Media Passkey.*

Internet Exercises. Including the text exercises with updates as necessary as well as additional exercises, these reinforce chapter concepts by guiding students through specific websites and asking them to assess the information from a marketing perspective. Available with the *"Guide to an 'A'" Media Passkey.*

Company links. Hot links to companies featured in the text are provided so that students can further their research and understanding of the marketing practices of these companies.

Online glossary, chapter summary, and flashcards. These sections help students review key concepts and definitions.

Marketing plan worksheets. These worksheets take students step-by-step through the process of creating their own marketing plan. A sample marketing plan is also provided as a model. This is a project that will help students apply their knowledge of marketing theories.

Career Center. Downloadable "Personal Career Plan Worksheets" and links to various marketing careers web sites will help students explore their options and plan their job search.

- **"Your Guide to an 'A'" Media Passkey.** The *"Guide to an 'A'" Media Passkey* provides access to the premium web content available with this program, including online activity updates, ACE, Online Flash Study Tutorials, and Audio Chapter Review MP3 downloadable files. It will be packaged upon request with all new *Foundations of Marketing* texts. For students buying a used textbook, the ìGuide to an 'A'î passkey is available to purchase as a stand-alone item.

 ## We Value Your Comments and Suggestions

Our major focus is on teaching and preparing learning material for introductory marketing students. We have traveled extensively to work with students and understand the needs of professors of introductory marketing courses. We teach introductory marketing courses on a regular basis and test the materials included in this book, the *Test Bank,* and other ancillary materials to make sure they are effective in the classroom.

We invite your comments, questions, and criticisms regarding this text and the supplemental materials that accompany it. We want to do our best to provide materials that enhance the teaching and learning of marketing concepts and strategies. Your suggestions will be sincerely appreciated. Please write us, e-mail us at **w-pride@tamu.edu** or **oferrell@uwyo.edu**, or call **979-845-5857** (Pride) or **307-766-3444** (Ferrell). You can also send a feedback message through the website at **www.prideferrell.com**.

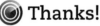 ## Thanks!

Like most textbooks, this one reflects the ideas of many academicians and practitioners who have contributed to the development of the marketing discipline. We appreciate the opportunity to present their ideas in this book.

Hundreds of reviewers have provided invaluable feedback over the years as we have written and revised our *Principles of Marketing* titles. Of course, those reviews have informed the creation of this book. In addition, over 500 faculty teaching introduction to marketing across the country responded to market research specifically designed to help create *Foundations of Marketing*. We sincerely appreciate that feedback. A special faculty advisory board assisted us in making decisions during the development of this text and its instructional package. For being "on-call" and available to answer questions and make valuable suggestions, we are grateful to those who participated: William Motz, *Lansing Community College;* Carol Rowey, *Community College of Rhode Island;* Morris A. Shapero, *University of South Florida;* Melodie Philhours, *Arkansas State University;* Patricia Bernson, *County College of Morris;* Eva Hyatt, *Appalachian State University;* Thomas Kanick, *Broome Community College;* Gayle Marco, *Robert Morris University;* Stanley Garfunkel, *Queensborough Community College;* Stephen Goodwin, *Illinois State University;*

William Carner, *University of Texas-Austin;* Mohan Agrawal, *California Polytechnic State University;* Jean-Luc Grosso, *University of South Carolina-Sumter;* Gloria Bemben, *Finger Lakes Community College;* Betty Jean Hebel, *Madonna University;* Barry McCarthy, *Irvine Valley College;* Donna Leonowich, *Middlesex Community College;* and Melissa Moore, *Mississippi State University.*

Gwyneth Walters assisted in research, editing, and content development for the text, supplements, and the Pride/Ferrell Marketing Learning Center. We deeply appreciate the assistance of Marian Wood for providing editorial suggestions, technical assistance, and support. For assistance in completing numerous tasks associated with the text and supplements, we express appreciation to Sarah Scott, Jonathan Bagwell, Deanna Ferreira, Brooke Arnold, Bridgett Burman, Rebekah Carter, Cheyne Morgan, Ben Siltman, and Clarissa Means.

We especially want to thank Linda Ferrell, *University of Wyoming,* who participated in all aspects of content and supplement development. Daniel Sherrell, *University of Memphis,* developed the framework used in Chapter 4. We especially appreciate his work in developing the six major characteristics of marketing on the Internet. Michael Hartline, *Florida State University,* helped in the development of the marketing plan outline and the sample marketing plan as well as the career worksheets on the web site. We want to thank V. Kumar, Chuck Tomkovick, Brian Jones, Todd Donavan, and John Eaton for developing supplementary modules for this edition. We also wish to thank Kirk Wakefield, *Baylor University,* for developing the class exercises included in the *Instructor's Resource Manual,* and John Drea, *Western Illinois University,* for developing the 'A' Student game.

We express appreciation for the support and encouragement given to us by our colleagues at *Texas A&M University* and *University of Wyoming.* We are also grateful for the comments and suggestions we receive from our own students, student focus groups, and student correspondents who provide ongoing feedback through the web site.

A number of talented professionals at Houghton Mifflin have contributed to the development of this book. We are especially grateful to George Hoffman, Mike Schenk, Suzanna Smith, Rachel D'Angelo Wimberly, Amy Galvin, Anthony D'Aries, Lisa Boden, and Marcy Kagan. Their inspiration, patience, support, and friendship are invaluable.

William M. Pride
w-pride@tamu.edu

O.C. Ferrell
oferrell@uwyo.edu

Strategic Marketing and Its Environment

Part 1 introduces the field of marketing and offers a broad perspective from which to explore and analyze various components of the marketing discipline. Chapter 1 defines *marketing* and explores some key concepts, including customers and target markets, the marketing mix, relationship marketing, the marketing concept, and value. Chapter 2 provides an overview of strategic marketing issues, such as the effect of organizational resources and opportunities on the planning process; the role of the mission statement; corporate, business-unit, and marketing strategies; and the creation of the marketing plan. These issues are profoundly affected by competitive, economic, political, legal and regulatory, technological, and sociocultural forces in the marketing environment. Chapter 3 deals with these environmental forces and with the role of social responsibility and ethics in marketing decisions.

1

Marketing's Role in Business and Society

OBJECTIVES

1 Define marketing.

2 Understand several important marketing terms, including *target market, marketing mix, marketing exchanges,* and *marketing environment.*

3 Be aware of the marketing concept and marketing orientation.

4 Understand the importance of building customer relationships.

5 Explain the major marketing functions that are part of the marketing management process.

6 Understand the role of marketing in our society.

Corvette Honored as Best Sports Car

Everyone is familiar with the Chevrolet Corvette and its success over the last 50 years. Although it is Chevrolet's most expensive car, with a starting price of $44,000, it is a relative bargain given its Porsche-like performance. The latest 'Vette, the 2005 C6 (for "sixth-generation Corvette"), features a full redesign that seems to have drawn the attention of two-seat sports performance car lovers. The C6's standard 6-liter V8 engine rates at 400 horsepower, and because of the car's modest 3,200-pound weight, it can achieve 186 miles per hour and go from standstill to 60 miles per hour in 4.1 seconds. A special-edition 2006 Z06 'Vette rates at 500 horsepower. Of course, you can add a navigation system, XM satellite radio, and other options. This Corvette C6 has push buttons instead of door handles, like General Motors' Cadillac XLR roadster, which is also built in the Corvette factory at Bowling Green, Kentucky.

When *Road and Track* magazine compared the Corvette C6 with the new Porsche 911, it gave the Corvette high praise. In testing, *Road and Track* compared a $54,000 Corvette with an $89,000 Porsche 911, a considerable price difference, but concluded that the two cars gave a "remarkably similar racetrack performance." In most of the comparisons, including speed, ability to maintain agility, and grip on the road, the cars are quite similar. The big difference is in terms of styling and design, and of course, brand name is very important to the consumer. *Road and Track* later named the Corvette C6 the best all-round sports car over tough competitors from Porsche, Dodge, BMW, Honda, Mercedes, and Nissan.

To promote the launch of the new car, which was unveiled at the Detroit Auto Show, Mattel released a large-scale (1:18) Hot Wheels model of the muscle car. Mattel and Chevrolet have had a marketing partnership for 36 years. GM also inked a deal with premium guitar maker Paul Reed Smith Guitars—favored by celebrities such as Carlos Santana and Melissa Ethridge—to put the Corvette logo on some custom-designed guitars and the PRS name on a C6 race car during the 2005 racing season.

GM predicts that the typical Corvette buyer is a male between the ages of 35 and 50, probably a college graduate with a $121,000 median household income. There will be only about 31,000 sold per year, and Chevrolet will use the Corvette as its flagship sports car to gain visibility and attention to its complete product line.[1] ◄

Like all organizations, GM's Chevrolet division must develop products that customers want, communicate useful information about them, price them appropriately, and make them available when and where customers may want to buy them. Even if it does these things well, competition from other automobile marketers, economic conditions, and other factors may affect the company's success.

This chapter introduces the strategic marketing concepts and decisions covered throughout the text. First, we develop a definition of *marketing* and explore each element of the definition in detail. Next, we introduce the marketing concept and consider several issues associated with implementing it. We also take a brief look at the concept of value, which customers are demanding today more than ever before. We then explore the process of marketing management, which includes planning, organizing, implementing, and controlling marketing activities to encourage marketing exchanges. Finally, we examine the importance of marketing in our global society.

Marketing Defined

stakeholders Constituents who have a "stake," or claim, in some aspect of a company's products, operations, markets, industry, and outcomes

marketing The process of creating, distributing, promoting, and pricing goods, services, and ideas to facilitate satisfying exchanges with customers and develop and maintain favorable relationships with stakeholders in a dynamic environment

If you ask several people what *marketing* is, you are likely to hear a variety of descriptions. Although many people think marketing is advertising or selling, marketing actually encompasses many more activities than most people realize. According to the American Marketing Association (AMA), "Marketing is an organizational function and a set of processes for creating, communicating, and delivering value to customers and for managing customer relationships in ways that benefit the organization and its stakeholders."[2] Stakeholders include those constituents who have a "stake," or claim, in some aspect of a company's products, operations, markets, industry, and outcomes; these include customers, employees, investors and shareholders, suppliers, governments, communities, and many others. In this book, we define marketing as the process of creating, distributing, promoting, and pricing goods, services, and ideas to facilitate satisfying exchanges with customers and develop and maintain favorable relationships with stakeholders in a dynamic environment. This definition includes most of the dimensions of the AMA's definition and guides the organization of this first chapter.

◉ Customers Are the Focus

As the purchasers of the products that organizations develop, price, distribute, and promote, customers are the focal point of all marketing activities (see Figure 1.1). Organizations have to define their products not as what the companies make or produce but as what they do to satisfy customers. The Walt Disney Company is not in the business of establishing theme parks; it is in the business of making people happy. At Disney World, customers are guests, the crowd is an audience, and employees are cast members. Customer satisfaction and enjoyment can come from anything received when buying and using a product. For instance, Procter & Gamble's Folger's Cafe Latte instant coffees—in flavors such as Mocha Fusion, Vanilla Vibe, and Chocolate Mint Mambo—provide an alternative to standing in line at the coffee shop, while its Tide HE helps keep clothes looking new even with today's high-efficiency washing machines.

The essence of marketing is to develop satisfying exchanges from which both customers and marketers benefit. The customer expects to gain a reward or

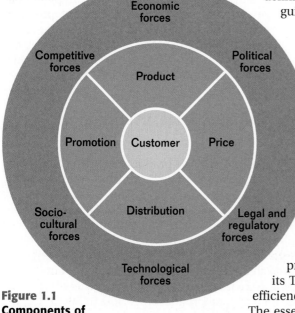

Figure 1.1
Components of Strategic Marketing

Give her
a boost!

Kellogg® introduces a
whole grain cereal
specially formulated to
help kids grow. Made with
a combination of...

Protein for
strong muscles,

Calcium for strong
bones and teeth,

And fiber to
aid digestion,

With a lightly sweet
taste kids love.

Kellogg's
NEW!
WHOLE GRAIN
Tiger
POWER

Gr-r-reat
for Growth!™

Appealing to a Target Market
Many children's cereals are positioned based on taste. Tiger Power is positioned as a healthier breakfast cereal.

benefit in excess of the costs incurred in a marketing transaction. The marketer expects to gain something of value in return, generally the price charged for the product. Through buyer-seller interaction, a customer develops expectations about the seller's future behavior. To fulfill these expectations, the marketer must deliver on promises made. Over time, this interaction results in relationships between the two parties. Fast-food restaurants such as Wendy's and Burger King depend on repeat purchases from satisfied customers—many often live or work a few miles from these restaurants—while customer expectations revolve around tasty food, value, and dependable service.

Organizations generally focus their marketing efforts on a specific group of customers, or target market. Marketing managers may define a target market as a vast number of people or a relatively small group. Rolls-Royce, for example, targets its automobiles at a small, very exclusive market: wealthy people who want the ultimate in prestige in an automobile. Other companies target multiple markets, with different products, prices, distribution systems, and promotion for each one. Nike uses this strategy, marketing different types of shoes to meet specific needs of cross-trainers, rock climbers, basketball players, aerobics enthusiasts, and other athletic-shoe buyers.

customers The purchasers of organizations' products; the focal point of all marketing activities

target market A specific group of customers on whom an organization focuses its marketing efforts

◉ Marketing Deals with Products, Price, Distribution, and Promotion

Marketing is more than simply advertising or selling a product; it involves developing and managing a product that will satisfy customer needs. It focuses on making the product available in the right place and at a price acceptable to buyers. It also requires communicating information that helps customers determine if the product will satisfy their needs. These activities are planned, organized, implemented, and controlled to meet the needs of customers within the target market. Marketers refer to these activities—product, pricing, distribution, and promotion—as the marketing mix because they decide what type of each element to use and in what amounts. A primary goal of a marketing manager is to create and maintain the right mix of these elements to satisfy customers' needs for a general product type. Note in Figure 1.1 that the marketing mix is built around the customer.

marketing mix Four marketing activities—product, pricing, distribution, and promotion—that a firm can control to meet the needs of customers within its target market

Expose the Truth

In the U.S. a woman will die from breast cancer, on average, every 13 minutes. We must stop this, here and around the world. Research today saves lives tomorrow.

The Breast Cancer

Research Foundation.

Funding the fight to prevent and cure breast cancer in our lifetime.

The Breast Cancer Research Foundation Founded in 1993 by Evelyn H. Lauder www.bcrfcure.org, 1.866.FIND.A.CURE

A Product Can Be An Idea
The Breast Cancer Research Foundation strives to create awareness of the impact of breast cancer and research initiatives.

product A good, a service, or an idea

Marketing managers strive to develop a marketing mix that matches the needs of customers in the target market. The marketing mix for Ralph Lauren's Polo brand of clothing, for example, combines a specific level of product design and quality with coordinated distribution, promotion, and price appropriate for the target market. The marketing mix for Ralph Lauren's Chaps clothing line differs from that for Polo, with lower prices and broader distribution.

Before marketers can develop a marketing mix, they must collect in-depth, up-to-date information about customer needs. Such information might include data about the age, income, ethnicity, gender, and educational level of people in the target market, their preferences for product features, their attitudes toward competitors' products, and the frequency with which they use the product. Such research helped convince Saturn to load its Ion sedan with stadium seating, a fold-down rear seat, and a multitude of options, including leopard-skin seats and brushed-steel interiors to appeal to Generation Y consumers (those born between 1977 and 1994).[3] Armed with market information, marketing managers are better able to develop a marketing mix that satisfies a specific target market.

Let's look more closely at the decisions and activities related to each marketing mix variable.

● **Product Variable.** Successful marketing efforts result in products that become part of everyday life. Consider the satisfaction customers have had over the years from Coca-Cola, Levi's jeans, Visa credit cards, Tylenol pain relievers, and 3M Post-it Notes. The product variable of the marketing mix deals with researching customers' needs and wants and designing a product that satisfies them. A product can be a good, a service, or an idea. A *good* is a physical entity you can touch. A Toyota Tacoma, an Usher compact disc, a Duracell battery, and a kitten available for adoption at an animal shelter are examples of goods. A *service* is the application of human and mechanical efforts to people or objects to provide intangible benefits to customers. Air travel, dry cleaning, haircutting, banking, medical care, and day care are examples of services. *Ideas* include concepts, philosophies, images, and issues. For instance, a marriage counselor, for a fee, gives spouses ideas to help improve their relationship. Other marketers of ideas include political parties, churches, and schools.

The product variable also involves creating or modifying brand names and packaging, and may include decisions regarding warranty and repair services. Even one of the world's best basketball players is a global brand. Yao Ming, the Houston Rockets center, has endorsed products from McDonald's, PepsiCo, and Reebok, many of which are marketed in his Chinese homeland.[4]

Product variable decisions and related activities are important because they are directly involved with creating products that address customers' needs and wants. To maintain an assortment of products that helps an organization achieve its goals, marketers must develop new products, modify existing ones, and eliminate those that no

MARKETING AROUND THE WORLD

PROCTER & GAMBLE PRODUCTS ARE NUMBER 1 AROUND THE WORLD

Consumers around the world trust Procter & Gamble (P&G) brands such as Always, Ariel, Bounty, Charmin, Crest, Downy, Folgers, Head & Shoulders, Iams, Olay, Pantene, Pringles, and Tide to improve their quality of life. P&G markets more than 300 branded products in more than 160 countries, with approximately 110,000 employees working in more than 80 countries. P&G's core product categories—baby care, fabric care, feminine care, and hair care—are number one in terms of both global sales and global market share and generate more than half of the company's total profits. One percentage point increase in market share across these four core businesses is worth about $1 billion in annual sales and more than $150 million in annual earnings. P&G is taking steps toward the strategic goal of having global category leadership and the number one global brand in every major category in which it competes.

Before its 2005 acquisition of Gillette, P&G had 16 brands with sales in excess of $1 billion per year. Tide, for example, is a $3 billion brand, and two others, Pantene and Ariel (a European detergent brand), are $2 billion brands. Health-care and baby-care business now represent nearly half of the company's sales and profits. Personal health-care sales have more than doubled in the past three years, significantly outpacing market growth. In China, P&G's laundry and oral-care market shares have more than doubled in the past three years. And in Russia, laundry, hair care, and oral care are all category leaders that have grown rapidly over the last three years. With the purchase of Gillette, P&G gained additional well-known

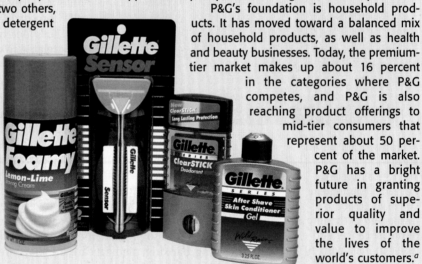

global brands including Gillette, Duracell, Oral-B, and Right Guard.

P&G enters world markets, such as China, Mexico, and Russia, in ways that minimize its risk. In China, for example, P&G's first products were shampoo, hair care, and personal cleansing. Once these products became market leaders, and the company developed distribution and supply chains to reach China's largest cities, it introduced fabric-care, feminine-care, and oral-care products. Then, it finally entered the baby-care market in the late 1990s. In markets like China, a premium price suggests a premium product, and consumers often want to be seen as using the best.

Sixteen countries account for 85 percent of P&G's sales. Current market shares by region include North America (50 percent), Western Europe (24 percent), Northeast Asia (5 percent), and developing countries (21 percent). Developing countries currently account for approximately 80 percent of long-term market potential.

P&G's foundation is household products. It has moved toward a balanced mix of household products, as well as health and beauty businesses. Today, the premium-tier market makes up about 16 percent in the categories where P&G competes, and P&G is also reaching product offerings to mid-tier consumers that represent about 50 percent of the market. P&G has a bright future in granting products of superior quality and value to improve the lives of the world's customers.[a]

longer satisfy enough buyers or that yield unacceptable profits. Microsoft, for example, introduced the Smartphone, which enables customers to access their e-mail, manage personal information, play music, and browse the Internet.[5] We consider such product issues and many more in Chapters 10 and 11.

● **Price Variable.** The price variable relates to decisions and actions associated with establishing pricing objectives and policies and determining product prices. Price is a critical component of the marketing mix because customers are concerned about the value obtained in an exchange. Price is often used as a competitive tool. For example, gardening products available at Lowe's home improvement stores cost 5 to 50 percent less than comparable products available at nurseries and small garden centers.[6] Intense price competition sometimes leads to price wars, but high prices can also be used competitively to establish a product's image. Waterman and Mont Blanc pens, for example, have an image of high quality and high price that has given them significant status. On the other hand, some luxury goods marketers are now offering lower priced versions of their products to appeal to middle-class consumers who want to "trade up" to prestigious brand names. Handbag maker Coach, for example, markets fabric wristlets for $78 as well as vintage leather wristlets, which sell for much more.[7] We explore pricing decisions in Chapters 12 and 13.

● **Distribution Variable.**   To satisfy customers, products must be available at the right time and in convenient locations. In dealing with the distribution variable, a marketing manager makes products available in the quantities desired to as many target market customers as possible, keeping total inventory, transportation, and storage costs as low as possible. With these objectives in mind, McDonald's expanded distribution by opening restaurants in Wal-Mart stores and in Amoco and Chevron service stations. This practice permits the fast-food giant to share costs with its partners and to reach more customers when and where hunger strikes. McDonald's now operates more than 30,000 restaurants in 119 countries, serving 47 million customers a day.[8] A marketing manager may also select and motivate intermediaries (wholesalers and retailers), establish and maintain inventory control procedures, and develop and manage transportation and storage systems. The advent of the Internet and electronic commerce has also dramatically influenced the distribution variable. Companies can now make their products available throughout the world without maintaining facilities in each country. The Great Southern Sauce Company, a small firm in Little Rock, Arkansas, for example, sells salsa, barbecue sauce, and other sauces through its website to buyers all over the United States and as far away as London and Saudi Arabia.[9] We examine distribution issues in Chapters 14 and 15.

● **Promotion Variable.**   The promotion variable relates to activities used to inform individuals or groups about the organization and its products. Promotion can aim to increase public awareness of the organization and of new or existing products. Procter & Gamble, for example, is using Nascar driver Tony Stewart to convey the masculinity and endurance of its Old Spice Red Zone antiperspirant.[10] Promotional activities can also educate customers about product features or urge people to take a particular stance on a political or social issue, such as smoking or drug abuse. Promotion can help sustain interest in established products that have been available for decades, such as Arm & Hammer baking soda or Ivory soap. Many companies are using the Internet and the World Wide Web to communicate information about themselves and their products. Ragu's website, for example, offers Italian phrases, recipes, and a sweepstakes, while Southwest Airlines' website enables customers to make flight reservations. In Chapters 16 through 18, we take a detailed look at promotion activities.

The marketing mix variables are often viewed as controllable because they can be modified. However, there are limits to how much marketing managers can alter them. Economic conditions, competitive structure, or government regulations may prevent a manager from adjusting prices frequently or significantly. Making changes in the size, shape, and design of most tangible goods is expensive; therefore, such product features cannot be altered very often. In addition, promotional campaigns and methods used to distribute products ordinarily cannot be rewritten or revamped overnight.

◉ Marketing Builds Satisfying Exchange Relationships

exchanges The provision or transfer of goods, services, or ideas in return for something of value

Individuals and organizations engage in marketing to facilitate exchanges, the provision or transfer of goods, services, or ideas in return for something of value. Any product (good, service, or even idea) may be involved in a marketing exchange. We assume only that individuals and organizations expect to gain a reward in excess of the costs incurred.

For an exchange to take place, four conditions must exist. First, two or more individuals, groups, or organizations must participate, and each must possess something of value that the other party desires. Second, the exchange should provide a benefit or satisfaction to both parties involved in the transaction. Third, each party must have confidence in the promise of the "something of value" held by the other. If you go to a Norah Jones concert, for example, you go with the expectation of a great performance. Finally, to build trust, the parties to the exchange must meet expectations.

Figure 1.2 depicts the exchange process. The arrows indicate that the parties communicate that each has something of value available to exchange. An exchange will not necessarily take place just because these conditions exist; marketing activities can occur even without an actual transaction or sale. You may see an ad for a Sub-Zero refrigerator, for instance, but you might never buy the product. When an exchange occurs, products are traded for other products or for financial resources.

Marketing activities should attempt to create and maintain satisfying exchange relationships. To maintain an exchange relationship, buyers must be satisfied with the obtained good, service, or idea, and sellers must be satisfied with the financial reward or something else of value received. A dissatisfied customer who lacks trust in the relationship often searches for alternative organizations or products.

◉ Marketing Occurs in a Dynamic Environment

marketing environment The competitive, economic, political, legal and regulatory, technological, and sociocultural forces that surround the customer and affect the marketing mix

Marketing activities do not take place in a vacuum. The marketing environment, which includes competitive, economic, political, legal and regulatory, technological, and sociocultural forces, surrounds the customer and affects the marketing mix (see Figure 1.1). The effects of these forces on buyers and sellers can be dramatic and difficult to predict. They can create threats to marketers, but can also generate opportunities for new products and new methods of reaching customers.

The forces of the marketing environment affect a marketer's ability to facilitate exchanges in three general ways. First, they influence customers by affecting their lifestyles, standards of living, and preferences and needs for products. Because a marketing manager tries to develop and adjust the marketing mix to satisfy customers, effects of environmental forces on customers also have an indirect impact on market-

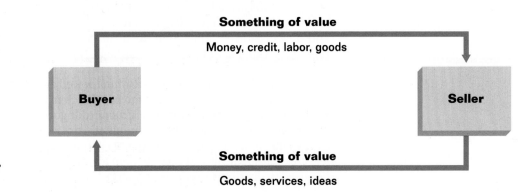

Figure 1.2
Exchange Between Buyer and Seller

WHAT IS MODERN LUXURY?

FORM THAT ACTUALLY FUNCTIONS.

An insanely comfortable bed that envelops you. A custom-designed shower that engulfs you. And 24-hour service that excels. This is the level of comfort where it stops being a business trip. Welcome to the age of modern luxury.

call your travel planner or 1 800 WESTIN1 or visit westin.com

WESTIN
HOTELS & RESORTS®

modern luxury.™

The Marketing Concept
Through research, Westin Hotels & Resorts has determined what business travelers desire and is providing it, as suggested in this advertisement.

ing mix components. For example, Ford and Mercury dealers can now use sophisticated technology to manage multiple communication methods for customer interaction. In addition to sending postcard reminders customized to each customer's vehicle service schedule, the dealers promote vehicles, accessories, and service through targeted phone contacts and Web-based campaigns. In the process, the dealers can gather marketing research information from customers and tailor offerings to meet customer needs.[11] Second, marketing environment forces help determine whether and how a marketing manager can perform certain marketing activities. Third, environmental forces may affect a marketing manager's decisions and actions by influencing buyers' reactions to the firm's marketing mix.

Marketing environment forces can fluctuate quickly and dramatically, which is one reason marketing is so interesting and challenging. Because these forces are closely interrelated, changes in one may cause changes in others. For example, evidence linking children's consumption of soft drinks and fast food to health issues such as obesity, diabetes, and osteoporosis has exposed marketers of such products to negative publicity and generated calls for legislation regulating the sale of soft drinks in public schools. Some companies have responded to these concerns by voluntarily reformulating products to make them healthier. PepsiCo, for example, has begun removing trans fats, which have been linked to heart disease, from its Frito-Lay snack foods, while the Ruby Tuesday restaurant chain has switched to frying with canola oil, which does not contain trans fats, and has urged suppliers to eliminate trans fats as well.[12] Even though changes in the marketing environment produce uncertainty for marketers and at times hurt marketing efforts, they also create opportunities. Marketers who are alert to changes in environmental forces not only adjust to and influence these changes but they can also capitalize on the opportunities such changes provide.

Marketing mix variables—product, price distribution, and promotion—are factors over which an organization has control; the forces of the environment, however, are subject to far less control. But even though marketers know they cannot predict changes in the marketing environment with certainty, they must nevertheless plan for them. Because these environmental forces have such a profound effect on marketing activities, we explore each of them in considerable depth in Chapter 3.

Understanding the Marketing Concept

Some firms have sought success by buying land, building a factory, equipping it with people and machines, and then making a product they believe buyers need. However, these firms frequently fail to attract customers with what they have to offer because they defined their business as "making a product" rather than as "helping potential customers satisfy their needs and wants." For example, when compact discs became more popular than vinyl records, turntable manufacturers had an opportunity to develop new products to satisfy customers' needs for home entertainment. Companies that did not pursue this opportunity, such as Dual and Empire, are no longer in business. Such organizations have failed to implement the marketing concept.

marketing concept   A managerial philosophy that an organization should try to satisfy customers' needs through a coordinated set of activities that also allows the organization to achieve its goals

According to the **marketing concept**, an organization should try to provide products that satisfy customers' needs through a coordinated set of activities that also allows the organization to achieve its goals. Customer satisfaction is the major focus of the marketing concept. To implement the marketing concept, an organization strives to determine what buyers want and uses this information to develop satisfying products. It focuses on customer analysis, competitor analysis, and integration of the firm's resources to provide customer value and satisfaction, as well as long-term profits.[13] The firm must also continue to alter, adapt, and develop products to keep pace with customers' changing desires and preferences. Ben & Jerry's, for example, constantly assesses customer demand for ice cream and sorbet. On its website, it maintains a "flavor graveyard" listing combinations that were tried and ultimately failed. It also notes its top ten flavors each month. Pharmaceutical companies such as Merck and Pfizer continually strive to develop new products to fight infectious diseases, viruses, cancer, and other medical problems. Drugs that lower cholesterol, control diabetes, alleviate depression, or improve the quality of life in other ways also provide huge profits for the drug companies. When new products—like Allegra, an allergy treatment—are developed, the companies must develop marketing activities to reach customers and communicate the products' benefits and side effects. Thus, the marketing concept emphasizes that marketing begins and ends with customers. Research has found a positive association between customer satisfaction and shareholder value.[14]

The marketing concept is not a second definition of marketing. It is a management philosophy guiding an organization's overall activities. This philosophy affects all organizational activities, not just marketing. Production, finance, accounting, human resources, and marketing departments must work together.

The marketing concept is also not a philanthropic philosophy aimed at helping customers at the expense of the organization. A firm that adopts the marketing concept must satisfy not only its customers' objectives but also its own, or it will not stay in business long. The overall objectives of a business might relate to increasing profits, market share, sales, or a combination of all three. The marketing concept stresses that an organization can best achieve these objectives by being customer oriented. Thus, implementing the marketing concept should benefit the organization as well as its customers.

MARKETING ENTREPRENEURS

Norman Ray Lambert & Family

THE BUSINESS: Lambert's Café: The only home of "Throwed Rolls"

FOUNDED: 1942

SUCCESS: Serves more than 226 tons of vegetables a year

Earl and Agnes Lambert, with just $1,500 in their pockets, opened a small café that seated 41 people on March 13, 1942. The Lambert's Café soon became a quaint eatery known for its healthy servings. Norman Ray, Earl's son, took over the café upon his father's death in 1976. While handing out oven-fresh rolls during one busy lunch hour on May 26 of that same year, a hungry patron, out of arms' reach, told Norman to just throw him the @$%# thing. Thus was born the slogan, "If it doesn't say Lambert's, it's not . . . Throwed Rolls." Since then, Lambert's has been throwing rolls to thousands of diners who come from all over just to catch them and to fill up on extras like white beans and fried okra, which servers ladle on your plate free of charge. Lambert's now operates out of three locations in two states and seats nearly 1,300 people.[b]

It is important for marketers to consider not only their current buyers' needs but also the long-term needs of society. Striving to satisfy customers' desires by sacrificing society's long-term welfare is unacceptable. For example, while many parents want disposable diapers that are comfortable, absorbent, and safe for their babies, society in general does not want nonbiodegradable disposable diapers that create tremendous landfill problems now and for the future. Marketers are expected to act in a socially responsible manner, an idea we discuss in more detail in Chapter 3.

◎ Evolution of the Marketing Concept

The marketing concept may seem like an obvious approach to running a business. However, businesspeople have not always believed that the best way to make sales and profits is to satisfy customers (see Figure 1.3).

● **The Production Orientation.**   During the second half of the nineteenth century, the Industrial Revolution was in full swing in the United States. Electricity, rail transportation, division of labor, assembly lines, and mass production made it possible to produce goods more efficiently. With new technology and new ways of using labor, products poured into the marketplace, where demand for manufactured goods was strong.

● **The Sales Orientation.**   In the 1920s, strong demand for products subsided, and businesses realized they would have to "sell" products to buyers. From the mid-1920s to the early 1950s, businesses viewed sales as the major means of increasing profits, and this period came to have a sales orientation. Businesspeople believed the most important marketing activities were personal selling, advertising, and distribution. Today some people incorrectly equate marketing with a sales orientation.

● **The Marketing Orientation.**   By the early 1950s, some businesspeople began to recognize that efficient production and extensive promotion did not guarantee that customers would buy products. These businesses, and many others since, found that they must first determine what customers want and then produce it rather than making the products first and then trying to persuade customers that they need them. As more organizations realized the importance of satisfying customers' needs, U.S. businesses entered the marketing era, one of marketing orientation.

marketing orientation An organizationwide commitment to researching and responding to customer needs

A marketing orientation requires the "organizationwide generation of market intelligence pertaining to current and future customer needs, dissemination of the intelligence across departments, and organizationwide responsiveness to it."[15] Top management, marketing managers, nonmarketing managers (those in production, finance, human resources, and so on), and customers are all important in developing and carrying out a marketing orientation. Unless marketing managers provide continuous customer-focused leadership with minimal interdepartmental conflict, achieving a marketing orientation will be difficult. Nonmarketing managers must

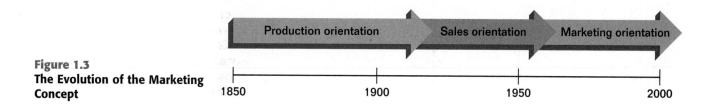

Figure 1.3
The Evolution of the Marketing Concept

Production orientation   Sales orientation   Marketing orientation

1850   1900   1950   2000

communicate with marketing managers to share information important to understanding the customer. Finally, a marketing orientation involves being responsive to ever-changing customer needs and wants. To accomplish this, Amazon.com, the online provider of books and compact discs, follows buyers' online purchases and recommends related topics. Trying to assess what customers want, which is difficult to begin with, is further complicated by the speed with which fashions and tastes can change. Today businesses want to satisfy customers and build meaningful long-term buyer-seller relationships. Doing so helps a firm boost its own financial value.[16]

◉ Implementing the Marketing Concept

A philosophy may sound reasonable and look good on paper, but that does not mean it can be put into practice easily. To implement the marketing concept, a marketing-oriented organization must accept some general conditions and recognize and deal with several problems. Consequently, the marketing concept has yet to be fully accepted by all businesses.

Management must first establish an information system to discover customers' real needs and then use the information to create satisfying products. For example, Parker Brothers encouraged customers to vote online for a new Monopoly game piece (a biplane, bag of money, or piggy bank). An information system is usually expensive; management must commit money and time for its development and maintenance. But without an adequate information system, an organization cannot be marketing oriented.

To satisfy customers' objectives as well as its own, a company must also coordinate all its activities. This may require restructuring the internal operations and overall objectives of one or more departments. If the head of the marketing unit is not a member of the organization's top-level management, he or she should be. Some departments may have to be abolished and new ones created. Implementing the marketing concept demands the support not only of top management but also of managers and staff at all levels.

◎ Managing Customer Relationships

Achieving the full profit potential of each customer relationship should be the fundamental goal of every marketing strategy. Marketing relationships with customers are the lifeblood of all businesses. At the most basic level, profits can be obtained through relationships in the following ways: (1) by acquiring new customers, (2) by enhancing the profitability of existing customers, and (3) by extending the duration of customer relationships. In addition to retaining customers, companies should also focus on regaining and managing relationships with customers who have abandoned the firm.[17] Implementing the marketing concept means optimizing the exchange relationship, which is the relationship between a company's financial investment in customer relationships and the return generated by customers responding to that investment.[18]

Maintaining positive relationships with customers is an important goal for marketers. The term **relationship marketing** refers to "long-term, mutually beneficial arrangements in which both the buyer and seller focus on value enhancement through the creation of more satisfying exchanges."[19] Relationship marketing continually deepens the buyer's trust in the company, and, as the customer's confidence grows, this in turn increases the firm's understanding of the customer's needs. Successful marketers respond to customer needs and strive to increase value to buyers over time. Eventually this interaction becomes a solid relationship that allows for cooperation and mutual dependency.

relationship marketing Establishing long-term, mutually satisfying buyer-seller relationships

customer relationship management (CRM) Using information about customers to create marketing strategies that develop and sustain desirable customer relationships

To build these long-term customer relationships, marketers are increasingly turning to marketing research and information technology. **Customer relationship management (CRM)** focuses on using information about customers to create marketing strategies that develop and sustain desirable customer relationships. By increasing customer value over time, organizations try to retain and increase long-term profitability through customer loyalty.[20] For example, AmSouth Bank, a financial institution with branches throughout the southeastern United States, promotes itself as "The Relationship Bank" and offers every financial service a business or a consumer could conceivably need. Instead of focusing on acquiring new customers, AmSouth strives to serve all the financial needs of each individual customer, thereby acquiring a greater share of each customer's financial business.[21]

Managing customer relationships requires identifying patterns of buying behavior and using that information to focus on the most promising and profitable customers.[22] Companies must be sensitive to customers' requirements and desires and establish communication to build their trust and loyalty. Consider that the lifetime value of a Taco Bell customer is approximately $12,000, while a lifelong Lexus customer is worth about $600,000.[23] A customer's lifetime value results from his or her frequency of purchases, average value of purchases, and brand-switching patterns.[24] In general, when marketers focus on customers chosen for their lifetime value, they earn higher profits in future periods than when they focus on customers selected for other reasons.[25] Because the loss of a loyal potential lifetime customer could result in lower profits, managing customer relationships has become a major focus of strategic marketing today.

Through the use of Internet-based marketing strategies (e-marketing), companies can personalize customer relationships on a nearly one-on-one basis. A wide range of products, such as computers, jeans, golf clubs, cosmetics, and greeting cards, can be tailored for specific customers. Customer relationship management provides a strategic bridge between information technology and marketing strategies aimed at long-term relationships. This involves finding and retaining customers using information to improve customer value and satisfaction. For example, Amazon.com uses e-mail to inform customers about books, music, or videos that may be of interest. Amazon analyzes each e-mail campaign to determine which strategies yield the greatest response rates and additional purchases. When the company offered a $5 or $10 gift certificate to 1 million new customers, 150,000 customers purchased again.[26] Thus, information technology helps Amazon manage customer relationship by making valuable offers to select customer groups, which in turn increases sales and customer satisfaction.

Value-Driven Marketing

value A customer's subjective assessment of benefits relative to costs in determining the worth of a product

Value is an important element of managing long-term customer relationships and implementing the marketing concept. We view **value** as a customer's subjective assessment of benefits relative to costs in determining the worth of a product (customer value = customer benefits – customer costs).

Customer benefits include anything a buyer receives in an exchange. Hotels and motels, for example, basically provide a room with a bed and bathroom, but each firm provides a different level of service, amenities, and atmosphere to satisfy its guests. Hampton Inns offers the minimum services necessary to maintain a quality, efficient, low-price overnight accommodation. In contrast, the Ritz-Carlton provides every imaginable service a guest might desire and strives to ensure that all service is of the highest quality. Customers judge which type of accommodation offers the best value

Value-Driven Marketing
Xerox understands its business customers need exceptional color prints and service.

according to the benefits they desire and their willingness and ability to pay for the costs associated with the benefits.

Customer costs include anything a buyer must give up to obtain the benefits the product provides. The most obvious cost is the monetary price of the product, but nonmonetary costs can be equally important in a customer's determination of value. Two nonmonetary costs are the time and effort customers expend to find and purchase desired products. To reduce time and effort, a company can increase product availability, thereby making it more convenient for buyers to purchase the firm's products. Another nonmonetary cost is risk, which can be reduced by offering good basic warranties or extended warranties for an additional charge.[27] Another risk reduction strategy is the offer of a 100 percent satisfaction guarantee. This strategy is increasingly popular in today's catalog/telephone/Internet shopping environment. L.L. Bean, for example, uses such a guarantee to reduce the risk involved in ordering merchandise from its catalogs.

The process people use to determine the value of a product is not highly scientific. All of us tend to get a feel for the worth of products based on our own expectations and previous experience. We can, for example, compare the value of tires, batteries, and computers directly with the value of competing products. We evaluate movies, sporting events, and performances by entertainers on the more subjective basis of personal preferences and emotions. For most purchases, we do not consciously try to calculate the associated benefits and costs. It becomes an instinctive feeling that Kellogg's Corn Flakes are a good value or that McDonald's is a good place to take children for a quick lunch. The purchase of an automobile or a mountain bike may have emotional components, but more conscious decision making may also figure in the process of determining value.

In developing marketing activities, it is important to recognize that customers receive benefits based on their experiences. For example, many computer buyers consider services such as fast delivery, ease of installation, technical advice, and training assistance to be important elements of the product. Customers also derive benefits from the act of shopping and selecting products. These benefits can be affected by the atmosphere or environment of a store, such as Red Lobster's nautical/seafood theme. Even the ease of navigating a website can have a tremendous impact on perceived value. For this reason, Cigna Health has joined with Yahoo! to create a user-friendly website where its health-care customers can quickly and easily check their benefits, submit claims, locate local medical providers, and update personal information. Also enhancing Cigna's value and customer service is the fact that customers can even order prescription drugs through this special website.[28]

The marketing mix can be used to enhance perceptions of value. A product that demonstrates value usually has a feature or an enhancement that provides benefits. Promotional activities can also help create an image and prestige characteristics that customers consider in their assessment of a product's value. In some cases, value may simply be perceived as the lowest price. Many customers may not care about the quality of the paper towels they buy; they simply want the cheapest ones for use in cleaning up spills because they plan to throw them in the trash anyway. On the other hand, more people are looking for the fastest, most convenient way to achieve a goal and therefore become insensitive to pricing. For example, many busy customers are buying more prepared meals in supermarkets to take home and serve quickly, even though these meals cost considerably more than meals prepared from scratch. In such cases, the products with the greatest convenience may be perceived as having the greatest value. The availability or distribution of products can also enhance their value. Taco Bell wants to have its Mexican fast-food products available at any time and any place people are thinking about consuming food. It has therefore introduced Taco Bell products into supermarkets, vending machines, college campuses, and other convenient locations. Thus, the development of an effective marketing strategy requires understanding the needs and desires of customers and designing a marketing mix to satisfy them and provide the value they want.

Marketing Management

marketing management The process of planning, organizing, implementing, and controlling marketing activities to facilitate exchanges effectively and efficiently

Marketing management is the process of planning, organizing, implementing, and controlling marketing activities to facilitate exchanges effectively and efficiently. Effectiveness and efficiency are important dimensions of this definition. *Effectiveness* is the degree to which an exchange helps achieve an organization's objectives. *Efficiency* refers to minimizing the resources an organization must spend to achieve a specific level of desired exchanges. Thus, the overall goal of marketing management is to facilitate highly desirable exchanges and to minimize the costs of doing so.

Planning is a systematic process of assessing opportunities and resources, determining marketing objectives, and developing a marketing strategy and plans for implementation and control. Planning determines when and how marketing activities are performed and who performs them. It forces marketing managers to think ahead, establish objectives, and consider future marketing activities and their impact on society. Effective planning also reduces or eliminates daily crises. We take a closer look at marketing strategies and plans in the next chapter.

Organizing marketing activities involves developing the internal structure of the marketing unit. The structure is the key to directing marketing activities. The marketing unit can be organized by functions, products, regions, types of customers, or a combination of all four.

Proper implementation of marketing plans hinges on coordination of marketing activities, motivation of marketing personnel, and effective communication within the unit. Marketing managers must motivate marketing personnel, coordinate their activities, and integrate their activities both with those in other areas of the company and with the marketing efforts of personnel in external organizations, such as advertising agencies and research firms. If McDonald's runs a promotion advertising Big Macs for 99 cents, proper implementation of this plan requires that each of the company's restaurants have enough staff and product on hand to handle the increased demand. An organization's communication system must allow the marketing manager to stay in contact with high-level management, with managers of other functional areas within the firm, and with personnel involved in marketing activities both inside and outside the organization.

The marketing control process consists of establishing performance standards, comparing actual performance with established standards, and reducing the difference between desired and actual performance. An effective control process has four requirements. It should ensure a rate of information flow that allows the marketing manager to detect quickly any differences between actual and planned levels of performance. It must accurately monitor various activities and be flexible enough to accommodate changes. The costs of the control process must be low relative to costs that would arise without controls. Finally, the control process should be designed so that both managers and subordinates can understand it.

The Importance of Marketing in Our Global Economy

Our definition of marketing and discussion of marketing activities reveal some of the obvious reasons the study of marketing is relevant in today's world. In this section, we look at how marketing affects us as individuals and at its role in our increasingly global society.

◉ Marketing Costs Consume a Sizable Portion of Buyers' Dollars

Studying marketing will make you aware that many marketing activities are necessary to provide satisfying goods and services. Obviously, these activities cost money. About one-half of a buyer's dollar goes for marketing costs. If you spend $16 on a new compact disc, 50 to 60 percent goes towards marketing expenses, including promotion and distribution, as well as profit margins. The production (pressing) of the CD represents about $1, or 6 percent of its price. A family with a monthly income of $3,000 that allocates $600 to taxes and savings spends about $2,400 for goods and services. Of this amount, $1,200 goes for marketing activities. If marketing expenses consume that much of your dollar, you should know how this money is used.

◉ Marketing Is Used in Nonprofit Organizations

Although the term *marketing* may bring to mind advertising for McDonald's, Chevrolet, and IBM, marketing is also important in organizations working to achieve goals other than ordinary business objectives such as profit. Government agencies at the federal, state, and local levels engage in marketing activities to fulfill their mission and goals. The U.S. Army, for example, uses promotion, including television advertisements and event sponsorships, to communicate the benefits of enlisting to potential recruits. The U.S. Treasury Department planned to spend $53 million over a five-year period to promote the release of redesigned $20, $50, and $100 bills. As part of the effort, the new bills were featured on episodes of *Wheel of Fortune, Jeopardy,* and *Who Wants to Be a Millionaire?*[29] Universities and colleges engage in marketing activities to recruit new students as well as to obtain donations from alumni and businesses.

In the private sector, nonprofit organizations also employ marketing activities to create, price, distribute, and promote programs that benefit particular segments of society. Habitat for Humanity, for example, must promote its philosophy of low-income housing to the public to raise funds and donations of supplies to build or renovate housing for low-income families who contribute "sweat equity" to the construction of their own homes. Such activities helped nonprofit organizations raise $241 billion a year in philanthropic contributions to assist them in fulfilling their missions.[30]

◉ Marketing Is Important to Businesses

Businesses must sell products to survive and grow, and marketing activities help sell their products. Financial resources generated from sales can be used to develop innovative products. New products allow a firm to satisfy customers' changing needs, which in turn enables the firm to generate more profits. Even nonprofit businesses need to "sell" to survive.

Marketing activities help produce the profits that are essential to the survival of individual businesses. Without profits, businesses would find it difficult, if not impossible, to buy more raw materials, hire more employees, attract more capital, and create additional products that in turn make more profits. Without profits, marketers cannot continue to provide jobs and contribute to social causes.

◉ Marketing Fuels Our Global Economy

Profits from marketing products contribute to the development of new products and technologies. Advances in technology, along with falling political and economic barriers and the universal desire for a higher standard of living, have made marketing across national borders commonplace while stimulating global economic growth. As a result of worldwide communications and increased international travel, many U.S. brands have achieved widespread acceptance around the world. At the same time, customers in the United States have greater choices among the products they buy because foreign brands such as Toyota (Japan), Bayer (Germany), and Nestlé (Switzerland) sell alongside U.S. brands such as General Motors, Tylenol, and Chevron. People around the world watch CNN and MTV on Toshiba and Sony televisions they purchased at Wal-Mart. Some well-known brands have been sold to foreign companies: Lenovo, a Chinese firm, purchased IBM's personal computer unit.[31] Electronic commerce via the Internet now enables businesses of all sizes to reach buyers around the world. We explore the international markets and opportunities for global marketing in Chapter 5.

◉ Marketing Knowledge Enhances Consumer Awareness

Besides contributing to the well-being of our economy, marketing activities help improve the quality of our lives. Studying marketing allows us to assess a product's value and flaws more effectively. We can determine which marketing efforts need improvement and how to attain that goal. For example, an unsatisfactory experience with a warranty may make you wish for stricter law enforcement so that sellers would fulfill their promises. You may also wish that you had more accurate information about a product before you purchased it. Understanding marketing enables us to evaluate corrective

What do CoPilot™ and a bloodhound have in common?

Both offer the best tracking system in the business.

But CoPilot can out-search even Ol' Duke. CoPilot is Pilot Air Freight's easy-to-use online shipping tool—and it's going to make your life a lot easier. It can give you fast, accurate price quotes, complete your airbills quickly, book your shipments instantly, swiftly track or trace them, even send you automatic e-mail alerts on shipment status, produce customized reports and much more.

Best of all, it comes from Pilot Air Freight—the worldwide transportation and logistics company that savvy shippers trust for speed, reliability, secure shipping and personalized service. If you've got a nose for saving time, reducing paperwork and eliminating hassles, start shipping with CoPilot online. Learn more by turning this page, calling 800-HI-PILOT (800-447-4568), or registering at: www.pilotair.com

PILOT AIR FREIGHT

www.pilotair.com

Marketing and the Growth of Technology
Pilot Air Freight provides sophisticated technology to improve the business shipping process.

measures (such as laws, regulations, and industry guidelines) that could stop unfair, damaging, or unethical marketing practices. Thus, understanding how marketing activities work can help you be a better consumer.

Marketing Connects People Through Technology

New technology, especially technology related to computers and telecommunications, helps marketers understand and satisfy more customers than ever before. Through toll-free telephone numbers, websites, and e-mail customers can provide feedback about their experiences with a company's products. Even bottled water products, such as Dannon Natural Spring Water, provide toll-free telephone numbers for questions or comments. This information can help marketers refine and improve their products to better satisfy consumer needs. The Internet, especially the World Wide Web, also allows companies to provide tremendous amounts of information about their products to consumers and to interact with them through e-mail and weblogs. A consumer shopping for a personal digital assistant, for example, can visit the websites of Palm and Handspring to compare the features of the PalmPilot and Visor, respectively. Although consumers are often reluctant to purchase products directly via the Internet, many value the Internet as a significant source of information for making purchasing decisions.

The Internet has also become a vital tool for marketing to other businesses. In fact, online sales now exceed $100 billion, accounting for more than 2 percent of all retail sales.[32] Successful companies are using technology in their marketing strategies to develop profitable relationships with these customers.

Socially Responsible Marketing Can Promote the Welfare of Customers and Stakeholders

The success of our economic system depends on marketers whose values promote trust and cooperative relationships in which customers and other stakeholders are treated with respect. The public is increasingly insisting that social responsibility and ethical concerns be considered in planning and implementing marketing activities. Although some marketers' irresponsible or unethical activities end up on the front pages of *USA Today* or *The Wall Street Journal*, more firms are working to develop a

The Nature Conservancy

In this half acre, 120 species are having a field day.

Sometimes, it's the things you don't see that matter most. For The Nature Conservancy, the small picture is often the big picture. Using science-based plans and innovative tools, we have protected 117 million acres around the world. With your support, that number will keep growing. Visit nature.org or call 1-888-2 JOIN TNC.

The Importance of Marketing
The Nature Conservancy works to protect millions of acres of natural habitat around the world.

ETHICS AND SOCIAL ISSUES
A GREENER FORD?

Ford Motor Company was founded in 1903 and grew into one of the world's largest corporations, selling nearly 7 million vehicles annually worldwide. During its century of operations, Ford has not been known for its environmental record, as evidenced most recently by environmentalists' ridicule of the gas-guzzling Ford Expedition sport-utility vehicle and the firm's failure to achieve a much-publicized goal of improving fuel efficiency on SUVs by 25 percent. Chairman and CEO William Clay Ford, Jr., wants to change that reputation for the company his grandfather founded.

When Bill Ford stepped into the CEO's office in 2001, he established far-reaching environmental, quality, and competitive goals for the company. Under his tenure, the company has improved quality, innovation, and cost efficiency. The company expects to launch 100 new models over five years, including several hybrid vehicles. The first of these hybrid vehicles—which employ an electric engine to augment the traditional gasoline engine to improve fuel efficiency—is the Escape SUV, which gets 36 miles to the gallon, about 50 percent more than a conventional Escape. The company is also aggressively pursuing fuel-cell technology, which may allow cars of the future to have great fuel efficiency and zero emissions.

Another example of Bill Ford's environmental focus is a new assembly plant in the Ford Rouge Center, which features efficient and flexible manufacturing processes as well as "breakthrough" environmental methods for storm-water management, energy use, air quality, and soil restoration. The roof of the Dearborn factory is a four-layer, mat-like system topped with drought-resistant plants, which acts like a giant sponge, absorbing rainfall and reducing polluted storm-water run-off, as well as an insulating blanket that helps sharply reduce energy consumption in all weather. Although the environmentally friendly roof added $3.6 million to the factory's cost, the firm will reap millions in savings by reducing energy expenses and eliminating the need for expensive storm sewers and storm-water treatment systems. The company has likewise invested in green facilities using solar, wind, and other technologies designed to reduce energy consumption and emissions.

Will these changes get environmentalists off of Bill Ford's back? He believes that being more environmentally responsible will ultimately result in a better reputation with stakeholders—particularly customers and employees, a stronger bottom line, and a safer environment. [c]

responsible approach to developing long-term relationships with customers *and* society. For example, Russell Simmons, who owns Phat Fashions, the Simmons-Lathan Media Group, and *OneWorld* magazine through his Rush Communications holding company, created the Rush Philanthropic Arts Foundation to donate funds to organizations that help underprivileged youth gain access to the arts.[33] By being concerned about the impact of marketing on society, a firm can protect the interests of the general public and the natural environment.

◉ Marketing Offers Many Exciting Career Prospects

From 25 to 33 percent of all civilian workers in the United States perform marketing activities. The marketing field offers a variety of interesting and challenging career opportunities throughout the world, such as personal selling, advertising, packaging, transportation, storage, marketing research, product development, wholesaling, and retailing. In addition, many individuals working for nonbusiness organizations engage in marketing activities to promote political, educational, cultural, church, civic, and charitable activities. Whether a person earns a living through marketing activities or performs them voluntarily for a nonprofit group, marketing knowledge and skills are valuable personal and professional assets.

CHAPTER REVIEW

❶ Define marketing.

Marketing is the process of creating, pricing, distributing, and promoting goods, services, and ideas to facilitate satisfying exchange relationships with customers and other stakeholders in a dynamic environment. The essence of marketing is to develop satisfying exchanges from which both customers and marketers benefit.

❷ Understand several important marketing terms, including _target market, marketing mix, marketing exchanges_, and _marketing environment._

A target market is the group of customers toward which a company directs a set of marketing efforts.

The variables—product, price, distribution, and promotion—are known as the marketing mix because marketing managers decide what type of each element to use and in what amounts. Marketing managers strive to develop a marketing mix that matches the needs of customers in the target market. Before marketers can develop a marketing mix, they must collect in-depth, up-to-date information about customer needs.

Individuals and organizations engage in marketing to facilitate exchanges—the provision or transfer of goods, services, and ideas in return for something of value. Four conditions must exist for an exchange to occur: (1) two or more individuals, groups, or organizations must participate, and each must possess something of value that the other party desires; (2) the exchange should provide a benefit or satisfaction to both parties involved in the transaction; (3) each party must have confidence in the promise of the "something of value" held by the other; and (4) to build trust, the parties to the exchange must meet expectations. Marketing activities should attempt to create and maintain satisfying exchange relationships.

The marketing environment, which includes competitive, economic, political, legal and regulatory, technological, and sociocultural forces, surrounds the customer and the marketing mix. These forces can create threats to marketers, but they also generate opportunities for new products and new methods of reaching customers.

❸ Be aware of the marketing concept and marketing orientation.

According to the marketing concept, an organization should try to provide products that satisfy customers' needs through a coordinated set of activities that also allows the organization to achieve its goals. Customer satisfaction is the marketing concept's major objective. The philosophy of the marketing concept emerged in the United States during the 1950s after the production and sales eras. Organizations that develop activities consistent with the marketing concept become marketing-oriented organizations.

❹ Understand the importance of building customer relationships.

Relationship marketing involves establishing long-term, mutually satisfying buyer-seller relationships. Customer relationship management (CRM) focuses on using information about customers to create marketing strategies that develop and sustain desirable customer relationships. Managing customer relationships requires identifying patterns of buying behavior and using that information to focus on the most promising and profitable customers.

Value is a customer's subjective assessment of benefits relative to costs in determining the worth of a product. Benefits include anything a buyer receives in an exchange, while costs include anything a buyer must give up to obtain the benefits the product provides.

⑤ Explain the major marketing functions that are part of the marketing management process.

Marketing management is the process of planning, organizing, implementing, and controlling marketing activities to facilitate effective and efficient exchanges. Planning is a systematic process of assessing opportunities and resources, determining marketing objectives, developing a marketing strategy, and preparing for implementation and control. Organizing marketing activities involves developing the marketing unit's internal structure. Proper implementation of marketing plans depends on coordinating marketing activities, motivating marketing personnel, and communicating effectively within the unit. The marketing control process consists of establishing performance standards, comparing actual performance with established standards, and reducing the difference between desired and actual performance.

⑥ Understand the role of marketing in our society.

Marketing costs absorb about half of each buyer's dollar. Marketing activities are performed in both business and nonprofit organizations. Marketing activities help business organizations generate profits, and they help fuel the increasingly global economy. A knowledge of marketing enhances consumer awareness. New technology improves marketers' abilities to connect with customers. Socially responsible marketing can promote the welfare of customers and society. Finally, marketing offers many exciting career opportunities.

✓ Please visit the student website at www.prideferrell.com
ACE self-test for ACE Self-Test questions that will help you prepare for exams.

KEY CONCEPTS

stakeholders	product	marketing orientation	value
marketing	exchanges	relationship marketing	marketing management
customers	marketing environment	customer relationship	
target market	marketing concept	management (CRM)	
marketing mix			

ISSUES FOR DISCUSSION AND REVIEW

1. What is marketing? How did you define the term before you read this chapter?

2. What is the focus of all marketing activities? Why?

3. What are the four variables of the marketing mix? Why are these elements known as variables?

4. What conditions must exist before a marketing exchange can occur? Describe a recent exchange in which you participated.

5. What are the forces in the marketing environment? How much control does a marketing manager have over these forces?

6. Discuss the basic elements of the marketing concept. Which businesses in your area use this philosophy? Explain why.

7. How can an organization implement the marketing concept?

8. What is customer relationship management? Why is it so important to "manage" this relationship?

9. What is value? How can marketers use the marketing mix to enhance the perception of value?

10. What types of activities are involved in the marketing management process?

11. Why is marketing important in our society? Why should you study marketing?

MARKETING APPLICATIONS

1. Identify several businesses in your area that have not adopted the marketing concept. What characteristics of these organizations indicate nonacceptance of the marketing concept?

2. Identify possible target markets for the following products:
   a. Kellogg's Corn Flakes
   b. Wilson tennis rackets
   c. Disney World
   d. Diet Pepsi

3. Discuss the variables of the marketing mix (product, price, promotion, and distribution) as they might relate to each of the following:
   a. A trucking company
   b. A men's clothing store
   c. A skating rink
   d. A campus bookstore

ONLINE EXERCISE

4. The American Marketing Association (AMA) is the marketing discipline's primary professional organization. In addition to sponsoring academic research, publishing marketing literature, and organizing meetings of local businesspeople with student members, it helps individual members find employment in member firms. Visit the AMA website at **www.marketingpower.com**.
   a. What type of information is available on the AMA website to assist students in planning their careers and finding jobs?
   b. If you joined a student chapter of the AMA, what benefits would you receive?
   c. What marketing mix variable does the AMA's Internet marketing effort exemplify?

VIDEO CASE

Finagle A Bagel

Finagle A Bagel, a fast-growing New England small business co-owned by Alan Litchman and Laura Trust, is at the forefront of one of the freshest concepts in the food service business: fresh food. The stores bake a new batch of bagels every hour and receive new deliveries of cheeses, vegetables, and other ingredients every day. Rather than prepackaging menu items, store employees make everything to order to satisfy the specific needs of each *guest* (Finagle A Bagel's term for a customer). Customers like this arrangement because they get fresh food prepared to their exact preferences—whether it's extra cheese on a bagel pizza or no onions in a salad—along with prompt, friendly service.

"Every sandwich, every salad is built to order, so there's a lot of communication between the customers and the cashiers, the customers and the sandwich makers, the customers and the managers," explains Trust. As a result, Finagle A Bagel's store employees have ample opportunity to build customer relationships and encourage repeat business. Many, like Mirna Hernandez of the Tremont Street store in downtown Boston, are so familiar with

what certain customers order that they spring into action when regulars enter the store. "We know what they want, and we just ring it in and take care of them," she says. Some employees even know their customers by name and make conversation as they create a sandwich or fill a coffee container.

Over time, the owners have introduced a wide range of bagels, sandwiches, and salads linked to the core bagel product. Some of the most popular offerings include a breakfast bagel pizza, salads with bagel chip croutons, and BLT (bacon, lettuce, tomato) bagel sandwiches. Round, flat, seeded, plain, crowned with cheese, or cut into croutons, bagels form the basis of every menu item at Finagle A Bagel. "So many other shops will just grab onto whatever is hot, whatever is trendy, in a 'me-too' strategy," observes Heather Robertson, director of marketing, human resources, and research and development. In contrast, she says, "We do bagels—that's what we do best. And any menu item in our stores really needs to reaffirm that as our core concept." That's the first of Finagle A Bagel's marketing rules.

To identify a new product idea, Robertson and her colleagues conduct informal research by talking with both customers and employees. They also browse food magazines and cookbooks for ideas about out-of-the-ordinary flavors, taste combinations, and preparation methods. When developing a new bagel variety, for example, Robertson looks for ideas that are innovative yet appealing: "If someone else has a sun-dried tomato bagel, that's all the more reason for me not to do it. People look at Finagle A Bagel as kind of the trendsetter."

Once the marketing staff comes up with a promising idea, the next step is to write up a formula or recipe, walk downstairs to the dough factory, and mix up a test batch. Through trial and error, they refine the idea until they like the way the bagel or sandwich looks and tastes. Occasionally Finagle A Bagel has to put an idea on hold until it can find just the right ingredients.

To further reinforce the brand and reward customer loyalty, Finagle A Bagel created the Frequent Finagler card. Cardholders receive one point for every dollar spent in a Finagle A Bagel store and can redeem accumulated points for coffee, juice, sandwiches, or a dozen bagels (actually a baker's dozen, meaning 13 instead of 12). To join, customers visit the company's website (**www.finagleabagel. com**) and complete a registration form asking for name, address, and other demographics. From then on, says Litchman, "It's a web-based program where customers can log on, check their points, and receive free gifts by mail. The Frequent Finagler is our big push right now to use technology as a means of generating store traffic."

Pricing is an important consideration in the competitive world of quick-serve food. This is where another of Finagle A Bagel's marketing rules comes in. Regardless of cost, the company will not compromise quality. Therefore, the first step in pricing a new product is to find the best possible ingredients and then examine the costs and calculate an approximate retail price. After thinking about what a customer might expect to pay for such a menu item, shopping the competition, and talking with some customers, the company settles on a price that represents "a great product for a fair value," says Robertson.

Although Finagle A Bagel's rental costs vary, the owners price menu items the same in both higher-rent and lower-rent stores. "We have considered adjusting prices based upon the location of the store, but we haven't done it because it can backfire in a very significant way," owner Laura Trust explains. "People expect to be treated fairly, regardless of where they live."

Although Finagle A Bagel competes with other bagel chains in and around Boston, its competition goes well beyond restaurants in that category. "You compete with a person selling a cup of coffee, you compete with a grocery store selling a salad," Litchman notes. "People only have so many 'dining dollars' and you need to convince them to spend those dining dollars in your store." Finagle A Bagel's competitive advantages are high-quality, fresh products, courteous and competent employees, and clean, attractive, and inviting restaurants.

Social responsibility is an integral part of Finagle A Bagel's operations. Rather than simply throwing away unsold bagels at the end of the day, the owners donate the bagels to schools, shelters, and other nonprofit organizations. When local nonprofit groups hold fundraising events, the owners contribute bagels to feed the volunteers. Over the years, Finagle A Bagel has provided bagels to bicyclists raising money for St. Jude Children's Research Hospital, to swimmers raising money for breast cancer research, and to people building community playgrounds. Also, the owners are strongly committed to being fair to their customers by offering good value and a good experience. "Something that we need to remember and instill in our people all the time," Trust emphasizes, "is that customers are coming in and your responsibility is to give them the best that you can give them."

Even with 400-plus employees, the owners find that owning a business is a nonstop proposition. "Our typical day never ends," says Trust. They are constantly visiting stores, dealing with suppliers, reviewing financial results, and planning for the future. Despite all these responsibilities, this husband-and-wife entrepreneurial team enjoys applying their educational background and business experience to build a business that satisfies thousands of customers every day.[34]

QUESTIONS FOR DISCUSSION
1. Describe Finagle A Bagel's marketing mix.
2. What forces from the marketing environment provide opportunities for Finagle A Bagel? What forces might threaten the firm's marketing strategy?
3. Does Finagle A Bagel appear to be implementing the marketing concept? Explain your answer.

Planning Marketing Strategies

▶ **Sears and Kmart Join Forces to Compete**

Just 18 months after emerging from bankruptcy protection, Kmart stunned the business world when it announced that it would pay $11 billion to purchase Sears & Roebuck. The merged firm, Sears Holdings, has 3,500 stores, making it the number 3 retailer, after Wal-Mart and Home Depot. Before the acquisition, Sears was the number 5 retailer and Kmart was the number 8 retailer, based on sales. Although most individual Sears and Kmart stores will retain their current names, some Kmart stores may become Sears stores, and both stores will promote each other's brands. Many believe that the merged company will be able to achieve tremendous cost savings, which will result in lower prices for consumers, and give retail giant Wal-Mart much more competition. The goal is to improve gross profit by $200 million per year and to save $300 million a year with more efficient purchasing and merchandising operations.

Both Kmart and Sears needed a new long-term strategy for reversing years of declines. The challenge will be to blend the two retail organizations into one customer-focused culture to compete with Wal-Mart and Target. The new enterprise will have to demonstrate that it can provide better value for customers than the competition. One way to accomplish this is through the leveraging of current brands and reputations for service. Sears is well known for its Kenmore appliances, Craftsman tools, Diehard batteries, and Lands' End apparel. Kmart home and fashion lines include Martha Stewart Everyday, Sesame Street, and Thalia Sodi. If the companies merge into one culture with one focused strategy, these brands could be a key force in attracting customers.

Allowing Sears and Kmart to sell each other's exclusive products is only one part of the strategy. Sears' long-time business model had relied on mall locations, but the retailing landscape has shifted to stand-alone "big box" retail stores in recent years. Many Kmart stores are located in prime locations outside malls and can now be converted to Sears stores.

It is ironic that Sears, Roebuck & Co. and its competitor Montgomery Ward were the leading retailers from the nineteenth century until Kmart overtook Sears as the nation's largest retailer in 1986. In 1900, Sears surpassed Montgomery Ward as the nation's largest retailer and retained that title for 86 years. In 1992, Wal-Mart assumed the title as the largest retailer. For Sears Holdings to be successful, it will need to engage in the strategic planning process, establishing its organizational mission, goals, corporate strategy, marketing objectives, and marketing strategy. Only with success in assessing opportunities and appropriate implementation of strategies can the new company be successful.[1] ◀

OBJECTIVES

1 Describe the strategic planning process.

2 Explain how organizational resources and opportunities affect the planning process.

3 Understand the role of the mission statement in strategic planning.

4 Examine corporate, business-unit, and marketing strategies.

5 Understand the process of creating the marketing plan.

6 Describe the marketing implementation process and the major approaches to marketing implementation.

With competition increasing, Sears Holdings and many other companies are spending more time and resources on strategic planning, that is, on determining how to use their resources and abilities to achieve their objectives. Although most of this book deals with specific marketing decisions and strategies, this chapter focuses on "the big picture," on all the functional areas and activities—finance, production, human resources, and research and development, as well as marketing—that must be coordinated to reach organizational goals. Effectively implementing the marketing concept of satisfying customers and achieving organizational goals requires that all organizations engage in strategic planning.

strategic planning The process of establishing an organizational mission and formulating goals, corporate strategy, marketing objectives, marketing strategy, and a marketing plan

We begin this chapter with an overview of the strategic planning process. Next, we examine how organizational resources and opportunities affect strategic planning and the role played by the organization's mission statement. After discussing the development of both corporate and business-unit strategy, we explore the nature of marketing strategy and the creation of the marketing plan. These elements provide a framework for the development and implementation of marketing strategies, as we will see throughout the remainder of this book.

Understanding the Strategic Planning Process

Through the process of **strategic planning**, a firm establishes an organizational mission and formulates goals, corporate strategy, marketing objectives, marketing strategy, and, finally, a marketing plan.[2] A marketing orientation should guide the process of strategic planning to ensure that a concern for customer satisfaction is an integral part of the process. A marketing orientation is also important for the successful implementation of marketing strategies.[3] Figure 2.1 shows the components of strategic planning.

The process begins with a detailed analysis of the organization's strengths and weaknesses and identification of opportunities and threats within the marketing environment. Based on this analysis, the firm can establish or revise its mission and goals, and then develop corporate strategies to achieve these goals. Next, each functional area of the organization (marketing, production, finance, human resources, etc.) establishes its own objectives and develops strategies to achieve them.[4] The objectives and strategies of each functional area must support the organization's overall goals and mission. The strategies of each functional area should also be coordinated with a focus on marketing orientation.

Because our focus is marketing, we are most interested, of course, in the development of marketing objectives and strategies. Marketing objectives should be designed so that their achievement will contribute to the

Marketing Plan
Prophesy emphasizes the need to plan ahead.

Figure 2.1
Components of Strategic Planning

Source: From *Marketing Strategy*, 2nd edition, by Ferrell. © 2002. Reprinted with permission of South-Western, a division of Thomson Learning: www.thomsonrights.com. Fax 800-730-2215.

marketing strategy   A plan of action for identifying and analyzing a target market and developing a marketing mix to meet the needs of that market

corporate strategy and can be accomplished through efficient use of the firm's resources. To achieve its marketing objectives, an organization must develop a **marketing strategy**, which includes identifying and analyzing a target market and developing a marketing mix to satisfy individuals in that market. Thus, a marketing strategy includes a plan of action for developing, distributing, promoting, and pricing products that meet the needs of the target market. Marketing strategy is best formulated when it reflects the overall direction of the organization and is coordinated with all the firm's functional areas. When properly implemented and controlled, a marketing strategy will contribute to the achievement not only of marketing objectives but also of the organization's overall goals. For example, the Chrysler Crossfire, which competes in the two-seat sports-car market, contains many Mercedes SLK parts. DaimlerChrysler executives hope this plan will improve the image of the Chrysler brand and help drive sales for DaimlerChrysler.

marketing plan   A written document that specifies the activities to be performed to implement and control an organization's marketing activities

The strategic planning process ultimately yields a marketing strategy that is the framework for a **marketing plan**, a written document that specifies the activities to be performed to implement and control the organization's marketing activities. In the remainder of this chapter, we discuss the major components of the strategic planning process: organizational opportunities and resources, organizational mission and goals, corporate and business-unit strategy, marketing strategy, and the role of the marketing plan.

Assessing Organizational Resources and Opportunities

The strategic planning process begins with an analysis of the marketing environment. As we shall see in Chapter 3, competitive, economic, political, legal and regulatory,

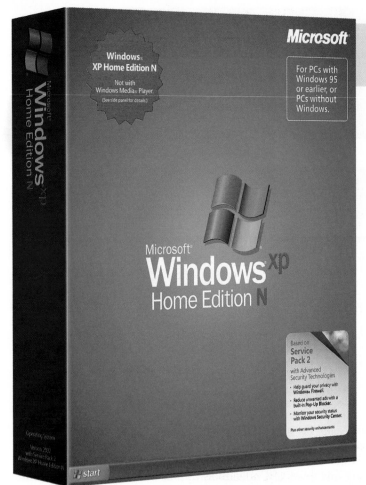

Core Competency
Microsoft maintains its core competency in software and devices.

technological, and sociocultural forces can threaten an organization and influence its overall goals; they also affect the amount and type of resources the firm can acquire. However, these environmental forces can create favorable opportunities as well—opportunities that can be translated into overall organizational goals and marketing objectives.

Any strategic planning effort must assess the organization's available financial and human resources and capabilities, as well as how the level of these factors is likely to change in the future. Additional resources may be needed to achieve the organization's goals and mission.[5] Resources affect marketing and financial performance indirectly by helping to create customer satisfaction and loyalty.[6] They can also include goodwill, reputation, and brand names. The reputation and well-known brand names of Rolex watches and BMW automobiles, for example, are resources that give these firms an advantage over their competitors. Such strengths also include **core competencies**, things a firm does extremely well—sometimes so well that they give the company an advantage over its competition. For example, the Chipotle fast-casual restaurant chain has built an advantage over competitors such as Baja Fresh Mexican Grill and Moe's Southwest Grill through a simple menu and fast, public food-preparation line with competitive prices.[7]

core competencies Things a firm does extremely well, which sometimes give it an advantage over its competition

market opportunity A combination of circumstances and timing that permits an organization to take action to reach a target market

strategic windows Temporary periods of optimal fit between the key requirements of a market and a firm's capabilities

competitive advantage The result of a company's matching a core competency to opportunities in the marketplace

Analysis of the marketing environment involves not only an assessment of resources but also identification of opportunities in the marketplace. When the right combination of circumstances and timing permits an organization to take action to reach a particular target market, a **market opportunity** exists. For example, advances in computer technology and the growth of the Internet have made it possible for real estate firms to provide prospective home buyers with databases of homes for sale all over the country. At **www.realtor.com**, the website of the National Association of Realtors, buyers have access to a wealth of online information about homes for sale, including photos, floor plans, and details about neighborhoods, schools, and shopping. The World Wide Web represents a great market opportunity for real estate firms because its visual nature is perfectly suited to the task of shopping for a home. Such opportunities are often called **strategic windows**, temporary periods of optimal fit between the key requirements of a market and the particular capabilities of a firm competing in that market.[8]

When a company matches a core competency to opportunities it has discovered in the marketplace, it is said to have a **competitive advantage**. In some cases, a company may possess manufacturing, technical, or marketing skills that it can match to market opportunities to create a competitive advantage. For example, eBay pioneered

MARKETING ENTREPRENEURS

Ryan Garman

THE BUSINESS: AllDorm.com

FOUNDED: 2000

SUCCESS: $25 million in sales

Two years after an arduous half-day journey in a U-Haul van from his Las Vegas home to his dorm room at Santa Clara University in California, Ryan Garman had an epiphany. Instead of hauling all of the things he would need for his dorm room across the country, it would have been nice if he could have had them delivered there before he even arrived. So, in 2000 he and a couple of dorm buddies founded AllDorm.com, an e-commerce site that caters to college students across the nation by allowing them to purchase items online such as beanbags, microwaves, mini-fridges, and bed sheets and then have them delivered to their dorm before they arrive on campus. By eliminating inventory, having minimal office space and few employees, AllDorm maintains its edge. AllDorm is now partnered with more than 250 universities and offers more than 6,000 items to choose from on its website.[a]

the online auction and built the premier site where 75 million users around the world buy and sell products. By analyzing its customer base, eBay found an opportunity to improve growth by targeting the nearly 23 million small businesses in the United States, many of which already use the auction site to buy and sell construction, restaurant, and other business equipment. To appeal to this important market, eBay sought ways to improve customers' online shopping experience.[9]

◉ SWOT Analysis

One tool that marketers use to assess an organization's strengths, weaknesses, opportunities, and threats is the **SWOT analysis**. Strengths and weaknesses are internal factors that can influence an organization's ability to satisfy its target markets. *Strengths* refer to competitive advantages or core competencies that give the firm an advantage in meeting the needs

SWOT analysis A tool that marketers use to assess an organization's strengths, weaknesses, opportunities, and threats

of its target markets. John Deere, for example, promotes its service, experience, and reputation in the farm equipment business to emphasize the craftsmanship it uses in its lawn tractors and mowers for city dwellers. *Weaknesses* refer to any limitations that a company faces in developing or implementing a marketing strategy. Consider that America Online, the leading Internet service provider, brings in half the online advertising revenue of other online services such as Google, MSN, and Yahoo! at a time when online advertising has accelerated dramatically.[10] Both strengths and weaknesses should be examined from a customer perspective because they are meaningful only when they help or hinder the firm in meeting customer needs. Only those strengths that relate to satisfying customers should be considered true competitive advantages. Likewise, weaknesses that directly affect customer satisfaction should be considered competitive disadvantages. To boost online ad revenue, AOL has redesigned its website and added more content, such as a news ticker and more sports and music, to boost usage by members and thereby make it more attractive to online advertisers.[11]

Opportunities and threats exist independently of the firm and therefore represent issues to be considered by all organizations, even those that do not compete with the firm. *Opportunities* refer to favorable conditions in the environment that could produce rewards for the organization if acted upon properly. That is, opportunities are situations that exist but must be acted upon if the firm is to benefit from them. *Threats,* on the other hand, refer to conditions or barriers that may prevent the firm from reaching its objectives. For example, consumers today are buying fewer music CDs, in part because many believe CD prices are too high. CD sales declined by 31 percent over a three-year period as consumers downloaded more music from online sharing networks such as Kazoo or shifted their entertainment dollars to video games and DVDs.[12] Threats must be acted upon to prevent them from limiting the organization's capabilities. To counter the threat of declining music sales, Universal Music Group slashed the wholesale price of CDs by artists such as Jay-Z and Shania Twain by

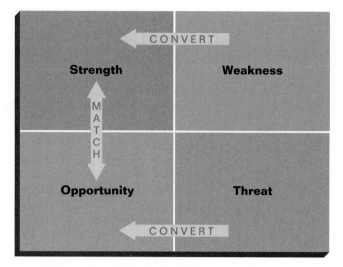

Figure 2.2
The Four-Cell SWOT Matrix
Source: Reprinted from *Market-Led Strategic Change,* by Nigel F. Piercy, p. 371, Copyright 1992 with permission from Elsevier Science.

as much as 31 percent.[13] Opportunities and threats can stem from many sources within the environment. When a competitor's introduction of a new product threatens a firm, a defensive strategy may be required. If the firm can develop and launch a new product that meets or exceeds the competition's offering, it can transform the threat into an opportunity.[14]

Figure 2.2 depicts a four-cell SWOT matrix that can help managers in the planning process. When an organization matches internal strengths to external opportunities, it creates competitive advantages in meeting the needs of its customers. In addition, an organization should act to convert internal weaknesses into strengths and external threats into opportunities. Ford Motor Company, for instance, converted the threats posed by rising gasoline prices and the growing acceptance of hybrid gas-electric cars from Japanese automakers into opportunities when it introduced a hybrid version of its Escape sport-utility vehicle, making the 36-mile-per-gallon Escape the first hybrid SUV available.[15] A firm that lacks adequate marketing skills can hire outside consultants to help convert a weakness into a strength.

Establishing an Organizational Mission and Goals

mission statement   A long-term view of what the organization wants to become

Once an organization has assessed its resources and opportunities, it can begin to establish goals and strategies to take advantage of those opportunities. The goals of any organization should derive from its **mission statement**, a long-term view, or vision, of what the organization wants to become. Herbal tea marketer Celestial Seasonings, for example, says that its mission is "To create and sell healthful, naturally oriented products that nurture people's bodies and uplift their souls."[16]

When an organization decides on its mission, it really answers two questions: Who are our customers? What is our core competency? Although these questions seem very simple, they are two of the most important questions any firm must answer. Defining customers' needs and wants gives direction to what the company must do to satisfy them.

An organization's goals and objectives, derived from its mission statement, guide the remainder of its planning efforts. Goals focus on the end results that the organi-

Our mission:
Deliver superior quality products and services for our customers and communities through leadership, innovation and partnerships.

Every day in Wendy's restaurants worldwide, we are focused on serving the very best. It's the foundation of our business – serve quality food, provide excellent service, superior value and a sparkling clean atmosphere.

Wendy's has a strong commitment to giving back. From corporate-sponsored initiatives, to the neighborhoods where the hard work and community service efforts of Wendy's employees make their corner of the world a little brighter, it's our responsibility to serve… and give back.

Wendy's International, Inc.

Tim Hortons. **WENDY'S** BAJA FRESH
MEXICAN-GRILL

Diversity & Ethics Department
P.O. Box 256
Dublin, OH 43017

Mission Statement
Wendy's International, Inc., communicates its mission.

marketing objective A statement of what is to be accomplished through marketing activities

zation seeks. Starbucks's mission statement, for example, incorporates the company's goals of striving for a high-quality product, a sound financial position, and community responsibility.

A **marketing objective** states what is to be accomplished through marketing activities. A marketing objective of Ritz-Carlton hotels, for example, is to have more than 90 percent of its customers indicate they had a memorable experience at the hotel. Marketing objectives should be based on a careful study of the SWOT analysis and should relate to matching strengths to opportunities and/or the conversion of weaknesses or threats. These objectives can be stated in terms of product introduction, product improvement or innovation, sales volume, profitability, market share, pricing, distribution, advertising, or employee training activities.

Marketing objectives should possess certain characteristics. First, a marketing objective should be expressed in clear, simple terms so that all marketing personnel understand exactly what they are trying to achieve. Second, an objective should be written so that it can be measured accurately. This allows the organization to determine if and when the objective has been achieved. If an objective is to increase market share by 10 percent, the firm should be able to measure market share changes accurately. Third, a marketing objective should specify a time frame for its accomplishment. A firm that sets an objective of introducing a new product should state the time period in which to do this. Finally, a marketing objective should be consistent with both business-unit and corporate strategy. This ensures that the firm's mission is carried out at all levels of the organization. General Motors, for example, may have an overall marketing objective of maintaining a 28 percent share of the U.S. auto market. To achieve this objective, some GM divisions may have to increase market share while the shares of other divisions decline.

Developing Corporate, Business-Unit, and Marketing Strategies

In any organization, strategic planning begins at the corporate level and proceeds downward to the business-unit and marketing levels. Corporate strategy is the broadest of these three levels and should be developed with the organization's overall mission in mind. Business-unit strategy should be consistent with the corporate strategy, and marketing strategy should be consistent with both the business-unit and corporate strategies. Figure 2.3 shows the relationships among these planning levels.

Corporate Strategy

corporate strategy A strategy that determines the means for utilizing resources in the various functional areas to reach the organization's goals

Corporate strategy determines the means for utilizing resources in the functional areas of marketing, production, finance, research and development, and human resources to reach the organization's goals. A corporate strategy determines not only the scope of the business but also its resource deployment, competitive advantages, and overall coordination of functional areas. It addresses the two questions posed in the organization's mission statement: Who are our customers? What is our core competency? The term *corporate* in this context does not apply solely to corporations; corporate strategy is used by all organizations, from the smallest sole proprietorship to the largest multinational corporation.

Corporate strategy planners are concerned with broad issues such as corporate culture, competition, differentiation, diversification, interrelationships among business units, and environmental and social issues. They attempt to match the resources of the organization with the opportunities and threats in the environment. Starbucks, for example, is attempting to capitalize on its strong brand appeal and loyal following by expanding beyond coffee and tea beverages into breakfast and lunch menu items as well as CD-burning stations.[17] Corporate strategy planners are also concerned with defining the scope and role of the firm's business units so that they are coordinated to reach the ends desired. A firm's corporate strategy may affect its technological competence and ability to innovate.[18]

strategic business unit (SBU) A division, product line, or other profit center within a parent company

Mission statement

↓

Corporate strategy

↓

Business-unit strategy

↓

Marketing strategy

↓

Marketing mix elements
- ▶ Product
- ▶ Distribution
- ▶ Promotion
- ▶ Pricing

Figure 2.3
Levels of Strategic Planning

Business-Unit Strategy

After analyzing corporate operations and performance, the next step in strategic planning is to determine future business directions and develop strategies for individual business units. A strategic business unit (SBU) is a division, product line, or other profit center within the parent company. Borden's strategic business units, for example, consist of dairy products, snacks, pasta, niche grocery products like ReaLemon juice and Cremora coffee creamer, and other units such as glue and paints. Each of these units sells a distinct set of products to an identifiable group of customers, and each competes with a well-defined set of competitors. The revenues, costs, investments, and strategic plans of each SBU can be separated from those of the parent company and evaluated. SBUs

market   A group of individuals and/or organizations that have needs for products in a product class and have the ability, willingness, and authority to purchase those products

market share   The percentage of a market that actually buys a specific product from a particular company

market-growth/market-share matrix   A strategic planning tool based on the philosophy that a product's market growth rate and market share are important in determining marketing strategy

Figure 2.4
Growth-Share Matrix Developed by the Boston Consulting Group
Source: Growth-Share Matrix Developed by the Boston Consulting Group, *Perspectives,* No. 66, "The Product Portfolio." Copyright © 1970. Reprinted by permission of Boston Consulting Group.

operate in a variety of markets, which have differing growth rates, opportunities, degrees of competition, and profit-making potential.

Strategic planners should recognize the different performance capabilities of each SBU and carefully allocate scarce resources among those divisions. Several tools allow a firm's portfolio of strategic business units, or even individual products, to be classified and visually displayed according to the attractiveness of various markets and the business's relative market share within those markets. A market is a group of individuals and/or organizations that have needs for products in a product class and have the ability, willingness, and authority to purchase those products. The percentage of a market that actually buys a specific product from a particular company is referred to as that product's (or business unit's) market share.[19] Microsoft, for example, controls 95 percent of the market for Internet Web browsers, but security issues with Internet Explorer have enabled Mozilla's Firefox to gain some of Microsoft's market share. Product quality, order of entry into the market, and market share have been associated with SBU success.[20]

One of the most helpful tools is the market-growth/market-share matrix, the Boston Consulting Group (BCG) approach, which is based on the philosophy that a product's market growth rate and its market share are important considerations in determining its marketing strategy. All the firm's SBUs and products should be integrated into a single, overall matrix and evaluated to determine appropriate strategies for individual products and overall portfolio strategies. Managers can use this model to determine and classify each product's expected future cash contributions and future cash requirements. Generally, managers who use this model should examine the competitive position of a product (or SBU) and the opportunities for improving that product's contribution to profitability and cash flow.[21] The BCG analytical approach is more of a diagnostic tool than a guide for making strategy prescriptions.

Figure 2.4, which is based on work by the BCG, enables the strategic planner to classify a firm's products into four basic types: stars, cash cows, dogs, and question marks.[22] *Stars* are products with a dominant share of the market and good prospects for growth. However, they use more cash than they generate to finance growth, add capacity, and increase market share. An example of a star might be Apple's iPod MP3 player. *Cash cows* have a dominant share of the market but low prospects for growth; typically, they generate more cash than is required to maintain market share. Bounty, the best-selling paper towels in the United States, represents a cash cow for Procter & Gamble. *Dogs* have a subordinate share of the market and low prospects for growth;

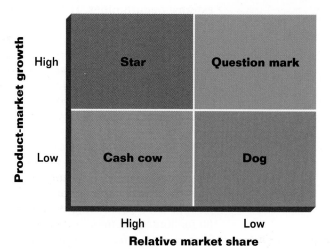

THE ONLY THING THAT WILL GROW FASTER IS THE COST OF A COLLEGE EDUCATION.

Kids grow up fast, and soon it's time for college. State Farm® can help you plan for the cost of your child's education. With investment choices such as education savings plans and mutual funds, your State Farm agent is ready to help. So call today. WE LIVE WHERE YOU LIVE.™

LIKE A GOOD NEIGHBOR   STATE FARM   STATE FARM IS THERE.™

Providing Insurance and Financial Services

Securities offered by registered representatives of State Farm VP Management Corp., Bloomington, IL. State Farm VP Management Corp. is a separate entity from those State Farm entities that provide insurance products. Consult your tax or legal advisor for specific advice.

ML2003-39 05/03

Target Market Selection
State Farm targets parents for its financial services.

these products are often found in established markets. The Oldsmobile brand may be considered a dog at General Motors; its declining profits and market share contributed to GM's decision to eliminate the brand. *Question marks,* sometimes called "problem children," have a small share of a growing market and generally require a large amount of cash to build market share. Mercedes mountain bikes, for example, are a question mark relative to Mercedes's automobile products.

The long-term health of an organization depends on having some products that generate cash (and provide acceptable profits) and others that use cash to support growth. Among the indicators of overall health are the size and vulnerability of the cash cows; the prospects for the stars, if any; and the number of question marks and dogs. Particular attention should be paid to those products with large cash appetites. Unless the company has an abundant cash flow, it cannot afford to sponsor many such products at one time. If resources, including debt capacity, are spread too thin, the company will end up with too many marginal products and will be unable to finance promising new-product entries or acquisitions in the future.

◉ Marketing Strategy

The next phase in strategic planning is the development of sound strategies for each functional area of the organization. Within the marketing area, a strategy is typically designed around two components: (1) the selection of a target market and (2) the creation of a marketing mix that will satisfy the needs of the chosen target market. A marketing strategy articulates the best use of the firm's resources and tactics to achieve its marketing objectives. It should also match customers' desire for value with the organization's distinctive capabilities. Internal capabilities should be used to maximize external opportunities. The planning process should be guided by a marketing-oriented culture and processes in the organization.[23] A comprehensive strategy involves a thorough search for information, the analysis of many potential courses of action, and the use of specific criteria for making decisions regarding strategy development and implementation.[24] When properly implemented, a good marketing strategy also enables a company to achieve its business-unit and corporate objectives. Although corporate, business-unit, and marketing strategies all overlap to some extent, the marketing strategy is the most detailed and specific of the three.

● **Target Market Selection.**   Selecting an appropriate target market may be the most important decision a company has to make in the planning process because the target market must be chosen before the organization can adapt its marketing mix to meet this market's needs and preferences. Defining the target market and developing an appropriate marketing mix are the keys to strategic success. Consider that there are 80 million consumers in "Generation Y" those born between 1977 and 1994 in the United States, and they command about $170 billion a year in spending power. These

MARKETING AROUND THE WORLD

DIGITAL REVOLUTION FORCES KODAK TO REFOCUS ITS STRATEGY

The Eastman Kodak Company was the pioneer in popular photography, bringing cameras and film into popular use starting as early as 1888. Kodak has long been an industry leader in film and related products, which in the past provided about 70 percent of the company's revenue. However, the twenty-first century brought the digital revolution to popular photography, and in 2003, digital cameras outsold film cameras for the first time. Worldwide, 69 million digital cameras were sold in 2004, with global sales reaching $16.5 billion. Kodak, like other traditional film manufacturers, has been forced to change its business strategy.

The change to digital photography poses many challenges for Kodak. The film industry traditionally provided high profit margins, while profit margins are typically low for digital products. Also, while Kodak is recognized as the brand name market leader in film, its brand name is not assured supremacy in the digital market. In addition, while consumers tend to take more pictures with digital cameras, they tend to make fewer prints. Photo printing historically has been a major source of revenue for Kodak.

Kodak's new digital strategy has forced the company to radically change its manufacturing plants, which necessitated the elimination of 15,000 jobs worldwide—about 20 percent of the company's total workforce. However, the company also had to build new facilities, which placed a huge demand on Kodak's cash reserves. Kodak spent $40 million on one plant alone, which will begin production of ribbon used in the company's digital photo kiosks by the end of 2005.

Several new products and features are at the core of Kodak's new digital strategy. One is the EasyShare digital camera line, which focuses on ease of use in transferring photos to computers and printers. Kodak has also started a campaign to place kiosks in markets around the world where consumers can make prints directly from their digital cameras. A new online service from Kodak, called Ofoto, will allow consumers to share pictures online and order prints from digital photos. Kodak's digital strategy also involves expansion into new international markets such as China. While Kodak has had a manufacturing presence in China for years, workers there were not able to afford to buy and use Kodak products. Now, China's growing middle class, estimated by some to comprise at least 100 million consumers, combined with the falling prices of digital products, has allowed the Chinese market for cameras and related products to grow tremendously.

How successful is the new digital strategy at Kodak? With the EasyShare digital camera, Kodak is aiming to be the number 1 seller of point-and-shoot digital cameras. By 2004, Kodak had almost closed the gap with Sony in digital camera sales, with Canon ranking third in shipments. Selling cameras is important because they generate sales of printers, paper, ink, and other high-margin accessories. Kodak's digital camera business is profitable, with many domestic and foreign opportunities from people who haven't made the switch to digital.[b]

"Ys" are skeptical and resourceful, and more comfortable with cell phones, instant messaging, and Internet shopping than any other market. This represents a significant opportunity for marketers willing to adapt their marketing mixes to satisfy the needs of this important target market.[25]

Accurate target market selection is crucial to productive marketing efforts. Products and even companies sometimes fail because marketers do not identify appropriate customer groups at whom to aim their efforts. If a company selects the wrong target market, all other marketing decisions will be a waste of time. Ford Motor, for

HIGH PERFORMANCE.
CHICKS DIG IT.

Introducing the new Schick® Quattro® for Women.™ With four ultra-thin blades, two conditioning strips and a sleek metal handle, it's a close, smooth, high-performance shave just for women. At last.

See what's just as good as his at www.QuattroForWomen.com

Schick
Quattro
FOR WOMEN™
THE POWER OF 4™

Competitive Advantage
Schick promotes four blades in a razor just for women as a competitive advantage.

example, experienced poor sales of its reintroduced Thunderbird, in part because its $35,000 to $40,000 price tag was too steep for the retro-styled convertible's target market of younger baby boomers and older Generation Xers. However, the Thunderbird could not compete with luxury high-performance vehicles like the BMW Z4 and the Audi TT, which offer greater horsepower and more features.[26] Organizations that try to be all things to all people rarely satisfy the needs of any customer group very well. An organization's management therefore should designate which customer groups the firm is trying to serve and gather adequate information about those customers. Identification and analysis of a target market provide a foundation on which the firm can develop a marketing mix.

When exploring possible target markets, marketing managers try to evaluate how entering them would affect the company's sales, costs, and profits. Marketing information should be organized to facilitate a focus on the chosen target customers. Accounting and information systems, for example, can be used to track revenues and costs by customer (or group of customers). In addition, managers and employees need to be rewarded for focusing on profitable customers. Teamwork skills can be developed with organizational structures that promote a customer orientation that allows quick responses to changes in the marketing environment.[27] Marketers should also assess whether the company has the resources to develop the right mix of product, price, promotion, and distribution to meet the needs of a particular target market. In addition, they determine if satisfying those needs is consistent with the firm's overall objectives and mission. When Amazon.com, the number 1 Internet bookseller, began selling electronics on its website, it made the decision that efforts to target this market would increase profits and be consistent with its objectives to be the largest online retailer. The size and number of competitors already marketing products in possible target markets are of concern as well.

● **Creating the Marketing Mix.** The selection of a target market serves as the basis for creating a marketing mix to satisfy the needs of that market. The decisions made in creating a marketing mix are only as good as the organization's understanding of the target market. This understanding typically comes from careful, in-depth research into the characteristics of the target market. Thus, while demographic information is important, the organization should also analyze customer needs, preferences, and behavior with respect to product design, pricing, distribution, and promotion. For example, Toyota's marketing research about Generation Y drivers found that they practically live in their cars, and many even keep a change of clothes handy in their vehicles. As a result of this research, Toyota designed its Scion as a "home on wheels," with a 15-volt outlet for plugging in a computer, reclining front seats for napping, and a powerful audio system for listening to MP3 music files, all for a $12,500 price tag.[28]

MARKETING LEADERS

CEREAL-ITY

Although cereal is usually purchased in supermarkets, David Roth and Rick Bacher chose to open the first all-cereal restaurant in Arizona State University's Student Union. The firm's first sit-down, café-style restaurant was opened in a retail district near the University of Pennsylvania. Why not, since more than 95 percent of all Americans like cereal! Roth and Bacher have plans for more cafés, targeting campuses, hospitals, train stations, arenas, airports, and office buildings across the United States.

Cereality: Cereal Bar and Cafe offers more than 30 varieties of brand name, hot and cold cereals, plus regular, flavored, or soy milk for about $2.95 per serving. In addition, the cafés offer toppings bars with more than 30 toppings such as cherries and marshmallows, as well as made-to-order cereal, yogurt blend smoothies ("Slurreali-

ties"), and homemade breakfast bars. The inspiration for the concept came from the cereal-loving characters on *Seinfeld*.

How does Cereality create an "out-of-home" atmosphere and retail experience to attract customers? First, the retail cafés are designed with kitchen-style cabinets, and employees dress in pajamas and robes to enhance the retail appeal. From Corn Chex to Wheaties, Cocoa Puffs to Lucky Charms and Cap'n Crunch, customers get good fast food, high in fiber and loaded with vitamins and minerals. Customers can even store their custom concoctions in an onsite computer for their next visit or they can purchase select mixes, such as "Devil Made Me Do It" consisting of Cocoa Puffs, Lucky Charms, chocolate-milk-flavored crystals, topped with malt balls. If you are perplexed as to how to combine the complex assortment of cereals and toppings, you can consult with an onsite "cereologist" who can make informed recommendations.

What helps fuel Cereality's success? With 65 percent repeat customers and the financial backing of Quaker, the company expects to be profitable in two to three years. For those who are "Koo Koo for Cocoa Puffs" or any other cereal, Cereality has your scoop. Cereality illustrates the idea that a new, innovative marketing strategy can be used to sell a product as simple and traditional as cereal.[c]

Marketing mix decisions should have two additional characteristics: consistency and flexibility. All marketing mix decisions should be consistent with the business-unit and corporate strategies. Such consistency allows the organization to achieve its objectives on all three levels of planning. Flexibility, on the other hand, permits the organization to alter the marketing mix in response to changes in market conditions, competition, and customer needs. Marketing strategy flexibility has a positive influence on organizational performance. Marketing orientation and strategic flexibility complement each other to help the organization manage varying environmental conditions.[29]

The concept of the four marketing mix variables has stood the test of time, providing marketers with a rich set of questions for the four most important decisions in strategic marketing. Consider the efforts of Harley-Davidson to improve its competitive position. The company worked to improve its product by eliminating oil leaks and other problems and set prices that customers consider fair. The firm used promotional tools to build a community of Harley riders renowned for their camaraderie. Harley-Davidson also fostered strong relationships with the dealers who distribute the company's motorcycles and related products and who reinforce the firm's promotional messages. Even the Internet has not altered the importance of finding the right marketing mix, although it has affected specific marketing mix elements. Amazon.com, for example, has exploited information technology to facilitate sales promotion by offering product feedback from other customers to help shoppers make a purchase decision.[30]

At the marketing mix level, a firm can detail how it will achieve a competitive advantage. To gain an advantage, the firm must do something better than its competition. In other words, its products must be of higher quality, its prices must be consistent with the level of quality (value), its distribution methods must be efficient and cost as little as possible, and its promotion must be more effective than the competition's. It is also important that the firm attempt to make these advantages sustainable. A **sustainable competitive advantage** is one that the competition cannot copy. Wal-Mart, for example, maintains a sustainable competitive advantage in toys over Toys 'R' Us because of its very efficient and low-cost distribution system. This advantage allows Wal-Mart to offer lower prices and resulted in Toys 'R' Us retreating from the toy segment of its business. Maintaining a sustainable competitive advantage requires flexibility in the marketing mix when facing uncertain competitive environments.[31]

sustainable competitive advantage An advantage that the competition cannot copy

Creating the Marketing Plan

marketing planning The process of assessing opportunities and resources, determining objectives, defining strategies, and establishing guidelines for implementation and control of the marketing program

A major concern in the strategic planning process is **marketing planning**, the systematic process of assessing marketing opportunities and resources, determining marketing objectives, defining marketing strategies, and establishing guidelines for implementation and control of the marketing program. The outcome of marketing planning is the development of a marketing plan. As noted earlier, a marketing plan is a written document that outlines and explains all the activities necessary to implement marketing strategies. It describes the firm's current position or situation, establishes marketing objectives for the product or product group, and specifies how the organization will attempt to achieve these objectives.

Developing a clear, well-written marketing plan, though time consuming, is important. The plan is the basis for internal communication among employees. It covers the assignment of responsibilities and tasks, as well as schedules for implementation. It presents objectives and specifies how resources are to be allocated to achieve those objectives. Finally, it helps marketing managers monitor and evaluate the performance of a marketing strategy.

Marketing planning and implementation are inextricably linked in successful companies. The marketing plan provides a framework to stimulate thinking and provide strategic direction, while implementation occurs as an adaptive response to day-to-day issues, opportunities, and unanticipated situations—for example, increasing interest rates or an economic slowdown—that cannot be incorporated into marketing plans. Implementation-related adaptations directly affect an organization's marketing orientation, rate of growth, and strategic effectiveness.[32]

Organizations use many different formats when devising marketing plans. Plans may be written for strategic business units, product lines, individual products or brands, or specific markets. Most plans share some common ground, however, by including many of the same components. Table 2.1 describes the major parts of a typical marketing plan.

Implementing Marketing Strategies

marketing implementation The process of putting marketing strategies into action

Marketing implementation is the process of executing marketing strategies. Although implementation is often neglected in favor of strategic planning, the implementation process itself can determine whether a marketing strategy succeeds. It is also impor-

Table 2.1   Components of the Marketing Plan

Plan Component	Component Summary	Highlights
Executive Summary	One- to two-page synopsis of the entire marketing plan	
Environmental Analysis	Information about the company's current situation with respect to the marketing environment	1. Assessment of marketing environment factors 2. Assessment of target market(s) 3. Assessment of current marketing objectives and performance
SWOT Analysis	Assessment of the organization's strengths, weaknesses, opportunities, and threats	1. Strengths 2. Weaknesses 3. Opportunities 4. Threats
Marketing Objectives	Specification of the firm's marketing objectives	1. Qualitative measures of what is to be accomplished
Marketing Strategies	Outline of how the firm will achieve its objectives	1. Target market(s) 2. Marketing mix
Marketing Implementation	Outline of how the firm will implement its marketing strategies	1. Marketing organization 2. Activities and responsibilities 3. Implementation timetable
Evaluation and Control	Explanation of how the firm will measure and evaluate the results of the implemented plan	1. Performance standards 2. Financial controls 3. Monitoring procedures (audits)

intended strategy   The strategy the company decides on during the planning phase

realized strategy   The strategy that actually takes place

tant to recognize that marketing strategies almost always turn out differently than expected. In essence, all organizations have two types of strategy: intended strategy and realized strategy.[33] The **intended strategy** is the strategy the organization decided on during the planning phase and wants to use, whereas the **realized strategy** is the strategy that actually takes place. The difference between the two is often the result of how the intended strategy is implemented. For example, Chrysler's PT Cruiser was originally marketed to young drivers, but the retro-styled vehicle ultimately proved more popular with their nostalgic baby boomer parents. Just 4 percent of the PT Cruiser's buyers were from the car's intended target market of drivers under 25.[34] The realized strategy, though not necessarily any better or worse than the intended strategy, often does not live up to planners' expectations.

◉ Approaches to Marketing Implementation

Just as organizations can achieve their goals by using different marketing strategies, they can implement their marketing strategies by using different approaches. In this section, we discuss two general approaches to marketing implementation: internal marketing and total quality management. Both approaches represent mindsets that marketing managers may adopt when organizing and planning marketing activities. These approaches are not mutually exclusive; indeed, many companies adopt both when designing marketing activities.

● **Internal Marketing.** External customers are the individuals who patronize a business—the familiar definition of customers—whereas internal customers are the company's employees. For implementation to succeed, the needs of both groups of customers must be addressed. If internal customers are not satisfied, it is likely that external customers will not be either. Thus, in addition to targeting marketing activities at external customers, a firm uses internal marketing to attract, motivate, and retain qualified internal customers by designing internal products (jobs) that satisfy their wants and needs. Internal marketing is a management philosophy that coordinates internal exchanges between the organization and its employees to achieve successful external exchanges between the organization and its customers.[35]

Generally speaking, internal marketing refers to the managerial actions necessary to make all members of the marketing organization understand and accept their respective roles in implementing the marketing strategy. Thus, marketing managers need to focus internally on employees as well as externally on customers.[36] This means everyone, from the president of the company down to the hourly workers on the shop floor, must understand the role they play in carrying out their jobs and implementing the marketing strategy. In short, anyone invested in the firm, both marketers and those who perform other functions, must recognize the tenet of customer orientation and service that underlies the marketing concept.

Like external marketing activities, internal marketing may involve market segmentation, product development, research, distribution, and even public relations and sales promotion.[37] For example, an organization may sponsor sales contests to inspire sales personnel to boost their selling efforts. This helps employees (and ultimately the company) to understand customers' needs and problems, teaches them valuable new skills, and heightens their enthusiasm for their regular jobs. In addition, many companies use planning sessions, websites, workshops, letters, formal reports, and personal conversations to ensure that employees comprehend the corporate mission, the organization's goals, and the marketing strategy. The ultimate results are more satisfied employees and improved customer relations.

● **Total Quality Management.** Quality has become a major concern in many organizations, particularly in light of intense foreign competition, more demanding customers, and poorer profit performance owing to reduced market share and higher costs. To regain a competitive edge, a number of firms have adopted a total quality management approach. Total quality management (TQM) is a philosophy that uniform commitment to quality in all areas of the organization will promote a culture that meets customers' perceptions of quality. Indeed, research has shown that both quality orientation and marketing orientation are sources of superior performance.[38] TQM involves coordinating efforts to improve customer satisfaction, increase employee participation and empowerment, form and strengthen supplier partnerships, and facilitate an organizational culture of continuous quality improvement. TQM requires continuous quality improvement and employee empowerment.

Continuous improvement of an organization's goods and services is built around the notion that quality is free; by contrast, *not* having high-quality goods and services can be very expensive, especially in terms of dissatisfied customers.[39] A

external customers Individuals who patronize a business

internal customers A company's employees

internal marketing Coordinating internal exchanges between the firm and its employees to achieve successful external exchanges between the firm and its customers

total quality management (TQM) A philosophy that uniform commitment to quality in all areas of the organization will promote a culture that meets customers' perceptions of quality

benchmarking Comparing the quality of the firm's goods, services, or processes with that of the best-performing competitors

primary tool of the continuous improvement process is benchmarking, the measuring and evaluating of the quality of the organization's goods, services, or processes as compared with the quality produced by the best-performing companies in the industry.[40] Benchmarking fosters organizational "learning" by helping firms identify and enhance valuable marketing capabilities.[41] It also helps an organization to assess where it stands competitively in its industry, thus giving it a goal to aim for over time.

Ultimately TQM succeeds or fails because of the efforts of the organization's employees. Thus, employee recruitment, selection, and training are critical to the success of marketing implementation. Empowerment gives customer-contact employees the authority and responsibility to make marketing decisions without seeking the approval of their supervisors.[42] Although employees at any level in an organization can be empowered to make decisions, empowerment is used most often at the front-line, where employees interact daily with customers.

empowerment Giving customer-contact employees authority and responsibility to make marketing decisions on their own

One characteristic of empowerment is that employees can perform their jobs the way they see fit, as long as their methods and outcomes are consistent with the organization's mission. However, empowering employees is successful only if the organization is guided by an overall corporate vision, shared goals, and a culture that supports the TQM effort.[43] For example, Ritz-Carlton hotels give each customer-contact employee permission to take care of customer needs as he or she observes issues. A great deal of time, effort, and patience are needed to develop and sustain a quality-oriented culture in an organization.

◉ Organizing Marketing Activities

The structure and relationships of a marketing unit, including lines of authority and responsibility that connect and coordinate individuals, strongly affect marketing activities. Firms that truly adopt the marketing concept develop a distinct organizational culture: a culture based on a shared set of beliefs that makes the customer's needs the pivotal point of the firm's decisions about strategy and operations.[44] Instead of developing products in a vacuum and then trying to persuade customers to purchase them, companies using the marketing concept begin with an orientation toward their customers' needs and desires. Recreational Equipment, Inc. (REI), for example, gives customers a chance to try out sporting goods in conditions that approximate how the products will actually be used. Customers can try out hiking boots on a simulated hiking path with a variety of trail surfaces and inclines or test climbing gear on an indoor climbing wall.

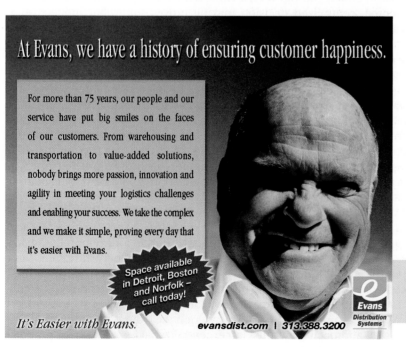

At Evans, we have a history of ensuring customer happiness.

For more than 75 years, our people and our service have put big smiles on the faces of our customers. From warehousing and transportation to value-added solutions, nobody brings more passion, innovation and agility in meeting your logistics challenges and enabling your success. We take the complex and we make it simple, proving every day that it's easier with Evans.

Space available in Detroit, Boston and Norfolk – call today!

It's Easier with Evans.   evansdist.com I 313.388.3200

Evans Distribution Systems

Customer Relationship Marketing
Evans Distribution Systems focuses on service in logistics solutions.

In addition, REI offers clinics to customers, such as "Rock Climbing Basics," "Basic Backpacking," and "REI's Outdoor School."[45]

If the marketing concept serves as a guiding philosophy, the marketing unit will be closely coordinated with other functional areas such as production, finance, and human resources. Marketing must interact with other departments in a number of key areas. It needs to work with manufacturing in determining the volume and variety of the company's products. Those in charge of production rely on marketers for accurate sales forecasts. Research and development departments depend heavily on information gathered by marketers about product features and benefits consumers desire. Decisions made by the physical distribution department hinge on information about the urgency of delivery schedules and cost/service tradeoffs. Information technology is often a crucial ingredient in effectively managing customer relationships, but successful customer relationship management (CRM) programs must include every department involved in customer relations.[46]

How effectively a firm's marketing management can plan and implement marketing strategies also depends on how the marketing unit is organized. Effective organizational planning can give the firm a competitive advantage. The organizational structure of a marketing department establishes the authority relationships among marketing personnel and specifies who is responsible for making certain decisions and performing particular activities. This internal structure helps direct marketing activities.

One crucial decision regarding structural authority is centralization versus decentralization. In a **centralized organization**, top-level managers delegate very little authority to lower levels. In a **decentralized organization**, decisionmaking authority is delegated as far down the chain of command as possible. The decision to centralize or decentralize the organization directly affects marketing. Most traditional organizations are highly centralized. In these organizations, most, if not all, marketing decisions are made at the top levels. However, as organizations become more marketing oriented, centralized decision making proves somewhat ineffective. In these organizations, decentralized authority allows the company to respond to customer needs more quickly.

No single approach to organizing a marketing unit works equally well in all businesses. The best approach or approaches depends on the number and diversity of the firm's products, the characteristics and needs of the people in the target market, and many other factors. A marketing unit can be organized according to (1) functions, (2) products, (3) regions, or (4) types of customers. Firms often use some combination of these organizational approaches. Product features may dictate that the marketing unit be structured by products, whereas customer characteristics require that it be organized by geographic region or by types of customers. By using more than one type of structure, a flexible marketing unit can develop and implement marketing plans to match customers' needs precisely.

● **Organizing by Functions.** Some marketing departments are organized by general marketing functions, such as marketing research, product development, distribution, sales, advertising, and customer relations. The personnel who direct these functions report directly to the top-level marketing executive. This structure is fairly common because it works well for some businesses with centralized marketing operations, such as Ford and General Motors. In more decentralized firms, such as grocery store chains, functional organization can cause serious coordination problems. However, the functional approach may suit a large, centralized company whose products and customers are neither numerous nor diverse.

centralized organization   A structure in which top management delegates little authority to levels below it

decentralized organization   A structure in which decision-making authority is delegated as far down the chain of command as possible

- **Organizing by Products.**   An organization that produces and markets diverse products may find the functional approach inadequate. The decisions and problems related to a single marketing function for one product may be quite different from those related to the same marketing function for another product. As a result, businesses that produce diverse products sometimes organize their marketing units according to product groups. Organizing by product groups gives a firm the flexibility to develop special marketing mixes for different products. Procter & Gamble, like many firms in the consumer packaged goods industry, is organized by product group. Although organizing by products allows a company to remain flexible, this approach can be rather expensive unless efficient categories of products are grouped together to reduce duplication and improve coordination of product management.

- **Organizing by Regions.**   A large company that markets products nationally (or internationally) may organize its marketing activities by geographic regions. Managers of marketing functions for each region report to their regional marketing manager; all the regional marketing managers report directly to the executive marketing manager. Frito-Lay, for example, is organized into four regional divisions, allowing the company to get closer to its customers and respond more quickly and efficiently to regional competitors. This form of organization is especially effective for a firm whose customers' characteristics and needs vary greatly from one region to another. Firms that try to penetrate the national market intensively may divide regions into subregions.

- **Organizing by Types of Customers.**   Sometimes a company's marketing unit is organized according to types of customers. This form of internal organization works well for a firm that has several groups of customers whose needs and problems differ significantly. For example, Bic may sell pens to large retail stores, wholesalers, and institutions. Retailers may want more rapid delivery of small shipments and more personal selling by the producer than do either wholesalers or institutional buyers. Because the marketing decisions and activities required for these two groups of customers differ considerably, the company may find it efficient to organize its marketing unit by types of customers.

◉ Controlling Marketing Activities

marketing control process
Establishing performance standards and trying to match actual performance to those standards

To achieve both marketing and general organizational objectives, marketing managers must effectively control marketing efforts. The marketing control process consists of establishing performance standards, evaluating actual performance by comparing it with established standards, and reducing the differences between desired and actual performance.

Although the control function is a fundamental management activity, it has received little attention in marketing. Organizations have both formal and informal control systems. The formal marketing control process, as mentioned before, involves performance standards, evaluation of actual performance, and corrective action to remedy shortfalls (see Figure 2.5). The informal control process involves self-control, social or group control, and cultural control through acceptance of a firm's value system. Which type of control system dominates depends on the environmental context of the firm.[47] We now discuss these steps in the formal control process and consider the major problems they involve.

- **Establishing Performance Standards.**   Planning and controlling are closely linked because plans include statements about what is to be accomplished. For purposes of control, these statements function as performance standards. A

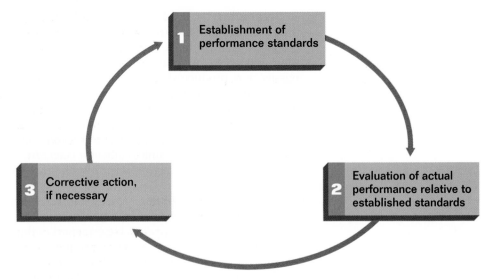

Figure 2.5
The Marketing Control Process

performance standard An expected level of performance

performance standard is an expected level of performance against which actual performance can be compared. A performance standard might be a reduction of customers' complaints by 20 percent, a monthly sales quota of $150,000, or a 10 percent increase per month in new-customer accounts. General Motors, for example, had a goal of selling 31,000 Corvette C6s in the United States in 2005.[48] As stated earlier, performance standards should be tied to organizational goals.

● **Evaluating Actual Performance.** To compare actual performance with performance standards, marketing managers must know what employees within the company are doing and have information about the activities of external organizations that provide the firm with marketing assistance. For example, Saturn, like many automakers, evaluates its product and service levels by how well it ranks on the J. D. Power and Associates Customer Service Index. In 2004, Saturn ranked number 6 among all automakers, down from number 2 in 2003, behind Lincoln, Buick, Infiniti, Cadillac, and Lexus.[49] Records of actual performance are compared with performance standards to determine whether and how much of a discrepancy exists. For example, if General Motors determines that only 25,000 Corvettes were sold in 2005, a discrepancy exists because its goal for the Corvette C6 was 31,000 vehicles sold annually.

Motivating Employees to Achieve Performance Standards
Accenture provides services to improve employee performance.

● **Taking Corrective Action.**   Marketing managers have several options for reducing a discrepancy between established performance standards and actual performance. They can take steps to improve actual performance, reduce or totally change the performance standard, or do both. At Wal-Mart, for example, managers implemented a strategy not to employ its usual steep discounts during the holiday shopping season, but when that strategy resulted in sluggish sales, they quickly slashed prices on key products and ran full-page newspaper ads to promote the lower prices.[50] To improve actual performance, the marketing manager may have to use better methods of motivating marketing personnel or find more effective techniques for coordinating marketing efforts.

● **Problems in Controlling Marketing Activities.**   In their efforts to control marketing activities, marketing managers frequently run into several problems. Often the information required to control marketing activities is unavailable or is available only at a high cost. Even though marketing controls should be flexible enough to allow for environmental changes, the frequency, intensity, and unpredictability of such changes may hamper control. In addition, the time lag between marketing activities and their results limits a marketing manager's ability to measure the effectiveness of specific marketing activities. This is especially true for all advertising activities.

Because marketing and other business activities overlap, marketing managers often cannot determine the precise costs of marketing activities. Without an accurate measure of marketing costs, it is difficult to know if the outcome of marketing activities is worth the expense. Finally, marketing control may be difficult because it is very hard to develop exact performance standards for marketing personnel.

CHAPTER REVIEW

❶ Describe the strategic planning process.

Through the process of strategic planning, a firm identifies or establishes its organizational mission and goals, corporate strategy, marketing goals and objectives, marketing strategy, and marketing plan. To achieve its marketing objectives, an organization must develop a marketing strategy, which includes identifying a target market and developing a plan of action for developing, distributing, promoting, and pricing products that meet the needs of customers in that target market. The strategic planning process ultimately yields the framework for a marketing plan, which is a written document that specifies the activities to be performed for implementing and controlling an organization's marketing activities.

❷ Explain how organizational resources and opportunities affect the planning process.

The marketing environment, including competitive, economic, political, legal and regulatory, technological, and sociocultural forces, can affect the resources a firm can acquire and create favorable opportunities. Resources may include core competencies, which are things that a firm does extremely well, sometimes so well that it gives the company an advantage over its competition. When the right combination of circumstances and timing permits an organization to take action toward reaching a particular target market, a market opportunity exists. Strategic windows are temporary periods of optimum fit between the key requirements of a market and the particular capabilities of a firm competing in that market. When a company matches a core competency to opportunities it has discovered in the marketplace, it is said to have a competitive advantage.

❸ Understand the role of the mission statement in strategic planning.

An organization's goals should be derived from its mission statement, which is a long-term view, or vision, of what the organization wants to become. A well-formulated mission statement helps give an organization a clear purpose and direction, distinguish it from competitors, provide direction for strategic planning, and foster a focus on customers. An organization's goals and objectives, which focus on the end results sought, guide the remainder of its planning efforts.

④ **Examine corporate, business-unit, and marketing strategies.**

Corporate strategy determines the means for utilizing resources in the areas of production, finance, research and development, human resources, and marketing to reach the organization's goals. Business-unit strategy focuses on strategic business units (SBUs)—divisions, product lines, or other profit centers within the parent company used to define areas for consideration in a specific strategic market plan. The Boston Consulting Group's market-growth/market-share matrix integrates a firm's products or SBUs into a single, overall matrix for evaluation to determine appropriate strategies for individual products and business units. Marketing strategies, the most detailed and specific of the three levels of strategy, are composed of two elements: the selection of a target market and the creation of a marketing mix that will satisfy the needs of the chosen target market. The selection of a target market serves as the basis for the creation of the marketing mix to satisfy the needs of that market. Marketing mix decisions should also be consistent with business-unit and corporate strategies and be flexible enough to respond to changes in market conditions, competition, and customer needs. Different elements of the marketing mix can be changed to accommodate different marketing strategies.

⑤ **Understand the process of creating the marketing plan.**

The outcome of marketing planning is the development of a marketing plan, which outlines all the activities necessary to implement marketing strategies. The plan fosters communication among employees, assigns responsibilities and schedules, specifies how resources are to be allocated to achieve objectives, and helps marketing managers monitor and evaluate the performance of a marketing strategy.

⑥ **Describe the marketing implementation process and the major approaches to marketing implementation.**

Marketing implementation is the process of executing marketing strategies. Marketing strategies do not always turn out as expected. Realized marketing strategies often differ from the intended strategies because of issues related to implementation. Proper implementation requires efficient organizational structures and effective control and evaluation.

One major approach to marketing implementation is internal marketing, a management philosophy that coordinates internal exchanges between the organization and its employees to achieve successful external exchanges between the organization and its customers. For strategy implementation to be successful, the needs of both internal and external customers must be met. Another approach is total quality management (TQM), which relies heavily on the talents of employees to improve continually the quality of the organization's goods and services.

Please visit the student website at www.prideferrell.com for ACE Self-Test questions that will help you prepare for exams.

KEY CONCEPTS

strategic planning
marketing strategy
marketing plan
core competencies
market opportunity
strategic windows
competitive advantage
SWOT analysis
mission statement

marketing objective
corporate strategy
strategic business unit (SBU)
market
market share
market-growth/market-share matrix

sustainable competitive advantage
marketing planning
marketing implementation
intended strategy
realized strategy
external customers
internal customers
internal marketing

total quality management (TQM)
benchmarking
empowerment
centralized organization
decentralized organization
marketing control process
performance standard

ISSUES FOR DISCUSSION AND REVIEW

1. Identify the major components of strategic planning, and explain how they are interrelated.

2. What are the two major parts of a marketing strategy?

3. What are some issues to consider in analyzing a firm's resources and opportunities? How do these issues affect marketing objectives and marketing strategy?

4. How important is the SWOT analysis to the marketing planning process?

5. How should organizations set marketing objectives?

6. Explain how an organization can create a competitive advantage at the corporate, business-unit, and marketing strategy levels.

7. Refer to question 6. How can an organization make its competitive advantages sustainable over time? How difficult is it to create sustainable competitive advantages?

8. What benefits do marketing managers gain from planning? Is planning necessary for long-run survival? Why or why not?

9. Why does an organization's intended strategy often differ from its realized strategy?

10. Why might an organization use multiple bases for organizing its marketing unit?

11. What are the major steps of the marketing control process?

MARKETING APPLICATIONS

1. Contact three organizations that appear to be successful. Talk with one of the managers or executives in the company, and ask if he or she would share with you the company's mission statement or organizational goals. Obtain as much information as possible about the statement and the organizational goals. Discuss how the statement matches the criteria outlined in the text.

2. Assume you own a new family-style restaurant that will open for business in the coming year. Formulate a long-term goal for the company, and then develop short-term goals that will assist you in achieving the long-term goal.

3. Amazon.com identified an opportunity to capitalize on a desire of many consumers to shop at home. This strategic window gave Amazon.com a very competitive position in a new market. Consider the opportunities that may be present in your city, region, or the United States as a whole. Identify a strategic window, and discuss how a company could take advantage of this opportunity. What kind of core competencies are necessary?

4. Marketing units may be organized according to functions, products, regions, or types of customers.

Describe how you would organize the marketing units for the following:
a. Toothpaste with whitener; toothpaste with extra-strong nicotine cleaners; toothpaste with bubble-gum flavor
b. National line offering all types of winter and summer sports clothing for men and women
c. Life insurance company that provides life, health, and disability insurance

ONLINE EXERCISE

5. Internet analysts have praised Sony's website as one of the best organized and most informative on the Internet. See why by accessing **www.sony.com.**
a. Based on the information provided at the website, describe Sony's strategic business units.
b. Based on your existing knowledge of Sony as an innovative leader in the consumer electronics industry, describe the company's primary competitive advantage. How does Sony's website support this competitive advantage?
c. Assess the quality and effectiveness of Sony's website. Specifically, perform a preliminary SWOT analysis comparing Sony's website with other high-quality websites you have visited.

VIDEO CASE

The Global Expansion of Subway Sandwich Shops

The Subway story began in 1965 when Dr. Peter Buck loaned Fred DeLuca $1,000 to open a sandwich shop in Bridgeport, Connecticut, which DeLuca hoped would help fund his college education. Since that time, Subway Sandwich Shops has grown to more than 22,350 restaurants in 78 countries, ranking it first in number of outlets in the United States and making its founder a billionaire. Subway remains a 100 percent franchised organization, and all Subway restaurants are individually owned and operated. Opening a Subway franchise store requires a $12,000 franchise fee to acquire the Subway name and $69,000 to $191,000 to build a store, depending on location. The company has been named the number 1 franchise opportunity in every category by *Entrepreneur* magazine, won a Restaurants and Institutions (Choice and Chains) Gold Award in the sandwich category, and received a *Nation's Restaurant News* Menu Masters Award for the best menu/line extension.

More than 3,700 Subway stores have opened outside the United States. Initially Subway did not seek to expand internationally, but when an entrepreneur from Bahrain approached the company about opening a sandwich shop on the Persian Gulf island, Subway decided to accept the challenge of global expansion. Expanding a food venture into a foreign country involves many issues, such as finding quality supplies for use in making sandwiches. Subway insists on a "gold standard of quality" when adapting to international environments. To properly train new franchise owners in locations around the globe, Subway has had to adapt to different languages and cultures. Initially international franchisees were trained in English in the United States; now the company has training facilities in Puerto Rico, Australia, and China.

When Subway enters a new market, the first issues it faces are building brand awareness and learning about potential customers' eating preferences and customs. Rather than second-guessing cultural differences, Subway attempts to adapt quickly to a new restaurant's immediate service area. In Israel, for example, the company omits pork items from its menu to avoid violating religious dietary customs. In countries where people are not used to eating sandwiches, Subway has had to educate consumers about this uniquely American product.

In addition to established markets, Subway is expanding into developing nations. In 2001, Subway opened its first restaurant in Croatia. Located in a 1929 building shared with the Capital Hotel Dubrovnik, the restaurant's entrance faces a busy pedestrian street with many shops and open terraces in one of the most beautiful areas of Zagreb. The franchisees chose to open a Subway because they wanted to offer Croatians something new and recognized an opportunity in the dynamic Croatian market to serve a need for affordable fast food with friendly service. The company plans to open additional shops in other major Croatian cities.

Subway also opened its first restaurant in Oman in 2001, where it joins other fast-food restaurants such as Fuddruckers, McDonald's, and Pizza Hut. Oman is one of the fastest-growing economies in the Middle East, with many international businesses in operation. Subway hopes to fill a void for those in the market for health-conscious food. In Oman, Subway offers its traditional menu and plans to include specialized items to meet local preferences.

France became the twenty-third European country to have a Subway sandwich shop in 2001. France's first Subway is situated near the Bastille in Paris. By day, the area's rich history attracts many tourists; at night, the area is renowned for its night life. The French are passionate about food, and they like submarine sandwiches. Subway believes the restaurant will fill a void for those looking for more health-conscious food choices. Although both Oman and France were slow to embrace the Subway concept, the brand's healthy attributes appear to have been a major factor in this expansion.

Subway had begun to position its menu as a more health-conscious alternative to fast food when it learned about the unique weight loss plan of one of its customers. Jared S. Fogle had been a regular Subway customer, but after reaching 425 pounds, he noticed the store's "7 under 6" promotion, which highlighted seven sandwiches with fewer than 6 grams of fat. Fogle began to eat a 6-inch turkey sandwich (no oil, mayo, condiments, or cheese) for lunch and a 12-inch veggie sandwich (no condiments or cheese) for dinner every day. His initial weight loss reinforced his commitment to eating more of the low-fat sandwiches. Jared Fogle ultimately lost 245 pounds on his

"Subway diet." His story turned Fogle into a national celebrity, with appearances on *Oprah* and NBC's *Today* with Katie Couric, an article in *USA Today,* and numerous TV commercials for Subway. Subway's TV ads make it clear that Fogle's diet was his own creation and may not be appropriate for everyone. Fogle, who has maintained his weight loss, continues to do TV commercials and make special appearances for Subway.

Subway has translated the Jared Fogle commercials into other languages for some international markets. The message is that Subway sandwiches are not only tasty but also healthier than offerings from competing fast-food restaurants. For example, one quarter-pound hamburger at another leading fast-food restaurant contains more than 62 grams of fat, whereas Subway offers a number of items with fewer than 10 grams of fat. Promoting the healthy benefits of its products has helped Subway develop its concept into the largest submarine sandwich franchise in the world.[51]

QUESTIONS FOR DISCUSSION
1. What market opportunities and strategic windows has Subway been able to capitalize on?
2. Based on the facts presented in the case, conduct a brief SWOT analysis for Subway.
3. Describe Subway's apparent marketing mix and target market.

The Marketing Environment, Social Responsibility, and Ethics

3

▶ Model Train Companies Collide

A legal dispute between Lionel LLC, the number 1 manufacturer of model trains, and MTH Electric Trains, Inc., the number 2 model train manufacturer, over designs for toy locomotives threatens the survival of both companies. MTH filed a lawsuit accusing Lionel of "misusing" stolen drawings and production schedules from one of MTH's subcontractors. The case has polarized a community of thousands of middle-aged men that prides itself on civility and a relaxed environment of collecting model trains.

Founded in 1900, Lionel was once the world's largest toy company, and it dominated the model train market for much of the twentieth century. However, its sales and business dwindled as Americans moved to the suburbs at a time when trains had become primarily an urban phenomenon, and teenagers turned to videogames and other toys. The lawsuit ultimately resulted in a judgment that Lionel had misused MTH's blueprints and thus damaged the number 2 firm's competitive position. Lionel, insisting it could not pay the $40.8 million judgment, filed for federal bankruptcy court protection.

The judgment against Lionel may have distracted the company from a major marketing opportunity that could have reinvigorated its customer base of model train collectors. That opportunity related to a "Polar Express" model licensed from Warner Brothers for the movie *The Polar Express*. The $249 train sets have sold out in many stores. However, the firm's bankruptcy filing is likely to prevent it from getting sufficient inventory into stores to take full advantage of the movie's publicity.

MTH executives believe that their company has been hurt badly by the Lionel's actions, forcing the rival company to slash its workforce by more than half over the past four years. MTH's revenues have declined from more than $60 million to $30 million, and if Lionel's bankruptcy precludes paying the $40.8 million judgment, MTH's financial situation will continue to worsen despite its reputation for providing customers with better-quality products than those offered by competitors. MTH has been an innovator in adding microchips that improve sound effects, synchronizing smoke-spouting, and introducing other special features.

The lawsuit has also sparked conflict among model train collectors and has the potential to stifle the entire train-collecting market. With the Polar Express train

OBJECTIVES

1 Recognize the importance of environmental scanning and analysis.

2 Explore the effects of competitive, economic, political, legal and regulatory, technological, and sociocultural factors on marketing strategies.

3 Understand the concept and dimensions of social responsibility.

4 Differentiate between ethics and social responsibility.

currently the best-selling item in Lionel's history, the lawsuit judgment threatens the survival of the company. It is obvious that improved leadership and compliance with ethical, legal, and regulatory requirements are necessary for survival and long-term success.[1]   ◀

To succeed in today's highly competitive marketplace, companies like Lionel and MTH must respond to changes in the marketing environment, particularly changes in customer desires and competitors' actions. Increasingly, success also requires that marketers act responsibly and ethically. Because recognizing and responding to such changes in the marketing environment are crucial to marketing success, this chapter explores in some detail the forces that contribute to these changes.

The first half of this chapter explores the competitive, economic, political, legal and regulatory, technological, and sociocultural forces that comprise the marketing environment. This discussion addresses the importance of scanning and analyzing the marketing environment as well as how each of these forces influences marketing strategy decisions. The second half of the chapter considers the role of social responsibility and ethics. These increasingly important forces raise several issues that pose threats and opportunities to marketers, such as the natural environment and consumerism.

The Marketing Environment

The marketing environment consists of external forces that directly or indirectly influence an organization's acquisition of inputs (human, financial, natural resources and raw materials, and information) and creation of outputs (goods, services, or ideas). As indicated in Chapter 1, the marketing environment includes six such forces: competitive, economic, political, legal and regulatory, technological, and sociocultural.

Whether fluctuating rapidly or slowly, environmental forces are always dynamic. Changes in the marketing environment create uncertainty, threats, and opportunities for marketers. Marketing managers who fail to recognize changes in environmental forces leave their firms unprepared to capitalize on marketing opportunities or cope with threats created by changes in the environment. Monitoring the environment is therefore crucial to an organization's survival and to the long-term achievement of its goals.

environmental scanning   The process of collecting information about forces in the marketing environment

To monitor changes in the marketing environment effectively, marketers engage in environmental scanning and analysis. **Environmental scanning** is the process of collecting information about forces in the marketing environment. Scanning involves observation; secondary sources such as business, trade, government, and Internet sources; and marketing research. The Internet has become a popular scanning tool because it makes data more accessible and allows companies to gather needed information quickly.

environmental analysis   The process of assessing and interpreting the information gathered through environmental scanning

Environmental analysis is the process of assessing and interpreting the information gathered through environmental scanning. A manager evaluates the information for accuracy, tries to resolve inconsistencies in the data, and, if warranted, assigns significance to the findings. By evaluating this information, the manager should be able to identify potential threats and opportunities linked to environmental changes.

Understanding the current state of the marketing environment and recognizing threats and opportunities arising from changes within it help companies with strate-

Sticking it on a Honda LEV would be redundant.

When it comes to a clean environment, there's nothing wrong with repetition. Fortunately, we're not alone in this thinking. Over one million Hondas have been sold with low-emission technology, and every car we build is now LEV-rated or cleaner.

This commitment to clean air took off in 1975. That's when our Civic CVCC became the first car without a catalytic converter to comply with the emission standards set by the 1970 U.S. Clean Air Act. However, we didn't stop there. In 1995, we voluntarily reduced smog-contributing hydrocarbons by 70% and became the first to meet California's strict Low-Emission Vehicle (LEV) standard. And in 2001, the Civic became an Ultra-Low-Emission Vehicle (ULEV).

Not too long ago, the California Air Resources Board issued an even stricter emissions standard for 2004: Super-Ultra-Low-Emission Vehicle (SULEV). Naturally, we've decided there's no reason to wait. The 2000 Accord SULEV' was the first gasoline-powered vehicle to meet this standard. And our dedication to the environment was recently recognized by the Union of Concerned Scientists, who named Honda Motor Co. the cleanest car company in the world.'

HONDA
The power of dreams.

Responding to Environmental Forces Honda is producing hybrid (gas and electric) powered cars in response to both customer demand and its own desire to exceed regulatory agency emissions standards.

gic planning. In particular, they can help marketing managers assess the performance of current marketing efforts and develop future marketing strategies.

◉ Responding to the Marketing Environment

Marketing managers take two general approaches to environmental forces: accepting them as uncontrollable or attempting to influence and shape them.[2] An organization that views environmental forces as uncontrollable remains passive and reactive toward the environment. Instead of trying to influence forces in the environment, its marketing managers adjust current marketing strategies to environmental changes. They approach with caution market opportunities discovered through environmental scanning and analysis. On the other hand, marketing managers who believe that environmental forces can be shaped adopt a more proactive approach. For example, if a market is blocked by traditional environmental constraints, proactive marketing managers may apply economic, psychological, political, and promotional skills to gain access to and operate within it. Once they identify what is blocking a market opportunity, they assess the power of the various parties involved and develop strategies to overcome the obstructing environmental forces. Microsoft and Intel, for example, have responded to political, legal, and regulatory concerns about their power in the computer industry by communicating the value of their competitive approaches to various publics. The computer giants contend that their competitive success results in superior products for their customers.

A proactive approach can be constructive and bring desired results. To exert influence on environmental forces, marketing managers seek to identify market opportunities or to extract greater benefits relative to costs from existing market opportunities. Political action is another way to affect environmental forces. The pharmaceutical industry, for example, has lobbied very effectively for fewer restrictions on prescription drug marketing. However, managers must recognize that there are limits on how much environmental forces can be shaped. Microsoft, for example, can take a proactive approach because of its financial resources and the highly visible image of its founder, Bill Gates. Although an organization may be able to influence legislation through lobbying, it is unlikely that a single organization can significantly increase the national birthrate or move the economy from recession to prosperity.

◉ Competitive Forces

Few firms, if any, operate free of competition. In fact, for most products, customers have many alternatives from which to choose. For example, the five best-selling soft drinks in 2003 were Coke Classic, Pepsi-Cola, Diet Coke, Mountain Dew, and Sprite.[3] Thus, when marketing managers define the target market(s) their firm will serve, they simultaneously establish a set of competitors.[4] The number of firms that supply a product may affect the strength of competitors. When just one or a few firms control supply, competitive factors exert a different sort of influence on marketing activities than when many competitors exist.

Competition
Wendy's, as a fast-food competitor, monitors the actions of other fast-food chains and adjusts its strategy accordingly.

Marketers need to monitor the actions of major competitors to determine what specific strategies competitors are using and how those strategies affect their own. Price is one of the marketing strategy variables that most competitors monitor. When Frontier or Southwest Airlines lowers the fare on a route, most major airlines attempt to match the price. Monitoring guides marketers in developing competitive advantages and aids them in adjusting current marketing strategies and planning new ones.

In monitoring competition, it is not enough to analyze available information; the firm must develop a system for gathering ongoing information about competitors. Understanding the market and what customers want, as well as what the competition is providing, will assist in maintaining a marketing orientation.[5] Information about competitors allows marketing managers to assess the performance of their own marketing efforts and to recognize the strengths and weaknesses in their own marketing strategies. Data about market shares, product movement, sales volume, and expenditure levels can be useful. However, accurate information on these matters is often difficult to obtain. We explore how marketers collect and organize such data in Chapter 6.

◉ Economic Forces

Economic forces in the marketing environment influence both marketers' and customers' decisions and activities. In this section, we examine the effects of buying power and willingness to spend, as well as general economic conditions.

● Buying Power and Willingness to Spend.

The strength of a person's **buying power** (see definition on p. 55) depends on economic conditions and the size of the resources—money, goods, and services that can be traded in an exchange—that enable the individual to make purchases. The major financial sources of buying power are income, credit, and wealth.

SPORT UTILITY? DEFINE SPORT.

Wealth
Companies such as Hummer target wealthy customers.

buying power   Resources, such as money, goods, and services, that can be traded in an exchange

disposable income   After-tax income

discretionary income   Disposable income available for spending and saving after an individual has purchased the basic necessities of food, clothing, and shelter

willingness to spend   An inclination to buy because of expected satisfaction from a product, influenced by the ability to buy and numerous psychological and social forces

For an individual, *income* is the amount of money received through wages, rents, investments, pensions, and subsidy payments for a given period, such as a month or a year. Normally this money is allocated among taxes, spending for goods and services, and savings.

Marketers are most interested in the amount of money left after payment of taxes because this **disposable income** is used for spending or saving. Because disposable income is a ready source of buying power, the total amount available in a nation is important to marketers. Several factors determine the size of total disposable income, including the total amount of income—which is affected by wage levels, the rate of unemployment, interest rates, and dividend rates—and the number and amount of taxes. Disposable income that is available for spending and saving after an individual has purchased the basic necessities of food, clothing, and shelter is called **discretionary income**. People use discretionary income to purchase entertainment, vacations, automobiles, education, pets, furniture, appliances, and so on. Changes in total discretionary income affect sales of these products, especially automobiles, furniture, large appliances, and other costly durable goods.

Credit is also important because it enables people to spend future income now or in the near future. However, credit increases current buying power at the expense of future buying power. Several factors determine whether people use or forgo credit. Interest rates affect buyers' decisions to use credit, especially for expensive purchases such as homes, appliances, and automobiles. When interest rates are low, the total cost of automobiles and houses becomes more affordable. In contrast, when interest rates are high, consumers are more likely to delay buying such expensive items. Use of credit is also affected by credit terms, such as size of the down payment and amount and number of monthly payments.

Wealth is the accumulation of past income, natural resources, and financial resources. It exists in many forms, including cash, securities, savings accounts, jewelry, and real estate. The significance of wealth to marketers is that as people become wealthier, they gain buying power in three ways: they can use their wealth to make current purchases, to generate income, and to acquire large amounts of credit.

People's **willingness to spend**—their inclination to buy because of expected satisfaction from a product—is related, to some degree, to their ability to buy. That is, people are sometimes more willing to buy if they have the buying power. However, several other elements also influence willingness to spend. Some elements affect specific products; others influence spending in general. A product's price and value influence almost all of us. Rolex watches, for example, appeal to customers who are willing to spend more for fine timepieces even when lower-priced watches are readily available. Increasingly, middle-class consumers seem more willing to spend on high-price luxury products, such as Coach purses, BMW automobiles, and spa vacations, although they may shop for discounted groceries and other basic products at Wal-Mart and Target in order to afford the upscale products.[6] The amount of satisfaction received from a product already owned may also influence customers' desire to buy other products. Satisfaction depends not only on the quality of the currently owned product but also on numerous psychological and social forces. The American Customer Satisfaction Index, computed by the National Quality Research Center at the University of Michigan (see Figure 3.1), offers an indicator of customer satisfaction with a wide variety of businesses. Among other things, the index suggests that if customers become more dissatisfied, they may curtail their overall spending, which could stifle economic growth.[7] Other factors that affect customers' general willingness to spend are expectations about future employment, income levels, prices, family size, and general economic conditions.

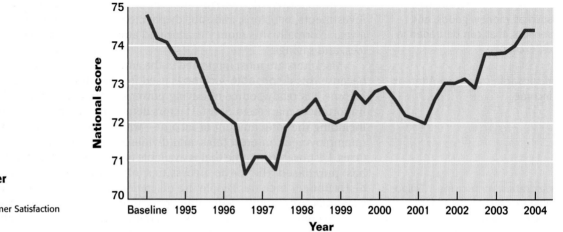

Figure 3.1
American Customer
Satisfaction Index
Source: American Customer Satisfaction
Index, August 24, 2004,
www.theasci.org/.

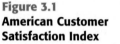

business cycle   A pattern of economic fluctuations that has four stages: prosperity, recession, depression, and recovery

● **Economic Conditions.**   The overall state of the economy fluctuates in all countries. Changes in general economic conditions affect (and are affected by) supply and demand, buying power, willingness to spend, consumer expenditure levels, and the intensity of competitive behavior. Therefore, current economic conditions and changes in the economy have a broad impact on the success of organizations' marketing strategies.

Fluctuations in the economy follow a general pattern, often referred to as the **business cycle**. In the traditional view, the business cycle consists of four stages: prosperity, recession, depression, and recovery. During *prosperity,* unemployment is low and total income is relatively high. Assuming a low inflation rate, this combination ensures high buying power. During a *recession,* however, unemployment rises while total buying power declines. Pessimism accompanying a recession often stifles both consumer and business spending. A prolonged recession may become a *depression,* a period in which unemployment is extremely high, wages are very low, total disposable income is at a minimum, and consumers lack confidence in the economy. During *recovery,* the economy moves from depression or recession to prosperity. During this period, high unemployment begins to decline, total disposable income increases, and the economic gloom that reduced consumers' willingness to buy subsides. Both the ability and willingness to buy increase.

The business cycle can influence the success of marketing strategies. In the prosperity stage, for example, marketers may expand their product offerings to take advantage of increased buying power. They may be able to capture a larger market share by intensifying distribution and promotion efforts. In times of recession or depression, when buying power decreases, many customers may become more price conscious and seek more basic, functional products. During economic downturns, a company should focus its efforts on determining precisely what functions buyers want and ensure that these functions are available in its product offerings. Promotional efforts should emphasize value and utility. Some firms make the mistake of drastically reducing their marketing efforts during a recession, harming their ability to compete. During a recession in Mexico, the Coca-Cola Company chose to continue its marketing efforts while most of its competitors cut back or even abandoned the Mexican market. By maintaining a high level of marketing, Coca-Cola increased its share of the Mexican market by 4 to 6 percent.[8] During recovery periods, marketers should maintain as much flexibility in their marketing strategies as possible so that they can make the needed adjustments.

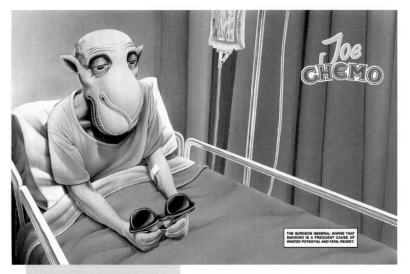

Combating Cigarette Company Advertising The Foundation for a Smokefree America's youth-oriented website NoTobacco.org promotes the health dangers associated with tobacco use.

Political Forces

Political, legal, and regulatory forces of the marketing environment are closely inter-related. Legislation is enacted, legal decisions are interpreted by courts, and regulatory agencies are created and operated, for the most part, by elected or appointed officials. Legislation and regulations (or their lack) reflect the current political outlook. Consequently the political forces of the marketing environment have the potential to influence marketing decisions and strategies.

Reactive marketers view political forces as beyond their control and simply adjust to conditions arising from those forces. Some firms are more proactive, however, and seek to influence the political process. In some cases, organizations publicly protest the actions of legislative bodies. More often, organizations help elect to political offices individuals who regard them positively. Much of this help is in the form of campaign contributions. Although laws restrict direct corporate contributions to campaign funds, corporate influence may be channeled into campaigns through executives' or stockholders' personal contributions. Such actions violate the spirit of corporate campaign contribution laws. Companies can also participate in the political process through lobbying to persuade public and/or government officials to favor a particular position in decision making. Many companies concerned about the threat of legislation or regulation that may negatively affect their operations employ lobbyists to communicate their concerns to elected officials. Microsoft, for example, established a Washington office with a staff of 14 lobbyists and spent $4.6 million to persuade federal officials that breaking up the company for antitrust violations would harm the computer industry and the U.S. economy.[9]

Legal and Regulatory Forces

A number of federal laws influence marketing decisions and activities. Table 3.1 lists some of the most significant pieces of legislation. Regulatory agencies and self-regulatory forces also affect marketing efforts.

● **Regulatory Agencies.** Federal regulatory agencies influence many marketing activities, including product development, pricing, packaging, advertising, personal selling, and distribution. Usually these bodies have the power to enforce specific laws, as well as some discretion in establishing operating rules and regulations to guide certain types of industry practices.

Of all the federal regulatory units, the **Federal Trade Commission (FTC)** influences marketing activities most. Although the FTC regulates a variety of business practices, it allocates considerable resources to curbing false advertising, misleading pricing, and deceptive packaging and labeling. When it receives a complaint or otherwise has reason to believe a firm is violating a law, the commission issues a complaint stating that the business is in violation. For example, the FTC filed suit against Transdermal Products International Marketing Corporation for making unsubstantiated claims that its skin patch enables buyers to achieve substantial weight loss. The FTC's

Federal Trade Commission (FTC) An agency that regulates a variety of business practices and curbs false advertising, misleading pricing, and deceptive packaging and labeling

Table 3.1   Major Federal Laws Affecting Marketing Decisions

Act (Date Enacted)	Purpose
Procompetitive Legislation	
Sherman Antitrust Act (1890)	Prohibits contracts, combinations, or conspiracies to restrain trade; calls monopolizing or attempting to monopolize a misdemeanor offense.
Clayton Act (1914)	Prohibits specific practices such as price discrimination, exclusive dealer arrangements, and stock acquisitions in which the effect may notably lessen competition or tend to create a monopoly.
Federal Trade Commission Act (1914)	Created the Federal Trade Commission; also gives the FTC investigatory powers to be used in preventing unfair methods of competition.
Robinson-Patman Act (1936)	Prohibits price discrimination that lessens competition among wholesalers or retailers; prohibits producers from giving disproportionate services of facilities to large buyers.
Wheeler-Lea Act (1938)	Prohibits unfair and deceptive acts and practices, regardless of whether competition is injured; places advertising of foods and drugs under the jurisdiction of the FTC.
Celler-Kefauver Act (1950)	Prohibits any corporation engaged in commerce from acquiring the whole or any part of the stock or other share of the capital assets of another corporation when the effect substantially lessens competition or tends to create a monopoly.
Consumer Goods Pricing Act (1975)	Prohibits the use of price maintenance agreements among manufacturers and resellers in interstate commerce.
Antitrust Improvements Act (1976)	Requires large corporations to inform federal regulators of prospective mergers or acquisitions so that they can be studied for any possible violations of the law.
Consumer Protection Legislation	
Pure Food and Drug Act (1906)	Prohibits the adulteration and mislabeling of food and drug products; established the Food and Drug Administration.
Fair Packaging and Labeling Act (1966)	Makes illegal the unfair or deceptive packaging or labeling of consumer products.
Consumer Product Safety Act (1972)	Established the Consumer Product Safety Commission; protects the public against unreasonable risk of injury and death associated with products.
Magnuson-Moss Warranty (FTC) Act (1975)	Provides for minimum disclosure standards for written consumer product warranties; defines minimum consent standards for written warranties; allows the FTC to prescribe interpretive rules in policy statements regarding unfair or deceptive practices.
Nutrition Labeling and Education Act (1990)	Prohibits exaggerated health claims and requires all processed foods to contain labels showing nutritional information.
Telephone Consumer Protection Act (1991)	Establishes procedures to avoid unwanted telephone solicitations; prohibits marketers from using automated telephone dialing system or an artificial or prerecorded voice to certain telephone lines.
Children's Online Privacy Protection Act (2000)	Regulates the online collection of personally identifiable information (name, mailing address, e-mail address, hobbies, interests, or information collected through cookies) from children under age 13.
Do Not Call Implementation Act (2003)	Directs the FCC and the FTC to coordinate so that their rules are consistent regarding telemarketing call practices including the Do Not Call Registry and other lists, as well as call abandonment.

Table 3.1   Continued

Act (Date Enacted)	Purpose
Trademark and Copyright Protection Legislation	
Lanham Act (1946)	Provides protections and regulation of brand names, brand marks, trade names, and trademarks.
Trademark Law Revision Act (1988)	Amends the Lanham Act to allow brands not yet introduced to be protected through registration with the Patent and Trademark Office.
Federal Trademark Dilution Act (1995)	Gives trademark owners the right to protect trademarks and requires relinquishment of names that match or parallel existing trademarks.
Digital Millennium Copyright Act (1998)	Refines copyright laws to protect digital versions of copyrighted materials, including music and movies.

complaint further charged the patch's manufacturer with falsely claiming that a key ingredient in the patch had been approved by the Food and Drug Administration and providing retailers with deceptive marketing materials.[10] If a company continues the questionable practice, the FTC can issue a cease-and-desist order demanding that the business stop doing whatever caused the complaint. The firm can appeal to the federal courts to have the order rescinded. However, the FTC can seek civil penalties in court, up to a maximum penalty of $10,000 a day for each infraction if a cease-and-desist order is violated. The commission can require companies to run corrective advertising in response to previous ads considered misleading. The FTC also assists businesses in complying with laws, and it evaluates new marketing methods every year.

Unlike the FTC, other regulatory units are limited to dealing with specific products, services, or business activities. For example, the Food and Drug Administration (FDA) enforces regulations prohibiting the sale and distribution of adulterated, misbranded, or hazardous food and drug products. The Consumer Product Safety Commission (CPSC) ensures compliance with the Consumer Product Safety Act and protects the public from unreasonable risk of injury from any consumer product not covered by other regulatory agencies.

In addition, all states, as well as many cities and towns, have regulatory agencies that enforce laws and regulations regarding marketing practices within their states or municipalities. State and local regulatory agencies try not to establish regulations that conflict with those of federal regulatory agencies. They generally enforce laws dealing with the production and sale of particular goods and services. Utility, insurance, financial, and liquor industries are commonly regulated by state agencies. Among these agencies' targets are misleading advertising and pricing.

● **Self-Regulation.** In an attempt to be good corporate citizens and to prevent government intervention, some businesses try to regulate themselves. Several trade associations have developed self-regulatory programs. Though these programs are not a direct outgrowth of laws, many were established to stop or stall the development of laws and governmental regulatory groups that would regulate the associations' marketing practices.

Better Business Bureau A local, nongovernmental regulatory agency, supported by the local businesses, that helps settle problems between customers and specific business firms

Perhaps the best-known nongovernmental regulatory group is the **Better Business Bureau**, a local regulatory agency supported by local businesses. More than 140 bureaus help settle problems between consumers and specific business firms. Each bureau also acts to preserve good business practices in a locality, although it usually lacks strong enforcement tools for dealing with firms that employ questionable practices. When a firm continues to violate what the Better Business Bureau believes to be good business practices, the bureau warns consumers through local newspapers or broadcast media. If the offending organization is a BBB member, it may be expelled from the local bureau.

The National Advertising Division (NAD) of the Council of Better Business Bureaus operates a self-regulatory program that investigates claims regarding alleged deceptive advertising. For example, after NAD received a complaint from Pfizer, a pharmaceutical firm, it asked the FTC and the FDA to further investigate whether Aventis's advertising for its Allegra prescription allergy medicine misleads consumers about the effectiveness of Pfizer's Benadryl, an over-the-counter allergy medicine.[11]

Another self-regulatory entity, the **National Advertising Review Board (NARB)**, considers cases in which an advertiser challenges issues raised by the National Advertising Division about an advertisement. Cases are reviewed by panels drawn from NARB members representing advertisers, agencies, and the public. The NARB, sponsored by the Council of Better Business Bureaus and three advertising trade organizations, has no official enforcement powers. However, if a firm refuses to comply with its decision, the NARB may publicize the questionable practice and file a complaint with the FTC.

National Advertising Review Board (NARB) A self-regulatory unit that considers challenges to issues raised by the National Advertising Division (an arm of the Council of Better Business Bureaus) about an advertisement

technology The application of knowledge and tools to solve problems and perform tasks more efficiently

Self-regulatory programs have several advantages over governmental laws and regulatory agencies. Establishment and implementation are usually less expensive, and guidelines are generally more realistic and operational. In addition, effective self-regulatory programs reduce the need to expand government bureaucracy. However, these programs have several limitations. When a trade association creates a set of industry guidelines for its members, nonmember firms do not have to abide by them. Furthermore, many self-regulatory programs lack the tools or authority to enforce guidelines. Finally, guidelines in self-regulatory programs are often less strict than those established by government agencies.

◉ Technological Forces

The word *technology* brings to mind scientific advances such as computers, spacecraft, DVDs, cell phones, cloning, lifestyle drugs, the Internet, radio frequency identification tags, and more. Such developments make it possible for marketers to operate ever more efficiently and to provide an exciting array of products for consumers. However, even though these innovations are outgrowths of technology, none of them *is* technology. Technology is the application of knowledge and tools to solve problems and perform tasks more efficiently.

The Impact of Technology
Diverse companies like Dell, through research and development, create technologically advanced products.

Technology determines how we, as members of society, satisfy our physiological needs. In various ways and to varying degrees, eating and drinking habits, sleeping patterns, sexual activities, health care, and work performance are all influenced by both existing technology and advances in technology. Because of the technological revolution in communications, for example, marketers can now reach vast numbers of people more efficiently through a variety of media. Electronic mail, voice mail, cell phones, PDAs, and computers help marketers interact with customers, make appointments, and handle last-minute orders or cancellations. Some companies, including Ford Motor, are even abandoning the use of traditional wired telephones in favor of exclusive use of cell phones in the workplace.[12]

Personal computers are now in more than 60 percent of all U.S. consumers' homes, and millions of them include broadband or modems for accessing the Internet. Although we enjoy the benefits of communicating through the Internet, we are increasingly concerned about protecting our privacy and intellectual property. Likewise, although health and medical research has created new drugs that save lives, cloning and genetically modified foods have become controversial issues to many segments of society. In various ways and to varying degrees, home environments, health care, leisure, and work performance are all influenced by both current technology and advances in technology.[13]

The effects of technology relate to such characteristics as dynamics, reach, and the self-sustaining nature of technological progress. The *dynamics* of technology involve the constant change that often challenges the structures of social institutions, including social relationships, the legal system, religion, education, business, and leisure. *Reach* refers to the broad nature of technology as it moves through society. Consider the impact of cellular and wireless telephones. The ability to call from almost any location has many benefits but also has negative side effects, including increases in traffic accidents, increased noise pollution, and fears about potential health risks.[14] The *self-sustaining* nature of technology relates to the fact that technology acts as a catalyst to spur even faster development. As new innovations are introduced, they stimulate the need for more advancements to facilitate further development. For example, the Internet has created the need for ever-faster transmission of signals through broadband connections such as high-speed phone lines (DSL), satellites, and cable. Technology initiates a change process that creates new opportunities for new technologies in every industry segment or personal life experience that it touches. At some point, there is even a multiplier effect that causes still greater demand for more change to improve performance.[15]

It is important for firms to determine when a technology is changing an industry and to define the strategic influence of the new technology. For example, wireless devices in use today include radios, cell phones, notebook computers, TVs, pagers,

MARKETING ENTREPRENEURS

Jo Waldron

THE BUSINESS: Able Planet Inc.

FOUNDED: 2003

SUCCESS: Allows the 34+ million Americans and 500 million worldwide with mild to severe to profound hearing loss to communicate through telecommunications

After a lifetime of silence and 18 months of research and development, Jo Waldron, together with veteran audiologist Dr. Joan Burleigh, invented a revolutionary micro technology called Able Planet. Smaller than a grain of rice, the micro-tech device is easily integrated into any phone, wireless, cell, or handheld set and interacts directly with the T-coil component of hearing aids. Instead of using a magnetic field to amplify the sound, Able Planet creates audio within the hearing aid itself, allowing users to hear up to 80 percent better. Soon we could be seeing Able Planet technology in devices such as stereos, computers, TVs, and more. Jo Waldron saw a need, helped create a new product, and has established effective distribution.[a]

and car keys. In the future, most long-distance communication will likely occur through fiber optics, and short-distance communication will be wireless.[16] To remain competitive, companies today must keep up with and adapt to these technological advances. Through a procedure known as *technology assessment,* managers try to foresee the effects of new products and processes on their firm's operation, on other business organizations, and on society in general. With information obtained through a technology assessment, management tries to estimate whether benefits of adopting a specific technology outweigh costs to the firm and to society at large. The degree to which a business is technologically based also influences its managers' response to technology.

◉ Sociocultural Forces

sociocultural forces The influences in a society and its culture(s) that change people's attitudes, beliefs, norms, customs, and lifestyles

Sociocultural forces are the influences in a society and its culture(s) that bring about changes in attitudes, beliefs, norms, customs, and lifestyles. Profoundly affecting how people live, these forces help determine what, where, how, and when people buy products. Like the other environmental forces, sociocultural forces present marketers with both challenges and opportunities.

Changes in a population's demographic characteristics—age, gender, race, ethnicity, marital and parental status, income, and education—have a significant bearing on relationships and individual behavior. These shifts lead to changes in how people live and ultimately in their consumption of products such as food, clothing, housing, transportation, communication, recreation, education, and health services. We look at a few of the changes in demographics and diversity that are affecting marketing activities.

One demographic change affecting the marketplace is the increasing proportion of older consumers. According to the U.S. Bureau of the Census, the number of people age 65 and older is expected to more than double by the year 2050, reaching 87 million.[17] Consequently, marketers can expect significant increases in the demand for health-care services, recreation, tourism, retirement housing, and selected skin-care products.

The United States is entering another baby boom, with nearly 82 million Americans age 19 or younger. The new baby boom represents 28 percent of the total population; the original baby boomers, born between 1946 and 1964, account for nearly 31 percent.[18] The children of the original baby boomers differ from one another radically in terms of race, living arrangements, and socioeconomic class. Thus, the newest baby boom is much more diverse than previous generations.

Another noteworthy population trend is the increasingly multicultural nature of U.S. society. The number of immigrants into the United States has steadily risen dur-

Kashi® Heart to Heart® is powered by six natural antioxidants, including grape seed and green tea. They actually fight free radicals to help keep arteries healthy. And our whole grain, honey-toasted oats are low in sodium to help promote healthy blood pressure. No other cereal has more for your heart. Guard dog on duty at kashi.com/heart.

Sociocultural Forces
Kashi Cereal Company has success appealing to the health conscious consumer.

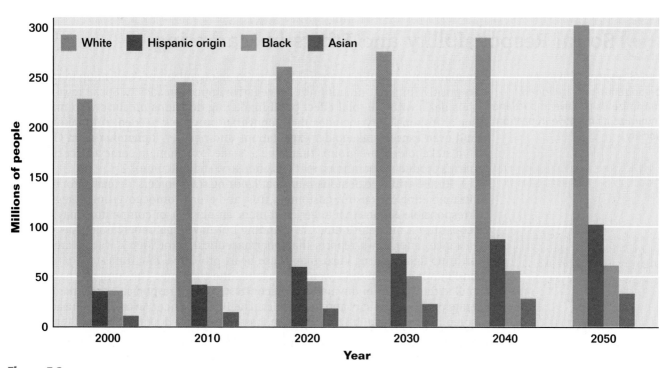

Figure 3.2
U.S. Population Projections by Race

Source: U.S. Bureau of the Census, *Statistical Abstract of the United States*, 2003 (Washington, DC: Government Printing Office, 2004), p. 18.

The U.S. government compiles a staggering amount of demographic data on U.S. citizens that marketers can mine for information about specific target markets. Much of this information is available in the annual *Statistical Abstract of the United States* (http://www.census.gov/statab/www/).

ing the last 40 years. By the turn of the twentieth century, the U.S. population had shifted from one dominated by whites to one consisting largely of three racial and ethnic groups: whites, blacks, and Hispanics. The U.S. government projects that by the year 2025, nearly 66 million Hispanics, 48 million blacks, and 20 million Asians will call the United States home.[19] Figure 3.2 depicts how experts believe the U.S. population will change over the next 50 years.

Changes in social and cultural values have dramatically influenced people's needs and desires for products. Although these values do not shift overnight, they do change at varying speeds. Marketers try to monitor these changes because knowing this information can equip them to predict changes in consumers' needs for products at least in the near future.

People today are more concerned about the foods they eat and thus are choosing more low-fat, organic, natural, and healthy products. Marketers have responded with a proliferation of foods, beverages, and exercise products that fit this new lifestyle. Celestial Seasonings, for example, has developed herbal teas like Mama Bear's Cold Care, with echinacea and mint, and Sleepytime, with chamomile.

The major source of values is the family. Values about the permanence of marriage are changing, but children remain important. Marketers have responded with safer, upscale baby gear and supplies, children's electronics, and family entertainment products. Marketers are also aiming more marketing efforts directly at children because children often play pivotal roles in purchasing decisions. Children and family values are also a factor in the trend toward more eat-out and takeout meals. Busy families are usually eager to spend less time in the kitchen and more time together enjoying themselves.[20] Beneficiaries of this trend have primarily been fast-food and casual restaurants like McDonald's, Taco Bell, Boston Market, and Applebee's, but most grocery stores have added more ready-to-cook or ready-to-serve meal components to meet the needs of busy customers. In Texas, H.E.B.'s Central Market grocery stores also offer eat-in gourmet cafés.

⟳ Social Responsibility and Ethics in Marketing

social responsibility   An organization's obligation to maximize its positive impact and minimize its negative impact on society

In marketing, social responsibility refers to an organization's obligation to maximize its positive impact and minimize its negative impact on society. Social responsibility thus deals with the total effect of all marketing decisions on society. In marketing, social responsibility includes the managerial processes needed to monitor, satisfy, and even exceed stakeholder expectations and needs.[21] Remember from Chapter 1 that stakeholders are groups that have a "stake," or claim, in some aspect of a company's products, operations, markets, industry, and outcomes.

Ample evidence demonstrates that ignoring stakeholders' demands for responsible marketing can destroy customers' trust and even prompt government regulations. Irresponsible actions that anger customers, employees, or competitors may not only jeopardize a marketer's financial standing but have legal repercussions as well. For instance, after news reports that pharmaceutical giant Merck was aware that its arthritis-fighting drug Vioxx may cause heart problems, the firm's stock plummeted and hundreds of lawsuits were filed against the company. The company had already pulled the drug from the market.[22] In contrast, socially responsible activities can generate positive publicity and boost sales. The Breast Cancer Awareness Crusade sponsored by Avon Products, for example, has helped raised nearly $300 million to fund community-based breast cancer education and early detection services. Hundreds of stories about Avon's efforts have appeared in major media, which contributed to an increase in company sales.[23]

Socially responsible efforts like Avon's have a positive impact on local communities; at the same time, they indirectly help the sponsoring organization by attracting goodwill, publicity, and potential customers and employees. Thus, while social responsibility is certainly a positive concept in itself, most organizations embrace it in the expectation of indirect long-term benefits.

marketing citizenship   The adoption of a strategic focus for fulfilling the economic, legal, ethical, and philanthropic social responsibilities expected by stakeholders

Socially responsible organizations strive for marketing citizenship by adopting a strategic focus for fulfilling the economic, legal, ethical, and philanthropic social responsibilities that their stakeholders expect of them. Companies that consider the diverse perspectives of stakeholders in their daily operations and strategic planning are said to have a *stakeholder orientation,* an important element of corporate citizenship.[24] A stakeholder orientation in marketing goes beyond customers, competitors, and regulators to include understanding and addressing the needs of all stakeholders, including communities and special-interest groups. As a result, organizations are now under pressure to undertake initiatives that demonstrate a balanced perspective on stakeholder interests.[25] Ford Motor, for example, has secured stakeholder input on a number of issues including human rights and climate change.[26] As Figure 3.3 shows, the economic, legal, ethical, and philanthropic dimensions of social responsibility can be viewed as a pyramid.[27] The economic and legal aspects have long been acknowledged, but philanthropic and ethical issues have gained recognition more recently.

◉ Economic Dimension

At the most basic level, all companies have an economic responsibility to be profitable so they can provide a return on investment to their owners and investors, create jobs for the community, and contribute goods and services to the economy. How organizations relate to stockholders, employees, competitors, customers, the community, and the natural environment affects the economy.

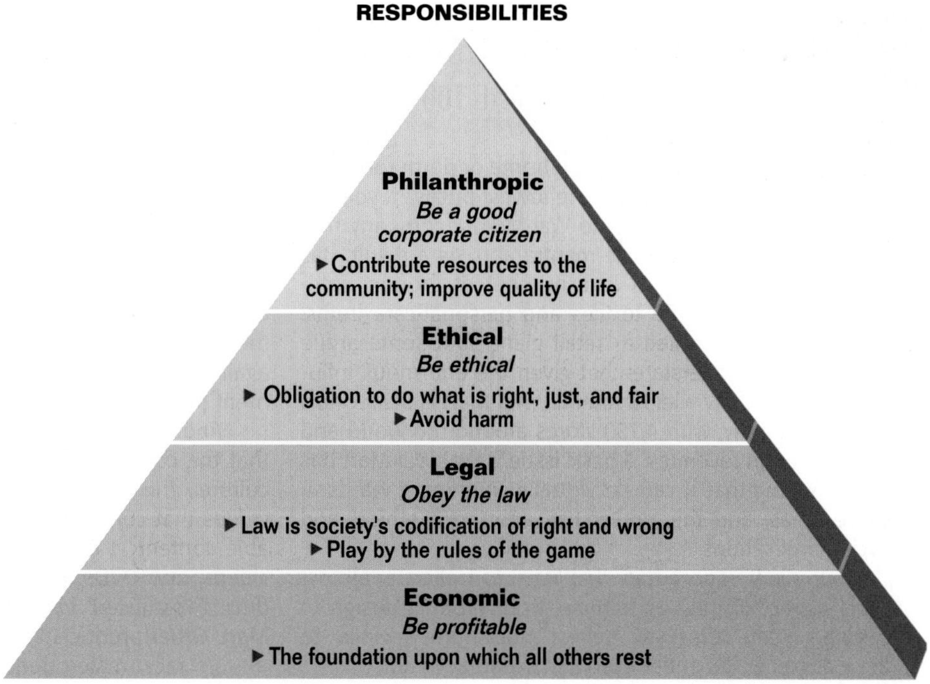

RESPONSIBILITIES

Figure 3.3
The Pyramid of Corporate Social Responsibility

Source: *Reprinted from Business Horizons,* July/August 1991, Archie B. Carroll, "The Pyramid of Corporate Social Responsibility: Toward the Moral Management of Organizational Stakeholders," adaptation of Figure 3, p. 42. Reprinted from *Business Horizons,* July/August 1991. Copyright © 1991 with permission from Elsevier Science.

Marketers also have an economic responsibility to compete fairly. Size frequently gives companies an advantage over others. Large firms can often generate economies of scale that allow them to put smaller firms out of business. Consequently, small companies and even whole communities may resist the efforts of firms like Wal-Mart, Home Depot, and Best Buy to open stores in their vicinity. These firms can operate at such low costs that small, local firms often cannot compete. Such issues create concerns about social responsibility for organizations, communities, and consumers.

◉ Legal Dimension

Marketers are also expected, of course, to obey laws and regulations. The efforts of elected representatives and special-interest groups to promote responsible corporate behavior have resulted in laws and regulations designed to keep U.S. companies' actions within the range of acceptable conduct. When marketers engage in deceptive practices to advance their own interests over those of others, charges of fraud may result. In general, fraud is any purposeful communication that deceives, manipulates, or conceals facts in order to create a false impression. It is considered a crime, and convictions may result in fines, imprisonment, or both. Fraud costs U.S. companies more than $600 billion a year; the average company loses about 6 percent of total revenues to fraud and abuses committed by its own employees.[28]

When customers, interest groups, or businesses become outraged over what they perceive as irresponsibility on the part of a marketing organization, they may urge their legislators to draft new legislation to regulate the behavior, or they may engage in litigation to force the organization to "play by the rules." For example, Shirley Slesinger Lasswell, whose late husband acquired the rights to Winnie the Pooh and his friends from creator A. A. Milne in 1930, filed a lawsuit against the Walt Disney Company over merchandising rights to the characters. Although Lasswell

ETHICS AND SOCIAL ISSUES

HAS WAL-MART BECOME TOO POWERFUL?

When you shop for items for your home or dorm room, do you consider where to go for the lowest prices? If you do, chances are you have gone to Wal-Mart, a company that lives strictly by its low-price mantra and, as a result, has come to dominate sales in a number of product categories, including home textiles and personal-care items. Wal-Mart is often called a "retail giant," but some argue that this is an understatement given the enormous influence the company wields. After all, Wal-Mart is the world's largest company, with 4,750 stores around the world and $245 billion in revenues. A basic issue is that Wal-Mart has grown so big that it can do virtually anything it wants in some areas, and this power has enormous ethical and social implications.

Suppliers report that Wal-Mart can dictate almost every aspect of their operations—from product design to pricing—in an effort to deliver maximum savings to the consumer. To meet Wal-Mart's demands for lower prices, some suppliers have been forced to lay off employees or move operations to countries where production costs are lower. Companies that balk risk finding their products quickly replaced by a competitor's on Wal-Mart's lucrative shelves.

Wal-Mart stores can also wreak havoc on businesses and workers in communities. Soon after Wal-Mart entered the Oklahoma City market, 30 supermarkets closed their doors. The demise of local businesses means the loss of jobs, and although Wal-Mart may rehire some workers, Wal-Mart employees generally receive lower pay and fewer benefits than workers at other retail stores. Because of the vast Wal-Mart workforce, these policies have been blamed for driving down retail wages across the United States. Other employment issues that have ethical and legal ramifications are allegations that Wal-Mart workers have been forced to work "off the clock" and that the company has discriminated against women and minorities in promotions to management positions.

Another consequence of Wal-Mart's dominance is that the company has become, in essence, an arbiter of culture. The retailer is famous for banning music and videos that contain what the company deems objectionable content; it is nonetheless the biggest seller of CDs, videos, and DVDs. Record companies are therefore producing "sanitized" versions of albums exclusively for Wal-Mart. Other products Wal-Mart has chosen not to sell are racy, male-oriented magazines, such as *Maxim,* and the "morning-after" pill that prevents unwanted pregnancy.

Unquestionably there are benefits to Wal-Mart's philosophy: it has compelled suppliers to concentrate on efficiency and to innovate with new products (to avoid fewer competitors), revived more than one floundering company, and directly and indirectly saved consumers an estimated $100 billion a year. But the real costs of Wal-Mart's philosophy have yet to be tallied up. As the world's largest company, it must accept the public scrutiny and social responsibilities that come with the territory.[b]

granted rights to use the characters to Walt Disney, she contended that the company cheated her and her family out of millions of dollars in royalties on video sales for two decades. Disney asserted that video sales were not specified in its agreement with Lasswell and declined to pay her a percentage of those sales. A California superior court judge dismissed the case after 13 years of proceedings, effectively siding with Disney in the dispute.[29]

ETHICS AND SOCIAL ISSUES

WILL THE MARTHA STEWART BRAND SURVIVE A LEGAL SCANDAL?

Martha Stewart is arguably America's most famous home-maker and one of its richest women executives. She left a position as a successful stockbroker to start a gourmet-food shop and catering business that evolved into Martha Stewart Living Omnimedia Inc. (MSLO), a company with interests in publishing, television, merchandising, electronic commerce, and related international partnerships. In 2001, however, Stewart became the center of head-lines, speculations, and eventually a much-publicized trial on criminal charges related to her sales of 4,000 shares of ImClone stock one day before that firm's stock price plummeted.

In June 2003, a federal grand jury indicted Stewart on charges of securities fraud, conspiracy, making false state-ments, and obstruction of justice, but not insider trading. The 41-page indictment alleged that she lied to federal investigators about the stock sale, attempted to cover up her activities, and defrauded Martha Stewart Living Omnimedia shareholders by misleading them about the gravity of the situation and thereby keeping the stock price from falling. The indictment further accused Stewart of deleting a computer log of the telephone message from her broker informing her that he thought ImClone's stock "was going to start trading downward." Ms. Stewart pleaded "not guilty" to all charges, but she resigned her positions as chief executive officer and chairman of the board of Martha Stewart Living Omnimedia hours after the indictment.

In February 2004, the judge threw out the most seri-ous of the charges against Stewart—securities fraud. How-ever, just one week later, a jury convicted Stewart on four remaining charges of making false statements and con-spiracy to obstruct justice. She was sentenced to serve five months in jail and five months in home detention. She finished her jail time in March 2005.

When Martha Stewart was convicted, her company shares hit a low of $10.86 per share and her flagship tel-evision show, *Martha Stewart Living,* was taken off the air. After a few months in prison, her company's share price had nearly tripled, increasing the value of her per-sonal stake to $827 million from $318 million. She signed a contract with Mark Burnett, the producer of *Survivor,* to appear in a reality television program, and she is planning a daily live-audience program for NBC beginning in Fall 2005. Although many were skeptical that the Martha Stewart brand could survive the scandal, Stewart herself says, "I think that my role is Walt Disney. There are very few brands that were really started by a person, with a person's name, that have survived as nicely as that."[c]

◉ Ethical Dimension

marketing ethics Principles and standards that define acceptable marketing conduct as determined by various stakeholders

Economic and legal responsibilities are the most basic levels of social responsibility for a good reason: failure to consider them may mean that a marketer is not around long enough to engage in ethical or philanthropic activities. Beyond these dimensions is **marketing ethics**, principles and standards that define acceptable conduct in mar-keting as determined by various stakeholders, including the public, government reg-ulators, private-interest groups, consumers, industry, and the organization itself. The most basic of these principles have been codified as laws and regulations to encour-age marketers to conform to society's expectations of conduct. However, marketing ethics goes beyond legal issues. Ethical marketing decisions foster trust, which helps to build long-term marketing relationships.

Marketers should be aware of ethical standards for acceptable conduct from sev-eral viewpoints—company, industry, government, customers, special-interest groups, and society at large. When marketing activities deviate from accepted standards, the exchange process can break down, resulting in customer dissatisfaction, lack of trust, and lawsuits. In fact, 78 percent of consumers say that they avoid certain businesses or products because of negative perceptions about them.[30] Arthur Andersen, for example, was convicted of obstruction of justice for destroying sensitive documents related to the Enron scandal. As a result of questions surrounding the auditor's role in

Enron's collapse, the venerable firm lost numerous major accounting clients, was suspended from filing audit results with the Securities and Exchange Commission, and ultimately went out of business.[31] When managers engage in activities that deviate from accepted principles, continued marketing exchanges become difficult, if not impossible. The best time to deal with such problems is during the strategic planning process, not after major problems materialize.

ethical issue An identifiable problem, situation, or opportunity requiring a choice among several actions that must be elevated as right or wrong, ethical or unethical

An **ethical issue** is an identifiable problem, situation, or opportunity requiring an individual or organization to choose from among several actions that must be evaluated as right or wrong, ethical or unethical. Any time an activity causes marketing managers or customers in their target market to feel manipulated or cheated, a marketing ethical issue exists, regardless of the legality of that activity. For example, organizational objectives that call for increased profits or market share may pressure marketers to bring an unsafe product to market, even if they know the product is unsafe. Such pressures represent ethical issues and may have led managers from Global Crossing, which operates a fiber-optic network, to create fake transactions when buying and selling network capacity and thus boost revenues. Although the telecommunications firm denied the allegations, the company is under federal investigation and has declared bankruptcy.[32] Regardless of the reasons behind specific ethical issues, marketers must be able to identify these issues and decide how to resolve them. To do so requires familiarity with the many kinds of ethical issues that may arise in marketing. Research suggests that the greater the consequences associated with an issue, the more likely it will be recognized as an ethics issue and the more important it will be to making an ethical decision.[33] Some examples of ethical issues related to product, promotion, price, and distribution (the marketing mix) appear in Table 3.2.

Table 3.2	**Ethical Issues in Marketing**
Issue Category	**Examples**
Product	• Failing to disclose risks associated with a product
	• Failing to disclose information about a product's function, value, or use
	• Failing to disclose information about changes in the nature, quality, or size of a product
Distribution	• Failing to live up to the rights and responsibilities associated with specific intermediary roles
	• Manipulating product availability
	• Using coercion to force other intermediaries to behave in a certain way
Promotion	• False or misleading advertising
	• Using manipulative or deceptive sales promotions, tactics, and publicity
	• Offering or accepting bribes in personal selling situations
Pricing	• Price fixing
	• Predatory pricing
	• Failing to disclose the full price of a purchase

◉ Philanthropic Dimension

cause-related marketing   The practice of linking products to a particular social cause on an ongoing or short-term basis

strategic philanthropy   The synergistic use of organizational core competencies and resources to address key stakeholders' interests and achieve both organizational and social benefits

At the top of the pyramid are philanthropic responsibilities. These responsibilities, which go beyond marketing ethics, are not required of a company, but they promote human welfare or goodwill, as do the economic, legal, and ethical dimensions of social responsibility. That many companies have demonstrated philanthropic responsibility is evidenced by the nearly $13.5 billion in annual corporate donations and contributions to environmental and social causes.[34] For example, after a tsunami killed more than 250,000 people and devastated parts of South Asia and Indonesia, many corporations—including 3M, American Express, Bristol-Myers Squibb, Coca-Cola, Kellogg, Kimberly-Clark, Microsoft, Nike, Starbucks, and many more—donated millions of dollars in cash, supplies, equipment, food, and medicine to help victims. Other firms matched employee donations or provided mechanisms through which customers could donate funds and supplies to help with relief efforts.[35] Even small companies participate in philanthropy through donations and volunteer support of local causes and national charities, such as the Red Cross and the United Way.

More companies than ever are adopting a strategic approach to corporate philanthropy. Many firms link their products to a particular social cause on an ongoing or short-term basis, a practice known as cause-related marketing. American Express, for example, donated $1 to the St. Jude's Research Hospital for every American Express Gift Card purchased.[36] Some companies are beginning to extend the concept of corporate philanthropy beyond financial contributions by adopting a strategic philanthropy approach, the synergistic use of organizational core competencies and resources to address key stakeholders' interests and achieve both organizational and social benefits. Strategic philanthropy involves employees, organizational resources and expertise, and the ability to link these assets to the concerns of key stakeholders, including employees, customers, suppliers, and social needs. Strategic philanthropy involves both financial and nonfinancial contributions to stakeholders (employee time, goods and services, and company technology and equipment, as well as facilities), but it also benefits the company. Home Depot, for example, has been progressive in aligning its expertise and resources to address community needs. Its relationship with Habitat for Humanity gives employees a chance to improve their skills and bring direct

If you think it works on salad, try it on steak or chicken. That's the sweetest cross-dressing.

Paul Newman

Shockingly, the whole idea of using my salad dressing for something other than salad is not as unnatural as it seems. I use virgin olive oil and herbs and spices so fresh you'll be tempted to slap them. But don't. Instead, turn a humble chicken breast into "poulet," dress up a London broil, and give the slightest shrimp a superiority complex. So next time you're having doubts about dinner, just cross-dress.

NEWMAN'S OWN®

Paul Newman donates all his profits to charity. Over $175 million donated by Paul Newman to thousands of charities since 1982.

For great recipe ideas, visit www.newmansown.com
©2005 Newman's Own Inc.

Strategic Philanthropy
Paul Newman donates all of his profits to charity, over $200 million to thousands of charities since 1982.

TECHNOLOGY IN ACTION

Trout survive only in the cleanest waters. With breakthroughs in water purification, Hitachi is using technology to sustain this precious natural resource. And to address other important environmental issues, including the reduction of atmospheric CO_2. From advanced battery solutions and electric vehicle management systems to energy-saving solutions for buildings and manufacturing facilities, Hitachi believes in a simple idea: that technology is never for its own sake but for the benefit of all. As an innovative global solutions company, Hitachi touches your life in so many ways. To understand how Hitachi is benefiting your world, visit us on the Web and see technology in action.

HITACHI
Inspire the Next

www.hitachi.com/inspire/

Green Marketing
Hitachi addresses environmental issues such as the reduction of atmospheric CO_2 in efforts to preserve the environment.

Green marketing The specific development, pricing, promotion, and distribution of products that do not harm the natural environment

consumerism Organized efforts by individuals, groups, and organizations to protect consumers' rights

knowledge back into the workplace to benefit customers. It also enhances Home Depot's image of expertise as the "do-it-yourself" center.[37]

Although social responsibility may seem to be an abstract ideal, managers make decisions related to social responsibility every day. To be successful, a business must determine what customers, government regulators, and competitors, as well as society in general, want or expect in terms of social responsibility. Two major categories of social responsibility issues are the natural environment and consumerism.

● **The Natural Environment.** One of the more common ways marketers demonstrate social responsibility is through programs designed to protect and preserve the natural environment. A recent survey indicates that 83.5 percent of *Fortune* 500 companies have a written environmental policy, 74.7 percent engage in recycling activities, and 69.7 percent have made investments in waste reduction efforts.[38] Many companies are making contributions to environmental protection organizations, sponsoring and participating in clean-up events, promoting recycling, retooling manufacturing processes to minimize waste and pollution, and generally reevaluating the effects of their products on the natural environment.

Green marketing refers to the specific development, pricing, promotion, and distribution of products that do not harm the natural environment. Toyota and Honda, for example, have succeeded in marketing "hybrid" cars that use electric motors to augment their internal-combustion engines, improving the vehicles' fuel economy without reducing their power. Ford Motor introduced the first hybrid SUV, the Escape, in 2004.[39] Herman Miller, Inc., has replaced several of the glues and finishes used in its ergonomic furniture with more environmentally friendly compounds and chooses woods carefully to ensure they come from renewable sources. The company also encourages its suppliers to switch to reusable packaging materials and designs its production facilities to function as efficiently as possible, thereby reducing waste and energy use.[40] On the other hand, some stakeholders, including customers, try to dictate companies' use of responsible suppliers and sources of products.[41] Aveda, for example, requires magazines in which it places ads for its earth-friendly personal-care products to be printed on recycled paper. The requirement has already prompted *Natural Health* to switch to recycled paper.[42]

● **Consumerism.** **Consumerism** consists of organized efforts by individuals, groups, and organizations seeking to protect consumers' rights. The movement's major forces are individual consumer advocates, consumer organizations and other interest groups, consumer education, and consumer laws.

To achieve their objectives, consumers and their advocates write letters or send e-mails to companies, lobby government agencies, broadcast public-service announcements, and boycott companies whose activities they deem irresponsible.

Some consumers choose to boycott firms and products out of a desire to support a cause and make a difference.[43] For example, several organizations evaluate children's products for safety, often announcing dangerous products before Christmas so parents can avoid them. Other actions by the consumer movement have resulted in seat belts and air bags in automobiles, dolphin-safe tuna, the banning of unsafe three-wheel motorized vehicles, and numerous laws regulating product safety and information.

Also of great importance to the consumer movement are four basic rights spelled out in a "consumer bill of rights" drafted by President John F. Kennedy. These rights include the right to safety, the right to be informed, the right to choose, and the right to be heard. Ensuring consumers' *right to safety* means marketers have an obligation not to market a product that they know could harm consumers. This right can be extended to imply that all products must be safe for their intended use, include thorough and explicit instructions for proper and safe use, and have been tested to ensure reliability and quality. Consumers' *right to be informed* means consumers should have access to and the opportunity to review all relevant information about a product before buying it. Many laws require specific labeling on product packaging to satisfy this right. In addition, labels on alcoholic and tobacco products inform consumers that these products may cause illness and other problems. The *right to choose* means consumers should have access to a variety of products and services at competitive prices. They should also be assured of satisfactory quality and service at a fair price. Activities that reduce competition among businesses in an industry might jeopardize this right. The *right to be heard* ensures that consumers' interests will receive full and sympathetic consideration in the formulation of government policy. The right to be heard also promises consumers fair treatment when they complain to marketers about products. This right benefits marketers too because when consumers complain about a product, the manufacturer can use this information to modify the product and make it more satisfying.

◉ Incorporating Social Responsibility and Ethics into Strategic Planning

Although the concepts of marketing ethics and social responsibility are often used interchangeably, it is important to distinguish between them. *Ethics* relates to individual and group decisions—judgments about what is right or wrong in a particular decisionmaking situation—whereas *social responsibility* deals with the total effect of marketing decisions on society. The two concepts are interrelated because a company that supports socially responsible decisions and adheres to a code of conduct is likely to have a positive effect on society. Because ethics and social responsibility programs can be profitable as well, an increasing number of companies are incorporating them into their overall strategic market planning.

Without compliance programs and uniform standards and policies regarding conduct, it is hard for a company's employees to determine what conduct is acceptable within the company. In the absence of such programs and standards, employees will generally make decisions based on their observations of how their peers and superiors behave. To improve ethics, many organizations have developed **codes of conduct** (also called *codes of ethics*) consisting of formalized rules and standards that describe what the company expects of its employees. The New York Stock Exchange now requires every member corporation to have a formal code of conduct. Codes of conduct promote ethical behavior by reducing opportunities for unethical behavior; employees know both what is expected of them and what kind of punishment they face if they violate the rules. Codes help marketers deal with ethical issues or dilemmas that develop in daily operations by prescribing or limiting specific activities.

codes of conduct Formalized rules and standards that describe what the company expects of its employees

Codes of conduct often include general ethical values such as honesty and integrity, general legal compliance, discreditable or harmful acts, and obligations related to social values, as well as more marketing-specific issues such as confidentiality, responsibilities to employers and clients, obligations to the profession, independence and objectivity, and marketing-specific legal and technical compliance issues.[44]

It is important that companies consistently enforce standards and impose penalties or punishment on those who violate codes of conduct. In addition, the company must take reasonable steps in response to violations of standards and, as appropriate, revise the compliance program to diminish the likelihood of future misconduct. To succeed, a compliance program must be viewed as part of the overall marketing strategy implementation. If ethics officers and other executives are not committed to the principles and initiatives of marketing ethics and social responsibility, the program's effectiveness will be in question.

Increasing evidence indicates that being ethical and socially responsible pays off. Research suggests that a relationship exists between a marketing orientation and an organizational climate that supports marketing ethics and social responsibility. This relationship implies that being ethically and socially concerned is consistent with meeting the demands of customers and other stakeholders. By encouraging their employees to understand their markets, companies can help them respond to stakeholders' demands.[45]

A survey of marketing managers found a direct association between corporate social responsibility and profits.[46] In a survey of consumers, nearly 90 percent indicated that when quality, service, and price are equal among competitors, they would be more likely to buy from the company with the best reputation for social responsibility. In addition, 54 percent would pay more for a product that supported a cause they care about, 66 percent would switch brands to support such a cause, and 62 percent would switch retailers.[47]

Thus, recognition is growing that the long-term value of conducting business in a socially responsible manner far outweighs short-term costs.[48] Companies that fail to develop strategies and programs to incorporate ethics and social responsibility into their organizational culture may pay the price with poor marketing performance and the potential costs of legal violations, civil litigation, and damaging publicity when questionable activities are made public.

CHAPTER REVIEW

1 Recognize the importance of environmental scanning and analysis.

Environmental scanning is the process of collecting information about the forces in the marketing environment; environmental analysis is the process of assessing and interpreting the information gathered through environmental scanning. This information helps marketing managers minimize uncertainty and threats, and capitalize on opportunities presented by environmental factors.

2 Explore the effects of competitive, economic, political, legal and regulatory, technological, and sociocultural factors on marketing strategies.

Marketers need to monitor the actions of competitors to determine what strategies competitors are using and how those strategies affect their own. Economic conditions influence consumers' buying power and willingness to spend. Legislation is enacted, legal decisions are interpreted by courts, and regulatory agencies are created and operated by elected or appointed officials. Marketers can also choose to regulate themselves. Technology determines how members of society satisfy needs and wants and helps improve the quality of life. Sociocultural forces are the influences in a society that bring about changes in attitudes, beliefs, norms, customs, and lifestyles. Changes in any of these forces can create opportunities and threats for marketers.

3 Understand the concept and dimensions of social responsibility.

Social responsibility refers to an organization's obligation to maximize its positive impact and minimize its negative impact on society. At the most basic level, companies have an economic responsibility to be profitable so they can provide a return on investment to their stockholders, create jobs for the community, and contribute goods and services to the economy. Marketers are also expected to obey laws and regulations. Marketing ethics refers to principles and standards that define acceptable conduct in marketing as determined by various stakeholders. Philanthropic responsibilities go beyond marketing ethics; they are not required of a company but promote human welfare or goodwill.

4 Differentiate between ethics and social responsibility.

Whereas social responsibility is achieved by balancing the interests of all stakeholders in an organization, ethics relates to acceptable standards of conduct in making individual and group decisions.

Please visit the student website at www.prideferrell.com for ACE Self-Test questions that will help you prepare for exams.

KEY CONCEPTS

environmental scanning	business cycle	technology	cause-related marketing
environmental analysis	Federal Trade Commission (FTC)	sociocultural forces	strategic philanthropy
buying power		social responsibility	Green marketing
disposable income	Better Business Bureau	marketing citizenship	consumerism
discretionary income	National Advertising Review Board (NARB)	marketing ethics	codes of conduct
willingness to spend		ethical issue	

ISSUES FOR DISCUSSION AND REVIEW

1. Why are environmental scanning and analysis important to marketers?

2. Define *income, disposable income,* and *discretionary income.* How does each type of income affect consumer buying power?

3. What factors influence a buyer's willingness to spend?

4. What are the goals of the Federal Trade Commission? List the ways in which the FTC affects marketing activities. Do you think a single regulatory agency should have such broad jurisdiction over so many marketing practices? Why or why not?

5. Name several nongovernmental regulatory forces. Do you believe self-regulation is more or less effective than governmental regulatory agencies? Why?

6. Discuss the impact of technology on marketing activities.

7. In what ways are cultural values changing? How are marketers responding to these changes?

8. What is social responsibility, and why is it important?

9. What are four dimensions of social responsibility? What impact do they have on marketing decisions?

10. What are some major social responsibility issues? Give an example of each.

11. Describe consumerism. Analyze some active consumer forces in your area.

12. What is the difference between ethics and social responsibility?

MARKETING APPLICATIONS

1. Assume you are opening *one* of the following retail businesses. Identify publications at the library or online that provide information about the environmental forces likely to affect the business. Briefly summarize the information each provides.
   a. Convenience store
   b. Women's clothing store
   c. Grocery store
   d. Fast-food restaurant
   e. Furniture store

2. Identify at least one technological advancement and one sociocultural change that has affected you as a consumer. Explain the impact of each on your needs as a customer.

3. Identify an organization in your community that has a reputation for being ethical and socially responsible. What activities account for this image? Is the company successful? Why or why not?

ONLINE EXERCISE

4. Business for Social Responsibility (BSR) is a nonprofit organization for companies desiring to operate responsibly and demonstrate respect for ethical values, people, communities, and the natural environment. Founded in 1992, BSR offers members practical information, research, educational programs, and technical assistance as well as the opportunity to network with peers on current social responsibility issues. Visit **http://www.bsr.org.**
   a. What types of businesses join BSR, and why?
   b. Pick three recent news articles that deal with social responsibility issues in marketing. For each article, explain how these issues relate to a concept covered in Chapter 3.
   c. In the Resources section, find the White Paper on ethics codes. Using this report, list some examples of corporate codes of ethics and describe the benefits of establishing a code of ethics.

VIDEO CASE

Social Responsibility at New Belgium Brewing Company

The idea for New Belgium Brewing Company (NBB) began with a bicycling trip through Belgium, where some of the world's finest ales have been brewed for centuries. As Jeff Lebesch, an American electrical engineer, cruised around the country on a fat-tired mountain bike, he wondered if he could produce such high-quality ales in his home state of Colorado. After returning home, Lebesch began to experiment in his Fort Collins basement. When his home-brewed experiments earned rave reviews from friends, Lebesch and his wife, Kim Jordan, decided to open the New Belgium Brewing Company in 1991. They named their first brew Fat Tire Amber Ale in honor of Lebesch's Belgian biking adventure.

Today New Belgium is the third-largest craft brewer. It markets a variety of ales and pilsners, including Sunshine Wheat, Blue Paddle Pilsner, Abbey Ale, Trippel Ale, and 1554 Black Ale, as well as the firm's number 1 seller, the

original Fat Tire Amber Ale. NBB also markets seasonal beers, such as Frambozen and Abbey Grand Cru—released at Thanksgiving—and Christmas and Farmhouse Ale, which are sold during the early fall months. The firm also occasionally offers one-time-only brews—such as LaFolie, a wood-aged beer—that are sold only until the batch runs out. Bottle label designs employ "good ol' days" nostalgia. The Fat Tire label, for example, features an old-style cruiser bike with fat tires, a padded seat, and a basket hanging from the handlebars.

Although Fat Tire was initially sold only in Fort Collins, distribution quickly expanded throughout the rest of Colorado. Customers can now find Fat Tire and other New Belgium offerings in 15 states, including Washington, Montana, Texas, New Mexico, and Arizona. The brewery regularly receives e-mails and telephone inquiries about when New Belgium beers will be available elsewhere, and tourists who visit the brewery often purchase beer to take back home.

NBB's most effective promotion has been via word-of-mouth advertising by devoted customers. The company initially avoided mass advertising, relying instead on small-scale, local promotions, such as print advertisements in alternative magazines, participation in local festivals, and sponsorship of alternative sports events. However, with expanding distribution, especially to California, the brewery has invested in a $10 million advertising campaign, created by Amalgamated, an independent New York agency. The campaign targets high-end beer drinkers, men ages 25 to 44, and highlights the brewery's image as being down to earth. The ads focus on a man building a bike out of used parts and then riding it along pastoral country roads. Through event sponsorships, such as the Tour de Fat and Ride the Rockies, NBB has raised thousands of dollars for various environmental, social, and cycling nonprofit organizations.

New Belgium beers are priced to reflect their quality, at about $7 per six-pack. This pricing strategy conveys the message that the products are special and of consistently higher quality than macrobrews, such as Budweiser and Coors, but also keeps them competitive with other microbrews, such as Pete's Wicked Ale, Pyramid Pale Ale, and Sierra Nevada. To demonstrate its appreciation for its retailers and business partners, New Belgium does not sell beer to consumers on-site at the brewhouse for less than the retailers charge.

New Belgium's marketing strategy also includes a concern for how the company's activities affect the natural environment. The brewery looks for cost-efficient, energy-saving alternatives to conducting business and reducing its impact on the environment. Thus, the company's employee-owners invested in a wind turbine, making New Belgium the first fully wind-powered brewery in the United States. The company further reduces its energy use with a steam condenser that captures and reuses the hot water from boiling the barley and hops in the production process to start the next brew; the steam is redirected to heat the floor tiles and de-ice the loading docks in cold weather. New Belgium strives to recycle as many supplies as possible, including cardboard boxes, keg caps, office materials, and the amber glass used in bottling. The brewery also stores spent barley and hop grains in an on-premise silo and invites local farmers to pick up the grains, free of charge, to feed their pigs. Another way NBB conserves energy is through the use of "sun tubes," which provide natural daytime lighting throughout the brewhouse all year long. NBB encourages employees to reduce air pollution through alternative transportation. As an incentive, NBB gives each employee a "cruiser bike" just like the one on the Fat Tire Amber Ale label—after one year of employment to encourage biking to work.

Beyond its use of environment-friendly technologies and innovations, New Belgium Brewing Company strives to improve communities and enhance lives through corporate giving, event sponsorship, and philanthropic involvement. The company donates $1 per barrel of beer sold to various cultural, social, environmental, and drug and alcohol awareness programs across the ten western states in which it distributes beer. Involvement is spread equally among the ten states, unless a special need requires greater participation or funding. The brewhouse also maintains a community board on which organizations can post community involvement activities and proposals. This board allows tourists and employees to see opportunities to help out the community, and it provides nonprofit organizations with a forum for making their needs known.

New Belgium's commitment to quality, the environment, and its employees and customers is clearly expressed in its stated purpose. "To operate a profitable brewery which makes our love and talent manifest." This dedication has been well rewarded with loyal customers and industry awards. The company received an award for best mid-size brewing company of the year and best mid-size brewmaster at the Great American Beer Festival in 1999. New Belgium also took home medals for three different brews: Abbey Belgian Style Ale, Blue Paddle Pilsner, and LaFolie specialty ale. Jeff Lebesch and Kim Jordan were named the recipients of the Rocky Mountain Region Entrepreneur of the Year Award for manufacturing. In 2000, NBB received the Better Business Bureau's Marketplace Ethics Award. For many people, the Fat Tire Brand has come to represent a reduction of anxiety, fat-tire bikes, and environmental friendliness.[49]

QUESTIONS FOR DISCUSSION

1. What steps has New Belgium Brewing Company taken to be socially responsible?

2. As a smaller business, how can New Belgium justify donating $1 per barrel of beer sold to environmental and community causes?

3. Some segments of society contend that companies selling alcoholic beverages cannot be socially responsible organizations because of the inherent nature of their products. Do you believe New Belgium Brewing Company's actions and initiatives make it a socially responsible business? Why or why not?

Using Technology for Customer Relationships in a Global Environment

Part 2 expands the marketing environment by examining technological and global issues in greater detail. Chapter 4 explores how marketers use information technology to build long-term relationships with customers by targeting them more precisely than ever before. Both e-marketing and customer relationship management are presented in the context of building an effective marketing strategy. Chapter 5 examines factors within the global marketing environment that create challenges and opportunities in international markets. Both the environmental variables and strategic alternatives for organizing marketing strategy are discussed.

4

E-Marketing and Customer Relationship Management

OBJECTIVES

1 Define electronic marketing and electronic commerce and recognize their increasing importance in strategic planning.

2 Understand the characteristics of electronic marketing—addressability, interactivity, memory, control, accessibility, and digitalization—and how they differentiate electronic marketing from traditional marketing activities.

3 Examine how the characteristics of electronic marketing affect marketing strategy.

4 Understand how electronic marketing and information technology can facilitate customer relationship management.

5 Identify the legal and ethical considerations in electronic marketing.

▶ Amazon.com Finds Success with Technology and Positive Relationships

Amazon.com, one of the few survivors of the dot-com demise, was founded in 1994 by Jeffrey P. Bezos. The company has grown from its garage birthplace into a leading Internet retailer with revenues of nearly $7 billion. Although stock shares of the Seattle-based company hit a low of $6 during the dot-com meltdown, they had recovered to as high as $58 by 2004. Bezos even claimed that Amazon had reached a milestone of a full-year profit of $35 million, although some analysts questioned that figure. The company's profit margins have been falling because of continued price cutting and the company's free shipping offer to customers.

For most of its first decade, the company continually reinvented itself. Although the company started out calling itself "the Earth's biggest bookstore," Bezos early on recognized the Internet's potential link to just about anyone who wanted to buy just about any product without the costly overhead of building multiple stores and employing large numbers of salespersons. Amazon soon branched out into additional product categories, including music, movies, toys, electronics, Web-based services, auctions, and apparel. Amazon's foray into online apparel marketing has been facilitated by relationships with merchants such as eBags, Eddie Bauer, Guess?, OshKosh, and Spiegel. These relationships allow Amazon to charge a sales-based fee to take care of the technology side of the transaction.

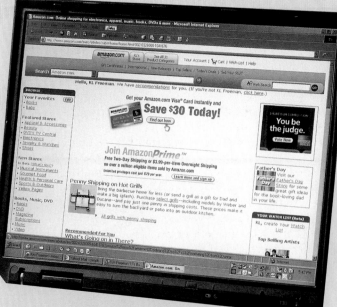

Amazon continues to tweak many of its selling initiatives, such as its effort to have other companies sell their products through Amazon. Now customers see offerings from Amazon and other companies together. Amazon insists that it can earn the same level of profit regardless of which option customers choose.

Bezos claims that he knows when to forge ahead and when to pull the plug on new products and ventures.

In the future, Bezos sees Amazon's greatest growth potential in international markets, especially in countries in which the company already operates, such as Germany and Japan. China, with more and more consumers logging onto the Internet, also looms as a tremendous opportunity. Bezos claims that Amazon focuses more on customers than its competitors do, but increasingly sophisticated search engines could make it easier for potential customers to find each other and bypass Amazon. Amazon has always wanted to become an online Wal-Mart or an e-business hub like Yahoo! and other Web portals. Only time will tell whether Amazon can continue to reinvent itself and remain one of the most successful online retailers.[1] ◀

The phenomenal growth of the Internet presents exciting opportunities for companies such as Amazon.com to forge interactive relationships with consumers and business customers. The interactive nature of the Internet, particularly the World Wide Web, has made it possible to target markets more precisely and even reach markets that previously were inaccessible. It also facilitates customer relationship management, allowing companies to network with manufacturers, wholesalers, retailers, suppliers, and outsource firms to serve customers more efficiently. Because of its ability to enhance the exchange of information between customer and marketer, the Internet has become an important component of most firms' marketing strategies.

We devote this chapter to exploring this new frontier. We begin by defining *electronic marketing* and exploring its context within marketing strategies. Next, we examine the characteristics that differentiate electronic marketing activities from traditional ones and explore how marketers are using the Internet strategically to build competitive advantage. Then, we take a closer look at the role of the Internet and electronic marketing in managing customer relationships. Finally, we consider some of the ethical and legal implications that affect Internet marketing.

Marketing on the Internet

electronic commerce (e-commerce) "Sharing . . . business information, maintaining business relationships, and conducting business transactions by means of telecommunications networks"

electronic marketing (e-marketing) The strategic process of creating, distributing, promoting, and pricing products for targeted customers in the virtual environment of the Internet

A number of terms have been coined to describe marketing activities and commercial transactions on the Internet. One of the most popular terms is electronic commerce (or e-commerce), which has been defined as "the sharing of business information, maintaining business relationships, and conducting business transactions by means of telecommunications networks."[2] In this chapter, we focus on how the Internet, especially the World Wide Web, relates to all aspects of marketing, including strategic planning. Thus, we use the term electronic marketing (or e-marketing) to refer to the strategic process of creating, distributing, promoting, and pricing products for targeted customers in the virtual environment of the Internet.

One of the most important benefits of e-marketing is the ability of marketers and customers to share information. Through company websites, consumers can learn about firms' products, including features, specifications, and prices. Many websites also provide feedback mechanisms through which customers can ask questions, voice complaints, indicate preferences, and otherwise communicate about their needs and desires. The Internet has changed the way marketers communicate and develop relationships not only with their customers but also with their employees and suppliers. Lockheed Martin, for example, created a global network linking

Electronic Marketing
Through Expedia.com buyers and sellers can learn about travel services, destinations, and prices.

80 suppliers to help build a new stealth fighter jet. The company expects the project to save about $25 million a year during product development.[3] Many companies use e-mail, groupware (software that allows people in different locations to access and work on the same file or document over the Internet), and videoconferencing to coordinate activities and communicate with employees. Because such technology facilitates and lowers the cost of communications, the Internet can contribute significantly to any industry. Indeed, the adoption of the Internet as a communications channel has been found to positively influence business performance.[4]

Telecommunications technology offers additional benefits to marketers, including rapid response, expanded customer service capability (e.g., 24 hours a day, 7 days a week, or 24/7), decreased operating costs, and reduced geographic barriers. Data networks have decreased cycle and decision times and permitted companies to treat customers more efficiently.[5] In today's fast-paced world, the ability to shop for books, clothes, and other merchandise at midnight, when traditional stores are usually closed, is a benefit for both buyers and sellers. Indeed, research by comScore Networks found that 20 percent of online shopping occurs between 9 P.M. and 9 A.M.[6] The Internet allows even small firms to reduce the impact of geography on their operations. For example, Coastal Tool & Supply, a small power tool and supply store in Connecticut, has generated sales from around the world through its website.

Despite these benefits, many companies that chose to make the Internet the core of their marketing strategies— often called "dot-coms"—failed to earn profits or acquire sufficient resources to remain in business. Many dot-coms failed because they thought the only thing that mattered was brand awareness. In reality, however, Internet markets are more similar to traditional markets than they are different.[7] Thus, successful e-marketing strategies, like traditional marketing ones, depend on creating, distributing, promoting, and pricing products that customers need or want, not merely developing a brand name or reducing the costs associated with online transactions. In fact, traditional retailers continue to do quite well in some areas that many people just a few years ago thought the Internet would dominate. For example, although many marketers believed there would be a shift to buying cars online, less than 3 percent of all new cars are sold through the Internet. Few consumers are willing to spend $30,000 online to purchase a new automobile. However, consumers are increasingly making car-buying decisions on the basis of information found at manufacturers' websites and other online sources and then making their purchase at a dealership.

Indeed, e-marketing has not changed all industries, although it has had more of an impact in some industries in which the costs of business and customer transactions are very high. For example, trading stock has become significantly easier and less expensive for customers who can go online and execute their own orders. Firms such as E*Trade and Charles Schwab have been innovators in this area, and traditional brokerage firms such as Merrill Lynch have had to introduce online trading for their customers to remain competitive. In many other industries, however, the impact of e-marketing may be incremental.

⊚ Basic Characteristics of Electronic Marketing

Although e-marketing is similar to traditional marketing, it is helpful to understand the basic characteristics that distinguish this environment from the traditional marketing environment. These characteristics include addressability, interactivity, memory, control, accessibility, and digitalization.

● **Addressability.** The technology of the Internet makes it possible for visitors to a website to identify themselves and provide information about their product needs and wants before making a purchase. The ability of a marketer to identify customers before they make a purchase is called addressability. Many websites encourage visitors to register to maximize their use of the site or to gain access to premium areas; some even require it. Registration forms typically ask for basic information, such as name, e-mail address, age, and occupation, from which marketers can build user profiles to enhance their marketing efforts. CDNow, for example, asks music lovers to supply information about their listening tastes so the company can recommend new releases. Some websites even offer contests and prizes to encourage users to register. Marketers can also conduct surveys to learn more about the people who access their websites, offering prizes as motivation for participation.

addressability A marketer's ability to identify customers before they make a purchase

Addressability represents the ultimate expression of the marketing concept. With the knowledge about individual customers garnered through the Web, marketers can tailor marketing mixes more precisely to target customers with narrow interests, such as recorded blues music or golf. Addressability also facilitates tracking website visits and online buying activity, which makes it easier for marketers to accumulate data about individual customers to enhance future marketing efforts. Amazon.com, for example, stores data about customers' purchases and uses that information to make recommendations the next time they visit the site.

Some website software can store a cookie, an identifying string of text, on a visitor's computer. Marketers use cookies to track how often a particular user visits the website, what he or she may look at while there, and in what sequence. Cookies also permit website visitors to customize services, such as virtual shopping carts, as well as the particular content they see when they log onto a web page. CNN, for example, allows visitors to its website to create a custom news page tailored to their particular interests. The use of cookies to store customer information can be an ethical issue, however, depending on how the data are used. If a website owner can use cookies to link a visitor's interests to a name and address, that information could be sold to advertisers and other parties without the visitor's consent or even knowledge. The potential for misuse of cookies has made many consumers wary of this technology. Because technology allows access to large quantities of data about customers' use of websites, companies must carefully consider how the use of such information affects individuals' privacy, as we discuss in more detail later in this chapter.

cookie An identifying string of text stored on a website visitor's computer

● **Interactivity.** Another distinguishing characteristic of e-marketing is interactivity, which allows customers to express their needs and wants directly to a firm in response to its marketing communications. This means marketers can interact with prospective customers in real time (or at least a close approximation of it). Of course, salespeople have always been able to do this, but at a much greater cost. The Web provides the advantages of a virtual sales representative, with broader market coverage and at lower cost.

interactivity The ability to allow customers to express their needs and wants directly to the firm in response to the firm's marketing communications

One implication of interactivity is that a firm's customers can also communicate with other customers (and noncustomers). For this reason, differences in the amount and type of information possessed by marketers and their customers are not as pronounced as in the past. One result is that the new- and used-car businesses have become considerably more competitive because buyers are coming into dealerships armed with more complete product and cost information obtained through comparison shopping on the Net. By providing information, ideas, and a context for interacting with other customers, e-marketers can enhance customers' interest and involvement with their products.

Interactivity enables marketers to capitalize on the concept of community to help customers derive value from the firm's products and website. **Community** refers to a sense of group membership or feeling of belonging by individual members of a group.[8] One such community is Tripod, a website where Generation Xers can create their own webpages and chat or exchange messages on bulletin boards about topics ranging from cars and computers to health and careers. Much of the site's content has been developed by members of the Tripod community. Like many online communities, Tripod is free but requires members to register to access the site. Such sites encourage visitors to "hang out" and contribute to the community (and see the website's advertising) instead of clicking elsewhere. Because such communities have well-defined demographics and common interests, they represent a valuable audience for advertisers, which typically generate the funds to maintain such sites.[9]

Another way to interact with customers is through **blogs**, web-based journals in which writers can editorialize and interact with other Internet users. There are an estimated 5 million blogs on a variety of topics, including companies, brands, and products, and they can be positive—raves about Manolo shoes, for example—or negative—such as rages against Wal-Mart, Kmart, and Best Buy. When Shayne McQuade invented a backpack with solar panels that let backpackers keep their gadgets charged, a friend mentioned the product on his blog, which soon led to references and discussions on other blogs, and ultimately, created a positive "buzz" and orders for the new product. Companies are increasingly establishing blogs to interact with customers. General Motors, for example, hosts the GM Smallblock Engine blog, where employees and customers marvel over Corvettes and other GM vehicles.[10]

● **Memory.** **Memory** refers to a firm's ability to access databases or data warehouses containing individual customer profiles and past purchase histories and to use these data in real time to customize its marketing offer to a specific customer. A **database** is a collection of information arranged for easy access and retrieval. Although companies have had database systems for many years, the information these systems contain did not become available on a real-time basis until fairly recently. Current software technology allows a marketer to identify a specific visitor to its website instantaneously, locate that customer's profile in its database, and then display the customer's past purchases or suggest new products based on past purchases while he or

community   A sense of group membership or feeling of belonging

blogs   Web-based journals in which writers editorialize and interact with other Internet users

memory   The ability to access databases or data warehouses containing individual customer profiles and past purchase histories and to use these data in real time to customize a marketing offer

database   A collection of information arranged for easy access and retrieval

Memory
Iomega provides software and disks to create memory for saving data.

she is still visiting the site. For example, Bluefly, an online clothing retailer, asks visitors to provide their e-mail addresses, clothing preferences, brand preferences, and sizes so it can create a customized online catalog ("My Catalog") of clothing that matches the customer's specified preferences. The firm uses customer purchase profiles to manage its merchandise buying. Whenever it adds new clothing items to its inventory, it checks them against its database of customer preferences and, if it finds a match, alerts the individual in an e-mail message. Applying memory to large numbers of customers represents a significant advantage when a firm uses it to learn more about individual customers each time they visit the firm's website.

control Customers' ability to regulate the information they view and the rate and sequence of their exposure to that information

● **Control.** In the context of e-marketing, control refers to customers' ability to regulate the information they view as well as the rate and sequence of their exposure to that information. The Web is sometimes referred to as a *pull* medium because users determine what they view at websites; website operators' ability to control the content users look at and in what sequence is limited. In contrast, television can be characterized as a *push* medium because the broadcaster determines what the viewer sees once he or she has selected a particular channel. Both television and radio provide "limited exposure control" (you see or hear whatever is broadcast until you change the station).

For e-marketers, the primary implication of control is that attracting—and retaining—customers' attention is more difficult. Marketers have to work harder and more creatively to communicate the value of their websites clearly and quickly, or viewers will lose interest and click to other sites. With literally hundreds of millions of unique pages of content available to any web surfer, simply putting a website on the Internet does not guarantee anyone will visit it or make a purchase. Publicizing the website may require innovative promotional activities. For this reason, many firms pay millions of dollars to advertise their products or websites on high-traffic sites such as America Online (AOL). Because of AOL's growing status as a portal (a multiservice website that serves as a gateway to other websites), firms are eager to link to it and other such sites to help draw attention to their own sites. Indeed, consumers spend most of their time online on portal sites such as MSN and Yahoo!, checking e-mail; tracking stocks; and perusing news, sports, and weather.

portal A multiservice website that serves as a gateway to other websites

accessibility The ability to obtain information available on the Internet

● **Accessibility.** An extraordinary amount of information is available on the Internet. The ability to obtain it is referred to as accessibility. Because customers can access in-depth information about competing products, prices, reviews, blog opinions, and so forth, they are much better informed about a firm's products and their relative value than ever before. Someone looking to buy a new truck, for example, can go to the websites of Ford, General Motors, and Toyota to compare the features of the Ford F-150, the GMC Sierra, and the Toyota Tundra. The truck buyer can also access online magazines and pricing guides to get more specific information about product features, performance, and prices.

MARKETING ENTREPRENEURS

Matt Drudge

THE BUSINESS: Drudge, Inc.

FOUNDED: 1995

SUCCESS: $800,000/year

In 1995, with only an e-mail address, a website, and a knack for uncovering and "telling" stories, Matt Drudge started one of the most successful and controversial online newspapers of our time, the *Drudge Report*. With a staff of two (including himself), Drudge compiles his "news" and "gossip"—such as the President Clinton/Monica Lewinsky scandal, which he scooped from *Newsweek*—from a variety of daily newspapers, wire services, and most importantly, thousands of daily e-mail tips. The site can then direct its readers via web links to online news sources that are already reporting on the stories. With the majority of the *Drudge Report*'s revenue coming from advertising, which accounts for around $100,000 monthly, and with minimal overhead, Drudge can clear around $3,500 a day and still have time for leisure.[a]

Digitalization
Napster.com provides downloads of over 1.5 million songs for a fee.
To learn more about Napster visit www.napster.com

digitalization The ability to represent a product, or at least some of its benefits, as digital bits of information

Accessibility also dramatically increases the competition for Internet users' attention. Without significant promotion, such as advertising on portals like AOL, MSN, Yahoo!, and other high-traffic sites, it is becoming increasingly difficult to attract a visitor's attention to a particular website. Consequently, e-marketers are having to become more creative and innovative to attract visitors to their sites.

● **Digitalization.** Digitalization is the ability to represent a product, or at least some of its benefits, as digital bits of information. Digitalization allows marketers to use the Internet to distribute, promote, and sell those features apart from the physical item itself. FedEx, for example, has developed web-based software that allows consumers and business customers to track their own packages from starting point to destination. Distributed over the Web at very low cost, the online tracking system adds value to FedEx's delivery services. Digitalization can be enhanced for users who have broadband access to the Internet because broadband's faster connections allow streaming audio and video and other new technologies.

In addition to providing distribution efficiencies, digitizing part of a product's features allows new combinations of features and services to be created quickly and inexpensively. For example, a service station that keeps a customer's history of automotive oil changes in a database can e-mail that customer when the next oil change is due and at the same time suggest other types of preventive maintenance, such as tire rotations or a tune-up. Digital features are easy to mix and match to meet the demands of individual customers.

◉ E-Marketing Strategies

Now that we have examined some distinguishing characteristics of doing business on the Internet, it is time to consider how these characteristics affect marketing strategy. Marketing strategy involves identifying and analyzing a target market and creating a marketing mix to satisfy individuals in that market, regardless of whether those individuals are accessible online or through more traditional avenues. However, there are significant differences in how the marketing mix components are developed and combined into a marketing strategy in the electronic environment of the Web. As we continue this discussion, keep in mind that the Internet is a very dynamic environment, meaning that e-marketing strategies may need to be modified frequently to keep pace.

● **Target Markets.** Marketing strategy involves identifying and analyzing a target market and creating a marketing mix to satisfy individuals in that market. With more than half of Americans online, the Internet has become an important medium for reaching consumers. Although Internet access outside the United States has lagged behind, people around the world are rapidly discovering the Web's potential for communication and e-marketing, as shown in Table 4.1

Although Internet usage statistics have long been dominated by men, American women are turning to the Internet in greater numbers for work and to save time and

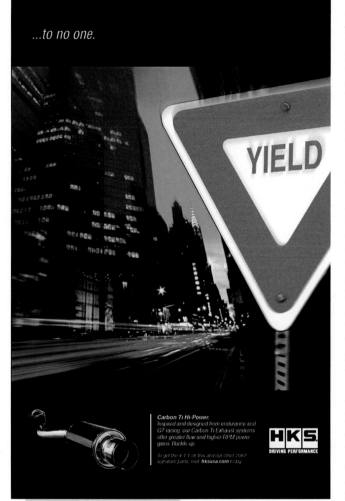

...to no one.

Carbon Ti Hi-Power.
Inspired and designed from endurance and
GT racing, our Carbon Ti Exhaust systems
offer greater flow and higher-RPM power
gains. Buckle up

To get the 4-1-1 on this and our other 2007
signature parts, visit **hksusa.com** *today*

HKS
DRIVING PERFORMANCE

Target Markets
HKS maintains a website, hksusa.com, for buyers who desire information on automobile exhaust systems.

money. About 52 percent of Internet users in the United States are women, compared to only 42 percent of European Internet users.[11] American children are increasingly using the Internet to communicate with peers, do homework, and entertain themselves. Three-quarters of American 14- to 17-year-olds and 65 percent of 10- to 13-year-olds spend time online.[12] Although Americans 55 and older account for just 18 percent of the adult online population, their numbers are growing rapidly, making them a valuable demographic market for marketers.[13]

Rather than using demographics such as age, gender, education, and so on, e-marketing can target customers based on their behavior, identifying potential customer groups based on their desires and interests. To use behavioral targeting, it is necessary to track behaviors so that an appropriate advertisement or other marketing message can be delivered. Panasonic, for example, identified customers shopping for electronics at various websites and sent an ad for a Panasonic phone to their web browsers. However, some people view this approach as too intrusive, and thus it may create ethical issues related to privacy, as well as increased potential for lawsuits and further legislation to protect consumers. The challenge is to devise communications that allow the marketer to send a message while respecting customers' choices.[14]

About 45 percent of Americans use e-mail, and one-third search for product information online.[15] More than half (53 percent) of U.S. Internet users have made a purchase online. Increasing numbers of Americans are using the Internet for online banking and other financial transactions. As Lee Rainie, director of the Pew Internet & American Life Project, says, "The Internet has gone from novelty to utility for many Americans."[16] Although many Americans continue to access the Internet through a telephone modem, broadband access at home (primarily via DSL or cable modem) accounts for 55 percent of at-home Internet users.[17]

● **Product Considerations.**   The growth of the Internet and the World Wide Web presents exciting opportunities for marketing products to both consumers and organizations. Computers and computer peripherals, industrial supplies, and packaged software are the leading business purchases online. Consumer products account for a small but growing percentage of Internet transactions, with food and beverage, sporting goods, and home goods among the fastest-growing online consumer purchases. Through e-marketing, companies can provide products, including goods, services, and ideas, that offer unique benefits and improve customer satisfaction.

The online marketing of goods such as computer hardware and software, books, videos, DVDs, CDs, toys, automobiles, and even groceries is accelerating rapidly. Dell Computer sold more than $49 billion worth of computers and related software and hardware last year, about half of that amount through its website.[18] Autobytel has established an effective model for online auto sales by helping consumers find the best price on their preferred models and then arranging for local delivery. However,

Table 4.1	Internet Use Around the World, by Selected Country	
Country	Users (In Millions)	Estimated Percentage of the Population
Australia	13.0	65.9
United States	185.6	63.9
Canada	20.5	63.5
Japan	78.1	61.4
United Kingdom	33.1	55.1
Israel	3.1	51.2
Germany	41.9	50.8
Chile	5.0	32.2
Russia	21.2	14.7
Mexico	13.9	13.2
Argentina	4.7	12.0
South Africa	4.8	11.0
Turkey	7.3	10.7
China	99.8	7.8
India	37.0	3.6

Source: "Population Explosion!" ClickZ, February 8, 2005,
www.clickz.com/stats/sectors/geographics/article.php/151151.

e-site

Anything associated with the Internet seems to move at the speed of light: thus, statistics on Internet access and usage are obsolete almost as soon as they appear in print. One valuable source of up-to-date statistics for marketers is ClickZ Network (www.clickz.com/stats/), which provides an easily accessible clearing-house of Internet data from leading research firms such as Forrester Research, Jupiter Research, Gartner Dataquest, and Nielsen/NetRatings. The award-winning site offers the latest demographic and geographic, usage, and traffic statistics, as well as articles about Internet advertising, business-to-business markets, retailing, and more.

low profit margins due to customized deliveries have challenged the ability of firms to deliver tangible goods.

Services may have the greatest potential for online marketing success. Many websites offer or enhance services ranging from home- and car-buying assistance to travel reservations and stock trading. At Century 21's website, consumers can search for the home of their dreams anywhere in the United States, get information about mortgages and credit and tips on buying real estate, and learn about the company's relocation services. Airlines are increasingly booking flights via their websites. Southwest Airlines, for example, now books 59 percent of its passenger revenue online.[19]

The proliferation of information on the World Wide Web has itself spawned new services. Web search engines and directories such as Google, Excite, Lycos, and Yahoo! are among the most heavily accessed sites on the Internet. Without these services, which track and index the vast quantity of information available on the Web, the task of finding something of interest would be tantamount to searching for the proverbial needle in a haystack. Many of these services, most notably Yahoo!, have evolved into portals by offering additional services, including news, weather, chat rooms, free e-mail accounts, and shopping.

Even ideas have potential for success on the Internet. Web-based distance learning and educational programs are becoming increasingly popular. Corporate employee training is a $55 billion industry, and online training modules are growing

MARKETING AROUND THE WORLD
INTERNET BANKING AT ING

ING Direct has become the largest Internet-based bank in the United States by not acting like a traditional "brick and mortar" bank. More than 1.5 million customers leave their money at ING Direct in the United States, and 8 million customers are served by ING Direct in Canada, Australia, France, Spain, Italy, Germany, and the United Kingdom. ING Direct's U.S. operations are headquartered in Wilmington, Delaware, with innovative ING Direct cafés in Philadelphia, New York, and Los Angeles, where you can drop by for coffee, call a sales associate, or visit INGDirect.com to learn about the bank and how to use it.

A subsidiary of the Amsterdam-based ING Group, ING Direct has built a reputation as an easy-to-use, reliable bank. It has rejected the notion of building branches with high-service contact on every corner; instead it exploits a range of technological innovations that make it possible to move money around the world electronically. It doesn't shower customers with free toasters and other gifts but rather offers them low-cost, simple banking products. It doesn't spend a lot of time coddling or directly interacting with its customers; such one-on-one service would be expensive and time-consuming. ING instead relies on paperless transactions, which reduce costs and improve speed, efficiency, and service to its clients.

To improve its success, ING studied the lifestyles and habits of its most profitable customers and applied what it learned to targeting prospects with similar behavior. Its ideal customers are savings-minded parents, age 30 to 50, who are comfortable using the Internet to order products and communicate with others about their buying experiences and what they've learned from searching Internet information resources. The average customer is comfortable but not wealthy, with average deposits of around $14,000.

ING Direct tries to carry out its theme of low-cost, simple transactions by letting savers open accounts with no fees, no minimums, and one of the best interest rates in the United States. Its mortgages have no application fee; a simple, no-hassle application; and great rates that can save customers thousands of dollars on their mortgage compared to the 30-year fixed mortgages offered by traditional banks. Although its operation is simple now, the Amsterdam holding company is suggesting that it might need to provide more services, including online brokerages and other services.[b]

rapidly. Additional ideas being marketed online include marriage and personal counseling; medical, tax, and legal advice; and even psychic services.

● **Distribution Considerations.** The role of distribution is to make products available at the right time at the right place in the right quantities. The Internet can be viewed as a new distribution channel. Physical distribution is especially compatible with e-marketing. The ability to process orders electronically and increase the speed of communications via the Internet reduces inefficiencies, costs, and redundancies throughout the marketing channel.

More firms are exploiting advances in information technology to synchronize the relationships between their manufacturing or product assembly and their customer contact operations. This increase in information sharing among various operations of the firm makes product customization easier to accomplish. Marketers can use their websites to query customers about their needs and then manufacture products that

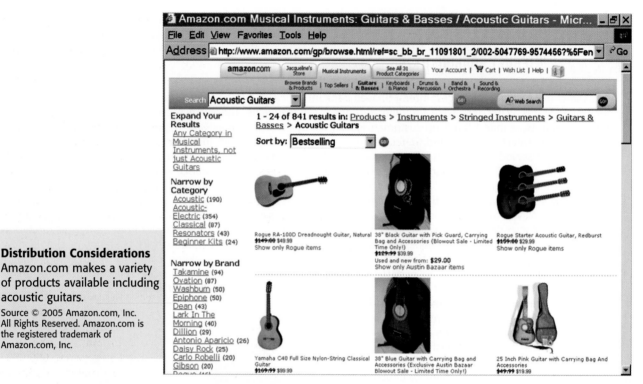

exactly fit those needs. Gateway and Dell, for example, help their customers build their own computers by asking them to specify what components to include; these firms then assemble and ship the customized product directly to the customer in a few days. Imperial Sugar lets business customers place orders, check stock, and track shipments via its website, which now accounts for 10 percent of the firm's sales.[20] Now business customers even have their own search engine, ThomasNet, where they can search for goods, services, and suppliers on a local, regional, and national level.[21]

One of the most visible members of any marketing channel is the retailer, and the Internet is increasingly becoming a retail venue. Online retail sales are expected to grow from $144 billion in 2004 to $316 billion in 2010 and account for 12 percent of total retail sales.[22] The Internet provides an opportunity for marketers of everything from computers to travel reservations to encourage exchanges. Amazon.com, for example, sold nearly $7 billion of books, CDs, DVDs, videos, toys, games, and electronics directly from its website in 2004.[23] Indeed, Amazon.com's success at marketing books online has been so phenomenal that many imitators have adopted its retailing model for everything from CDs to toys. Another retailing venture is online auctioneers, such as eBay and Haggle Online, which auction everything from fine wines and golf clubs to computer goods and electronics.

● **Promotion Considerations.**   The Internet is an interactive medium that can be used to inform, entertain, and persuade target markets to accept an organization's products. In fact, gathering information about goods and services is one of the main reasons people go online. The accessibility and interactivity of the Internet allow marketers to complement their traditional media usage for promotional efforts. The control characteristic of e-marketing means that customers who visit a firm's website are there because they choose to be, which implies that they are interested in the firm's products and therefore can be at least somewhat involved in the message and dialog provided by the firm. For these reasons, the Internet represents a highly cost-effective communication tool for small businesses. Results of Verizon's Annual Small Business Internet Survey suggest that 37 percent of small businesses now have a website, and these marketers are primarily using the Internet as a tool to foster customer relations, advertising, and communications.[24]

Many companies augment their TV and print advertising campaigns with web-based promotions. Both Kraft and Ragu, for example, have created websites with recipes and entertaining tips to help consumers get the most out of their products. Many movie studios have set up websites at which visitors can view clips of their latest releases, and television commercials for new movies often encourage viewers to visit these sites. Some companies have even created fake websites to entertain customers, such as Burger King's Subservient Chicken—where visitors seem to control a person dressed in a chicken costume by typing in commands—and Alaska Airlines' parody website, skyhighairlines.com.[25] In addition, many companies choose to advertise their goods, services, and ideas on portals, search engines, and even other firms' websites. Table 4.2 describes the most common types of advertisements found on websites.

Many marketers are also offering buying incentives and adding value to their products online through the use of sales promotions, especially coupons. Several websites, including **www.coolsavings.com, www.valupage.com,** and **www.valpak. com,** offer online coupons for their members. Val-pak, for example, offers about 30,000 coupons through its site, and its (free) membership has grown to 600,000. Val-pak has succeeded by offering coupons for a variety of local merchants, including restaurants, dry cleaners, video stores, fitness centers, and car washes.[26]

The characteristics of e-marketing make promotional efforts on the Internet significantly different than those using more traditional media. First, because Internet users can control what they see, customers who visit a firm's website are there because they choose to be, which implies, as pointed out previously, that they are interested in the firm's products and therefore may be more involved in the message and dialog provided by the firm. Second, the interactivity characteristic allows marketers to enter

Table 4.2	**Types of Advertising on Websites**
Banner Ads	Small, rectangular, static or animated ads that typically appear at the top of a webpage.
Keyword Ads	Ads that relate to text or subject matter specified in a web search.
Button Ads	Small square or rectangular ads bearing a corporate or brand name or logo and usually appearing at the bottom or side of a webpage.
Pop-up Ads	Large ads that open in a separate web browser window on top of the website being viewed.
Pop-under Ads	Large ads that open in a new browser window underneath the website being viewed.
Sponsorship Ads	Ads that integrate companies' brands and products with the editorial content of certain websites.

into dialogs with customers to learn more about their interests and needs. This information can then be used to tailor promotional messages to the individual customer. Finally, addressability can make marketing efforts directed at specific customers more effective. Indeed, direct marketing combined with effective analysis of customer databases may become one of e-marketing's most valuable promotional tools.

● **Pricing Considerations.**   Pricing relates to perceptions of value and is the most flexible element of the marketing mix. E-marketing enables firms to charge different prices for customers purchasing through different channels such as retail stores, catalogs, and Internet. This ability to have multiple-channel price options can provide value to the customer and improve marketing performance.[27] E-marketing facilitates both price and nonprice competition because the accessibility characteristic of e-marketing gives consumers access to more information about the cost and price of products than has ever been available to them before. For example, car shoppers can access automakers' webpages, configure an ideal vehicle, and get instant feedback on its cost. They can also visit Autobytel, Edmund's, and other websites to obtain comparative pricing information on both new and used cars to help them find the best value. They can then purchase a vehicle online or at a dealership.

Customer Relationship Management

One characteristic of companies engaged in e-marketing is a renewed focus on relationship marketing by building customer loyalty and retaining customers—in other words, on customer relationship management (CRM). As we noted in Chapter 1, CRM focuses on using information about customers to create marketing strategies that develop and sustain desirable long-term customer relationships. Procter & Gamble, for example, encourages Oil of Olay customers to join Club Olay, an online community with some 4 million members. In exchange for beauty tips, coupons, and special offers, the website collects some information about customers and their use of the skin-care product.[28] A focus on CRM is possible in e-marketing because of marketers' ability to target individual customers. This effort is enhanced over time as customers invest time and effort into "teaching" the firm what they want. This investment in the firm also increases the costs that a customer would incur by switching to another company. Once a customer has learned to trade stocks online through Charles Schwab, for example, there is a cost associated with leaving to find a new brokerage firm: another firm may offer less service, and it may take time to find a new firm and learn a new system. Any time a marketer can learn more about its customers to strengthen the match between its marketing mix and target customers' desires and preferences, it increases the perceived costs of switching to another firm.

E-marketing permits companies to target customers more precisely and accurately than ever before. The addressability, interactivity, and memory characteristics of e-marketing allow marketers to identify specific customers, establish interactive dialogs with them to learn about their needs, and combine this information with their purchase histories to customize products to meet those needs. Amazon.com, for example, stores and analyzes purchase data to understand each customer's interests. This information helps the online retailer improve its ability to satisfy individual customers and thereby increase sales of books, music, movies, and other products to each customer. The ability to identify individual customers allows marketers to shift their focus from targeting groups of similar customers to increasing their share of an individual customer's purchases. Thus, the emphasis shifts from *share of market* to

If only you **knew** the REAL me...

...you could have my business for life. Know your customers and keep them for life. That's what Surado SCM SQL is all about. By providing seamless coordination between customer care, help desk, sales, marketing and other functions that touch your customers, your team has a comprehensive view of customer preferences and experiences, transforming them into knowledge workers who are able to provide consistent, effective and *personalized* service. And with management analytics, you're able to monitor the health of your business and maximize your most profitable relationships.

Want to keep customers for life? Visit www.scmsql.com/inc or call 1-800-4SURADO for more info.

SURADO
SCM SQL   CRM for Growing Companies
Enterprise CRM Solution   © 2002 Surado Solutions. All Rights Reserved.
SCM SQL is a trademark of Surado Solutions, Inc.

Customer Relationship Management
Surado SCMSQL provides customer relationship management solutions for organizations.

share of customer. In moving to a share-of-customer perspective, however, a firm should ensure that individual target customers have sufficient potential to justify such specialized efforts. Indeed, one benefit arising from the addressability characteristic of e-marketing is that firms can track and analyze individual customers' purchases and identify the most profitable and loyal customers. However, a firm must balance its resources between customer-acquisition efforts and customer-retention efforts in order to maximize profits.[29]

Focusing on share of customer requires recognizing that all customers have different needs and that all customers do not have equal value to a firm. The most basic application of this idea is the 80/20 rule: 80 percent of business profits come from 20 percent of customers. Although this idea is not new, advances in technology and data collection techniques now permit firms to profile customers in real time. The goal is to assess the worth of individual customers and thus estimate their lifetime value (LTV) to the firm. Some customers—those who require considerable hand-holding or who return products frequently—may simply be too expensive to retain given the low level of profits they generate. Companies can discourage these unprofitable customers by requiring them to pay higher fees for additional services. For example, many banks and brokerages charge hefty maintenance fees on small accounts. Such practices allow firms to focus their resources on developing and managing long-term relationships with more profitable customers.[30]

Technology Drives CRM

CRM focuses on building satisfying exchange relationships between buyers and sellers by gathering useful data at all customer-contact points—telephone, fax, online, and personal—and analyzing those data to better understand customers' needs and desires. Indeed, the term *m-commerce* has been applied to the use of portable handheld devices—such as PDAs and cell phones—to reach customers at every possible location.[31] Companies are increasingly automating and managing customer relationships through technology. Indeed, one fast-growing area of CRM is customer-support and call-center software, which helps companies capture information about all interactions with customers and provides a profile of the most important aspects of the customer experience on the Web and on the phone. Using technology, marketers can analyze interactions with customers to identify performance issues and even build a library of "best practices" for customer interaction.[32] Customer-support and call-center software can focus on those aspects of customer interaction that are most relevant to performance, such as how long customers have to wait on the phone to ask a question of a service representative or how long they must wait to receive a response from an online request. This technology can also help marketers determine whether call-center personnel are missing opportunities to promote additional products or to provide better service. For example, after buying a new Saab automobile, the customer is supposed to meet a service mechanic who can answer any technical questions about the new car during the first service visit. Saab follows up this visit with a telephone survey to determine whether the new car buyer met the Saab mechanic and to learn about the buyer's experience with the first service call.

Sales automation software can link a firm's sales force to e-marketing applications that facilitate selling and providing service to customers. Often these applications enable customers to assist themselves instead of using traditional sales and service organizations. At Cisco, for example, 80 percent of all customer-support questions can be answered online through the firm's website, eliminating 75,000 phone calls a month.[33] In addition, CRM systems can provide sales managers with information that helps provide the best product solution for customers and thus maximize service. Dell Computer employs CRM data to identify those customers with the greatest needs for computer hardware and then provides these select customers with additional value in the form of free, secure, customized websites. These "premier pages" allow customers—typically large companies—to check their order status, arrange deliveries, and troubleshoot problems. Although Dell collects considerable data about its customers from its online sales transactions, the company avoids selling customer lists to outside vendors.[34] CRM applications like that used by Dell include software for marketing automation, sales automation, and customer support and call centers. The market for CRM applications is expected to reach $16.5 billion in the United States by 2006.[35]

◉ Customer Satisfaction Is the End Result of CRM

Although technology drives CRM and can help companies build relationships with desirable customers, it is used too often as a cost-reduction tactic or a tool for selling, with little thought toward developing and sustaining long-term relationships. Some companies spend millions to develop CRM systems yet fail to achieve the associated benefits. These companies often see themselves as sophisticated users of technology to manage customers, but they do not view customers as assets. Customer relationship management cannot be effective, however, unless it is developed as a relationship-building tool. CRM is a process of reaching out to customers and building trust, not a technology solution for customer sales.[36]

Perhaps because of the software and information technology associated with collecting information from consumers and responding to their desires, some critics view CRM as a form of manipulation. It is possible to use information about customers at their expense to obtain quick results—for example, charging higher prices whenever possible and using available data to maximize profits. However, using CRM to foster customer loyalty does not require collecting every conceivable piece of data from consumers or trying to sell customers products they don't want. Marketers should not try to control customers; they should try to develop relationships that derive from the trust gained over many transactions and are sustained by customers' belief that the company genuinely desires their continued patronage.[37] Trust reduces the costs associated with worrying about whether expectations will be honored and simplifies the customers' buying efforts in the future.

What marketers can do with CRM technology is identify their most valuable customers so that they can make an investment in building long-term relationships with those customers.[38] Building on this information about customer preferences can permit customized offers to create a one-to-one marketing relationship.[39] To be effective, marketers must measure the effectiveness of CRM systems in terms of their progress toward developing satisfactory customer relationships. Less than 20 percent of companies track customer retention, but developing and assessing customer loyalty is important in managing long-term customer relationships.

The most important component of CRM is remembering that it is not about technology but about relationships with customers. CRM systems should ensure that marketers listen to customers and then respond to their needs and concerns to build long-term relationships. The Internet can provide a valuable listening post and serve as a medium to manage customer relationships.[40]

Legal and Ethical Issues in E-Marketing

How marketers use technology to gather information—both online and off—to foster long-term relationships with customers has raised numerous legal and ethical issues. The popularity and widespread use of the Internet grew so quickly that global legal systems have not been able to keep pace with advances in technology. Among the issues of concern are personal privacy, unsolicited e-mail, and the misappropriation of copyrighted intellectual property.

One of the most significant privacy issues involves the personal information companies collect from website visitors. A survey by the Progress and Freedom Foundation found that 96 percent of popular commercial websites collect personally identifying information from visitors.[41] Cookies are the most common means of obtaining such information. Some people fear the collection of personal information from website users may violate users' privacy, especially if done without their knowledge.

In response to privacy concerns, some companies are cutting back on the amount of information they collect. The 96 percent of websites identified by the Progress and Freedom Foundation survey as collectors of personal information was down from 99 percent two years before, and 84 percent of the surveyed sites indicated that they are collecting less data than before.[42] Public concerns about online privacy remain, however, and many in the industry are urging self-policing on this issue to head off potential regulation. One effort toward self-policing is the online privacy program developed by the BBBOnLine subsidiary of the Council of Better Business Bureaus (see Figure 4.1). The program awards a privacy seal to companies that clearly disclose to their website visitors what information they are collecting and how they are using it.[43]

stop spam now

Legal and Ethical Issues in E-Marketing
SurfControl stops unwanted e-mails, blocks inappropriate content, and secures confidential data.

E-MARKETING AND TECHNOLOGY
YELLOW FREIGHT MANAGES CUSTOMER RELATIONSHIPS WITH TECHNOLOGY

Shipping costs are a major expense in the physical distribution process, and companies around the world are always looking for the most efficient, reliable, and convenient means of moving supplies and products and thus satisfy their own customers. To help marketers fulfill these objectives, Yellow Freight, a global transportation company, has introduced new high-tech services, including Electronic Data Interchange (EDI), E-Tools, Yellow Live/Voice, and E-Channels.

EDI allows Yellow Freight and its customers to share documents over the Internet. This service can be useful for transferring invoices, bills of lading, shipment tracking, and other data files. The use of EDI almost eliminates the need for paper communications and establishes a new medium for communication between Yellow Freight and its customers.

My Yellow E-Tools is a system designed to simplify business interactions by allowing customers to use the Internet to create bills of lading, schedule pickups, track shipments, view account information and invoices, and, if necessary, dispute invoices. Through E-Tools, customers can obtain instant quotes, and then complete bills of lading and schedule pickups if the quoted rates are satisfactory. Registered E-Tools customers can also grant designated partners access to their application information. The customer chooses what information to share and to whom it can be provided.

With Yellow Live/Voice, Yellow Freight becomes the first transportation firm to offer live voice capability through its website. This service allows customers to have real-time audio conversations with customer-service representatives by downloading voice-enabling software. Customers using a computer equipped with a microphone and speakers can engage in two-way audio communication, while those whose computers lack a microphone can type

text questions and then listen to audio feedback from customer service.

E-Channels, which includes Yellow Live/Voice, helps customers stay connected to Yellow Freight via the Internet. This service allows customers to track shipments sent through Yellow Freight from any mobile phone that has wireless Internet capabilities. Customers can also track shipments through a Palm VII organizer. These features grant customers greater options and control over how, when, and how often they access information about their shipments.

Yellow Freight's new e-commerce services provide customers with greater control over their accounts and efficiency in shipping. The entire shipping process, from price quotes to pickup to tracking, can now be accomplished online. By expanding the options available to customers who need to track their shipments, Yellow Freight has gained a competitive advantage in the global shipping industry.[c]

Few laws specifically address personal privacy in the context of e-marketing, but the standards for acceptable marketing conduct implicit in other laws and regulations can generally be applied to e-marketing. Personal privacy is protected by the U.S. Constitution; various Supreme Court rulings; and laws such as the 1971 Fair Credit Reporting Act, the 1978 Right to Financial Privacy Act, and the 1974 Privacy Act, which deals with the release of government records. However, with few regulations on how businesses use information, companies can legally buy and sell information about customers to gain competitive advantage. Some have suggested that if personal data were treated as property, customers would have greater control over their use.

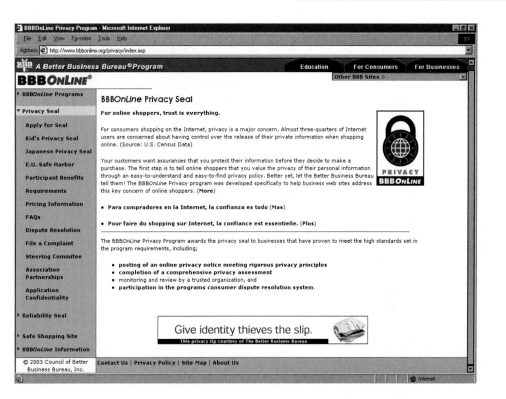

Figure 4.1
The BBBOnLine Privacy Seal and Program Explanation

Source: Reprinted with permission of the Council of Better Business Bureaus, Inc., Copyright 2003. Council of Better Business Bureaus, Inc. 4200 Wilson Blvd., Arlington, VA 22203. World Wide Web: http://www.bbb.org.

spam   Unsolicited commercial e-mail

The most serious strides toward regulating privacy issues associated with e-marketing are emerging in Europe. The 1998 European Union Directive on Data Protection specifically requires companies that want to collect personal information to explain how the information will be used and to obtain the individual's permission. Companies must make customer data files available on request, just as U.S. credit reporting firms must grant customers access to their personal credit histories. The law also bars website operators from selling e-mail addresses and using cookies to track visitors' movements and preferences without first obtaining permission. Because of this legislation, no company may deliver personal information about EU citizens to countries whose privacy laws do not meet EU standards.[44] The directive may ultimately establish a precedent for Internet privacy that other nations emulate.

Spam, or unsolicited commercial e-mail (UCE), has become a major source of frustration with the Internet. Many Internet users believe spam violates their privacy and steals their resources. Many companies despise spam because it costs them nearly $22 billion a year in lost productivity, new equipment, antispam filters, and man power. By some estimates, spam accounts for more than 75 percent of all e-mail.[45] Spam has been likened to receiving a direct-mail promotional piece with postage due. While some recipients of spam appreciate the opportunity to learn about new products (see Figure 4.2), others have become so angry that they have organized boycotts against companies that advertise in this manner. Most commercial online services (e.g., America Online) and Internet service providers offer their subscribers the option to filter out e-mail from certain Internet addresses that generate a large volume of spam. Businesses are installing software to filter out spam from outside their networks. Some firms have filed lawsuits against spammers under the Controlling the Assault of Non-Solicited Pornography and Marketing (CAN-SPAM) Law, which went into effect in 2004 and bans fraudulent or deceptive unsolicited

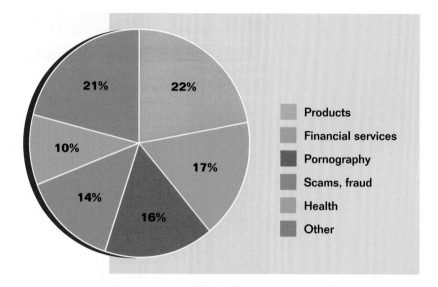

Figure 4.2
Types of Goods and Services Marketed Through Spam
Source: Ferris Research, in "Spam for Everyone," *The New York Times,* January 31, 2005, www.nytimes.com.

commercial e-mail and requires senders to provide information on how recipients can opt out of receiving additional messages. However, spammers appear to be ignoring the law and finding creative ways to get around spam filters.[46] Increasingly, spam originates from outside the United States.

The Internet has also created issues associated with intellectual property, the copyrighted or trademarked ideas and creative materials developed to solve problems, carry out applications, and educate and entertain others. Intellectual property losses relate to lost revenue from the illegal copying of computer programs, movies, compact discs, and books. This issue has become a global concern because of disparities in enforcement of laws throughout the world. The Business Software Alliance estimates that global losses from software piracy amount to $13 billion a year, including movies, music, and software downloaded from the Internet.[47] The Digital Millennium Copyright Act (DMCA) was passed to protect copyrighted materials on the Internet.

Protecting trademarks can also be problematic. For example, some companies have discovered that another firm has registered a URL (website address) that duplicates or is very similar to their own trademarks. The "cyber-squatter" then attempts to sell the right to use the URL to the legal trademark owner. Companies such as Taco Bell, MTC, and KFC have paid thousands of dollars to gain control of domain names that match or parallel their company trademarks.[48] To help companies address this conflict, Congress passed the Federal Trademark Dilution Act of 1995, which gives trademark owners the right to protect their trademarks, prevents the use of trademark-protected entities, and requires the relinquishment of names that duplicate or closely parallel registered trademarks.

As the Internet continues to evolve, more legal and ethical issues will certainly arise. Recognizing this, the American Marketing Association has developed a Code of Ethics for Marketing on the Internet (see Table 4.3) Such self-regulatory policies may help head off government regulation of electronic marketing and commerce. Marketers and all other users of the Internet should make an effort to learn and abide by basic "netiquette" (Internet etiquette) to ensure they get the most out of the resources available on this growing medium. Fortunately, most marketers recognize the need for mutual respect and trust when communicating in any public medium. They know that doing so will allow them to maximize the tremendous opportunities the Internet offers to foster long-term relationships with customers.

Table 4.3   American Marketing Association Code of Ethics for Marketing on the Internet

Preamble

The Internet, including online computer communications, has become increasingly important to marketers' activities, as they provide exchanges and access to markets worldwide. The ability to interact with stakeholders has created new marketing opportunities and risks that are not currently specifically addressed in the American Marketing Association Code of Ethics. The American Marketing Association Code of Ethics for Internet marketing provides additional guidance and direction for ethical responsibility in this dynamic area of marketing. The American Marketing Association is committed to ethical professional conduct and has adopted these principles for using the Internet, including online marketing activities utilizing network computers.

General Responsibilities

Internet marketers must assess the risks and take responsibility for the consequences of their activities. Internet marketers' professional conduct must be guided by:

1. Support of professional ethics to avoid harm by protecting the rights of privacy, ownership and access.

2. Adherence to all applicable laws and regulations with no use of Internet marketing that would be illegal, if conducted by mail, telephone, fax or other media.

3. Awareness of changes in regulations related to Internet marketing.

4. Effective communication to organizational members on risks and policies related to Internet marketing, when appropriate.

5. Organizational commitment to ethical Internet practices communicated to employees, customers and relevant stakeholders.

Privacy

Information collected from customers should be confidential and used only for expressed purposes. All data, especially confidential customer data, should be safeguarded against unauthorized access. The expressed wishes of others should be respected with regard to the receipt of unsolicited e-mail messages.

Ownership

Information obtained from the Internet sources should be properly authorized and documented. Information ownership should be safeguarded and respected. Marketers should respect the integrity and ownership of computer and network systems.

Access

Marketers should treat access to accounts, passwords, and other information as confidential, and only examine or disclose content when authorized by a responsible party. The integrity of others' information systems should be respected with regard to placement of information, advertising or messages.

Source: Reprinted by permission of the American Marketing Association.

CHAPTER REVIEW

1 Define electronic marketing and electronic commerce and recognize their increasing importance in strategic planning.

Electronic commerce (e-commerce) refers to sharing business information, maintaining business relation- ships, and conducting business transactions by means of telecommunications networks. Electronic market- ing (e-marketing) is the strategic process of creating, distributing, promoting, and pricing products for tar- geted customers in the virtual environment of the

Internet. The Internet has changed the way marketers communicate and develop relationships with their customers, employees, and suppliers. Telecommunications technology offers marketers potential advantages, including rapid response, expanded customer-service capability, reduced costs of operation, and reduced geographic barriers. Despite these benefits, many Internet companies have failed because they did not realize that Internet markets are more similar to traditional markets than they are different and thus require the same marketing principles.

2   **Understand the characteristics of electronic marketing—addressability, interactivity, memory, control, accessibility, and digitalization—and how they differentiate electronic marketing from traditional marketing activities.**

A marketer's ability to identify customers before they make a purchase is called addressability. One way websites achieve addressability is through the use of cookies, strings of text placed on a visitor's computer. Interactivity allows customers to express their needs and wants directly to a firm in response to its marketing communications. It also enables marketers to capitalize on the concept of community and customers to derive value from the use of the firm's products and websites. Memory refers to a firm's ability to access collections of information in databases or data warehouses containing individual customer profiles and past purchase histories. Firms can then use these data in real time to customize their marketing offer to a specific customer. Control refers to customers' ability to regulate the information they view as well as the rate and sequence of their exposure to that information. Accessibility refers to customers' ability to obtain the vast amount of information available on the Internet. This is enhanced by the recognition value of a firm's URL, or website address. Digitalization is the representation of a product, or at least some of its benefits, as digital bits of information.

The addressability, interactivity, and memory characteristics of e-marketing enable marketers to identify specific customers, establish interactive dialogs with them to learn their needs, and combine this information with their purchase histories to customize products to meet their needs. E-marketers can thus focus on building customer loyalty and retaining customers.

3   **Examine how the characteristics of electronic marketing affect marketing strategy.**

The growth of the Internet and the World Wide Web presents opportunities for marketing products (goods, services, and ideas) to both consumers and organizations. The Internet can also be viewed as a new distribution channel. The ability to process orders electronically and to increase the speed of communications via the Internet reduces inefficiencies, costs, and redundancies throughout the marketing channel. The Internet is an interactive medium that can be used to inform, entertain, and persuade target markets to accept an organization's products. The accessibility of the Internet presents marketers with an opportunity to expand and complement their traditional media promotional efforts. The Internet gives consumers access to more information about the cost and price of products than has ever been available to them before.

4   **Understand how electronic marketing and information technology can facilitate customer relationship management.**

One of the characteristics of companies engaged in e-marketing is a focus on customer relationship management (CRM), which employs information about customers to create marketing strategies that develop and sustain desirable long-term customer relationships. The addressability, interactivity, and memory characteristics of e-marketing allow marketers to identify specific customers, establish interactive dialogs with them to learn about their needs, and combine this information with customers' purchase histories to tailor products that meet those needs. It also permits marketers to shift their focus from share of market to share of customer. Although technology drives CRM and can help companies build relationships with desirable customers, customer relationship management cannot be effective unless it is developed as a relationship-building tool.

5   **Identify the legal and ethical considerations in electronic marketing.**

One of the most controversial issues is personal privacy, especially the personal information that companies collect from website visitors, often through the use of cookies. Additional issues relate to spam, or unsolicited commercial e-mail, and the misappropriation of copyrighted or trademarked intellectual property. More issues are likely to emerge as the Internet and e-marketing continue to evolve.

Please visit the student website at **www.prideferrell.com** for ACE Self-Test questions that will help you prepare for exams.

KEY CONCEPTS

electronic commerce
  (e-commerce)
electronic marketing
  (e-marketing)

addressability
cookie
interactivity
community

blogs
memory
database
control

portal
accessibility
digitalization
spam

ISSUES FOR DISCUSSION AND REVIEW

1. How does addressability differentiate e-marketing from the traditional marketing environment? How do marketers use cookies to achieve addressability?

2. Define *interactivity* and explain its significance. How can marketers exploit this characteristic to improve relations with customers?

3. Memory gives marketers quick access to customers' purchase histories. How can a firm use this capability to customize its product offerings?

4. Explain the distinction between *push* and *pull* media. What is the significance of control in terms of using websites to market products?

5. What is the significance of digitalization?

6. How can marketers exploit the characteristics of the Internet to improve the product element of the marketing mix?

7. How do the characteristics of e-marketing affect the promotion element of the marketing mix?

8. How does e-marketing facilitate customer relationship management?

9. How can technology help marketers improve their relationships with customers?

10. Electronic marketing has raised several ethical questions related to consumer privacy. How can cookies be misused? Should the government regulate the use of cookies by marketers?

MARKETING APPLICATIONS

Online Exercises

1. Amazon.com is one of the Web's most recognizable marketers. Visit the company's site at **www.amazon.com,** and describe how the company adds value to its customers' buying experience.

2. Some products are better suited than others to electronic marketing activity. For example, Art.com specializes in selling art prints via its online store. The ability to display a variety of prints in many different categories gives customers a convenient and efficient way to search for art. On the other hand, GE has a website displaying its appliances, but customers must visit a retailer to purchase them. Visit **www.art.com** and **www.geappliances.com,** and compare how each firm uses the electronic environment of the Internet to enhance its marketing efforts.

3. Visit the web site **www.covisint.com** and evaluate the nature of the business customers attracted. Who

is the target audience for this business marketing site? Describe the types of firms that are currently doing business through this exchange. What other types of organizations might be attracted? Is it appropriate to sell any banner advertising on a site such as this? What other industries might benefit from developing similar e-marketing exchange hubs?

4. iVillage is an example of an online community. Explore the content of this website at **www.ivillage.com.**
   a. What target market can marketers access through this community?
   b. How can marketers target this community to market their goods and services?
   c. Based on your understanding of the characteristics of e-marketing, analyze the advertisements you observe on this website.

VIDEO CASE

4SURE.com Targets Business Customers

One company that has succeeded in the dot-com arena is 4SURE.com, which rang up $200 million in sales in 2000. Founded in 1998 by Bruce Martin and Linwood Lacy, 4SURE.com markets technology products online primarily to business customers through two distinct websites: solutions4SURE.com and computers4SURE.com. Solutions4SURE.com caters to the needs of large businesses and of government and educational customers, while computers4SURE.com targets individuals and small office and home office (SOHO) customers. Both websites serve as online technology superstores featuring more than 60,000 brand name products, including computers, hardware, software, and supplies. Among the characteristics that distinguish these sites from competitors are a powerful search engine, fast checkout, the ability to pay with credit cards and wire transfers, and a bill-when-shipped policy.

4SURE.com is committed to offering customers an extensive selection of products at competitive prices with first-rate customer service. Its easy-to-navigate website is backed by well-trained, knowledgeable customer-service representatives, hassle-free exchanges and returns, and guaranteed secure transactions. The company alerts customers about sale prices and new items via e-mail and provides technical customer service for more knowledgeable buyers. To foster a close working relationship with customer-contact personnel, the company has kept sales and customer-service teams in-house. The firm even installed giant digital clocks to count down the time customers are kept on hold. The company is also linked electronically to all of its major distributors and partners, which include Compaq Computer and Sony Electronics. Although the company outsources much of its logistics needs, it has built its own warehouse to ensure that it can supply customers quickly—even overnight when necessary. By leveraging extensive relationships with manufacturers and suppliers, 4SURE.com grants customers the opportunity to "buy with confidence—guaranteed." To reinforce business customers' confidence, the company's websites carry the TRUSTe trustmark logo, as well as certifications from Bizrate.com, VeriSign, and the BBBOnline Reliability Program.

Thanks to the strong focus on customer service of the company, computers4SURE.com has received three prestigious awards—from Bizrate.com, Gomez.com, and RatingWonders.comfor its site's product selection, ease of use, privacy policy, and customer support. Bizrate.com, which rates online stores on the basis of customer feedback, gave the computers4SURE.com site 4.5 stars out of a potential 5, the highest rating achieved by any company reviewed by that site. RatingWonders.com also gave computers4SURE.com a score of 4.5 out of 5.

In 2001, 4SURE.com was acquired by Office Depot, the world's largest retailer of office products. Office Depot's own websites, including nine international sites, have already been recognized as industry leaders in the online retailing of office products. Office Depot hopes that 4SURE.com's brand name and success will help the firm reach new markets and achieve its goal of being the industry leader in providing knowledge, solutions, and products through multiple channels. According to Office Depot's CEO, Bruce Nelson, "This acquisition strategically positions Office Depot to grow in an online customer/product segment we have not successfully reached."[49]

QUESTIONS FOR DISCUSSION

1. How does 4SURE.com exploit the characteristics of electronic marketing to serve its customers? Which of these characteristics are most important to 4SURE.com's success?

2. Describe 4SURE.com's marketing mix. How does this mix differ from that of a more traditional, "brick-and-mortar" office supply store?

3. 4SURE.com has focused primarily on business markets, but it does market to consumers through its computers4SURE.com site. Assess this strategy in light of the firm's apparent success at a time when so many other dot-coms have failed.

Global Markets and International Marketing

▶ Foreign Brands Challenge Cola Giants

The Coca-Cola Company and PepsiCo have battled for decades over market share in countries around the world. The two companies now face growing competition from small, regional firms capitalizing on weaknesses in the two giants' marketing strategy.

Coca-Cola has long dominated store shelves in Latin America. Mexico, where Coke has a 70 percent market share, is the second-largest market for soft drinks after the United States and generates annual sales of about $15 billion. It is no surprise then that the market has attracted private retail brands, like Wal-Mart, as well as regional brands. One of the fastest growing upstarts is Kola Real (officially called Industrias Añaños), which was established in Peru by the Añaños family after they observed that the hijacking of delivery trucks by local militants resulted in routine shortages of Coca-Cola products. At first, the family bottled its Big Cola in recycled bottles with hand-pasted labels and hired third-party trucks to deliver it to local stores, allowing it to keep costs low. This low-cost strategy helped Big Cola make sharp inroads into the soft drink markets in Peru, and later in Ecuador, Venezuela, and Mexico. Other regional firms have also debuted in Latin America, including Fiemex SA's El Gallito and the Guadalajara soccer club's Chica Cola.

In China, the leading domestic beverage producer, Hangzhou Wahaha Group Co., introduced Feichang Kele ("Future Cola") in 1998. Although Coca-Cola has invested $14 billion in the Chinese market, where it holds 24 percent of the market share, Future Cola has already gained a 7 percent market share by focusing first on rural areas where the company had a good distribution system. Wahaha also promotes Future Cola as a patriotic brand and prices the product very competitively. The company has expanded distribution to include Hong Kong, Taiwan, France, Japan, Germany, Italy, the Netherlands, Spain, and the United States.

Qibla-Cola was founded to give British consumers an alternative to Coca-Cola and Pepsi; it contributes 10 percent of its profits to charitable causes. The company has expanded its distribution of cola and flavored carbonated drinks to Canada, Poland, the Netherlands, and Belgium, and plans to introduce them into Pakistan, Bangladesh, and India as well.

Despite the growth of these regional brands, Coca-Cola insists that its sales in

OBJECTIVES

1 Understand the nature of global markets and international marketing.

2 Analyze the environmental forces affecting international marketing efforts.

3 Identify several important regional trade alliances, markets, and agreements.

4 Examine methods of involvement in international marketing activities.

5 Recognize that international marketing strategies fall along a continuum from customization to globalization.

Europe have risen by 5 to 8 percent. In Latin America, regional brands have hurt PepsiCo far more than Coca-Cola. However, both giants have made concessions to retain their appeal. PepsiCo has twice cut prices to better compete with Big Cola, leading to a price war. Although Coke has not reduced prices, it has stepped up promotions, such as offering free cases of product to retailers. However, two Mexican stores complained to the country's antitrust commission that Coca-Cola has used unfair tactics to get stores to agree not to carry Big Cola, charges that Coca-Cola denies.[1] ◄

international marketing
Developing and performing marketing activities across national boundaries

Technological advances and rapidly changing political and economic conditions are making it easier than ever for companies like Coca-Cola to market their products overseas as well as at home. **International marketing** involves developing and performing marketing activities across national boundaries. With most of the world's population and two-thirds of total purchasing power outside the United States, international markets represent tremendous opportunities for growth. MTV, for example, now operates 100 MTV, VH1, and Nickelodeon channels worldwide. The company tailors the content of each channel to match local language and culture. MTV Indonesia, for example, has a regular call to prayer for its Muslim viewers, while MTV in Japan is very edgy and techoriented. Eight out of ten MTV Network viewers live outside the United States.[2] Accessing these markets can promote innovation, while intensifying global competition spurs companies to market better, less expensive products.

Adapting Products and Promotion
Nokia introduced the 1100 model specifically for the Indian market. The phone doubles as a flashlight and along with other models, generated $2 billion in sales in India.
Source: Reprinted courtesy of Nokia.

MARKETING ENTREPRENEURS

Tom Monaghan

THE BUSINESS: Domino's Pizza

FOUNDED: 1960

SUCCESS: $4 billion in annual sales

In 1960 Tom Monaghan and his brother bought Dominick's Pizza in Ypsilanti, Michigan, for $900. One year later Tom Monaghan traded his Volkswagen Beetle for his brother's half of the business. Over the next 13 years, Monaghan worked 100 hours a week, seven days a week, and took just one six-day vacation in order to help grow his business. Along the way, he developed many innovative tools for the pizza industry such as dough trays, corrugated pizza boxes, and insulated pizza delivery bags. Domino's is now the second largest pizza chain in the world with 7,000 locations in 61 international markets, more than 111,000 employees, and $4 billion in annual sales. Tom Monaghan sold his interest in Domino's in 1999 for a reported $1 billion.[a]

Because of the increasingly global nature of marketing, we devote this chapter to the unique features of global markets and international marketing. We begin by exploring the environmental forces that create opportunities and threats for international marketers. Next, we consider several regional trade alliances, markets, and agreements. Finally, we consider the levels of commitment that U.S. firms have toward international marketing and their degree of involvement in it. These factors are significant and must be considered in any marketing plan that includes an international component.

Environmental Forces in International Markets

Firms that enter foreign markets often find they must make significant adjustments in their marketing strategies. The environmental forces that affect foreign markets may differ dramatically from those affecting domestic markets. Thus, a successful international marketing strategy requires a careful environmental analysis. Conducting research to understand the needs and desires of foreign customers is crucial to international marketing success. Consider that urban Mexicans, who spend an average of two hours per day on transportation, are increasingly resorting to snacks at convenience stores. Recognizing this trend has encouraged Oxxo and 7-Eleven to open thousands of new convenience stores in recent years to cater to this market.[3] Many firms have demonstrated that such efforts can generate tremendous financial rewards, increase market share, and heighten customer awareness of their products around the world. In this section, we explore how differences in the sociocultural, economic, political, legal, and technological forces of the marketing environment in other countries can profoundly affect marketing activities.

Cultural and Social Forces

Cultural and social differences among nations can have significant effects on marketing activities. Because marketing activities are primarily social in purpose, they are influenced by beliefs and values regarding family, religion, education, health, and recreation. By identifying major sociocultural deviations among countries, marketers lay groundwork for an effective adaptation of marketing strategy. For instance, when Little Caesars opened new franchise pizza outlets abroad, it made some menu changes to accommodate local tastes and social norms. In Japan, Little Caesars'

When you do business in more than 60 countries, you learn the value of diversity.

Each day Cargill does business in food, nutrition, agriculture and supply chain management. With more than 100,000 employees in 60 countries around the world, our work in such diverse communities has made us very aware of the importance of diversity. We've learned that no one has a monopoly on good ideas and that they can come from anyone, anywhere. We're committed to employee and supplier diversity because we know it adds value to what we do for our customers...as well as promoting prosperity in communities everywhere. For more information, visit Cargill.com.

Cargill
Nourishing Ideas. Nourishing People."

www.cargill.com
©2005 Cargill, Incorporated

Cultural and Social Forces
Cargill recognizes the value of diversity in doing business in over 60 countries with more than 100,000 employers.

pizzas are garnished with asparagus, potatoes, squid, or seaweed. Turkish menus include a local pastry for dessert, while Middle Eastern menus exclude pork.[4] Although football is a popular sport in the United States and a major opportunity for many television advertisers, soccer is the most popular televised sport in Europe. And, of course, marketing communications often must be translated into other languages. Sometimes, however, the true meaning of translated messages can be misinterpreted or lost. Consider some translations that went awry in foreign markets: KFC's long-running slogan, "Finger lickin' good," was translated into Spanish as "Eat your fingers off," while Coors' "Turn it loose" campaign was translated into Spanish as "Drink Coors and get diarrhea."[5]

It can be difficult to transfer marketing symbols, trademarks, logos, and even products to international markets, especially if these are associated with objects that have profound religious or cultural significance in a particular culture. For example, when Big Boy opened a new restaurant in Bangkok, it quickly became popular with European and American tourists, but the local Thais refused to eat there. Instead, they placed gifts of rice and incense at the feet of the Big Boy statue—a chubby boy holding a hamburger—which reminded them of Buddha. In Japan, customers were forced to tiptoe around a logo painted on the floor at the entrance to an Athlete's Foot store because in Japan it is taboo to step on a crest.[6]

Buyers' perceptions of other countries can influence product adoption and use. Research indicates that consumer preferences for domestic products depend on both the country of origin and the product category of competing products.[7] Japanese consumers evaluate products from Japan more favorably than those from other countries regardless of product superiority. Americans, however, evaluate domestic products more favorably than foreign ones only when the U.S. products are superior to products from other countries.[8] When people are unfamiliar with products from another country, their perceptions of the country itself may affect their attitude toward the product and help determine whether they will buy it. If a country has a reputation for producing quality products and therefore has a positive image in consumers' minds, marketers of products from that country will want to make the country of origin well known. For example, a generally favorable image of Western computer technology has fueled sales of U.S.-made personal computers and Microsoft software in Japan. On the other hand, marketers may want to dissociate themselves from a particular country. Because the world has not always viewed Mexico as producing quality products, Volkswagen may not want to advertise that some of the models it sells in the United States, including the Beetle, are made in Mexico. The extent to which a product's brand image and country of origin influence purchases is subject to considerable variation based on national culture characteristics.[9]

When products are introduced from one nation into another, acceptance is far more likely if similarities exist between the two cultures. In fact, there are many similar cultural characteristics across countries. For international marketers, cultural differences have implications for product development, advertising, packaging, and pricing. In Indonesia, for example, McDonald's restaurants serve meals certified as "halal," meaning they contain no pork and are prepared according to Muslim law.[10]

◉ Economic Forces

Global marketers need to understand the international trade system, particularly the economic stability of individual nations, as well as trade barriers that may stifle marketing efforts. Economic differences among nations—differences in standards of living, credit, buying power, income distribution, national resources, exchange rates, and the like—dictate many of the adjustments that must be made in marketing abroad.

The United States and western Europe are more stable economically than many other regions of the world. In recent years, several countries, including Russia, Japan, Korea, Colombia, Argentina, and Singapore, have experienced economic problems such as recession, high unemployment, corporate bankruptcies, instability in currency markets, trade imbalances, and financial systems that need major reforms. Even more stable developing countries, such as Mexico and Brazil, tend to have greater fluctuations in their business cycles than the United States does. Economic instability can disrupt the markets for U.S. products in places that otherwise might be great marketing opportunities.

gross domestic product (GDP)
The market value of a nation's total output of goods and services for a given period; an overall measure of economic standing

In terms of the value of all products produced by a nation, the United States has the largest gross domestic product in the world, more than $10 trillion. Gross domestic product (GDP) is an overall measure of a nation's economic standing; it is the market value of a nation's total output of goods and services for a given period. However, it does not take into account the concept of GDP in relation to population (GDP per capita). The United States has a GDP per capita of $36,121. Switzerland is roughly 230 times smaller than the United States—a little larger than the state of Maryland—but its population density is nearly six times greater than that of the United States. Although Switzerland's GDP is about one-fortieth the size of the U.S. GDP, its GDP per capita is about the same. Even Canada, which is comparable in size to the United States, has a lower GDP and GDP per capita.[11] Table 5.1 provides a comparative economic analysis of Canada, Switzerland, and the United States. Knowledge about per capita income, credit, and the distribution of income provides general insights into market potential.

Opportunities for international trade are not limited to countries with the highest incomes. Some nations are progressing at a much faster rate than they

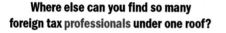

Economic Differences
Companies such as Ernst & Young assist business customers in dealing with economic differences.

Table 5.1	A Comparative Economic Analysis of Canada, Switzerland, and the United States		
	Canada	**Switzerland**	**United States**
Land area (sq. mi.)	3,560,219	15,355	3,539,227
Population (millions)	32.21	7.41	290.34
Population density (persons per sq. mi.)	9	482	82
GDP, 2002 ($ billions)	$725	$268	$10,383
GDP per capita	$23,074	$36,722	$36,121

Source: U.S. Bureau of the Census, *Statistical Abstract of the United States,* 2004 (Washington, DC: Government Printing Office, 2005), pp. 841–843, 853.

were a few years ago, and these countries—especially in Africa, eastern Europe, Latin America, and the Middle East—have great market potential. However, marketers must understand the political and legal environment before they can convert buying power of customers in these countries into actual demand for specific products.

◉ Political, Legal, and Ethical Forces

A nation's political system, laws, regulatory bodies, special-interest groups, and courts all have great impact on international marketing. A government's policies toward public and private enterprise, consumers, and foreign firms influence marketing across national boundaries. Some countries have established trade restrictions, such as tariffs. An **import tariff** is any duty levied by a nation on goods bought outside its borders and brought in. Because they raise the prices of foreign goods, tariffs impede free trade between nations. Tariffs are usually designed either to raise revenue for a country or to protect domestic products.

Nontariff trade barriers include quotas and embargoes. A **quota** is a limit on the amount of goods an importing country will accept for certain product categories in a specific time period. An **embargo** is a government's suspension of trade in a particular product or with a given country. Embargoes are generally directed at specific goods or countries and are established for political, health, or religious reasons. For example, the United States forbids the importation of cigars from Cuba for political reasons. However, demand for Cuban cigars is so strong that many enter the U.S. market illegally.

Exchange controls, government restrictions on the amount of a particular currency that can be bought or sold, may also limit international trade. They can force businesspeople to buy and sell foreign products through a central agency, such as a central bank. On the other hand, to promote international trade, some countries have joined together to form free trade zones—multinational economic communities that eliminate tariffs and other trade barriers. Such regional trade alliances are discussed later in the chapter. Foreign currency exchange rates also affect the prices marketers can charge in foreign markets. Fluctuations in the international monetary market can change the prices charged across national boundaries on a daily basis. Consequently these fluctuations must be considered in any international marketing strategy.

import tariff   A duty levied by a nation on goods bought outside its borders and brought in

quota   A limit on the amount of goods an importing country will accept for certain product categories in a specific time period

embargo   A government's suspension of trade in a particular product or with a given country

exchange controls   Government restrictions on the amount of a particular currency that can be bought or sold

balance of trade   The difference in value between a
nation's exports and its imports

Countries may limit imports to maintain a favorable balance of trade. The **balance of trade** is the difference in value between a nation's exports and its imports. When a nation exports more products than it imports, a favorable balance of trade exists because money is flowing into the country. The United States has a negative balance of trade—a trade deficit—for goods and services of $618 billion.[12] A negative balance of trade is considered harmful because it means U.S. dollars are supporting foreign economies at the expense of U.S. companies and workers. Table 5.2 lists the countries with which the United States has the greatest trade deficits.

Many nontariff barriers, such as quotas and minimum price levels set on imports, taxes, and health and safety requirements, can make it difficult for U.S. companies to export their products. For example, the collectivistic nature of Japanese culture and the high-context nature of Japanese communication make some types of direct marketing messages less effective there and may predispose many Japanese to support greater regulation of direct marketing practices.[13] A government's attitude toward importers has a direct impact on the economic feasibility of exporting to that country.

Differences in ethical values and legal standards can also affect marketing efforts. China and Vietnam, for example, have different standards regarding intellectual property than does the United States. These differences create an issue for marketers of computer software, music CDs, books, and many other products. In fact, the World Customs Organization estimates that pirated and counterfeit goods comprise as much as 5 to 7 percent of worldwide merchandise trade, particularly in China, resulting in lost sales of $512 billion a year. Among the products routinely counterfeited are consumer electronics, pharmaceuticals, cell phones, cigarettes, watches, shoes, motorcycles, and automobiles.[14] General Motors has filed a lawsuit accusing the

Table 5.2   Top Ten Countries with Which the United States Has a Trade Deficit

Country	Trade Deficit (Millions of U.S. Dollars)
China	161,978
Japan	75,195
Canada	66,827
Germany	45,855
Mexico	45,068
Venezuela	20,181
South Korea	19,829
Ireland	19,276
Italy	17,378
Malaysia	17,288

Source: "Top Ten Countries with Which the U.S. Has a Trade Deficit," U.S. Bureau of the Census, www.census.gov/foreign-trade/top/dst/current/deficit.html (accessed February 21, 2005).

Chinese-based Chery Automobile Company of using proprietary information stolen from GM Daewoo to develop its QQ minicar, which GM says is a virtual clone of its Chevrolet Spark.[15]

Because of differences in legal and ethical standards, many companies are working both individually and collectively to establish ethics programs and standards for international business conduct.[16] Levi Strauss's code of ethics, for example, bars the firm from manufacturing in countries where workers are known to be abused. Starbucks's global code of ethics strives to protect agricultural workers who harvest coffee. Many companies choose to standardize their ethical behavior across national boundaries to maintain a consistent and well-integrated corporate culture.

Differences in national standards of ethics are illustrated by what the Mexicans call *la mordida,* "the bite." The use of payoffs and bribes is deeply entrenched in many governments. Because U.S. trade and corporate policy, as well as U.S. law, prohibits direct involvement in payoffs and bribes, U.S. companies may have a hard time competing with foreign firms that do engage in these practices. Some U.S. businesses that refuse to make payoffs are forced to hire local consultants, public relations firms, or advertising agencies, which results in indirect payoffs. The ultimate decision about whether to give small tips or gifts where they are customary must be based on a company's code of ethics. Under the Foreign Corrupt Practices Act of 1977, however, it is illegal for U.S. firms to attempt to make large payments or bribes to influence policy decisions of foreign governments. Nevertheless, facilitating payments, or small payments to support the performance of standard tasks, are often acceptable. The act also subjects all publicly held U.S. corporations to rigorous internal controls and record keeping requirements for their overseas operations.

◉ Technological Forces

Advances in technology have made international marketing much easier. Voice mail, e-mail, fax, cellular phones, and the Internet make international marketing activities more affordable and convenient. Internet use has accelerated dramatically within the United States and abroad. In Europe, 50 percent of households have Internet access at home or work, pushing e-commerce revenues to $16.4 billion.[17] In Japan, 78 million have Internet access, and 100 million Chinese are logging on to the Internet.[18]

In many developing countries that lack the level of technological infrastructure found in the United States and Japan, marketers are beginning to capitalize on opportunities to "leapfrog" existing technology. For example, cellular and wireless phone technology is reaching many countries at less expense than traditional hard-wired telephone systems. Nearly one-quarter of the world's population uses mobile phones, and growth in cell phone subscriptions has now surpassed that for fixed lines.[19] Opportunities for growth in the cell phone market remain strong in Africa, the Middle East, and Southeast Asia. In war-torn Iraq, for example, many firms are competing fiercely for opportunities to rebuild the nation's telecommunications infrastructure, and MCI and Motorola have already won contracts to develop cell phone networks there.[20]

◎ Regional Trade Alliances, Markets, and Agreements

Although many more firms are beginning to view the world as one huge marketplace, various regional trade alliances and specific markets affect companies engaging in international marketing. Some create opportunities; others impose constraints. In this section, we examine several regional trade alliances, markets, and changing conditions affecting markets, including the North American Free Trade Agreement among the United States, Canada, and Mexico; the European Union; the Common Market of the Southern Cone; Asia-Pacific Economic Cooperation; the General Agreement on Tariffs and Trade; and the World Trade Organization.

The North American Free Trade Agreement (NAFTA)

North American Free Trade Agreement (NAFTA) An alliance that merges Canada, Mexico, and the United States into a single market

The **North American Free Trade Agreement (NAFTA)**, implemented in 1994, effectively merged Canada, Mexico, and the United States into one market of more than 428 million consumers. NAFTA will eliminate almost all tariffs on goods produced and traded among Canada, Mexico, and the United States to create a free trade area by 2009. The estimated annual output for this trade alliance is $11 trillion.[21]

NAFTA makes it easier for U.S. businesses to invest in Mexico and Canada; provides protection for intellectual property (of special interest to high-technology and entertainment industries); expands trade by requiring equal treatment of U.S. firms in both countries; and simplifies country-of-origin rules, hindering Japan's use of Mexico as a staging ground for further penetration into U.S. markets. Although most tariffs on products coming to the United States will be lifted, duties on more sensitive products, such as household glassware, footware, and some fruits and vegetables, will be phased out over a 15-year period.

Canada's 32 million consumers are relatively affluent, with a per capita GDP of $23,074.[22] Trade between the United States and Canada totals nearly $450 billion.[23] Currently exports to Canada support approximately 1.5 million U.S. jobs. Canadian investments in U.S. companies are also increasing, and various markets, including air travel, are opening as regulatory barriers dissolve.[24]

With a per capita GDP of $6,342, Mexico's 106 million consumers are less affluent than Canadian consumers. However, they bought nearly $100 billion worth of U.S. products last year. In fact, Mexico has become the United States' second-largest trading market, after Canada.[25] Many U.S. companies, including Hewlett-Packard, IBM, and General Motors, have taken advantage of Mexico's low labor costs and close proximity to the United States to set up production facilities, sometimes called *maquiladoras*. Production at the *maquiladoras*, especially in the automotive, electronics, and apparel industries, tripled between 1994 and 2000 as companies as diverse as Ford, John Deere, Motorola, Sara Lee, Kimberly-Clark, and VF Corporation set up facilities in north-central Mexican states. With the *maquiladoras* accounting for roughly half of Mexico's exports, Mexico has risen to become the world's ninth-largest exporter.[26]

Mexico's membership in NAFTA links the United States and Canada with other Latin American countries, providing additional opportunities to integrate trade among all the nations in the Western Hemisphere. Indeed, efforts to create a free trade agreement among the 34 nations of North and South America are underway. Like NAFTA, the Free Trade Area of the Americas (FTAA) would progressively eliminate trade barriers and create the world's largest free trade zone; however, the negotiations to complete the agreement have been contentious, and the agreement itself has become a lightning rod for antiglobalization activists.

-site

One excellent source for country-specific information may be somewhat surprising: the U.S. Central Intelligence Agency (CIA). For years, the CIA has published an annual *World Fact Book* (www.cia.gov/cia/publications/factbook/index.html), which profiles every country in the world. This useful guide offers detailed information on each country's geography (including maps and climate information), population, government and military, economy, infrastructure, and significant transnational issues. Before doing business in a specific country, marketers will need to conduct further research, and the *World Fact Book* can be an excellent place to begin.

The European Union (EU)

European Union (EU) An alliance that promotes trade among its member countries in Europe

The **European Union (EU)**, also called the European Community or Common Market, was established in 1958 to promote trade among its members, which initially included Belgium, France, Italy, West Germany, Luxembourg, and the Netherlands. In 1991, East and West Germany united, and by 1995 the United Kingdom, Spain,

Denmark, Greece, Portugal, Ireland, Austria, Finland, and Sweden had joined as well. (Cyprus, Poland, Hungary, the Czech Republic, Slovenia Estonia, Latvia, Lithuania, Slovakia, and Malta joined in 2004; Romania, Bulgaria, and Turkey have requested membership as well.[27]) Until 1993 each nation functioned as a separate market, but at that time the members officially unified into one of the largest single world markets, which today includes nearly half a billion consumers with a combined GDP of $11 trillion.[28]

To facilitate free trade among members, the EU is working toward standardization of business regulations and requirements, import duties, and value-added taxes; the elimination of customs checks; and the creation of a standardized currency for use by all members. Many European nations (Austria, Belgium, Finland, France, Germany, Greece, Ireland, Italy, Luxembourg, the Netherlands, Portugal, and Spain) trade in a common currency, the euro; however, several EU members have rejected use of the euro in their countries. Although the common currency requires many marketers to modify their pricing strategies and will subject them to increased competition, the use of a single currency frees companies that sell goods among European countries from the nuisance of dealing with complex exchange rates.[29] The long-term goals are to eliminate all trade barriers within the EU, improve the economic efficiency of the EU nations, and stimulate economic growth, thus making the union's economy more competitive in global markets, particularly against Japan and other Pacific Rim nations, and North America. Several disputes and debates still divide the member nations, however, and many barriers to completely free trade remain. Consequently it may take many years before the EU is truly one deregulated market.

As the EU nations attempt to function as one large market, consumers in the EU may become more homogeneous in their needs and wants. Most residents of the EU strongly desire, however, to maintain their national cultures and traditions.[30] As a result, marketers may need to adjust their marketing mixes for customers within each nation to reflect their differences in tastes and preferences as well as primary language. Gathering information about these distinct tastes and preferences is likely to remain a very important factor in developing marketing mixes that satisfy the needs of European customers.

◉ The Common Market of the Southern Cone (MERCOSUR)

Common Market of the Southern Cone (MERCOSUR) An alliance that promotes the free circulation of goods, services, and production factors and has a common external tariff and commercial policy among member nations in South America

The **Common Market of the Southern Cone** (also known as Mercado Comun del Sur or MERCOSUR) was established in 1991 under the Treaty of Asunción to unite Argentina, Brazil, Paraguay, and Uruguay as a free trade alliance; Bolivia and Chile joined as associates in 1996. The alliance represents two-thirds of South America's population and has a combined GDP of (U.S.) $800 billion, making it the third-largest trading bloc behind NAFTA and the EU. Like NAFTA, MERCOSUR promotes "the free circulation of goods, services and production factors among the countries" and established a common external tariff and commercial policy.[31]

◉ Asia-Pacific Economic Cooperation (APEC)

Asia-Pacific Economic Cooperation (APEC) An alliance that promotes open trade and economic and technical cooperation among member nations throughout the world

The **Asia-Pacific Economic Cooperation (APEC)**, established in 1989, promotes open trade and economic and technical cooperation among member nations, which initially included Australia, Brunei Darussalam, Canada, Indonesia, Japan, Korea, Malaysia, New Zealand, the Philippines, Singapore, Thailand, and the United States. Since then the alliance has grown to include Chile, China, Chinese Taipei, Hong Kong, Mexico, Papua New Guinea, Peru, Russia, and Vietnam. The 21-member alliance rep-

Asian-Pacific Expansion
YUM! Brands, which owns KFC, is growing rapidly in Southeast Asia. This store in Bangkok, Thailand, is just one example.

resents 2.6 billion consumers, has a combined GDP of (U.S.) $19 trillion, and accounts for nearly 47 percent of global trade. APEC differs from other international trade alliances in its commitment to facilitating business and its practice of allowing the business/private sector to participate in a wide range of APEC activities.[32]

Despite economic turmoil and a recession in Asia in recent years, companies of APEC have become increasingly competitive and sophisticated in global business in the last three decades. South Korea, for example, has become the fifth largest producer of cars and trucks in the world, exporting more than half a million vehicles to the United States. Hyundai and Kia have gained market share in the United States by expanding their product lines and improving their quality and brand image.[33] The most important emerging economic power is China, which has become one of the most productive manufacturing nations. The markets of APEC offer tremendous opportunities to marketers who understand them. For example, YUM! Brands, the number 2 fast-food chain after McDonald's, opened its first KFC fast-food restaurant in China in 1987 and has since opened 1,200 KFC outlets in China, as well as Pizza Hut and Taco Bell stores. China accounts for about one-third of the company's more than $3 billion in international sales.[34]

◉ General Agreement on Tariffs and Trade (GATT) and World Trade Organization (WTO)

General Agreement on Tariffs and Trade (GATT) An agreement among nations to reduce worldwide tariffs and increase international trade

Like NAFTA and the European Union, the General Agreement on Tariffs and Trade (GATT) is based on negotiations among member countries to reduce worldwide tariffs and increase international trade. Originally signed by 23 nations in 1947, GATT provides a forum for tariff negotiations and a place where international trade problems can be discussed and resolved. GATT negotiations currently involve some 124 nations and have had far-reaching ramifications for the international marketing strategies of U.S. firms. GATT sponsors rounds of negotiations aimed at reducing trade restrictions. The most recent round, the Uruguay Round (1986–1994), reduced trade barriers for most products and provided new rules to prevent dumping, the selling of products at unfairly low prices.

dumping Selling products at unfairly low prices

MARKETING AROUND THE WORLD

CHINA: THE NEW ECONOMIC POWERHOUSE

Companies around the world are coming to grips with the developing economic power of China. With 25 percent of the world's total population, China's 1.3 billion people confer considerable market power, and its economy is growing at an astounding 9.5 percent a year. The development and expansion of China's manufacturing sector has also become a major source of competition for manufacturers in North America and Europe. China also accounts for a large portion of the United States' total trade deficit.

The United States and other industrialized nations have overcome challenges from other countries on the manufacturing front before, such as South Korea and Mexico. Although these developing nations were able to provide low-cost alternatives, other industrialized nations remained dominant in high-tech industries because they could provide skilled workers and proximity to customers. However, the current situation with China is different. For the first time, a country is competing with both low costs *and* advanced technology. China can produce goods at a cost of 30 to 50 percent lower than the cost of production in the United States. Even in industries in which the Chinese penetrate at a very low level, such as advanced networking equipment, they are able to substantially affect price competition.

This high level of productivity has drawn foreign companies into China. Many U.S. industries, including apparel, electronics, and plastics, have been shuttering U.S. factories for decades and moving their operations to China. Some blame China's expansion as a major factor in the loss of 2.7 million manufacturing jobs in the United States since 2000. However, despite this rapidly occurring expansion, some critics say that the growth of China's infrastructure will lag far behind the growth of industry for some time. While the Chinese government is investing in building roads, railways, and ports, the existing infrastructure is not extensive enough to accommodate the country's dramatic level of growth. Although manufacturing and labor costs remain lower in China, cargo transportation costs may remain considerably higher than in other countries.

Despite U.S. losses in the manufacturing sector, the expansion of trade with China has helped other industries. U.S. corporations, such as Procter & Gamble, Amway, Avon, and Motorola, have greatly increased their profits by manufacturing products in China and selling them directly to the growing Chinese middle class, which now comprises 100 million consumers. The demand for raw materials for manufacturing in China has also created a boom in the world commodity markets, boosting profits for U.S. steelmakers and lumber companies. General Motors plans to sell as many Buicks in China as in the United States. China is also the largest broadband DSL market with Motorola and Intel expecting to cash in on this opportunity.[b]

World Trade Organization (WTO)   An entity that promotes free trade among member nations

The most significant outcome of the Uruguay Round was the establishment of the World Trade Organization (WTO) to promote free trade among 148 member nations. Fulfilling this purpose requires eliminating trade barriers; educating individuals, companies, and governments about trade rules around the world; and assuring global markets that no sudden changes of policy will occur. The WTO also serves as a forum for trade negotiations and dispute resolution. At the heart of the WTO are agreements that provide legal ground rules for international commerce and trade policy.[35]

International Involvement

Marketers engage in international marketing activities at several levels of involvement covering a wide spectrum, as Figure 5.1 shows. Domestic marketing involves marketing strategies aimed at markets within the home country; at the other extreme, global marketing entails developing marketing strategies for major regions or for the entire world. Many firms with an international presence start as small companies serving local and regional markets and expand to national markets before considering opportunities in foreign markets. The level of commitment to international marketing is a major variable in international marketing strategies. In this section, we examine importing and exporting, trading companies, licensing and franchising, contract manufacturing, joint ventures, direct ownership, and other approaches to international involvement.

Importing and Exporting

importing The purchase of products from a foreign source

exporting The sale of products to foreign markets

Importing and exporting require the least amount of effort and commitment of resources. Importing is the purchase of products from a foreign source. Exporting, the sale of products to foreign markets, enables businesses of all sizes to participate in global business. Limited exporting may occur even if a firm makes little or no effort to obtain foreign sales. Foreign buyers may seek the company and/or its products, or a distributor may discover the firm's products and export them. A firm may find an exporting intermediary to take over most marketing functions associated with selling to other countries. This approach entails minimal effort and cost. Modifications in packaging, labeling, style, or color may be the major expenses in adapting a product for the foreign market. Having sound objectives and maintaining product quality are important in attaining a competitive advantage in exporting.[36]

Figure 5.1
Levels of Involvement in Global Marketing

Domestic marketing
All marketing strategies focus on the market in the country of origin.

Limited exporting
The firm develops no international marketing strategies, but international distributors or foreign firms purchase some of its products.

International marketing
International markets are a consideration in the marketing strategy.

Globalized marketing
Marketing strategies are developed for major regions or the entire world so firms can compete globally.

MARKETING LEADERS

ARISTOCRAT ANGUS

The Aristocrat Angus Ranch was founded in 1965 by Ben and Anita Houston near Denver, Colorado. Over the years, the ranch grew as the Houstons experienced success showing their Angus bulls at prestigious venues such as the International Livestock Show and the National Western Stock Show. The Houstons developed a breeding program focused on quality, productivity, and longevity, using sophisticated breeding and performance records. Today, their Aristocrat Land and Cattle Company has grown to include a purebred Angus herd, a commercial herd of Angus, a feedlot with a capacity of 2,500 head, and a state-of-the-art embryo transplant center. Ben and Anita Houston continue to operate the ranch, with the assistance of their four children; their son Skylar handles the day-to-day management responsibilities at the ranch.

The company has developed a close relationship with nearby Colorado State University, which has allowed Aristocrat to be a part of the development of new technologies and veterinary treatments. One such project, involving Colorado State, Aristocrat Angus, and Colorado Genetics, Inc., was the export of live cattle and frozen embryos to the Ukraine in 1992. In May of that year, 14 bulls, 71 heifers, and 2,000 frozen embryos were shipped on a specially modified airplane—the first ever direct export of cattle made by air from Denver. The cattle were delivered to Kiev, where Skylar Houston and Sam Woody of Aristocrat spent six weeks exhibiting the cattle at the Kiev World Expo. This initial shipment was followed by a second shipment of almost 500 head of cattle in the fall, which were transported by road and waterways to the Ukraine. The development of artificial insemination and embryo transfer helped Aristocrat to broaden the channels for marketing its products around the world.

Aristocrat Angus is an example of a small entrepreneurial firm that has created opportunities for exporting its products to foreign markets such as the Ukraine, Mexico, and Japan. The small family business has become a specialist at understanding the needs of cattle ranchers around the world. The embryo transfer of a cattle breed such as Black Angus to other countries provides a unique opportunity for ranchers in other countries to improve productivity. Ranchers from other nations also come to the ranch in Colorado to observe Aristocrat's operation so that they can get ideas for improving their own ranches at home. As Aristocrat Angus learns more about marketing and related activities associated with selling to other countries, it can become a better exporter and continue to expand its sales and profits. It can be extremely meaningful for a small family business to be able to reach buyers in other countries who need and want a specialty product such as a cattle embryo transplant to enhance their ability not only to make a profit, but also to contribute to the food supply for their country.[c]

Export agents bring together buyers and sellers from different countries and collect a commission for arranging sales. Export houses and export merchants purchase products from different companies and then sell them abroad. They are specialists at understanding foreign customers' needs. Using exporting intermediaries involves limited risk because no direct investment in the foreign country is required.

Marketers sometimes employ a trading company, which links buyers and sellers in different countries but is not involved in manufacturing and does not own assets related to manufacturing. Trading companies buy goods in one country at the lowest price consistent with quality and sell them to buyers in another country. The best-known U.S. trading company is Sears World Trade, which specializes in consumer goods, light industrial items, and processed foods. Trading companies reduce risk for firms seeking to get involved in international marketing. A trading company provides producers with information about products that meet quality and price expectations in domestic and international markets.

◉ Licensing and Franchising

licensing An alternative to direct investment requiring a licensee to pay commissions or royalties on sales or supplies used in manufacturing

When potential markets are found across national boundaries, and when production, technical assistance, or marketing know-how is required, **licensing** is an alternative to direct investment. The licensee (the owner of the foreign operation) pays commissions or royalties on sales or supplies used in manufacturing. The licensee may also pay an initial down payment or fee when the licensing agreement is signed. Exchanges of management techniques or technical assistance are primary reasons for licensing agreements. Yoplait is a French yogurt that is licensed for production in the United States; the Yoplait brand tries to maintain a French image.

Licensing is an attractive alternative to direct investment when the political stability of a foreign country is in doubt or when resources are unavailable for direct investment. Licensing can also be a valuable strategy for enhancing a firm's brand while generating additional revenue. PepsiCo has licensed many products, including T-shirts, men's and women's apparel, footwear, and accessories, under its well-known name. The company views licensing as a significant tool for building awareness of and extending the Pepsi brand.[37]

franchising A form of licensing in which a franchiser, in exchange for a financial commitment, grants a franchisee the right to market its product in accordance with the franchiser's standards

Franchising is a form of licensing in which a company (the franchiser) grants a franchisee the right to market its product, using its name, logo, methods of operation, advertising, products, and other elements associated with the franchiser's business, in return for a financial commitment and an agreement to conduct business in accordance with the franchiser's standard of operations. This arrangement allows franchisers to minimize the risks of international marketing in four ways: (1) the franchiser does not have to put up a large capital investment; (2) the franchiser's revenue stream is fairly consistent because franchisees pay a fixed fee and royalties; (3) the franchiser retains control of its name and increases global penetration of its product; and (4) franchise agreements ensure a certain standard of behavior from franchisees,

Licensing and Franchising
Subway, with over 23,500 restaurants in 82 countries, was voted the top franchise opportunity by *Entrepreneur* magazine.

Source: world.subway.com/ countries/frmMainPage.aspx?cc=SWE. Reprinted courtesy of Doctor's Associates, Inc.

which protects the franchise name.[38] KFC, Wendy's, McDonald's, Holiday Inn, and Marriott are well-known franchisers with international visibility. In Indonesia, for example, Bambang Rachmadi owns McDonald's Indonesia, which operates 85 franchised McDonald's restaurants.[39]

◉ Contract Manufacturing

contract manufacturing The practice of hiring a foreign firm to produce a designated volume of product to specification

Contract manufacturing occurs when a company hires a foreign firm to produce a designated volume of the firm's product to specification, and the final product carries the domestic firm's name. The Gap, for example, relies on contract manufacturing for some of its apparel; Reebok uses Korean contract manufacturers to manufacture many of its athletic shoes. Marketing may be handled by the contract manufacturer or by the contracting company.

◉ Joint Ventures

joint venture A partnership between a domestic firm and a foreign firm or government

In international marketing, a **joint venture** is a partnership between a domestic firm and a foreign firm or government. Joint ventures are especially popular in industries that call for large investments, such as natural resources extraction or automobile manufacturing. Control of the joint venture may be split equally or one party may control decision making. Joint ventures are often a political necessity because of nationalism and government restrictions on foreign ownership. They also provide legitimacy in the eyes of the host country's citizens. Local partners have firsthand knowledge of the economic and sociopolitical environment and of distribution networks, and they may have privileged access to local resources (raw material, labor management, and so on). Entrepreneurs in many less developed countries actively seek associations with a foreign partner as a ready means of implementing their own corporate strategy.[40]

Joint ventures are assuming greater global importance because of cost advantages and the number of inexperienced firms entering foreign markets. They may be the result of a tradeoff between a firm's desire for completely unambiguous control of an enterprise and its quest for additional resources. They may occur when acquisition or internal development is not feasible or when the risks and constraints leave no other alternative. As project sizes increase in the face of global competition and firms attempt to spread the huge costs of technological innovation, the impetus to form joint ventures is stronger.[41]

strategic alliances Partnerships formed to create a competitive advantage on a worldwide basis

Strategic alliances, the newest form of international business structure, are partnerships formed to create competitive advantage on a worldwide basis. They are very similar to joint ventures. What distinguishes international strategic alliances from other business structures is that partners in the alliance may have been traditional rivals competing for market share in the same product class. An example of such an alliance is New United Motor Manufacturing, Inc. (NUMMI), formed by Toyota and General Motors, which today manufactures the popular Toyota Tacoma compact pickup, as well as the Toyota Corolla, Pontiac Vibe, and the right-hand-drive Toyota Voltz for sale in Japan. This alliance united the quality engineering of Japanese cars with the marketing expertise and market access of General Motors.[42] Partners in international strategic alliances often retain their distinct identities, and each brings a core competency to the union.

◉ Direct Ownership

direct ownership A situation in which a company owns subsidiaries or other facilities overseas

Once a company makes a long-term commitment to marketing in a foreign nation that has a promising political and economic environment, **direct ownership** of a foreign subsidiary or division is a possibility. Mexico's Gigante grocery chain, for example, has opened stores in Los Angeles and southern California, where it hopes its name will

Leadership. Reliability.
Commitment to clients.

A winning combination in
Latin America.

With local offices throughout Latin America, and over
100 years of experience in the region, JPMorgan is
dedicated to providing advice, capital and a complete
range of global products to meet the needs of
corporations, financial institutions and sovereigns.
If you seek global strength, local expertise and
proven commitment, turn to JPMorgan.

jpmorgan.com

JPMorgan

JPMorgan is a marketing name for investment banking businesses of J.P. Morgan Chase & Co. and its subsidiaries worldwide. Investment banking activities are performed by securities affiliates of J.P. Morgan Chase & Co., including J.P. Morgan Securities Inc., member NYSE/SIPC. Lending, derivative, and commercial banking activities are performed by banking affiliates of J.P. Morgan Chase & Co. ©2003 J.P. Morgan Chase & Co. All rights reserved.

Direct Ownership
JPMorgan Chase is a leading global financial services firm with operations in over 50 countries. As such, it offers local expertise in many regions where its clients might want to do business.

multinational enterprise   A firm that has operations or subsidiaries in many countries

appeal to the 11 million Latinos who live there.[43] Most foreign investment covers only manufacturing equipment or personnel because the expense of developing a separate foreign distribution system can be tremendous. The opening of retail stores in Canada, Europe, or Mexico can require a staggering financial investment in facilities, research, and management.

The term **multinational enterprise** refers to firms that have operations or subsidiaries in many countries. Often the parent company is based in one country and carries on production, management, and marketing activities in other countries. The firm's subsidiaries may be mostly autonomous so they can respond to the needs of individual international markets. Table 5.3 lists the ten largest global corporations.

A wholly owned foreign subsidiary may be allowed to operate independently of the parent company to give its management more freedom to adjust to the local environment. Cooperative arrangements are developed to assist in marketing efforts, production, and management. A wholly owned foreign subsidiary may export products to the home country. Some U.S. automobile manufacturers, for example, import cars built by their foreign subsidiaries. A foreign subsidiary offers important tax, tariff, and other operating advantages. One of the greatest advantages is the cross-cultural approach. A subsidiary usually operates under foreign management so that it can develop a local identity. The greatest danger in such an arrangement comes from political uncertainty: a firm may lose its foreign investment.

Table 5.3   The Ten Largest Global Corporations

Rank	Company	Country	Revenues (In Millions)
1.	Wal-Mart	United States	$263,009
2.	BP	Britain	$232,571
3.	ExxonMobil	United States	$222,883
4.	Royal Dutch/ Shell	Britain/Netherlands	$201,728
5.	General Motors	United States	$195,324
6.	Ford Motors	United States	$164,505
7.	DaimlerChrysler	Germany	$156,602
8.	Toyota Motor	Japan	$153,111
9.	General Electric	United States	$134,187
10.	Total	France	$118,441

Source: "The Fortune Global 500," *Fortune,* July 26, 2004, pp. 163–182.

Customization Versus Globalization of International Marketing Strategies

Like domestic marketers, international marketers develop marketing strategies to serve specific target markets. Traditionally, international marketing strategies have customized marketing mixes according to cultural, regional, and national differences. Many soap and detergent manufacturers, for example, adapt their products to local water conditions, equipment, and washing habits. Ford Motor Company has customized its F-series truck to accommodate global differences in roads, product use, and economic conditions. The strategy has been quite successful, with millions of Ford trucks sold around the world. Ford's strategy may best be described as *mass customization,* the use of standard platforms with custom applications. This practice dissolves the oxymoron of efficiency of mass production with effectiveness of customization of a product or service.[44]

globalization The development of marketing strategies that treat the entire world (or its major regions) as a single entity

At the other end of the spectrum, **globalization** of marketing involves developing marketing strategies as though the entire world (or its major regions) were a single entity; a globalized firm approaches the world market with as much standardization in the marketing strategy as possible. Nike and Adidas shoes, for example, are standardized worldwide. Other examples of globalized products include electronic communications equipment, American clothing, movies, soft drinks, rock and alternative music CDs, cosmetics, and toothpaste. Sony televisions, Levi jeans, and American cigarette brands post year-to-year gains in the world market. Today, technological advancement, particularly with regard to computers and telecommunications, has the potential to facilitate globalization.[45]

For many years, organizations have attempted to globalize their marketing mixes as much as possible by employing standardized products, promotion campaigns, prices, and distribution channels for all markets. The economic and competitive payoffs for globalized marketing strategies are certainly great. Brand name, product characteristics, packaging, and labeling are among the easiest marketing mix variables to standardize; media allocation, retail outlets, and price may be more difficult. In the end, the degree of similarity among the various environmental and market conditions determines the feasibility and degree of globalization. A successful globalization strategy often depends on the extent to which a firm can implement the idea of "think globally, act locally."[46] Even take-out food lends itself to globalization: McDonald's, KFC, and Taco Bell restaurants seem to satisfy hungry cus-

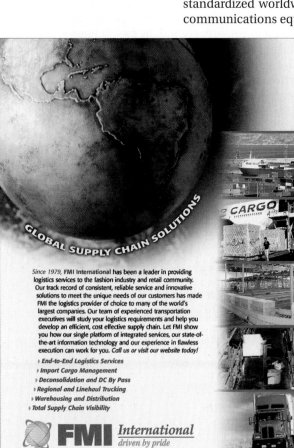

Globalization
Companies such as FMI International help global clients coordinate their supply chains and logistics.

tomers in every hemisphere, although menus are customized to some degree to satisfy local tastes.

International marketing demands some strategic planning if a firm is to incorporate foreign sales into its overall marketing strategy. Although globalization has been viewed as a mechanism for world economic development, advances may be challenging if marketers ignore unique nation-specific factors.[47] International marketing activities often require customized marketing mixes to achieve the firm's goals. Globalization requires a total commitment to the world, regions, or multinational areas as an integral part of the firm's markets; world or regional markets become as important as domestic ones. Regardless of the extent to which a firm chooses to globalize its marketing strategy, extensive environmental analysis and marketing research are necessary to understand the needs and desires of the target market(s) and successfully implement the chosen marketing strategy. A global presence does not automatically result in a global competitive advantage. However, a global presence generates five opportunities for creating value: (1) to adapt to local market differences, (2) to exploit economies of global scale, (3) to exploit economies of global scope, (4) to mine optimal locations for activities and resources, and (5) to maximize the transfer of knowledge across locations.[48] To exploit these opportunities, marketers need to conduct marketing research, the topic of the next chapter.

CHAPTER REVIEW

① Understand the nature of global markets and international marketing.

International marketing involves developing and performing marketing activities across national boundaries. International markets can provide tremendous opportunities for growth.

② Analyze the environmental forces affecting international marketing efforts.

Environmental aspects of special importance include cultural, social, economic, political, legal, ethical, and technological forces. Because marketing activities are primarily social in purpose, they are influenced by beliefs and values regarding family, religion, education, health, and recreation. Cultural differences may affect decision-making behavior, product adoption, and product use. Gross domestic product (GDP) and GDP per capita are common measures of a nation's economic standing. Political and legal forces include a nation's political and ethics systems, laws, regulatory bodies, special-interest groups, and courts. Significant trade barriers include import tariffs, quotas, embargoes, and exchange controls. Advances in technology have greatly facilitated international marketing.

③ Identify several important regional trade alliances, markets, and agreements.

Various regional trade alliances and specific markets, such as the North American Free Trade Agreement, the European Union, the Common Market of the Southern Cone, Asia-Pacific Economic Cooperation, the General Agreement on Tariffs and Trade, and the World Trade Organization, create both opportunities and constraints for companies engaged in international marketing.

④ Examine methods of involvement in international marketing activities.

Importing (the purchase of products from a foreign source) and exporting (the sale of products to foreign markets) are the easiest and most flexible methods of entering international markets. Licensing and franchising are arrangements whereby one firm pays fees to another for the use of its name, expertise, and supplies. Contract manufacturing occurs when a company hires a foreign firm to produce a designated volume of the firm's product to specification and the final product carries the domestic firm's name. Joint ventures are partnerships between a domestic firm and a foreign firm or a government; strategic alliances are partnerships formed to create competitive advantage on a worldwide basis. A firm can also establish its own marketing or production facilities overseas. When companies have direct ownership of facilities in many countries, they may be considered multinational enterprises.

⑤ **Recognize that international marketing strategies fall along a continuum from customization to globalization.**

Although most firms adjust their marketing mixes for differences in target markets, some firms standardize their marketing efforts worldwide. Traditional full-scale international marketing involvement is based on products customized according to cultural, regional, and national differences. Globalization, however, involves developing marketing strategies as if the entire world (or regions of it) were a single entity; a globalized firm markets standardized products in the same way everywhere. International marketing demands some strategic planning if a firm is to incorporate foreign sales into its overall marketing strategy.

✓ Please visit the student website at **www.prideferrell.com** for ACE Self-Test questions that will help you prepare for ACE self-test exams.

KEY CONCEPTS

international marketing
gross domestic product (GDP)
import tariff
quota
embargo
exchange controls
balance of trade

North American Free Trade Agreement (NAFTA)
European Union (EU)
Common Market of the Southern Cone (MERCOSUR)
Asia-Pacific Economic Cooperation (APEC)

General Agreement on Tariffs and Trade (GATT)
dumping
World Trade Organization (WTO)
importing
exporting
licensing

franchising
contract manufacturing
joint venture
strategic alliances
direct ownership
multinational enterprise
globalization

ISSUES FOR DISCUSSION AND REVIEW

1. How does international marketing differ from domestic marketing?

2. What factors must marketers consider as they decide whether to become involved in international marketing?

3. Why do you think this chapter focuses on an analysis of the international marketing environment?

4. A manufacturer recently exported peanut butter with a green label to a nation in the Far East. The product failed because it was associated with jungle sickness. How could this mistake have been avoided?

5. If you were asked to provide a small tip (or bribe) to have a document approved in a foreign nation where this practice is customary, what would you do?

6. How will NAFTA affect marketing opportunities for U.S. products in North America (the United States, Mexico, and Canada)?

7. In marketing dog food to Latin America, what aspects of the marketing mix would a U.S. firm need to alter?

8. What should marketers consider as they decide whether to license or enter into a joint venture in a foreign nation?

9. Discuss the impact of strategic alliances on marketing strategies.

10. Contrast globalization with customization of marketing strategies. Is one practice better than the other? Explain.

MARKETING APPLICATIONS

1. Which environmental forces (sociocultural, economic, political/legal, or technological) might a marketer need to consider when marketing the following products in the international marketplace, and why?
   a. Barbie dolls
   b. Beer
   c. Financial services
   d. Televisions

2. Which would be the best organizational approach to international marketing of the following products, and why?
   a. Construction equipment manufacturing
   b. Cosmetics
   c. Automobiles

3. Describe how a shoe manufacturer would go from domestic marketing, to limited exporting, to international marketing, and finally to globalization of marketing. Give examples of some activities that might be involved in this process.

ONLINE EXERCISE

4. Founded in 1910 as "Florists' Telegraph Delivery," FTD was the first company to offer a "flowers-by-wire" service. FTD does not itself deliver flowers but depends on local florists to provide this service. In 1994, FTD expanded its toll-free telephone-ordering service by establishing a website. Visit the site at **www.ftd.com.**
   a. Click on International Deliveries. Select a country to which you would like to send flowers. Summarize the delivery and pricing information that would apply to that country.
   b. Determine the cost of sending fresh-cut seasonal flowers to Germany.
   c. What are the benefits of this global distribution system for sending flowers worldwide? What other consumer products could be distributed globally through the Internet?

VIDEO CASE

BMW International

Bayerische Motoren Werke (better known as BMW) is one of Europe's top automakers. The Munich-based company manufactures vehicles under several brand names, including BMW, Mini, and Rolls-Royce Motor Cars, as well as BMW Motorcycles, which also offers a line of motorcycling apparel such as leather suits, gloves, and boots. The company sold more than 1 million vehicles in 2003.

In the United States, the BMW Group has grown to include marketing, sales, and financial service organizations for the BMW, to Mini, and Rolls-Royce brands; DesignworksUSA, an industrial design firm in California; a technology office in Silicon Valley; and various other operations throughout the country. BMW Manufacturing Corporation in South Carolina is part of BMW Group's global manufacturing network and is the exclusive manufacturer for all Z4 roadster and X5 Sports Activity Vehicles, supplying these products to more than 100 countries. The BMW Group sales organization markets vehicles in the United States through networks of 340 BMW car, 327 BMW Sports Activity Vehicle, 148 BMW Motorcycle, and 70 Mini dealers. BMW (US) Hold-ing Corporation, the BMW Group's sales headquarters for North, Central, and South America, is located in Woodcliff Lake, New Jersey.

In Germany, the United States, and abroad, BMW concentrates exclusively on selected premium segments in the automobile market, making it the only multibrand automobile manufacturer in the world that is not active in the mass market. With the BMW, Mini, and (since 2003) Rolls-Royce brands, BMW covers the premium segments ranging from the small car to the absolute-luxury category. BMW's premium brand strategy allows it to focus on achieving higher revenues per vehicle on the basis of a high value and a distinctive brand profile. The premium brand strategy therefore positions BMW for further profitable growth. The company expects the premium segments of the automobile market to grow worldwide by about 50 percent in the next ten years, while the mass volume automobile segments will increase by about 25 percent. The BMW Group is aiming to exploit this growth by assessing consumer behavior and meeting consumers' expectations for premium-branded automobiles.

Consumers are increasingly status and brand conscious. They are willing to pay more than $3 for a latte at Starbucks, yet clip coupons for the grocery store and shop at wholesale clubs for discounted household items. According to Michael Silverstein and Neil Fiske in their book *Trading Up,* people are willing to pay more for quality products that matter to them, even if that requires making sacrifices in other areas. Mercedes recognized this in the early 1990s and responded by introducing less expensive "entry-level" luxury autos—such as the M class and the C class automobiles, which sold for $26,000 to $40,000—with the hope that buyers would "trade up" to more expensive vehicles as they matured. The phenomenon of trading up affects a variety of income levels—from $50,000 to $200,000—and all demographics—singles, seniors, families, and so on. Part of Mercedes' strategy stemmed from its recognition that the average age of its customers was over 50, but it wanted to reach a younger target market. BMW has also benefited from customers' desire for status and quality. BMW recognized the lifetime value of its customers and sought to encourage them to get into BMW-branded vehicles as early as possible. Thus, BMW introduced the 318i, which as a retail price in the mid-$20,000s, reached a whole new segment for the company.

Luxury goods can be broken down into several categories, including "accessible superpremium" and "old luxury brand extensions." Accessible superpremium products are priced at the high end of their category (e.g., high-end liquors, pet foods, cosmetics), while old luxury brand extensions reflect the strategic orientation that BMW has adopted in global markets. This strategy involves offering lower-priced versions of existing products, which previously were accessible only to affluent buyers, to attract new market segments.

The best example of making a luxury brand accessible is the Mini. The brand's association with BMW makes it a premium small-car product, while its $17,000 entry price in the United States makes it affordable. The car also appeals to the nostalgia for small British roadsters and fun cars. Publicity from the film *The Italian Job* may also have helped the car reach record sales of 170,000 in 2003. The Mini will gain a competitor in 2006 when Daimler-Chrysler launches the Smart minicar brand. Daimler-Chrysler hopes to sell about 60,000 Smart-brand vehicles once the brand is established.

The BMW Group is following a worldwide strategy that can best be described as mass customization: tailoring products, prices, and distribution for customers' personal selection in the premium brand market. Although such customizing is more complex than mass-producing computers and cars, BMW, as well as other automakers, desires to custom-build more vehicles to match specific customer needs.

The best example of success through product diversification is the various BMW product lines. The 3-series is available in the mid-$20,000 to $50,000 range and includes sedans, coupes, and convertibles as well as the X3 All-Activity vehicle. The 5-series caters to the core luxury market with prices beginning in the low $40,000s to mid-$50,000s. This series is complemented by the X5 All-Activity vehicle. The 6-series is a luxury coupe that sells in the $60,000 to $70,000 range. It is considered a "grand turismo," which represents the combination of sports car spirit and luxury-salon comfort. The high-tech car of the future, the 7-series, embodies all the features of the ultimate luxury brand. But for those who might not consider the 7-series sufficiently luxurious, BMW's recently purchased Rolls-Royce brand should certainly satisfy their desire for the best in an automobile.

As a German company, BMW has developed an international brand and reputation that has become a role model for other organizations engaging in global marketing. Its key to success is acquiring an understanding of its demanding target market and developing a marketing mix that produces customer satisfaction. Consumers around the world aspire to the pride of owning and driving a BMW.[49]

QUESTIONS FOR DISCUSSION

1. How has BMW developed such a successful international marketing strategy?
2. How would you compare BMW's worldwide marketing strategy with that of U.S. car manufacturers, such as Ford and General Motors?
3. Do you think BMW's global marketing strategy meets the requirements of the concept of globalization as described in the chapter?

Target Market Selection and Research

Part 3 focuses on researching and selecting target customers. The development of a marketing strategy begins with the customer. Chapter 6 provides a foundation for analyzing customers through a discussion of marketing information systems and the basic steps in the marketing research process. Chapter 7 focuses on one of the major steps in the development of a marketing strategy: selecting and analyzing target markets.

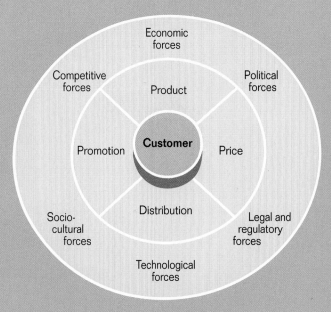

6

Marketing Research and Information Systems

OBJECTIVES

1 Define marketing research and understand its importance.

2 Describe the basic steps in conducting market research.

3 Explore the fundamental methods of gathering data for marketing research.

4 Describe how tools such as databases, decision support systems, and the Internet facilitate marketing information systems and research.

5 Identify key ethical and international considerations in marketing research.

McDonald's Responds to Changing Customer Desires

The fast-food industry has long concentrated on getting customers in and out as quickly as possible. McDonald's, however, has uncovered information that customers might be interested in a more relaxing interior environment where they can hang out for a while. Facing competition from relaxing environment specialists such as Starbucks, McDonald's developed a McCafe coffee shop concept in Chicago, but it never took off. McDonald's continued to tinker with the concept, opening a Starbucks-style coffee bar McCafe restaurant inside a Mountain View McDonald's in Raleigh, North Carolina. A West Coast location followed in Palo Alto, California. If the concept catches on, McDonald's plans to roll out McCafes all over the country. Already, 500 McCafes are doing well outside the United States, particularly in New Zealand and Australia.

Research at McDonald's suggests that the McCafe concept will appeal to the "veto vote," the person in a group of diners who typically vetoes McDonald's because there is nothing on its regular menu that appeals to that person. Research also indicates that high-end coffee consumers have different expectations from those of the average McDonald's customer. Thus McCafe's baristas are separate from McDonald's regular counter workers; they dress differently, and they are trained to educate the average cheeseburger-buyer who might be intimidated by ordering a cappuccino.

Because not all McCafe franchise owners have previously worked for the company, there is a new policy to give McDonald's owner-operators the freedom to define their décor, style, and offerings according to the local environment and customer base. Ideas other than McCafe are surfacing, such as a diner home-style food environment. McDonald's is trying a lot of different things and gathering information to make the most of the good ideas. The best information is coming from franchisees who engage in change and provide information about successes. One interesting statistic is that overhauls that change the look of a restaurant 100 percent are almost guaranteed to increase sales by one-third.

Change and innovation has been a part of McDonald's business plan for decades. With public concern about the healthfulness of fast food and the ever-increasing demand for fast-paced meals, there is a need for change in the fast-food industry. Part of the change for McDonald's is to integrate its ownership of Boston Market restaurants with McDonald's restaurants by testing Boston Market dinner items inside McDonald's restaurants. Bringing Boston Market into McDonald's could create more of a diner environment and greatly expand the food menu. McDonald's has to be careful that it maintains a strong marketing information system that can gain consumer reaction to its innovative plans.[1]   ◄

The marketing research conducted by McDonald's illustrates that implementing the marketing concept requires that marketers obtain information about the characteristics, needs, and desires of target market customers. When used effectively, such information facilitates customer relationship management by helping marketers focus their efforts on meeting and even anticipating the needs of their customers. Marketing research and information systems that can provide practical and objective information to help firms develop and implement marketing strategies therefore are essential to effective marketing.

In this chapter, we focus on how marketers gather information needed to make marketing decisions. First, we define marketing research and examine the individual steps of the marketing research process, including various methods of collecting data. Next, we look at how technology aids in collecting, organizing, and interpreting marketing research data. Finally, we consider ethical and international issues in marketing research.

The Importance of Marketing Research

marketing research The systematic design, collection, interpretation, and reporting of information to help marketers solve specific marketing problems or take advantage of marketing opportunities

Marketing research is the systematic design, collection, interpretation, and reporting of information to help marketers solve specific marketing problems or take advantage of marketing opportunities. As the word *research* implies, it is a process for gathering information not currently available to decision makers. The purpose of marketing research is to inform an organization about customers' needs and desires, marketing opportunities for particular goods and services, and changing attitudes and purchase patterns of customers. Market information increases marketers' ability to respond to customer needs, which leads to improved organizational performance.[2] Detecting shifts in buyers' behaviors and attitudes helps companies stay in touch with the ever-changing marketplace. Fast-food marketers, for example, would be very interested to know that young men ages 18 to 24 average 20 trips a month to fast-food establishments, compared with about 15 trips a month for all fast-food diners. The billions that consumers spend dining out represent a tremendous opportunity for those companies willing to invest the resources to understand this market.[3] Strategic planning requires marketing research to facilitate the process of assessing such opportunities or threats.

All sorts of organizations use marketing research to help them develop marketing mixes to match the needs of customers. Marketing research can help a firm better understand market opportunities, ascertain the potential for success for new products, and determine the feasibility of a particular marketing strategy. JCPenney, for example, conducted extensive research to learn more about a core segment of shoppers who weren't being adequately reached by department stores: middle-income

IT professionals, B.S. degree, $100K HH income, with an earring.

They're out there. You can find them at SurveySavvy. Your distinct group is easy to find in our SurveySavvy online panel. That's because SurveySavvy is made up of more than 3 million people worldwide. We built it using patented technology and insight gained from 27 years in market research. SurveySavvy is just one of our services – from all methodologies of data collection to sample-only solutions – that help you get the precise market intelligence you need. To find the people you're looking for, visit luthresearch.com or call 800-465-5884.

LUTH research

mothers between the ages of 35 and 54. The research involved asking 900 women about their casual clothes preferences. Later the firm conducted in-depth interviews with 30 women about their clothing needs, feelings about fashion, and their shopping experiences. The research helped the company recognize that this "missing middle" segment of shoppers was frustrated with the choices and quality of clothing available in their price range and stressed out by the experience of shopping for clothes for themselves. Armed with this information, Penney launched two new lines of moderately priced, quality casual women's clothing, including one by designer Nicole Miller.[4] A study by SPSS Inc. found that the most common reasons for conducting marketing research surveys included determining satisfaction (43 percent), product development (29 percent), branding (23 percent), segmentation (18 percent), business markets (11 percent), and awareness, trend tracking, and concept testing (18 percent).[5]

The real value of marketing research is measured by improvements in a marketer's ability to make decisions. Marketers should treat information in the same manner as they use other resources, and they must weigh the costs of obtaining information against the benefits derived. Information should be judged worthwhile if it results in marketing activities that better satisfy the firm's target customers, lead to increased sales and profits, or help the firm achieve some other goal.

The Marketing Research Process

To maintain the control needed to obtain accurate information, marketers approach marketing research as a process with logical steps: (1) locating and defining issues or problems, (2) designing the research project, (3) collecting data, (4) interpreting research findings, and (5) reporting research findings (Figure 6.1). These steps should be viewed as an overall approach to conducting research rather than as a rigid set of rules to be followed in each project. In planning research projects, marketers must consider each step carefully and determine how they can best adapt them to resolve the particular issues at hand.

Locating and Defining Research Issues or Problems

The first step in launching a research study is issue or problem definition, which focuses on uncovering the nature and boundaries of a situation or question related to marketing strategy or implementation. The first sign of a problem is typically a depar-

Figure 6.1
The Five Steps of the
Marketing Research Process

ture from some normal function, such as failure to attain objectives. If a corporation's objective is a 12 percent sales increase and the current marketing strategy resulted in a 6 percent increase, this discrepancy should be analyzed to help guide future marketing strategies. Declining sales, increasing expenses, and decreasing profits also signal problems. Armed with this knowledge, a firm could define a problem as finding a way to adjust for biases stemming from existing customers when gathering data or to develop methods for gathering information to help find new customers. Conversely, when an organization experiences a dramatic rise in sales or some other positive event, it may conduct marketing research to discover the reasons and maximize the opportunities stemming from them.

Marketing research often focuses on identifying and defining market opportunities or changes in the environment. When a firm discovers a market opportunity, it may need to conduct research to understand the situation more precisely so it can craft an appropriate marketing strategy. That is exactly what Dunkin' Donuts is doing to remain competitive against Krispy Kreme and Starbucks as well as McDonald's, which recently entered the espresso-drink market. A survey of Dunkin' Donuts customers revealed that they welcomed menu changes such as iced beverages, espresso drinks, and scrambled eggs and cheese on a bagel. The firm's research also suggested that it should continue its strategy of targeting workday on-the-go customers and not take on Starbucks directly.[6] The company can use this information to focus its efforts on specific target markets and refine its marketing strategy appropriately.

To pin down the specific boundaries of a problem or an issue through research, marketers must define the nature and scope of the situation in a way that requires probing beneath the superficial symptoms. The interaction between the marketing manager and the marketing researcher should yield a clear definition of the research need. Researchers and decision makers should remain in the issue or problem definition stage until they have determined precisely what they want from marketing research and how they will use it. Deciding how to refine a broad, indefinite issue or problem into a precise, researchable statement is a prerequisite for the next step in the research process.

◉ Designing the Research Project

research design An overall plan for obtaining the information needed to address a research problem or issue

Once the problem or issue has been defined, the next step is research design, an overall plan for obtaining the information needed to address it. This step requires formulating a hypothesis and determining what type of research is most appropriate for testing the hypothesis to ensure the results are reliable and valid.

hypothesis An informed guess or assumption about a certain problem or set of circumstances

● **Developing a Hypothesis.** The objective statement of a marketing research project should include hypotheses based on both previous research and expected research findings. A hypothesis is an informed guess or assumption about a certain problem or set of circumstances. It is based on all the insight and knowledge available about the problem or circumstances from previous research studies and other sources. As information is gathered, a researcher can test the hypothesis. For example, a food marketer like H. J. Heinz might propose the hypothesis that children today have considerable influence on their families' buying decisions regarding ketchup

exploratory research
Research conducted to gather more information about a problem or to make a tentative hypothesis more specific

descriptive research   Research conducted to clarify the characteristics of certain phenomena and thus solve a particular problem

causal research   Research in which it is assumed that a particular variable X causes a variable Y

reliability   A condition existing when a research technique produces almost identical results in repeated trials

validity   A condition existing when a research method measures what it is supposed to measure

and other grocery products. A marketing researcher would then gather data, perhaps through surveys of children and their parents, and draw conclusions about whether the hypothesis is correct. Sometimes several hypotheses are developed during an actual research project; the hypotheses that are accepted or rejected become the study's chief conclusions.

● **Types of Research.**   The hypothesis being tested determines whether an exploratory, descriptive, or causal approach will be used to gather data. When marketers need more information about a problem or want to make a tentative hypothesis more specific, they may conduct **exploratory research**. For instance, they may review the information in the firm's own records or examine publicly available data. Questioning knowledgeable people inside and outside the organization may yield new insights into the problem. Information about industry trends or demographics may also be an excellent source for exploratory research. For example, finding data indicating that inner-city household incomes grew by 20 percent to $35,000 a year between 1990 and 2000 while the national median household income grew by just 14 percent could be useful to consider in marketing plans to serve specific market segments.[7]

If marketers need to understand the characteristics of certain phenomena to solve a particular problem, **descriptive research** can aid them. Such studies may range from general surveys of customers' education, occupation, or age to specifics on how often teenagers eat at fast-food restaurants after school or how often customers buy new pairs of athletic shoes. For example, if Nike and Reebok want to target more young women, they might ask 15- to 35-year-old females how often they work out, how frequently they wear athletic shoes for casual use, and how many pairs of athletic shoes they buy in a year. Such descriptive research can be used to develop specific marketing strategies for the athletic-shoe market. Descriptive studies generally demand much prior knowledge and assume the issue or problem is clearly defined. Some descriptive studies require statistical analysis and predictive tools. The marketer's major task is to choose adequate methods for collecting and measuring data.

Hypotheses about causal relationships call for a more complex approach than a descriptive study. In **causal research**, it is assumed that a particular variable X causes a variable Y. Marketers must plan the research so that the data collected determine whether X influences Y. To do so, marketers must try to hold constant all variables except X and Y. For example, to determine whether new carpeting, pet-friendly policies, or outside storage increases the number of rentals in an apartment complex, researchers need to keep all variables constant except one of these three variables in a specific time period.

● **Research Reliability and Validity.**   In designing research, marketing researchers must ensure that research techniques are both reliable and valid. A research technique has **reliability** if it produces almost identical results in repeated trials. But a reliable technique is not necessarily valid. To have **validity**, the research method must measure what it is supposed to measure, not something else. For example, although a group of customers may express the same level of satisfaction based on a rating scale, the individuals may not exhibit the same repurchase behavior because of different personal characteristics. This result might cause the researcher to question the validity of the satisfaction scale if the purpose of rating satisfaction was to estimate potential repurchase behavior.[8] A study to measure the effect of advertising on sales would be valid if advertising could be isolated from other factors or variables that affect sales. The study would be reliable if replications of it produced the same results.

Primary Data Collection
CfMC Research Software assists companies in personal interviewing and Internet surveys.

◉ Collecting Data

The next step in the marketing research process is collecting data to help prove (or disprove) the research hypothesis. The research design must specify what types of data to collect and how they will be collected.

● **Types of Data.**   Marketing researchers have two types of data at their disposal. **Primary data** are observed and recorded or collected directly from respondents. This type of data must be gathered by observing phenomena or surveying people of interest. **Secondary data** are compiled both inside and outside the organization for some purpose other than the current investigation. Secondary data include general reports supplied to an enterprise by various data services and internal and online databases. Such reports might concern market share, retail inventory levels, and customers' buying behavior. Secondary data are commonly available in private or public reports or have been collected and stored by the organization itself. Due to the opportunity to obtain data via the Internet, more than half of all marketing research now comes from secondary sources.

primary data   Data observed and recorded or collected directly from respondents

secondary data   Data compiled both inside and outside the organization for some purpose other than the current investigation

● **Sources of Secondary Data.**   Marketers often begin the data collection phase of the marketing research process by gathering secondary data. They may use available reports and other information from both internal and external sources to study a marketing problem.

Internal sources of secondary data can contribute tremendously to research. An organization's own database may contain information about past marketing activities, such as sales records and research reports, which can be used to test hypotheses and pinpoint problems. From sales reports, for example, a firm may be able to determine

Table 6.1 **Internal Sources of Secondary Data**

- Sales data, which may be broken down by geographical area, product type, or even type of customer

- Accounting information, such as costs, prices, and profits, by product category

- Competitive information gathered by the sales force

Source: "Internal Secondary Market Research," Lycos Small Business, http://business.lycos.com/cch/ guidebook.html?lpv=1&docNumber=PO3_3020, February 6, 2002.

not only which product sold best at certain times of the year but also which colors and sizes customers preferred. Such information may have been gathered for management or financial purposes.[9] Table 6.1 lists some commonly available internal company information that may be useful for marketing research purposes.

Accounting records are also an excellent source of data but, strangely enough, are often overlooked. The large volume of data an accounting department collects does not automatically flow to other departments. As a result, detailed information about costs, sales, customer accounts, or profits by product category may not be easily accessible to the marketing area. This condition develops particularly in organizations that do not store marketing information on a systematic basis.

External sources of secondary data include periodicals, government publications, unpublished sources, and online databases. Periodicals such as *Business Week, The Wall Street Journal, Sales & Marketing Management, Marketing Research,* and *Industrial Marketing* publish general information that can help marketers define problems and develop hypotheses. *Survey of Buying Power,* an annual supplement to *Sales & Marketing Management,* contains sales data for major industries on a county-by-county basis. Many marketers also consult federal government publications such as the *Statistical Abstract of the United States,* the *Census of Business,* the *Census of Agriculture,* and the *Census of Population;* some of these government publications are available through online information services or the Internet. Although the government still conducts its primary census every ten years, it now surveys 250,000 households every month, providing decision makers with a more up-to-date demographic picture of the nation's population every year. Such data helps Target executives make merchandising and marketing decisions as well as identify promising locations for new Target stores.[10]

In addition, companies may subscribe to services, such as ACNielsen or Information Resources, Inc., that track retail sales and other information. IRI, for example, tracks consumer purchases using in-store, scanner-based technology. Marketers can purchase information from IRI about a product category, such as frozen orange juice, as secondary data.[11] Small businesses may be unable to afford such services, but they can still find a wealth of information through industry publications and trade associations.[12] Table 6.2 summarizes the major external sources of secondary data, excluding syndicated services.

● **Methods of Collecting Primary Data.** The collection of primary data is a more lengthy, expensive, and complex process than the collection of secondary data. To gather primary data, researchers use sampling procedures, survey methods, observation, and experimentation. These efforts can be handled in-house by the firm's own research department or contracted to a private research firm such as ACNielsen, Information Resources, Inc., IMS International, and Quality Controlled Services.

E-MARKETING AND TECHNOLOGY
TAKING A LOOK-LOOK AT YOUTH TRENDS

Look-Look.com is an online, real-time service that provides accurate and reliable information, research, news, trends, and photos about global trendsetting youths ages 14 to 30. With youth spending estimated at $140 billion annually and growing, many companies are willing to pay an annual subscription fee of about $20,000 for access to this valuable data.

Look-Look pays more than 20,000 handpicked, pre-screened young people from all over the world to e-mail information about their styles, trends, opinions, and ideas. These trendsetting young people are forward thinkers, innovative, and influential to their peers. Although trendsetters account for only about 20 percent of the youth population, they influence the other 80 percent. Look-Look also has 20 photographers who travel the globe capturing youth trends in photos.

Look-Look clients have instant access to online surveys and polls and the results. They also can key in research questions and instantly reach a worldwide focus group 24 hours a day. Clients include an apparel company, video game manufacturers, a cosmetics company, beverage firms, and movie studios. Look-Look delivers fast, accurate, and timely information through the Internet and the company's own intranet and database.

Look-Look co-presidents DeeDee Gordon and Sharon Lee believe that full understanding of the youth culture requires a constant dialog with youth—not just once- or twice-a-year focus groups or market research. Look-Look provides information on the latest fashion, entertainment, technology, activities, eating and drinking habits, health and beauty trends, youth mindsets, and *City Guide* suggestions (the best shops, hangouts, and restaurants in selected cities). The "living research" provided by Look-Look means they never stop listening and observing and that their information is alive and always moving. Whether it's cropped cherry red hair, skintight leather hip-huggers, tattoos, or body piercing, Look-Look knows what the youth market likes, and for a fee, they'll help youth marketers stay on top of the latest trends.[a]

Table 6.2   External Sources of Secondary Data

- Trade associations (e.g., American Marketing Association)

- Industry publications and databases (e.g., *Inbound Logistics, Sales & Marketing Management*)

- Government databases (e.g., Census Bureau, Department of Commerce)

- Sales, volume, and brand market share measurement systems (e.g., ACNielsen Company, Information Resources, Inc.)

Source: "External Secondary Market Research," Lycos Small Business, http://business.lycos.com/cch/guidebook.html?lpv=1&docNumber=PO3_3011, February 6, 2002.

population   All the elements, units, or individuals of interest to researchers for a specific study

sample   A limited number of units chosen to represent the characteristics of the population

sampling   The process of selecting representative units from a total population

probability sampling   A sampling technique in which every element in the population being studied has a known chance of being selected for study

random sampling   A type of probability sampling in which all units in a population have an equal chance of appearing in a sample

stratified sampling   A type of probability sampling in which the population is divided into groups according to a common attribute and a random sample is then chosen within each group

nonprobability sampling   A sampling technique in which there is no way to calculate the likelihood that a specific element of the population being studied will be chosen

quota sampling   A nonprobability sampling technique in which researchers divide the population into groups and then arbitrarily choose participants from each group

Sampling.   Because the time and resources available for research are limited, it is almost impossible to investigate all the members of a target market or other population. A **population**, or "universe," includes all the elements, units, or individuals of interest to researchers for a specific study. For a Gallup poll designed to predict the results of a presidential election, all registered voters in the United States would constitute the population. By systematically choosing a limited number of units—a **sample**—to represent the characteristics of a total population, researchers can project the reactions of a total market or market segment. **Sampling** in marketing research, therefore, is the process of selecting representative units from a total population. Sampling techniques allow marketers to predict buying behavior fairly accurately on the basis of the responses from a representative portion of the population of interest. Most types of marketing research employ sampling techniques.

There are two basic types of sampling: probability sampling and nonprobability sampling. With **probability sampling**, every element in the population being studied has a known chance of being selected for study. Random sampling is a kind of probability sampling. When marketers employ **random sampling**, all the units in a population have an equal chance of appearing in the sample. The various events that can occur have an equal or known chance of taking place. For example, a specific card in a regulation deck should have a 1/52 probability of being drawn at any one time. Sample units are ordinarily chosen by selecting from a table of random numbers statistically generated so that each digit, 0 through 9, will have an equal probability of occurring in each position in the sequence. The sequentially numbered elements of a population are sampled randomly by selecting the units whose numbers appear in the table of random numbers.

Another kind of probability sampling is **stratified sampling**, in which the population of interest is divided into groups according to a common attribute and a random sample is then chosen within each group. The stratified sample may reduce some of the error that could occur in a simple random sample. By ensuring that each major group or segment of the population receives its proportionate share of sample units, investigators avoid including too many or too few sample units from each group. Samples are usually stratified when researchers believe there may be variations among different types of respondents. For example, many political opinion surveys are stratified by gender, race, age, and/or geographic location.

The second type of sampling, **nonprobability sampling**, is more subjective than probability sampling because there is no way to calculate the likelihood that a specific element of the population being studied will be chosen. Quota sampling, for example, is highly judgmental because the final choice of participants is left to the researchers. In **quota sampling**, researchers divide the population into groups and then arbitrarily choose participants from each group. A study of people who wear eyeglasses, for example, may be conducted by interviewing equal numbers of men and women who wear eyeglasses. In quota sampling, there are some controls—usually limited to two or three variables, such as age, gender, or race—over the selection of participants. The controls attempt to ensure that representative categories of respondents are interviewed. Because quota samples are not probability samples, not everyone has an equal chance of being selected, and sampling error therefore cannot be measured statistically. Quota samples are used most often in exploratory studies, when hypotheses are being developed. Often a small quota sample will not be projected to the total population, although the findings may provide valuable insights into a problem. Quota samples are useful when people with some common characteristic are found and questioned about the topic of interest. A probability sample used to study people allergic to cats would be highly inefficient.

Survey Methods.   Marketing researchers often employ sampling to collect primary data through mail, telephone, online, or personal interview surveys. The results of such surveys are used to describe and analyze buying behavior. Selection of a survey method depends on the nature of the problem or issue; the data needed to test the hypothesis; and the resources, such as funding and personnel, available to the researcher. Marketers may employ more than one survey method depending on the goals of the research. The SPSS Inc. survey of American Marketing Association members found that 43.8 percent use telephone surveys; 39.3 percent, web-based surveys; 36.8 percent, focus groups; 19 percent, mail surveys; 11.8 percent, e-mail surveys; and 9.6 percent, in-person interviews.[13] Table 6.3 summarizes and compares the advantages of the various survey methods.

Gathering information through surveys is becoming increasingly difficult because fewer people are willing to participate. Many people believe responding to surveys takes up too much scarce personal time, especially as surveys become longer

Table 6.3   Comparison of the Four Basic Survey Methods

	Mail Surveys	Telephone Surveys	Online Surveys	Personal Interview Surveys
Economy	Potentially lower in cost per interview than telephone or personal surveys if there is an adequate response rate.	Avoids interviewers' travel expenses; less expensive than in-home interviews.	The least expensive method if there is an adequate response rate.	The most expensive survey method; shopping mall and focus group interviews have lower costs than in-home interviews.
Flexibility	Inflexible; questionnaire must be short and easy for respondents to complete.	Flexible because interviewers can ask probing questions but observations are impossible.	Less flexible; survey must be easy for online users to receive and return; short, dichotomous, or multiple-choice questions work best.	Most flexible method; respondents can react to visual materials; demographic data are more accurate; in-depth probes are possible.
Interviewer Bias	Interviewer bias is eliminated; questionnaires can be returned anonymously.	Some anonymity; may be hard to develop trust in respondents.	Interviewer bias is eliminated, but e-mail address on the return eliminates anonymity.	Interviewers' personal characteristics or inability to maintain objectivity may result in bias.
Sampling and Respondents' Cooperation	Obtaining a complete mailing list is difficult; nonresponse is a major disadvantage.	Sample limited to respondents with telephones; devices that screen calls, busy signals, and refusals are a problem.	Sample limited to respondents with computer access; the available e-mail address list may not be a representative sample for some purposes.	Not-at-homes are a problem, which may be overcome by focus-group and shopping mall interviewing.

Marketing Decision Support
Directions Research provides a library of product testing research on over 3,800 products across 50 categories.

and more detailed. Others have concerns about how much information marketers are gathering and whether their privacy is being invaded. The unethical use of selling techniques disguised as marketing surveys has also led to decreased cooperation. These factors contribute to non-response rates for any type of survey. Most researchers consider nonresponse the greatest threat to valid survey research.[14]

In a **mail survey**, questionnaires are sent to respondents, who are encouraged to complete and return them. Mail surveys are used most often when the individuals in the sample are spread over a wide area and funds for the survey are limited. A mail survey is potentially the least expensive survey method as long as the response rate is high enough to produce reliable results. The main disadvantages of this method are the possibilities of a low response rate and of misleading results if respondents differ significantly from the population being sampled. Research has found that providing a monetary incentive to respond to a mail survey has a significant impact on response rates for both consumer and business samples. However, such incentives may reduce the cost effectiveness of this survey method.[15]

In a **telephone survey**, an interviewer records respondents' answers to a questionnaire over a phone line. A telephone survey has some advantages over a mail survey. The rate of response is higher because it takes less effort to answer the telephone and talk than to fill out and return a questionnaire. If there are enough interviewers, a telephone survey can be conducted very quickly. Thus, political candidates or organizations seeking an immediate reaction to an event may choose this method. In addition, a telephone survey permits interviewers to gain rapport with respondents and ask probing questions.

However, only a small proportion of the population likes to participate in telephone surveys. Just one-third of Americans are willing to participate in telephone interviews, down from two-thirds 20 years ago.[16] This poor image can significantly limit participation and distort representation in a telephone survey. Moreover, telephone surveys are limited to oral communication; visual aids or observation cannot be included. Many households are excluded from telephone directories by choice (unlisted numbers) or because the residents moved after the directory was published. Potential respondents often use telephone answering machines, voice mail, or caller ID to screen or block calls. Moreover, an increasing number of younger Americans have given up their fixed phone lines in favor of wireless phones.[17] These issues have serious implications for the use of telephone samples in conducting surveys.

Online surveys are evolving as an alternative to telephone surveys. In an **online survey**, questionnaires can be transmitted to respondents who have agreed to be contacted and have provided their e-mail addresses. More firms are using their websites

mail survey A research method in which respondents answer a questionnaire sent through the mail

telephone survey A research method in which respondents' answers to a questionnaire are recorded by interviewers on the phone

online survey A research method in which respondents answer a questionnaire via e-mail or on a website

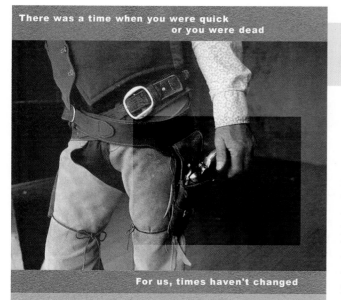

Online Surveys
Western Wats provides quick and accurate data collection solutions with online surveys.

to conduct surveys. Online surveys can also make use of online communities—such as chat rooms, web-based forums, and newsgroups—to identify trends in interests and consumption patterns. Movies, consumer electronics, food, and computers are popular topics in many online communities.[18] Indeed, by "listening in" on these ongoing conversations, marketers may be able to identify new product opportunities and consumer needs. Moreover, this type of online data can be gathered at little incremental cost compared to alternative data sources.[19] Evolving technology and the interactive nature of the Internet allow for considerable flexibility in designing questionnaires for online surveys.

Given the growing number of households that have computers with Internet access, marketing research is likely to rely heavily on online surveys in the future. Indeed, experts predict that Internet-based marketing research will account for about 50 percent, or around $3 billion, of marketing research spending in 2005 compared to just 2 percent of marketing research revenues in 1998.[20] Furthermore, as negative attitudes toward telephone surveys render that technique less representative and more expensive, the integration of e-mail, fax, and voice-mail functions into one computer-based system provides a promising alternative for survey research. E-mail surveys have especially strong potential within organizations whose employees are networked and for associations that publish members' e-mail addresses. College students in particular are often willing to provide their e-mail address and other personal information in exchange for incentives such as T-shirts and other giveaways.[21] However, there are some ethical issues to consider when using e-mail for marketing research, such as "spam" (unsolicited e-mail) and privacy.

personal interview survey
A research method in which participants respond to survey questions face to face

In a **personal interview survey**, participants respond to questions face to face. Various audiovisual aids—pictures, products, diagrams, or prerecorded advertising copy—can be incorporated in a personal interview. Rapport gained through direct interaction usually permits more in-depth interviewing, including probes, follow-up questions, or psychological tests. In addition, because personal interviews can be longer, they may yield more information. Finally, respondents can be selected more carefully, and reasons for nonresponse can be explored.

in-home (door-to-door) interview A personal interview that takes place in the respondent's home

One such research technique is the **in-home (door-to-door) interview**. The in-home interview offers a clear advantage when thoroughness of self-disclosure and elimination of group influence are important. In an in-depth interview of 45 to 90 minutes, respondents can be probed to reveal their real motivations, feelings, behaviors, and aspirations.

Twenty years after his birth, a graffiti artist named Marc Milecofsky started a clothing line with six hand-painted T-shirt designs. The line: Ecko Unlimited. The line took off when rapper Chuck D and director Spike Lee were seen in Ecko's shirts. Now, with annual revenue in the neighborhood of $400 million a year, Ecko Unlimited has become one of the hottest urban apparel firms on the market. Ecko stays up to date on what consumers want by hanging out and talking with people in social hot spots and focuses on point-of-sale instead of mass-media advertising in order to connect with the consumer. Ecko now offers a variety of lines and products that include gloves, hats, watches, outerwear, underwear, and shoes.[b]

focus-group interview
A research method involving observation of group interaction when members are exposed to an idea or a concept

telephone depth interview
An interview that combines the traditional focus group's ability to probe with the confidentiality provided by telephone surveys

shopping mall intercept interview   A research method that involves interviewing a percentage of persons passing by "intercept" points in a mall

The object of a **focus-group interview** is to observe group interaction when members are exposed to an idea or a concept. The state of Nebraska used focus groups as part of its effort to develop a formal marketing campaign. Among other things, focus groups suggested the state promote its history and natural beauty.[22] Often these interviews are conducted informally, without a structured questionnaire, in small groups of 8 to 12 people. They allow customer attitudes, behavior, lifestyles, needs, and desires to be explored in a flexible and creative manner. Questions are open-ended and stimulate respondents to answer in their own words. Researchers can ask probing questions to clarify something they do not fully understand or something unexpected and interesting that may help explain buying behavior. For example, Ford Motor Company may use focus groups to determine whether to change its advertising to emphasize a vehicle's safety features rather than its style and performance. It may be necessary to use separate focus groups for each major market segment studied—men, women, and age groups—and experts recommend the use of at least two focus groups per segment in case one group is unusually idiosyncratic.[23] Focus groups have been found to be especially useful to set new product prices.[24]

Still another option is the **telephone depth interview**, which combines the traditional focus group's ability to probe with the confidentiality provided by telephone surveys. This type of interview is most appropriate for qualitative research projects among a small targeted group that is difficult to bring together for a traditional focus group because of members' profession, location, or lifestyle. Respondents can choose the time and day for the interview. Although this method is difficult to implement, it can yield revealing information from respondents who otherwise would be unwilling to participate in marketing research.[25]

The nature of personal interviews has changed. In the past, most personal interviews, which were based on random sampling or prearranged appointments, were conducted in the respondent's home. Today most personal interviews are conducted outside the home. **Shopping mall intercept interviews** involve interviewing a percentage of individuals passing by certain "intercept" points in a mall. Like any face-to-face interviewing method, mall intercept interviewing has many advantages. The interviewer is in a position to recognize and react to respondents' nonverbal indications of confusion. Respondents can be shown product prototypes, videotapes of commercials, and the like, and asked for their reactions. The mall environment lets the researcher deal with complex situations. For example, in taste tests, researchers know that all the respondents are reacting to the same product, which can be prepared and monitored from the mall test kitchen. In addition to the ability to conduct tests requiring bulky equipment, lower cost and greater control make shopping mall intercept interviews popular.

Questionnaire Construction.   A carefully constructed questionnaire is essential to the success of any survey. Questions must be clear, easy to understand, and directed toward a specific objective; that is, they must be designed to elicit information that meets the study's data requirements. Researchers need to define the objective before trying to develop a questionnaire because the objective determines the substance of the questions and the amount of detail. A common mistake in constructing questionnaires is to ask questions that interest the researchers but do not yield information useful in deciding whether to accept or reject a hypothesis. Finally, the most important rule in composing questions is to maintain impartiality.

The questions are usually of three kinds: open-ended, dichotomous, and multiple-choice.

Open-Ended Question

What is your general opinion about broadband Internet access?

_____

_____

Dichotomous Question

Do you presently have broadband access at home, work, or school?

Yes _____ No _____

Multiple-Choice Question

What age group are you in?

   Under 20 _____

   20–35 _____

   36 and over _____

Researchers must be very careful about questions that a respondent might consider too personal or that might require an admission of activities that other people are likely to condemn. Questions of this type should be worded to make them less offensive.

Observation Methods.   In using observation methods, researchers record individuals' overt behavior, taking note of physical conditions and events. Direct contact with them is avoided; instead, their actions are examined and noted systematically. For instance, researchers might use observation methods to answer the question "How long does the average McDonald's restaurant customer have to wait in line before being served?" Observation may include the use of ethnographic techniques, such as watching customers interact with a product in a real-world environment. Bissell, Inc., employed ethnographic techniques when it observed how a very small sample of consumers used its Steam Gun, a hot-water-based cleaning appliance, in the home. Based on this research, the company made several changes to the product, including its name, before launching the Steam N Clean.[26]

Observation may also be combined with interviews. For example, during a personal interview, the condition of a respondent's home or other possessions may be observed and recorded. The interviewer can also directly observe and confirm demographic information such as race, approximate age, and sex.

Data gathered through observation can sometimes be biased if the person is aware of the observation process. However, an observer can be placed in a natural market environment, such as a grocery store, without biasing or influencing shoppers' actions. If the presence of a human observer is likely to bias the outcome or if human sensory abilities are inadequate, mechanical means may be used to record behavior. Mechanical observation devices include cameras, recorders, counting machines, scanners, and equipment that records physiological changes. The electronic scanners used in supermarkets are very useful in marketing research. They provide accurate data on sales and customers' purchase patterns, and marketing researchers may obtain such data from the supermarkets.

Observation is straightforward and avoids a central problem of survey methods: motivating respondents to state their true feelings or opinions. However, observation tends to be descriptive. When it is the only method of data collection, it may not provide insights into causal relationships. Another drawback is that analyses based on observation are subject to the biases of the observer or the limitations of the mechanical device.

experiment A research method that attempts to maintain certain variables while measuring the effects of experimental variables

Experimentation. Another method for gathering primary data is experimentation. In an **experiment**, marketing researchers attempt to maintain certain variables while measuring the effects of experimental variables. Experimentation requires that an independent variable (one not influenced by or dependent on other variables) be manipulated and the resulting changes in a dependent variable (one contingent on, or restricted to, one value or set of values assumed by the independent variable) be measured. PepsiCo, for example, used experimentation to test the taste, color, and packaging of its new Mountain Dew Code Red soft drink on a sample from its target market.[27] Experimentation is used primarily in marketing research to improve hypothesis testing.

◉ Interpreting Research Findings

statistical interpretation Analysis of what is typical or what deviates from the average

After collecting data to test their hypotheses, marketers need to interpret the research findings. Interpretation of the data is easier if marketers carefully plan their data analysis methods early in the research process. They should also allow for continual evaluation of the data during the entire collection period. They can then gain valuable insight into areas that should be probed during the formal interpretation.

The first step in drawing conclusions from most research is to display the data in table format. If marketers intend to apply the results to individual categories of the things or people being studied, cross-tabulation may be quite useful, especially in tabulating joint occurrences. For example, using the two variables gender and purchase rates of automobile tires, a cross-tabulation could show how men and women differ in purchasing automobile tires.

After the data are tabulated, they must be analyzed. Statistical interpretation focuses on what is typical or what deviates from the average. It indicates how widely responses vary and how they are distributed in relation to the variable being measured. When marketers interpret statistics, they must take into account estimates of expected error or deviation from the true values of the population. The analysis of data may lead researchers to accept or reject the hypothesis being studied.

Interpreting Research Findings
Decision Analyst assists companies in interpreting research to develop new products, services, ads, and promotions.

◉ Reporting Research Findings

The final step in the marketing research process is to report the research findings. Before preparing the report, the marketer must take a clear, objective look at the findings to see how well the gathered facts answer the research question or support or negate the initial hypotheses. In most cases, it is extremely unlikely that the study can provide everything needed to answer the research question. Thus, the researcher must point out the deficiencies, along with the reasons for them, in the report.

The report of research results is usually a formal, written document. Researchers must allow time for the writing task when they plan and schedule the project. Because the report is a means of communicating with the decision makers who will use the research findings, researchers need to determine beforehand how much detail and supporting data to include. They should keep in mind that corporate executives prefer reports that are short, clear, and simply expressed. Researchers often give their summary and recommendations first, especially if decision makers do not have time to study how the results were obtained. A technical report allows its users to analyze data and interpret recommendations because it describes the research methods and procedures and the most important data gathered. Thus, researchers must recognize the needs and expectations of the report user and adapt to them.

))) Using Technology to Improve Marketing Information Gathering and Analysis

Technology is making information for marketing decisions increasingly accessible. The ability of marketers to track customer buying behavior and to discern what buyers want is changing the nature of marketing. Customer relationship management is being enhanced by integrating data from all customer contacts and combining that information to improve customer retention. Information technology permits internal research and quick information gathering to understand and satisfy customers. For example, company responses to e-mail complaints as well as to communications through mail, telephone, and fax can be used to improve customer satisfaction, retention, and value.[28] Armed with such information, marketers can fine-tune marketing mixes to satisfy the needs of their customers.

The integration of telecommunications and computer technologies is allowing marketers to access a growing array of valuable information sources related to industry forecasts, business trends, and customer buying behavior. Electronic communication tools can be effectively utilized to gain accurate information with minimal customer interaction. Most marketing researchers have e-mail, voice mail, teleconferencing, and fax machines at their disposal. In fact, many firms use marketing information systems to network all these technologies and organize all the marketing data available to them. In this section, we look at marketing information systems and specific technologies that are helping marketing researchers obtain and manage marketing research data.

◉ Marketing Information Systems

marketing information system (MIS) A framework for the management and structuring of information gathered regularly from sources inside and outside an organization

A **marketing information system (MIS)** is a framework for the day-to-day management and structuring of information gathered regularly from sources both inside and outside an organization. An MIS provides a continuous flow of information about prices, advertising expenditures, sales, competition, and distribution expenses. Anheuser-Bush, for example, uses a system called BudNet that compiles information about past sales at individual stores, inventory, competitors' displays and prices, and a host of other information collected by distributors' sales representatives on hand-held computers. BudNet allows managers to respond quickly to changes in social trends of competitors' strategies with an appropriate promotional message, package, display, or discount.[29]

The main focus of the MIS is on data storage and retrieval, as well as on computer capabilities and management's information requirements. Regular reports of sales by product or market categories, data on inventory levels, and records of salespeople's activities are examples of information that is useful in making decisions. In the MIS, the means of *gathering* data receive less attention than do the procedures for expediting the *flow* of information.

An effective MIS starts by determining the objective of the information, that is, by identifying decision needs that require certain information. The firm can then specify an information system for continuous monitoring to provide regular, pertinent information on both the external and internal environment. FedEx, for example, has developed interactive marketing systems to provide instantaneous communication between the company and its customers. Through the telephone and Internet, customers can track their packages and receive immediate feedback concerning delivery. The company's website provides valuable information about customer usage, and it allows customers to express directly what they think about company services. The evolving telecommunications and computer technology is allowing marketing information systems to cultivate one-to-one relationships with customers.

◎ Databases

Most marketing information systems include internal databases. As we saw in Chapter 4, databases allow marketers to tap into an abundance of information useful in making marketing decisions: internal sales reports, newspaper articles, company news releases, government economic reports, bibliographies, and more, typically accessed through a computer system. Information technology has made it possible to develop databases to guide strategic planning and help improve customer services. Many commercial websites require consumers to register and provide personal information to access the site or make a purchase. Frequent flier programs permit airlines to ask loyal customers to participate in surveys about their needs and desires, and the airlines can track their best customers' flight patterns by time of day, week, month, and year. Grocery stores gain a significant amount of data through checkout scanners tied to store discount cards. According to ACNielsen, 78 percent of U.S. households now use at least one store discount card.[30] In fact, one of the best ways to predict market behavior is the use of database information gathered through loyalty programs or other transaction-based processes.[31]

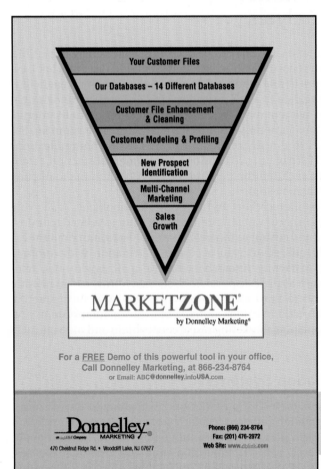

Databases
Donnelley Marketing provides 19 different databases to solve their customers' marketing research needs.

E-MARKETING AND TECHNOLOGY
WAL-MART'S DATA WAREHOUSE BRINGS EFFICIENCY AND PROFITS

Wal-Mart is not only the world's largest retailer, but also operates the world's largest data warehouse, an organizationwide data collection and storage system that gathers data from all of a firm's critical operation systems as well as from selected external data sources. Wal-Mart's data warehouse contains more than 460 terabytes of data stored on mainframe computers; experts believe the Internet comprises less than half that amount of data. Wal-Mart's data warehouse is operated by Teradata, a division of NCR.

Wal-Mart collects reams of data about products and customers primarily from checkout scanners at its Wal-Mart discount and Sam's Club membership stores. Clerks and managers may also use wireless handheld units to gather additional inventory data. The company stores the detailed data for an infinite period of time and classifies it into categories, for example, by product, individual store, or region. The system also serves as a basis for the Retail Link decision-support system between Wal-Mart and its suppliers. Retail Link permits some vendors, like Kraft, to access data about how well their products are selling at Wal-Mart stores.

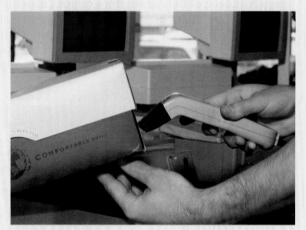

The mountain of data Wal-Mart collects helps boost efficiency dramatically by matching product supplies to demand. This information, for example, helped the firm determine to stock not only flashlights but also extra strawberry Pop-Tarts prior to a hurricane in Florida. It seems that Pop-Tart sales increase as much as seven times their normal rate ahead of a hurricane. The data may also help the company track supplier performance, set ideal prices, and even determine how many cashiers to schedule at a certain store on a certain day. Most importantly, it helps the retailer avoid carrying too much inventory or not having enough to satisfy demand.

Although some people are concerned about the amount of personal information Wal-Mart collects, the company contends that it safeguards this information carefully. In fact, Linda Dillman, Wal-Mart's chief information officer, insists that the retailer is far more interested in information on products than on consumers. "Me knowing what you specifically buy is not necessarily going to help me get the right merchandise into the store. Knowing collectively what goes into one shopping cart together tells us a lot more."[c]

Marketing researchers can also use commercial databases developed by information research firms, such as Lexis-Nexis, to obtain useful information for marketing decisions. Many of these commercial databases are accessible online for a fee. They can also be obtained in printed form or on CD-ROMs. In most commercial databases, the user typically does a computer search by keyword, topic, or company, and the database service generates abstracts, articles, or reports that can be printed out. Accessing multiple reports or a complete article may cost extra.

single-source data Information provided by a single marketing research firm

Information provided by a single firm on household demographics, purchases, television viewing behavior, and responses to promotions such as coupons and free samples is called **single-source data**.[32] For example, Behavior Scan, offered by Information Resources, Inc., screens about 60,000 households in 26 U.S. markets. This single-source information service monitors consumer household televisions and records the programs and commercials watched. When buyers from these households shop in stores equipped with scanning registers, they present Hotline cards (similar to credit cards) to cashiers. This enables each customer's identification to be electronically coded so the firm can track each product purchased and store the information in a database.

⊙ Marketing Decision Support Systems

marketing decision support
system (MDSS)   Customized
computer software that aids
marketing managers in decision
making

A **marketing decision support system (MDSS)** is customized computer software that aids marketing managers in decision making by helping them anticipate the effects of certain decisions. Some MDSSs have a broader range and offer greater computational and modeling capabilities than spreadsheets; they let managers explore a greater number of alternatives. For example, a MDSS can determine how sales and profits might be affected by higher or lower interest rates or how sales forecasts, advertising expenditures, production levels, and the like, might affect overall profits. For this reason, MDSS software is often a major component of a company's marketing information system. For example, both Oracle and Ford Motor Company use a software product called NeuroServer that acts as a customer interface to solve problems and answer questions for customers. Based on customized parameters, it allows marketers to acquire specific information on customers that can go into the MDSS.[33] Some MDSSs incorporate artificial intelligence and other advanced computer technologies.

⊙ The World Wide Web

Table 6.4 lists several websites that can be valuable resources for marketing research. The U.S. Bureau of the Census, for example, uses the World Wide Web to disseminate information that may be useful to marketing researchers, particularly through the *Statistical Abstract of the United States*, and data from the most recent census. Among the companies that exploit census data for marketing decisions are Starbucks, which analyzes the data to assess potential coffee shop sites, and Blockbuster, which mines

Table 6.4	Online Resources for Marketing Information
Government Sources	
U.S. Bureau of the Census	www.census.gov
U.S. Department of State	www.state.gov
FedWorld	www.fedworld.gov
Commercial Sources	
ACNielsen	www.acnielsen.com
Information Resources, Inc.	www.infores.com
Gallup	www.gallup.com
Arbitron	www.arbitron.com
Periodicals and Books	
Advertising Age	www.adage.com
Sales & Marketing Management	www.salesandmarketing.com
Fortune	www.fortune.com
Inc.	www.inc.com
Business Week	www.businessweek.com
Bloomberg Report	www.bloomberg.com

the data to help determine how many copies of a particular movie or video game to offer at each store.[34]

Companies can also mine their own websites for useful information. Amazon.com, for example, has built a relationship with its customers by tracking the types of books and music they purchase. Each time a customer logs onto the website, the company can offer recommendations based on the customer's previous purchases. Such a marketing system helps the company track the changing desires and buying habits of its most valued customers.

Issues in Marketing Research

The Importance of Ethical Marketing Research

Marketing managers and other professionals are relying more and more on marketing research, marketing information systems, and new technologies to make better decisions. It is therefore essential that professional standards be established by which to judge the reliability of such research. Such standards are necessary because of the ethical and legal issues that develop in gathering marketing research data. In addition, the relationships between research suppliers, such as marketing research agencies, and the marketing managers who make strategy decisions require ethical behavior. Organizations like the Marketing Research Association have developed codes of conduct and guidelines to promote ethical marketing research. To be effective, such guidelines must instruct those who participate in marketing research on how to avoid misconduct. Table 6.5 recommends explicit steps interviewers should follow when introducing a questionnaire.

International Issues in Marketing Research

Sociocultural, economic, political, legal, and technological forces vary in different regions of the world, and these variations create challenges for organizations attempting to understand foreign customers through marketing research. The marketing research process we described in this chapter is used globally, but to ensure that the research is valid and reliable, data-gathering methods may have to be modified to allow for regional differences. For example, experts have found that Latin Americans do not respond well to focus groups or in-depth interviews lasting more than 90 minutes. Researchers therefore need to adjust their tactics to generate information useful for marketing products in Latin America.[35] To ensure that global and regional differences are satisfactorily addressed, many companies retain a research firm with experience in the country of interest. Most of the largest marketing

Ethical Marketing Research
Opinion Place recognizes some of the key ethical issues in marketing research: currency of data and the lack of bias in analysis.

Table 6.5	Guidelines for Questionnaire Introduction

Questionnaire introduction should:

- Allow interviewers to introduce themselves by name.

- State the name of the research company.

- Indicate that this questionnaire is a marketing research project.

- Explain there will be no sales involved.

- Note the general topic of discussion (if this is a problem in a "blind" study, a statement such as "consumer opinion" is acceptable).

- State the likely duration of the interview.

- Assure the anonymity of the respondent and confidentiality of all answers.

- State the honorarium if applicable (for many business-to-business and medical studies, this is done up front for both qualitative and quantitative studies).

- Reassure the respondent with a statement such as, "There are no right or wrong answers, so please give thoughtful and honest answers to each question" (recommended by many clients).

Source: Reprinted with permission of The Marketing Research Association, P.O. Box 230, Rocky Hill, CT 06067-0230, (860) 257-4008.

research firms derive a significant share of their revenues from research conducted outside the United States. VNU, the largest marketing research firm in the world, received 47 percent of its revenues from outside the United States.[36]

Experts recommend a two-pronged approach to international marketing research. The first phase involves a detailed search for and analysis of secondary data to gain greater understanding of a particular marketing environment and to pinpoint issues that must be taken into account in gathering primary research data. Secondary data can be particularly helpful in building a general understanding of the market, including economic, legal, cultural, and demographic issues, as well as in assessing the risks of doing business in that market and in forecasting demand.[37] Marketing researchers often begin by studying country trade reports from the U.S. Department of Commerce as well as country-specific information from local sources, such as a country's website, and trade and general business publications such as *The Wall Street Journal*. These sources can offer insight into the marketing environ-

International Issues in Marketing Research
GMI helps businesses understand various cultural norms and values.

ment in a particular country and can even indicate untapped market opportunities abroad.

The second phase involves field research using many of the methods described earlier, including focus groups and telephone surveys, to refine a firm's understanding of specific customer needs and preferences. Specific differences among countries can have a profound influence on data gathering. For example, in-home (door-to-door) interviews are illegal in some countries. In China, few people have regular telephone lines, making telephone surveys both impractical and nonrepresentative of the total population. Primary data gathering may have a greater chance of success if the firm employs local researchers who better understand how to approach potential respondents and can do so in their own language.[38] Regardless of the specific methods used to gather primary data, whether in the United States or abroad, the goal is to understand the needs of specific target markets and thus craft the best marketing strategy to satisfy the needs of customers in each market, as we will see in the next chapter.

CHAPTER REVIEW

① Define marketing research and understand its importance.

Marketing research is the systematic design, collection, interpretation, and reporting of information to help marketers solve specific marketing problems or take advantage of marketing opportunities. Marketing research and information systems that furnish practical, unbiased information help firms avoid the assumptions and misunderstandings that could lead to poor marketing performance. The value of marketing research is measured by improvements in a marketer's ability to make decisions.

② Describe the basic steps in conducting market research.

To maintain the control needed to obtain accurate information, marketers approach marketing research as a process with logical steps: (1) defining and locating issues or problems, (2) designing the research project, (3) collecting data, (4) interpreting research findings, and (5) reporting research findings. The first step, issue or problem definition, focuses on uncovering the nature and boundaries of a situation or question related to marketing strategy or implementation. The second step involves designing a research project to obtain needed information, formulating a hypothesis, and determining what type of research to employ that will test the hypothesis so that the results are reliable and valid. The type of hypothesis being tested dictates whether exploratory, descriptive, or causal studies will be used. Research is considered reliable if it produces almost identical results in suc-

cessive repeated trials; it is valid if it measures what it is supposed to measure and not something else. The third step is the data-gathering phase. To apply research data to decision making, marketers must interpret and report their findings properly—the final two steps in the research process. Statistical interpretation focuses on what is typical or what deviates from the average. After interpreting the research findings, the researchers must prepare a report on the findings that the decision makers can understand and use.

③ Explore the fundamental methods of gathering data for marketing research.

For the third step in the marketing research process, two types of data are available. Primary data are observed and recorded or collected directly from subjects; secondary data are compiled inside or outside the organization for some purpose other than the current investigation. Secondary data may be collected from an organization's database and other internal sources, or from periodicals, government publications, and unpublished sources. Methods for collecting primary data include sampling, surveys, observation, and experimentation. Sampling involves selecting representative units from a total population. In probability sampling, every element in the population being studied has a known chance of being selected for study. Nonprobability sampling is more subjective because there is no way to calculate the likelihood that a specific element of the population being studied will be chosen. Marketing researchers employ sampling to collect primary data through surveys by mail, telephone, or the Internet or through personal or group interviews. A carefully constructed questionnaire is essential to the success of any survey. In using observation methods, researchers record respondents' overt behavior and take note of physical conditions and events, but avoid direct contact with respondents. In an experiment, marketing researchers attempt to maintain certain variables while measuring the effects of experimental variables.

(4) **Describe how tools such as databases, decision support systems, and the Internet facilitate marketing information systems and research.**
Many firms use computer technology to create a marketing information system (MIS), which is a framework for gathering and managing information from sources both inside and outside an organization. A database is a collection of information arranged for easy access and retrieval. A marketing decision sup-

port system (MDSS) is customized computer software that aids marketing managers in decision making by helping them anticipate what effect certain decisions will have. The World Wide Web also enables marketers to communicate with customers and obtain information.

(5) **Identify key ethical and international considerations in marketing research.**
Eliminating unethical marketing research practices and establishing generally acceptable procedures for conducting research are important goals of marketing research. International marketing uses the same marketing research process, but data-gathering methods may require modification to address differences.

Please visit the student website at **www.prideferrell.com** for ACE Self-Test questions that will help you prepare for exams.

KEY CONCEPTS

marketing research
research design
hypothesis
exploratory research
descriptive research
causal research
reliability
validity
primary data

secondary data
population
sample
sampling
probability sampling
random sampling
stratified sampling
nonprobability sampling
quota sampling

mail survey
telephone survey
online survey
personal interview survey
in-home (door-to-door) interview
focus-group interview
telephone depth interview

shopping mall intercept interview
experiment
statistical interpretation
marketing information system (MIS)
single-source data
marketing decision support system (MDSS)

ISSUES FOR DISCUSSION AND REVIEW

1. What is marketing research? Why is it important?

2. Describe the five steps in the marketing research process.

3. What is the difference between defining a research problem and developing a hypothesis?

4. Describe the different types of approaches to marketing research and indicate when each should be used.

5. Where are data for marketing research obtained? Give examples of internal and external data.

6. What is the difference between probability sampling and nonprobability sampling? In what situation

would it be best to use random sampling? Stratified sampling? Quota sampling?

7. Suggest some ways to encourage respondents to cooperate in mail surveys.

8. Describe some marketing problems that could be solved through information gained from observation.

9. What is a marketing information system, and what should it provide?

10. How does marketing research in other countries differ from marketing research in the United States?

MARKETING APPLICATIONS

1. After observing customers' traffic patterns, Bashas Markets repositioned the greeting card section in its stores, and card sales increased substantially. To increase sales for the following types of companies, what information might marketing researchers want to gather from customers?
   a. Furniture stores
   b. Gasoline outlets/service stations
   c. Investment companies
   d. Medical clinics

2. Choose a company in your city or town that you think might benefit from a research project. Develop a research question and outline a method to approach this question. Explain why you think the research question is relevant to the organization and why the particular methodology is suited to the question and the company.

3. Input for marketing information systems can come from internal or external sources. Indicate two firms or companies in your city that might benefit from internal sources and two that would benefit from external sources, and explain why they would benefit. Suggest the type of information each should gather.

4. Suppose you were opening a health insurance brokerage firm and wanted to market your services to small businesses with fewer than 50 employees. Determine which database for marketing information you would use in your marketing efforts, and explain why you would use it.

ONLINE EXERCISE

5. The World Association of Opinion and Marketing Research Professionals (founded as the European Society for Opinion and Marketing Research, ESOMAR, in 1948) is a nonprofit association for marketing research professionals. The European organization promotes the use of opinion and marketing research to improve marketing decisions in companies worldwide and works to protect personal privacy in the research process. Visit the association's website at **www.esomar.org/.**
   a. How can ESOMAR help marketing professionals conduct research to guide marketing strategy?
   b. How can ESOMAR help marketers protect the privacy of research subjects when conducting marketing research in other countries?
   c. ESOMAR introduced the first professional code of conduct for marketing research professionals in 1948. The association continues to update the document to address new technology and other changes in the marketing environment. According to ESOMAR's code, what are the specific professional responsibilities of marketing researchers?

VIDEO CASE

IRI Provides Marketing Research Data from Multiple Sources

One of today's leading marketing research firms is Information Resources, Inc. (IRI), which provides sales data to customers indicating how much of their products have been sold, where, and at what price. Such information is critical to planning market strategies and managing the movement of products through the supply chain. The Chicago-based firm's customers include manufacturers, retailers, and sales/marketing agencies in the United States and throughout the world. Now a subsidiary of Gingko Acquisition Corporation, IRI offers its customers vital marketing intelligence to help them make sound strategic marketing decisions.

One of IRI's most renowned research tools is the InfoScan store-tracking service. Through InfoScan, IRI collects sales data from a system of checkout scanners in supermarkets, drugstores, and mass merchandisers. Every week, data collected from more than 20,000 stores are input into IRI's huge database for analysis. IRI breaks this information down into client-specific databases. The company sells the analyzed information to customers, which include manufacturers such as Nestlé, Procter & Gamble, PepsiCo, and Lever Bros., as well as retailers like Kroger's, Albertson's, Walgreen's, and Target.

Databases developed by IRI allow marketers to tap into an abundance of information on sales, market share, distribution, pricing, and promotion for hundreds of consumer product categories. For example, InfoScan can track new products to assess their performance and gauge competitors' reactions to their marketing strategy. Once new products are on store shelves, IRI monitors related information such as prices and market share of competing products. This information helps the products' marketers gauge the effect of competitors' tactics so they can adjust their marketing strategies as necessary. InfoScan can also help marketers assess customers' reactions to changes in a product's price, packaging, display, and other marketing mix elements. By tracking a product's sales in relation to promotional efforts, InfoScan data also help marketers assess the effect of their own advertising as well as that of competitors.

Another IRI product, Behavior Scan, provides single-source data on household demographics, television viewing behavior, purchases, and responses to promotions such as coupons and free samples. Through Behavior Scan, IRI screens about 70,000 households in 26 U.S. markets. Behavior Scan monitors participating households' television viewing habits, recording the programs and commercials each household watches. When consumers from these households shop in a store equipped with scanning registers, they present credit-card-size hotline cards, which allow the store to electronically identify them so IRI can track their purchases and store the information in a database for analysis. With this information, IRI can relate the purchases of a household to the commercials viewed on television, further allowing the companies to assess the effects of their promotional strategies.

Although IRI specializes primarily in scanner-based data collection that documents what consumers buy under certain conditions—that is, behavioral research—the company also recognizes the value of attitudinal research to explain the "why behind the buy." Thus, IRI sought an alliance with Sorensen Associates to observe and interview shoppers at the point of purchase in supermarkets and other retail outlets. These in-store research methods provide valuable insights into shopping behavior and attitudes in a real-life retail environment. To expand its portfolio of client services, IRI has also partnered with Mosaic Group to conduct field surveys. By providing survey research, IRI can introduce new services to help clients make better and more timely marketing decisions. As companies develop databases, the various data sources can be merged to improve efficiency and develop and improve customer satisfaction.

All of IRI's services facilitate customer relationship management using marketing research and information technology to provide profiles of consumers, including behavior and attitudes. IRI also employs information technology to deliver information over the Internet. In 2000 the company launched CPGNetwork.com, through which customers can access marketing intelligence in the form of data-driven analyses, alerts, key performance indicators, "best practices," and case studies via the Web.

In addition to its services to client customers, IRI occasionally provides public relations information to the retail industry. For example, the company recently released a study indicating that 23 percent of online consumers have purchased consumer packaged goods online, and 99 percent of those customers planned to maintain or increase their online spending levels over the next year. Although just 12 percent of shoppers who buy online consumer packaged goods spent more than 25 percent of their budget online, that number is expected to increase by 35 percent. Such information is important to retailers because it indicates that purchases of consumer packaged goods via the Internet are increasing and represent an opportunity for online retailers.

IRI tailors its information services to the unique information needs of each customer. The research it provides arms these customers with marketing intelligence to help them match their marketing mixes to the needs of their customers. With timely and accurate information about what products are selling, where they are selling, the most effective prices, and competitors' activities, marketers can make sound decisions about the marketing strategy for specific products.[39]

QUESTIONS FOR DISCUSSION

1. How are the data gathered by IRI useful in customer relationship management?
2. What is the advantage of integrating scanner data with television viewing behavior?
3. Compare the usefulness of behavioral scanner data with data collected through surveys.

Target Markets: Segmentation and Evaluation

▶ Nickelodeon Targets Tots, Tweens, and Teens

So many target markets, so many marketing mixes. The cable television network Nickelodeon—Nick for short—is seeking to satisfy a number of tough target markets. Tots want fun, engaging programs such as *Blue's Clues* and *Dora the Explorer.* School-age viewers enjoy slightly wacky cartoons such as *SpongeBob SquarePants.* Preteen children—also known as tweens—tune in for programs like *All That* while older teens watch the celebrity specials. And parents want to be sure that Nick's programs entertain without violence or sex when a child is holding the remote control. Nick's marketing mix includes programming, advertising, and branded products for each market. The result: high ratings and annual revenues exceeding $4 billion.

Every program presents new opportunities to give viewers a good experience and encourage them to tune in again and again. Nick is known for its in-depth marketing research and its careful control of animation and production. Because no one can predict precisely which characters and shows will resonate with viewers, the network has had both tremendous successes and big disappointments. Management was surprised by the immediate and immense popularity of *SpongeBob SquarePants,* a phenomenon that has gone beyond television to spawn a full-length motion picture. However, children did not take to either the *Animorphs* series or the *Noah Knows Best* series. One Nick executive says these programs were "too talky and a little too old."

Even though millions of children and teens tune in every week, Nick's future growth will have to come from sources other than television advertising revenue. "There are only so many hours in the network day," explains the president of Nickelodeon Enterprises. "It's constraining. At some point, you reach the limit of what you can do there."

One lucrative approach is licensing Nick's program-related brands for an ever-widening mix of goods and services, such as Nick Zone departments within

OBJECTIVES

1 Learn what a market is.

2 Understand the differences among general targeting strategies.

3 Become familiar with the major segmentation variables.

4 Know what segment profiles are and how they are used.

5 Understand how to evaluate market segments.

6 Identify the factors that influence the selection of specific market segments for use as target markets.

7 Become familiar with sales forecasting methods.

JCPenney stores. Another is creating and licensing new brands that are unconnected with any of Nick's shows. Nick's EverGirl brand targeting tween girls, for example, is being licensed to manufacturers of clothing, school supplies, games, and bedroom accessories. EverGirl products are sold exclusively through Kohl's department stores. Nick's first video game, *Tak and the Power of Juju*, targets tween boys. Although the company expected to sell 1 million *Tak* games in its first year, it reached that sales level after only six months. And Curious Buddies is Nick's brand for toddler videos that compete with Walt Disney's Baby Einstein videos.

Can Nick profitably expand by selling branded products without television tie-ins to its target markets? Stay tuned.[1]   ◄

To compete effectively, Nickelodeon has singled out specific customer groups toward which it will direct its marketing efforts. Any organization that wants to succeed must identify its customers and develop and maintain marketing mixes that satisfy the needs of these customers.

In this chapter, we explore markets and market segmentation. Initially we define the term *market* and discuss the major requirements of a market. Then we examine the steps in the target market selection process, including identifying the appropriate targeting strategy, determining which variables to use for segmenting consumer and business markets, developing market segment profiles, evaluating relevant market segments, and selecting target markets. Finally, we discuss various methods for developing sales forecasts.

))) What Is a Market?

In Chapter 2, we defined a market as a group of people who, as individuals or as organizations, have needs for products in a product class and have the ability, willingness, and authority to purchase such products. Students, for example, are part of the market for textbooks; they are also part of the markets for computers, clothes, food, music, and other products. Individuals can have the desire, the buying power, and the willingness to purchase certain products but may not have the authority to do so. For example, teenagers may have the desire, the money, and the willingness to buy liquor, but a liquor producer does not consider them a market because teenagers are prohibited by law from buying alcoholic beverages. A group of people that lacks any one of the four requirements thus does not constitute a market.

Markets fall into one of two categories: consumer markets and business markets. These categories are based on the characteristics of the individuals and groups that make up a specific market and the purposes for which they buy products. A **consumer market** consists of purchasers and household members who intend to consume or benefit from the purchased products and do not buy products for the main purpose of making a profit. Consumer markets are sometimes also referred to as business-to-consumer (B2C) markets. Each of us belongs to numerous consumer markets. The millions of individuals with the ability, willingness, and authority to buy make up a multitude of consumer markets for products such as housing, food, clothing, vehicles, personal services, appliances, furniture, recreational equipment, and so on.

consumer market Purchasers and household members who intend to consume or benefit from the purchased products and do not buy products to make profits

Ideas move faster in color

Fast forward your company's best ideas. Share them
in striking Ricoh color. Ricoh's full line of networked
color laser printers. From tiny marvels to complete
high speed printing systems. Full finishing options.
Faster than ever duplexing. Ricoh dependability.
Sharing in Ricoh color really makes an impact.

How well do you share?

RICOH
Image Communication

ricoh-usa.com

introducing Diet Coke with Lime

Consumer and Business Markets
Coca-Cola is aiming this Diet Coke advertisement at consumer markets. Ricoh
promotes its products to business markets.

business market Individuals
or groups that purchase a
specific kind of product for
resale, direct use in producing
other products, or use in general
daily operations

A **business market** consists of individuals or groups that purchase a specific kind of product for one of three purposes: resale, direct use in producing other products, or use in general daily operations. For example, a lamp producer that buys electrical wire to use in the production of lamps is part of a business market for electrical wire. This same firm purchases dust mops to clean its office areas. Although the mops are not used in the direct production of lamps, they are used in the operations of the firm; thus, this manufacturer is part of a business market for dust mops. Business markets may also be called business-to-business (B2B), industrial, or organizational markets. They can also be classified into producer, reseller, government, and institutional markets, as we shall see in Chapter 9.

 ## Target Market Selection Process

In Chapter 1 we indicate that the first of two major components for developing a marketing strategy is to select a target market. Although marketers may employ several methods for target market selection, generally they use a five-step process. This process is shown in Figure 7.1 and we discuss it in the following sections.

| 1 Identify the appropriate targeting strategy | 2 Determine which segmentation variables to use | 3 Develop market segment profiles | 4 Evaluate relevant market segments | 5 Select specific target markets |

Figure 7.1
Target Market Selection Process

⊙ Step 1: Identify the Appropriate Targeting Strategy

A target market is a group of people or organizations for which a business creates and maintains a marketing mix specifically designed to satisfy the needs of group members. The strategy used to select a target market is affected by target market characteristics, product attributes, and the organization's objectives and resources. Figure 7.2 illustrates the three basic targeting strategies: undifferentiated, concentrated, and differentiated.

● **Undifferentiated Strategy.**   An organization sometimes defines an entire market for a particular product as its target market. When a company designs a single marketing mix and directs it at the entire market for a particular product, it is using an **undifferentiated targeting strategy**. As Figure 7.2 shows, the strategy assumes that all customers in the target market for a specific kind of product have similar needs, and so the organization can satisfy most customers with a single marketing mix. This mix consists of one type of product with little or no variation, one price, one promotional program aimed at everybody, and one distribution system to reach most customers in the total market. Products marketed successfully through the undifferentiated strategy include staple food items, such as sugar and salt, and certain kinds of farm produce.

undifferentiated targeting strategy   A strategy in which an organization defines an entire market for a particular product as its target market, designs a single marketing mix, and directs it at that market

The undifferentiated targeting strategy is effective under two conditions. First, a large proportion of customers in a total market must have similar needs for the product, a situation termed a **homogeneous market**. A marketer using a single marketing mix for a total market of customers with a variety of needs would find that the marketing mix satisfies very few people. A "universal car" meant to satisfy everyone would satisfy very few customers' needs for cars because it would not provide the specific attributes a specific person wants. Second, the organization must be able to develop and maintain a single marketing mix that satisfies customers' needs. The company must be able to identify a set of needs common to most customers in a total market and have the resources and managerial skills to reach a sizable portion of that market.

homogeneous market   A market in which a large proportion of customers have similar needs for a product

Although customers may have similar needs for a few products, for most products their needs decidedly differ. In such instances, a company should use a concentrated or a differentiated strategy.

● **Concentrated Strategy Through Market Segmentation.**   Markets made up of individuals or organizations with diverse product needs are called **heterogeneous markets**. Not everyone wants the same type of car, furniture, or clothes. For example, some individuals want an economical car, others desire a status symbol, and still others seek a roomy and comfortable vehicle. Thus, the automobile market is heterogeneous.

heterogeneous markets
Markets made up of individuals or organizations with diverse needs for products in a specific product class

For such heterogeneous markets, market segmentation is appropriate. **Market segmentation** is the process of dividing a total market into groups, or segments, consisting of people or organizations with relatively similar product needs. The purpose

market segmentation   The process of dividing a total market into groups with relatively similar product needs to design a marketing mix that matches those needs

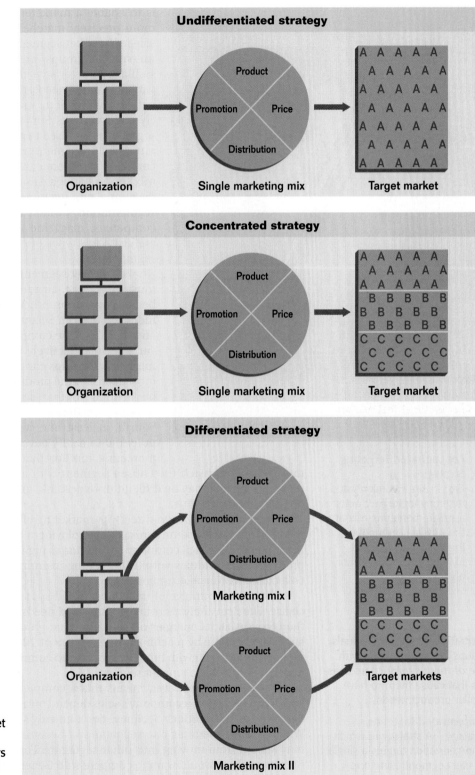

Figure 7.2
Targeting Strategies
The letters in each target market represent potential customers. Customers with the same letters have similar characteristics and similar product needs.

Introducing Apogee

CROSS.

Concentrated Targeting Strategies
Cross uses a concentrated targeting strategy. It aims a single marketing mix at the upscale segment of the writing instrument market, which is primarily a gift segment.

market segment Individuals, groups, or organizations with one or more similar characteristics that cause them to have similar product needs

concentrated targeting strategy A strategy in which an organization targets a single market segment using one marketing mix

is to enable a marketer to design a marketing mix that more precisely matches the needs of customers in the selected market segment. A **market segment** consists of individuals, groups, or organizations with one or more similar characteristics that cause them to have relatively similar product needs. For example, the automobile market is divided into many different market segments. Hyundai aims its Sonata at the mid-size sedan market segment as opposed to aiming at all car buyers.[2] The main rationale for segmenting heterogeneous markets is that a company can more easily develop a satisfying marketing mix for a relatively small portion of a total market than develop a mix meeting the needs of all people. Market segmentation is widely used. Fast-food chains, soft-drink companies, magazine publishers, hospitals, and banks are just a few types of organizations that employ market segmentation.

For market segmentation to succeed, five conditions must exist. First, customers' needs for the product must be heterogeneous; otherwise, there is little reason to segment the market. Second, segments must be identifiable and divisible. The company must find a characteristic or variable for effectively separating individuals in a total market into groups containing people with relatively uniform needs for the product. Third, the total market should be divided so that segments can be compared with respect to estimated sales potential, costs, and profits. Fourth, at least one segment must have enough profit potential to justify developing and maintaining a special marketing mix for that segment. Finally, the company must be able to reach the chosen segment with a particular marketing mix. Some market segments may be difficult or impossible to reach because of legal, social, or distribution constraints.

When an organization directs its marketing efforts toward a single market segment using one marketing mix, it is employing a **concentrated targeting strategy**. Mont Blanc, a German company famous for its high quality writing pens, targets their products to individuals within the writing instrument market who value high-end, collectable writing instruments.[3]

The chief advantage of the concentrated strategy is that it allows a firm to specialize. The firm analyzes characteristics and needs of a distinct customer group and then focuses all its energies on satisfying that group's needs. A firm may generate a large sales volume by reaching a single segment. Also, concentrating on a single segment permits a firm with limited resources to compete with larger organizations that may have overlooked smaller segments.

Specialization, however, means that a company puts all its eggs in one basket, which can be risky. If a company's sales depend on a single segment and the segment's demand for the product declines, the company's financial strength also declines. When a firm penetrates one segment and becomes well entrenched, its popularity may keep it from moving into other segments. For example, it is very unlikely that Bentley could or would want to compete with General Motors in the pickup truck and sport-utility vehicle market segment.

MARKETING LEADERS

LITTLEMISSMATCHED PAIRS SOCKS

Mix, not match, is the name of the marketing game for LittleMissMatched, a San Francisco–based company started by four entrepreneurs using a concentrated targeting strategy aimed at preteen girls. One reason the four started the company was to solve the purely practical problem of what happens when socks are separated from their mates. "We thought, 'Wouldn't it be amazing if someone made mismatched socks?'" says co-founder Arielle Eckstut. "That way, you would never have to worry about losing a sock."

That's why LittleMissMatched offers a package with one sock for $2, a package with three mixed-up socks for $5, and a package with seven mixed-up socks for $10. The idea is that customers can put together pairs from 134 sock designs in four-color groupings: Fabulous, Marvelous, Kooky, and Zany.

The second reason for starting the company was to let girls be girls for a little longer. "So much of the stuff being marketed to them is oversexualized," Eckstut observes. "We want to encourage girls to be playful and have fun, not to truncate their girlhood." When they wear LittleMissMatched socks, customers are expressing their personalities and—in a small way—flouting convention.

Each package describes three customer profiles to help girls make buying decisions. Girls who identify with the "Alota" profile will enjoy pairing wildly different combinations, such as one pink-and-black star sock and one yellow-and-purple fish sock. Girls who see themselves as more conservative, like the "Kinda" profile, will choose socks with different patterns within the same color grouping. Girls who fit the "Sorta" profile will want pairs that are neither wild nor conservative but "sorta" in between.

The inside band of each sock shows the color grouping and pattern number, such as Fabulous 33 (red with pink hearts). Marking the products in this way not only helps customers keep track of which socks they own, it encourages them to collect and trade socks. Soon LittleMissMatched will be marketing flip-flops, pajamas, and other garments that can be mismatched for fun and fashion for its preeten target market.[a]

differentiated targeting strategy   A strategy in which an organization targets two or more segments by developing a marketing mix for each

● **Differentiated Strategy Through Market Segmentation.**   With a **differentiated targeting strategy**, an organization directs its marketing efforts at two or more segments by developing a marketing mix for each (see Figure 7.2). After a firm uses a concentrated strategy successfully in one market segment, it sometimes expands its efforts to include additional segments. For example, Fruit of the Loom underwear has traditionally been aimed at one segment: men. However, the company now markets underwear for women and children as well. Marketing mixes for a differentiated strategy may vary according to product features, distribution methods, promotion methods, and prices.

A firm may increase sales in the aggregate market through a differentiated strategy because its marketing mixes are aimed at more people. For example, the Gap, which established its retail clothes reputation by targeting people under 25, now targets several age groups, from infants to people over 60. A company with excess production capacity may find a differentiated strategy advantageous because the sale of products to additional segments may absorb excess capacity. On the other hand, a differentiated strategy often demands more production processes, materials, and people. Thus, production and costs may be higher than with a concentrated strategy.

◉ Step 2: Determine Which Segmentation Variables to Use

segmentation variables   Characteristics of individuals, groups, or organizations used to divide a market into segments

Segmentation variables are the characteristics of individuals, groups, or organizations used to divide a market into segments. For example, location, age, gender, or rate of product usage can all be bases for segmenting markets.

To select a segmentation variable, several factors are considered. The segmentation variable should relate to customers' needs for, uses of, or behavior toward the product. Stereo marketers might segment the stereo market based on income and age, but not on religion, because people's stereo needs do not differ due to religion. If individuals or organizations in a total market are to be classified accurately, the segmentation variable must be measurable. Age, location, and gender are measurable because such information can be obtained through observation or questioning. But segmenting a market on the basis of, say, intelligence is extremely difficult because this attribute is harder to measure accurately. Furthermore, a company's resources and capabilities affect the number and size of segment variables used. The type of product and degree of variation in customers' needs also dictate the number and size of segments targeted. In short, there is no best way to segment markets.

Marketers try to segment markets in ways that may help them build and manage relationships with targeted customers. Marketing research is often necessary to acquire information about customers' preferences and interests; basic demographic information about target customers' age, income, employment status, household structure, and family roles may also be revealing. Marketers are using customer relationship management techniques more often now to track customers' purchases over time and to mine their databases to uncover trends about repeat customers.[4]

Choosing a segmentation variable or variables is a critical step in targeting a market. Selecting an inappropriate variable limits the chances of developing a successful marketing strategy. To help you better understand potential segmentation variables, we examine the major types of variables used to segment consumer markets and business markets.

● **Variables for Segmenting Consumer Markets.**   A marketer using segmentation to reach a consumer market can choose one or several variables from an assortment of possibilities. As Figure 7.3 shows, segmentation variables can be grouped into four categories: demographic, geographic, psychographic, and behavioristic.

Demographic Variables.   Demographic characteristics that marketers commonly use in segmenting markets include age, gender, race, ethnicity, income, education,

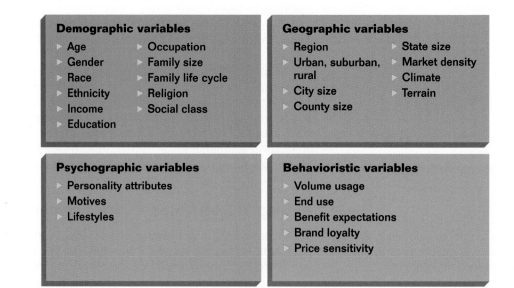

Figure 7.3
Segmentation Variables for Consumer Markets

Gender-Based Segmentation
As shown in this advertisement, some brands of razors are aimed at women, whereas others may be aimed at men.

occupation, family size, family life cycle, religion, and social class. Marketers rely on these demographic characteristics because they are often closely linked to customers' needs and purchasing behavior and can be readily measured. Like demographers, a few marketers even use mortality rates. Service Corporation International (SCI), the largest U.S. funeral services company, attempts to locate its facilities in higher-income suburban areas with high mortality rates. SCI operates more than 2,800 funeral service locations, cemeteries, and crematoriums.[5]

Age is a commonly used variable for segmentation purposes. For example, Disney has created a free online game called *Virtual Magic Kingdom* aimed primarily at 7- to 12-year-olds. This game is targeted to those consumers who will appreciate the online multiplayer game, namely vacation-influencing children.[6] Marketers need to be aware of age distribution and how that distribution is changing. All age groups under 55 are expected to decrease by the year 2025, and all age categories 55 and older are expected to increase. In 1970, the average age of a U.S. citizen was 27.9; currently, it is about 35.3. As Figure 7.4 shows, Americans 65 and older spend as much or more on health care and entertainment compared to Americans in the two younger age groups.

Gender is another demographic variable commonly used to segment markets, including the markets for clothing, soft drinks, nonprescription medications, toiletries, magazines, and even cigarettes. The U.S. Census Bureau reports that girls and women account for 50.8 percent and boys and men for 49.2 percent of the total U.S. population.[7] Some deodorant marketers use gender segmentation: Secret deodorant is marketed specifically to women, whereas Old Spice deodorant is directed toward men. A number of websites are aimed at females, including Girl Tech, Moms Online, Women.com, and Online Women's Business Center. Effective online targeting of women relies heavily on personalization, sense of community, and trust.[8]

Marketers also use race and ethnicity as variables for segmenting markets for products such as food, music, clothing, and cosmetics and for services like banking and insurance. The U.S. Hispanic population illustrates the importance of ethnicity as a segmentation variable. Made up of people of Mexican, Cuban, Puerto Rican, and Central and South American heritage, this ethnic group is growing five times faster than the general population. Hispanics now comprise 12.5 percent of the U.S. population, a 60 percent increase in just a decade.[9] Consequently, Campbell Soup, Procter & Gamble, and other companies target Hispanic consumers, viewing this segment as attractive because of its size and growth potential. Procter & Gamble, for example, spent some $90 million on Hispanic advertising in 2003, a 28 percent increase over the amount spent the previous year.[10] Asian Americans are another important subculture for many companies. Sears, for example, in an effort to better market to Asian Americans, African Americans, and Hispanics, has redesigned its apparel departments in stores located in cities with large multiethnic populations. These revisions include new in-store signage, updated merchandising displays, and new brands that appeal to an ethnically diverse audience.[11]

Income often provides a way to divide markets because it strongly influences people's product needs. It affects their ability to buy and their desires for certain lifestyles.

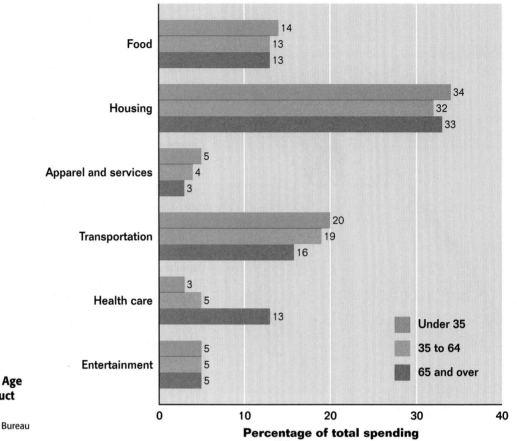

Figure 7.4
Spending Levels of Three Age Groups for Selected Product Categories
Source: U.S. Department of Labor, Bureau of Statistics, 2003.

Product markets segmented by income include sporting goods, housing, furniture, cosmetics, clothing, jewelry, home appliances, automobiles, and electronics.

Among the factors influencing household income and product needs are marital status and the presence and ages of children. These characteristics, often combined and called the *family life cycle,* affect needs for housing, appliances, food and beverages, automobiles, and recreational equipment. Family life cycles can be broken down in a number of ways. Figure 7.5 shows a breakdown into nine categories. The composition of the U.S. household in relation to the family life cycle has changed significantly over the last several decades. Single-parent families are on the rise, meaning that the "typical" family no longer consists of a married couple with children. Since 1970, households headed by a single mother increased from 12 percent to 26 percent of total family households, and that number grew from 1 percent to 6 percent for families headed by a single father. Another factor influencing the family life cycle is the increase in median marrying age for both women and men. The median marrying age for women has increased from 20.8 years to 25.3 years since 1970, while for men it increased to 27.1 years from 23.2 years. More significantly, the proportion of women ages 20 to 24 who have never been married has more than doubled over this time, and for women ages 30 to 34 this number has nearly tripled. Other important changes in the family life cycle include the rise in the number of people living alone and the number of unmarried couples living together.[12] Tracking these changes helps marketers satisfy the needs of particular target markets through new marketing mixes. For example,

CUSTOMER RELATIONSHIP MANAGEMENT
TARGETING MATURE CUSTOMERS

Forget the old stereotypes and meet the new senior segment. By 2025, at least 100 million Americans will have passed their fiftieth birthday. Their buying power and behavior present a huge marketing opportunity for companies that study and target this sizable group.

Consider the psychographic variable of lifestyle. Research shows that today's seniors think and feel about seven to ten years younger than their real ages. Knowing this, car advertisements rarely feature people who appear to be near retirement age. For example, the average age of consumers who buy new Lincoln Town Cars is 67. Yet the brand is projecting a more youthful image through its spokesperson, Magic Johnson, a former basketball star turned successful businessman.

Lifestyle is another key psychographic variable. Many adults over 50 are grandparents (or great-grandparents) and enjoy indulging younger family members with gifts of toys and other products. In fact, seniors buy 25 percent of toys sold during any given year. The influence of lifestyle extends to major purchases as well. As an example, minivan commercials showing families with young children appeal to seniors because, says one expert, grandparents realize that minivans are perfect for transporting grandchildren and their belongings.

Today's seniors are healthier and more active than ever before, and they are seeking specific benefits from the products they buy. Retired seniors in particular have the time and money to play sports, travel, attend cultural events, go back to school, and pursue other interests. As they get ready for retirement, seniors need a wide variety of financial services, creating more opportunity for insurance firms, banks, brokers, and financial planners. Finally, seniors of all ages want to stay as healthy as possible for as long as possible. Therefore, segmenting this market in terms of specific health benefits is a top priority for pharmaceutical firms and others in the health-care industry.[b]

MicroMarketing, Inc. helps companies target customers through what it calls Lifestage Marketing. MicroMarketing can create a direct mail campaign aimed at groups such as people who recently moved, soon-to-be newlyweds, recent high school and college graduates, and expectant parents. By focusing on such narrow target markets, Micro-Marketing boasts a return on investments of up to 2,000 percent.[13]

Marketers also use many other demographic variables. For instance, dictionary publishing companies segment markets by education level. Some insurance companies segment markets using occupation, targeting health insurance at college students and at younger workers with small employers that do not provide health coverage.

Geographic Variables. Geographic variables—climate, terrain, city size, population density, and urban/rural areas—also influence customer product needs. Markets may be divided into regions because one or more geographic variables can cause customers to differ from one region to another. A company selling products to a national market might divide the United States into the following regions: Pacific, Southwest, Central, Midwest, Southeast, Middle Atlantic, and New England. A firm operating in one or several states might regionalize its market by counties, cities, zip code areas, or other units.

Family Life Cycle Segmentation
Saab aims its 9-5 wagon at individuals in a specific stage of the family life cycle.

City size can be an important segmentation variable. Some marketers focus efforts on cities of a certain size. For example, one franchised restaurant organization will not locate in cities of fewer than 200,000 people. It concluded that a smaller population base would result in inadequate profits. Other firms actively seek opportunities in smaller towns. A classic example is Wal-Mart, which initially located only in small towns.

Market density refers to the number of potential customers within a unit of land area, such as a square mile. Although market density relates generally to population density, the correlation is not exact. For example, in two different geographic markets of approximately equal size and population, market density for office supplies would be much higher in one area if it contained a much greater proportion of business customers than the other area. Market density may be a useful segmentation variable because low-density markets often require different sales, advertising, and distribution activities compared to high-density markets.

Several marketers are using geodemographic segmentation. **Geodemographic**

market density The number of potential customers within a unit of land area

geodemographic segmentation Marketing segmentation that clusters people in zip code areas and smaller neighborhood units based on lifestyle and demographic information

micromarketing An approach to market segmentation in which organizations focus precise marketing efforts on very small geographic markets

segmentation clusters people in zip code areas and even smaller neighborhood units based on lifestyle information and especially demographic data, such as income, education, occupation, type of housing, ethnicity, family life cycle, and level of urbanization. These small, precisely described population clusters help marketers isolate demographic units as small as neighborhoods where the demand for specific products is strongest. Geodemographic segmentation allows marketers to engage in micromarketing. **Micromarketing** is the focusing of precise marketing efforts on very small geodemographic markets, such as community and even neighborhood markets. Providers of financial and health-care services, retailers, and consumer products companies use micromarketing. Special advertising campaigns, promotions, retail-site location analyses, special pricing, and unique retail product offerings are a few examples of micromarketing facilitated through geodemographic segmentation.

Climate is commonly used as a geographic segmentation variable because of its broad impact on people's behavior and product needs. Product markets affected by climate include air-conditioning and heating equipment, clothing, gardening equipment, recreational products, and building materials.

Psychographic Variables. Marketers sometimes use psychographic variables, such as personality characteristics, motives, and lifestyles, to segment markets. A psycho-

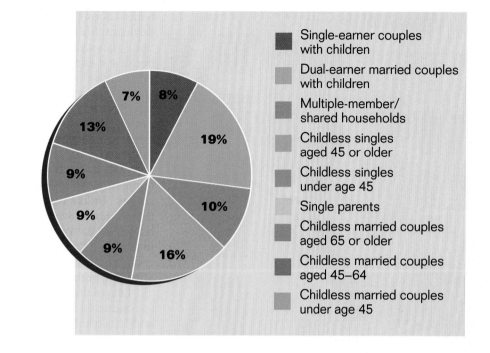

Figure 7.5
Family Life Cycle Stages as a Percentage of All Households
Source: U.S. Bureau of the Census, *Current Population Survey.*

graphic dimension can be used by itself to segment a market or combined with other types of segmentation variables.

Personality characteristics can be useful for segmentation when a product resembles many competing products and consumers' needs are not significantly related to other segmentation variables. However, segmenting a market according to personality traits can be risky. Although marketing practitioners have long believed consumer choice and product use vary with personality, until recently marketing research had indicated only weak relationships. It is hard to measure personality traits accurately, especially since most personality tests were developed for clinical use, not for segmentation purposes.

When appealing to a personality characteristic, marketers almost always select one that many people view positively. Individuals with this characteristic, as well as those who would like to have it, may be influenced to buy that marketer's brand. Marketers taking this approach do not worry about measuring how many people have the positively valued characteristic; they assume a sizable proportion of people in the target market either have or want to have it.

When motives are used to segment a market, the market is divided according to consumers' reasons for making a purchase. Personal appearance, affiliation, status, safety, and health are examples of motives affecting the types of products purchased and the choice of stores in which they are bought. Marketing efforts based on health and fitness motives can be a point of competitive advantage. For example, Yum! Brands, Inc. (Taco Bell, Long John Silver's, Pizza Hut, KFC, and A&W Restaurants) has teamed up with Bally Total Fitness to pair a free trial membership, valued at $50, with each restaurant's better-for-you menu items. This partnership will appeal to fitness-motivated individuals and will create a link between fitness and the restaurants of Yum! Brands.[14]

Lifestyle segmentation groups individuals according to how they spend their time, the importance of things in their surroundings (homes or jobs, for example),

Lifestyle Segmentation
Recreation-related products are often segmented on the basis of lifestyle, as illustrated in this advertisement.

beliefs about themselves and broad issues, and some demographic characteristics, such as income and education.[15] Lifestyle analysis provides a broad view of buyers because it encompasses numerous characteristics related to people's activities (work, hobbies, entertainment, sports), interests (family, home, fashion, food, technology), and opinions (politics, social issues, education, the future). For example, homeownership is valued by most income and age segments. Recent studies show, however, that 49 percent of Generation Xers (born between 1964 and 1973) own homes and account for 16.5 percent of the home furnishing market and 19.9 percent of furniture purchases. Unlike baby boomers (born 1946–1963), Generation X homeowners often research products for their homes on the Web and later buy those products in-store. In addition, their decisions on major home improvements are often decided based on how those improvements will affect the home's resale value.[16]

One of the more popular programs studying lifestyles is conducted by the Stanford Research Institute's Value and Lifestyle Program (VALS). This program surveys U.S. consumers to select groups with identifiable values and lifestyles. Initially, VALS identified three broad consumer groups: Outer-Directed, Inner-Directed, and Need-Driven consumers. The current VALS classification categorizes consumers into eight basic lifestyle groups: Innovators, Thinkers, Believers, Achievers, Strivers, Experiencers, Makers, and Survivors. Figure 7.6 shows the proportion of each group that was involved in various sports activities in a recent year, according to a VALS/Mediamark Research Inc. survey. Marketers of products related to hunting would most likely focus on the Maker, whereas marketers of products related to mountain biking would most likely target the Experiencer lifestyle segments.[17] The VALS studies have been used to create products as well as to segment markets.

Behavioristic Variables. Firms can divide a market according to some feature of consumer behavior toward a product, commonly involving some aspect of product use. For example, a market may be separated into users—classified as heavy, moderate, or light—and nonusers. To satisfy a specific group, such as heavy users, marketers may create a distinctive product, set special prices, or initiate special promotion and distribution activities. Per capita consumption data help to identify different levels of usage. For example, the Beverage Market Index of 2003 shows that per capita consumption of bottled water varies from 9.0 gallons in the East Central states (Illinois, Indiana, Kentucky, Michigan, Ohio, West Virginia, and Wisconsin) to 34.5 gallons in the Southwest (Arizona, New Mexico, Oklahoma, and Texas).[18]

How customers use or apply products may also determine segmentation. To satisfy customers who use a product in a certain way, some feature—packaging, size, texture, or color—may be designed precisely to make the product easier to use, safer, or more convenient.

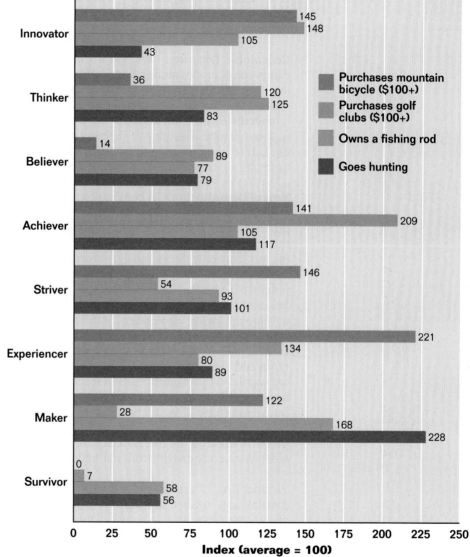

Figure 7.6
Types and Sports Preferences
Source: VALS/Mediamark Research Inc. survey. SRI Consulting Business Intelligence. www.sric-bi.com/VALS. Reprinted with permission.

benefit segmentation The division of a market according to benefits that customers want from the product

Benefit segmentation is the division of a market according to benefits that consumers want from the product. Although most types of market segmentation assume a relationship between the variable and customers' needs, benefit segmentation differs because the benefits customers seek *are* their product needs. For example, a customer who purchases toothpaste may be interested in cavity protection, whiter teeth, natural ingredients, or sensitive gum protection. Thus, individuals are segmented directly according to their needs. By determining the desired benefits, marketers may be able to divide people into groups seeking certain sets of benefits. The effectiveness of such segmentation depends on three conditions: the benefits sought must be identifiable; using these benefits, marketers must be able to divide people into recognizable segments; and one or more of the resulting segments must be accessible to the firm's marketing efforts. Both Timberland and Avia, for example, segment the foot apparel market based on benefits sought by purchasers.

● **Variables for Segmenting Business Markets.**   Like consumer markets, business markets are frequently segmented. Marketers segment business markets according to geographic location, type of organization, customer size, and product use.

Geographic Location.   We noted that the demand for some consumer products varies considerably among geographic areas because of differences in climate, terrain, customer preferences, and similar factors. Demand for business products also varies according to geographic location. For example, producers of certain types of lumber divide their markets geographically because their customers' needs vary from region to region. Geographic segmentation may be especially appropriate for reaching industries concentrated in certain locations. Furniture and textile producers, for example, are concentrated in the Southeast.

Type of Organization.   A company sometimes segments a market by types of organizations within that market. Different types of organizations often require different product features, distribution systems, price structures, and selling strategies. Given these variations, a firm may either concentrate on a single segment with one marketing mix (concentration strategy) or focus on several groups with multiple mixes (a differentiated targeting strategy). A carpet producer, for example, could segment potential customers into several groups, such as automobile makers, commercial carpet contractors (firms that carpet large commercial buildings), apartment complex developers, carpet wholesalers, and large retail carpet outlets.

Customer Size.   An organization's size may affect its purchasing procedures and the types and quantities of products it wants. Size can thus be an effective variable for segmenting a business market. To reach a segment of a particular size, marketers may have to adjust one or more marketing mix components. For example, customers who buy in extremely large quantities are sometimes offered discounts. In addition, marketers often must expand personal selling efforts to serve large organizational buyers properly. Because the needs of large and small buyers tend to be quite distinct, marketers frequently use different marketing practices to reach various customer groups.

Product Use.   Certain products, especially basic raw materials like steel, petroleum, plastics, and lumber, are used in numerous ways. How a company uses products affects the types and amounts of products purchased, as well as the purchasing method. For example, computers are used for engineering purposes, basic scientific research, and business operations such as word processing, accounting, and telecommunications. A computer maker therefore may segment the computer market by types of use because organizations' needs for computer hardware and software depend on the purpose for which products are purchased.

◉ Step 3: Develop Market Segment Profiles

A market segment profile describes the similarities among potential customers within a segment and explains the differences among people and organizations in different segments. A profile may cover aspects such as demographic characteristics, geographic factors, product benefits sought, lifestyles, brand preferences, and usage rates. Individuals and organizations within segments should be quite similar with respect to several characteristics and product needs and differ considerably from those within other market segments. Marketers use market segment profiles to assess the degree to which the organization's possible products can match or fit potential customers' product needs. Market segment profiles help marketers understand how a business can use its capabilities to serve potential customer groups.

The use of market segment profiles benefits marketers in several ways. Such profiles help a marketer determine which segment or segments are most attractive to the organization relative to the firm's strengths, weaknesses, objectives, and resources. While marketers may initially believe certain segments are quite attractive, development of market segment profiles may yield information that indicates the opposite. For the market segment or segments chosen by the organization, the information included in market segment profiles can be highly useful in making marketing decisions.

◉ Step 4: Evaluate Relevant Market Segments

After analyzing the market segment profiles, a marketer is likely to identify several relevant market segments that require further analysis and eliminate certain segments from consideration. To assess relevant market segments further, several important factors, including sales estimates, competition, and estimated costs associated with each segment, should be analyzed.

● **Sales Estimates.**   Potential sales for a segment can be measured along several dimensions, including product level, geographic area, time, and level of competition.[19] With respect to product level, potential sales can be estimated for a specific product item (for example, Diet Coke) or an entire product line (for example, Coca-Cola Classic, Caffeine-Free Coke, Diet Coke, Caffeine-Free Diet Coke, Cherry Coca-Cola, Diet Cherry Coca-Cola, Vanilla Coke, and Diet Vanilla Coke). A manager must also determine the geographic area to be included in the estimate. In relation to time, sales estimates can be short range (one year or less), medium range (one to five years), or long range (longer than five years). The competitive level specifies whether sales are being estimated for a single firm or for an entire industry.

market potential   The total amount of a product that customers will purchase within a specified period at a specific level of industrywide marketing activity

Market potential is the total amount of a product, for all firms in an industry, that customers will purchase within a specified period at a specific level of industrywide marketing activity. Market potential can be stated in terms of dollars or units. For example, with the aging of the large baby boomer generation, the market potential for medical instruments and medications to treat congestive heart failure, hypertension, and other cardiovascular conditions is estimated to reach over $20 billion by 2013.[20] A segment's market potential is affected by economic, sociocultural, and other environmental forces. Marketers must assume a certain general level of marketing effort in the industry when they estimate market potential. The specific level of marketing effort varies from one firm to another, but the sum of all firms' marketing activities equals industrywide marketing efforts. A marketing manager must also consider whether and to what extent industry marketing efforts will change.

company sales potential   The maximum percentage of market potential that an individual firm can expect to obtain for a specific product

Company sales potential is the maximum percentage of market potential that an individual firm within an industry can expect to obtain for a specific product. Several factors influence company sales potential for a market segment. First, the market potential places absolute limits on the size of the company's sales potential. Second, the magnitude of industrywide marketing activities has an indirect but definite impact on the company's sales potential. Those activities have a direct bearing on the size of the market potential. When Domino's Pizza advertises home-delivered pizza, for example, it indirectly promotes pizza in general; its commercials may also help sell Pizza Hut's and other competitors' home-delivered pizza. Third, the intensity and effectiveness of a company's marketing activities relative to those of its competitors affect the size of the company's sales potential. If a company spends twice as much as any of its competitors on marketing efforts and if each dollar spent is more effective in generating sales, the firm's sales potential will be quite high compared to its competitors'.

breakdown approach
Measuring company sales potential based on a general economic forecast for a specific period and the market potential derived from it

buildup approach Measuring company sales potential by estimating how much of a product a potential buyer in a specific geographic area will purchase in a given period, multiplying the estimate by the number of potential buyers, and adding the totals of all the geographic areas considered

There are two general approaches to measuring company sales potential: breakdown and buildup. In the **breakdown approach**, the marketing manager first develops a general economic forecast for a specific time period. Next, market potential is estimated on the basis of this economic forecast. The company's sales potential is then derived from the general economic forecast and estimate of market potential. In the **buildup approach**, the marketing manager begins by estimating how much of a product a potential buyer in a specific geographic area, such as a sales territory, will purchase in a given period. The manager then multiplies that amount by the total number of potential buyers in that area. The manager performs the same calculation for each geographic area in which the firm sells products and then adds the totals for each area to calculate market potential. To determine company sales potential, the manager must estimate, based on planned levels of company marketing activities, the proportion of the total market potential the company can obtain.

● **Competitive Assessment.** Besides obtaining sales estimates, it is crucial to assess competitors already operating in the segments being considered. Without competitive information, sales estimates may be misleading. A market segment that seems attractive based on sales estimates may prove to be much less so following a competitive assessment. Such an assessment should ask several questions about competitors: How many exist? What are their strengths and weaknesses? Do several competitors have major market shares and together dominate the segment? Can our company create a marketing mix to compete effectively against competitors' marketing mixes? Is it likely that new competitors will enter this segment? If so, how will they affect our firm's ability to compete successfully? Answers to such questions are important for proper assessment of the competition in potential market segments. For example, using the data in Table 7.1, a pet food company could develop a marketing mix to target a market segment that views dogs as family members. Even so, the company would have to consider the strength of competing brands, such as Purina and Iams, that already target pet owners.

● **Cost Estimates.** To fulfill the needs of a target segment, an organization must develop and maintain a marketing mix that precisely meets the wants and needs of

Table 7.1 **Dog Owners' Attitudes Toward Their Pets**	
Activity	**Percentage of Owners Who Say They Engage in Activity**
Pet and hug dog daily	95
Play with dog daily	92
Take dog on vacation	45
Celebrate dog's birthday	42
Take dog shopping or to a pet store	35
Visit health-care facilities or schools with dog	28
Take dog to work	19
Take dog to store/restaurant/bar	16

Source: Ralston Purina, reported in "In the Doghouse," *American Demographics*, January 2002, p. 7.

individuals and organizations in that segment. Developing and maintaining such a mix can be expensive. Distinctive product features, attractive package design, generous product warranties, extensive advertising, attractive promotional offers, competitive prices, and high-quality personal service consume considerable organizational resources. Indeed, to reach certain segments, the costs may be so high that a marketer may see the segment as inaccessible. Another cost consideration is whether the organization can effectively reach a segment at costs equal to or below competitors' costs. If the firm's costs are likely to be higher, it will be unable to compete in that segment in the long run.

◎ Step 5: Select Specific Target Markets

An important initial issue to consider in selecting a target market is whether customers' needs differ enough to warrant the use of market segmentation. If segmentation analysis shows customer needs to be fairly homogeneous, the firm's management may decide to use the undifferentiated approach, discussed earlier. However, if customer needs are heterogeneous, which is much more likely, one or more target markets must be selected. On the other hand, marketers may decide not to enter and compete in any of the segments.

Assuming one or more segments offer significant opportunities for the organization to achieve its objectives, marketers must decide in which segments to participate. Ordinarily, information gathered in the previous step—information about sales estimates, competitors, and cost estimates—requires careful consideration in this final step to determine long-term profit opportunities. Also, the firm's management must investigate whether the organization has the financial resources, managerial skills, employee expertise, and facilities to enter and compete effectively in selected segments. Furthermore, the requirements of some market segments may be at odds with the firm's overall objectives, and the possibility of legal problems, conflicts with stakeholders, and technological advancements could make certain segments unattractive. In addition, when prospects for long-term growth are taken into account, some segments may appear very attractive and others less desirable.

Selecting appropriate target markets is important to an organization's adoption and use of the marketing concept philosophy. Identifying the right target market is the key to implementing a successful marketing strategy, whereas failure to do so can lead to low sales, high costs, and severe financial losses. A careful target market analysis places an organization in a better position both to serve customers' needs and to achieve its objectives.

e-site

Being well informed about current developments in the marketplace is crucial when deciding which market segments to target. Bizjournals.com (**www. bizjournals.com**) is a website where marketers and marketing students can get breaking marketplace news. The site has current and archived top news stories from dozens of regional business journals, as well as information on industry-specific trends and demographics.

◉ Developing Sales Forecasts

sales forecast The amount of a product a company expects to sell during a specific period at a specified level of marketing activities

A **sales forecast** is the amount of a product the company actually expects to sell during a specific period at a specified level of marketing activities. The sales forecast differs from the company sales potential. It concentrates on what actual sales will be at a certain level of company marketing effort, whereas the company sales potential assesses what sales are possible at various levels of marketing activities, assuming certain environmental conditions will exist. Businesses use the sales forecast for planning, organizing, implementing, and controlling their activities. The success of numerous activities depends on this forecast's accuracy. Common problems in companies that fail are improper planning and lack of realistic sales forecasts. Overly optimistic sales forecasts can lead to overbuying, overinvestment, and higher costs.

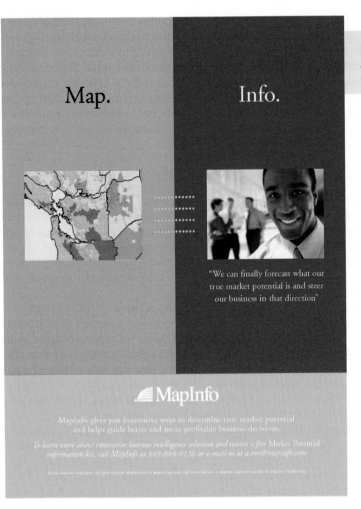

Map.

Info.

"We can finally forecast what our true market potential is and steer our business in that direction"

MapInfo

MapInfo gives you innovative ways to determine true market potential and helps guide better and more profitable business decisions.

To learn more about innovative business intelligence solutions and receive a free Market Potential information kit, call MapInfo at 888-889-0136 or e-mail us at acrm@mapinfo.com

To forecast sales, a marketer can choose from several forecasting methods, some arbitrary and others more scientific, complex, and time consuming. A firm's choice of method or methods depends on the costs involved, type of product, market characteristics, time span of the forecast, purposes of the forecast, stability of the historical sales data, availability of required information, managerial preferences, and forecasters' expertise and experience.[21] Common forecasting techniques fall into five categories: executive judgment, surveys, time series analysis, regression analysis, and market tests.

◉ Executive Judgment

At times, a company forecasts sales chiefly on the basis of executive judgment, the intuition of one or more executives. This approach is unscientific but expedient and inexpensive. Executive judgment may work reasonably well when product demand is relatively stable and the forecaster has years of market-related experience. However, because intuition is swayed most heavily by recent experience, the forecast may be overly optimistic or overly pessimistic. Another drawback to intuition is that the forecaster has only past experience as a guide for deciding where to go in the future.

◉ Surveys

executive judgment Sales forecasting based on the intuition of one or more executives

customer forecasting survey A survey of customers regarding the types and quantities of products they intend to buy during a specific period

sales force forecasting survey A survey of a firm's sales force regarding anticipated sales in their territories for a specified period

Another way to forecast sales is to question customers, sales personnel, or experts regarding their expectations about future purchases. In a customer forecasting survey, marketers ask customers what types and quantities of products they intend to buy during a specific period. This approach may be useful to a business with relatively few customers. For example, Intel, which markets to a limited number of companies (primarily computer manufacturers), could conduct customer forecasting surveys effectively. PepsiCo, in contrast, has millions of customers and could not feasibly use a customer survey to forecast future sales.

In a sales force forecasting survey, the firm's salespeople estimate anticipated sales in their territories for a specified period. The forecaster combines these territorial estimates to arrive at a tentative forecast. A marketer may survey the sales staff for several reasons. The most important is that the sales staff is closer to customers on a daily basis than other company personnel and therefore should know more about customers' future product needs. When sales representatives assist in developing the forecast, they are more likely to work toward its achievement. Another advantage of

MARKETING ENTREPRENEURS

Tim Keck and Chris Johnson

THEIR BUSINESS: *The Onion*

FOUNDED: as juniors in college

SUCCESS: Revenues of $7 million a year

Tim Keck and Chris Johnson, students at the University of Wisconsin, took out an $8,000 loan to start *The Onion*, a free paper spoofing university events that they distributed in their dorm. The paper immediately began to profit and after the first year, the pair decided to sell *The Onion* to a couple of their collaborators. Since then, printed versions of the weekly have been launched in five cities, and the company now has an online version (**www. theonion.com**). The bulk of the paper's revenues stem from newspaper and Web advertisers.[c]

expert forecasting survey
Sales forecasts prepared by experts such as economists, management consultants, advertising executives, college professors, or other persons outside the firm

Delphi technique   A procedure in which experts create initial forecasts, submit them to the company for averaging, and then refine the forecasts

time series analysis   A forecasting method that uses historical sales data to discover patterns in the firm's sales over time and generally involves trend, cycle, seasonal, and random factor analyses

trend analysis   An analysis that focuses on aggregate sales data over a period of many years to determine general trends in annual sales

cycle analysis   An analysis of sales figures for a period of three to five years to ascertain whether sales fluctuate in a consistent, periodic manner

this method is that forecasts can be prepared for single territories, divisions consisting of several territories, regions made up of multiple divisions, and the total geographic market. Thus, the method provides sales forecasts from the smallest geographic sales unit to the largest.

When a company wants an **expert forecasting survey**, it hires professionals to help prepare the sales forecast. These experts are usually economists, management consultants, advertising executives, college professors, or other persons outside the firm with solid experience in a specific market. Drawing on this experience and their analyses of available information about the company and the market, experts prepare and present forecasts or answer questions regarding a forecast. Using experts is expedient and relatively inexpensive. However, because they work outside the firm, these forecasters may be less motivated than company personnel to do an effective job.

A more complex form of the expert forecasting survey incorporates the Delphi technique. The **Delphi technique** is a procedure in which experts create initial forecasts, submit them to the company for averaging, and have the results returned to them so that they can make individual refined forecasts. The premise is that the experts will use the averaged results when making refined forecasts and that these forecasts will be in a narrower range. The procedure may be repeated several times until the experts, each working separately, reach a consensus on the forecasts. The ultimate goal in using the Delphi technique is to develop a highly accurate sales forecast.

◉ Time Series Analysis

With **time series analysis**, the forecaster uses the firm's historical sales data to discover a pattern or patterns in the firm's sales over time. If a pattern is found, it can be used to forecast sales. This forecasting method assumes that past sales patterns will continue in the future. The accuracy, and thus usefulness, of time series analysis hinges on the validity of this assumption.

In a time series analysis, a forecaster usually performs four types of analyses: trend, cycle, seasonal, and random factor. **Trend analysis** focuses on aggregate sales data, such as the company's annual sales figures, covering a period of many years to determine whether annual sales are generally rising, falling, or staying about the same. Through **cycle analysis**, a forecaster analyzes sales figures (often monthly sales data) from a period of three to five years to ascertain whether sales fluctuate in a consistent, periodic manner. When performing **seasonal analysis** (definition on p. 170), the analyst studies daily, weekly, or monthly sales figures to evaluate the degree to which seasonal factors, such as climate and holiday activities, influence sales. In a **random factor analysis** (definition on p. 170), the forecaster attempts to attribute erratic sales variations to random, nonrecurrent events, such as a regional power failure, a natural disaster, or political unrest in a foreign market. After performing each of

seasonal analysis   An analysis of daily, weekly, or monthly sales figures to evaluate the degree to which seasonal factors influence sales

random factor analysis   An analysis attempting to attribute erratic sales variation to random, nonrecurrent events

regression analysis   A method of predicting sales based on finding a relationship between past sales and one or more variables, such as population or income

these analyses, the forecaster combines the results to develop the sales forecast. Time series analysis is an effective forecasting method for products with reasonably stable demand, but not for products with highly erratic demand.

Regression Analysis

Like time series analysis, regression analysis requires the use of historical sales data. In **regression analysis**, the forecaster seeks to find a relationship between past sales (the dependent variable) and one or more independent variables, such as population, per capita income, or gross domestic product. Simple regression analysis uses one independent variable, whereas multiple regression analysis includes two or more independent variables. The objective of regression analysis is to develop a mathematical formula that accurately describes a relationship between the firm's sales and one or more variables; however, the formula indicates only an association, not a causal relationship. Once an accurate formula is established, the analyst plugs the necessary information into the formula to derive the sales forecast.

Regression analysis is useful when a precise association can be established. However, a forecaster seldom finds a perfect one. Furthermore, this method can be used only when available historical sales data are extensive. Thus, regression analysis is futile for forecasting sales of new products.

Market Tests

market test   Making a product available to buyers in one or more test areas and measuring purchases and consumer responses

A **market test** involves making a product available to buyers in one or more test areas and measuring purchases and consumer responses to distribution, promotion, and price. Test areas are often cities with populations of 200,000 to 500,000, but can be larger metropolitan areas or towns with populations of 50,000 to 200,000. Acxiom's Best/Worst list ranks the top 150 metropolitan areas from best to worst as test markets; Albany, New York, and the surrounding area is considered to be the best test market, and New York City was ranked as the worst test market in America.[22]

A market test provides information about consumers' actual, rather than intended, purchases. In addition, purchase volume can be evaluated in relation to the intensity of other marketing activities—advertising, in-store promotions, pricing, packaging, and distribution. For example, 7-Eleven can market test new products in its convenience stores and generate hourly data from the firm's cash registers to help suppliers such as Coca-Cola assess consumers' responses to changes in their marketing mixes.[23] Forecasters base their sales estimates for larger geographic units on customer response in test areas.

Because it does not require historical sales data, a market test is effective for forecasting sales of new products or sales of existing products in new geographic areas. A market test also gives a marketer an opportunity to test various elements of the marketing mix. However, these tests are often time consuming and expensive. In addition, a marketer cannot be certain that consumer response during a market test represents the total market response or that such a response will continue in the future.

Multiple Forecasting Methods

Although some businesses depend on a single sales forecasting method, most firms use several techniques. Sometimes a company is forced to use several methods when marketing diverse product lines, but even for a single product line several forecasts may be needed, especially when the product is sold to different market segments. Thus, a producer of automobile tires may rely on one technique to forecast tire sales for new cars and on another to forecast sales of replacement tires. Variation in the length of needed forecasts may call for several forecasting methods. A firm that employs one method for a short-range forecast may find it inappropriate for long-range forecasting. Sometimes a marketer verifies results of one method by using one or more other methods and comparing outcomes.

CHAPTER REVIEW

1 Learn what a market is.

A market is a group of people who, as individuals or as organizations, have needs for products in a product class and have the ability, willingness, and authority to purchase such products.

2 Understand the differences among general targeting strategies.

The undifferentiated targeting strategy involves designing a single marketing mix directed toward the entire market for a particular product. This strategy is effective in a homogeneous market, whereas a concentrated targeting strategy or differentiated targeting strategy is more appropriate for a heterogeneous market. The concentrated strategy and differentiated strategy both divide markets into segments consisting of individuals, groups, or organizations that have one or more similar characteristics and so can be linked to similar product needs. The concentrated strategy involves targeting a single market segment with one marketing mix. The differentiated targeting strategy targets two or more market segments with marketing mixes customized for each.

3 Become familiar with the major segmentation variables.

Segmentation variables are the characteristics of individuals, groups, or organizations used to segment a total market. The variable(s) used should relate to customers' needs for, uses of, or behavior toward the product. Segmentation variables for consumer markets can be grouped into four categories: demographic (age, gender, income, ethnicity, family life cycle), geographic (population, market density, climate), psychographic (personality traits, motives, lifestyles), and behavioristic (volume usage, end use, expected benefits, brand loyalty, price sensitivity). Variables for segmenting business markets include geographic location, type of organization, customer size, and product use.

4 Know what segment profiles are and how they are used.

Segment profiles describe the similarities among potential customers within a segment and explain the differences among people and organizations in different market segments. They are used to assess the degree to which the firm's products can match potential customers' product needs.

5 Understand how to evaluate market segments.

Marketers evaluate relevant market segments by analyzing several important factors associated with each segment, such as sales estimates (including market potential and company sales potential), competitive assessments, and cost estimates.

6 Identify the factors that influence the selection of specific market segments for use as target markets.

Actual selection of specific target market segments requires an assessment of whether customers' needs differ enough to warrant segmentation and which segments to focus on. Sales estimates, competitive assessments, and cost estimates for each potential segment, and the firm's financial resources, managerial skills, employee expertise, facilities, and objectives are important factors in this decision, as are legal issues, potential conflicts with stakeholders, technological advancements, and the long-term prospects for growth.

7 Become familiar with sales forecasting methods.

A sales forecast is the amount of a product the company expects to sell during a specific period at a specified level of marketing activities. To forecast sales, marketers can choose from several techniques, including executive judgment, surveys, time series analysis, regression analysis, and market tests. Executive judgment is based on the intuition of one or more executives. Surveys include customer, sales force, and expert forecasting surveys. Time series analysis uses the firm's historical sales data to discover patterns in the firm's sales over time and employs four major types of analyses: trend, cycle, seasonal, and random factor. With regression analysis, forecasters attempt to find a relationship between past sales and one or more independent variables. Market testing involves making a product available to buy-

ers in one or more test areas and measuring purchases and consumer responses to distribution, promotion, and price. Many companies employ multiple forecasting methods.

Please visit the student website at **www.prideferrell.com** for ACE Self-Test questions that will help you prepare for exams.

KEY CONCEPTS

consumer market
business market
undifferentiated targeting strategy
homogeneous market
heterogeneous markets
market segmentation
market segment
concentrated targeting strategy

differentiated targeting strategy
segmentation variables
market density
geodemographic segmentation
micromarketing
benefit segmentation
market potential
company sales potential

breakdown approach
buildup approach
sales forecast
executive judgment
customer forecasting survey
sales force forecasting survey
expert forecasting survey
Delphi technique

time series analysis
trend analysis
cycle analysis
seasonal analysis
random factor analysis
regression analysis
market test

ISSUES FOR DISCUSSION AND REVIEW

1. In your local area, identify a group of people with unsatisfied product needs who represent a market. Could this market be reached by a business organization? Why or why not?

2. Outline the five major steps in the target market selection process.

3. What is an undifferentiated strategy? Under what conditions is it most useful? Describe a present market situation in which a company is using an undifferentiated strategy. Is the business successful? Why or why not?

4. What is market segmentation? Describe the basic conditions required for effective segmentation. Identify several firms that use market segmentation.

5. List the differences between concentrated and differentiated strategies, and describe the advantages and disadvantages of each.

6. Identify and describe four major categories of variables that can be used to segment consumer markets. Give examples of product markets that are segmented by variables in each category.

7. What dimensions are used to segment business markets?

8. What is a market segment profile? Why is it an important step in the target market selection process?

9. Describe the important factors that marketers should analyze to evaluate market segments.

10. Why is a marketer concerned about sales potential when trying to select a target market?

11. Why is selecting appropriate target markets important to an organization that wants to adopt the marketing concept philosophy?

12. What is a sales forecast? Why is it important?

MARKETING APPLICATIONS

1. MTV Latino targets the growing Hispanic market in the United States. Identify another product marketed to a distinct target market. Describe the target market, and explain how the marketing mix appeals specifically to that group.

2. Locate an article that describes the targeting strategy of a particular organization. Describe the target market, and explain the strategy being used to reach that market.

3. The stereo market may be segmented according to income and age. Name two ways the market for each of the following products might be segmented.
   a. Candy bars
   b. Travel agency services
   c. Bicycles
   d. Hair spray

ONLINE EXERCISE

4. iExplore is an Internet company that offers a variety of travel and adventure products. Visit its website at **www.iexplore.com.**
   a. Based on the information provided at the website, what are some of iExplore's basic products?
   b. What market segments does iExplore appear to be targeting with its website? What segmentation variables are being used to segment these markets?
   c. How does iExplore appeal to comparison shoppers?

VIDEO CASE

BuyandHold.com Targets Smaller Investors

The strategy of targeting smaller, more cost-conscious investors is paying dividends for BuyandHold.com, a division of Freedom Investments. When Peter E. Breen co-founded BuyandHold.com as an online brokerage site in 1999, his goal was to offer consumers affordable access to stocks and mutual funds. "Wall Street put up a lot of different barriers for people," he says. "BuyandHold.com came along and took all those barriers down."

Today, BuyandHold.com's pricing is low even when compared with the commissions charged by deep-discount, Web-only brokers. There is no minimum balance requirement to open an account, and customers pay as little as $2.99 per trade to buy or sell securities. Customers can also buy securities according to the amount they have to invest, even if this means buying a fraction of a share. In contrast, traditional brokerages charge $15 or more for one order to buy or sell securities, and they prefer trades made in 100-share blocks or at least full-share lots.

Pricing isn't the only difference between BuyandHold.com and other brokerage firms. The company also focuses on an unusual target market. Merrill Lynch and other full-service firms generally target investors with larger portfolios who want considerable investment advice and personal assistance. Discount brokerage firms like Charles Schwab are targeting the "mass affluent," experienced investors who handle their own accounts and forgo personalized help in exchange for lower trading fees. In contrast, BuyandHold.com aims for lower-income consumers who can afford to build a portfolio only little by little and are investing to meet a long-term need such as financing a child's college education or saving for retirement.

This target market of small investors is far from insignificant. By one estimate, 63 million U.S. households hold no stocks or bonds—yet, 11 million of these households have at least $50,000 that could be invested. Small wonder that BuyandHold.com faces competitive pressure from a growing number of rivals including ShareBuilder, Portfolio Builder, and MyStockFund. All three offer a variety of low-commission programs that encourage investors to invest a few dollars every week or month, year in and year out.

The only way BuyandHold.com can offer rock-bottom pricing to serve its target segment is to keep costs as low as possible. One way it does this is by bundling all the orders it receives and going into the market to buy and sell just twice a day, once in mid-morning and again in mid-afternoon. Although this minimizes trading costs, it also limits the customer's ability to take advantage of changing market conditions and place trades at specific prices. Another way BuyandHold.com keeps costs down is by limiting its selection of stocks and mutual funds. Unlike mainstream brokers, who allow investors to choose from a much wider selection of securities, BuyandHold.com offers stock from fewer than 5,000 public companies.

Low cost, however, doesn't mean no service. BuyandHold.com maintains an online library to educate consumers about investing, posts business headlines on its webpage, and offers investing tips from experts. The company also promotes an automated plan that enables customers to transfer funds electronically and make small investments on a set schedule throughout the year.

By targeting a single consumer segment, BuyandHold.com's management has been able to learn a great deal about its market. For example, the company found through feedback that some customers wanted a pricing alternative for more active trading. As a result, it changed its pricing strategy to add a $14.99 flat monthly fee covering unlimited trades.

Management also realized that many cost-conscious investors were saving money by buying shares directly from public companies rather than through brokers. In response, the firm established the Virtual Direct Stock Purchase Plan. Under this plan, participating companies like Walt Disney post an online link to a special BuyandHold.com webpage where consumers can set up accounts and buy stock. The companies save money because they don't have to prepare and mail customer statements, and consumers can stick with their investment choices or trade in additional securities at a low price.

Once BuyandHold.com customers accumulate a sizable nest egg and decide they want more investment advice and guidance, they can switch to the full brokerage services of parent company Freedom Investments. This helps BuyandHold.com continue to attract cost-conscious consumers who are committed to achieving a better financial future.[24]

Questions for Discussion

1. What type of general targeting strategy is BuyandHold.com using? Explain.
2. What segmentation variables does BuyandHold.com use?
3. As more competitors start marketing to the cost-conscious segment, would you recommend that BuyandHold.com change its targeting strategy? Why or why not?

Customer Behavior

Part 4 continues the focus on the customer. Understanding elements that affect buying decisions enables marketers to analyze customers' needs and evaluate how specific marketing strategies can satisfy those needs. Chapter 8 examines consumer buying decision processes and factors that influence buying decisions. Chapter 9 stresses business markets, organizational buyers, the buying center, and the organizational buying decision process.

8

Consumer Buying Behavior

OBJECTIVES

1 Describe the level of involvement and types of consumer problem-solving processes.

2 Recognize the stages of the consumer buying decision process.

3 Explain how situational influences may affect the consumer buying decision process.

4 Understand the psychological influences that may affect the consumer buying decision process.

5 Be familiar with the social influences that affect the consumer buying decision process.

Buying Cars with a Click at AutoTrader.com

Who buys a car without checking under the hood or kicking the tires? Since 1997, millions of people have bought cars through the AutoTrader.com website (**www.autotrader.com**) without leaving their computer keyboards. At any one time, the site features classified ads for more than 2.5 million cars, both new and used, offered by 40,000 dealers and 250,000 individuals across the United States. Buyers and sellers make contact through the site to negotiate the final terms for purchases. Buyers pay no fee to browse or buy, which encourages visitors to surf the site often.

When AutoTrader first opened its online business, few people had ever bought or sold a vehicle on the Internet. Therefore, the company's initial challenge was to change the habits of dealers and consumers who were accustomed to using newspaper classified advertising for used-car transactions. Instead of charging dealers for every listing, as newspapers did, AutoTrader set a flat monthly fee for posting any number of descriptions and photos.

The next step was to educate AutoTrader's primary target market, 25- to 49-year-old men, about buying and selling cars online. The company did this by running informative television commercials showing how to use its site step by step. The result: the number of visitors surged to more than 5.5 million every month. Also, for the past few years, AutoTrader has sponsored television's *Monday Night Football* to reach this target market throughout the late summer and fall. During the two days following a *Monday Night Football* game, AutoTrader's website consistently increases by 10 percent, and the company sends auto dealers 12 percent more sales leads than it does during other periods.

At one time, AutoTrader cooperated with eBay, the world's largest auction site, to allow consumers to search for cars on either site. However, after monitoring buyer behavior, AutoTrader ended the agreement and set up its own vehicle auctions in direct competition with eBay. "We did a lot of research and studied very closely the behavior of auction-style users on our site," says Chip Perry, AutoTrader's CEO. He acknowledges that eBay is the "current major player in an extremely small niche segment of the car business," but he sees plenty of room for AutoTrader in this fast-growing segment.

As AutoTrader's annual vehicle sales accelerate past $135 million, Perry has observed new behavior patterns emerging. "Online car shopping and selling has made it possible for people to be a little more cavalier about buying and selling cars," he says. "People are much more willing to buy and sell on a regular basis as opposed to feeling like they're stuck with a car."[1]   ◄

buying behavior   The decision processes and acts of people involved in buying and using products

consumer buying behavior   Buying behavior of people who purchase products for personal or household use and not for business purposes

Marketers at successful organizations like AutoTrader go to great efforts to understand their customers' needs and gain a better grasp of customers' buying behavior. A firm's ability to establish and maintain satisfying customer relationships requires an understanding of buying behavior. **Buying behavior** is the decision processes and acts of people involved in buying and using products. **Consumer buying behavior** refers to the buying behavior of ultimate consumers, those who purchase products for personal or household use and not for business purposes. Marketers attempt to understand buying behavior for several reasons. First, buyers' reactions to a firm's marketing strategy have a great impact on the firm's success. Second, as indicated in Chapter 1, the marketing concept stresses that a firm should create a marketing mix that satisfies customers. To find out what satisfies buyers, marketers must examine the main influences on what, where, when, and how consumers buy. Third, by gaining a better understanding of the factors that affect buying behavior, marketers are in a better position to predict how consumers will respond to marketing strategies.

In this chapter, we first examine how the customer's level of involvement affects the type of problem solving employed and discuss the types of consumer problem-solving processes. Then we analyze the major stages of the consumer buying decision process, beginning with problem recognition, information search, and evaluation of alternatives and proceeding through purchase and postpurchase evaluation. Next, we examine situational influences that affect purchasing decisions: surroundings, time, purchase reason, and buyer's mood and condition. We go on to consider psychological influences on purchasing decisions: perception, motives, learning, attitudes, personality and self-concept, and lifestyles. We conclude with a discussion of social influences that affect buying behavior: roles, family, reference groups and opinion leaders, social classes, and culture and subcultures.

Level of Involvement and Consumer Problem-Solving Processes

level of involvement   An individual's intensity of interest in a product and the importance of the product for that person

Consumers generally try to acquire and maintain an assortment of products that satisfy their current and future needs. To do so, consumers engage in problem solving. When purchasing products such as food, clothing, shelter, medical care, education, recreation, and transportation, people engage in different types of problem-solving processes. The amount of effort, both mental and physical, that buyers expend in solving problems varies considerably. A major determinant of the type of problem-solving process employed depends on the customer's **level of involvement**, the degree of interest in a product and the importance the individual places on this product. High-involvement products tend to be those visible to others (such as clothing, furniture, or automobiles) and which are expensive. Expensive bicycles, for example, are usually high-involvement products. High-importance issues, such as health care, are associated with high levels of involvement. Low-involvement products tend to be those which are less expensive and have less associated social risk, such as many grocery items. When a person's interest in a product category is ongoing and long term, it is referred to as *enduring involvement*. In contrast, *situational involvement* is temporary and dynamic, and results from a particular set of circumstances. Involvement level, as well as other factors, affects a person's selection of one of three types of

Levels of Involvement
Buying decisions about numerous grocery products, such as olives, are associated with low levels of involvement. Buying decisions regarding recreational equipment, such as kayaks, are associated with high levels of involvement.

routinized response behavior
A type of consumer problem-solving process used when buying frequently purchased, low-cost items that require very little search-and-decision effort

limited problem solving A type of consumer problem-solving process that buyers use when purchasing products occasionally or when they need information about an unfamiliar brand in a familiar product category

extended problem solving A type of consumer problem-solving process employed when purchasing unfamiliar, expensive, or infrequently bought products

consumer problem solving: routinized response behavior, limited problem solving, or extended problem solving.

A consumer uses **routinized response behavior** when buying frequently purchased, low-cost items needing very little search-and-decision effort. When buying such items, a consumer may prefer a particular brand but is familiar with several brands in the product class and views more than one as being acceptable. Typically, low-involvement products are bought through routinized response behavior, that is, almost automatically. For example, most buyers spend little time or effort selecting a soft drink or a brand of cereal.

Buyers engage in **limited problem solving** when buying products occasionally or when they need to obtain information about an unfamiliar brand in a familiar product category. This type of problem solving requires a moderate amount of time for information gathering and deliberation. For example, if Procter & Gamble introduces an improved Tide laundry detergent, buyers will seek additional information about the new product, perhaps by asking a friend who has used it or watching a commercial about it, before making a trial purchase.

The most complex type of problem solving, **extended problem solving**, occurs when purchasing unfamiliar, expensive, or infrequently bought products—for instance, a car, home, or college education. The buyer uses many criteria to evaluate alternative brands or choices and spends much time seeking information and deciding on the purchase. Extended problem solving is frequently used for purchasing high-involvement products.

Purchase of a particular product does not always elicit the same type of problem-solving process. In some instances, we engage in extended problem solving the first time we buy a certain product but find that limited problem solving suffices when we buy it again. If a routinely purchased, formerly satisfying brand no longer satisfies us, we may use limited or extended problem solving to switch to a new brand. Thus, if we notice that the brand of pain reliever we normally buy is not working, we may seek out a different brand through limited problem solving. Most consumers occasionally make purchases solely on impulse, and not on the basis of any of these three problem-solving processes. **Impulse buying** involves no conscious planning but results from a powerful urge to buy something immediately.

impulse buying   An unplanned buying behavior resulting from a powerful urge to buy something immediately

Consumer Buying Decision Process

consumer buying decision process   A five-stage purchase decision process that includes problem recognition, information search, evaluation of alternatives, purchase, and postpurchase evaluation

The **consumer buying decision process**, shown in Figure 8.1, includes five stages: problem recognition, information search, evaluation of alternatives, purchase, and postpurchase evaluation. Before we examine each stage, consider these important points. First, the act of purchasing is only one stage in the process and usually not the first stage. Second, even though we indicate that a purchase occurs, not all decision processes lead to a purchase. Individuals may end the process at any stage. Finally, not all consumer decisions include all five stages. People engaged in extended problem solving usually go through all stages of this decision process, whereas those engaged in limited problem solving and routinized response behavior may omit some stages.

Figure 8.1
Consumer Buying Decision Process and Possible Influences on the Process

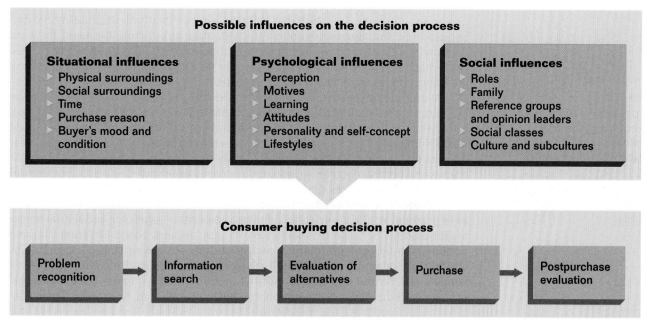

Possible influences on the decision process

Situational influences
- Physical surroundings
- Social surroundings
- Time
- Purchase reason
- Buyer's mood and condition

Psychological influences
- Perception
- Motives
- Learning
- Attitudes
- Personality and self-concept
- Lifestyles

Social influences
- Roles
- Family
- Reference groups and opinion leaders
- Social classes
- Culture and subcultures

Consumer buying decision process

Problem recognition → Information search → Evaluation of alternatives → Purchase → Postpurchase evaluation

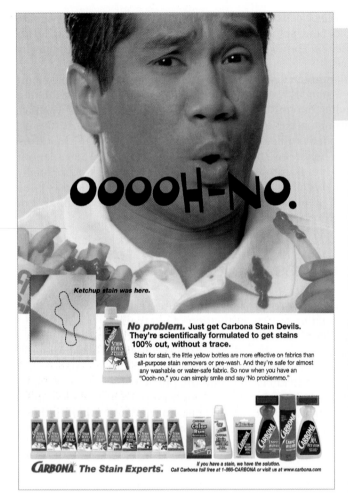

Ketchup stain was here.

No problem. Just get Carbona Stain Devils. They're scientifically formulated to get stains 100% out, without a trace.

Stain for stain, the little yellow bottles are more effective on fabrics than all-purpose stain removers or pre-wash. And they're safe for almost any washable or water-safe fabric. So now when you have an "Oooh-no," you can simply smile and say 'No problemmo.'

If you have a stain, we have the solution.
CARBONA. The Stain Experts.   Call Carbona toll free at 1-866-CARBONA or visit us at www.carbona.com

Problem Recognition
The maker of Carbona cleaning products employs advertising to encourage problem recognition that certain stains are difficult to remove and that its products will remove them.

◉ Problem Recognition

Problem recognition occurs when a buyer becomes aware of a difference between a desired state and an actual condition. Consider a student who owns a non-programmable calculator and learns she needs a programmable one for her math course. She recognizes that a difference exists between the desired state—having a programmable calculator—and her actual condition. She therefore decides to buy a new calculator.

The speed of consumer problem recognition can be quite rapid or rather slow. Sometimes a person has a problem or need but is unaware of it. Marketers use sales personnel, advertising, and packaging to help trigger recognition of such needs or problems. For example, a university bookstore may advertise programmable calculators in the school newspaper at the beginning of the term. Students who see the advertisement may recognize that they need these calculators for their course work.

◉ Information Search

After recognizing the problem or need, a buyer (if continuing the decision process) searches for product information that will help resolve the problem or satisfy the need. For example, the above-mentioned student, after recognizing the need for a programmable calculator, may search for information about different types and brands of calculators. She acquires information over time from her surroundings. However, the information's impact depends on how she interprets it.

internal search An information search in which buyers search their memories for information about products that might solve their problem

external search An information search in which buyers seek information from outside sources

An information search has two aspects. In an **internal search**, buyers search their memories for information about products that might solve the problem. If they cannot retrieve enough information from memory to make a decision, they seek additional information from outside sources in an **external search**. The external search may focus on communication with friends or relatives, comparison of available brands and prices, marketer-dominated sources, and/or public sources. For example, a recent survey indicates that the Internet is the most preferred information source of car shoppers in online households, especially for pricing information.[2] An individual's personal contacts—friends, relatives, associates—often are influential sources of information because the person trusts and respects them. Utilizing marketer-dominated sources of information, such as salespeople, advertising, package labeling, and in-store demonstrations and displays, typically requires little effort on the consumer's part. Buyers also obtain information from public sources—for instance, government reports, news presentations, publications such as *Consumer Reports,* and

Cleaning used to be easy.

But now it's

...ruff.

Make cleaning a little easier

with America's best cleaning bagless by Hoover.

The new WindTunnel™ Bagless, featuring powerful WindTunnel™ Technology, picks up more dirt than any other clean-air upright...period.*

Its unique Twin Chamber™ Bagless System maintains superior cleaning power, and features HEPA filtration.

And its conveniently stored hand tool cleans carpeted stairs and upholstery with powered brushing action.

Now, cleaning is even easier, thanks to your new best friend.

HOOVER

DEEP DOWN,
YOU WANT HOOVER.

The New WindTunnel™ Bagless by Hoover

*As tested per American Society for Testing Materials - Test F608-97, the only recognized industry standard.

Framing Product Attributes
Hoover helps frame product attributes by highlighting product features such as vacuuming power, twin chambers, no bags, HEPA filtration, and powered brushing action.

consideration set A group of brands that a buyer views as alternatives for possible purchase

evaluative criteria Objective and subjective characteristics that are important to a buyer

reports from product-testing organizations. Consumers frequently view information from public sources as highly credible because of its factual and unbiased nature. Repetition, a technique well known to advertisers, increases consumers' learning of information. When seeing or hearing an advertising message for the first time, recipients may not grasp all its important details, but learn more details as the message is repeated.

◉ Evaluation of Alternatives

A successful information search yields a group of brands that a buyer views as possible alternatives. This group of brands is sometimes called a **consideration set** (also called an *evoked set*). For example, a consideration set of calculators might include those made by Texas Instruments, Hewlett-Packard, Sharp, and Casio.

To assess the products in a consideration set, the buyer uses **evaluative criteria**, which are objective (such as an EPA mileage rating) and subjective (such as style) characteristics that are important to the buyer. For example, one calculator buyer may want a rechargeable unit with a large display and large buttons, whereas another may have no size preferences but dislikes rechargeable calculators. The buyer also assigns a certain level of importance to each criterion; some features and characteristics carry more weight than others. Using the criteria, the buyer rates and eventually ranks brands in the consideration set. The evaluation stage may yield no brand the buyer is willing to purchase. In that case, a further information search may be necessary.

Marketers may influence consumers' evaluations by *framing* the alternatives, that is, by describing the alternatives and their attributes in a certain manner. Framing can make a characteristic seem more important to a consumer and facilitate its recall from memory. For example, by stressing a car's superior comfort and safety features over those of a competitor's, an automaker can direct consumers' attention toward these points of superiority. Framing probably influences the decision processes of inexperienced buyers more than those of experienced ones.

◉ Purchase

In the purchase stage, the consumer chooses the product to be bought. Selection is based on the outcome of the evaluation stage and on other dimensions. Product availability may influence which brand is purchased. For example, if a consumer wants a black pair of Nikes and cannot find them in her size, she might buy a black pair of Reeboks.

During this stage, buyers also pick the seller from whom they will buy the product. The choice of seller may affect final product selection—and so may the terms of sale, which, if negotiable, are determined at this stage. Other issues, such as price, delivery, warranties, maintenance agreements, installation, and credit arrangements, are also settled. Finally, the actual purchase takes place during this stage, unless the consumer decides to terminate the buying decision process.

◉ Postpurchase Evaluation

After the purchase, the buyer begins evaluating the product to ascertain if its actual performance meets expected levels. Many criteria used in evaluating alternatives are applied again during postpurchase evaluation. The outcome of this stage is either satisfaction or dissatisfaction, which influences whether the consumer complains, communicates with other possible buyers, and repurchases the product.

cognitive dissonance A buyer's doubts shortly after a purchase about whether the decision was the right one

Shortly after purchase of an expensive product, evaluation may result in **cognitive dissonance**, doubts in the buyer's mind about whether purchasing the product was the right decision. For example, after buying a pair of $169 inline skates, a person may feel guilty about the purchase or wonder whether she purchased the right brand and quality. Cognitive dissonance is most likely to arise when a person has recently bought an expensive, high-involvement product that lacks some of the desirable features of competing brands. A buyer experiencing cognitive dissonance may attempt to return the product or seek positive information about it to justify choosing it. Marketers sometimes attempt to reduce cognitive dissonance by having salespeople contact recent purchasers to make sure they are satisfied with their new purchases.

As Figure 8.1 shows, three major categories of influences are believed to affect the consumer buying decision process: situational, psychological, and social. In the remainder of this chapter, we focus on these influences. Although we discuss each major influence separately, their effects on the consumer decision process are interrelated.

⟲ Situational Influences on the Buying Decision Process

situational influences Influences resulting from circumstances, time, and location that affect the consumer buying decision process

Situational influences result from circumstances, time, and location that affect the consumer buying decision process. For example, buying an automobile tire after noticing while washing your car that the tire is badly worn is a different experience from buying a tire right after a blowout on the highway derails your vacation. Situational factors can influence the buyer during any stage of the consumer buying decision process and may cause the individual to shorten, lengthen, or terminate the process.

Situational factors can be classified into five categories: physical surroundings, social surroundings, time perspective, reason for purchase, and the buyer's momentary mood and condition.[3] Physical surroundings include location, store atmosphere, aromas, sounds, lighting, weather, and other factors in the physical environment in which the decision process occurs. Numerous restaurant chains, such as Olive Garden and Chili's, invest heavily in facilities, often building from the ground up, to provide special surroundings that enhance customers' dining experiences.

Clearly, in some settings, dimensions, such as weather, traffic sounds, and odors, are beyond the marketers' control. Yet they must try to make customers more comfortable. General climatic conditions, for example, may influence a customer's decision to buy a specific type of vehicle (such as an SUV) and certain accessories (such as four-wheel drive). Current weather conditions, depending on whether they are favorable or unfavorable, may either encourage or discourage consumers to go shopping and to seek out specific products.

Social surroundings include characteristics and interactions of others, such as friends, relatives, salespeople, and other customers, who are present when a purchase decision is being made. Buyers may feel pressured to behave in a certain way because they are in public places such as restaurants, stores, or sports arenas. Thoughts about who will be around when the product is used or consumed is also a dimension of the social setting. An overcrowded store or an argument between a customer and a salesperson may cause consumers to stop shopping or even leave the store.

The time dimension, such as the amount of time required to become knowledgeable about a product, to search for it, and to buy it, also influences the buying decision process in several ways. For instance, to make an informed decision at their own convenience, more men than ever are buying diamond engagement rings online. A high-end Internet jeweler like Blue Nile features interactive tools on its website to help men educate themselves about diamonds and then select a unique combination from its large inventory of diamonds and settings.[4] Time plays a major role because the buyer considers the possible frequency of product use, the length of time required to use the product, and the length of the overall product life. Other time dimensions that influence purchases include time of day, day of the week or month, seasons, and holidays. The amount of time pressure a consumer is under affects how much time is devoted to purchase decisions. A customer under severe time constraints is likely either to make quick purchase decisions or to delay them.

The purchase reason raises the questions of what exactly the product purchase should accomplish and for whom. Generally, consumers purchase an item for their own use, for household use, or as a gift. For example, people who are buying a gift may buy a different product than if they were purchasing the product for themselves. If you own a Cross pen, for example, it is unlikely that you bought it for yourself.

The buyer's momentary moods (such as anger, anxiety, contentment) or momentary conditions (fatigue, illness, being flush with cash) may have a bearing on the consumer buying decision process. These moods or conditions immediately precede the current situation and are not chronic. Any of these moods or conditions can affect a person's ability and desire to search for information, receive information, or seek and evaluate alternatives. They can also significantly influence a consumer's postpurchase evaluation.

Psychological Influences on the Buying Decision Process

psychological influences Factors that partly determine people's general behavior, thus influencing their behavior as consumers

Psychological influences partly determine people's general behavior and thus influence their behavior as consumers. Primary psychological influences on consumer behavior are perception, motives, learning, attitudes, personality and self-concept, and lifestyles. Even though these psychological factors operate internally, they are very much affected by social forces outside the individual.

Perception

perception   The process of selecting, organizing, and interpreting information inputs to produce meaning

information inputs   Sensations received through the sense organs

selective exposure   The process of selecting inputs to be exposed to our awareness while ignoring others

Different people perceive the same thing at the same time in different ways. When you first look at Figure 8.2, do you see fish or birds? Similarly, an individual at different times may perceive the same item in a number of ways. **Perception** is the process of selecting, organizing, and interpreting information inputs to produce meaning. **Information inputs** are sensations received through sight, taste, hearing, smell, and touch. When we hear an advertisement, see a friend, smell polluted air or water, or touch a product, we receive information inputs.

As the definition indicates, perception is a three-step process. Although we receive numerous pieces of information at once, only a few reach our awareness. We select some inputs and ignore others because we do not have the ability to be conscious of all inputs at one time. This phenomenon is sometimes called **selective exposure** because an individual selects which inputs will reach awareness. If you are

Figure 8.2
Fish or Birds?
Do you see fish or birds?

concentrating on this paragraph, you probably are not aware that cars outside are making noise, that the room light is on, or that you are touching this page. Even though you receive these inputs, they do not reach your awareness until they are pointed out.

An individual's current set of needs affects selective exposure. Information inputs that relate to one's strongest needs at a given time are more likely to be selected to reach awareness. It is not by random chance that many fast-food commercials are aired near mealtimes. Customers are more likely to tune in to these advertisements at these times.

The selective nature of perception may result not only in selective exposure but also in two other conditions: selective distortion and selective retention. **Selective distortion** is changing or twisting currently received information; it occurs when a person receives information inconsistent with personal feelings or beliefs. For example, on seeing an advertisement promoting a disliked brand, a viewer may distort the information to make it more consistent with prior views. This distortion substantially lessens the effect of the advertisement on the individual. In **selective retention**, a person remembers information inputs that support personal feelings and beliefs and forgets inputs that do not. After hearing a sales presentation and leaving a store, a customer may forget many selling points if they contradict personal beliefs.

The second step in the process of perception is perceptual organization. Information inputs that reach awareness are not received in an organized form. To produce meaning, an individual must mentally organize and integrate new information with what is already stored in memory. People use several methods to organize. One method, called *closure,* occurs when a person mentally fills in missing elements in a pattern or statement. In an attempt to draw attention to its brand,

selective distortion An individual's changing or twisting of information when it is inconsistent with personal feelings or beliefs

selective retention Remembering information inputs that support personal feelings and beliefs and forgetting inputs that do not

an advertiser will capitalize on closure by using incomplete images, sounds, or statements in its advertisements.

Interpretation, the third step in the perceptual process, is the assignment of meaning to what has been organized. A person bases interpretation on what he or she expects or what is familiar. For this reason, a manufacturer that changes a product or its package faces a major problem. When people are looking for the old, familiar product or package, they may not recognize the new one. Unless a product or package change is accompanied by a promotional program that makes people aware of the change, an organization may suffer a sales decline.

◉ Motives

motive   An internal energizing force that directs a person's behavior toward satisfying needs or achieving goals

A **motive** is an internal energizing force that orients a person's activities toward satisfying needs or achieving goals. Buyers' actions are affected by a set of motives rather than by just one motive. At a single point in time, some of a person's motives are stronger than others. For example, a person's motives for having a cup of coffee are much stronger right after waking up than just before going to bed. Motives also affect the direction and intensity of behavior. Some motives may help an individual achieve his or her goals, whereas others create barriers to goal achievement.

Maslow's hierarchy of needs The five levels of needs that humans seek to satisfy, from most to least important

Abraham Maslow, an American psychologist, conceived a theory of motivation based on a hierarchy of needs. According to Maslow, humans seek to satisfy five levels of needs, from most important to least important, as shown in Figure 8.3. This sequence is known as **Maslow's hierarchy of needs**. Once needs at one level are met, humans seek to fulfill needs at the next level up in the hierarchy. At the most basic level are *physiological needs,* requirements for survival such as food, water, sex, clothing, and shelter, which people try to satisfy first. Food and beverage marketers often appeal to physiological needs. At the next level are *safety needs,* which include security and freedom from physical and emotional pain and suffering. Next are *social needs,* the human requirements for love and affection and a sense of belonging. Ads for cosmetics and other beauty products, jewelry, and even cars often suggest that purchasing these products will bring love. At the level of *esteem needs,* people require respect and recognition from others as well as self-esteem, a sense of their own worth. Owning a Lexus automobile, having a beauty makeover, or flying first class can satisfy esteem needs. At the top of the hierarchy are *self-actualization needs.* These refer to people's need to grow and develop and to become all they are capable of becoming. In its recruiting advertisements, the U.S. Army told potential enlistees to "be all that you can be in the Army."

Figure 8.3
Maslow's Hierarchy of Needs
Maslow believed that people seek to fulfill five categories of needs.

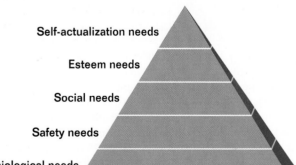

Self-actualization needs

Esteem needs

Social needs

Safety needs

Physiological needs

patronage motives Motives that influence where a person purchases products on a regular basis

Motives that influence where a person purchases products on a regular basis are called **patronage motives**. A buyer may shop at a specific store because of patronage motives such as price, service, location, product variety, or friendliness of salespeople. To capitalize on patronage motives, marketers try to determine why regular customers patronize a particular store and to emphasize these characteristics in the store's marketing mix.

◉ Learning

learning Changes in an individual's thought processes and behavior caused by information and experience

Learning refers to changes in a person's thought processes and behavior caused by information and experience. Consequences of behavior strongly influence the learning process. Behaviors that result in satisfying consequences tend to be repeated. For example, a consumer who buys a Snickers candy bar and enjoys the taste is more likely to buy a Snickers again. In fact, the individual will probably continue to purchase that brand until it no longer provides satisfaction. When effects of the behavior are no longer satisfying, the person may switch brands or stop eating candy bars altogether.

When making purchasing decisions, buyers process information. Individuals have differing abilities to process information. The type of information inexperienced buyers use may differ from the type used by experienced shoppers familiar with the product and purchase situation. Thus, two potential purchasers of an antique desk may use different types of information in making their purchase decisions. The inexperienced buyer may judge the desk's value by price, whereas the more experienced buyer may seek information about the manufacturer, period, and place of origin to judge the desk's quality and value. Consumers lacking experience may seek information from others when making a purchase and even take along an informed "purchase pal." More experienced buyers have greater self-confidence and more knowledge about the product and can recognize which product features are reliable cues to product quality. For example, Safeway decided to launch its Safeway.com online grocery shopping service in Portland, Oregon, and Vancouver, Washington, because consumers in those two cities were already familiar with the operation and offerings of Web-based grocery stores. As a result, these consumers had the experience and knowledge and thus were more likely to understand and use Safeway.com.[5]

Marketers help customers learn about their products by helping them gain experience with them. Free samples, sometimes coupled with coupons, can successfully encourage trial and reduce purchase risk. For example, because some consumers may be wary of exotic menu items, restaurants sometimes offer free samples. In-store demonstrations foster knowledge of product uses. Test drives give potential new-car purchasers some experience with the automobile's features. Consumers also learn by experiencing products indirectly through information from salespeople, advertisements, friends, and relatives. Through sales personnel and advertisements, marketers offer information before (and sometimes after) purchases to influence what consumers learn and to create more favorable attitudes toward the product.

MARKETING ENTREPRENEURS

Melissa and Mallory Gollick

THEIR BUSINESSES: MelMaps and Jungle Beans

FOUNDED AT AGES: 7 and 9

SUCCESS: Loyal customers

Melissa and Mallory Gollick of Denver, Colorado, share more in common than your average siblings: they both became entrepreneurs by the ripe age of 9. Melissa, now 18, is the founder and operator of MelMaps, a computer graphics firm specializing in location, vicinity, site, and floor maps. Over the past 9 years, she has established a loyal clientele of local real estate agents and bankers. Her younger sister Mallory, who is now 16, owns and operates Jungle Beans, a company that sells gourmet Costa Rican coffee beans to the tune of 40 kilos (88 pounds) a week.[a]

⊚ Attitudes

attitude An individual's enduring evaluation of, feelings about, and behavioral tendencies toward an object or idea

An **attitude** is an individual's enduring evaluation of, feelings about, and behavioral tendencies toward an object or idea. The objects toward which we have attitudes may be tangible or intangible, living or nonliving. For example, we have attitudes toward sex, religion, politics, and music, just as we do toward cars, football, and breakfast cereals. Although attitudes can change, they tend to remain stable and do not vary from moment to moment. However, all of a person's attitudes do not have equal impact at any one time; some are stronger than others. Individuals acquire attitudes through experience and interaction with other people.

An attitude consists of three major components: cognitive, affective, and behavioral. The cognitive component is the person's knowledge and information about the object or idea. The affective component comprises feelings and emotions toward the object or idea. The behavioral component manifests itself in the person's actions regarding the object or idea. Changes in one of these components may or may not alter the other components. Thus, a consumer may become more knowledgeable about a specific brand without changing the affective or behavioral components of his or her attitude toward that brand.

Consumer attitudes toward a company and its products greatly influence success or failure of the firm's marketing strategy. When consumers have strong negative attitudes toward one or more aspects of a firm's marketing practices, they may not only stop using its products, but also urge relatives and friends to do likewise.

Because attitudes play such an important part in determining consumer behavior, marketers should measure consumer attitudes toward prices, package designs, brand names, advertisements, salespeople, repair services, store locations, features of existing or proposed products, and social responsibility efforts. Several methods help marketers gauge these attitudes. One of the simplest ways is to question people directly. Press Ganey Associates, in South Bend, Indiana, researches patient opinions about their hospitalization, one of the factors being hospital food. Marion General Hospital in Marion, Indiana, found satisfaction with its food service ranked in the 40th percentile. To help increase its score, the hospital consulted with a Fort Wayne hospital whose food service ranked in the 90th percentile. Instituting several ideas from the consultation, Marion General's score rose to the 70th percentile and eventually reached a rating in the 90s.[6] Marketers also evaluate attitudes through attitude scales. An **attitude scale** usually consists of a series of adjectives, phrases, or

attitude scale Means of measuring consumer attitudes by gauging the intensity of individuals' reactions to adjectives, phrases, or sentences about an object

Attempting to Change Attitudes
A number of organizations attempt to convince smokers to quit smoking and to inform them about the effects of secondhand smoke.

sentences about an object. Respondents indicate the intensity of their feelings toward the object by reacting to the adjectives, phrases, or sentences in a certain way. For example, a marketer measuring people's attitudes toward shopping might ask respondents to indicate the extent to which they agree or disagree with a number of statements, such as "Shopping is more fun than watching television."

When marketers determine that a significant number of consumers have negative attitudes toward an aspect of a marketing mix, they may try to change those attitudes to make them more favorable. This task is generally lengthy, expensive, and difficult, and may require extensive promotional efforts. For example, the California Prune Growers, an organization of prune producers, has tried to use advertising to change consumers' attitudes toward prunes by presenting them as a nutritious snack high in potassium and fiber. To alter consumers' responses so that more of them buy a given brand, a firm might launch an information-focused campaign to change the cognitive component of a consumer's attitude or a persuasive (emotional) campaign to influence the affective component. Distributing free samples might help change the behavioral component. Both business and nonbusiness organizations try to change people's attitudes about many issues, from health and safety to prices and product features.

◉ Personality and Self-Concept

personality   A set of internal traits and distinct behavioral tendencies that result in consistent patterns of behavior

Personality is a set of internal traits and distinct behavioral tendencies that result in consistent patterns of behavior in certain situations. An individual's personality arises from hereditary characteristics and personal experiences that make the person unique. Personalities typically are described as having one or more characteristics such as compulsiveness, ambition, gregariousness, dogmatism, authoritarianism, introversion, extroversion, and competitiveness. Marketing researchers look for relationships between such characteristics and buying behavior. Even though a few links between several personality traits and buyer behavior have been determined, results of many studies have been inconclusive. The weak association between personality and buying behavior may be the result of unreliable measures rather than a lack of a relationship. Some marketers are convinced that consumers' personalities do influence types and brands of products purchased. For example, the type of clothing, jewelry, or automobile a person buys may reflect one or more personality characteristics.

At times marketers aim advertising at certain types of personalities. For example, ads for certain cigarette brands are directed toward specific personality types. Marketers focus on positively valued personality characteristics, such as security consciousness, sociability, independence, or competitiveness, rather than on negatively valued ones like insensitivity or timidity.

self-concept   Perception or view of oneself

A person's self-concept is closely linked to personality. **Self-concept** (sometimes called *self-image*) is a person's view or perception of him- or herself. Individuals develop and alter their self-concepts based on an interaction of psychological and social dimensions. Research shows that a buyer purchases products that reflect and enhance the self-concept and that purchase decisions are important to the development and maintenance of a stable self-concept. Consumers' self-concepts may influence whether they buy a product in a specific product category and may affect brand selection as well as where they buy. For example, home improvement retailer Lowe's is targeting women—who make 90 percent of household decisions about home decor and home improvement—using self-concept as the basis of its advertising message. "Only Lowe's has everything and everyone to help your house tell the story about who you really are," says the company's advertising tag line.[7]

Self-Concept
This Adidas advertisement is designed to appeal to individuals whose self-concept includes being strong and persevering.

⊚ Lifestyles

lifestyle An individual's pattern of living expressed through activities, interests, and opinions

A **lifestyle** is an individual's pattern of living expressed through activities, interests, and opinions. Lifestyle patterns include the ways people spend time, the extent of their interaction with others, and their general outlook on life and living. People partially determine their own lifestyles, but the pattern is also affected by personality, as well as by demographic factors such as age, education, income, and social class. Lifestyles are measured through a lengthy series of questions.

Lifestyles have a strong impact on many aspects of the consumer buying decision process, from problem recognition to postpurchase evaluation. Lifestyles influence consumers' product needs, brand preferences, types of media used, and how and where they shop.

⦾ Social Influences on the Buying Decision Process

social influences The forces other people exert on one's buying behavior

Forces that other people exert on buying behavior are called **social influences**. As Figure 8.1 shows, they are grouped into five major areas: roles, family, reference groups and opinion leaders, social classes, and culture and subcultures.

⊚ Roles

role Actions and activities that a person in a particular position is supposed to perform based on expectations of the individual and surrounding persons

All of us occupy positions within groups, organizations, and institutions. Associated with each position is a **role**, a set of actions and activities a person in a particular position is supposed to perform based on expectations of both the individual and surrounding persons. Because people occupy numerous positions, they have many roles. For example, a man may perform the roles of son, husband, father, employee

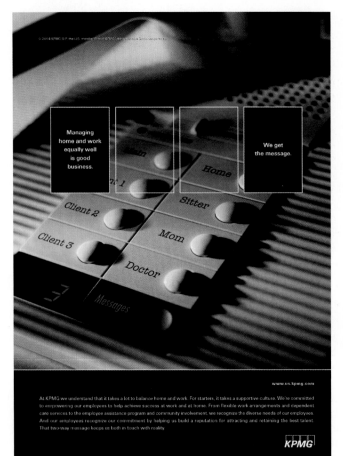

Role Influences
Some organizations, such as KPMG, recognize the existence of multiple role influences and express sensitivity toward them.

consumer socialization The process through which a person acquires the knowledge and skills to function as a consumer

or employer, church member, civic organization member, and student in an evening college class. Thus, multiple sets of expectations are placed on each person's behavior.

An individual's roles influence both general behavior and buying behavior. The demands of a person's many roles may be diverse and even inconsistent. Consider the various types of clothes that you buy and wear depending on whether you are going to class, to work, to a party, to church or synagogue, or to an aerobics class. You and others involved in these settings have expectations about what is acceptable clothing for these events. Thus, the expectations of those around us affect our purchases of clothing and many other products.

◉ Family Influences

Family influences have a very direct impact on the consumer buying decision process. Parents (and other household adults) teach children how to cope with various problems, including those dealing with purchase decisions. **Consumer socialization** is the process through which a person acquires the knowledge and skills to function as a consumer. Often children gain this knowledge and set of skills by observing parents and older siblings in purchase situations, as well as through their own purchase experiences. Children observe brand preferences and buying practices in their families and, as adults, maintain some of these brand preferences and buying practices as they establish households and raise their own families. Buying decisions made by a family are a combination of group and individual decision making.

Although female roles continue to change, women still make buying decisions related to many household items, including health-care products, laundry supplies, paper products, and foods. Spouses participate jointly in the purchase of several products, especially durable goods. Due to changes in men's roles, a significant proportion of men are the primary grocery shoppers. Children make many purchase decisions and influence numerous household purchase decisions. Knowing that children wield considerable influence over food brand preferences, H. J. Heinz targeted them a few years ago with EZ Squirt ketchup in a squeeze bottle designed for small hands to grasp and in a rainbow of colors such as green, purple, blue, teal, pink, and orange.[8] Also, many advertising messages are targeted at teens. For example, Britney Spears speaks for Pepsi, Brandy for Covergirl, Jennifer Love Hewitt for Neutrogena, and Jessica Biel for L'Oreal.[9]

The extent to which adult family members take part in family decision making varies among families and product categories. Traditionally family decision making processes have been grouped into four categories: autonomic, husband-dominant, wife-dominant, and syncratic. Autonomic decision making means that an equal number of decisions are made by each adult household member. In husband-dominant or wife-dominant decision making, the husband or the wife, respectively, makes most of the family decisions. Syncratic decision making means most decisions concerning purchases are made jointly by both partners. The type of family decision making employed depends on the composition of the family as well as the values and attitudes of family members.

When two or more family members participate in a purchase, their roles may dictate that each is responsible for performing certain purchase-related tasks, such as initiating the idea, gathering information, determining if the product is affordable, deciding whether to buy the product, or selecting the specific brand. The specific purchase tasks performed depend on the types of products being considered, the kind of family purchase decision process typically employed, and the amount of influence children have in the decision process. Thus, different family members may play different roles in the family buying process. To develop a marketing mix that meets the needs of target market members precisely, marketers must know not only who does the actual buying but also which other family members perform purchase-related tasks.

The family life cycle stage affects individual and joint needs of family members. (Family life cycle stages are discussed in Chapter 7.) For example, consider how the car needs of recently married twenty-somethings differ from those of the same couple when they are forty-somethings with a 13-year-old daughter and a 17-year-old son. Family life cycle changes can affect which family members are involved in purchase decisions and the types of products purchased.

◉ Reference Groups and Opinion Leaders

reference group   Any group that positively or negatively affects a person's values, attitudes, or behavior

A **reference group** is any group that positively or negatively affects a person's values, attitudes, or behavior. Reference groups can be large or small. Most people have several reference groups, such as families, work-related groups, fraternities or sororities, civic clubs, professional organizations, or church-related groups.

In general, there are three major types of reference groups: membership, aspirational, and disassociative. A membership reference group is one to which an individual actually belongs; the individual identifies with group members strongly enough to take on the values, attitudes, and behaviors of people in that group. An aspirational reference group is a group to which one aspires to belong; one desires to be like those group members. A group that a person does not wish to be associated with is a disassociative reference group; the individual does not want to take on the values, attitudes, and behavior of group members.

A reference group may serve as an individual's point of comparison and source of information. A customer's behavior may change to be more in line with actions and beliefs of group members. For example, a person might stop buying one brand of shirts and switch to another based on reference group members' advice. An individual may also seek information from the reference group about other factors regarding a prospective purchase, such as where to buy a certain product.

The extent to which a reference group affects a purchase decision depends on the product's conspicuousness and on the individual's susceptibility to reference group influence. Generally, the more conspicuous a product, the more likely that the purchase decision will be influenced by reference groups. A product's conspicuousness is determined by whether others can see it and whether it can attract attention. Reference groups can affect whether a person does or does not buy a product at all, buys a type of product within a product category, or buys a specific brand. A marketer sometimes tries to use reference group influence in advertisements by suggesting that people in a specific group buy a product and are highly satisfied with it.

opinion leader   A reference group member who provides information about a specific sphere that interests reference group participants

In most reference groups, one or more members stand out as opinion leaders. An **opinion leader** provides information about a specific sphere that interests reference group participants who seek information. Opinion leaders are viewed by other group members as being well informed about a particular area and as easily accessible. An opinion leader is not the foremost authority on all issues. Because such individuals know they are opinion leaders, however, they feel a responsibility to remain informed about their sphere of interest and thus seek out advertisements, manufacturers'

E-MARKETING AND TECHNOLOGY
MARKETING "COOL" BEFORE THE FRENZY FIZZLES

Marketers that target teenagers and young adults know that the quest for cool drives much of the buying done by these segments. However, products based on the newest trend or the latest pop culture development can go from frenzy to fizzle quickly and without warning. This is why many companies hire trend consultants or specialized researchers to help them spot the new, new thing before it becomes the old, old thing.

Often what teenagers think is cool is heavily influenced by media. "Each season, teens get more fashionable," says Erin Conroy of Brown Shoe, a fashion shoe company. "They are tuned in to MTV and Hollywood and follow celebrities and other trend-setters rather than setting the trends." Yet media coverage contributes to the speedy death of trends as well as to their birth. Almost immediately after a celebrity wears a new style, the word spreads through the Internet, television, magazines, and newspapers. Teens want what's cool right now, not what was cool yesterday. Long-time trend analyst Irma Zandl stresses the importance of timing: being the first to introduce a product in the hope of making it trendy is just as risky as being the last to market.

Moreover, teen tastes influence what preteens and young adults will buy. As other groups start to buy what teens in the vanguard are buying, trendy products become mainstream and much less appealing to the superhip. This is the signal for companies to put once-cool items on sale and gear up for the next trend.

Firms that cater to trendy teens cannot afford the luxury of waiting months for items to be manufactured and shipped from the Far East or other distant sources because the window of opportunity closes much sooner these days. When teens want a cool product, they want it *now.* Price is a secondary consideration.

Keeping up with cool also means keeping advertising up to date. Andrew Keller, creative director at ad agency CP+B, says that "advertising is disposable" and yet, he adds, "the faster we react to fads, the faster they'll go away." The bottom line for marketers is that the quest for cool never ends. Now more than ever, companies need to know their customers and look carefully for clues to the next cool thing.[b]

brochures, salespeople, and other sources of information. An opinion leader is likely to be most influential when consumers have high product involvement but low product knowledge, when they share the opinion leader's values and attitudes, and when the product details are numerous or complicated.

◉ Social Classes

social class An open group of individuals with similar social rank

In all societies, people rank others into higher or lower positions of respect. This ranking results in social classes. A **social class** is an open group of individuals with similar social rank. A class is referred to as "open" because people can move into and out of it. Criteria for grouping people into classes vary from one society to another. In the United States, we take into account many factors, including occupation, education, income, wealth, race, ethnic group, and possessions. A person who is ranking someone does not necessarily apply all of a society's criteria. Sometimes, too, the role of income in social class determination tends to be overemphasized. Although income does help determine social class, the other factors also play a role. Within social classes, both incomes and spending habits differ significantly among members.

Analyses of social class in the United States commonly divide people into three to seven categories. Social scientist Richard P. Coleman suggests that, for purposes of consumer analysis, the population be divided into the four major status groups shown in Table 8.1. However, he cautions marketers that considerable diversity exists in people's life situations within each status group.

To some degree, individuals within social classes develop and assume common behavioral patterns. They may have similar attitudes, values, language patterns, and possessions. Social class influences many aspects of people's lives. For example, it affects their chances of having children and their children's chances of surviving infancy. It influences their childhood training, choice of religion, selection of occupation, and leisure time activities. Because social class has a bearing on so many aspects of a person's life, it also affects buying decisions.

Table 8.1   Social Class Behavioral Traits and Purchasing Characteristics

Class (% of Population)	Behavioral Traits	Buying Characteristics
Upper (14%); includes upper-upper, lower-upper, upper-middle	Income varies among the groups, but goals are the same; various lifestyles: preppy, conventional, intellectual, etc; neighborhood and prestigious schooling important.	Prize quality merchandise; favor prestigious brands; products purchased must reflect good taste; invest in art; spend money on travel, theater, books, tennis, golf, and swimming clubs.
Middle (32%)	Often in management; considered white collar; prize good schools; desire an attractive home in a nice, well-maintained neighborhood; often emulate the upper class; enjoy travel and physical activity; often very involved in children's school and sports activities.	Like fashionable items; consult experts via books, articles, etc., before purchasing; spend for experiences they consider worthwhile for their children (e.g., ski trips, college education); tour packages, weekend trips; attractive home furnishings.
Working (38%)	Emphasis on family, especially for economic and emotional supports (e.g., job opportunity tips, help in times of trouble); blue collar; earn good incomes; enjoy mechanical items and recreational activities; enjoy leisure time after working hard.	Buy vehicles and equipment related to recreation, camping, and selected sports; strong sense of value; shop for best bargains at off price and discount stores; purchase automotive equipment for making repairs; enjoy local travel, recreational parks.
Lower (16%)	Often unemployed due to situations beyond their control (e.g., layoffs, company takeover); can include individuals on welfare and homeless individuals; often have strong religious beliefs; may be forced to live in less desirable neighborhoods; in spite of their problems, often good-hearted toward others; enjoy everyday activities when possible.	Most products purchased are for survival; ability to convert good discards into usable items.

Source: Adapted from Richard P. Coleman, "The Continuing Significance of Social Class to Marketing," *Journal of Consumer Research,* December 1983, pp. 265–280. Reprinted by permission of the publisher, The University of Chicago Press, and reprinted by permission of The McGraw-Hill Companies from J. Paul Peter and Jerry C. Olson, *Consumer Behavior Marketing Strategy Perspective,* p. 433. Copyright © 1987.

Social class influences people's spending, saving, and credit practices. It determines to some extent the type, quality, and quantity of products a person buys and uses. For example, it affects purchases of clothing, foods, financial and health-care services, travel, recreation, entertainment, and home furnishings. Social class also affects an individual's shopping patterns and types of stores patronized. In some instances, marketers attempt to focus on certain social classes through store location and interior design, product design and features, pricing strategies, personal sales efforts, and advertising.

◉ Culture and Subcultures

culture   The values, knowledge, beliefs, customs, objects, and concepts of a society

Culture is the accumulation of values, knowledge, beliefs, customs, objects, and concepts that a society uses to cope with its environment and passes on to future generations. Examples of objects are foods, furniture, buildings, clothing, and tools. Concepts include education, welfare, and laws. Culture also includes core values and the degree of acceptability of a wide range of behaviors in a specific society. For example, in our culture, customers as well as businesspeople are expected to behave ethically.

Culture influences buying behavior because it permeates our daily lives. Our culture determines what we wear and eat and where we reside and travel. Society's interest in the healthfulness of food affects food companies' approaches to developing and promoting their products. Culture also influences how we buy and use products and our satisfaction from them.

When U.S. marketers sell products in other countries, they realize the tremendous impact those cultures have on product purchases and use. Global marketers find that people in other regions of the world have different attitudes, values, and needs, which call for different methods of doing business as well as different types of marketing mixes. Some international marketers fail because they do not or cannot adjust to cultural differences.

subculture   A group of individuals whose characteristic values and behavior patterns are similar and differ from those of the surrounding culture

A culture consists of various subcultures. **Subcultures** are groups of individuals whose characteristic values and behavior patterns are similar and differ from those of the surrounding culture. Subcultural boundaries are usually based on geographic designations and demographic characteristics, such as age, religion, race, and ethnicity. Our culture is marked by several different subcultures, among them West Coast, gay, Asian American, and college students. Within subcultures, greater similarities exist in people's attitudes, values, and actions than within the broader culture. Relative to other subcultures, individuals in one subculture may have stronger preferences for specific types of clothing, furniture, or foods. It is important to understand that a person can be a member of more than one subculture and that the behavioral patterns and values attributed to specific subcultures do not necessarily apply to all group members.

The percentage of the U.S. population comprising ethnic and racial subcultures is expected to grow. By 2050, about one-half of the people of the United States will be members of racial and ethnic minorities. The Bureau of the Census reports that the three largest and fastest-growing ethnic U.S. subcultures are African Americans, Hispanics, and Asians. The population growth of these subcultures interests marketers. To target these groups more precisely, marketers are striving to become increasingly sensitive to and knowledgeable about their differences. Businesses recognize that to succeed, their marketing strategies will have to take into account the values, needs, interests, shopping patterns, and buying habits of various subcultures.

● **African American Subculture.**   In the United States, the African American subculture represents 12 percent of the population.[10] Like all subcultures, African American consumers possess distinct buying patterns. For example, African American

Subcultures Based on Age

Marketers sometimes aim marketing mixes at age-based subcultures.

consumers spend more money on telephone service, shoes, children's apparel, groceries, and housing than do white consumers.[11] Conversely, African Americans tend to spend much less on health insurance, health care, entertainment, education, alcoholic beverages, and eating out.[12]

Recently, Procter & Gamble began an initiative to increase marketing aimed at the African American community.[13] By including African American actors in their ads, the company believes it can encourage a positive response to its products, increasing sales among African American consumers, while still maintaining ties with white consumers.[14] For example, if an African American family is featured in an ad, the white consumers will see a heartwarming bond between family members. The African American viewers will note the inclusion of their race and feel a stronger connection to the product.[15]

Other corporations are reaching out to the African American community by celebrating Black History Month. Chrysler Group, partnering with DaimlerChrysler African American Network, organized an assortment of festivities to commemorate Black History Month. Exhibits, concerts, and guest speakers helped increase awareness about the African American community and its vital contributions to present-day society.[16] Hawaiian Punch also supports Black History Month with a national contest inviting schoolchildren to learn about historical African American figures.[17] In 2002, McDonald's launched 365Black, a program that celebrates Black History all year round. The following year, they introduced 365Black Awards. At these annual awards, modern-day African Americans are honored for their outstanding achievements.

● **Hispanic Subculture.** Hispanics represent 13 percent of the U.S. population.[18] Because of the group's growth and purchasing power, understanding the Hispanic subculture is critical to marketers. In general, Hispanics have strong family values, concern for product quality, and strong brand loyalty.[19] Studies reveal that the majority of Hispanic consumers not only are brand loyal, but also will pay more for a well-known brand.[20] Like African American consumers, Hispanics spend more on groceries, telephone services, and children's apparel and shoes. But they also spend more on small appliances and housewares.[21]

White consumers, especially between the ages of 12 and 34, continue to be influenced by minority cultures, especially in areas such as fashion, entertainment, dining, sports, and music.[22] Thanks to this increasing appeal, advertisers have made a beneficial discovery. They can target both white and Hispanic consumers by hiring famous Hispanic people to appear in their ad campaigns.[23] Pepsi put Latina pop star Shakira in its ads. Bell South hired actress Daisy Fuentes to appear in a telephone company commercial discussing the importance of friends and family.[24] The ad was aired both in English and Spanish. This is crucial since 61 percent of bilingual households are Spanish speaking.[25]

-site

"Everything Consumer"
Consumerworld.org offers a variety of free information to those interested in consumer buying behavior. Articles and other resources make this an interesting and helpful site for marketers. See www. consumerworld.org.

CUSTOMER RELATIONSHIP MANAGEMENT
CELEBRATE THE SIMILARITIES AND DIFFERENCES OF SUBCULTURES

One nation, many subcultures—and many marketing possibilities. PepsiCo, McDonald's, and Allstate are among the growing number of U.S. companies that market to members of subcultures by celebrating both the similarities and differences. PepsiCo's director of multicultural marketing emphasizes that "the multicultural mind-set is more about your interests, like music, than whether you're African American or Latino." PepsiCo uses music as a way to appeal to what it calls "the multicultural heart." Pepsi commercials featuring Shakira and Beyoncé Knowles cross cultural boundaries and link the brand with two of the music world's hottest stars.

The company has created specific products for particular subcultures, such as Gatorade Xtremo geared to Hispanic tastes. However, it often promotes Pepsi beverages and Doritos snacks in one campaign, adjusting the tone and the product mix for different subcultures. As an example, its advertisements for Hispanic audiences create a fiesta-like atmosphere, whereas its ads for African American audiences highlight barbecue-flavored snacks.

Fast-food marketer McDonald's is known for its promotional efforts targeting individual subcultures, including the urban youth subculture. "Today's younger generation is far more aware of diversity," notes one of McDonald's ad agency executives. Therefore, he says, companies should "offer a multicultural connection in order to be relevant, with people from different ethnic backgrounds having fun and playing together." In one commercial for the Big Mac sandwich, a diverse group of actors sang hip-hop music in English and Spanish. Big Mac sales rose more than 30 percent during the six weeks this commercial aired on the ABC, CBS, NBC, Univision, Telemundo, and Black Entertainment Television networks.

As another example, consider how Allstate adapted its "You're in good hands with Allstate" insurance slogan for the Chinese American market. The company's advertising agency developed dozens of versions in Chinese dialects to find wording that made sense while retaining the slogan's emotional appeal. After months of research, Allstate launched an ad campaign using a new slogan that translated as "turn over to our hands, relax, and be free of worry." The result: awareness of the Allstate brand among Chinese Americans doubled in markets where the campaign ran for six months.[c]

When considering the buying behavior of Hispanics, marketers must keep in mind that this subculture is really composed of nearly two dozen nationalities, including Cuban, Mexican, Puerto Rican, Caribbean, Spanish, and Dominican. Each has its own history and unique culture that affect consumer preferences and buying behavior.

To attract this powerful subculture, marketers are taking Hispanic values and preferences into account when developing products and creating advertising and promotions. Kmart focuses major marketing efforts on Hispanics, and it expects Hispanics to emerge as its number one core shoppers by 2020.[26] The company launched a monthly Spanish magazine and a Sunday advertising circular. Kmart has roughly one-third of its stores in urban markets.[27]

● **Asian American Subculture.** The term *Asian American* includes people from more than 15 ethnic groups, including Filipinos, Chinese, Japanese, Asian Indians, Koreans, and Vietnamese. Asian Americans are the fastest-growing U.S. subculture. They also have the most money, the best education, and the largest percentage of professionals and managers of all U.S. minorities.[28] The individual language, religion, and value system of each group influences its members' purchasing decisions. Some traits of this subculture, however, carry across ethnic divisions, including an emphasis on hard work, strong family ties, and a high value placed on education.[29]

Retailers with a large population of Chinese shoppers have begun to capitalize on this group's celebration of the Lunar New Year. For example, during this period in the Los Angeles area, supermarkets stock traditional Chinese holiday foods and items used in the celebration, such as candles, greeting cards, and party goods. The McDonald's website features a link about the Chinese New Year and traditional ways of celebrating the important holiday. The website also features an extensive assortment of facts about different Asian cultures and the holidays they celebrate. Catering to the tastes of Asians living in the United States, Maria's Bakery (based in Hong Kong), Ten Ren (based in Taiwan), and Woo Lae Oak (based in South Korea) have opened restaurants in Washington, D.C., and other areas. With a few menu changes, they are also successfully introducing their foods to other U.S. customers.[30]

CHAPTER REVIEW

① Describe the level of involvement and types of consumer problem-solving processes.

An individual's level of involvement—the importance and intensity of his or her interest in a product in a particular situation—affects the type of problem-solving processes used. Enduring involvement is an ongoing interest in a product class because of personal relevance, whereas situational involvement is a temporary interest stemming from the particular circumstance or environment in which buyers find themselves. There are three kinds of consumer problem solving: routinized response behavior, limited problem solving, and extended problem solving. Consumers rely on routinized response behavior when buying frequently purchased, low-cost items requiring little search-and-decision effort. Limited problem solving is used for products purchased occasionally or when buyers need to acquire information about an unfamiliar brand in a familiar product category. Consumers engage in extended problem solving when purchasing an unfamiliar, expensive, or infrequently bought product.

② Recognize the stages of the consumer buying decision process.

The consumer buying decision process includes five stages: problem recognition, information search, evaluation of alternatives, purchase, and post-purchase evaluation. Not all decision processes culminate in a purchase, nor do all consumer decisions include all five stages. Problem recognition occurs when buyers become aware of a difference between a desired state and an actual condition. After recognizing the problem or need, buyers search for information about products to help resolve the problem or satisfy a need. A successful search yields a group of brands, called a consideration set, that a buyer views as possible alternatives. To evaluate the product in the consideration set, the buyer establishes certain criteria by which to compare, rate, and rank different products. Marketers can influence consumers' evaluation by framing alternatives. In the purchase stage, consumers select products or brands on the basis of results from the evaluation stage and on other dimensions. Buyers also choose the seller from whom they will buy the product. After the purchase, buyers evaluate the product to determine if its actual performance meets expected levels.

③ Explain how situational influences may affect the consumer buying decision process.

Situational influences are external circumstances or conditions existing when a consumer makes a purchase decision. Situational influences include surroundings, time, reason for purchase, and the buyer's mood and condition.

④ Understand the psychological influences that may affect the consumer buying decision process.

Psychological influences partly determine people's general behavior, thus influencing their behavior as consumers. The primary psychological influences on consumer behavior are perception, motives, learning, attitudes, personality and self-concept, and lifestyles. Perception is the process of selecting, organizing, and interpreting information inputs (sensations received through sight, taste, hearing, smell, and touch) to produce meaning. The three steps in the perceptual process are selection, organization, and interpretation. An individual has numerous perceptions of packages, products, brands, and organizations, all of which affect the buying decision process. A motive is an internal energizing force that orients a person's activities toward satisfying needs or achieving goals. Learning refers to changes in a person's thought processes and behavior caused by information and experience. Marketers try to shape what consumers learn to influence what they buy. An attitude is an individual's enduring evaluation, feelings, and behavioral tendencies toward an object or idea and consists of three major components: cognitive, affective, and behavioral. Personality is the set of traits and behaviors that make a person unique. Self-concept, closely linked to personality, is a person's view of perception of him- or herself. Research indicates that a buyer purchases products that reflect and enhance self-concept. Lifestyle is an individual's pattern of living expressed through activities, interests, and opinions.

5 Be familiar with the social influences that affect the consumer buying decision process.

Social influences are forces that other people exert on buying behavior. They include roles, family, reference groups and opinion leaders, social class, and culture and subcultures. Everyone occupies positions within groups, organizations, and institutions, and each position has a role—a set of actions and activities that a person in a particular position is supposed to perform based on expectations of both the individual and surrounding persons. In a family, children learn from parents (other household adults) and older siblings how to make decisions, such as purchase decisions. Consumer socialization is the process through which a person acquires the knowledge and skills to function as a consumer. The consumer socialization process is partially accomplished through family influences. A reference group is any group that positively or negatively affects a person's values, attitudes, or behavior. The three major types of reference groups are membership, aspirational, and disassociative. In most reference groups, one or more members stand out as opinion leaders by furnishing requested information to reference group participants. A social class is an open group of individuals with similar social rank. Social class influences people's spending, saving, and credit practices. Culture is the accumulation of values, knowledge, beliefs, customs, objects, and concepts that a society uses to cope with its environment and passes on to future generations. A culture is made up of subcultures. A subculture is a group of individuals whose characteristics, values, and behavior patterns are similar and differ from those of the surrounding culture. U.S. marketers focus on three major ethnic subcultures: African American, Hispanic, and Asian American.

Please visit the student website at **www.prideferrell.com** for ACE Self-Test questions that will help you prepare for exams.

KEY CONCEPTS

buying behavior	internal search	selective distortion	self-concept
consumer buying behavior	external search	selective retention	lifestyle
level of involvement	consideration set	motive	social influences
routinized response behavior	evaluative criteria	Maslow's hierarchy of needs	role
limited problem solving	cognitive dissonance	patronage motives	consumer socialization
extended problem solving	situational influences	learning	reference group
impulse buying	psychological influences	attitude	opinion leader
consumer buying decision process	perception	attitude scale	social class
	information inputs	personality	culture
	selective exposure		subculture

ISSUES FOR DISCUSSION AND REVIEW

1. How does a consumer's level of involvement affect his or her choice of problem-solving process?

2. Name the types of consumer problem-solving processes. List some products you have bought using each type. Have you ever bought a product on impulse? If so, describe the circumstances.

3. What are the major stages in the consumer buying decision process? Are all these stages used in all consumer purchase decisions? Why or why not?

4. What are the categories of situational factors that influence consumer buying behavior? Explain how each of these factors influences buyers' decisions.

5. What is selective exposure? Why do people engage in it?

6. How do marketers attempt to shape consumers' learning?

7. Why are marketers concerned about consumer attitudes?

8. In what ways do lifestyles affect the consumer buying decision process?

9. How do roles affect a person's buying behavior? Provide examples.

10. What are family influences, and how do they affect buying behavior?

11. What are reference groups? How do they influence buying behavior? Name some of your own reference groups.

12. How does an opinion leader influence the buying decision process of reference group members?

13. In what ways does social class affect a person's purchase decisions?

14. What is culture? How does it affect a person's buying behavior?

15. Describe the subcultures to which you belong. Identify buying behavior that is unique to one of your subcultures.

MARKETING APPLICATIONS

1. Describe three buying experiences you have had—one for each type of problem solving—and identify which problem-solving process you used. Discuss why that particular process was appropriate.

2. Interview a classmate about the last purchase he or she made. Report the stages of the consumer buying process used and those skipped, if any.

3. Briefly describe how a beer company might alter the cognitive and affective components of consumer attitudes toward beer products and toward the company.

4. Identify two of your roles and give an example of how they have influenced your buying decisions.

5. Select five brands of toothpaste and explain how the appeals used in advertising these brands relate to Maslow's hierarchy of needs.

ONLINE EXERCISES

6. Some mass-market e-commerce sites, such as Amazon.com, have extended the concept of customization to their customer base. Amazon has created an affinity group by drawing on certain users' likes and dislikes to make product recommendations to other users. Check out this pioneering online retailer at **www.amazon.com.**
   a. What might motivate some consumers to read a "Top Selling" list?
   b. Is the consumer's level of involvement with online book purchase likely to be high or low?
   c. Discuss the consumer buying decision process as it relates to a decision to purchase from Amazon.com.

VIDEO CASE

Build-A-Bear Builds Memorable Customer Experiences

Stitch and stuff a special furry friend in one fun visit—that's the attraction of going to a Build-A-Bear Workshop store. Since 1997, this retail chain has sold more than 17 million stuffed animals by turning the point-of-sale buying process into a hands-on, interactive experience. The chief executive bear (CEB) of this rapidly expanding retail empire is Maxine Clark, who honed her keen sense of consumer behavior during 25 years as an executive with May Department Stores.

Clark left the corporate world to become an entrepreneur in 1997. Thinking back to her much-loved teddy bear and to the magic she remembered in special shopping trips as a child, Clark focused her new business on a very smart niche: entertainment retailing designed to please children of all ages. She was determined to make memories, not simply sell an everyday, off-the-shelf product. So she created a store-based workshop environment and invited buyers to participate in crafting their own stuffed animals.

Master Bear Builders (store employees) help buyers choose the types of animals they want. Bears, bunnies, dogs, ponies, and frogs, available in small or large sizes, are just some of the choices. Next, buyers select the fake-fur color and the amount of stuffing, insert the heart, help stitch the seams, gently fluff the fur, and name their new friends. Finally, they dress their animals in miniature cowboy gear, angel wings, or another cute outfit and pick out accessories to create one-of-a-kind, personalized furry friends. A typical purchase consists of the basic stuffed animal, priced at $10 to $35, plus outfits and accessories, priced at $5 and up. Each cuddly friend goes home in a house-shaped package, complete with a birth certificate signed by Clark.

As part of the buying procedure, customers enter their animals' and their own names, addresses, e-mail addresses, gender, and birthdates at computer stations in each store. This information is used to generate a birth certificate for every toy. The information is then pooled with sales data and other details, carefully analyzed, and used to plan newsletters and other communications and promotions. In addition, because each animal contains a unique bar-coded tag, the company can send lost toys back to their owners by consulting the database to determine ownership. Build-A-Bear's database holds more than 8 million names; it also collects data from the 4 million people who browse its website every month.

Before opening the first Build-A-Bear store in St. Louis, Missouri, Clark tested the idea on the 10-year-old daughter of a friend, who was enthusiastic about the concept. As the chain grows, she continues to stay in touch with changes in her market's needs and behavior through a Cub Advisory Board composed of 20 children, ages 6 to 14. The group meets every three months to discuss new programs and review proposals for new stuffed animals, fur colors, accessories, and fashions. Clark also requests board feedback on specific questions via mail and e-mail and combs through customer letters and e-mail messages to learn more about what customers like and don't like. A newly formed Web-based advisory board helps her tap the ideas of a broader cross-section of customers as well.

The special retail atmosphere Clark wants to create requires lots of behind-the-scenes planning. Build-A-Bear's retail employees must complete an intensive three-week training course at World Bearquarters in St. Louis before they start work in a store. Yet the company doesn't take itself too seriously. The organization weaves a "bear" theme throughout its official activities. For example, managers hold titles such as "bearitory leader," and employees are entitled to "honey days," 15 days of paid vacation and personal time off every year.

Build-A-Bear has grown into a bear-size success story. The company currently operates 165 U.S. stores and eight international franchise stores, with total annual sales topping $213 million. Each store rings up $600 per square foot in annual sales, roughly twice the average of a typical mall store. To keep customers coming back, Clark and her marketing experts are constantly changing the chain's offerings. "We add new products monthly to stay in step with the latest fashions and trends," she says. "More than 80 percent of our line changes at least twice a year." This ensures that buyers have new choices and new experiences each time they visit a Build-A-Bear store.[31]

QUESTIONS FOR DISCUSSION

1. Which situational influences would you expect to be most important for customers in a Build-A-Bear Workshop?

2. What role does learning play in shaping the buying behavior of Build-A-Bear's customers?

3. How does Build-A-Bear influence the level of involvement that customers might attach to stuffed animals? Does the level of involvement depend on whether the customer is a child or a parent?

Business Markets and Buying Behavior

Using the 3Rs to Drive Product Innovation at 3M

3M, the $16 billion company formerly known as Minnesota Mining and Manufacturing, drives new-product development by carefully managing the 3Rs: risk, reward, and responsibility. 3M has more than a century of experience in successfully developing and managing a diverse mix of consumer and business products. Post-it Notes and Scotch-Brite scouring pads are just two of 3M's well-known brand names. The company also creates products for very specific uses, such as light-reflective coatings for street signs and medicinal creams for fighting skin-based viruses.

Day in and day out, 6,500 employees follow the 3R system as they search for new technologies and applications that could conceivably become 3M's next blockbuster product. The first *R*, risk, is a vital element in decisions about whether a product idea is promising enough to be developed into a prototype, test marketed, and ultimately brought to market through commercialization. Rather than take the safer path of incrementally improving existing products, 3M is taking calculated risks in its search for major breakthroughs. Its ambitious goals are to introduce twice the number of new products and triple the number of successful products as it has in the past.

Risks are evaluated relative to the second *R*, reward. Through the 3M Acceleration system, managers filter out ideas with lower profit potential and concentrate company resources on the few hundred ideas with higher profit potential. The point is to more productively support corporate growth by bringing high-potential products to market more quickly. Executives monitor all the ideas that make it into the Acceleration program to ensure speedy progress toward commercialization and measure the rewards in terms of revenue and profits.

With respect to the third *R*, responsibility, Lead User Teams—cross-functional groups of up to six employees—are responsible for new-product development. In addition to technical and marketing staff, a team may have members from manufacturing, finance, procurement, or other departments, depending on its focus. Each team investigates product ideas to satisfy the unspoken or unrecognized needs of its customer segment. "They are taught to set their sights on exploring the areas where the possibilities for discovery are greatest because the pre-existing knowledge is most slim," says one 3M manager. This entails systematically examining trends that barely register today to consider products so advanced that "even the 'early adopters' have not yet arrived."

In addition to team responsibility, 3M has a long-standing tradition of nurturing independent research into potential new products. This encourages innovation from within and has led to new products and processes

OBJECTIVES

1 Be familiar with the various types of business markets.

2 Identify the major characteristics of business customers and transactions.

3 Understand several attributes of demand for business products.

4 Be familiar with the major components of a buying center.

5 Understand the stages of the business buying decision process and the factors that affect this process.

6 Describe industrial classification systems and explain how they can be used to identify and analyze business markets.

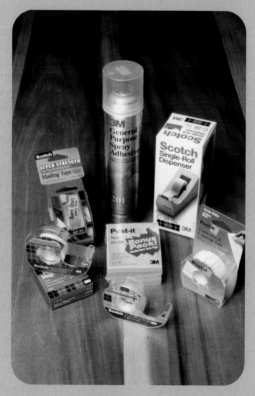

that benefited the company as well as its customers. Staff scientists are allowed to spend up to 15 percent of their time on self-directed projects that they think will blossom into commercially feasible products. They can request funding from their own business units or any other 3M unit to pursue the best ideas. If they are unable to obtain funding from a business unit, they can apply for a company-sponsored independent research grant of up to $100,000. Employees are also eligible for awards that honor outstanding achievement in new-product development, technology, and quality.

Along with the 3Rs, 3M is relying on DFSS—Design for Six Sigma—to boost product quality and development efficiency. The Six Sigma program takes quality far beyond simple error measurement and reduction: it teaches employees to incorporate the customer perspective early in the development process. More than 20,000 managers and scientists around the world have already received training in Six Sigma. These techniques "allow us to be more closely connected to the market and give us a much higher probability of success in our new-product designs," says 3M's vice president of research and development. The program has been so successful that the company is teaching its customers to apply Six Sigma techniques to improve their processes and products.

Finally, 3M is expediting new-product development by transferring 400 scientists from the corporate research and development department to specific business units. "By bringing more of our technical people into 3M businesses, we are strengthening our ability to commercialize new products now and well into the future," explains the CEO. "Now technical people can play more of a role in transforming pipeline projects into marketplace realities."[1] ◄

Serving business markets effectively requires business marketers like 3M to understand business customers. Business marketers go to considerable lengths to understand and to reach their customers so they can provide better services and develop and maintain long-term customer relationships. Like consumer marketers, business marketers are concerned about satisfying their customers.

In this chapter, we look at business markets and business buying decision processes. We first discuss various kinds of business markets and the types of buyers making up these markets. Next, we explore several dimensions of business buying, such as characteristics of transactions, attributes and concerns of buyers, methods of buying, and distinctive features of demand for products sold to business purchasers. We then examine how business buying decisions are made and who makes the purchases. Finally, we consider how business markets are analyzed.

Business Markets

business markets Individuals or groups that purchase a specific kind of product for resale, direct use in producing other products, or use in general daily operations

A **business market** (also called a *business-to-business, or B2B, market*) consists of individuals or groups that purchase a specific kind of product for one of three purposes: resale, direct use in producing other products, or use in general daily operations. The four categories of business markets are producer, reseller, government, and institutional. In the remainder of this section, we discuss each of these types of markets.

New Concepts In Ingredient Technology

TRI-K INDUSTRIES

YOUR SOURCE FOR

INNOVATION

TRI-K INDUSTRIES, INC. 151 Veterans Dr. Northvale, NJ 07647 201.750.1055 www.tri-k.com

Producer Markets
TRI-K Industries makes ingredients for skin care products and hair care products. These ingredients are sold to manufacturers.

◉ Producer Markets

Individuals and business organizations that purchase products for the purpose of making a profit by using them to produce other products or using them in their operations are classified as **producer markets**. Producer markets include buyers of raw materials, as well as purchasers of semifinished and finished items used to produce other products. For example, manufacturers buy raw materials and component parts for direct use in product production. Supermarkets are part of producer markets for numerous support products such as paper and plastic bags, counters, and scanners. Farmers are part of producer markets for farm machinery, fertilizer, seed, and livestock. Producer markets include a broad array of industries, ranging from agriculture, forestry, fisheries, and mining to construction, transportation, communications, and utilities. As Table 9.1 indicates, the number of business establishments in national producer markets is enormous.

producer markets   Individuals and business organizations that purchase products to make profits by using them to produce other products or using them in their operations

Table 9.1 **Number of Establishments in Industry Groups**	
Industry	**Number of Establishments**
Agriculture, forestry, fishing, and hunting	26,000
Mining	24,000
Construction	699,000
Manufacturing	353,000
Transportation and warehousing	191,000
Finance, insurance, and real estate	732,000
Professional, scientific, technical, and educational services	808,000
Accommodation and food services	549,000
Other Services	1,082,000

Source: U.S. Bureau of the Census, *Statistical Abstract of the United States,* 2004–2005 (Washington, DC: Government Printing Office, 2005), p. 493.

Reseller Markets
American Valve produces valves and sells them through wholesalers and industrial distributors, which are resellers.

reseller markets Intermediaries who buy finished goods and resell them for profit

government markets Federal, state, county, and local governments that buy goods and services to support their internal operations and provide products to their constituencies

Manufacturers are geographically concentrated. More than half are located in only seven states: California, New York, Texas, Ohio, Illinois, Pennsylvania, and Michigan (arranged in descending order). This concentration sometimes enables businesses that sell to producer markets to serve them more efficiently. Within certain states, production in a specific industry may account for a sizable proportion of that industry's total production.

◉ Reseller Markets

Reseller markets consist of intermediaries, such as wholesalers and retailers, who buy finished goods and resell them for profit. Aside from making minor alterations, resellers do not change the physical characteristics of the products they handle. Except for items that producers sell directly to consumers, all products sold to consumer markets are first sold to reseller markets, consisting of wholesalers and retailers. Wholesalers purchase products for resale to retailers, to other wholesalers, and to producers, governments, and institutions. Of the 438,000 wholesalers in the United States, a large percentage are located in California, New York, Florida, Texas, Illinois, Pennsylvania, and Ohio (arranged in descending order).[2] Although some products are sold directly to end users, some manufacturers sell their products to wholesalers, who in turn sell the products to other firms in the distribution system. Retailers purchase products and resell them to final consumers. There are approximately 1.1 million retailers in the United States, employing more than 15 million people and generating more than $3.1 trillion in annual sales.[3] Some retailers carry a large number of items. Supermarkets may handle as many as 30,000 different products. In small, individually owned retail stores, owners or managers make purchasing decisions.

When making purchase decisions, resellers consider several factors. They evaluate the level of demand for a product to determine in what quantity and at what prices the product can be resold. Retailers assess the amount of space required to handle a product relative to its potential profit. In fact, they sometimes evaluate products on the basis of sales per square foot of selling area. Because customers often depend on resellers to have products available when needed, resellers typically appraise a supplier's ability to provide adequate quantities when and where wanted. Resellers also take into account the ease of placing orders and the availability of technical assistance and training programs from the producer. These types of concerns distinguish reseller markets from other markets.

◉ Government Markets

Federal, state, county, and local governments make up **government markets**. These markets spend billions of dollars annually for a variety of goods and services to support their internal operations and provide citizens with products such as highways, education, water, energy, and national defense. The federal government spends about $454 billion annually on national defense alone. Government expenditures annually account for about 20 percent of the U.S. gross domestic product.[4]

Besides the federal government, there are 50 state governments, 3,034 county governments, and 87,525 local governments.[5] The amount spent by federal, state, and local units during the last 30 years has increased rapidly because the total number of government units and the services they provide have both increased. Costs of providing these services have also risen. The federal government spends more than half the total amount spent by all governments.

MARKETING LEADERS

BRIGHTON SUPPORTS SPECIAL MARKETING FOR SPECIALTY RETAILERS

CEO Jerry Kohl had a bright idea when he decided to treat his business customers—6,000 independent retailers—like "valued customers." Brighton is a California-based company that produces coordinating head-to-toe accessories for women, some men's accessories, fragrances, sunglasses, jewelry, gifts, and home accessories.

What makes Brighton really stand out is the CEO's decision to do business almost exclusively with independent specialty stores. Having owned a small store in the past, Kohl was convinced that Brighton would prosper if it focused on building special relationships with smaller stores. He and his managers continually research what their resellers need to satisfy customers and boost profits. Studying shoppers' buying behavior has led to bright new ideas for increasing store traffic, encouraging brand loyalty, and boosting sales.

Equally important, Brighton gives resellers the tools they need to serve their customers more effectively. For example, Brighton sales representatives travel the country visiting retailers and educating their sales staffs about Brighton products—how a handbag or belt is made, why it lasts longer, and how customers benefit. They update store owners on the latest promotions and gather retailers' sales tips and success stories to share with Brighton's entire reseller network.

In addition, retailers receive useful reference books such as *M.I.S.S. (Marketing Is Simply Smart)* and a subscription to the colorful *Brighton View* newsletter. Each newsletter offers insights into customer behavior, describes new products, explains promotions such as the "Think Pink Too" bracelet raising money for breast cancer research, and helps owners learn to analyze Brighton products sales and inventory levels. Finally, owners of stores that sell at least $150,000 worth of Brighton products in a year receive a free trip to the company's annual convention in Hawaii.

By marketing through smaller specialty stores and pampering his retail customers, Kohl has built Brighton into a major accessories company. The retailers also benefit. A Brighton retailer in Bryan, Texas, says, "I have close to 60 different vendors and I would put Brighton right at the top because of the support from its sales representatives, the product quality, the value, and the overall assistance in helping me build my business. Brighton treats us as their customers and this helps us learn how to better treat our customers."[a]

The types and quantities of products bought by government markets reflect societal demands on various government agencies. As citizens' needs for government services change, so does the demand for products by government markets. For example, Identix was recently granted a contract with the U.S. Department of State to supply large-scale facial recognition systems for visa processing, a capability that has become increasingly important in today's world.[6] Although it is common to hear of large corporations being awarded government contracts, in fact businesses of all sizes market to government agencies. In recent years, the Internet has helped small businesses earn more government contracts than ever before by providing venues for small businesses to learn about and bid on government contracting opportunities. For example, VM Manufacturing, a small Holbrook, New York–based company specializing in aircraft and commercial parts, used ePublicBids to help it win contracts of up to $100,000 with defense supply centers in Philadelphia and Richmond.[7]

Because government agencies spend public funds to buy the products needed to provide services, they are accountable to the public. This accountability explains their relatively complex set of buying procedures. Some firms do not even try to sell to government buyers because they want to avoid the tangle of red tape. However, many marketers have learned to deal efficiently with government procedures and do not find them a stumbling block. For certain products, such as defense-related items, the government may be the only customer. The U.S. Government Printing Office publishes and distributes several documents explaining buying procedures and describing the types of products various federal agencies purchase.

◉ Institutional Markets

institutional markets Organizations with charitable, educational, community, or other nonbusiness goals

Organizations with charitable, educational, community, or other nonbusiness goals constitute **institutional markets**. Members of institutional markets include churches, some hospitals, fraternities and sororities, charitable organizations, and private colleges. Institutions purchase millions of dollars' worth of products annually to provide goods, services, and ideas to congregations, students, patients, and others. Because institutions often have different goals and fewer resources than other types of organizations, marketers may use special marketing efforts to serve them. For example, Hussey Seating in Maine sells bleacher stadium seating to schools, colleges, and other institutions, as well as to sports arenas. The family-owned business shows its support for institutional customers through assistance with school funding and reduced-cost construction of local economic development projects.[8]

◉ Dimensions of Marketing to Business Customers

Having considered different types of business customers, we now look at several dimensions of marketing to business customers. We examine several characteristics of transactions with business customers, and then discuss attributes of business customers and some of their primary concerns when making purchase decisions. Next, we consider buying methods and major types of purchases. Finally, we discuss the characteristics of demand for business products.

◉ Characteristics of Transactions with Business Customers

Transactions between businesses differ from consumer sales in several ways. Orders by business customers tend to be much larger than individual consumer sales. Suppliers often must sell products in large quantities to make profits; consequently, they prefer not to sell to customers who place small orders. Some business purchases involve expensive items, such as computers. Other products, such as raw materials and component items, are used continuously in production, and the supply may need frequent replenishing. The contract regarding terms of sale of these items is likely to be a long-term agreement.

Discussions and negotiations associated with business purchases can require considerable marketing effort. Purchasing decisions are often made by committee. Orders are frequently large and expensive. Products may be custom built. Several people or departments in the purchasing organization may be involved.

reciprocity An arrangement unique to business marketing in which two organizations agree to buy from each other

One practice unique to business markets is **reciprocity**, an arrangement in which two organizations agree to buy from each other. Reciprocal agreements that threaten

Building Long-Term Relationships with Business Customers
Like many other companies, ERB industries attempts to build
long-term customer relationships. In this advertisement, the
company states "our mission at ERB Safety is to develop and
maintain long-term customer relationships by providing
exceptional service and value."

competition are illegal. The Federal Trade Commission and the
Justice Department take actions to stop anticompetitive reciprocal practices. Nonetheless, a certain amount of reciprocal activity
occurs among small businesses and, to a lesser extent, among
larger companies. Because reciprocity influences purchasing
agents to deal only with certain suppliers, it can lower morale
among agents and lead to less than optimal purchases.

◉ Attributes of Business Customers

Business customers differ from consumers in their purchasing
behavior because they are better informed about the products
they purchase. They demand detailed information about products' functional features and technical specifications to ensure
that the products meet the organization's needs. Personal goals,
however, may also influence business buying behavior. Most
purchasing agents seek the psychological satisfaction that
comes with organizational advancement and financial rewards.
Agents who consistently exhibit rational business buying behavior are likely to attain these personal goals because they help
their firms achieve organizational objectives. Today many suppliers and their customers build and maintain mutually beneficial relationships, sometimes called *partnerships*. Researchers
have found that even in a partnership between a small vendor
and a large corporate buyer, a strong partnership exists because high levels of interpersonal trust can lead to higher levels of commitment to the partnership by both
organizations.[9]

◉ Primary Concerns of Business Customers

When making purchasing decisions, business customers take into account a variety
of factors. Among their chief considerations are price, product quality, and service.
Price matters greatly to business customers because it influences operating costs and
costs of goods sold, which in turn affect selling price, profit margin, and ultimately the
ability to compete. When purchasing major equipment, a business customer views
price as the amount of investment necessary to obtain a certain level of return or savings. A business customer is likely to compare the price of a product with the benefits
the product will provide to the organization.

Most business customers try to achieve and maintain a specific level of quality in
the products they buy. To achieve this goal, most firms establish standards (usually
stated as a percentage of defects allowed) for these products and buy them on the
basis of a set of expressed characteristics, commonly called *specifications*. A customer
evaluates the quality of the products being considered to determine whether they

meet specifications. If a product fails to meet specifications or malfunctions for the ultimate consumer, the customer may drop that product's supplier and switch to a different one. On the other hand, customers are ordinarily cautious about buying products that exceed specifications because such products often cost more, thus increasing the organization's overall costs. Specifications are designed to meet a customer's wants, and anything that does not contribute to meeting those wants is considered wasteful.

Business buyers value service. Services offered by suppliers directly and indirectly influence customers' costs, sales, and profits. In some instances, the mix of customer services is the major means by which marketers gain a competitive advantage. Typical services desired by customers are market information, inventory maintenance, on-time delivery, repair services, and online communication capabilities. Business buyers are likely to need technical product information, data regarding demand, information about general economic conditions, or supply and delivery information. Maintaining adequate inventory is critical because it helps make products accessible when a customer needs them and reduces the customer inventory requirements and costs. Since business customers are usually responsible for ensuring that products are on hand and ready for use when needed, on-time delivery is crucial. Furthermore, reliable, on-time delivery saves business customers money because it enables them to carry less inventory. For example, Dell recently opened an enterprise command center similar to those it operates in the United States and in Limerick, Ireland, to provide around-the-clock support for its business customers in Europe, the Middle East, and Africa.[10] Purchasers of machinery are especially concerned about obtaining repair services and replacement parts quickly because inoperable equipment is costly. Caterpillar Inc., manufacturer of earth-moving, construction, and materials-handling machinery, has built an international reputation, as well as a competitive advantage, by providing prompt service and replacement parts for its products around the world. Communication channels that allow customers to ask questions, voice complaints, submit orders, and trace shipments are indispensable components of service. Marketers should strive for uniformity of service, simplicity, truthfulness, and accuracy.

Marketers should develop customer service objectives and monitor customer service programs. Firms can monitor service by formally surveying customers or informally calling on customers and asking questions about the quality of the services they receive. Expending the time and effort to ensure that customers are happy can greatly benefit marketers by increasing customer retention. One study found that boosting customer retention by 5 percent could double a small firm's profitability.[11]

⦿ Methods of Business Buying

Although no two business buyers do their jobs the same way, most use one or more of the following purchase methods: *description, inspection, sampling,* and *negotiation.* When products are standardized according to certain characteristics (such as size, shape, weight, and color) and graded using such standards, a business buyer may be able to purchase simply by describing or specifying quantity, grade, and other attributes. Agricultural products often fall into this category. Sometimes buyers specify a particular brand or its equivalent when describing the desired product. Purchases on the basis of description are especially common between a buyer and seller with an ongoing relationship built on trust.

Certain products, such as industrial equipment, used vehicles, and buildings, have unique characteristics and may vary with regard to condition. For example, a particular used truck may have a bad transmission. Consequently, business buyers of such products must base purchase decisions on inspection.

E-MARKETING AND TECHNOLOGY
THE BUSINESS OF ONLINE AUCTIONS

Whether they're buying or selling, more companies are participating in online business-to-business (B2B) auctions. Auction technology helps business buyers locate new suppliers and find bargains on numerous products, from computers and dental supplies to commercial refrigerators and cattle. On the other side of the virtual gavel, online auctions are a good way for marketers to attract bids from buyers anywhere in the world.

Before an auction starts, bidders can inspect online digital photos or video files of the products being sold. Some auctions accept bids over the course of several hours or days. Others take place at a specified time, with participants logging on to bid against one another for a few minutes. Major auction sites such as eBay and Yahoo! host hundreds of B2B auctions every day. In addition, businesses can offer goods and services through industry-specific auction sites such as those in construction, landscaping, and aviation.

The rise of online auctions has led to higher demand for software that helps businesses manage bidding and fulfillment. Atlanta-based Auctionworks, for example, makes the system that Home Depot and other corporations use to manage online auctions. Richland Equipment, which sells John Deere agricultural machinery, is an Auctionworks customer. Within 18 months of its first foray into online auctions, the retailer was ringing up nearly one-third of its revenues through auctions. "It pretty much opens up a new client base for us because I'm able to get in front of people all across the country," says Richland's CEO.

Getting a good price is important, but buyers also want to know whom they're buying from. Suppliers should therefore build relationships with potential buyers before the bidding begins. Says Bob VanFleteren of Doane Pet Care in Tennessee: "Buyers want to make good buying decisions, and while cost management is always a goal, they still want strong suppliers who are concerned with category growth, strategic positioning and planning, new products, marketing, and merchandising. Face contact gives both the buyer and the seller the opportunity to determine the relative value of each supply option."[b]

Sampling entails taking a specimen of the product from the lot and evaluating it on the assumption that its characteristics represent the entire lot. This method is appropriate when the product is homogeneous—for instance, grain—and examining the entire lot is not physically or economically feasible.

Some purchases by businesses are based on negotiated contracts. In certain instances, buyers describe exactly what they need and ask sellers to submit bids. They then negotiate with the suppliers who submit the most attractive bids. This approach may be used when acquiring commercial vehicles, for example. In other cases, the buyer may be unable to identify specifically what is to be purchased but can provide only a general description, as might be the case for a piece of custom-made equipment. A buyer and seller might negotiate a contract that specifies a base price and provides for the payment of additional costs and fees. These contracts are most commonly used for one-time projects such as buildings, custom-made equipment, and special projects.

◉ Types of Business Purchases

new-task purchase An initial purchase by an organization of an item to be used to perform a new job or solve a new problem

Most business purchases are one of three types: new-task, straight rebuy, or modified rebuy purchase. In a **new-task purchase**, an organization makes an initial purchase of an item to be used to perform a new job or solve a new problem. A new-task purchase may require development of product specifications, vendor specifications, and procedures for future purchases of that product. To make the initial purchase, the business buyer usually needs much information. For example, if Heineken were introducing a

straight rebuy purchase   A routine purchase of the same products by a business buyer

modified rebuy purchase   A new-task purchase that is changed on subsequent orders or when the requirements of a straight rebuy purchase are modified

derived demand   Demand for industrial products that stems from demand for consumer products

> **Purchases Through Negotiated Contracts**
> The purchases of business services are sometimes made through negotiated contracts.

salty, spicy, beer-flavored snack and were purchasing automated packaging equipment, that would be a new-task purchase.

A **straight rebuy purchase** occurs when buyers purchase the same products routinely under approximately the same terms of sale. Buyers require little information for these routine purchase decisions and tend to use familiar suppliers that have provided satisfactory service and products in the past. These suppliers try to set up automatic reordering systems to make reordering easy and convenient for business buyers.

In a **modified rebuy purchase**, a new-task purchase is changed the second or third time it is ordered or requirements associated with a straight rebuy purchase are modified. A business buyer might seek faster delivery, lower prices, or a different quality level of product specifications. A modified rebuy situation may cause regular suppliers to become more competitive to keep the account, since other suppliers could obtain the business. For example, when a firm buys a slightly different set of communication services, it has made a modified rebuy purchase.

◉ Demand for Business Products

Unlike consumer demand, demand for business products (also called *industrial demand*) can be characterized as (1) derived, (2) inelastic, (3) joint, or (4) fluctuating.

● **Derived Demand.**   Because business customers, especially producers, buy products for direct or indirect use in the production of goods and services to satisfy consumers' needs, the demand for business products derives from the demand for consumer products. It is therefore called **derived demand**. In the long run, no demand for business products is totally unrelated to the demand for consumer products. The derived nature of demand is usually multilevel. Business marketers at different levels are affected by a change in consumer demand for a particular product. For instance, consumers have become concerned with health and good nutrition, and as a result are purchasing more products with less fat, cholesterol, and sodium. When consumers reduced their purchases of high-fat foods, a change occurred in the demand for products marketed by food processors, equipment manufacturers, and suppliers of raw materials associated with these products. When consumer demand for a product changes, a wave is set in motion that affects demand for all firms involved in the production of that product.

● **Inelastic Demand.**   **Inelastic demand** (definition on p. 211) means that a price increase or decrease will not significantly alter demand for a business product. Because some business products contain a number of parts, price increases affecting only one or two parts may yield only a slightly higher per-unit production cost. When

Types of Business Purchases
The purchase of office supplies likely would be a modified rebuy purchase or a new-task purchase.

inelastic demand   Demand that is not significantly altered by a price increase or decrease

joint demand   Demand involving the use of two or more items in combination to produce a product

a sizable price increase for a component represents a large proportion of the product's cost, demand may become more elastic because the price increase in the component causes the price at the consumer level to rise sharply. For example, if aircraft engine manufacturers substantially increase the price of engines, forcing Boeing to raise the prices of the aircraft it manufactures, the demand for airliners may become more elastic as airlines reconsider whether they can afford to buy new aircraft. An increase in the price of windshields, however, is unlikely to affect greatly either the price of or the demand for airliners.

Inelasticity applies only to industry demand for business products, not to the demand curve that an individual firm faces. Suppose a spark plug producer increases the price of spark plugs sold to manufacturers of small engines, but its competitors continue to maintain lower prices. The spark plug company will probably experience reduced unit sales because most small-engine producers will switch to lower-priced brands. A specific firm is vulnerable to elastic demand, even though industry demand for a specific business product is inelastic.

● **Joint Demand.** Demand for certain business products, especially raw materials and components, is subject to joint demand. Joint demand occurs when two or more items are used in combination to produce a product. For example, a firm that manufactures axes needs the same number of ax handles as it does ax blades. These two products thus are demanded

MARKETING ENTREPRENEURS

Shazad Mohamed

HIS BUSINESS: GlobalTek Solutions

FOUNDED AT AGE: 12

SUCCESS: Revenues of over $1 million a year

When someone hears that Shazad Mohamed was able to carry his company through the dot-com bust of the late 1990s and the technology downturn, they might assume him to be a seasoned CEO with years of experience. What might come as a surprise, however, is that Mohamed is still not even old enough to vote. His company, GlobalTek Solutions, develops software for use in the health-care industry. He plans to initiate international projects in countries such as India and Pakistan in upcoming years.[c]

Bread is strictly optional.

A friendly reminder from America's Peanut Farmers™
www.nationalpeanutboard.org

A two-tablespoon serving of peanut butter contains 12.2 grams of unsaturated fat and 3.3 grams of saturated fat, and 0 cholesterol.

Derived Demand
The National Peanut Board promotes additional uses of peanut butter beyond the traditional peanut butter and jelly sandwich, because a portion of the demand for peanuts derives from the consumer demand for peanut butter.

jointly. If a shortage of ax handles exists, the producer buys fewer ax blades. Understanding the effects of joint demand is particularly important for a marketer selling multiple jointly demanded items. Such a marketer realizes that when a customer begins purchasing one of the jointly demanded items, a good opportunity exists to sell related products.

● **Fluctuating Demand.** Because it is derived from consumer demand, the demand for business products may fluctuate enormously. In general, when particular consumer products are in high demand, their producers buy large quantities of raw materials and components to ensure meeting long-run production requirements. In addition, these producers may expand production capacity, which entails acquiring new equipment and machinery, more workers, and more raw materials and component parts. Conversely, a decline in demand for certain consumer goods significantly reduces demand for business products used to produce those goods. Sometimes price changes lead to surprising temporary changes in demand. A price increase for a business product may initially cause business customers to buy more of the item because they expect the price to rise further. Similarly, demand for a business product may be significantly lower following a price cut because buyers are waiting for further price reductions. Fluctuations in demand can be substantial in industries in which prices change frequently.

Business Buying Decisions

business (organizational) buying behavior The purchase behavior of producers, government units, institutions, and resellers

buying center The people within an organization, including users, influencers, buyers, deciders, and gatekeepers, who make business purchase decisions

Business (organizational) buying behavior refers to the purchase behavior of producers, government units, institutions, and resellers. Although several factors affecting consumer buying behavior (discussed in the previous chapter) also influence business buying behavior, several factors are unique to the latter. We first analyze the buying center to learn who participates in business purchase decisions. We then focus on the stages of the buying decision process and the factors affecting it.

The Buying Center

Relatively few business purchase decisions are made by just one person; mostly they are made through a buying center. The **buying center** is the group of people within the organization who make business purchase decisions. They include users, influencers, buyers, deciders, and gatekeepers.[12] One person may perform several roles.

Users are the organization members who actually use the product being acquired. They frequently initiate the purchase process and/or generate purchase specifications. After the purchase, they evaluate product performance relative to the specifications. Influencers are often technical personnel, such as engineers, who help develop the specifications and evaluate alternative products. Technical personnel are especially important influencers when products being considered involve new, advanced technology. Buyers select suppliers and negotiate terms of purchase. They may also become involved in developing specifications. Buyers are sometimes called purchasing agents or purchasing managers. Their choices of vendors and products, especially for new-task purchases, are heavily influenced by people occupying other roles in the buying center. Deciders actually choose the products. Although buyers may be deciders, it is not unusual for different people to occupy these roles. For routinely purchased items, buyers are commonly deciders. However, a buyer may not be authorized to make purchases exceeding a certain dollar limit, in which case higher-level management personnel are deciders. Gatekeepers, such as secretaries and technical personnel, control the flow of information to and among people occupying other roles in the buying center. Buyers who deal directly with vendors may also be gatekeepers because they can control information flows.

The number and structure of an organization's buying centers are affected by the organization's size and market position, the volume and types of products being purchased, and the firm's overall managerial philosophy regarding exactly who should be involved in purchase decisions. The size of a buying center is influenced by the stage of the buying decision process and the type of purchase (new-task, straight rebuy, or modified rebuy).[13] For example, when Siebel Systems began talking with Fleetwood Enterprises about purchasing its customer relationship management software—a new-task buy—Siebel personnel had to consider the needs and influence of the executives who would make the final buying decision as well as those of the influencers (including Fleetwood's information technology experts) and the actual users (Fleetwood's marketing, sales, and customer-service personnel).[14]

A marketer attempting to sell to a business customer should determine who is in the buying center, the types of decisions each individual makes, and which individuals are most influential in the decision process. Because in some instances many people make up the buying center, marketers cannot feasibly contact all participants. Instead, they must be certain to contact a few of the most influential.

◉ Stages of the Business Buying Decision Process

Like consumers, businesses follow a buying decision process. This process is summarized in the lower portion of Figure 9.1. In the first stage, one or more individuals recognize that a problem or need exists. Problem recognition may arise under a variety of circumstances—for instance, when machines malfunction or a firm modifies an existing product or introduces a new one. Individuals in the buying center, such as users, influencers, or buyers, may be involved in problem recognition, but it may be stimulated by external sources, such as sales representatives or advertisements.

The second stage of the process, development of product specifications, requires that buying center participants assess the problem or need and determine what is necessary to resolve or satisfy it. During this stage, users and influencers, such as engineers, often provide information and advice for developing product specifications. By assessing and describing needs, the organization should be able to establish product specifications.

Diversity + Inclusion = Innovation + Opportunity

The Altria family of companies encourages diversity in every part of our business. For over thirty years, our family of companies has built partnerships with thousands of minority-owned and women-owned firms. We believe that we couldn't be as successful without their support and we're proud to partner with them.

Diversity and innovation are hallmarks of the community-based programs sponsored by the Altria family of companies. Through contributions supporting hunger relief, domestic violence prevention, the arts, and the battle against AIDS, we've been making a difference in communities around the world for more than forty-five years.

The people of Altria are committed to helping those in need, and to supporting visionary individuals and organizations

Altria
Kraft Foods
Philip Morris International
Philip Morris USA
altria.com

Vendor Search
Altria has a vendor diversity program focused on partnering with minority- and women-owned businesses.

value analysis   An evaluation of each component of a potential purchase

vendor analysis   A formal, systematic evaluation of current and potential vendors

multiple sourcing   An organization's decision to use several suppliers

sole sourcing   An organization's decision to use only one supplier

Searching for and evaluating potential products and suppliers is the third stage in the decision process. Search activities may involve looking in company files and trade directories, contacting suppliers for information, soliciting proposals from known vendors, and examining websites, catalogs, and trade publications. To facilitate vendor searches, some organizations, such as Wal-Mart, advertise their desire to build partnerships with specific types of vendors, such as those owned by women or by minorities. During this stage, some organizations engage in value analysis, an evaluation of each component of a potential purchase. Value analysis examines quality, designs, materials, and possibly item reduction or deletion to acquire the product in the most cost-effective way. Products are evaluated to make sure they meet or exceed product specifications developed in the second stage. Usually suppliers are judged according to multiple criteria. A number of firms employ vendor analysis, a formal, systematic evaluation of current and potential vendors focusing on characteristics such as price, product quality, delivery service, product availability, and overall reliability. Some vendors may be deemed unacceptable because they are not large enough to supply needed quantities. Others may be excluded because of poor delivery and service records. Sometimes the product is not available from any existing vendor and the buyer must find an innovative company, like 3M, to design and make the product.

Results of deliberations and assessments in the third stage are used during the fourth stage to select the product to be purchased and the supplier from which to buy it. In some cases, the buyer selects and uses several suppliers, a process known as multiple sourcing. In others, only one supplier is selected, a situation known as sole sourcing. For example, Best Buy and UPS recently agreed to an exclusive shipping relationship that resulted in greater savings, efficiencies, and customer loyalty for both companies.[15] Firms with federal government contracts are required to have several sources for an item. Sole sourcing has traditionally been discouraged except when a product is available from only one company. Sole sourcing is much more common today, however, partly because such an arrangement means better communications between buyer and supplier, stability and higher profits for suppliers, and often lower prices for buyers. However, many organizations still prefer multiple sourcing because this approach lessens the possibility of disruption caused by strikes, shortages, or bankruptcies. The actual product is ordered in this fourth stage, and specific details regarding terms, credit arrangements, delivery dates and methods, and technical assistance are finalized.

During the fifth stage, the product's performance is evaluated by comparing it with specifications. Sometimes the product meets the specifications, but its performance does not adequately solve the problem or satisfy the need recognized in the first stage. In that case, product specifications must be adjusted. The supplier's performance is also evaluated during this stage. If supplier performance is inadequate,

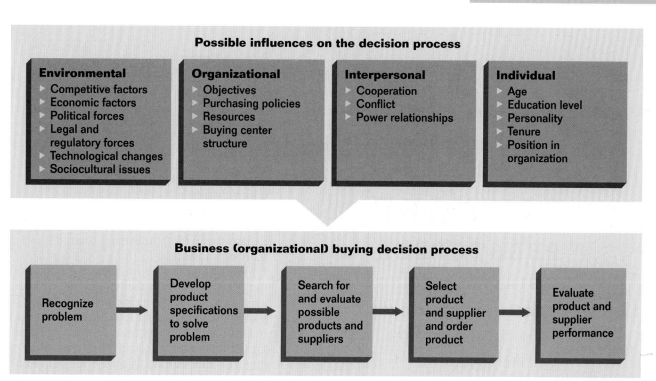

Figure 9.1
Business (Organizational) Buying Decision Process and Factors That May Influence It

the business purchaser seeks corrective action from the supplier or searches for a new one. Results of the evaluation become feedback for the other stages in future business purchase decisions.

This business buying decision process is used in its entirety primarily for new-task purchases. Several stages, but not necessarily all, are used for modified rebuy and straight rebuy situations.

◉ Influences on the Business Buying Decision Process

Figure 9.1 also lists four major categories of factors that influence business buying decisions: environmental, organizational, interpersonal, and individual.

Environmental factors include competitive and economic factors, political forces, legal and regulatory forces, technological changes, and sociocultural issues. These factors generate considerable uncertainty for an organization, which can make individuals in the buying center apprehensive about certain types of purchases. Changes in one or more environmental forces can create new purchasing opportunities and threats. For example, changes in competition and technology can make buying decisions difficult in the case of products like software, computers, and telecommunications equipment.

Organizational factors influencing the buying decision process include the company's objectives, purchasing policies, and resources, as well as the size and composition of its buying center. An organization may have certain buying policies to which buying center participants must conform. For instance, a firm's policies may mandate long-term contracts, perhaps longer than most sellers desire. An organization's financial resources may require special credit arrangements. Any of these conditions could affect purchase decisions.

Read the IT chart. You've got serious problems.

Porn may be the most visible, but it's only one of your worries. See more clearly with Websense Enterprise®, the most comprehensive solution for protecting your network from threats that appear as employee computing and the Internet converge. You don't have to rely on 20/20 hindsight.

For a **free white paper** on *Emerging Threats in Employee Computing* or to assess your risks visit **www.websense.com/checkup.**

WEBSENSE

FILTER | PROTECT | OPTIMIZE

©2004, Websense Inc. All rights reserved. Websense and Websense Enterprise are registered trademarks of Websense, Inc. in the United States and certain international markets. Websense has numerous other unregistered trademarks in the United States and internationally. All other trademarks are the property of their respective owners.

Interpersonal factors are the relationships among people in the buying center. Use of power and level of conflict among buying center participants influence business buying decisions. Certain individuals in the buying center may be better communicators than others and may be more persuasive. Often these interpersonal dynamics are hidden, making them difficult for marketers to assess.

Individual factors are personal characteristics of participants in the buying center, such as age, education, personality, and tenure and position in the organization. For example, a 55-year-old manager who has been in the organization for 25 years may affect decisions made by the buying center differently than a 30-year-old person employed only 2 years. How influential these factors are depends on the buying situation, the type of product being purchased, and whether the purchase is new-task, modified rebuy, or straight rebuy. Negotiating styles of people vary within an organization and from one organization to another. To be effective, marketers must know customers well enough to be aware of these individual factors and the effects they may have on purchase decisions.

Industrial Classification Systems

Standard Industrial Classification (SIC) System   The federal government system for classifying selected economic characteristics of industrial, commercial, financial, and service organizations

North American Industry Classification System (NAICS)   An industry classification system that will generate comparable statistics among the United States, Canada, and Mexico

Marketers have access to a considerable amount of information about potential business customers, since much of this information is available through government and industry publications and websites. Marketers use this information to identify potential business customers and to estimate their purchase potential.

Much information about business customers is based on industrial classification systems. In the United States, marketers traditionally have relied on the Standard Industrial Classification (SIC) System, which the federal government developed to classify selected economic characteristics of industrial, commercial, financial, and service organizations. However, the SIC system is being replaced by a new industry classification system called the North American Industry Classification System (NAICS). NAICS is a single industry classification system that all three NAFTA partners (the United States, Canada, and Mexico) will use to generate comparable statistics among all three countries. The NAICS classification is based on the types of production activities performed.[16] NAICS is similar to the International Standard Industrial

Table 9.2   Comparison of the SIC System and NAICS for Manufacturers of Magnetic and Optical Media

SIC Hierarchy		NAICS Hierarchy	
Division D	Manufacturing	Sector 31–33	Manufacturing
Major Group 36	Manufacturers of electronic and other electrical equipment, except computer equipment	Subsector 334	Computer and electronic manufacturing
Industry Subgroup 369	Manufacturers of miscellaneous electrical machinery, equipment, and supplies	Industry Group 3346	Manufacturing and reproduction of optical media
Detailed Industry 3695	Manufacturers of magnetic and optical recording media	Industry 33461	Manufacturing and reproduction of magnetic and optical media
		U.S. Industry 334611	U.S. specific-reproduction of software

 *-site*

The Thomas Register of Manufacturers (www.thomasnet.com) is an online database of nearly 650,000 U.S. and Canadian manufacturers. This website allows quick searches by company name, product, or brand name. Results include links to company websites, fax-back literature, and online commerce when available. Registration is required and free.

Classification (ISIC) system used in Europe and many other parts of the world. Whereas the SIC system divides industrial activity into 10 divisions, NAICS divides it into 20 sectors. NAICS contains 1,172 industry classifications, compared with 1,004 in the SIC system. NAICS is more comprehensive and will be more up to date. All three countries have agreed to update it every five years. In addition, NAICS will provide considerably more information about service industries and high-tech products. A comparison of the SIC system and NAICS appears in Table 9.2. Over the next few years, all three NAFTA countries will convert from previously used industrial classification systems to NAICS.

Industrial classification systems are ready-made tools that allow marketers to divide organizations into groups based mainly on the types of goods and services provided. Although an industrial classification system is a vehicle for segmentation, it is most appropriately used in conjunction with other types of data to determine exactly how many and which customers a marketer can reach.

A marketer can take several approaches to determine the identities and locations of organizations in specific industrial classification groups. One approach is to use state directories or commercial industrial directories, such as *Standard & Poor's Register* and Dun & Bradstreet's *Million Dollar Directory.* These sources contain information about a firm, such as its name, industrial classification, address, phone number, and annual sales. By referring to one or more of these sources, marketers isolate business customers with industrial classification numbers, determine their locations, and develop lists of potential customers by desired geographic area. A more expedient, although more expensive, approach is to use a commercial data service. Dun & Bradstreet, for example, can provide a list of organizations that fall into a particular industrial classification group. For each company on the list, Dun & Bradstreet gives the name, location, sales volume, number of employees, type of products handled, names of chief executives, and other pertinent information. Either method can effectively identify and locate a group of potential customers. However, a marketer probably cannot pursue all organizations on the list. Because some companies have greater purchasing potential than others, marketers must determine which customer or customer group to pursue.

To estimate the purchase potential of business customers or groups of customers, a marketer must find a relationship between the size of potential customers' purchases and a variable available in industrial classification data, such as the number of employees. For example, a paint manufacturer might attempt to determine the average number of gallons purchased by a specific type of potential customer relative to the number of employees. A marketer with no previous experience in this market segment will probably have to survey a random sample of potential customers to establish a relationship between purchase sizes and numbers of employees. Once this relationship is established, it can be applied to potential customer groups to estimate their purchases. After deriving these estimates, the marketer is in a position to select the customer groups with the most sales and profit potential.

Despite their usefulness, industrial classification data pose several problems. First, a few industries do not have specific designations. Second, because a transfer of products from one establishment to another is counted as part of total shipments, double counting may occur when products are shipped between two establishments within the same firm. Third, because the U.S. Bureau of the Census is prohibited from providing data that identify specific business organizations, some data, such as value of total shipments, may be understated. Finally, because government agencies provide industrial classification data, a significant lag usually exists between data collection time and the time the information is released.

CHAPTER REVIEW

1 Be familiar with the various types of business markets.

Business markets consist of individuals and groups that purchase a specific kind of product for resale, direct use in producing other products, or use in day-to-day operations. Producer markets include those individuals and business organizations purchasing products for the purpose of making a profit by using them to produce other products or as part of their operations. Intermediaries that buy finished products and resell them to make a profit are classified as reseller markets. Government markets consist of federal, state, county, and local governments, which spend billions of dollars annually for goods and services to support internal operations and to provide citizens with services. Organizations with charitable, educational, community, or other not-for-profit goals constitute institutional markets.

2 Identify the major characteristics of business customers and transactions.

Transactions involving business customers differ from consumer transactions in several ways. Such transactions tend to be larger, and negotiations occur less frequently, though they are often lengthy when they do occur. They often involve more than one person or department in the purchasing organization. They may also involve reciprocity, an arrangement in which two organizations agree to buy from each other. Business customers are usually better informed than ultimate consumers and more likely to seek information about a product's features and technical specifications.

3 Understand several attributes of demand for business products.

Business customers are particularly concerned about quality, service, and price. Quality is important because it directly affects the quality of products the buyer's firm produces. To achieve an exact level of quality, organizations often buy products on the basis of a set of expressed characteristics, called specifications. Because services have such a direct influence on a firm's costs, sales, and profits, matters such as market information, on-time delivery, availability of parts, and communication capabilities are crucial to a business buyer. Although business customers do not depend solely on price to decide which products to buy, price is of prime concern because it directly influences profitability.

Business buyers use several purchasing methods, including description, inspection, sampling, and negotiation. Most organizational purchases are new-task, straight rebuy, or modified rebuy. In a new-task purchase, an organization makes an initial purchase of items to be used to perform new jobs or to solve new problems. A straight rebuy purchase occurs when a buyer purchases the same products routinely under approximately the same terms of sale. In a modified rebuy purchase, a new-task purchase is changed the second or third time it is ordered or requirements associated with a straight rebuy purchase are modified.

Industrial demand differs from consumer demand along several dimensions. Industrial demand derives from demand for consumer products. At the industry level, industrial demand is inelastic. Some business products are subject to joint demand, which occurs when two or more items are used in combination to make a product. Finally, because organizational demand derives from consumer demand, the demand for business products can fluctuate widely.

4 **Be familiar with the major components of a buying center.**
Business purchase decisions are made through a buying center, the group of people involved in making such purchase decisions. Users are those in the organization who actually use the product. Influencers help develop specifications and evaluate alternative products for possible use. Buyers select suppliers and negotiate purchase terms. Deciders choose the products. Gatekeepers control the flow of information to and among individuals occupying other roles in the buying center.

5 **Understand the stages of the business buying decision process and the factors that affect this process.**
The stages of the business buying decision process are problem recognition, development of product specifications to solve problems, search for and evaluation of products and suppliers, selection and ordering of the most appropriate product, and evaluation of the product's and supplier's performance.

Four categories of factors influence business buying decisions. Environmental factors include competitive forces, economic conditions, political forces, laws and regulations, technological changes, and sociocultural factors. Organizational factors include the company's objectives, purchasing policies, and resources, as well as the size and composition of its buying center. Interpersonal factors are the relationships among people in the buying center. Individual factors are personal characteristics of members of the buying center, such as age, education, personality, tenure, and position in the organization.

6 **Describe industrial classification systems and explain how they can be used to identify and analyze business markets.**
An industrial classification system categorizes businesses into major industry groups, industry subgroups, and detailed industry categories. Currently the United States is converting from the traditional SIC system to NAICS. An industrial classification system provides marketers with information needed to identify business customer groups. It is best used for this purpose in conjunction with other information. After identifying target industries, a marketer can obtain the names and locations of potential customers by using government and commercial data sources. Marketers then must estimate potential purchases of business customers by finding a relationship between a potential customer's purchases and a variable available in industrial classification data.

Please visit the student website at **www.prideferrell.com** for ACE Self-Test questions that will help you prepare for exams.

KEY CONCEPTS

business markets
producer markets
reseller markets
government markets
institutional markets
reciprocity
new-task purchase

straight rebuy purchase
modified rebuy purchase
derived demand
inelastic demand
joint demand
business (organizational)
   buying behavior

buying center
value analysis
vendor analysis
multiple sourcing
sole sourcing

Standard Industrial
   Classification (SIC)
   System
North American Industry
   Classification System
   (NAICS)

ISSUES FOR DISCUSSION AND REVIEW

1. Identify, describe, and give examples of the four major types of business markets.

2. Regarding purchasing behavior, why might business customers generally be considered more rational than ultimate consumers?

3. What are the primary concerns of business customers?

4. List several characteristics that differentiate transactions involving business customers from consumer transactions.

5. What are the commonly used methods of business buying?

6. Why do buyers involved in a straight rebuy purchase require less information than those making a new-task purchase?

7. How does demand for business products differ from consumer demand?

8. What are the major components of a firm's buying center?

9. Identify the stages of the business buying decision process. How is this decision process used when making straight rebuys?

10. How do environmental, business, interpersonal, and individual factors affect business purchases?

11. What function does an industrial classification system help marketers perform?

12. List some sources that a business marketer can use to determine the names and addresses of potential customers.

MARKETING APPLICATIONS

1. Identify organizations in your area that fit each business market category—producer, reseller, government, and institutional. Explain your classifications.

2. Indicate the method of buying (description, inspection, sampling, negotiation) an organization would be most likely to use when purchasing each of the following items. Defend your selection.
   a. A building for the home office of a light bulb manufacturer
   b. Wool for a clothing manufacturer

   c. An Alaskan cruise for a company retreat, assuming a regular travel agency is used
   d. One-inch nails for a building contractor

3. Categorize the following purchase decisions as new-task, modified rebuy, or straight rebuy and explain your choice.
   a. Bob has purchased toothpicks from Smith Restaurant Supply for 25 years and recently placed an order for yellow toothpicks rather than the usual white ones.

b. Jill's investment company has been purchasing envelopes from AAA Office Supply for a year and now needs to purchase boxes to mail year-end portfolio summaries to clients. Jill calls AAA to purchase these boxes.

c. Reliance Insurance has been supplying its salespeople with small personal computers to assist in their sales efforts. The company recently agreed to begin supplying them with faster, more sophisticated computers.

4. Identifying qualified customers is important to the survival of any organization. NAICS provides helpful information about many different businesses. Find the NAICS manual at the library and identify the NAICS code for the following items:

a. Chocolate candy bars
b. Automobile tires
c. Men's running shoes

ONLINE EXERCISE

5. General Electric Company is a highly diversified, global corporation with many divisions GEPolymerland.com is the online site for GE's resins business. Visit the site at **www.GEPolymerland.com.**

a. At what type of business markets are GE's resin products targeted?
b. How does GEPolymerland address some of the concerns of business customers?
c. What environmental factors do you think affect demand for GE resin products?

VIDEO CASE

VIPdesk.com Serves Business Customers

Concierge service is not just for hotel guests any more. A growing number of companies are hiring specialized concierge firms such as VIPdesk to help customers make restaurant reservations, obtain sports tickets, arrange for home repairs, or find that perfect gift—at any hour of the day and on any day of the week. Web-based VIPdesk evolved from CEO Mary Naylor's years of experience providing on-site concierge services for the employees of corporations in major office complexes around metropolitan Washington, D.C. Recognizing the opportunity to cost effectively serve a wider corporate customer base through technology, Naylor established her first concierge website in 1996 and upgraded it to VIPdesk in 2000.

Today VIPdesk is the leading provider of "live" Web-based concierge services with 20 million users. It is also building a reputation as a full-service provider of "experience-based" rewards for employees of companies such as Van Kampen. VIPdesk can arrange for the employees of clients to take circus lessons, have a fashion makeover, take a trip, or enjoy some other experience as a bonus for good performance.

In recent years, the main market on which Naylor is focusing, however, is corporate clients such as Master-Card and Citibank that want to provide concierge services to their customers. For example, when MasterCard was planning to launch its platinum World Card, management realized that offering VIPdesk's high-tech yet very personalized concierge service to cardholders would be a good way to help member banks differentiate the new credit card. Alice Droogan, vice president of worldwide cardholder services, notes that VIPdesk's around-the-clock concierge services cost MasterCard "pennies a card, and as enhancements go, that's quite valuable." Seventeen financial institutions have begun using the service to attract new cardholders and reinforce cardholder loyalty, and Droogan expects demand to increase.

MasterCard is particularly enthusiastic about VIPdesk's flexibility in responding to just about any request rather than simply offering a limited menu of preset options from which customers can choose. Although "most of the other companies we looked at were just basically travel assistance services," Droogan was impressed with VIPdesk's wider capabilities. Given the highly competitive environment in the credit card field, where MasterCard must battle Visa, American Express, Discover, and Diner's Club, VIPdesk is playing an important role because it helps MasterCard "support our initiatives to offer more services to our issuers," says Droogan.

Depending on her business customers' requirements and budget constraints, Naylor offers access to concierge services in many ways. Users can search the VIPdesk website for information, initiate a live text chat or phone call with a concierge, send e-mail messages requesting help, access customized information via Web-enabled cell phones, or contact a concierge via a handheld computer such as a Palm Pilot. Among the most common requests are help with travel arrangements, auto rentals, local entertainment options, last-minute theater and sports tickets, personal shopping, and other errands. VIPdesk needs just 30 minutes to complete a typical request. The buying cycle of its business customers, however, is much longer, with negotiations stretching over 6 to 12 months.

In addition to maintaining two call centers staffed with dozens of concierges, VIPdesk hires former hotel concierges to work part time from home during periods of peak demand. These part-timers bring an in-depth knowledge of local resources they can tap to satisfy requests from callers in their area.

Instead of paying for each use of VIPdesk's services, business customers pay a flat annual fee. This means customers can set a definite budget for the expense rather than worrying about being billed different amounts every month if usage varies. The price, says Naylor, ranges "anywhere from $25 a person a year to as low as 25 cents per person per year." In exchange, she says, the business customer benefits "by decommoditizing its products and extending the relationship well beyond the core products to the everyday life of the customer. It can cost less than a key chain or some token item that a corporation may give as a gift to a customer, and yet it keeps giving every day and keeps that brand identity in front of that end user."[17]

QUESTIONS FOR DISCUSSION

1. Are VIPdesk's business customers members of producer markets, reseller markets, government markets, or institutional markets?

2. What would be the primary concerns of a credit card company that is considering offering VIPdesk's services to its cardholders? What is VIPdesk doing to address these concerns?

3. How might a company use methods of description, inspection, sampling, and negotiating when making a buying decision about offering VIPdesk's services to its customers?

Product Decisions

We are now prepared to analyze the decisions and activities associated with developing and maintaining effective marketing mixes. In Parts 5 through 8, we focus on the major components of the marketing mix: product, pricing, distribution, and promotion. Part 5 explores the product ingredient of the marketing mix. Chapter 10 focuses on basic product concepts and on branding and packaging decisions. Chapter 11 analyzes various dimensions regarding product management, including line extensions and product modification, new-product development, product deletions, and the management of services as products.

10

Product, Branding, and Packaging Concepts

OBJECTIVES

1 Understand the concept of a product and how products are classified.

2 Explain the concepts of product item, product line, and product mix, and understand how they are connected.

3 Understand the product life cycle and its impact on marketing strategies.

4 Describe the product adoption process.

5 Explain the value of branding and the major components of brand equity.

6 Recognize the types of brands and how they are selected and protected.

7 Identify two types of branding policies and explain brand extensions, co-branding, and brand licensing.

8 Describe the major packaging functions and design considerations and how packaging is used in marketing strategies.

9 Understand the functions of labeling and selected legal issues.

Dell Mixes It Up with Customers, Electronics, and More

From MP3 music players and an online music store to flat-screen televisions to home theater projectors, Dell is filling out its product mix with goods and services for the entire household. The company formerly known as Dell Computer wants to build on its dominance of the personal computer market by making inroads into the lucrative, $100 billion world of consumer electronics. Based in Austin, Texas, Dell made its name selling computers directly to customers through its website. In the future, the company expects to derive an ever-larger portion of revenues and profits from a wider mix of products for use beyond the home office.

This drive for diversification started with the introduction of the Dell Axim hand-held computer—in direct competition with Palm and other established rivals—followed one year later by a second Axim model. Because the Axims are priced lower than most comparable products, Dell's entry has forced Hewlett-Packard and other competitors to lower prices to protect their market share. The company used the same approach when it began selling printers and ink cartridges on its website, again competing directly with Hewlett-Packard. Even some Dell insiders were surprised when printer sales in the first six months were two times higher than forecasted sales.

Now the stage was set for a more comprehensive move into electronics designed for the digital home. Founder Michael Dell and his team envisioned consumers using a personal computer (from Dell, of course) to control televisions, music players, and other products all around the house. They began the planning process by carefully examining electronics products made by nearly 90 manufacturers. They also analyzed consumers' needs, buying patterns, and complaints about incompatibility problems between new and older products. Based on all of this research, they developed an ultra-bright, flat-screen LCD television, a Dell Digital Jukebox (DJ) to store and play music files, and a home theater projector for viewing DVDs and other entertainment. These new products were introduced in time for the holiday

buying season, along with the Dell Music Store (selling downloadable music files) and software preloaded on Dell computers to help consumers manage digital entertainment files.

These new products, like the printers and handheld computers before them, put Dell squarely in the middle of a competitive battle with well-established rivals. The Dell DJ competes with Apple's iPod digital music player. The Dell Music Store sells downloadable music files in competition with Apple's iTunes store and other online retailers of digital music. The LCD television not only challenges Sony's television business but also sets up a different kind of confrontation about which appliance will serve as the control center of home entertainment. Dell is putting its brand and money behind the computer as the controlling appliance, whereas Sony is putting its resources behind the television as the controlling appliance. "Now is the time for TVs to be reborn," comments a Sony spokesperson.

Although Dell started with only a product or two in each new line, it is gradually adding depth and expanding the width of its product mix. The company is not looking to pioneer new lines; it specializes in applying new technology, adding new features, and making production more efficient. As Dell gains experience with consumer electronics products, it finds ways to lower costs while enhancing each new model. Meanwhile Hewlett-Packard is focusing more on consumer products with the introduction of more than 150 new products, including digital cameras designed for compatibility with its color printers. Samsung and Sony are aggressively targeting segments of the home entertainment market with plasma televisions, home theater projectors, and other products.

Can Dell triumph in such a dynamic and competitive environment? The company certainly knows how to keep prices low by wringing the most productivity out of its direct distribution method. It also knows how to stay close to customers and find out what they want. Finally, with a 20-year history of marketing technology-based products, Dell is among the best-known brands in the country. "We've come out of nowhere to be the number-three consumer brand in the U.S. in less than five years, while Coca-Cola has been doing it for 100 years," says Dell's general manager of consumer business for the United States. "We're not in this to be number three. Number one is the only target around here."[1]   ◄

Products are an important variable in the marketing mix. The mix of products offered by a company like Dell can be a firm's most important competitive tool. If a company's products do not meet customers' desires and needs, the company will fail unless it makes adjustments. Developing successful products like Dell personal computers requires knowledge of fundamental product concepts.

In this chapter, we first define a product and discuss how products are classified. Next, we examine the concepts of product line and product mix. We then explore the stages of the product life cycle and the effect of each life cycle stage on marketing strategies. Next, we outline the product adoption process. Then, we discuss branding, its value to customers and marketers, brand loyalty, and brand equity. Next, we examine the various types of brands. We then consider how companies choose and protect brands, the various branding policies employed, brand extensions, co-branding, and brand licensing. We look at the critical role packaging plays as part of the product. We then explore the functions of packaging, issues to consider in packaging design, and how the package can be a major element in marketing strategy. We conclude with a discussion of labeling.

What Is a Product?

As defined in Chapter 1, a *product* is a good, a service, or an idea received in an exchange. It can be either tangible or intangible and includes functional, social, and psychological utilities or benefits. It also includes supporting services, such as installation, guarantees, product information, and promises of repair or maintenance. Thus, the 5-year/60,000-mile warranty that covers some new automobiles is part of the product itself. A **good** is a tangible physical entity, such as a Dell personal computer or a Big Mac. A **service**, in contrast, is intangible; it is the result of the application of human and mechanical efforts to people or objects. Examples of services include a performance by Ozzy Osbourne, online travel agencies, medical examinations, child day care, real estate services, and martial arts lessons. An **idea** is a concept, philosophy, image, or issue. Ideas provide the psychological stimulation that aids in solving problems or adjusting to the environment. For example, MADD (Mothers Against Drunk Driving) promotes safe consumption of alcohol and stricter enforcement of laws against drunk driving.

When buyers purchase a product, they are really buying the benefits and satisfaction they think the product will provide. A Rolex watch, for example, is purchased to make a statement of success, not just for telling time. Services in particular are purchased on the basis of expectations. Expectations, suggested by images, promises, and symbols, as well as processes and delivery, help consumers make judgments about tangible and intangible products. Products are formed by the activities and processes that help satisfy expectations. Starbucks did not originate the coffee shop,

good   A tangible physical entity

service   An intangible result of the application of human and mechanical efforts to people or objects

idea   A concept, philosophy, image, or issue

What Is a Product?
Besides tangible goods, products can be services or ideas such as this idea marketed by Women Against Handgun Violence.

It's time there was something new on the lips of American women. Rage. WOMEN AGAINST HANDGUN VIOLENCE

but it did develop standardized and inviting stores with high-quality coffee beverages that have become a stylish way to enjoy what traditionally was a commodity product.[2] Often symbols and cues are used to make intangible products more tangible, or real, to the consumer. Allstate Insurance Company, for example, uses giant hands to symbolize security, strength, and friendliness.

Classifying Products

consumer products Products purchased to satisfy personal and family needs

business products Products bought to use in an organization's operations, to resell, or to make other products

Products fall into one of two general categories. Products purchased to satisfy personal and family needs are **consumer products**. Those bought to use in a firm's operations, to resell, or to make other products are **business products**. Consumers buy products to satisfy their personal wants, whereas business buyers seek to satisfy the goals of their organizations. Product classifications are important because they may influence pricing, distribution, and promotion decisions. In this section, we examine the characteristics of consumer and business products and explore the marketing activities associated with some of these products.

Consumer Products

convenience products Relatively inexpensive, frequently purchased items for which buyers exert minimal purchasing effort

The most widely accepted approach to classifying consumer products is based on characteristics of consumer buying behavior. It divides products into four categories: convenience, shopping, specialty, and unsought products. However, not all buyers behave in the same way when purchasing a specific type of product. Thus, a single product can fit into several categories. To minimize this problem, marketers think in terms of how buyers *generally* behave when purchasing a specific item. Examining the four traditional categories of consumer products can provide further insight.

● **Convenience Products.** Convenience products are relatively inexpensive, frequently purchased items for which buyers exert only minimal purchasing effort. They range from bread, soft drinks, and chewing gum to gasoline and newspapers. The buyer spends little time planning the purchase or comparing available brands or sellers. Even a buyer who prefers a specific brand will readily choose a substitute if the preferred brand is not conveniently available. A convenience product is normally marketed through many retail outlets. Because sellers experience high inventory turnover, per-unit gross margins can be relatively low. Producers of convenience products, such as Altoid mints, expect little promotional effort at the retail level and thus must provide it themselves with advertising and sales promotion. Packaging is also important because many convenience items are available only on a self-service basis at the retail level, and thus the package plays a major role in selling the product.

Consumer Products
Shoes are usually seen as shopping products.

shopping products Items for which buyers are willing to expend considerable effort in planning and making purchases

● **Shopping Products.** Shopping products are items for which buyers are willing to expend considerable effort in planning and making the purchase. Buyers spend much time comparing stores and brands with respect to prices, product features, qualities, services, and perhaps warranties. Appliances, bicycles, furniture, stereos, cameras, and shoes exemplify shopping products. These products are expected to last a fairly long time and thus are purchased less frequently than convenience items. Even though shopping products are more expensive than convenience products, few buyers of shopping products are particularly brand-loyal. If they were, they would be unwilling to shop and compare among brands. Shopping products require fewer retail outlets than convenience products. Because shopping products are purchased less frequently, inventory turnover is lower, and marketing channel members expect to receive higher gross margins. In certain situations, both shopping products and convenience products may be marketed in the same location. HEB, a privately held Texas grocery chain, recently implemented a new store concept called HEB Plus. These stores carry everything from toys and home entertainment products to area rugs and high-end televisions as well as the traditional groceries and ethnic foods in which HEB excels.[3]

specialty products Items with unique characteristics that buyers are willing to expend considerable effort to obtain

● **Specialty Products.** Specialty products possess one or more unique characteristics, and generally buyers are willing to expend considerable effort to obtain them. Buyers actually plan the purchase of a specialty product; they know exactly what they want and will not accept a substitute. Examples of specialty products include a Mont Blanc pen and a one-of-a-kind piece of baseball memorabilia, such as a ball signed by Babe Ruth. When searching for specialty products, buyers do not compare alternatives. They are concerned primarily with finding an outlet that has the preselected product available. Bentley automobiles, for example, are very expensive, ranging from $215,000 to $360,000. Suppose a Bentley dealer invites a prospective buyer to test-drive a vehicle at a racetrack. If the prospect decides to make a purchase, he or she has a Bentley "personally commissioned" and typically flies to the automaker's plant in Crewe, England, to observe its manufacture.[4] Specialty products are often distributed through a limited number of retail outlets. Like shopping products, they are purchased infrequently, causing lower inventory turnover and thus requiring relatively high gross margins.

unsought products Products purchased to solve a sudden problem, products of which customers are unaware, and products that people do not necessarily think about buying

● **Unsought Products.** Unsought products are products purchased when a sudden problem must be solved, products of which customers are unaware, and products that people do not necessarily think of purchasing. Emergency medical services and automobile repairs are examples of products needed quickly to solve a problem. A consumer who is sick or injured has little time to plan to go to an emergency medical center or hospital. Likewise, in the event of a broken fan belt on the highway, a consumer will likely seek the nearest auto repair facility to get back on the road as quickly as possible. In such cases, speed and problem resolution are far more important than price and other features buyers might normally consider if they had more time for making decisions. Companies such as ServiceMaster (Rescue Rooter and Furniture Medic) and First Service (Colliers International and CMN International) are making the purchases of these unsought products more bearable by building trust with consumers through recognizable brands and superior functional performance.[5]

◉ Business Products

Business products are usually purchased on the basis of an organization's goals and objectives. Generally the functional aspects of the product are more important than

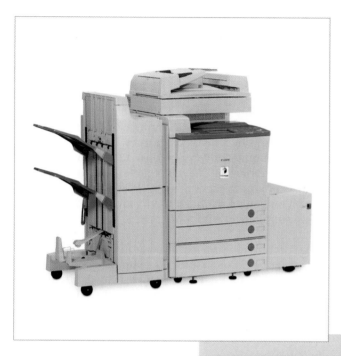

A logo does not
a brand make.

It helps to think of a logo as the shirt a brand wears.
Without something underneath, the shirt is lifeless.

Business Products
A copier, such as the one shown here, is classified as accessory equipment since it does not become a part of the final product, but is used for office activities. Coates Kokes is an advertising agency. Its products are classified as business services.

the psychological rewards sometimes associated with consumer products. Business products can be classified into seven categories according to their characteristics and intended uses: installations, accessory equipment, raw materials, component parts, process materials, MRO supplies, and business services.

installations Facilities and nonportable major equipment

● **Installations.**   Installations include facilities, such as office buildings, factories, and warehouses, and major equipment that is nonportable, such as production lines and very large machines. Normally, installations are expensive and intended to be used for a considerable length of time. Because they are so expensive and typically involve a long-term investment of capital, purchase decisions are often made by high-level management. Marketers of installations frequently must provide a variety of services, including training, repairs, maintenance assistance, and even aid in financing such purchases.

accessory equipment Equipment used in production or office activities

● **Accessory Equipment.**   Accessory equipment does not become part of the final physical product but is used in production or office activities. Examples include file cabinets, fractional-horsepower motors, calculators, and tools. Compared with major equipment, accessory items are usually much cheaper, purchased routinely with less negotiation, and treated as expense items rather than capital items because they are not expected to last as long. More outlets are required for distributing accessory equipment than for installations, but sellers do not have to provide the multitude of services expected of installations marketers.

raw materials   Basic natural materials that become part of a physical product

● **Raw Materials.**   Raw materials are the basic natural materials that actually become part of a physical product. They include minerals, chemicals, agricultural products, and materials from forests and oceans. They are usually bought and sold according to grades and specifications, and in relatively large quantities. Rose oil and jasmine are examples of raw materials in making perfume.

component parts   Items that become part of the physical product and are either finished items ready for assembly or products that need little processing before assembly

● **Component Parts.**   Component parts become part of the physical product and are either finished items ready for assembly or products that need little processing before assembly. Although they become part of a larger product, component parts can often be easily identified and distinguished. Spark plugs, tires, clocks, and switchers are all component parts of the automobile. Buyers purchase such items according to their own specifications or industry standards. They expect the parts to be of specified quality and delivered on time so that production is not slowed or stopped. Producers that are primarily assemblers, such as most lawn mower and computer manufacturers, depend heavily on suppliers of component parts.

process materials   Materials that are used directly in the production of other products but are not readily identifiable

● **Process Materials.**   Process materials are used directly in the production of other products. Unlike component parts, however, process materials are not readily identifiable. For example, a salad dressing manufacturer includes vinegar in its salad dressing. The vinegar is a process material because it is included in the salad dressing but is not identifiable. As with component parts, process materials are purchased according to industry standards or the purchaser's specifications.

MRO supplies   Maintenance, repair, and operating items that facilitate production and operations but do not become part of the finished product

● **MRO Supplies.**   MRO supplies are maintenance, repair, and operating items that facilitate production and operations but do not become part of the finished product. Paper, pencils, oils, cleaning agents, and paints are in this category. MRO supplies are commonly sold through numerous outlets and are purchased routinely. To ensure supplies are available when needed, buyers often deal with more than one seller.

business services   The intangible products that many organizations use in their operations

● **Business Services.**   Business services are the intangible products that many organizations use in their operations. They include financial, legal, marketing research, information technology, and janitorial services. Firms must decide whether to provide their own services internally or obtain them from outside the organization. This decision depends on the costs associated with each alternative and how frequently the services are needed.

Product Line and Product Mix

product item   A specific version of a product

product line   A group of closely related product items viewed as a unit because of marketing, technical, or end-use considerations

Marketers must understand the relationships among all the products of their organization to coordinate the marketing of the total group of products. The following concepts help describe the relationships among an organization's products. A product item is a specific version of a product that can be designated as a distinct offering among an organization's products. A Gillette M3 Power Razor represents a product item. A product line is a group of closely related product items that are considered to be a unit because of marketing, technical, or end-use considerations. For example, Procter & Gamble, which acquired Gillette in early 2005, has over 300 brands that fall into one of 22 product lines ranging from deodorants to paper products.[6] The exact

Product Mix
Hain Pure Foods' product mix consists of several product lines of natural foods that are free of artificial colors, flavors, and preservatives.

product mix The total group of products that an organization makes available to customers

width of product mix The number of product lines a company offers

depth of product mix The average number of different product items offered in each product line

boundaries of a product line (although sometimes blurred) are usually indicated by using descriptive terms such as "frozen dessert" product line or "shampoo" product line. To come up with the optimal product line, marketers must understand buyers' goals. Specific product items in a product line usually reflect the desires of different target markets or the different needs of consumers.

A **product mix** is the composite, or total, group of products that an organization makes available to customers. For example, all the health-care, beauty-care, laundry and cleaning, food and beverage, paper, cosmetic, and fragrance products that Procter & Gamble manufactures constitute its product mix. The **width of product mix** is measured by the number of product lines a company offers. For example, Krispy Kreme, known for its signature doughnuts, recently announced plans to widen its product mix by introducing a line of frozen, blended beverages including chocolate, latte, and raspberry flavors.[7] The **depth of product mix** is the average number of different product items offered in each product line. Figure 10.1 shows the width and depth of part of Procter & Gamble's product mix.

Laundry detergents	Toothpastes	Bar soaps	Deodorants	Shampoos	Tissue/Towel
Ivory Snow 1930	Gleem 1952	Ivory 1879	Old Spice 1948	Pantene 1947	Charmin 1928
Dreft 1933	Crest 1955	Camay 1926	Secret 1956	Head & Shoulders 1961	Puffs 1960
Tide 1946		Zest 1952	Sure 1972	Vidal Sassoon 1974	Bounty 1965
Cheer 1950		Safeguard 1963		Pert Plus 1979	
Bold 1965		Oil of Olay 1993		Ivory 1983	
Gain 1966				Infusium 23 1986	
Era 1972				Physique 2000	
Febreze Clean Wash 2000				Herbal Essence 2001	

Depth (vertical axis label on left)
Width (horizontal axis label at bottom)

Figure 10.1
The Concepts of Product Mix Width and Depth Applied to Selected U.S. Procter & Gamble Products
Source: © The Procter & Gamble Company. Used by permission.

Product Life Cycles and Marketing Strategies

product life cycle The progression of a product through four stages: introduction, growth, maturity, and decline

Just as biological cycles progress from birth through growth and decline, so do product life cycles. As Figure 10.2 shows, a **product life cycle** has four major stages: introduction, growth, maturity, and decline. As a product moves through its cycle, the strategies relating to competition, pricing, distribution, promotion, and market information must be periodically evaluated and possibly changed. Astute marketing managers use the life cycle concept to make sure the introduction, alteration, and deletion of a product are timed and executed properly. By understanding the typical life cycle pattern, marketers can maintain profitable product mixes.

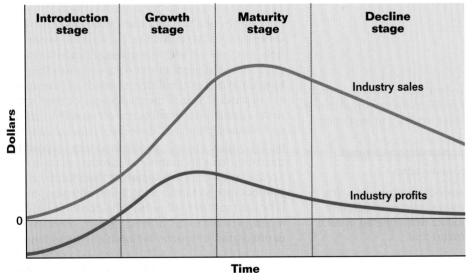

Figure 10.2
The Four Stages of the Product Life Cycle

◉ Introduction

introduction stage The initial stage of a product's life cycle—its first appearance in the market-place—when sales start at zero and profits are negative

The **introduction stage** of the product life cycle begins at a product's first appearance in the marketplace, when sales start at zero and profits are negative. Profits are below zero because initial revenues are low, and the company generally must cover large expenses for product development, promotion, and distribution. Notice in Figure 10.2 how sales should move upward from zero, and profits should also move upward from a position in which they are negative because of high expenses.

Potential buyers must be made aware of new product features, uses, and advantages. Two difficulties may arise at this point. First, sellers may lack the resources, technological knowledge, and marketing know-how to launch the product successfully. Entrepreneurs without large budgets can still attract attention, however, by giving away free samples, as Essence of Vali does with its aromatherapy products. Another technique is to gain visibility through media appearances. Dave Dettman, also known as Dr. Gadget, specializes in promoting new products on television news and talk programs. Companies such as Sony, Disney, Warner Bros., and others have hired Dr. Gadget to help with the introduction of new products.[8] Second, the initial product price may have to be high to recoup expensive marketing research or development costs. Given these difficulties, it is not surprising that many products never get beyond the introduction stage.

Most new products start off slowly and seldom generate enough sales to bring immediate profits. As buyers learn about the new product, marketers should be alert for product weaknesses and make corrections quickly to prevent the product's early demise. As the sales curve moves upward, the breakeven point is reached, and competitors enter the market, the growth stage begins.

◉ Growth

growth stage The stage of a product's life cycle when sales rise rapidly and profits reach a peak and then start to decline

During the **growth stage**, sales rise rapidly; profits reach a peak and then start to decline (see Figure 10.2). The growth stage is critical to a product's survival because competitive reactions to the product's success during this period will affect the product's life expectancy. For example, Palm marketed the first successful personal digital assistant (PDA), the PalmPilot, but today competes against numerous other brands such as Handspring, Casio, and Hewlett-Packard. Profits begin to decline late in the growth stage as more competitors enter the market, driving prices down.

As sales increase, management must support the momentum by adjusting the marketing strategy. The goal is to establish and fortify the product's market position by encouraging brand loyalty. To achieve greater market penetration, segmentation may have to be used more intensely. That requires developing product variations to satisfy the needs of people in several different market segments. Apple, for example, recently introduced two variations on its wildly popular iPod MP3 player. The iPod Mini, a slimmer, more colorful device, and the iPod Shuffle, a more affordable iPod, have helped expand Apple's market penetration in the competitive MP3 player industry.[9] Marketers should also analyze the competing brands' product positions relative to their own brands and take corrective actions, if needed.

As sales volume increases, efficiencies in production may result in lower costs, thus providing an opportunity for lower prices. For example, when satellite navigation systems for cars were initially introduced, the price was $5,000 or more. As demand soared, manufacturers were able to take advantage of economies of scale to reduce production costs and lower prices to less than $2,000 within several years.[10] If price cuts are feasible, they can help a brand gain market share and discourage new competitors from entering the market. Gaps in geographic market coverage should be

MARKETING AROUND THE WORLD
NOKIA IS CALLING ALL GAME PLAYERS

Seeking to extend the maturity stage of the cell phone life cycle, Nokia is packing a pocketful of gadgets into its N-Gage models. Users can make phone calls and send text messages with the N-Gage and N-Gage QD, but the main attraction is the ability to play popular video games such as *The Sims, Tony Hawk's Pro Skater,* and *Pocket Kingdom* alone or with other players. Adding to the appeal, N-Gage phones also can play MP3 music files and pick up FM radio signals.

Why is Finland's Nokia, the leader in mobile communications, interested in video games? The company commands 31 percent of the $500 billion global market for cell phones, selling 167 million handsets each year. However, it is facing more competition as the product category matures and international rivals such as Motorola (United States) and Samsung (South Korea) launch multiple products. Even as Nokia opens facilities in India and other regions where economic expansion supports higher sales, global competition is driving down handset prices and profits. This has prompted Nokia to move into the $30 billion video game market, which—along with the cell phone market—targets teenagers and young adults as a key segment.

The N-Gage takes phone-based gaming to an entirely new level. Earlier, users were limited to downloading basic games (for a small fee) from mobile phone carriers. In contrast, the Nokia phone can run more sophisticated 3D video games stored on memory cards. Users simply switch memory cards when they want to play a different game. Perhaps the biggest innovation is the option for multiplayer gaming. N-Gage models incorporate Bluetooth wireless communication, allowing people in one room to play against each other. N-Gage phones also serve as wireless gateways to the N-Gage Arena, a worldwide community of gamers playing interactively.

Customers bought one million units in the N-Gage's first 11 months on the market. However, more competition is ahead from handheld gaming units such as Nintendo's Game Boy and Sony's PlayStation Portable. Can Nokia count on video games to extend the cell phone's life cycle and keep profits rolling in?[a]

filled during the growth period. As a product gains market acceptance, new distribution outlets usually become easier to obtain. Promotion expenditures may be slightly lower than during the introductory stage but are still quite substantial. As sales increase, promotion costs should drop as a percentage of total sales. The advertising messages should stress brand benefits. Coupons and samples may be used to increase market share.

◉ Maturity

maturity stage The stage of a product's life cycle when the sales curve peaks and starts to decline as profits continue to fall

During the **maturity stage**, the sales curve peaks and starts to decline, and profits continue to fall (see Figure 10.2). This stage is characterized by intense competition because many brands are now in the market. Competitors emphasize improvements and differences in their versions of the product. As a result, during the maturity stage, weaker competitors are squeezed out of the market. The producers who remain in the market are likely to change their promotional and distribution efforts. Advertising and dealer-oriented promotions are typical during this stage of the product life cycle. Marketers must also take into account that as the product reaches maturity, buyers' knowledge of it attains a high level. Consumers are no longer inexperienced generalists. Instead, they are experienced specialists. Marketers of mature products sometimes expand distribution into global markets. Often the products have to be adapted to fit differing needs of global customers more precisely.

Because many products are in the maturity stage of their life cycles, marketers must know how to deal with these products and be prepared to adjust their marketing strategies. There are many approaches to altering marketing strategies during the maturity stage. To increase the sales of mature products, marketers may suggest new uses for them. Arm & Hammer has boosted demand for its baking soda by this method.

During the maturity stage, three objectives are sometimes pursued, including generating cash flow, maintaining share of market, and increasing share of customer. Generating cash flow is essential for recouping the initial investment and generating excess cash to support new products. Some firms simply strive to keep their current market shares. Companies with marginal market shares must decide whether they have a reasonable chance to improve their position or whether they should drop out. Whereas market share refers to the percentage of total customers served by a firm, share of customer relates to the percentage of each customer's needs being met by the firm. For example, many banks have added new services (brokerage, financial planning, and auto leasing) to gain more of each customer's financial services business.[11]

A greater mixture of pricing strategies is used during the maturity stage. Strong price competition is likely and may ignite price wars. Firms also compete in other ways besides price, such as through product quality or services. In addition, marketers develop price flexibility to differentiate offerings in product lines. Markdowns and price incentives are common. Prices may have to be increased, however, if distribution and production costs rise.

During the maturity stage, marketers go to great lengths to serve dealers and to provide incentives for selling their brands. Maintaining market share during the maturity stage requires moderate, and sometimes large, promotion expenditures. Advertising messages focus on differentiating a brand from the field of competitors, and sales promotion efforts may be aimed at both consumers and resellers.

◉ Decline

decline stage   The stage of a product's life cycle when sales fall rapidly

During the decline stage, sales fall rapidly (see Figure 10.2). When this happens, the marketer considers pruning items from the product line to eliminate those not earning a profit. The marketer may also cut promotion efforts, eliminate marginal distributors, and, finally, plan to phase out the product. Although Procter & Gamble's Oxydol detergent had been around for 90 years, the company phased it out and sold the brand name to Redox Brands for $7 million. Sales had declined from $64 million in 1950 to $5.5 million when the product was deleted.[12]

In the decline stage, marketers must determine whether to eliminate the product or try to reposition it to extend its life. Usually a declining product has lost its distinctiveness because similar competing products have been introduced. Competition engenders increased substitution and brand switching as buyers become insensitive to minor product differences. For these reasons, marketers do little to change a product's style, design, or other attributes during its decline. New technology or social trends, product substitutes, or environmental considerations may also indicate that the time has come to delete the product.

During a product's decline, outlets with strong sales volumes are maintained and unprofitable outlets are weeded out. An entire marketing channel may be eliminated if it does not contribute adequately to profits. An outlet not previously used, such as a factory outlet, will sometimes be used to liquidate remaining inventory of an obsolete product. As sales decline, the product becomes more inaccessible, but loyal buyers seek out dealers who still carry it. Spending on promotion efforts is usually considerably reduced. Advertising of special offers may slow the rate of decline. Sales promotions, such as coupons and premiums, may temporarily regain buyers' attention. As the product continues to decline, the sales staff shifts its emphasis to more profitable products.

Product Adoption Process

Acceptance of new products—especially new-to-the-world products—usually doesn't happen overnight. In fact, it can take a very long time. People are sometimes cautious or even skeptical about adopting new products, as indicated by some of the remarks quoted in Table 10.1. Customers who eventually accept a new product do so through an adoption process. The stages of the **product adoption process** are as follows:

product adoption process
The stages buyers go through in accepting a product

1. *Awareness:* The buyer becomes aware of the product.

2. *Interest:* The buyer seeks information and is receptive to learning about the product.

3. *Evaluation:* The buyer considers the product's benefits and decides whether to try it.

4. *Trial:* The buyer examines, tests, or tries the product to determine if it meets his or her needs.

5. *Adoption:* The buyer purchases the product and can be expected to use it again whenever the need for this general type of product arises.[13]

In the first stage, when individuals become aware that the product exists, they have little information about it and are not concerned about obtaining more. Con-

Stimulating Product Trial
The makers of Splenda, a sugar substitute, encourage customers to try their product by promoting it through free samples, as seen in this photo.

Table 10.1 Most New Ideas Have Their Skeptics

"I think there is a world market for maybe five computers."
—Thomas Watson, chairman of IBM, 1943

"This 'telephone' has too many shortcomings to be seriously considered as a means of communication. The device is inherently of no value to us."
—Western Union internal memo, 1876

"The wireless music box has no imaginable commercial value. Who would pay for a message sent to nobody in particular?"
—David Sarnoff's associates in response to his urgings for investment in the radio in the 1920s

"The concept is interesting and well-formed, but in order to earn better than a 'C,' the idea must be feasible."
—A Yale University management professor in response to Fred Smith's paper proposing reliable overnight delivery service (Smith went on to found Federal Express Corp.)

"Who the hell wants to hear actors talk?"
—H. M. Warner, Warner Brothers, 1927

"A cookie store is a bad idea. Besides, the market research reports say America likes crispy cookies, not soft and chewy cookies like you make."
—Banker's response to Debbie Fields's idea of starting Mrs. Fields' Cookies

"We don't like their sound, and guitar music is on the way out."
—Decca Recording Co. rejecting the Beatles, 1962

e-site

Founded in 1976, the Product Development & Management Association (PDMA) is a nonprofit organization of product developers, academics, and service providers dedicated to the support of product development research. PDMA sponsors an annual international conference on new-product development, highlighting the latest academic research, and offers members several publications devoted to product innovation. Many of these publications and other information related to new-product development and management are available on the organization's website at www.pdma.org/.

innovators First adopters of new products

early adopters Careful choosers of new products

sumers enter the interest stage when they are motivated to get information about the product's features, uses, advantages, disadvantages, price, or location. During the evaluation stage, individuals consider whether the product will satisfy certain criteria that are crucial to meeting their specific needs. In the trial stage, they use or experience the product for the first time, possibly by purchasing a small quantity, taking advantage of free samples, or borrowing the product from someone. Individuals move into the adoption stage by choosing a specific product when they need a product of that general type. Entering the adoption process does not mean the person will eventually adopt the new product. Rejection may occur at any stage, including the adoption stage. Both product adoption and product rejection can be temporary or permanent.

When an organization introduces a new product, people do not begin the adoption process at the same time, nor do they move through the process at the same speed. Of those who eventually adopt the product, some enter the adoption process rather quickly, whereas others start considerably later. For most products, there is also a group of nonadopters who never begin the process.

Depending on the length of time it takes them to adopt a new product, consumers fall into one of five major adopter categories: innovators, early adopters, early majority, late majority, and laggards.[14] Figure 10.3 illustrates each adopter category and the percentage of total adopters it typically represents. **Innovators** are the first to adopt a new product; they enjoy trying new products and tend to be venturesome. **Early adopters** choose new products carefully and are viewed as "the people to check

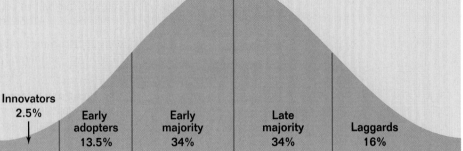

Figure 10.3
Distribution of Product Adopter Categories

Source: Reprinted with permission of The Free Press, a division of Simon & Schuster Adult Publishing Group, from *Diffusion of Innovations,* Fourth Edition, by Everett M. Rogers. Copyright © 1995 by Everett M. Rogers. Copyright © 1962, 1971, 1983 by The Free Press. All rights reserved.

Innovators 2.5% — Early adopters 13.5% — Early majority 34% — Late majority 34% — Laggards 16%

early majority Those adopting new products just before the average person

late majority Skeptics who adopt new products when they feel it is necessary

laggards The last adopters, who distrust new products

with" by those in the remaining adopter categories. People in the early majority adopt just prior to the average person; they are deliberate and cautious in trying new products. Individuals in the late majority are quite skeptical of new products but eventually adopt them because of economic necessity or social pressure. Laggards, the last to adopt a new product, are oriented toward the past. They are suspicious of new products, and when they finally adopt the innovation, it may already have been replaced by a new product.

Branding

brand An identifying name, term, design, or symbol

brand name The part of a brand that can be spoken

brand mark The part of a brand not made up of words

trademark A legal designation of exclusive use of a brand

trade name Full legal name of an organization

Marketers must make many decisions about products, including choices about brands, brand names, brand marks, trademarks, and trade names. A brand is a name, term, design, symbol, or any other feature that identifies one seller's good or service as distinct from those of other sellers. A brand may identify one item, a family of items, or all items of that seller.[15] A brand name is the part of a brand that can be spoken—including letters, words, and numbers—such as 7Up. A brand name is often a product's only distinguishing characteristic. Without the brand name, a firm could not differentiate its products. To consumers, a brand name is as fundamental as the product itself. Indeed, many brand names have become synonymous with the product, such as Scotch Tape and Xerox copiers. Through promotional activities, the owners of these brand names try to protect them from being used as generic names for tape and photocopiers.

The element of a brand that is not made up of words—often a symbol or design—is a brand mark. One example is the Golden Arches, which identify McDonald's restaurants and can be seen on patches worn by athletic teams—from U.S. Olympic teams to Little League softball teams—sponsored by McDonald's. A trademark is a legal designation indicating that the owner has exclusive use of a brand or a part of a brand and others are prohibited by law from using it. To protect a brand name or brand mark in the United States, an organization must register it as a trademark with the U.S. Patent and Trademark Office. In 2003, the Patent and Trademark Office registered over 167,000 new trademarks.[16] Finally, a trade name is the full and legal name of an organization, such as Ford Motor Company, rather than the name of a specific product.

◉ Value of Branding

Both buyers and sellers benefit from branding. Brands help buyers identify specific products that they do and do not like, which in turn facilitates the purchase of items that satisfy their needs and reduces the time required to purchase the product. Without brands, product selection would be quite random because buyers could have no assurance they were purchasing what they preferred. The purchase of certain brands can be a form of self-expression. For example, clothing brand names are important to many teenage boys. Names such as Tommy Hilfiger, Polo, Champion, Nike, and Guess? give manufacturers an advantage in the marketplace. Especially when a customer is unable to judge a product's quality, a brand may symbolize a certain quality level to the customer, and in turn the person lets that perception of quality represent the quality of the item. A brand helps reduce a buyer's perceived risk of purchase. In addition, a psychological reward may come from owning a brand that symbolizes status. The Mercedes-Benz brand in the United States is an example.

Sellers benefit from branding because each company's brands identify its products, which makes repeat purchasing easier for customers. Branding helps a firm introduce a new product that carries the name of one or more of its existing products because buyers are already familiar with the firm's existing brands. Branding also facilitates promotional efforts because the promotion of each branded product indirectly promotes all other similarly branded products. Branding also fosters brand loyalty. To the extent that buyers become loyal to a specific brand, the company's market share for that product achieves a certain level of stability, allowing the firm to use its resources more efficiently. Once a firm develops some degree of customer loyalty for a brand, it can maintain a fairly consistent price rather than continually cutting the price to attract customers.

brand equity The marketing and financial value associated with a brand's strength in a market

brand loyalty A customer's favorable attitude toward a specific brand

◉ Brand Equity

A well-managed brand is an asset to an organization. The value of this asset is often referred to as brand equity. Brand equity is the marketing and financial value associated with a brand's strength in a market. Besides the actual proprietary brand assets, such as patents and trademarks, four major elements underlie brand equity: brand name awareness, brand loyalty, perceived brand quality, and brand associations (see Figure 10.4).[17]

Being aware of a brand leads to brand familiarity, which in turn results in a level of comfort with the brand. A familiar brand is more likely to be selected than an unfamiliar brand because the familiar brand often is viewed as more reliable and of more acceptable quality. The familiar brand is likely to be in a customer's consideration set whereas the unfamiliar brand is not.

Brand loyalty is a customer's favorable attitude toward a specific brand. If brand loyalty is strong enough, customers may consistently purchase this brand when they need a product in that product category. Development of brand loyalty in a customer reduces his or her risks and shortens the time spent buying the product. However, the degree of brand loyalty for products

Figure 10.4
Major Elements of Brand Equity
Source: Adapted with the permission of The Free Press, a division of Simon & Schuster Adult Publishing Group, from *Managing Brand Equity: Capitalizing on the Value of a Brand Name* by David A. Aaker. Copyright © 1991 by David A. Aaker. All rights reserved.

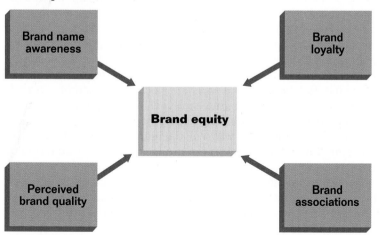

CUSTOMER RELATIONSHIP MANAGEMENT
HARLEY-DAVIDSON REVS UP BRAND EQUITY

Who would attend a birthday party for a brand? Harley-Davidson found out when it threw a one-hundredth anniversary bash—and 250,000 people showed up. Named for the two founders, the company started with one motorcycle built in a shed and today annually sells more than 290,000 motorcycles across the United States, Europe, and Japan.

The Harley-Davidson brand represents more than just two-wheeled transportation to its customers. When they line up to buy Harley-Davidson bikes, wear branded apparel, and participate in cross-country tours benefiting charities, customers are making a lifestyle choice. Nonmotorcycle products with the Harley-Davidson brand are so popular that they bring in revenues exceeding $10 million monthly. Some customers start out wearing Harley-Davidson clothing and then progress to buying Harley-Davidson motorcycles, becoming part of a brand-centered community. The Harley Owners Group—640,000 members strong—allows enthusiasts to connect with one another and with the brand.

Nevertheless, the company may face a bumpy ride as it searches for ways to encourage brand loyalty and fend off rivals. Fifteen years ago, the average age of a Harley-Davidson buyer was 35; today the average age is 46. Moreover, market share is beginning to slip as customers buy high-performance models from competitors. In response, Harley-Davidson is introducing sleek, speedy new models to showcase performance as a key brand association and is offering lower-priced models geared toward first-time buyers.

Harley-Davidson is also thinking ahead to keeping its brand in front of people who don't yet own one of its motorcycles. "We're trying to make our brand and products relevant in new and meaningful ways to a group we've loosely identified as 'dreamers' who say they want to ride some day and own a Harley-Davidson," says director of marketing Tom Watson. Any noncustomer who contacts the company by mail or online receives an "Attainability Program" package by mail with details about various models, financing alternatives, and dealer locations. "We want to get these people across the threshold," Watson explains. "They may not buy this year or next year, but this keeps them aware."[b]

---

brand recognition   A customer's awareness that the brand exists and is an alternative purchase

brand preference   The degree of brand loyalty in which a customer prefers one brand over competitive offerings

brand insistence   The degree of brand loyalty in which a customer strongly prefers a specific brand and will accept no substitute

varies from one product category to another. It is challenging to develop brand loyalty for some products, like bananas, because customers can judge the quality of these products and do not need to refer to a brand as an indicator of quality. Brand loyalty also varies by country. Customers in France, Germany, and the United Kingdom tend to be less brand-loyal than U.S. customers.

There are three degrees of brand loyalty: recognition, preference, and insistence. **Brand recognition** occurs when a customer is aware that the brand exists and views it as an alternative purchase if the preferred brand is unavailable or if the other available brands are unfamiliar. This is the mildest form of brand loyalty. The term *loyalty* clearly is being used very loosely here. **Brand preference** is a stronger degree of brand loyalty. A customer definitely prefers one brand over competitive offerings and will purchase this brand if available. However, if the brand is not available, the customer will accept a substitute brand rather than expending additional effort finding and purchasing the preferred brand. When **brand insistence** occurs, a customer strongly prefers a specific brand, will accept no substitute, and is willing to spend a great deal of time and effort to acquire that brand. If a brand-insistent customer goes to a store and finds the brand unavailable, he or she will seek the brand elsewhere rather than purchase a substitute brand. Brand insistence is the strongest degree of brand loyalty; it is a brander's dream. However, it is the least common type of brand loyalty.

Brand loyalty is an important component of brand equity because it reduces a brand's vulnerability to competitors' actions. Brand loyalty allows an organization to keep its existing customers and avoid spending an enormous amount of resources

Table 10.2
Top Ten Most Valuable Brands in the World

Brand	Brand Value (In Billion $)
Coca-Cola	67.4
Microsoft	61.4
IBM	53.8
GE	44.1
Intel	33.5
Disney	27.1
McDonald's	25.0
Nokia	24.0
Toyota	22.7
Marlboro	22.1

Source: "The 100 Top Brands," *BusinessWeek,* August 2, 2004, p. 68. The brand valuations draw on publicly available information, which has not been independently investigated by Interbrand. Data: Interbrand Corp., J. P. Morgan Chase & Co., Citigroup, Morgan Stanley, Business Week.

manufacturer brands Brands initiated by producers

private distributor brands Brands initiated and owned by resellers

generic brands Brands indicating only the product category

gaining new ones. Loyal customers provide brand visibility and reassurance to potential new customers. And because customers expect their brands to be available when and where they shop, retailers strive to carry the brands known for their strong customer following.

Customers associate a particular brand with a certain level of overall quality. A brand name may be used as a substitute for actual judgment of quality. In many cases, customers can't actually judge the quality of the product for themselves and instead must rely on the brand as a quality indicator. Perceived high brand quality helps support a premium price, allowing a marketer to avoid severe price competition. Also, favorable perceived brand quality can ease the introduction of brand extensions because the high regard for the brand will likely translate into high regard for the related products.

The set of associations linked to a brand is another key component of brand equity. At times a marketer works to connect a particular lifestyle or, in some instances, a certain personality type with a specific brand. For example, customers associate Michelin tires with protecting family members; a De Beers diamond with a loving, long-lasting relationship ("A Diamond Is Forever"); and Dr Pepper with a unique taste. These types of brand associations contribute significantly to the brand's equity. Brand associations are sometimes facilitated by using trade characters, such as the Jolly Green Giant, Pillsbury Dough Boy, and Charlie the Tuna. Placing these trade characters in advertisements and on packages helps consumers link the ads and packages to the brands.

Although difficult to measure, brand equity represents the value of a brand to an organization. Table 10.2 lists the top ten brands with the highest economic value. Any company that owns a brand listed in Table 10.2 would agree that the economic value of that brand is likely to be the greatest single asset in the organization's possession.

◉ Types of Brands

There are three categories of brands: manufacturer, private distributor, and generic. **Manufacturer brands** are initiated by producers and ensure that producers are identified with their products at the point of purchase—for example, Green Giant, Dell, and Levi's jeans. A manufacturer brand usually requires a producer to become involved in distribution, promotion, and, to some extent, pricing decisions.

Private distributor brands (also called *private brands, store brands,* or *dealer brands*) are initiated and owned by resellers—wholesalers or retailers. The major characteristic of private brands is that the manufacturers are not identified on the products. Retailers and wholesalers use private distributor brands to develop more efficient promotion, generate higher gross margins, and change store image. Familiar retailer brand names include Sears' Kenmore and JCPenney's Arizona. Some successful private brands, like Kenmore, are distributed nationally. Sometimes retailers with successful private distributor brands start manufacturing their own products to gain more control over product costs, quality, and design with the hope of increasing profits. Private brands account for more than 16 percent of dollar volume sales and approximately 21 percent of unit volume sales in supermarkets.[18]

Some marketers of traditionally branded products have embarked on a policy of not branding, often called *generic branding.* **Generic brands** indicate only the product category (such as aluminum foil) and do not include the company name or other identifying terms. Generic brands are usually sold at lower prices than comparable branded items. Although at one time generic brands may have represented as much as 10 percent of all retail grocery sales, today they account for less than a half of a percent.

Types of Brands
Shown here are examples of store brands, generic brands, and manufacturer brands.

⊙ Selecting a Brand Name

Marketers consider several factors in selecting a brand name. First, the name should be easy for customers (including foreign buyers, if the firm intends to market its products in other countries) to say, spell, and recall. Short, one-syllable names, such as Cheer, often satisfy this requirement. Second, the brand name should indicate the product's major benefits and, if possible, should suggest in a positive way the product's uses and special characteristics; negative or offensive references should be avoided. For example, the brand names of household cleaning products such as Ajax dishwashing liquid, Vanish toilet bowl cleaner, Formula 409 multipurpose cleaner, Cascade dishwasher detergent, and Wisk laundry detergent connote strength and effectiveness. Third, to set it apart from competing brands, the brand should be distinctive. If a marketer intends to use a brand for a product line, that brand must be compatible with all products in the line. Finally, a brand should be designed so that it can be used and recognized in all types of media. Finding the right brand name has become a challenging task because many obvious product names have already been used.

How are brand names devised? Brand names can be created from single or multiple words—for example, Bic or Dodge Grand Caravan. Letters and numbers are used to create brands such as IBM PC or Z71. Words, numbers, and letters are combined to yield brand names such as Mazda MX-5 Miata or BMW Z4 Roadster. To avoid terms that have negative connotations, marketers sometimes use fabricated words that have absolutely no meaning when created—for example, Kodak and Exxon.

Who actually creates brand names? Brand names can be created internally by the organization. Sometimes a name is suggested by individuals who are close to the development of the product. Some organizations have committees that participate in brand name creation and approval. Large companies that introduce numerous new products annually are likely to have a department that develops brand names. At times, outside consultants and companies that specialize in brand name development are used. For example, Philip Morris hired Landor Associates to develop its new name, Altria Group.[19]

⊙ Protecting a Brand

A marketer should also design a brand so that it can be protected easily through registration. A series of court decisions has created a broad hierarchy of protection based on brand type. From most protectable to least protectable, these brand types are fanciful (Exxon), arbitrary (Dr Pepper), suggestive (Spray 'n Wash), descriptive (Minute Rice), and generic (aluminum foil). Generic brands are not protectable. Surnames and descriptive, geographic, or functional names are difficult to protect.[20] However, research shows that overall, consumers prefer descriptive and suggestive brand names and find them easier to recall compared with fanciful and arbitrary brand names.[21] Because of their designs, some brands can be legally infringed on more easily than others. Although registration protects trademarks domestically for ten years, and trademarks can be renewed indefinitely, a firm should develop a system for ensuring that its trademarks are renewed as needed.

To protect its exclusive rights to a brand, a company must make certain the brand is not likely to be considered an infringement on any brand already registered with the U.S. Patent and Trademark Office. This task may be complex because infringement is determined by the courts, which base their decisions on whether a brand causes consumers to be confused, mistaken, or deceived about the source of the product. McDonald's is one company that aggressively protects its trademarks against infringement; it has brought charges against a number of companies with *Mc* names because it fears the use of that prefix will give consumers the impression that these companies are associated with or owned by McDonald's.

A marketer should guard against allowing a brand name to become a generic term used to refer to a general product category. Generic terms cannot be protected as exclusive brand names. For example, *aspirin, escalator,* and *shredded wheat*—all brand names at one time—eventually were declared generic terms that refer to product classes. Thus, they could no longer be protected. To keep a brand name from becoming a generic term, the firm should spell the name with a capital letter and use it as an adjective to modify the name of the general product class, as in Kool-Aid Brand Soft Drink Mix.[22] Including the word *brand* just after the brand name is also helpful. An organization can deal with this problem directly by advertising that its brand is a trademark and should not be used generically. The firm can also indicate that the brand is a registered trademark by using the symbol ®.

A U.S. firm that tries to protect a brand in a foreign country frequently encounters problems. In many countries, brand registration is not possible; the first firm to use a brand in such a country automatically has the rights to it. In some instances, U.S. companies actually have had to buy their own brand rights from a firm in a foreign country because the foreign firm was the first user in that country.

Marketers trying to protect their brands must also contend with brand counterfeiting. In the United States, for instance, one can purchase counterfeit General Motors parts, Cartier watches, Louis Vuitton handbags, Walt Disney character dolls, Warner Brothers Clothing, Mont Blanc pens, and a host of other products illegally marketed by manufacturers that do not own the brands. Losses caused by counterfeit products are estimated to be between $250 billion and $350 billion annually.

In the interest of strengthening trademark protection, Congress enacted the Trademark Law Revision Act in 1988, the only major federal trademark legislation since the Lanham Act of 1946. The purpose of this more recent legislation is to increase the value of the federal registration system for U.S. firms relative to foreign competitors and to protect the public from counterfeiting, confusion, and deception.[23]

> **MARKETING ENTREPRENEURS**
>
> **Elise and Evan MacMillan**
>
> **THEIR BUSINESS:** Chocolatefarm.com
>
> **FOUNDED AT AGES: 10 and 13**
>
> **SUCCESS: Revenues of $1 million a year**
>
> After her first chocolate-making session with her grandma at age 3, Elise MacMillan was hooked on the candy business. Over the next seven years, she experimented with chocolate until she perfected her signature product—chocolates in the shape of animals. Her brother Evan joined the venture when he drafted a financial plan. Shortly thereafter the two secured a bank loan and launched the business online.[c]

Branding Policies

Before establishing branding policies, a firm must decide whether to brand its products at all. If a company's product is homogeneous and is similar to competitors' products, it may be difficult to brand in a way that will generate brand loyalty. Raw materials such as coal, sand, and farm produce are hard to brand because of the homogeneity of such products and their physical characteristics.

If a firm chooses to brand its products, it may use individual branding, family branding, or a combination. **Individual branding** is a policy of naming each product

individual branding
A policy of naming each product differently

differently. For example, Unilever relies on an individual branding policy for its line of detergents, which includes Wisk, Persil, and All.[24] A major advantage of individual branding is that if an organization introduces an inferior product, the negative images associated with it do not contaminate the company's other products. An individual branding policy may also facilitate market segmentation when a firm wishes to enter many segments of the same market. Separate, unrelated names can be used and each brand aimed at a specific segment. Sara Lee uses individual branding among its many divisions, which include Hanes underwear, L'eggs pantyhose, Champion sportswear, Bali, Jimmy Dean, Ball Park, and other vastly different brands.

family branding   Branding all of a firm's products with the same name

When using **family branding**, all of a firm's products are branded with the same name or at least part of the name, such as Kellogg's Frosted Flakes, Kellogg's Rice Krispies, and Kellogg's Corn Flakes. In some cases, a company's name is combined with other words to brand items. Arm & Hammer uses its name on all its products, along with a general description of the item, such as Arm & Hammer Heavy Duty Detergent, Arm & Hammer Pure Baking Soda, and Arm & Hammer Carpet Deodorizer. Unlike individual branding, family branding means that the promotion of one item with the family brand promotes the firm's other products. Examples of other companies that use family branding include Mitsubishi, Heinz, and Sony.

An organization is not limited to a single branding policy. A company that uses primarily individual branding for many of its products may also use family branding for a specific product line. Branding policy is influenced by the number of products and product lines the company produces, the characteristics of its target markets, the number and types of competing products available, and the size of the firm's resources.

◉ Brand Extensions

brand extension   Using an existing brand to brand a new product in a different product category

A **brand extension** occurs when an organization uses one of its existing brands to brand a new product in a different product category. For example, Procter & Gamble employed a brand extension when it named a new product Ivory Body Wash. Another example is when Bic, the maker of disposable pens, introduced Bic disposable razors and Bic lighters. A brand extension should not be confused with a line extension. A line extension refers to using an existing brand on a new product in the same product category, such as new flavors or sizes. For example, when the maker of Tylenol, McNeil Consumer Products, introduced Extra Strength Tylenol P.M., the new product was a line extension since it was in the same category.

Marketers share a common concern that if a brand is extended too many times or extended too far outside its original product category, the brand can be significantly weakened. For example, the Nabisco Snackwell brand initially appeared only on crackers, cookies, and snack bars, all of which fall into the baked-snack category. However, extending the brand to yogurts and gelatin mixes goes further afield. Although some experts might caution Nabisco against extending the Snackwell brand to this degree, some evidence suggests that brands can be successfully extended to less closely related product categories through the use of advertisements that extend customers' perceptions of the original product category. For example, Waterford, an upscale Irish brand of crystal, extended its name to writing instruments when seeking sales growth beyond closely related product categories such as china, cutlery, and table linens.[25]

◉ Co-Branding

co-branding   Using two or more brands on one product

Co-branding is the use of two or more brands on one product. Marketers employ co-branding to capitalize on the brand equity of multiple brands. Co-branding is popular in several processed food categories and in the credit card industry. The brands used for co-branding can be owned by the same company. For example, Kraft's Lunchables product teams the Kraft cheese brand with Oscar Mayer lunchmeats, another Kraft-owned brand. The brands may also be owned by different companies. Credit card companies like American Express, Visa, and MasterCard, for instance, team up with other brands like General Motors, AT&T, and many airlines. Effective co-branding capitalizes on the trust and confidence customers have in the brands involved. The brands should not lose their identities, and it should be clear to customers which brand is the main brand. For example, it is fairly obvious that Kellogg owns the brand and is the main brander of Kellogg's Healthy Choice Cereal. It is important for marketers to understand that when a co-branded product is unsuccessful, both brands are implicated in the product failure. To gain customer acceptance, the brands involved must represent a complementary fit in the minds of buyers. Trying to link a brand like Harley-Davidson with a brand like Healthy Choice will not achieve co-branding objectives because customers are not likely to perceive these brands as compatible.

◉ Brand Licensing

brand licensing   An agreement whereby a company permits another organization to use its brand on other products for a licensing fee

A popular branding strategy involves **brand licensing**, an agreement in which a company permits another organization to use its brand on other products for a licensing fee. Royalties may be as low as 2 percent of wholesale revenues or higher than 10 percent. Mattel, for example, licensed Warner Brothers' Harry Potter brand for use on board games and toys to tie in with the first movie based on the popular book series. Warner was guaranteed royalties of $20 million from Mattel's licensing fee of 15 percent of gross revenues earned on these branded products.[26] The licensee is responsible for all manufacturing, selling, and advertising functions and bears the costs if the licensed product fails. The advantages of licensing range from extra revenues and low-cost or free publicity to new images and trademark protection. The major disadvantages are a lack of manufacturing control, which could hurt the company's name, and bombarding consumers with too many unrelated products bearing the same name.

◉ Packaging

Packaging involves the development of a container and a graphic design for a product. A package can be a vital part of a product, making it more versatile, safer, and easier to use. Like a brand name, a package can influence customers' attitudes toward a product and so affect their purchase decisions. For example, several producers of jellies, sauces, and ketchups have packaged their products in squeezable plastic containers to make use and storage more convenient. Package characteristics help shape buyers' impressions of a product at the time of purchase or during use. In this section, we examine the main functions of packaging and consider several major packaging decisions. We also analyze the role of the package in a marketing strategy.

◉ Packaging Functions

Effective packaging means more than simply putting products in containers and covering them with wrappers. First, packaging materials serve the basic purpose of protecting the product and maintaining its functional form. Fluids like milk and orange juice need packages that preserve and protect them. The packaging should prevent damage that could affect the product's usefulness and thus lead to higher costs. Since product tampering has become a problem, several packaging techniques have been developed to counter this danger. Some packages are also designed to deter shoplifting.

Another function of packaging is to offer convenience to consumers. For example, small aseptic packages—individual-size boxes or plastic bags that contain liquids and do not require refrigeration—strongly appeal to children and young adults with active lifestyles. The size or shape of a package may relate to the product's storage, convenience of use, or replacement rate. Small, single-serving cans of vegetables, for instance, may prevent waste and make storage easier. A third function of packaging is to promote a product by communicating its features, uses, benefits, and image. Sometimes a reusable package is developed to make the product more desirable. For example, the Cool Whip package doubles as a food-storage container.

◉ Major Packaging Considerations

As they develop packages, marketers must take many factors into account. Obviously, one major consideration is cost. Although a variety of packaging materials, processes, and designs are available, costs vary greatly. In recent years, buyers have shown a willingness to pay more for improved packaging, but there are limits.

Marketers should consider how much consistency is desirable among an organization's package designs. No consistency may be the best policy, especially if a firm's products are unrelated or aimed at vastly different target markets. To promote an overall company image, a firm may decide that all packages should be similar or include one major element of the design. This approach is called family packaging. Sometimes it is used only for lines of products, as with Campbell's soups, Weight Watcher's foods, and Planter's nuts.

A package's promotional role is an important consideration. Through verbal and nonverbal symbols, the package can inform potential buyers about the product's content, features, uses, advantages, and hazards. A firm can create desirable images and

family packaging Using similar packaging for all of a firm's products or packaging that has one common design element

Distinctive Packaging Shapes
Distinctive package shapes provide enhanced brand identities.

Unique glass packaging communicates brand image to the consumer. At Vitro Packaging, Inc., we specialize in custom bottles, special colors, and prelabeling options to create a premium image that makes that critical first statement. Its your brand out there on the shelf...don't just sit there. Say something!

Call us at 800-766-0600, email rfisher@vto.com, or visit our web site at www.vitropackaging.com

A SUBSIDIARY OF VITRO, SOCIEDAD ANONIMA, A MEXICAN CORPORATION

associations by its choice of color, design, shape, and texture. Many cosmetics manufacturers, for example, design their packages to create impressions of richness, luxury, and exclusiveness. To develop a package that has a definite promotional value, a designer must consider size, shape, texture, color, and graphics. Beyond the obvious limitation that the package must be large enough to hold the product, a package can be designed to appear taller or shorter. Light-colored packaging may make a package appear larger, whereas darker colors may minimize the perceived size.

Colors on packages are often chosen to attract attention, and color can positively influence customers' emotions. People often associate specific colors with certain feelings and experiences. Blue is soothing; it is also associated with wealth, trust, and security. Gray is associated with strength, exclusivity, and success. Orange can stand for low cost. Red connotes excitement and stimulation. Purple is associated with dignity and stateliness. Yellow connotes cheerfulness and joy. Black is associated with being strong and masterful.[27] When opting for color on packaging, marketers must judge whether a particular color will evoke positive or negative feelings when linked to a specific product. Rarely, for example, do processors package meat or bread in green materials because customers may associate green with mold. Marketers must also determine whether a specific target market will respond favorably or unfavorably to a particular color. Packages designed to appeal to children often use primary colors and bold designs.

Packaging must also meet the needs of resellers. Wholesalers and retailers consider whether a package facilitates transportation, storage, and handling. Resellers may refuse to carry certain products if their packages are cumbersome. Concentrated versions of laundry detergents and fabric softeners aid retailers in offering more product diversity within the existing shelf space.

◉ Packaging and Marketing Strategy

Packaging can be a major component of a marketing strategy. A new cap or closure, a better box or wrapper, or a more convenient container may give a product a competitive advantage. The developers of the SpinBrush, a $5 electric toothbrush, had this in mind when they created packaging that allowed shoppers to turn the brush on in the store to see how it worked. This bold strategy helped SpinBrush sell over 10 million units in its first year on the shelves.[28] The right type of package for a new product can help it gain market recognition very quickly. In the case of existing brands, marketers should reevaluate packages periodically. Marketers should view packaging as a major strategic tool, especially for consumer convenience products. For instance, in the food industry, jumbo and large package sizes for products such as hot dogs, pizzas, English muffins, frozen dinners, and biscuits have been very successful. When considering the strategic uses of packaging, marketers must also analyze the cost of packaging and package changes. In this section, we examine several ways in which packaging can be used strategically.

● **Altering the Package.**   At times a marketer changes a package because the existing design is no longer in style, especially when compared with the packaging of competitive products. Arm & Hammer now markets a refillable plastic shaker for its baking soda. Quaker Oats hired a package design company to redesign its Rice-A-Roni package to give the product the appearance of having evolved with the times while retaining its traditional taste appeal. A package may be redesigned because new product features need to be highlighted or because new packaging materials have become available. An organization may decide to change a product's packaging to make the product safer or more convenient to use. Nestlé USA, for example, changed its Coffee-Mate package to a new, easy-to-grip plastic container that features a pouring spout, eliminating the need to unscrew the lid and spoon out the creamer. Nestlé expects the new, more convenient package to give its powdered-creamer product a boost in the marketplace.[29]

● **Secondary-Use Packaging.**   A secondary-use package is one that can be reused for purposes other than its initial function. For example, a margarine container can be reused to store leftovers, and a jelly container can serve as a drinking glass. Customers often view secondary-use packaging as adding value to products, in which case its use should stimulate unit sales.

● **Category-Consistent Packaging.**   With category-consistent packaging, the product is packaged in line with the packaging practices associated with a particular product category. Some product categories—for example, mayonnaise, mustard, ketchup, and peanut butter—have traditional package shapes. Other product categories are characterized by recognizable color combinations, such as red and white for soup, and red, white, and blue for Ritz-like crackers. When an organization introduces a brand in one of these product categories, marketers will often use traditional package shapes and color combinations to ensure that customers will recognize the new product as being in that specific product category.

● **Innovative Packaging.**   Sometimes a marketer employs a unique cap, design, applicator, or other feature to make a product distinctive. Such packaging can be effective when the innovation makes the product safer or easier to use, or provides better protection for the product. In some instances, marketers use innovative or unique packages that are inconsistent with traditional packaging practices to make the brand stand out from its competitors. Unusual packaging sometimes requires spending considerable resources, not only on package design but also on making customers aware of the unique package and its benefits. The findings of a recent study suggest that uniquely shaped packages that attract attention are more likely to be perceived as containing a higher volume of product.[30]

● **Multiple Packaging.**   Rather than packaging a single unit of a product, marketers sometimes use twin packs, tri-packs, six-packs, or other forms of multiple packaging. For certain types of products, multiple packaging may increase demand because it increases the amount of the product available at the point of

Innovative Packaging
The maker of Folgers Coffee adds value to its brand by using a new canister design that keeps coffee fresh and is easier to hold.

consumption (in one's house, for example). It may also increase consumer acceptance of the product by encouraging the buyer to try the product several times. Multiple packaging can make products easier to handle and store, as in the case of six-packs for soft drinks.

● **Handling-Improved Packaging.** A product's packaging may be changed to make it easier to handle in the distribution channel—for example, by changing the outer carton or using special bundling, shrink-wrapping, or pallets. In some cases, the shape of the package is changed. Outer containers for products are sometimes changed so they will proceed more easily through automated warehousing systems.

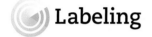 # Labeling

labeling Providing identifying, promotional, or other information on package labels

Labeling is very closely interrelated with packaging and is used for identification, promotional, and informational and legal purposes. Labels can be small or large relative to the size of the product and carry varying amounts of information. The sticker on a Chiquita banana, for example, is quite small and displays only the brand name of the fruit. A label can be part of the package itself or a separate feature attached to the package. The label on a can of Coke is actually part of the can, whereas the label on a two-liter bottle of Coke is separate and can be removed. Information presented on a label may include the brand name and mark, the registered trademark symbol, package size and content, product features, nutritional information, type and style of the product, number of servings, care instructions, directions for use and safety precautions, the name and address of the manufacturer, expiration dates, seals of approval, and other facts.

Labels can facilitate the identification of a product by displaying the brand name in combination with a unique graphic design. For example, Heinz ketchup is easy to identify on a supermarket shelf because the brand name is easy to read and the label has a distinctive, crownlike shape. By drawing attention to products and their benefits, labels can strengthen an organization's promotional efforts. Labels may contain promotional messages such as the offer of a discount or a larger package size at the same price, or information about a new or improved product feature.

Several federal laws and regulations specify information that must be included on the labels of certain products. Garments must be labeled with the name of the manufacturer, country of manufacture, fabric content, and cleaning instructions. Labels on nonedible items like shampoos and detergents must include both safety precautions and directions for use. The Nutrition Labeling Act of 1990 requires the Food and Drug Administration to review food labeling and packaging, focusing on nutrition content, label format, ingredient labeling, food descriptions, and health messages. This act regulates much of the labeling on more than 250,000 products made by 17,000 U.S. companies. Any food product for which a nutritional claim is made must have nutrition labeling that follows a standard format. Food product labels must state the number of servings per container, serving size, number of calories per serving, number of calories derived from fat, number of carbohydrates, and amounts of specific nutrients such as vitamins. In addition, new nutritional labeling requirements focus on the amounts of trans-fatty acids in food products.

The use of new technology in the production and processing of food has led to additional food labeling issues. The FDA now requires that a specific irradiation logo be used when labeling irradiated food products. In addition, the FDA also has issued voluntary guidelines for food companies to follow if they choose to label foods as biotech-free or promote biotech ingredients.[31]

Of concern to many manufacturers are the Federal Trade Commission's guidelines regarding "Made in U.S.A." labels, a growing problem due to the increasingly global nature of manufacturing. The FTC requires that "all or virtually all" of a product's components be made in the United States if the label says "Made in U.S.A."

CHAPTER REVIEW

① Understand the concept of a product and how products are classified.

A product is a good, a service, an idea, or any combination of the three received in an exchange. It can be either tangible or intangible and includes functional, social, and psychological utilities or benefits. When consumers purchase a product, they are buying the benefits and satisfaction they think the product will provide.

Products can be classified on the basis of the buyer's intentions. Consumer products are those purchased to satisfy personal and family needs. Business products are purchased for use in a firm's operations, to resell, or to make other products. Consumer products can be subdivided into convenience, shopping, specialty, and unsought products. Business products can be classified as installations, accessory equipment, raw materials, component parts, process materials, MRO supplies, and business services.

② Explain the concepts of product item, product line, and product mix, and understand how they are connected.

A product item is a specific version of a product that can be designated as a distinct offering among an organization's products. A product line is a group of closely related product items that are considered a unit because of marketing, technical, or end-use considerations. The composite, or total, group of products that an organization makes available to customers is called the product mix. The width of the product mix is measured by the number of product lines the company offers. The depth of a product mix is the average number of different products offered in each product line.

③ Understand the product life cycle and its impact on marketing strategies.

The product life cycle describes how product items in an industry move through four stages: introduction, growth, maturity, and decline. The sales curve is at zero at introduction, rises at an increasing rate during growth, peaks during the maturity stage, and then declines. Profits peak toward the end of the growth stage of the product life cycle.

④ Describe the product adoption process.

When customers accept a new product, they usually do so through a five-stage adoption process. The first stage is awareness, when buyers become aware that a product exists. Interest, the second stage, occurs when buyers seek information and are receptive to learning about the product. The third stage is evaluation; buyers consider the product's benefits and decide whether to try it. The fourth stage is trial; during this stage, buyers examine, test, or try the product to determine if it meets their needs. The last stage is adoption, when buyers actually purchase the product and use it whenever a need for this general type of product arises.

⑤ Explain the value of branding and the major components of brand equity.

A brand is a name, term, design, symbol, or any other feature that identifies one seller's good or service and distinguishes it from those of other sellers. Branding helps buyers identify and evaluate products, helps sellers facilitate product introduction and repeat purchasing, and fosters brand loyalty. Brand equity is the marketing and financial value associated with a brand's strength. It represents the value of a brand to an organization. The four major elements underlying brand equity include brand name awareness, brand loyalty, perceived brand quality, and brand associations.

⑥ Recognize the types of brands and how they are selected and protected.

A manufacturer brand is initiated by a producer. A private distributor brand is initiated and owned by a reseller, sometimes taking on the name of the store or distributor. A generic brand indicates only the product category and does not include the company name or other identifying terms. When selecting a brand name, a marketer should choose one that is easy to say, spell, and recall and that alludes to the product's uses, benefits, or special characteristics. Brand names can be devised from words, letters, numbers, nonsense words, or a combination of these. Companies protect ownership of their brands through registration with the U.S. Patent and Trademark Office.

7 **Identify two types of branding policies and explain brand extensions, co-branding, and brand licensing.**

Individual branding designates a unique name for each of a company's products. Family branding identifies all of a firm's products with a single name. A brand extension is the use of an existing name on a new or improved product in a different product category. Co-branding is the use of two or more brands on one product. Through a licensing agreement and for a licensing fee, a firm may permit another organization to use its brand on other products. Brand licensing enables producers to earn extra revenue, receive low-cost or free publicity, and protect their trademarks.

8 **Describe the major packaging functions and design considerations and how packaging is used in marketing strategies.**

Packaging involves the development of a container and a graphic design for a product. Effective packaging offers protection, economy, safety, and convenience. It can influence a customer's purchase decision by promoting features, uses, benefits, and image.

When developing a package, marketers must consider the value to the customer of efficient and effective packaging, offset by the price the customer is willing to pay. Other considerations include how to make the package tamper resistant, whether to use multiple packaging and family packaging, how to design the package as an effective promotional tool, and how best to accommodate resellers. Packaging can be an important part of an overall marketing strategy and can be used to target certain market segments. Modifications in packaging can revive a mature product and extend its product life cycle. Producers alter packages to convey new features or to make them safer or more convenient. If a package has a secondary use, the product's value to the consumer may increase. Category-consistent packaging makes products more easily recognized by consumers. Innovative packaging enhances a product's distinctiveness.

9 **Understand the functions of labeling and selected legal issues.**

Labeling is closely interrelated with packaging and is used for identification, promotional, and informational and legal purposes. Various federal laws and regulations require that certain products be labeled or marked with warnings, instructions, nutritional information, manufacturer's identification, and perhaps other information.

✓ Please visit the student website at www.prideferrell.com
ACE self-test for ACE Self-Test questions that will help you prepare for exams.

KEY CONCEPTS

good	process materials	product adoption process	brand recognition
service	MRO supplies	innovators	brand preference
idea	business services	early adopters	brand insistence
consumer products	product item	early majority	manufacturer brands
business products	product line	late majority	private distributor brands
convenience products	product mix	laggards	generic brands
shopping products	width of product mix	brand	individual branding
specialty products	depth of product mix	brand name	family branding
unsought products	product life cycle	brand mark	brand extension
installations	introduction stage	trademark	co-branding
accessory equipment	growth stage	trade name	brand licensing
raw materials	maturity stage	brand equity	family packaging
component parts	decline stage	brand loyalty	labeling

ISSUES FOR DISCUSSION AND REVIEW

1. Is a personal computer sold at a retail store a consumer product or a business product? Defend your answer.

2. How do convenience products and shopping products differ? What are the distinguishing characteristics of each type of product?

3. How does an organization's product mix relate to its development of a product line? When should an enterprise add depth to its product lines rather than width to its product mix?

4. How do industry profits change as a product moves through the four stages of its life cycle?

5. What are the stages in the product adoption process, and how do they affect the commercialization phase?

6. How does branding benefit consumers and marketers?

7. What is brand equity? Identify and explain the major elements of brand equity.

8. What are the three major degrees of brand loyalty?

9. Compare and contrast manufacturer brands, private distributor brands, and generic brands.

10. Identify the factors a marketer should consider in selecting a brand name.

11. What is co-branding? What major issues should be considered when using co-branding?

12. Describe the functions a package can perform. Which function is most important? Why?

13. What are the main factors a marketer should consider when developing a package?

14. In what ways can packaging be used as a strategic tool?

15. What are the major functions of labeling?

MARKETING APPLICATIONS

1. Choose a familiar clothing store. Describe its product mix, including its depth and width. Evaluate the mix and make suggestions to the owner.

2. Tabasco pepper sauce is a product that has entered the maturity stage of the product life cycle. Name products that would fit into each of the four stages (introduction, growth, maturity, and decline). Describe each product and explain why it fits in that stage.

3. Generally buyers go through a product adoption process before becoming loyal customers. Describe your experience in adopting a product you now use consistently. Did you go through all the stages?

4. Identify two brands for which you are brand insistent. How did you begin using these brands? Why do you no longer use other brands?

5. General Motors introduced the subcompact Geo with a name that appeals to a world market. Invent a brand name for a line of luxury sports cars that also would appeal to an international market. Suggest a name that implies quality, luxury, and value.

6. For each of the following product categories, choose an existing brand. Then, for each selected brand, suggest a co-brand and explain why the co-brand would be effective.
   a. Cookies
   b. Pizza
   c. Long-distance telephone service
   d. A sports drink

7. Identify a package that you believe to be inferior. Explain why you think the package is inferior, and discuss your recommendations for improving it.

ONLINE EXERCISE

GOODYEAR TIRE & RUBBER COMPANY

8. In addition to providing information about the company's products, Goodyear's website helps consumers find the exact products they want and even directs them to the nearest Goodyear retailer. Visit the Goodyear site at **www.goodyear.com**.

a. How does Goodyear use its website to communicate information about the quality of its tires?
b. How does Goodyear's website demonstrate product and design features?
c. Based on what you learned at the website, describe what Goodyear has done to position its tires.

VIDEO CASE

Sony's PlayStation Gets Personal

Although the PlayStation Portable weighs in at just 9 ounces, it holds the key to Sony's continued dominance of the $13 billion video game industry. Sony has long been the market leader, thanks in large part to its careful expansion of the PlayStation product line. Sony introduced the original PlayStation in the mid-1990s, followed by PlayStation 2 in 2000 and the handheld PlayStation Portable in 2004. PlayStation 3, its next-generation game console, features even more advanced technology to give players an extremely vivid and realistic playing experience.

Sony's PlayStation products face challenges from two main rivals: Nintendo and Microsoft. Nintendo's GameCube game console came to market a year after PlayStation 2, with a retail price $100 lower than the Sony console. Although Nintendo has sold more than 120 million GameBoy and GameBoy Advance units since 1989, it didn't compete directly with Sony before launching the GameCube. Now Nintendo has Sony in its sights once again with the introduction of the wireless-equipped DS (dual screen) handheld game console, geared to many of the same customers that Sony is targeting with its PlayStation Portable. Not only is the DS priced lower than the PlayStation Portable, it can run any of the Game Boy

Advance games, an important benefit for customers with large game libraries.

Sony's PlayStation Portable can play digital music and videos, display digital photos, connect players wirelessly, and make phone calls over the Internet. Despite all these features, the console is so small that it fits into a backpack with plenty of room to spare. However, because of its smaller size, the PlayStation Portable cannot run any of the games created for the PlayStation 1, 2, or 3. Sony, in fact, is counting on demand for PlayStation Portable games to boost revenues and profits in the coming years.

Sony's other rival, Microsoft, introduced its Xbox console in 2001 to challenge the PlayStation 2 on price, speed, and other features. However, unlike the PlayStation 2, it cannot play DVDs and CDs without a separate remote control. Microsoft, famed for its software, has sold 16 million Xbox units by emphasizing the user-friendly interface and unique games such as the *Halo* series. It has also started Xbox Live, a subscription-only online gaming platform that has attracted more than 1 million gamers in 11 countries. Users can play the latest version of 100 other video games by logging on to the Xbox Live site rather than buying each game individually.

Fueled by new game console technology and more lifelike graphics, consumers are snatching up fast-paced video games such as *Need for Speed* and *Halo 2*. Video games represent a product that is more intangible than tangible. Buyers search for performance and functional benefits. Every time they play a game, they have a different experience. The experience and excitement associated with playing the game are the ultimate product. Marketers can make video games more tangible and demonstrate their value through clever advertising, eye-popping packaging, consistent branding, and special hints for gamers.

On average, video games cost $50, including a fee of roughly $10 that the game publisher pays to the console maker (Sony, Nintendo, or Microsoft). Sony's decision to keep PlayStation 3 compatible with older video games allows any of the 70-million-plus PlayStation 2 customers who upgrade to PlayStation 3 to keep their favorite games instead of having to buy newer versions. This is a key benefit that Sony emphasizes when communicating the features, benefits, and uses of its PlayStation consoles. Moreover, it puts pressure on Microsoft and Nintendo to ensure that new versions of their game consoles can accept video games purchased for older versions. This adds another layer of complexity and expense to the product development process.

Sony continues to set the industry standard by developing innovative products that incorporate PlayStation technology. The PSX home entertainment center, for example, incorporates a television tuner, a DVD player and recorder, a digital video recorder and storage, a digital music player and storage, and a digital photo album. The company also has brought out a variety of accessories, including larger hard drives, network connectors, LCD monitors, and multimedia software. With tens of millions of customers around the world, the PlayStation brand is sure to play on and on.[32]

QUESTIONS FOR DISCUSSION

1. As a consumer product, how can PlayStation Portable be classified? Defend your classification.
2. Where in the life cycle is PlayStation Portable?
3. To which product adopter groups would Sony be most likely to promote PlayStation Portable? Why?

Developing and Managing Goods and Services

11

XM Satellite Radio Tunes in Extra-Special Features

The sky's the limit for XM Satellite Radio as it continues to tune into future profits by marketing an older product—radio—with a high-tech new twist. Traditionally, AM and FM radio stations have been free to all listeners, mainly because of commercial sponsorship. Now XM is offering, for a monthly fee, perfect 24-hour radio reception and a choice of more than 100 channels for customers' listening pleasure anywhere in the United States.

The company started on the road to static-free radio in 1997 by acquiring a license to broadcast digital radio. XM's management believed that commuters—and anyone traveling by car for long periods of time—would be interested in unique radio content and uninterrupted reception. In making satellite radio a reality, XM paid $1 billion for two satellite launches, satellite dishes to beam radio signals skyward, 800 antennas to bring signals to local listeners, and two studios to produce exclusive programming.

Another big challenge was developing the radio equipment for customers' cars. Since XM planned to encode its satellite signals to prevent noncustomers from listening to its channels, the radio had to be capable of receiving and decoding satellite signals yet compact enough to fit in a car. After building and testing prototypes, XM began manufacturing a suitcase-sized model for after-market installation. In time, the company signed with General Motors, Honda, Audi, Nissan, and several other big automakers to offer factory-installed XM radios as options in their new cars.

Prior to introduction, XM researched the target market's listening tastes. Based on this research, the company decided to devote most of its radio stations to specific types of music such as country, rap, jazz, blues, rock and roll, classic rock, international pop, instrumental classical music, and movie soundtracks. For more variety, it planned news-only, sports-only, talk-only, comedy-only, and children's stations among other special-interest stations.

OBJECTIVES

1 Understand how companies manage existing products through line extensions and product modifications.

2 Describe how businesses develop a product idea into a commercial product.

3 Know the importance of product differentiation and the elements that differentiate one product from another.

4 Explain product positioning and repositioning.

5 Understand how product deletion is used to improve product mixes.

6 Understand the characteristics of services and how these characteristics present challenges when developing marketing mixes for service products.

7 Be familiar with organizational structures used for managing products.

Today, XM has 3 million subscribers who pay $10 per month for its services, compared with the 1 million subscribers who pay $13 per month for competitor Sirius Satellite Radio's services. By 2010, the industry could be serving 30 million subscribers. XM's CEO expects to continue his company's market dominance by emphasizing program content. The company has signed an 11-year contract to broadcast Major League Baseball games and is investing more heavily in new music programming. "The technology is only the facilitator," he says. "Music connects so personally to people. We're putting the passion back into radio."[1] ◄

To compete effectively and achieve their goals, organizations like XM Satellite Radio must be able to adjust their product mixes in response to changes in customers' needs. A firm often has to introduce new products, modify existing products, or delete products that were successful perhaps only a few years ago. To provide products that satisfy target markets and achieve the organization's objectives, a marketer must develop, alter, and maintain an effective product mix. An organization's product mix may need several types of adjustments. Because customers' attitudes and product preferences change over time, their desire for certain products may wane.

In this chapter, we examine several ways to improve an organization's product mix. First, we discuss managing existing products through effective line extension and product modification. Next, we examine the stages of new-product development. Then we go on to discuss the ways companies differentiate their products in the marketplace and follow with a discussion of product positioning and repositioning. Next, we examine the importance of deleting weak products and the methods companies use to eliminate them. Then we explore the characteristics of services as products and how these services' characteristics affect the development of marketing mixes for services. Finally, we look at the organizational structures used to manage products.

Managing Existing Products

An organization can benefit by capitalizing on its existing products. By assessing the composition of the current product mix, a marketer can identify weaknesses and gaps. This analysis can then lead to improvement of the product mix through line extension and through product modification.

Line Extensions

line extension Development of a product that is closely related to existing products in the line but meets different customer needs

A **line extension** is the development of a product closely related to one or more products in the existing product line but designed specifically to meet somewhat different customer needs. Both Coca-Cola and Pepsi have created line extensions to their bottled water brands, Dasani and Aquafina. Both companies have launched berry and citrus flavored waters.[2]

Many of the so-called new products introduced each year are in fact line extensions. Line extensions are more common than new products because they are a less expensive, lower-risk alternative for increasing sales. A line extension may focus on a different market segment or may be an attempt to increase sales within the same market segment by more precisely satisfying the needs of people in that segment. Line extensions are also used to take market share from competitors. The bottled water category leader, Nestlé, is planning to release its own four-flavor line of water called

Pure Life Splash in direct response to Coca-Cola and Pepsi's latest line extensions.[3] However, one side effect of employing a line extension is that it may result in a less positive evaluation of the core product if customers are less satisfied with the line extension.

◉ Product Modifications

Product modification means changing one or more characteristics of a product. A product modification differs from a line extension because the original product does not remain in the line. For example, automakers use product modifications annually when they create new models of the same brand. Once the new models are introduced, the manufacturers stop producing last year's model. Like line extensions, product modifications entail less risk than developing new products.

Product modification can indeed improve a firm's product mix, but only under certain conditions. First, the product must be modifiable. Second, customers must be able to perceive that a modification has been made. Third, the modification should make the product more consistent with customers' desires so it provides greater satisfaction. There are three major ways to modify products: quality, functional, and aesthetic modifications.

product modification Change in one or more characteristics of a product

quality modifications Changes relating to a product's dependability and durability

● **Quality Modifications.** Quality modifications are changes relating to a product's dependability and durability. The changes usually are executed by altering the materials or the production process. For example, Energizer increased its product's durability by using better materials—a larger cathode and anode interface—that make batteries last longer.

Reducing a product's quality may allow an organization to lower its price and direct the item at a different target market. In contrast, increasing the quality of a product may give a firm an advantage over competing brands. Higher quality may enable a company to charge a higher price by creating customer loyalty and lowering customer sensitivity to price. However, higher quality may require the use of more expensive components and processes, thus forcing the organization to cut costs in other areas. Some firms, such as Caterpillar, are finding ways to increase quality while reducing costs.

functional modifications Changes affecting a product's versatility, effectiveness, convenience, or safety

● **Functional Modifications.** Changes that affect a product's versatility, effectiveness, convenience, or safety are called functional modifications; they usually require that the product be redesigned. Product categories that have undergone considerable

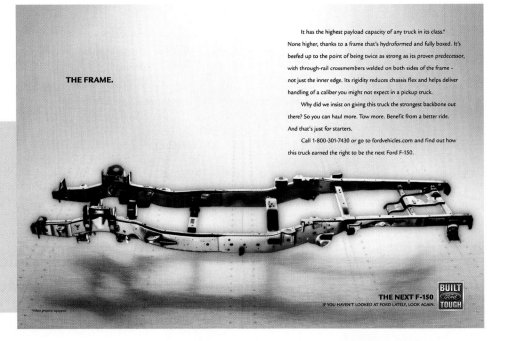

THE FRAME.

It has the highest payload capacity of any truck in its class.*
None higher, thanks to a frame that's hydroformed and fully boxed. It's
beefed up to the point of being twice as strong as its proven predecessor,
with through-rail crossmembers welded on both sides of the frame –
not just the inner edge. Its rigidity reduces chassis flex and helps deliver
handling of a caliber you might not expect in a pickup truck.

Why did we insist on giving this truck the strongest backbone out
there? So you can haul more. Tow more. Benefit from a better ride.
And that's just for starters.

Call 1-800-301-7430 or go to fordvehicles.com and find out how
this truck earned the right to be the next Ford F-150.

THE NEXT F-150
IF YOU HAVEN'T LOOKED AT FORD LATELY, LOOK AGAIN.

BUILT Ford TOUGH

Product Modifications
Automakers are major users of product modifications in order to manage their product mixes. In this advertisement, Ford is promoting a feature modification. With its new hydroformed frame, the F-150 has greater towing capacity and better handling.

functional modification include office and farm equipment, appliances, cleaning products, and consumer electronics. Functional modifications can make a product useful to more people and thus enlarge its market. They can place a product in a favorable competitive position by providing benefits that competing brands do not offer. They can also help an organization achieve and maintain a progressive image. Finally, functional modifications are sometimes made to reduce the possibility of product liability lawsuits.

aesthetic modifications
Changes to the sensory appeal of a product

● **Aesthetic Modifications.**   Aesthetic modifications change the sensory appeal of a product by altering its taste, texture, sound, smell, or appearance. A buyer making a purchase decision is swayed by how a product looks, smells, tastes, feels, or sounds. Procter & Gamble, for example, added a new Caribbean flavor to its Sunny Delight orange beverage product line. An aesthetic modification may strongly affect purchases. Automobile makers have relied on both quality and aesthetic modifications. For example, the Ford Mustang has been around in one form or another since April 1964. The latest model has a redesigned look that dates back to the Mustang's muscle car past. Also, it has several new safety features.[4]

Through aesthetic modifications, a firm can differentiate its product from competing brands and thus gain a sizable market share. The major drawback in using aesthetic modifications is that their value is determined subjectively. Although a firm may strive to improve the product's sensory appeal, customers may actually find the modified product less attractive.

Developing New Products

A firm develops new products as a means of enhancing its product mix. Developing and introducing new products is frequently expensive and risky. For example, Kellogg's management decided to discontinue Kellogg's Cereal Mates after two years of

MARKETING LEADERS

DEMETER MAKES SCENTS OF NEW PRODUCTS

Marketers at Demeter Fragrance Library, the originator of such fragrances as Dirt, Snow, Birthday Cake, and Sugar Cane, are always sniffing out ideas for new products. In an industry where well-known brands are supported by millions of dollars worth of packaging, sampling, and advertising, Demeter has made its name by concentrating on the development of offbeat scents. The company's goal is to boost sales beyond $50 million before the end of the decade by creating a series of new fragrances for the target segment of 15- to 30-year-olds.

Many of Demeter's ideas for new colognes, body lotions, and bath gels are sparked by aromas in the natural world. Some ideas are sparked by the smell of places such as New Zealand or of favorite foods such as apple pie. The most promising concepts eventually evolve into more than one product. "Our Wet Garden scent started out as a version of what became Greenhouse," explains fragrance maker and Demeter cofounder Christopher Gable. "It had the aroma of fresh green wetness, but not the humidity, so it became something else equally beautiful."

Customers sometimes provide inspiration for new scents, as well. Gable once asked a customer, "What aroma do you really want that you can't get?" When the customer responded, "It's the scent that comes when I first turn on my air conditioner in May," Gable recognized the aroma as mildew. The company proceeded to develop Mildew, which Gable says "is lovely and has quite a following."

Among Demeter's newest fragrances are scents that evoke a particular mood or experience. Its Natural Attraction Collection Cologne Sprays include Always Calm, Always Energetic, and Always Happy. Its Kahala fragrances, which include Guava Nectar and Hawaiian Surf, are intended to "deliver the Hawaiian context and concept in an authentic, original, and sophisticated way," says CEO Mark Crames.

Demeter now sells more than $10 million worth of fragrances yearly through Sephora, Liberty, and other retailers in the United States and Europe. If more people catch the scent of its new products, the company will stay on track toward its ambitious long-term sales goals.[a]

being in the marketplace. Cereal Mates, available in Corn Flakes, Fruit Loops, Mini Wheats, and Frosted Flakes, consisted of two components: cereal and aseptically packaged milk. The product failed because most U.S. consumers do not care for warm milk on cereal and therefore found the aseptically packaged milk unappealing; some customers viewed the product as slightly overpriced.[5] Although introducing new products is risky, failure to introduce new products is also risky. For example, the makers of Timex watches gained a large share of the U.S. watch market through effective marketing strategies during the 1960s and early 1970s. In the 1980s, Timex's market share slipped considerably, in part because Timex failed to introduce new products. In recent years, however, Timex has introduced new, technologically advanced products and has regained market share.

The term *new product* can have more than one meaning. A genuinely new product offers innovative benefits. But products that are different and distinctly better are often viewed as new. The following items are product innovations of the last 30 years: Post-it Notes, fax machines, cell phones, personal computers, PDAs, disposable razors, caller ID, and DVDs. A new product can be an innovative product that has

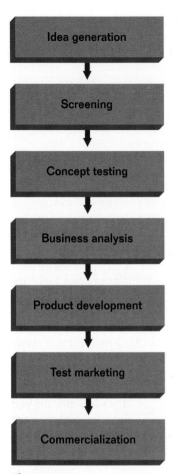

Figure 11.1
Phases of New-Product Development

new-product development process A seven-phase process for introducing products

idea generation Seeking product ideas to achieve objectives

never been sold by any organization, such as the digital camera when it was introduced for the first time. A radically new product involves a complex developmental process, including an extensive business analysis to determine the possibility of success.[6] A new product can also be one that a specific firm is currently launching even though other firms are already producing and marketing similar products. Finally, a product can be viewed as new when it is brought to one or more markets from another market. For example, making the Saturn VUE SUV available in Japan is viewed as a new-product introduction in Japan.

Before a product is introduced, it goes through the seven phases of the **new-product development process** shown in Figure 11.1: (1) idea generation, (2) screening, (3) concept testing, (4) business analysis, (5) product development, (6) test marketing, and (7) commercialization. A product may be dropped, and many are, at any stage of development. In this section, we look at the process through which products are developed, from idea inception to fully commercialized product.

◉ Idea Generation

Businesses and other organizations seek product ideas that will help them achieve their objectives. This activity is **idea generation**. The fact that only a few ideas are good enough to be commercially successful underscores the difficulty of the task. Although some organizations get their ideas almost by chance, firms that try to manage their product mixes effectively usually develop systematic approaches for generating new-product ideas. Indeed, there is a relationship between the amount of market information gathered and the number of ideas generated by work groups in organizations.[7] At the heart of innovation is a purposeful, focused effort to identify new ways to serve a market.

New-product ideas can come from several sources. They may come from internal sources—marketing managers, researchers, sales personnel, engineers, or other organizational personnel. Brainstorming and incentives or rewards for good ideas are typical intrafirm devices for stimulating development of ideas. For example, the idea for 3M Post-it Notes came from an employee. As a church choir member, he used slips of paper to mark songs in his hymnal. Because the pieces of paper fell out, he suggested developing an adhesive-backed note. New-product ideas may also arise from sources outside the firm, such as customers, competitors, advertising agencies, management consultants, and research organizations. For instance, Goodmark Foods and other companies have obtained new-product ideas from the U.S. Army, which researches technologies to solve problems such as how to feed soldiers in the field. After the army developed a way to keep bread fresh for three years, Goodmark worked with the researchers to create a line of bread-pocket sandwiches with a long shelf life.[8] Consultants are often used as sources for stimulating new-product ideas. The Eureka Ranch, also known as the "idea factory," charges clients as much as $150,000 for a three-day creativity session.[9] Developing new-product alliances with other firms has also been found to enhance the acquisition and utilization of information useful for creating new-product ideas.[10] A significant portion of this money is used to assess customers' needs. Asking customers what they want from products and organizations has helped many firms become successful and remain competitive.

◉ Screening

screening Choosing the most promising ideas for further review

In the process of **screening**, the ideas with the greatest potential are selected for further review. During screening, product ideas are analyzed to determine whether or not they match the organization's objectives and resources. If a product idea results in a product similar to the firm's existing products, marketers must assess the degree to which the new product could cannibalize the sales of current products. The company's overall abilities to produce and market the product are also analyzed. Other aspects of an idea to be weighed are the nature and wants of buyers and possible environmental changes. At times a checklist of new-product requirements is used when making screening decisions. This practice encourages evaluators to be systematic and thus reduces the chances of overlooking some pertinent fact. Compared with other phases, the largest number of new-product ideas are rejected during the screening phase.

◉ Concept Testing

concept testing Seeking potential buyers' responses to a product idea

To evaluate ideas properly, it may be necessary to test product concepts. In concept testing, a small sample of potential buyers is presented with a product idea through a written or oral description (and perhaps a few drawings) to determine their attitudes and initial buying intentions regarding the product. For a single product idea, an organization can test one or several concepts of the same product. Concept testing is a low-cost procedure that lets the organization determine customers' initial reactions to a product idea before it invests considerable resources in research and development. The results of concept testing can help product development personnel better understand which product attributes and benefits are most important to potential customers.

During concept testing, the concept is briefly described and then a series of questions is presented. The questions vary considerably depending on the type of product being tested. Typical questions are: In general, do you find this proposed product attractive? Which benefits are especially attractive to you? Which features are of little or no interest to you? Do you feel this proposed product would work better for you than the product you currently use? Compared with your current product, what are the primary advantages of the proposed product? If this product were available at an appropriate price, would you buy it? How often would you buy this product? How could this proposed product be improved?

◉ Business Analysis

business analysis Assessing the potential of a product idea for the firm's sales, costs, and profits

During the business analysis stage, the product idea is evaluated to determine its potential contribution to the firm's sales, costs, and profits. In the course of a business analysis, evaluators ask various questions: Does the product fit with the organization's existing product mix? Is demand strong enough to justify entering the market, and will the demand endure? What types of environmental and competitive changes can be expected, and how will these changes affect the product's future sales, costs, and profits? Are the organization's research, development, engineering, and production capabilities adequate to develop the product? If new facilities must be constructed, how quickly can they be built, and how much will they cost? Is the necessary financing for development and commercialization on hand or obtainable at terms consistent with a favorable return on investment?

In the business analysis stage, firms seek market information. The results of consumer polls, along with secondary data, supply the specifics needed to estimate potential sales, costs, and profits. For many products in this stage (when they are still just product ideas), forecasting sales accurately is difficult. This is especially true for innovative and completely new products. Organizations sometimes employ breakeven analysis to determine how many units they would have to sell to begin making a profit. At times an organization also uses payback analysis, in which marketers compute the time period required to recover the funds that would be invested in developing the new product. Because breakeven and payback analyses are based on estimates, they are usually viewed as useful but not particularly precise tools.

◉ Product Development

product development Determining if producing a product is feasible and cost effective

Product development is the phase in which the organization determines if it is technically feasible to produce the product and if it can be produced at costs low enough to make the final price reasonable. To test its acceptability, the idea or concept is converted into a prototype, or working model. The prototype should reveal tangible and intangible attributes associated with the product in consumers' minds. The product's design, mechanical features, and intangible aspects must be linked to wants in the marketplace. Through marketing research and concept testing, product attributes important to buyers are identified. These characteristics must be communicated to customers through the design of the product.

After a prototype is developed, its overall functioning must be tested. Its performance, safety, convenience, and other functional qualities are tested both in a laboratory and in the field. Functional testing should be rigorous and lengthy enough to test the product thoroughly.

A crucial question that arises during product development is how much quality to build into the product. For example, a major dimension of quality is durability. Higher quality often calls for better materials and more expensive processing, which increase production costs and, ultimately, the product's price. In determining the specific level of quality, a marketer must ascertain approximately what price the target market views as acceptable. In addition, a marketer usually tries to set a quality level consistent with that of the firm's other products. Obviously, the quality of competing brands is also a consideration.

The development phase of a new product is frequently lengthy and expensive; thus, a relatively small number of product ideas are put into development. If the product appears sufficiently successful during this stage to merit test marketing, then, during the latter part of the development stage, marketers begin to make decisions regarding branding, packaging, labeling, pricing, and promotion for use in the test marketing stage.

◉ Test Marketing

test marketing Introducing a product on a limited basis to measure the extent to which potential customers will actually buy it

A limited introduction of a product in geographic areas chosen to represent the intended market is called **test marketing**. Its aim is to determine the extent to which potential customers will buy the product. Test marketing is not an extension of the development stage; it is a sample launching of the entire marketing mix. Test marketing should be conducted only after the product has gone through development and initial plans regarding the other marketing mix variables have been made. Companies use test marketing to lessen the risk of product failure. The dangers of introducing an untested product include undercutting already profitable products and, should the new product fail, loss of credibility with distributors and customers.

Selection of appropriate test areas is very important because the validity of test market results depends heavily on selecting test sites that provide accurate representation of the intended target market. The top ten most often used U.S. test market cities appear in Table 11.1.

The criteria used for choosing test cities depend on the product's attributes, the target market's characteristics, and the firm's objectives and resources. Test marketing provides several benefits. It lets marketers expose a product in a natural marketing environment to measure its sales performance. While the product is being marketed

Table 11.1	
Top Ten U.S. Test Market Cities	
Rank	**City**
1	Albany, NY
2	Rochester, NY
3	Greensboro, NC
4	Birmingham, AL
5	Syracuse, NY
6	Charlotte, NC
7	Nashville, TN
8	Eugene, OR
9	Wichita, KS
10	Richmond, VA

Source: "Which American City Provides the Best Consumer Test Market?" *Business Wire,* May 24, 2004.

in a limited area, the company can strive to identify weaknesses in the product or in other parts of the marketing mix. A product weakness discovered after a nationwide introduction can be expensive to correct. If consumers' early reactions are negative, marketers may be unable to persuade consumers to try the product again. Thus, making adjustments after test marketing can be crucial to the success of a new product. On the other hand, testing results may be positive enough to accelerate the introduction of a new product. Test marketing also allows marketers to experiment with variations in advertising, pricing, and packaging in different test areas and to measure the extent of brand awareness, brand switching, and repeat purchases resulting from these alterations in the marketing mix.

Test marketing is not without risks. It is expensive, and competitors may try to interfere. A competitor may attempt to "jam" the test program by increasing its own advertising or promotions, lowering prices, and offering special incentives, all to combat the recognition and purchase of the new brand. Any such tactics can invalidate test results. Sometimes, too, competitors copy the product in the testing stage and rush to introduce a similar product. It is therefore desirable to move to the commercialization phase as soon as possible after successful testing. On the other hand, some firms have been known to promote new products heavily long before they are ready for the market to discourage competitors from developing similar new products.

Because of these risks, many companies use alternative methods to measure customer preferences. One such method is simulated test marketing. Typically consumers at shopping centers are asked to view an advertisement for a new product and are given a free sample to take home. These consumers are subsequently interviewed over the phone and asked to rate the product. The major advantages of simulated test marketing are greater speed, lower costs, and tighter security, which reduce the flow of information to competitors and reduce jamming. Gillette's Personal Care Division spends less than $200,000 for a simulated test that lasts three to five months. A live test market costs Gillette $2 million, counting promotion and distribution, and takes one to two years to complete. Several marketing research firms, such as ACNielsen Company, offer test marketing services to help provide independent assessment of proposed products.

Clearly not all products that are test marketed are launched. At times, problems discovered during test marketing cannot be resolved. Procter & Gamble, for example, test marketed a new plastic wrap product called Impress in Grand Junction, Colorado, but decided not to launch the brand nationally.[11]

◉ Commercialization

commercialization Deciding on full-scale manufacturing and marketing plans and preparing budgets

During the **commercialization** phase, plans for full-scale manufacturing and marketing must be refined and settled and budgets for the project prepared. Early in the commercialization phase, marketing management analyzes the results of test marketing to find out what changes in the marketing mix are needed before the product is introduced. The results of test marketing may tell marketers to change one or more of the product's physical attributes, modify the distribution plans to include more retail outlets, alter promotional efforts, or change the product's price. However, as more and more changes are made based on test marketing findings, the test marketing projections may become less valid.

During the early part of this stage, marketers must not only gear up for larger-scale production but also make decisions about warranties, repairs, and replacement parts. The type of warranty a firm provides can be a critical issue for buyers, especially when expensive, technically complex products are involved. Establishing an effective system for providing repair services and replacement parts is necessary to maintain favorable customer relationships. Although the producer may furnish these services directly to buyers, it is more common for the producer to provide such services through regional service centers. Regardless of how services are provided, it is important to customers that they be performed quickly and correctly.

The product enters the market during the commercialization phase. When introducing a product, a firm may spend enormous sums for advertising, personal selling, and other types of promotion, as well as for plant and equipment. Such expenditures may not be recovered for several years. Smaller organizations may find commercializing of a product especially difficult.

Products are not usually launched nationwide overnight but are introduced through a process called a *roll-out.* Through a roll-out, a product is introduced in stages, starting in one set of geographic areas and gradually expanding into adjacent areas. It may take several years to market the product nationally. Sometimes the test cities are used as initial marketing areas, and the introduction of the product becomes a natural extension of test marketing. A product test marketed in Albany, NY; Birmingham, AL; Eugene, OR; and Wichita, KS, as the map in Figure 11.2 shows, could be introduced first in those cities. After the stage 1 introduction is complete, stage 2 could include market coverage of the states where the test cities are located. In stage 3, marketing efforts might be extended into adjacent states. All remaining states would then be covered in stage 4. Gradual product introductions do not always occur state by state; other geographic combinations, such as groups of counties that cross state borders, are sometimes used. Products destined for multinational markets may also be rolled out one country or region at a time. Procter & Gamble test marketed its new Circ line of men's hair coloring products in several cities in the United Kingdom, gradually expanding the areas for the product's distribution.[12]

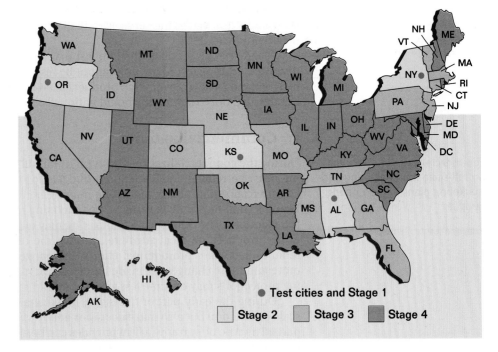

Figure 11.2
Stages of Expansion into a National Market During Commercialization

Gradual product introduction is desirable for several reasons. It reduces the risks of introducing a new product. If the product fails, the firm will experience smaller losses if it introduced the item in only a few geographic areas than if it marketed the product nationally. Furthermore, a company cannot introduce a product nationwide overnight because a system of wholesalers and retailers necessary to distribute the product cannot be established so quickly. The development of a distribution network may take considerable time. Also, the number of units needed to satisfy national demand for a successful product can be enormous, and a firm usually cannot produce the required quantities in a short time.

Despite the good reasons for introducing a product gradually, marketers realize this approach creates some competitive problems. A gradual introduction allows competitors to observe what the firm is doing and to monitor results, just as the firm's own marketers are doing. If competitors see that the newly introduced product is successful, they may quickly enter the same target market with similar products. In addition, as a product is introduced region by region, competitors may expand their marketing efforts to offset promotion of the new product.

Product Differentiation Through Quality, Design, and Support Services

product differentiation
Creating and designing products so that customers perceive them as different from competing products

Some of the most important characteristics of products are the elements that distinguish them from one another. **Product differentiation** is the process of creating and designing products so that customers perceive them as different from competing products. Customer perception is critical in differentiating products. Perceived differences might include quality, features, styling, price, or image. A crucial element used to differentiate one product from another is the brand. In this section, we examine three aspects of product differentiation that companies must consider when creating and offering products for sale: product quality, product design and features, and product support services. These aspects involve the company's attempt to create real differences among products. Later in this chapter, we discuss how companies position their products in the marketplace based on these three aspects.

quality The overall characteristics of a product that allow it to perform as expected in satisfying customer needs

Product Quality

Quality refers to the overall characteristics of a product that allow it to perform *as expected* in satisfying customer needs. The words *as expected* are very important to this definition because quality usually means different things to different customers. For some, durability signifies quality. For other customers, a product's ease of use may indicate quality.

OPEN OYSTER
Milk chocolate with hazelnut praliné

Differentiation Through Product Quality
The maker of Godiva Chocolates differentiates its product primarily based on quality.

-site

level of quality   The amount of quality a product possesses

consistency of quality   The degree to which a product has the same level of quality over time

product design   How a product is conceived, planned, and produced

styling   The physical appearance of a product

product features   Specific design characteristics that allow a product to perform certain tasks

The concept of quality also varies between consumer and business markets. According to one study, U.S. consumers consider high-quality products to have these characteristics (in order): reliability, durability, ease of maintenance, ease of use, a known and trusted brand name, and a reasonable price.[13] For business markets, technical suitability, ease of repair, and company reputation are important characteristics. Unlike consumers, most businesses place far less emphasis on price than on product quality.

One important dimension of quality is level of quality, the amount of quality a product possesses. The concept is a relative one because the quality level of one product is difficult to describe unless it is compared with that of other products. For example, most consumers would consider the quality level of Timex watches to be good, but when they compare Timex with Rolex, most consumers would say Rolex's level of quality is higher. How high should the level of quality be? It depends on the product and the costs and consequences of a product failure.

A second important dimension is consistency. Consistency of quality refers to the degree to which a product has the same level of quality over time. Consistency means giving customers the quality they expect every time they purchase the product. Like level of quality, consistency is a relative concept. It implies a quality comparison within the same brand over time. The quality level of McDonald's french fries is generally consistent from one location to another. The consistency of product quality can also be compared across competing products. At this stage, consistency becomes critical to a company's success. Companies that can provide quality on a consistent basis have a major competitive advantage over rivals.

Product Design and Features

Product design refers to how a product is conceived, planned, and produced. Design is a very complex topic because it involves the total sum of all the product's physical characteristics. Many companies are known for the outstanding designs of their products: Sony for personal electronics, Hewlett-Packard for laser printers, Levi Strauss for clothing, and JanSport for backpacks. Good design is one of the best competitive advantages any brand can possess.

One component of design is styling, or the physical appearance of the product. The style of a product is one design feature that can allow certain products to sell very rapidly. Good design, however, means more than just appearance; it also involves a product's functioning and usefulness. For example, a pair of jeans may look great, but if they fall apart after three washes, clearly the design was poor. Most consumers seek products that both look good and function well.

Product features are specific design characteristics that allow a product to perform certain tasks. By adding or subtracting features, a company can differentiate its products from those of the competition. Chrysler promotes its line of minivans as having more features related to passenger safety—dual air bags, steel-reinforced doors, and integrated child safety seats—than any other auto company. Product features can also be used to differentiate products within the same company. For example, Nike offers both a walking shoe and a run-walk shoe for specific consumer needs. In these cases, the company's products are sold with a wide range of features, from low-priced "base" or "stripped-down" versions to high-priced, prestigious "feature-packed" ones. The automotive industry regularly sells products with a wide range of features. In general, the more features a product has, the higher its price, and often, the higher the perceived quality. For a brand to have a sustainable competitive advantage, marketers must determine the product designs and features that customers desire. Information from marketing research efforts and from databases can help in assessing customers' product design and feature preferences. Being able to meet customers' desires for product design and features at prices they can afford is crucial to a product's long-term success.

◉ Product Support Services

customer services Human or mechanical efforts or activities that add value to a product

Many companies differentiate their product offerings by providing support services. Usually referred to as **customer services**, these services include any human or mechanical efforts or activities a company provides that add value to a product.[14] Examples of customer services include delivery and installation, financing arrangements, customer training, warranties and guarantees, repairs, layaway plans, convenient hours of operation, adequate parking, and information through toll-free numbers.

Whether as a major or minor part of the total product offering, all marketers of goods sell customer services. Providing good customer service may be the only way a company can differentiate its products when all products in a market have essentially the same quality, design, and features. This is especially true in the computer industry. When buying a laptop computer, for example, some customers are more concerned about fast delivery, technical support, warranties, and price than about product quality and design. Through research, a company can discover the types of services customers want and need. The level of customer service a company provides can profoundly affect customer satisfaction.

◉ Product Positioning and Repositioning

product positioning Creating and maintaining a certain concept of a product in customers' minds

Product positioning refers to the decisions and activities intended to create and maintain a certain concept of the firm's product (relative to competitive brands) in customers' minds. When marketers introduce a product, they try to position it so that it appears to have the characteristics that the target market most desires. This projected image is crucial. Crest is positioned as a fluoride toothpaste that fights cavities, and Close-Up is positioned as a whitening toothpaste that enhances the user's sex appeal.

◉ Perceptual Mapping

A product's position is the result of customers' perceptions of the product's attributes relative to those of competitive brands. Buyers make numerous purchase decisions on a regular basis. To avoid a continuous reevaluation of numerous products, buyers tend to group, or "position," products in their minds to simplify buying decisions. Rather than allowing customers to position products independently, marketers often try to influence and shape consumers' concepts or perceptions of products through advertising. Marketers sometimes analyze product positions by developing perceptual maps, as shown in Figure 11.3. Perceptual maps are created by questioning a sample of consumers about their perceptions of products, brands, and organizations with respect to two or more dimensions. To develop a perceptual map like the one in Figure 11.3, respondents would be asked how they perceive selected pain relievers in regard to price and type of pain for which the products are used. Also, respondents would be asked about their preferences for product features to establish "ideal points" or "ideal clusters," which represent a consensus about what a specific group of customers desires in terms of product features. Then marketers can compare how their brand is perceived compared with the ideal points.

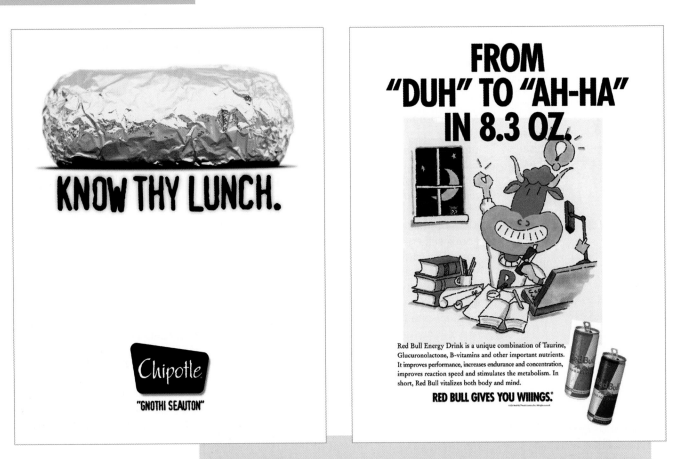

Product Positioning
Chipotle Mexican Grill positions its burritos as being large, custom made for the buyer, and a good value. Red Bull is positioned as the drink that improves performance, increases endurance, increases concentration, and improves reaction speed.

◉ Bases for Positioning

Marketers can use several bases for product positioning. A common basis for positioning products is to use competitors. A firm can position a product to compete head-on with another brand, as PepsiCo has done against Coca-Cola, or to avoid competition, as 7Up has done relative to other soft-drink producers. Head-to-head competition may be a marketer's positioning objective if the product's performance characteristics are at least equal to those of competitive brands and if the product is priced lower. Head-to-head positioning may be appropriate even when the price is higher if the product's performance characteristics are superior. For example, the no-calorie sweetener Splenda is positioned as a healthier sugar substitute through its campaign slogan "Made from sugar so it tastes like sugar." Splenda also competes head-to-head through advertisements that indicate how it is unlike other no-calorie sweeteners because it is heat tolerant and can be used in baking as a cup-for-cup sugar substitute.[15] Conversely, positioning to avoid competition may be best when the product's performance characteristics do not differ significantly from competing brands. Moreover, positioning a brand to avoid competition may be appropriate

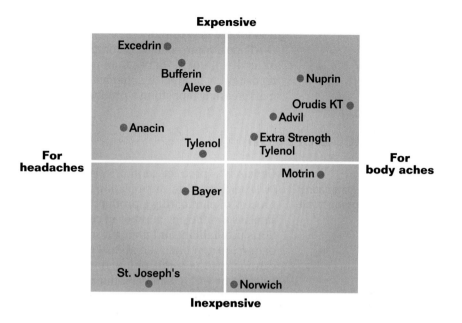

Figure 11.3
Hypothetical Perceptual Map for Pain Relievers

when that brand has unique characteristics that are important to some buyers. Volvo, for example, has for years positioned itself away from competitors by focusing on the safety characteristics of its cars. Whereas some auto companies mention safety issues in their advertisements, many are more likely to focus on style, fuel efficiency, performance, or terms of sale. Avoiding competition is critical when a firm introduces a brand into a market in which the company already has one or more brands. Marketers usually want to avoid cannibalizing sales of their existing brands, unless the new brand generates substantially larger profits.

A product's position can be based on specific product attributes or features. For example, the Apple iPod is positioned based on product attributes such as its unique shape, its storage capacity (stores thousands of tunes), and its access to iTunes. If a product has been planned properly, its features will give it the distinct appeal needed. Style, shape, construction, and color help create the image and the appeal. If buyers can easily identify the benefits, they are, of course, more likely to purchase the product. When the new product does not offer certain preferred attributes, there is room for another new product.

Other bases for product positioning include price, quality level, and benefits provided by the product. For example, Era laundry detergent provides stain treatment and stain removal. Also, the target market can be a positioning basis caused by marketing. This type of positioning relies heavily on promoting the types of people who use the product.

◉ Repositioning

Positioning decisions are not just for new products. Evaluating the positions of existing products is important because a brand's market share and profitability may be strengthened by product repositioning. For example, several years ago Kraft was on the verge of discontinuing Cheez Whiz because its sales had declined considerably. After Kraft marketers repositioned Cheez Whiz as a fast, convenient, microwavable cheese sauce, its sales rebounded to new heights. When introducing a new product into a product line, one or more existing brands may have to be repositioned to minimize cannibalization of established brands and thus ensure a favorable position for the new brand.

Repositioning can be accomplished by physically changing the product, its price, or its distribution. Rather than making any of these changes, marketers sometimes reposition a product by changing its image through promotional efforts. Finally a marketer may reposition a product by aiming it at a different target market.

Product Deletion

product deletion Eliminating a product from the product mix

Generally a product cannot satisfy target market customers and contribute to the achievement of an organization's overall goals indefinitely. **Product deletion** is the process of eliminating a product from the product mix, usually because it no longer satisfies a sufficient number of customers. A declining product reduces an organization's profitability and drains resources that could be used to modify other products or develop new ones. A marginal product may require shorter production runs, which can increase per-unit production costs. Finally, when a dying product completely loses favor with customers, the negative feelings may transfer to some of the company's other products.

Most organizations find it difficult to delete a product. A decision to drop a product may be opposed by managers and other employees who believe the product is necessary to the product mix. Salespeople who still have some loyal customers are especially upset when a product is dropped. For example, General Motors has had to endure many lawsuits and complaints from dealers, employees, and customers since it announced plans to phase out Oldsmobile, the nation's oldest automobile brand.[16] Considerable resources and effort are sometimes spent trying to change a slipping product's marketing mix to improve its sales and thus avoid having to eliminate it.

Some organizations delete products only after the products have become heavy financial burdens. A better approach is some form of systematic review in which each product is evaluated periodically to determine its impact on the overall effectiveness of the firm's product mix. Such a review should analyze the product's contribution to the firm's sales for a given period, as well as estimate future sales, costs, and profits associated with the product. It should also gauge the value of making changes in the marketing strategy to improve the product's performance. A systematic review allows an organization to improve product performance and ascertain when to delete products. Procter & Gamble, for example, discontinued its White Cloud brand of toilet tissue in the early 1990s after determining the product did not match customer needs. However, after Wal-Mart acquired the rights to the name, White Cloud was repositioned as a premium private label brand and expanded to include laundry detergent, fabric softener, and dryer sheets. Ironically, these products now compete head to head with Procter & Gamble's Tide laundry detergent and Downy fabric softener in Wal-Mart stores.[17]

There are three basic ways to delete a product: phase it out, run it out, or drop it immediately (see Figure 11.4). A *phase-out* allows the product to decline without a change in the marketing strategy; no attempt is made to give the product new life. A *run-out* exploits any strengths left in the product. Intensifying marketing efforts in core markets or eliminating some marketing expenditures, such as advertising, may cause a sudden jump in profits. This approach is commonly taken for technologically obsolete products, such as older models of computers and calculators. Often the price is reduced to get a sales spurt. The third alternative, an *immediate drop* of an unprofitable product, is the best strategy when losses are too great to prolong the product's life.

CUSTOMER RELATIONSHIP MANAGEMENT
GENERAL MOTORS TAKES SLOW-SELLING PRODUCTS OFF THE ROAD

No more Oldsmobile, Pontiac Grand Am, Pontiac Aztek, Chevrolet Cavalier, Cadillac Catera, or Cadillac Eldorado vehicles will ever roll out of General Motors' factories. Deleting one car is a momentous decision. Yet GM has deleted six in the past few years and could delete others as it systematically reassesses each product in its mix. What do these deletions mean for GM, its customers, and its dealers?

GM's overall market share has been only slightly affected by the deletions. By its final year of production, Oldsmobile's share was below 1 percent. The Catera's sales were so disappointing that GM deleted it just six years after introduction. The once-popular Grand Am was replaced by the Pontiac G6. Sales of the Cavalier spiked after GM announced that it would be replaced by the Cobalt, but the deletion decision stood. The Aztek never lived up to sales expectations and was deleted in less than five years, to be replaced by the Torrent.

The Oldsmobile deletion was a run-out supported by direct-mail advertising, price incentives, and other marketing activities. Still, GM was concerned about whether customers would buy the car in its final months on the market. To encourage purchasing, the company promised to honor all Oldsmobile warranties and to offer parts and service for seven more years. Nonetheless, as the deletion date approached, fewer dealers carried the cars and some Oldsmobile dealers went out of business.

GM also launched an aggressive retention campaign to counter the efforts of competitors that began approaching Oldsmobile customers. One mailing thanked Oldsmobile customers for their loyalty and promoted other GM cars. A later mailing highlighted the specific features and benefits of GM's Buicks. Where Oldsmobile dealers had closed, GM dealers contacted Oldsmobile owners to offer other GM cars.

Pontiac's product director notes that the deleted Aztek did support customer relationships. "It brought us some conquest buyers and had a cult following, though not enough of a following to continue it," he says. Now GM is monitoring market share and customer retention to see how the six deletions are affecting its progress on the road toward higher revenues and profits.[b]

Figure 11.4
Product Deletion Process

Source: Martin L. Bell, *Marketing: Concepts and Strategy,* 3rd ed., p. 267; copyright 1979, Houghton Mifflin Company; used by permission of Marcellette Bell Chapman.

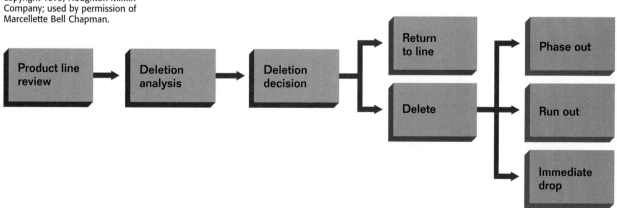

Managing Services as Products

Many products are services rather than tangible goods. The organizations that market service products include for-profit firms, such as those offering financial, personal, and professional services, and nonprofit organizations, such as educational institutions, churches, charities, and governments. In this section, we focus initially on the growing importance of service industries in our economy. Then we address the unique characteristics of services. Finally, we deal with the challenges these characteristics pose in developing and managing marketing mixes for services.

Nature and Importance of Services

service An intangible product involving a deed, performance, or effort that cannot be physically possessed

All products, whether goods, services, or ideas, are to some extent intangible. A **service** is an intangible product involving a deed, a performance, or an effort that cannot be physically possessed.[18] Services are usually provided through the application of human and/or mechanical efforts directed at people or objects. For example, a service like education involves the efforts of service providers (teachers) directed at people (students), whereas janitorial and interior decorating services direct their efforts at objects. Services can also involve the use of mechanical efforts directed at people (air transportation) or objects (freight transportation). A wide variety of services, such as health care and landscaping, involve both human and mechanical efforts. Although many services entail the use of tangibles like tools and machinery, the primary difference between a service and a good is that a service is dominated by the intangible portion of the total product. Services, as products, should not be confused with the related topic of customer services. While customer service is part of the marketing of goods, service marketers also provide customer services.

The increasing importance of services in the U.S. economy has led many people to call the United States the world's first service economy. Service industries account for about 80 percent of the country's gross domestic product (GDP). More than one-half of new businesses are service businesses, and service employment is expected to continue to grow. These industries have absorbed much of the influx of women and minorities into the work force.

Characteristics of Services

The issues associated with marketing service products are not exactly the same as those associated with marketing goods. To understand these differences, it is first necessary to understand the distinguishing characteristics of services. Services have six basic characteristics: intangibility, inseparability of production and consumption, perishability, heterogeneity, client-based relationships, and customer contact.[19]

intangibility A service that is not physical and cannot be touched

● **Intangibility.** As already noted, the major characteristic that distinguishes a service from a good is intangibility. **Intangibility** means a service is not physical and therefore cannot be touched. For example, it is impossible to touch the education that students derive from attending classes; the intangible benefit is becoming more knowledgeable. In addition, services cannot be physically possessed. Products range from pure goods (tangible) to pure services (intangible). Pure goods, if they exist at all, are rare since practically all marketers of goods also provide customer services. Intangible, service-dominant products like education or health care are clearly service products. Of course, some products, like a restaurant meal or a hotel stay, have both tangible and intangible dimensions.

WELCOME TO THE EYE OF THE HURRICANE.

The Grand Spa. Massage therapies. Aroma therapies. Facials. Wraps. Intensely therapeutic. Utterly decompressing. Some needed tranquility deep within a place that's anything but maximumVegas. MGM GRAND

mgmgrand.com 1-800-929-1111

Inseparability of Production and Consumption
The production and consumption of hotel-related services, such as those provided by the MGM Grand Hotel & Casino, are inseparable. Both production and consumption occur simultaneously.

● **Inseparability of Production and Consumption.** Another important characteristic of services that creates challenges for marketers is inseparability, which refers to the fact that the production of a service cannot be separated from its consumption by customers. For example, air passenger service is produced and consumed simultaneously. In other words, services are often produced, sold, and consumed at the same time. In goods marketing, a customer can purchase a good, take it home, and store it until ready to use it. The manufacturer of the good may never see an actual customer. Customers, however, often must be present at the production of a service (such as marriage counseling or surgery) and cannot take the service home. For instance, customers who use coin-counting machines in their local supermarkets must pour in their coins and then wait until all the change is tallied.

inseparability Being produced and consumed at the same time

perishability The inability of unused service capacity to be stored for future use

● **Perishability.** Services are characterized by perishability because the unused service capacity of one time period cannot be stored for future use. For example, empty seats on an air flight today cannot be stored and sold to passengers at a later date. Other examples of service perishability include unsold basketball tickets, unscheduled dentists' appointment times, and empty hotel rooms. Although some goods, such as meat, milk, and produce, are perishable, goods generally are less perishable than services. If a pair of jeans has been sitting on a department store shelf for a week, someone can still buy them the next day. Goods marketers can handle the supply-demand problem through production scheduling and inventory techniques. Service marketers do not have the same advantage, and they face several hurdles in trying to balance supply and demand. They can, however, plan for demand that fluctuates according to day of the week, time of day, or season.

heterogeneity Variation in quality

● **Heterogeneity.** Services delivered by people are susceptible to heterogeneity, or variation in quality. Quality of manufactured goods is easier to control with standardized procedures, and mistakes are easier to isolate and correct. Because of the nature of human behavior, however, it is very difficult for service providers to maintain a consistent quality of service delivery. This variation in quality can occur from one organization to another, from one service person to another within the same service facility, and from one service facility to another within the same organization. For example, the retail clerks in one bookstore may be more knowledgeable and therefore more helpful than those in another bookstore owned by the same chain. Heterogeneity usually increases as the degree of labor intensiveness increases. Many services, such as auto repair, education, and hairstyling, rely heavily on human labor. Other services,

Perishability
The inventories of service providers, such as JetBlue, are time sensitive and cannot be stored for later use. Unsold seats on a flight perish and have no value once the boarding for a specific flight is closed.

such as telecommunications, health clubs, and public transportation, are more equipment intensive. People-based services are often prone to fluctuations in quality from one time period to the next. For example, the fact that a hairstylist gives a customer a good haircut today does not guarantee that customer a haircut of equal quality from the same hairstylist at a later date. Equipment-based services, in contrast, suffer from this problem to a lesser degree than people-based services. For instance, automated teller machines have reduced inconsistency in the quality of teller services at banks, and bar-code scanning has improved the accuracy of service at the checkout counters in grocery stores.

● **Client-Based Relationships.**   The success of many services depends on creating and maintaining **client-based relationships**, interactions with customers that result in satisfied customers who use a service repeatedly over time.[20] In fact, some service providers, such as lawyers, accountants, and financial advisers, call their customers *clients* and often develop and maintain close, long-term relationships with them. For such service providers, it is not enough to attract customers. They are successful only to the degree to which they can maintain a group of clients who use their services on an ongoing basis. For example, an accountant may serve a family in his or her area for decades. If the members of this family like the quality of the accountant's services, they are likely to recommend the accountant to other families. If several families repeat this positive word-of-mouth communication, the accountant will likely acquire a long list of satisfied clients. This process is the key to creating and maintaining client-based relationships. To ensure that it actually occurs, the service provider must take steps to build trust, demonstrate customer commitment, and satisfy customers so well that they become very loyal to the provider and unlikely to switch to competitors.

client-based relationships
Interactions that result in satisfied customers who use a service repeatedly over time

WE TURNED

A CHILD WHO

COULDN'T HEAR INTO

A TYPICAL 2 YEAR

OLD WHO DOESN'T

LISTEN.

Level of Customer Contact
The services provided by hospitals require a considerable amount of customer contact.

customer contact The level of interaction between provider and customer needed to deliver the service

● **Customer Contact.**   Not all services require a high degree of customer contact, but many do. Customer contact refers to the level of interaction between the service provider and the customer that is necessary to deliver the service. High-contact services include health-care, real estate, legal, and hair-care services. Examples of low-contact services are tax preparation, auto repair, and dry cleaning. Note that high-contact services generally involve actions directed toward people, who must be present during production. A hairstylist's customer, for example, must be present during the styling process. When the customer must be present, the process of production may be just as important as its final outcome. Although it is sometimes possible for the service provider to go to the customer, high-contact services typically require that the customer go to the production facility.

Employees of high-contact service providers are part of a very important ingredient in creating satisfied customers. A fundamental precept of customer contact is that satisfied employees lead to satisfied customers. In fact, research indicates that employee satisfaction is the single most important factor in providing high service quality. Thus, to minimize the problems that customer contact can create, service organizations must take steps to understand and meet the needs of employees by adequately training them, empowering them to make more decisions, and rewarding them for customer-oriented behavior.[21] To provide the quality of customer service that has made it the fastest-growing coffee retailer in the world, Starbucks provides extensive employee training. Employees receive about 25 hours of initial training, which includes memorizing recipes and learning the differences among a variety of coffees, proper coffee making techniques, and many other skills that stress Starbucks's dedication to customer service.[22]

◉ Creating Marketing Mixes for Services

The characteristics of services create a number of challenges for service marketers (see Table 11.2). These challenges are especially evident in the development and management of marketing mixes for services. Although such mixes contain the four major marketing mix variables—product, price, distribution, and promotion—the characteristics of services require that marketers consider additional issues.

● **Development of Services.**   A service offered by an organization generally is a package, or bundle, of services consisting of a core service and one or more supplementary services. A core service is the basic service experience or commodity that a customer expects to receive. A supplementary service is a supportive one related to the core service and is used to differentiate the service bundle from that of competitors. For example, Hampton Inns provides a room as a core service. Bundled with the room are supplementary services such as free local phone calls, cable television, and a complimentary continental breakfast.

As discussed earlier, heterogeneity results in variability in service quality and makes it difficult to standardize services. However, heterogeneity provides one advantage to service marketers: it allows them to customize their services to match the

Table 11.2   Service Characteristics and Marketing Challenges

Service Characteristics	Resulting Marketing Challenges
Intangibility	Difficult for customer to evaluate Customer does not take physical possession Difficult to advertise and display Difficult to set and justify prices Service process usually not protectable by patents
Inseparability of production and consumption	Service provider cannot mass-produce services Customer must participate in production Other consumers affect service outcomes Services are difficult to distribute
Perishability	Services cannot be stored Balancing supply and demand is very difficult Unused capacity is lost forever Demand may be very time sensitive
Heterogeneity	Service quality is difficult to control Service delivery is difficult to standardize
Client-based relationships	Success depends on satisfying and keeping customers over the long term Generating repeat business is challenging Relationship marketing becomes critical
Customer contact	Service providers are critical to delivery Requires high levels of service employee training and motivation Changing a high-contact service into a low-contact service to achieve lower costs without reducing customer satisfaction

Sources: K. Douglas Hoffman and John E. G. Bateson, *Essentials of Services Marketing* (Mason, OH: Southwestern, 2001); Valarie A. Zeithaml, A. Parasuraman, and Leonard L. Berry, *Delivering Quality Service: Balancing Customer Perceptions and Expectations* (New York: Free Press, 1990); Leonard L. Berry and A. Parasuraman, *Marketing Services: Competing through Quality* (New York: Free Press, 1991), p. 5.

specific needs of individual customers. Health care is an example of an extremely customized service; the services provided differ from one patient to the next. Such customized services can be expensive for both provider and customer, and some service marketers therefore face a dilemma: how to provide service at an acceptable level of quality in an efficient and economic manner and still satisfy individual customer needs. To cope with this problem, some service marketers offer standardized packages. For example, a lawyer may offer a divorce package at a specified price for an uncontested divorce. When service bundles are standardized, the specific actions and activities of the service provider usually are highly specified. Automobile quick-lube providers frequently offer a service bundle for a single price; the specific actions to be taken are quite detailed about what will be done to a customer's car. Various other equipment-based services are also often standardized into packages. For instance, cable television providers frequently offer several packages, such as "Basic," "Standard," "Premier," and "Hollywood."

The characteristic of intangibility makes it difficult for customers to evaluate a service prior to purchase. Intangibility requires service marketers, like hairstylists, to market promises to customers. The customer is forced to place some degree of trust in the service provider to perform the service in a manner that meets or exceeds these promises. Service marketers must guard against making promises that raise customer expectations beyond what they can provide. To cope with the problem of intangibility, marketers employ tangible cues, such as well-groomed, professional-appearing contact personnel and clean, attractive physical facilities, to help assure customers about the quality of the service. Life insurance companies sometimes try to make the quality of their policies more tangible by putting them on very-high-quality paper and enclosing them in leather sheaths.

The inseparability of production and consumption and the level of customer contact also influence the development and management of services. The fact that customers are present during the production of a service means other customers can affect the outcome of the service. For instance, if a nonsmoker dines in a restaurant without a no-smoking section, the overall quality of service experienced by the non-smoking customer declines. Service marketers can reduce these problems by encouraging customers to share the responsibility of maintaining an environment that allows all participants to receive the intended benefits of the service.

● **Pricing of Services.**   Prices for services can be established on several different bases. The prices of pest control services, dry cleaning, carpet cleaning, and a physician's consultation are usually based on the performance of specific tasks. Other service prices are based on time. For example, attorneys, consultants, counselors, piano teachers, and plumbers often charge by the hour or day.

Some services use demand-based pricing. When demand for a service is high, the price is also high; when demand for a service is low, so is the price. The perishability of services means that when demand is low, the unused capacity cannot be stored and is therefore lost forever. Every empty seat on an airline flight or in a movie theater represents lost revenue. Some services are very time sensitive because a significant number of customers desire the service at a particular time. This point in time is called *peak demand*. A provider of time-sensitive services brings in most of its revenue during peak demand. For an airline, peak demand is usually early and late in the day. Providers of time-sensitive services often use demand-based pricing to manage the problem of balancing supply and demand. They charge top prices during peak demand and lower prices during off-peak demand to encourage more customers to use the service. This is why the price of a matinee movie is often half the price of the same movie shown at night.

When services are offered to customers in a bundle, marketers must decide whether to offer the services at one price, price them separately, or use a combination of the two methods. For example, some hotels offer a package of services at one price, while others charge separately for the room, phone service, and breakfast. Some service providers offer a one-price option for a specific bundle of services and make add-on bundles available at additional charges. For example, telephone services, such as call waiting and caller ID, are frequently bundled and sold as a package for one price.

Because of the intangible nature of services, customers rely heavily at times on price as an indicator of quality. If customers perceive the available services in a service category as being similar in quality, and if the quality of such services is difficult to judge even after these services are purchased, customers may seek out the lowest-priced provider. For example, many customers seek auto insurance providers with the lowest rates. If the quality of different service providers is likely to vary, customers may rely heavily on the price-quality association. For example, if you have to have an appendectomy, will you choose the surgeon who charges an average price of $1,500 or the surgeon who will take your appendix out for $399?

● **Distribution of Services.** Marketers deliver services in various ways. In some instances, customers go to a service provider's facility. For example, most health-care, dry cleaning, hair-care, and tanning services are delivered at service providers' facilities. Some services are provided at the customer's home or business. Lawn care, air conditioning and heating repair, and carpet cleaning are examples. Some services are delivered primarily at "arm's length," meaning no face-to-face contact occurs between the customer and the service provider. Several equipment-based services are delivered at arm's length, including electric, online, cable television, and telephone services. Providing high-quality customer service at arm's length can be costly but essential in keeping customers satisfied and maintaining market share. For example, many airlines, although trying to cut costs, are also increasing spending on refurbishing their websites to better serve customers. Companies such as United and American Airlines are working on user-friendly websites as a way to draw customers to their online services rather than going through an online travel agent like Orbitz or Travelocity.[23]

Marketing channels for services are usually short and direct, meaning that the producer delivers the service directly to the end user. Some services, however, use intermediaries. For example, travel agents facilitate the delivery of airline services, independent insurance agents participate in the marketing of various insurance policies, and financial planners market investment services.

Service marketers are less concerned with warehousing and transportation than are goods marketers. They are very concerned, however, about inventory management, especially balancing supply and demand for services. The service characteristics of inseparability and level of customer contact contribute to the challenges of demand management. In some instances, service marketers use appointments and reservations as approaches for scheduling the delivery of services. Health-care providers, attorneys, accountants, auto mechanics, and restaurants often use reservations or appointments to plan and pace the delivery of their services. To increase the supply of a service, marketers use multiple service sites and also increase the number of contact service providers at each site. National and regional eye-care and hair-care services are examples.

To make delivery more accessible to customers, and to increase the supply of a service, as well as reduce labor costs, some service providers have decreased the use of contact personnel and replaced them with equipment. In other words, they have changed a high-contact service into a low-contact one. The banking industry is an example. By installing ATMs, banks have increased production capacity and reduced customer contact. In addition, numerous automated banking services are now available by telephone 24 hours a day. Such services have helped lower costs by reducing the need for customer service representatives. Changing the delivery of services from human to equipment has created some problems, however.

MARKETING ENTREPRENEURS

Ercan Tutal

HIS BUSINESS: The Alternative Camp for Disabled Individuals

SUCCESS: Organization has served over 200,000 people

Located in Turkey, the Alternative Camp is a nonprofit organization that provides the disabled with an opportunity to participate in underwater sports such as diving. Tutal's organization has served over 200,000 people and is funded entirely from the donations of generous businesses. So successful is his organization that the World Young Business Association bestowed on him the Social Responsibility Award, and recently he was chosen to take part in the Olympic ceremonies as a torch bearer.[c]

● **Promotion of Services.**   The intangibility of services results in several promotion-related challenges to service marketers. Since it may not be possible to depict the actual performance of a service in an advertisement or to display it in a store, explaining a service to customers can be a difficult task. Promotion of services typically includes tangible cues that symbolize the service. For example, Trans America uses its pyramid-shaped building to symbolize strength, security, and reliability, important features associated with insurance and other financial services. Similarly, the hands Allstate uses in its ads symbolize personalized service and trustworthy, caring representatives. Although these symbols have nothing to do with the actual services, they make it much easier for customers to understand the intangible attributes associated with insurance services. To make a service more tangible, advertisements for services often show pictures of facilities, equipment, and service personnel.

Compared with goods marketers, service providers are more likely to promote price, guarantees, performance documentation, availability, and training and certification of contact personnel. The International Smart Tan Network, a trade association for indoor tanning salons, offers a certification course in professional standards for tanning facility operators. The association encourages salons to promote their "Smart Tan Certification" in advertising and throughout the salon as a measure of quality training.[24] When preparing advertisements, service marketers are careful to use concrete, specific language to help make services more tangible in the minds of customers. They are also careful not to promise too much regarding their services so that customer expectations do not rise to unattainable levels.

Through their actions, service contact personnel can be directly or indirectly involved in the personal selling of services. Personal selling is often important because personal influence can help the customer visualize the benefits of a given service.

Because of the heterogeneity and intangibility of services, word-of-mouth communication is important in service promotion. What other people say about a service provider can have a tremendous impact on whether an individual decides to use that provider. Some service marketers attempt to stimulate positive word-of-mouth communication by asking satisfied customers to tell their friends and associates about the service and may even provide incentives for doing so.

Organizing to Develop and Manage Products

After reviewing the concepts of product line and mix, life cycles, positioning, and repositioning, it should be obvious that managing products is a complex task. Often the traditional functional form of organization, in which managers specialize in business functions such as advertising, sales, and distribution, does not fit a company's needs. In this case, management must find an organizational approach that accomplishes the tasks necessary to develop and manage products. Alternatives to functional organization include the product or brand manager approach, the market manager approach, and the venture team approach.

A **product manager** is responsible for a product, a product line, or several distinct products that make up an interrelated group within a multiproduct organization. A **brand manager** is responsible for a single brand. General Foods, for example, has one brand manager for Maxim coffee and one for Maxwell House coffee. A product or brand manager operates cross-functionally to coordinate the activities, information, and strategies involved in marketing an assigned product. Product managers and brand managers plan marketing activities to achieve objectives by coordinating a mix

product manager   The person within an organization responsible for a product, a product line, or several distinct products that make up a group

brand manager   The person responsible for a single brand

of distribution, promotion (especially sales promotion and advertising), and price. They must consider packaging and branding decisions and work closely with personnel in research and development, engineering, and production. Marketing research helps product managers understand consumers and find target markets. The product or brand manager approach to organization is used by many large, multiple-product companies. General Motors, for example, is now supporting new vehicle introductions by assigning brand managers who previously worked on successful launches: "We've got some people who are good at launches, and we'll move them where the launches are going on for some additional expertise," says a GM executive.[25]

market manager The person responsible for managing the marketing activities that serve a particular group of customers

A **market manager** is responsible for managing the marketing activities that serve a particular group of customers. This organizational approach is particularly effective when a firm engages in different types of marketing activities to provide products to diverse customer groups. A company might have one market manager for business markets and another for consumer markets. These broad market categories might be broken down into more limited market responsibilities.

venture team A cross-functional group that creates entirely new products that may be aimed at new markets

A **venture team** creates entirely new products that may be aimed at new markets. Unlike a product or market manager, a venture team is responsible for all aspects of developing a product: research and development, production and engineering, finance and accounting, and marketing. Venture team members are brought together from different functional areas of the organization. In working outside established divisions, venture teams have greater flexibility to apply inventive approaches to develop new products that can take advantage of opportunities in highly segmented markets. Companies are increasingly using such cross-functional teams for product development in an effort to boost product quality. Quality may be positively related to information integration within the team, customers' influence on the product development process, and a quality orientation within the firm.[26] When a new product has demonstrated commercial potential, team members may return to their functional areas, or they may join a new or existing division to manage the product.

CHAPTER REVIEW

1 Understand how companies manage existing products through line extensions and product modifications.

Organizations must be able to adjust their product mixes to compete effectively and achieve their goals. Using existing products, a product mix can be improved through line extension and through product modification. A line extension is the development of a product closely related to one or more products in the existing line but designed specifically to meet different customer needs. Product modification is the changing of one or more characteristics of a product. This approach can be achieved through quality mod-

ifications, functional modifications, and aesthetic modifications.

2 Describe how businesses develop a product idea into a commercial product.

Before a product is introduced, it goes through a seven-phase new-product development process. In the idea generation phase, new-product ideas may come from internal or external sources. In the process of screening, ideas are evaluated to determine whether they are consistent with the firm's overall objectives and resources. Concept testing, the third phase, involves having a small sample of potential customers review a brief description of the product idea to determine their initial perceptions of the proposed product and their early buying intentions. During the business analysis stage, the product idea is evaluated to determine its potential contribution to the firm's sales, costs, and profits. In the product development stage, the organization determines if it is technically feasible to produce the product and if it can be produced at a cost low enough to make the final price reasonable. Test marketing is a limited introduction of a product in areas chosen to represent the intended market. Finally, in the commercialization phase, full-scale production of the product begins and a complete marketing strategy is developed.

③ Know the importance of product differentiation and the elements that differentiate one product from another.

Product differentiation is the process of creating and designing products so that customers perceive them as different from competing products. Product quality, product design and features, and product support services are three dimensions of product differentiation that companies consider when creating and marketing products.

④ Explain product positioning and repositioning.

Product positioning refers to the decisions and activities that create and maintain a certain concept of the firm's product in the customer's mind. Organizations can position a product to compete head to head with another brand if the product's performance is at least equal to the competitive brand's and if the product is priced lower. When a brand possesses unique characteristics that are important to some buyers, positioning it to avoid competition is appropriate. Companies also increase an existing brand's market share and profitability through product repositioning.

⑤ Understand how product deletion is used to improve product mixes.

Product deletion is the process of eliminating a product that no longer satisfies a sufficient number of customers. Although a firm's personnel may oppose product deletion, weak products are unprofitable, consume too much time and effort, may require shorter production runs, and can create an unfavorable impression of the firm's other products. A prod-

uct mix should be systematically reviewed to determine when to delete products. Products to be deleted can be phased out, run out, or dropped immediately.

⑥ Understand the characteristics of services and how these characteristics present challenges when developing marketing mixes for service products.

Services are intangible products involving deeds, performances, or efforts that cannot be physically possessed. They have six fundamental characteristics: intangibility, inseparability of production and consumption, perishability, heterogeneity, client-based relationships, and customer contact. Intangibility means that a service cannot be seen, touched, tasted, or smelled. Inseparability refers to the fact that the production of a service cannot be separated from its consumption. Perishability means unused service capacity of one time period cannot be stored for future use. Heterogeneity is variation in service quality. Client-based relationships are interactions with customers that lead to the repeated use of a service over time. Customer contact is the interaction needed to deliver a service between providers and customers.

⑦ Be familiar with organizational structures used for managing products.

Often the traditional functional form or organization does not lend itself to the complex task of developing and managing products. Alternative organizational forms include the product or brand manager approach, the market manager approach, and the venture team approach. A product manager is responsible for a product, a product line, or several distinct products that make up an interrelated group within a multiproduct organization. A brand manager is a product manager who is responsible for a single brand. A market manager is responsible for managing the marketing activities that serve a particular group or class of customers. A venture team is sometimes used to create entirely new products that may be aimed at new markets.

Please visit the student website at **www.prideferrell.com** for ACE Self-Test questions that will help you prepare for exams.

KEY CONCEPTS

line extension
product modification
quality modifications
functional modifications
aesthetic modifications
new-product development
  process
idea generation
screening

concept testing
business analysis
product development
test marketing
commercialization
product differentiation
quality
level of quality
consistency of quality

product design
styling
product features
customer services
product positioning
product deletion
service
intangibility
inseparability

perishability
heterogeneity
client-based relationships
customer contact
product manager
brand manager
market manager
venture team

ISSUES FOR DISCUSSION AND REVIEW

1. What is a line extension, and how does it differ from a product modification?

2. Compare and contrast the three major approaches to modifying a product.

3. Identify and briefly explain the seven major phases of the new-product development process.

4. Do small companies that manufacture just a few products need to be concerned about developing and managing products? Why or why not?

5. Why is product development a cross-functional activity within an organization? That is, why must finance, engineering, manufacturing, and other functional areas be involved?

6. What is the major purpose of concept testing, and how is it accomplished?

7. What are the benefits and disadvantages of test marketing?

8. Why can the process of commercialization take a considerable amount of time?

9. What is product differentiation, and how can it be achieved?

10. Explain how the term *quality* has been used to differentiate products in the automobile industry in recent years. What are some makes and models of automobiles that come to mind when you hear the terms *high quality* and *poor quality?*

11. What is product positioning? Under what conditions would head-to-head product positioning be appropriate? When should head-to-head positioning be avoided?

12. What types of problems does a weak product cause in a product mix? Describe the most effective approach for avoiding such problems.

13. How important are services in the U.S. economy?

14. Identify and discuss the major service characteristics.

15. For each marketing mix element, which service characteristics are most likely to have an impact?

16. What type of organization might use a venture team to develop new products? What are the advantages and disadvantages of such a team?

MARKETING APPLICATIONS

1. A company often test markets a proposed product in a specific area or location. Suppose you wish to test market your new revolutionary SuperWax car wax, which requires only one application for a lifetime finish. Where and how would you test market your new product?

2. Select an organization that you think should reposition itself in the consumer's eye. Identify where it is currently positioned, and make recommendations for repositioning. Explain and defend your suggestions.

3. Identify a familiar product that recently was modified, categorize the modification (quality, functional, or aesthetic), and describe how you would have modified it differently.

4. The characteristics of services affect the development of marketing mixes for services. Choose a specific service and explain how each marketing mix element could be affected by these service characteristics.

5. Identify three service organizations you see in outdoor, television, or magazine advertising. What symbols are used to represent their services? What message do the symbols convey to potential customers?

6. Visit a retail store in your area, and ask the manager what products he or she has had to discontinue in the recent past. Find out what factors influenced the decision to delete the product and who was involved in the decision. Ask the manager to identify any products that should be but have not been deleted, and try to ascertain the reason.

ONLINE EXERCISE

7. Merck, a leading global pharmaceutical company, develops, manufactures, and markets a broad range of health-care products. In addition, the firm's Merck-Medco Managed Care Division manages pharmacy benefits for more than 40 million Americans. The company has established a website to serve as an educational and informational resource for Internet users around the world. Visit Merck at **www.merck.com.**

   a. What products has Merck developed and introduced recently?

   b. What role does research play in Merck's success? How does research facilitate new-product development at Merck?

   c. Find Merck's mission statement. Is Merck's focus on research consistent with the firm's mission and values?

VIDEO CASE

Cali Cosmetics Offer the Benefits of Olive Oil

Around the world, more women (and men) are seeking out personal-care products based on natural botanical ingredients. For a smaller company like Cali Cosmetics, locked in competition with international beauty giants such as L'Oreal, Procter & Gamble, Unilever, Shiseido, and Estée Lauder, this back-to-nature trend is proving to be an important source of product differentiation.

Competition in the $32 billion global market for skin-care products is intense. Thousands of new products arrive on store shelves every year in the United States, and these are as likely to have been launched by lesser-known firms such as Hearts and Roses, Love Thy Hair, and Matahari as by well-established market leaders. In such a highly competitive industry, product differentiation is crucial. Typically companies accomplish this through brand name, product design, and styling as well as specific product features and ingredients.

For example, cosmetics companies have incorporated fruits, vegetables, herbs, vitamins, and just about anything else imaginable that can be safely applied to skin. Yet formulating beauty products with olive oil—the same ingredient favored by professional chefs and home cooks alike—is a relatively recent innovation. The ancient Romans called olive oil "liquid gold" and "nectar of the gods." The healthful benefits of olive oil for human skin and hair have long been recognized: ancient Egyptians used it as a moisturizer, Roman gladiators as a salve for wounds, and the Spanish as a primary ingredient of Castile soap.

As a cosmetic ingredient, experts believe the olive offers many benefits. Its skin, pulp, and oil contain glycerides and fatty acids that clean and moisturize, while its pit and bark make excellent exfoliants. Research also suggests that olive oil may have anti-aging and cancer-fighting properties. With the growing recognition of the benefits of olives and olive oil, many established companies are including olive oil as an ingredient or as the primary essence in a variety of personal-care products, including lip balms, shampoos, bath oils, hand lotions, nail soaks, massage oils, and more.

Some companies offer just one item infused with olive extracts, such as Philosophy's Amazing Grace perfumed olive oil body scrub and Bibo's O-live a Little hand and body lotion. Other companies are marketing entire collections of olive oil–based cosmetics, including The Thymes, which introduced Olive Leaf, a product line that incorporates every part of the olive into products designed to improve skin texture and protect from environmental damage.

An Italian firm, Cali Cosmetics has entered the industry with its Oliva brand of beauty products. Founded by Italy's Baronessa Consuelo Cali, Cali offers beauty products with vitamin-enriched extracts of Italian olive oil designed to protect and soften skin. Cali Cosmetics grew out of the Cali family's olive orchard and spa. Legend has it that the area, on the outskirts of Rome overlooking the Mediterranean Sea, was discovered by Roman nobles who enjoyed olive oil treatments there in the nineteenth century. The Cali Beauty Farm, housed in the Cali family's ancestral castle, has attracted customers ever since with olive-based food recipes and beauty treatments.

Baronessa Cali became the spa's primary owner in the late 1980s. In the late 1990s, she began to adapt generations-old family recipes and use modern technology to perfect them for home use by extracting vitamins from olive oil to create skin products that do not feel greasy. Now the line includes 11 "Scents of Italy" cleansers, moisturizers, and scrubs for the hair, face, body, and feet, formulated with aromas such as lavender and rose water. Over time, Baronessa Cali expects to introduce up to 100 new products based on her family's recipes.

In a market saturated with beauty products that smell good, feel good, and claim to promote healthy skin, Cali can succeed only by making its Oliva products stand out. To do this, the company focuses on linking its brand and image to the health and beauty benefits of its olive oil-based skin-care products. Customers are already responding: Cali achieved annual sales of more than $1 million a year during its first three years in the U.S. market. Cali products are also available in Belgium, Canada, Germany, Hong Kong, Saudi Arabia, Singapore, Switzerland, and the United Kingdom. Experts see a bright future for skin-care products, with demand especially strong in Europe and Asia. Cali is counting on its brand's distinctive appeal and the beauty benefits of olive oil ingredients to keep Oliva sales growing in the coming years.[27]

QUESTIONS FOR DISCUSSION
1. Are Oliva beauty products line extensions, modified products, or new products for the Cali family?
2. Describe the positioning of Oliva beauty products.
3. Assess Cali Cosmetics' strategy for differentiating its products from those of competitors.

Pricing Decisions

If an organization is to provide a satisfying marketing mix, the price must be acceptable to target market members. Pricing decisions can have numerous effects on other parts of the marketing mix. For example, price can influence how customers perceive the product, what types of marketing institutions are used to distribute the product, and how the product is promoted. Chapter 12 discusses the importance of price and looks at some characteristics of price and nonprice competition. It explores fundamental concepts such as demand, elasticity, marginal analysis, and breakeven analysis. Then it examines the major factors that affect marketers' pricing decisions. Chapter 13 discusses six major stages in the process marketers use to establish prices.

12

Pricing Fundamentals

OBJECTIVES

1 Understand the role of price.

2 Identify the characteristics of price and nonprice competition.

3 Be familiar with demand curves and the price elasticity of demand.

4 Understand the relationships among demand, costs, and profits.

5 Describe key factors that may influence marketers' pricing decisions.

6 Be familiar with the major issues that affect the pricing of products for business markets.

The New Napster Dances to a Different Tune

Napster, which began as free software for sharing music files, has forged a new life as a fee-based online music store challenging industry heavyweights such as Apple's iTunes and Microsoft's MSN Music. The original Napster functioned as a kind of clearinghouse where members could search for music by artist or song title and download songs for free from other members' hard drives. However, barely a year after Napster's launch, the Recording Industry Association of America filed suit, claiming that free file-swapping violated copyright laws and cost music publishers more than $300 million in lost sales. After a lengthy legal battle, Napster was found guilty and ultimately went bankrupt.

Then Napster's name and assets were purchased by Roxio, a company known for its CD-burning software. With much fanfare, Roxio introduced Napster 2.0 with 500,000 downloadable songs available for 99 cents each—at the time, the largest music catalog on the Web. Just as important, Napster's relaunch came with the blessing of five major music publishers. The service attracted so much interest that Roxio sold its other products and changed its name to Napster, signaling the company's concentration on digital music retailing.

Over time, more people have shown their willingness to pay for music downloads from official sources such as Napster. This trend is fueled, in part, by the publicity surrounding music industry lawsuits against people who download without payment or permission. Also, many consumers believe that CDs cost too much and would rather simply pay for one or two songs than buy entire albums.

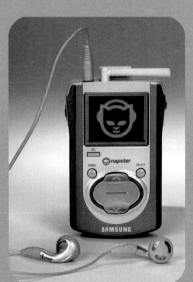

Today, Napster carries 1 million downloadable songs that can be purchased one by one or through a monthly subscription fee. Competitors include Apple's iTunes Music Store and Microsoft's MSN Music. Both offer similarly large music catalogs and price songs at 99 cents each, with monthly subscriptions available as well.

In the end, format and selection are likely to sway buyers more than price. Apple's AAC digital music format is compatible only with the stylish and successful iPod music player, whereas the WMA format used by Napster, MSN Music, Virgin, MusicMatch Jukebox, and other iTunes rivals is not. Napster's files are completely compatible with Windows Media software, and the store is particularly strong in country music. MSN Music features album exclusives from artists such as the Dave Matthews Band, and its Map of Music categorizes music by region and decade. Music fans who like jazz and blues may prefer iTunes, where they can also buy "mixtape" selections chosen by celebrities. Only time will tell whether Napster will play on and on.[1] ◀

Napster uses pricing as a tool to compete against its major competitors. However, to compete, Napster's rivals also employ pricing as a major competitive tool. In some industries, firms are very successful even if they don't have the lowest prices. The best price is not always the lowest price.

In this chapter, we focus first on the role of price. We then consider some characteristics of price and nonprice competition. Next, we discuss several pricing-related concepts such as demand, elasticity, and breakeven analysis. Then we examine in some detail the numerous factors that can influence pricing decisions. Finally, we discuss selected issues related to the pricing of products for business markets.

The Role of Price

price Value exchanged for products in a marketing transaction

barter The trading of products

The purpose of marketing is to facilitate satisfying exchange relationships between buyer and seller. **Price** is the value exchanged for products in a marketing transaction. Many factors may influence the assessment of value, including time constraints, price levels, perceived quality, and motivations to use available information about prices.[2] However, price does not always take the form of money paid. In fact, trading of products, or **barter**, is the oldest form of exchange. Money may or may not be involved.

Buyers' interest in price stems from their expectations about the usefulness of a product or the satisfaction they may derive from it. Because buyers have limited resources, they must allocate those resources to obtain the products they most desire. Buyers must decide whether the utility gained in an exchange is worth the buying power sacrificed. Almost anything of value—ideas, services, rights, and goods—can be assessed by a price. In our society, financial price is the measurement of value commonly used in exchanges. The purpose of price is to quantify and express the value of the items in marketing exchanges.

As pointed out in Chapter 11, developing a product may be a lengthy process. It takes time to plan promotion and to communicate benefits. Distribution usually requires a long-term commitment to dealers who will handle the product. Often price is the only thing a marketer can change quickly to respond to changes in demand or to actions of competitors. Under certain circumstances, however, the price variable may be relatively inflexible.

Price is a key element in the marketing mix because it relates directly to the generation of total revenue. The following equation is an important one for the entire organization:

$$\text{Profit} = \text{Total Revenue} - \text{Total Costs}$$

or

$$\text{Profits} = (\text{Price} \times \text{Quantity Sold}) - \text{Total Costs}$$

Prices affect an organization's profits in several ways because it is a key component of the profit equation and can be a major determinant of the quantities sold. For example, price is a top priority for Hewlett-Packard in gaining market share and improving financial performance.[3] Furthermore, total costs are influenced by quantities sold.

Because price has a psychological impact on customers, marketers can use it symbolically. By pricing high, they can emphasize the quality of a product and try to increase the prestige associated with its ownership. By lowering a price, marketers can emphasize a bargain and attract customers who go out of their way to save a small amount of money. Thus, as this chapter details, price can have strong effects on a firm's sales and profitability.

Price and Nonprice Competition

The competitive environment strongly influences the marketing mix decisions associated with a product. Pricing decisions are often made according to the price or nonprice competitive situation in a particular market. Price competition exists when consumers have difficulty distinguishing competitive offerings and marketers emphasize low prices. Nonprice competition involves a focus on marketing mix elements other than price.

Price Competition

price competition Emphasizing price and matching or beating competitors' prices

When engaging in **price competition**, a marketer emphasizes price as an issue and matches or beats the prices of competitors. To compete effectively on a price basis, a firm should be the low-cost seller of the product. If all firms producing the same product charge the same price for it, the firm with the lowest costs is the most profitable. Firms that stress low price as a key marketing mix element tend to market standardized products. A seller competing on price may change prices frequently or at least must be willing and able to do so. For example, Best Buy, a retail consumer electronic leader, engages in price competition. To attain sales growth, Best Buy has had to reduce its prices.[4] Whenever competitors change their prices, the seller usually responds quickly and aggressively.

Price competition gives a marketer flexibility. Prices can be altered to account for changes in the firm's costs or in demand for the product. If competitors try to gain market share by cutting prices, an organization competing on a price basis can react quickly to such efforts. However, a major drawback of price competition is that competitors also have the flexibility to adjust prices. If they quickly match or beat a company's price cuts, a price war may ensue. For example, a price war has developed in the market for high-speed Internet access, with prices for cable-modem service dropping below $20 a month in some areas.[5] Telecommunications companies often compete

Purex® gets clothes clean and smelling fresh for about half the price of more expensive brands. Don't waste money on dirt.™

Price Competition
The Dial Corporation, maker of Purex, competes on the basis of price.

E-MARKETING AND TECHNOLOGY

WILL THE PC PRICE WAR CONTINUE?

In the high-stakes world of personal computer marketing, a market share increase of even a fraction of a percentage point translates into hundreds of thousands of units sold. Small wonder that Dell, Hewlett-Packard, and other manufacturers are using price competition to score market share gains in this important product category.

IBM, which invented the PC, led the market during part of the 1980s and again in the early 1990s. Compaq took over as the world's number one PC maker until Dell took the top spot in 2001, followed closely by Hewlett-Packard. IBM has since dropped out of the race by selling its unprofitable PC division to China's Lenovo Group, which is working to turn the business around. Although Dell still holds a substantial market share lead, the rankings could change again at any time—especially if the PC price war continues.

Dell can be very price competitive because it controls costs by marketing directly to customers and making PCs to order. For years, Dell added low-

price, entry-level models and cut prices on high-end models in its quest for higher market share. However, to boost profit margins and cover the rising costs of key components such as memory chips and flat-panel displays, Dell's prices have inched up recently.

Hewlett-Packard, which owns Compaq, has been forced to respond with price cuts to defend its market share and remain competitive during the price war. Lately, Hewlett-Packard has been looking to digital cameras, photo printers, home media centers, and other consumer products for higher sales and profits.

Gateway, which lost share as Dell strengthened its leadership position in PCs, is now putting more emphasis on business markets. The company offers attractive prices and will also adapt its offerings to make big sales. Profitability remains the bottom line, however. This is why Gateway, Hewlett-Packard, and Dell are all paying close attention to competitive pricing and staying alert for signs that the profit-sapping price war is coming to an end.[a]

mainly on the basis of price reductions, per-second call billing, and free calls.[6] Chronic price wars such as this one can substantially weaken organizations. However, as a result of the sudden consolidation in telecommunications, customers could see an end to the price wars of recent years.[7]

◉ Nonprice Competition

nonprice competition
Emphasizing factors other than price to distinguish a product from competing brands

Nonprice competition occurs when a seller decides not to focus on price and instead emphasizes distinctive product features, service, product quality, promotion, packaging, or other factors to distinguish its product from competing brands. Thus, nonprice competition allows a company to increase its brand's unit sales through means other than changing the brand's price. A major advantage of nonprice competition is that a firm can build customer loyalty toward its brand. If customers prefer a brand because of nonprice factors, they may not be easily lured away by competing firms and brands. In contrast, when price is the primary reason customers buy a particular brand, a competitor is often able to attract these customers through price cuts. However, some surveys show that a fairly small proportion of customers base their purchase decisions solely on price.[8]

Nonprice competition is effective only under certain conditions. A company must be able to distinguish its brand through unique product features, higher product quality, promotion, packaging, or excellent customer service. Vermont Pure, a New England bottled water company, used superior service and the addition of a customer-oriented delivery service to compete against the bottled water behemoths Coca-Cola, Pepsi, and Nestlé. As a result of an increased focus on the service aspect of bottled water, Vermont Pure's sales were expected to rise about 15 percent.[9] Buyers not only must be able to perceive these distinguishing characteristics but must also view them as important. The distinguishing features that set a particular brand apart from competitors should be difficult, if not impossible, for competitors to imitate. Finally, the organization must extensively promote the distinguishing characteristics of the brand to establish its superiority and set it apart from competitors in the minds of buyers.

Even a marketer that is competing on a nonprice basis cannot ignore competitors' prices. It must be aware of them and sometimes be prepared to price its brand near or slightly above competing brands. Therefore, price remains a crucial marketing mix component even in environments that call for nonprice competition.

Analysis of Demand

Determining the demand for a product is the responsibility of marketing managers, who are aided in this task by marketing researchers and forecasters. Marketing research and forecasting techniques yield estimates of sales potential, or the quantity of a product that could be sold during a specific period. These estimates are helpful in establishing the relationship between a product's price and the quantity demanded.

The Demand Curve

demand curve   A graph of the quantity of products expected to be sold at various prices if other factors remain constant

For most products, the quantity demanded goes up as the price goes down, and as the price goes up, the quantity demanded goes down. Intel, for example, knows that lowering prices boosts demand for its Pentium PC chips. By cutting the price of its sophisticated Pentium 4 chip from $795 to $519 in less than five months, Intel was able to keep sales growing even as the PC market suffered a slowdown.[10] Thus, an inverse relationship exists between price and quantity demanded. As long as the marketing environment and buyers' needs, ability (purchasing power), willingness, and authority to buy remain stable, this fundamental inverse relationship holds.

Figure 12.1 illustrates the effect of one variable—price—on the quantity demanded. The classic **demand curve** (D_1) is a graph of the quantity of products expected to be sold at various prices if other factors remain constant.[11] It illustrates that as price falls, the quantity demanded usually rises. Demand depends on other factors in the marketing mix, including product quality, promotion, and distribution. An improvement in any of these factors may cause a shift to, say, demand curve D_2. In such a case, an increased quantity (Q_2) will be sold at the same price (P).

There are many types of demand, and not all conform to the classic demand curve shown in Figure 12.1. Prestige products, such as selected perfumes and jewelry, seem to sell better at high prices than at low ones. These products are desirable partly because their expense makes buyers feel elite. If the price fell drastically and many people owned these products, they would lose some of their appeal.

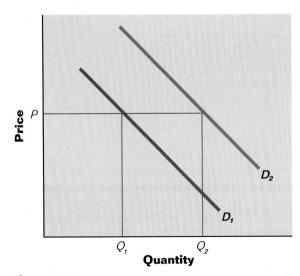

Figure 12.1
Demand Curve Illustrating the Price/Quantity Relationship and Increase in Demand

The demand curve in Figure 12.2 shows the relationship between price and quantity demanded for prestige products. Quantity demanded is greater, not less, at higher prices. For a certain price range—from P_1 to P_2—the quantity demanded (Q_1) goes up to Q_2. After a certain point, however, raising the price backfires. If the price goes too high, the quantity demanded goes down. The figure shows that if the price is raised from P_2 to P_3, the quantity demanded goes back down from Q_2 to Q_1.

◉ Demand Fluctuations

Changes in buyers' needs, variations in the effectiveness of other marketing mix variables, the presence of substitutes, and dynamic environmental factors can influence demand. Restaurants and utility companies experience large fluctuations in demand daily. Toy manufacturers, fireworks suppliers, and air-conditioning and heating contractors also face demand fluctuations because of the seasonal nature of their products. The demand for online services, beef, and flat-screen TVs has changed over the last few years. Building Customer Relationships examines changes in the demand and price of beef. In the case of the flat-screen plasma or LCD TVs, demand accelerated as prices dropped by as much as 30 percent.[12] In some cases, demand fluctuations are predictable. It is no surprise to restaurants and utility company managers that demand fluctuates. However, changes in demand for other products may be less predictable, and this leads to problems for some companies. Other organizations anticipate demand fluctuations and develop new products and prices to meet consumers' changing needs.

◉ Assessing Price Elasticity of Demand

Up to this point, we have seen how marketers identify the target market's evaluation of price and its ability to purchase and how they examine demand to learn whether price is related inversely or directly to quantity. The next step is to assess price elasticity of demand. **Price elasticity of demand** (see definition on p. 292) provides a measure of the sensitivity of demand to changes in price. It is formally defined as the percentage change in quantity demanded relative to a given percentage change in price (see Figure 12.3).[13] The percentage change in quantity demanded caused by a percentage change in price is much greater for elastic demand than for inelastic demand. For a product such as electricity, demand is relatively inelastic: when its price increases, say, from P_1 to P_2, quantity demanded goes down only a little, from Q_1 to Q_2. For products such as recreational vehicles, demand is relatively elastic: when price rises sharply, from P_1 to P_2, quantity demanded goes down a great deal, from Q_1 to Q_2.

If marketers can determine the price elasticity of demand, setting a price is much easier. By analyzing total revenues as prices change, marketers can determine whether a product is price elastic. Total revenue is price times quantity; thus, 10,000 rolls of wallpaper sold in one year at a price of $10 per roll equals $100,000 of total revenue. If demand is elastic, a change in price causes an opposite change in total revenue; an increase in price will decrease total revenue, and a decrease in price will increase total revenue. Inelastic demand results in a change in the same direction in total revenue. An increase in price will increase total revenue,

Prestige Products
The Steuben Hellenic Urn is an example of a prestige product.

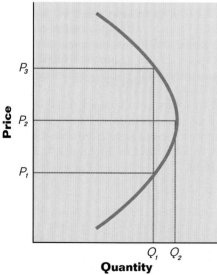

Figure 12.2
Demand Curve Illustrating the Relationship Between Price and Quantity for Prestige Products

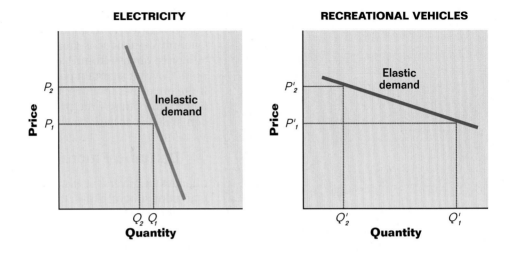

Figure 12.3
Elasticity of Demand

price elasticity of demand
A measure of the sensitivity of demand to changes in price

and a decrease in price will decrease total revenue. The following formula determines the price elasticity of demand:

$$\text{Price Elasticity of Demand} = \frac{(\% \text{ Change in Quantity Demanded})}{(\% \text{ Change in Price})}$$

For example, if demand falls by 8 percent when a seller raises the price by 2 percent, the price elasticity of demand is −4 (the negative sign indicating the inverse relationship between price and demand). If demand falls by 2 percent when price is increased by 4 percent, elasticity is −0.5. The less elastic the demand, the more beneficial it is for the seller to raise the price. Products without readily available substitutes and for which consumers have strong needs (for example, electricity or appendectomies) usually have inelastic demand.

Marketers cannot base prices solely on elasticity considerations. They must also examine the costs associated with different sales volumes and evaluate what happens to profits.

MARKETING ENTREPRENEURS

Pankaj Arora

HIS BUSINESSES: paWare and Pankaj Arora Software

FOUNDED AT AGE: 14

SUCCESS: Offered a salary of $100,000/year

A seemingly normal 16-year-old high school student, Pankaj Arora's extracurricular activities include heading up two technology-based businesses. Arora runs both paWare, a Web design and custom-computer company, and Pankaj Arora Software, which develops and distributes software with ZDNet. Already a business savvy entrepreneur, Arora is not seduced by the idea of making millions. In fact, he recently turned down a $100,000/year offer from a Minneapolis consulting firm so he could continue to improve his shareware and freeware technologies. Clearly, Arora has proven himself to be a hot commodity within the high-tech industry, but for now he says he is just doing what he likes to do.[b]

Demand, Cost, and Profit Relationships

The analysis of demand, cost, and profit is important because customers are becoming less tolerant of price increases, forcing manufacturers to find new ways to control costs. In the past, many customers desired premium brands and were willing to pay extra for these products. Today customers pass up certain brand names if they can pay less without sacrificing quality. To stay in business, a company has to set prices that not only cover its costs but also meet customers' expectations. In this section, we explore two approaches to understanding demand, cost, and profit relationships: marginal analysis and breakeven analysis.

fixed costs Costs that do not vary with changes in the number of units produced or sold

average fixed cost The fixed cost per unit produced

variable costs Costs that vary directly with changes in the number of units produced or sold

average variable cost The variable cost per unit produced

total cost The sum of average fixed and average variable costs times the quantity produced

average total cost The sum of the average fixed cost and the average variable cost

marginal cost (MC) The extra cost a firm incurs by producing one more unit of a product

◉ Marginal Analysis

Marginal analysis examines what happens to a firm's costs and revenues when production (or sales volume) changes by one unit. Both production costs and revenues must be evaluated. To determine the costs of production, it is necessary to distinguish among several types of costs. Fixed costs do not vary with changes in the number of units produced or sold. For example, an airplane manufacturer's cost of renting a building for use as a production facility does not change because of increased production of airplanes in this facility. Rent may go up when the lease is renewed, but not because the factory has increased production or revenue. Average fixed cost is the fixed cost per unit produced and is calculated by dividing fixed costs by the number of units produced.

Variable costs vary directly with changes in the number of units produced or sold. The wages for a second shift and the cost of more materials are extra costs that occur when production is increased. Average variable cost, the variable cost per unit produced, is calculated by dividing the variable costs by the number of units produced.

Total cost is the sum of average fixed costs and average variable costs times the quantity produced. The average total cost is the sum of the average fixed cost and the average variable cost. Marginal cost (MC) is the extra cost a firm incurs when it produces one more unit of a product.

Table 12.1 illustrates various costs and their relationships. Notice that average fixed cost declines as output increases. Average variable cost follows a U shape, as

Table 12.1	Costs and Their Relationships					
1	2	3	4	5	6	
Quantity	Fixed Cost	Average Fixed Cost (2) ÷ (1)	Average Variable Cost	Average Total Cost (3) + (4)	Total Cost (5) × (1)	Marginal Cost
1	$40	$40.00	$20.00	$60.00	$ 60	
						$10
2	40	20.00	15.00	35.00	70	
						2
3	40	13.33	10.67	24.00	72	
						18
4	40	10.00	12.50	22.50	90	
						20
5	40	8.00	14.00	22.00	110	
						30
6	40	6.67	16.67	23.34	140	
						40
7	40	5.71	20.00	25.71	180	

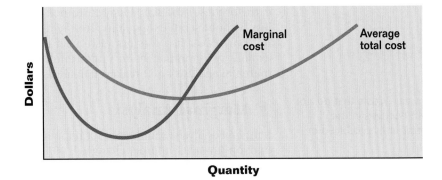

Figure 12.4
Typical Marginal Cost and Average Total Cost Relationship

does average total cost. Because average total cost continues to fall after average variable cost begins to rise, its lowest point is at a higher level of output than that of average variable cost. Average total cost is lowest at 5 units at a cost of $22.00, whereas average variable cost is lowest at 3 units at a cost of $10.67. As Figure 12.4 shows, marginal cost equals average total cost at the latter's lowest level. In Table 12.1, this occurs between 5 and 6 units of production. Average total cost decreases as long as marginal cost is less than average total cost, and it increases when marginal cost rises above average total cost.

marginal revenue (MR) The change in total revenue resulting from the sale of an additional unit of a product

Marginal revenue (MR) is the change in total revenue that occurs when a firm sells an additional unit of a product. Figure 12.5 depicts marginal revenue and a demand curve. Most firms in the United States face downward-sloping demand curves for their products. They must lower their prices to sell additional units. This situation means that each additional unit of product sold provides the firm with less revenue than the previous unit sold. MR then becomes less than average revenue, as Figure 12.5 shows. Eventually MR reaches zero, and the sale of additional units actually hurts the firm.

Before the firm can determine whether a unit makes a profit, it must know its cost, as well as its revenue, because profit equals revenue minus cost. If MR is a unit's addition to revenue and MC is a unit's addition to cost, MR minus MC tells us whether the unit is profitable. Table 12.2 illustrates the relationships among price, quantity sold, total revenue, marginal revenue, marginal cost, total cost, and profit for various combinations of price and quantity. Notice that the total cost and the marginal cost figures in Table 12.2 are calculated and appear in Table 12.1.

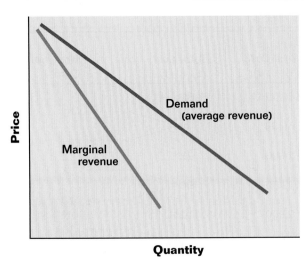

Figure 12.5
Typical Marginal Revenue and Average Revenue Relationship

Profit is the highest where MC = MR (see Table 12.2). In this table, note that at a quantity of 4 units, profit is the highest and MR − MC = 0. The best price is $33, and the profit is $42. Up to this point, the additional revenue generated from an extra unit sold exceeds the additional cost of producing it. Beyond this point, the additional cost of producing another unit exceeds the additional revenue generated, and profits decrease. If the price were based on minimum average total cost—$22 (Table 12.1)— it would result in a lower profit of $40 (Table 12.2) for 5 units priced at $30 versus a profit of $42 for 4 units priced at $33.

Graphically combining Figures 12.4 and 12.5 into Figure 12.6 shows that any unit for which MR exceeds MC adds to a firm's profits, and any unit for which MC exceeds MR subtracts from profits. The firm should produce at the point where MR equals MC because this is the most profitable level of production.

Table 12.2   Marginal Analysis Method for Determining the Most Profitable Price

1	2	3	4	5	6	7
Price	Quanitity Sold	Total Revenue (1) × (2)	Marginal Revenue	Marginal Cost	Total Cost	Profit (3) − (6)
$57	1	$ 57	$ 57	$ 60	$ 60	−$3
50	2	100	43	10	70	30
38	3	114	14	2	72	42
33*	**4**	**132**	**18**	**18**	**90**	**42**
30	5	150	18	20	110	40
27	6	162	12	30	140	22
25	7	175	13	40	180	−5

*Boldface indicates the best price-profit combination.

This discussion of marginal analysis may give the false impression that pricing can be highly precise. If revenue (demand) and cost (supply) remained constant, prices could be set for maximum profits. In practice, however, cost and revenue change frequently. The competitive tactics of other firms or government action can quickly undermine a company's expectations of revenue. Thus, marginal analysis is only a model from which to work. It offers little help in pricing new products before costs and revenues are established. On the other hand, in setting prices of existing products, especially in competitive situations, most marketers can benefit by understanding the relationship between marginal cost and marginal revenue.

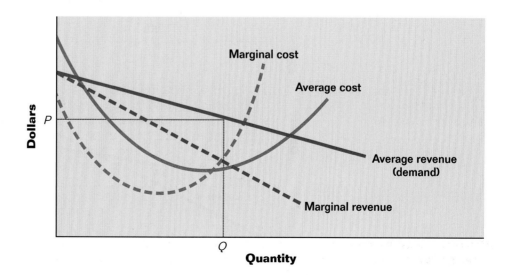

Figure 12.6
Combining the Marginal Cost and Marginal Revenue Concepts for Optimal Profit

◉ Breakeven Analysis

The point at which the costs of producing a product equal the revenue made from selling the product is the breakeven point. If a wallpaper manufacturer has total annual costs of $100,000 and sells $100,000 worth of wallpaper in the same year, the company has broken even.

Figure 12.7 illustrates the relationships among costs, revenue, profits, and losses involved in determining the breakeven point. Knowing the number of units necessary to break even is important in setting the price. If a product priced at $100 per unit has an average variable cost of $60 per unit, the contribution to fixed costs is $40. If total fixed costs are $120,000, the breakeven point in units is determined as follows:

$$\text{Breakeven Point} = \frac{\text{Fixed Costs}}{\text{Per-Unit Contribution to Fixed Costs}}$$

$$= \frac{\text{Fixed Costs}}{\text{Price-Variable costs}}$$

$$= \frac{\$120,000}{\$40}$$

$$= 3,000 \text{ Units}$$

To calculate the breakeven point in terms of dollar sales volume, multiply the breakeven point in units by the price per unit. In the preceding example, the breakeven point in terms of dollar sales volume is 3,000 (units) times $100, or $300,000.

To use breakeven analysis effectively, a marketer should determine the breakeven point for each of several alternative prices. This determination allows the marketer to compare the effects on total revenue, total costs, and the breakeven point for each price under consideration. Although this comparative analysis may not tell the marketer exactly what price to charge, it will identify highly undesirable price alternatives that should definitely be avoided.

Breakeven analysis is simple and straightforward. It does assume, however, that the quantity demanded is basically fixed (inelastic) and that the major task in setting prices is to recover costs. It focuses more on how to break even than on how to achieve a pricing objective, such as percentage of market share or return on investment. Nonetheless, marketing managers can use this concept to determine whether a product will achieve at least a breakeven volume.

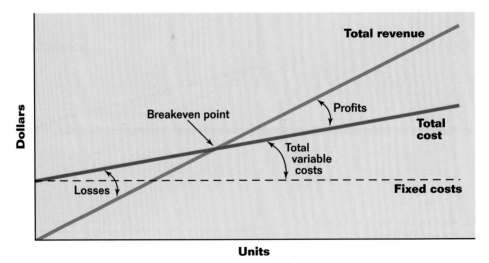

Figure 12.7
Determining the Breakeven Point

Factors Affecting Pricing Decisions

Pricing decisions can be complex because of the number of factors to be considered. Frequently there is considerable uncertainty about the reactions to price among buyers, distribution channel members, and competitors. Price is also an important consideration in marketing planning, market analysis, and sales forecasting. It is a major issue when assessing a brand's position relative to competing brands. Most factors that affect pricing decisions can be grouped into one of the eight categories shown in Figure 12.8. In this section, we explore how each of these eight groups of factors enters into price decision making.

◉ Organizational and Marketing Objectives

Marketers should set prices that are consistent with the organization's goals and mission. For example, a retailer trying to position itself as value oriented may wish to set prices that are quite reasonable relative to product quality. In this case, a marketer would not want to set premium prices on products but would strive to price products in line with this overall organizational goal.

Pricing decisions should also be compatible with the organization's marketing objectives. For instance, suppose one of a producer's marketing objectives is a 12 percent increase in unit sales by the end of the next year. Assuming buyers are price sensitive, increasing the price or setting a price above the average market price would not be in line with this objective.

◉ Types of Pricing Objectives

The type of pricing objectives a marketer uses obviously has considerable bearing on the determination of prices. For example, an organization that uses pricing to increase its market share would likely set the brand's price below competing brands of similar quality to attract competitors' customers. A marketer sometimes uses temporary price reductions in the hope of gaining market share. If a business needs to raise cash quickly, it will likely use temporary price reductions such as sales, rebates, and special discounts. We examine pricing objectives in more detail in the next chapter.

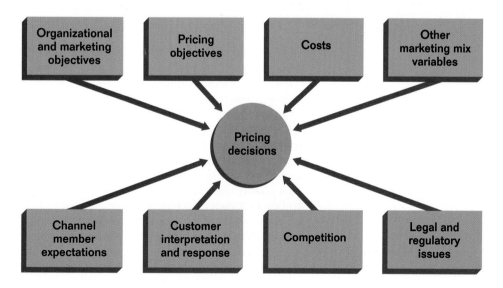

Figure 12.8
Factors That Affect Pricing Decisions

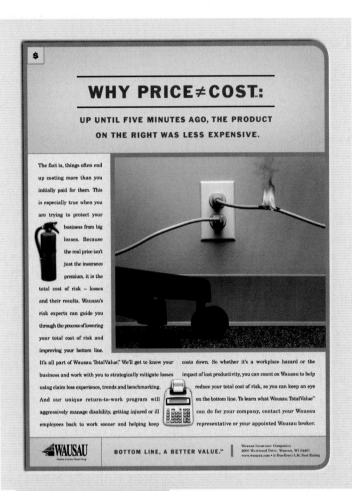

Cost as a Pricing Consideration
Wausau discusses the cost of risk in pricing its insurance services.

Costs

Clearly, costs must be an issue when establishing price. A firm may temporarily sell products below cost to match competition, to generate cash flow, or even to increase market share, but in the long run it cannot survive by selling its products below cost. Even when a firm has a high-volume business, it cannot survive if each item is sold slightly below what it costs. A marketer should be careful to analyze all costs so that they can be included in the total cost associated with a product.

To maintain market share and revenue in an increasingly price-sensitive market, many marketers have concentrated on reducing costs. In the highly competitive computer industry, for example, IBM constantly looks for ways to lower the cost of developing, producing, and marketing computers and related products. As a cost-cutting move, the company recently relocated 4,750 managerial and engineering jobs to India, where labor costs are significantly lower.[14] Labor-saving technologies, a focus on quality, and efficient manufacturing processes have brought productivity gains that translate into reduced costs and lower prices for customers.

Besides considering the costs associated with a particular product, marketers must take into account the costs that the product shares with others in the product line. Products often share some costs, particularly the costs of research and development, production, and distribution. Most marketers view a product's cost as a minimum, or floor, below which the product cannot be priced.

Other Marketing Mix Variables

All marketing mix variables are highly interrelated. Pricing decisions can influence decisions and activities associated with product, distribution, and promotion variables. A product's price frequently affects the demand for that item. A high price, for instance, may result in low unit sales, which in turn may lead to higher production costs per unit. Conversely, lower per-unit production costs may result from a low price. For many products, buyers associate better product quality with a high price and poorer product quality with a low price. This perceived price–quality relationship influences customers' overall image of products or brands. Sony, for example, prices its televisions higher than average to help communicate that Sony televisions are high-quality electronic products. Consumers recognize the Sony brand name, its reputation for quality, and the prestige associated with buying Sony products. Individuals who associate quality with a high price are likely to purchase products with well-established and recognizable brand names.[15]

The price of a product is linked to several dimensions of its distribution. Premium-priced products are often marketed through selective or exclusive distribution. Sony Ericsson is using more exclusive distribution for its line of diamond-studded, gold mobile phones, which are priced at $24,000 and up.[16] Lower-priced products in the same product category may be sold through intensive distribution. For example, Cross pens are distributed through selective distribution and Bic pens through intensive distribution. Moreover, an increase in physical distribution costs, such as shipping, may have to be passed on to customers. Soaring ocean-shipping rates, for example, increased the price of imported commodities and goods in the United States when the supply of ships trailed the demand for ocean-shipping services.[17] When setting a price, the profit margins of marketing channel members, such as wholesalers and retailers, must be considered. Channel members must be adequately compensated for the functions they perform.

Price may determine how a product is promoted. Bargain prices are often included in advertisements. Premium prices are less likely to be advertised, though they are sometimes included in advertisements for upscale items such as luxury cars or fine jewelry. Higher-priced products are more likely than lower-priced ones to require personal selling. Furthermore, the price structure can affect a salesperson's relationship with customers. A complex pricing structure takes longer to explain to customers, is more likely to confuse potential buyers, and may cause misunderstandings that result in long-term customer dissatisfaction. For example, the pricing structures of many airlines are complex and frequently confuse ticket sales agents and travelers alike.

◉ Channel Member Expectations

When making price decisions, a producer must consider what members of the distribution channel expect. A channel member certainly expects to receive a profit for the functions it performs. The amount of profit expected depends on what the intermediary could make if it were handling a competing product instead. Also, the amount of time and the resources required to carry the product influence intermediaries' expectations.

Channel members often expect producers to give discounts for large orders and prompt payment. At times, resellers expect producers to provide several support activities such as sales training, service training, repair advisory service, cooperative advertising, sales promotions, and perhaps a program for returning unsold merchandise to the producer. These support activities clearly have associated costs that a producer must consider when determining prices.

◉ Customer Interpretation and Response

When making pricing decisions, marketers should be concerned with a vital question: How will our customers interpret our prices and respond to them? *Interpretation* in this context refers to what

Value-Conscious Customers
By emphasizing both quality and price, this Xerox advertisement is aimed especially at value-conscious customers.

DC240 DIGITAL CAMERA
$477⁹⁵

PICTURE YOURSELF SAVING MONEY.

Ⓑ
BUY.COM
The Internet Superstore

COMPUTERS   SOFTWARE   BOOKS   VIDEOS   GAMES   MUSIC   CLEARANCE

Price-Conscious Customers
This advertisement primarily emphasizes price and thus is aimed at price-conscious customers.

internal reference price A price developed in the buyer's mind through experience with the product

external reference price A comparison price provided by others

the price means or what it communicates to customers. Does the price mean "high quality," "low quality," or "great deal," "fair price," or "rip-off"? Customer *response* refers to whether the price will move customers closer to the purchase of the product and the degree to which the price enhances their satisfaction with the purchase experience and with the product after purchase.

Customers' interpretation of and response to a price are determined to some degree by their assessment of what they receive compared with what they give up to make the purchase. In evaluating what they receive, customers will consider product attributes, benefits, advantages, disadvantages, the probability of using the product, and possibly the status associated with the product. In assessing the cost of the product, customers likely will consider its price, the amount of time and effort required to obtain it, and perhaps the resources required to maintain it after purchase.

At times customers interpret a higher price as an indication of higher product quality. They are especially likely to make this price–quality association when they cannot judge the quality of the product themselves. This is not always the case, however. Whether price is equated with quality depends on the types of customers and products involved. Obviously, marketers who rely on customers making a price–quality association and who provide moderate- or low-quality products at high prices will be unable to build long-term customer relationships.

When interpreting and responding to prices, how do customers determine if the price is too high, too low, or about right? In general, they compare prices with internal or external reference prices. An internal reference price is a price developed in the buyer's mind through experience with the product. It is a belief that a product should cost approximately a certain amount. As consumers, our experiences have given each of us internal reference prices for several products. For example, most of us have a reasonable idea of how much to pay for a six-pack of soft drinks, a loaf of bread, or a gallon of milk. For the product categories with which we have less experience, we rely more heavily on external reference prices. An external reference price is a comparison price provided by others, such as retailers or producers. For example, a retailer in an advertisement might state "while this product is sold for $100 elsewhere, our price is only $39.95." After Verizon Communications raised its pay phone price to 50 cents for each unlimited-time call in Virginia, it decided to target consumers who make short calls by dropping the price on one-minute and three-minute calls. Compared to the external reference price of 50 cents, a one-minute call for 10 cents or a three-minute call for 25 cents seemed like a bargain—especially when Verizon called attention to the price with a Special Discount Offer sign on each phone.[18] When attempting to establish a reference price in customers' minds by advertising a higher price against which to compare the company's real price, a marketer must make sure the higher price is realistic, because if it is not, customers will not use this price when establishing or altering their reference prices.[19] Customers' perceptions of prices are also influenced by their expectations about future price increases, by what they paid for the product recently, and by what they would like to pay for the product. Other factors affecting customers' perception of whether the price is right include time or financial constraints, the costs associated with searching for lower-priced products, and expectations that products will go on sale.

Buyers' perceptions of a product relative to competing products may allow the firm to set a price that differs significantly from rivals' prices. If the product is deemed superior to most of the competition, a premium price may be feasible. However, even products with superior quality can be overpriced. Strong brand loyalty sometimes provides the opportunity to charge a premium price. On the other hand, if buyers view a product less than favorably (though not extremely negatively), a lower price may generate sales.

In the context of price, buyers can be characterized according to their degree of value consciousness, price consciousness, and prestige sensitivity. Marketers who understand these characteristics are better able to set pricing objectives and policies. **Value-conscious** consumers are concerned about both price and quality of a product. To appeal to the value-conscious consumer, Tommy Hilfiger recently expanded his H Hilfiger brand into footwear to create a product that is both affordable and fashionable.[20] Similarly, Apple Computer recently introduced the Mac Mini and iPod Shuffle, more compact versions of their respective counterparts offered at discount prices.[21] **Price-conscious** individuals strive to pay low prices. **Prestige-sensitive** buyers focus on purchasing products that signify prominence and status.[22] For example, the Porsche Cayenne, one of the highest-priced sport-utility vehicles ever marketed, created record sales and profits for Porsche. Only 18 percent of Cayenne buyers had previously owned a Porsche; many of the rest were attracted to a vehicle with the prestige associated with the Porsche name.[23] In addition, some consumers vary in their degree of value, price, and prestige consciousness. In some segments, consumers are increasingly "trading up" to higher-status products in categories such as automobiles, home appliances, restaurants, and even pet food, yet remain price conscious regarding cleaning and grocery products. This trend has benefited marketers such as Starbucks, Sub-Zero, BMW, and Petco, which can charge premium prices for high-quality, prestige products, as well as Sam's Club and Costco, which offer basic household products at everyday low prices.[24]

value conscious Concerned about price and quality of a product

price conscious Striving to pay low prices

prestige sensitive Drawn to products that signify prominence and status

◎ Competition

A marketer needs to know competitors' prices so it can adjust its own prices accordingly. This does not mean a company will necessarily match competitors' prices; it may set its price above or below theirs. For some organizations, however, matching competitors' prices is an important strategy for survival.

When adjusting prices, a marketer must assess how competitors will respond. Will competitors change their prices, and if so, will they raise or lower them? In Chapter 3, we described several types of competitive market structures. The structure that characterizes the industry to which a firm belongs affects the flexibility of price setting. For example, because of reduced pricing regulation, firms in the telecommunications industry have moved from a monopolistic market structure to an oligopolistic one, which has resulted in significant price competition.

When an organization operates as a monopoly and is unregulated, it can set whatever prices the market will bear. However, the company may not price the product at the highest possible level to avoid government regulation or to penetrate

Pricing Decisions Are Affected by Competitors' Prices
Gorilla Mobile competes effectively with Verizon Wireless in its international pricing.

price discrimination
Providing price differentials that injure competition by giving one or more buyers a competitive advantage

a market by using a lower price. If the monopoly is regulated, it normally has less pricing flexibility; the regulatory body lets it set prices that generate a reasonable, but not excessive, return. A government-owned monopoly may price products below cost to make them accessible to people who otherwise could not afford them. Transit systems, for example, sometimes operate this way. However, government-owned monopolies sometimes charge higher prices to control demand. In some states with state-owned liquor stores, the price of liquor is higher than in states where liquor stores are not owned by a government body.

The automotive and aircraft industries exemplify oligopolies, in which there are only a few sellers and the barriers to competitive entry are high. Companies in such industries can raise their prices, hoping competitors will do the same. When an organization cuts its price to gain a competitive edge, other companies are likely to follow suit. Thus, very little advantage is gained through price cuts in an oligopolistic market structure.

A monopolistic competition market structure consists of numerous sellers with product offerings that are differentiated by physical characteristics, features, quality, and brand images. The distinguishing characteristics of its product may allow a company to set a different price than its competitors. However, firms in a monopolistic competitive market structure are likely to practice nonprice competition, discussed earlier in this chapter.

Under conditions of perfect competition, many sellers exist. Buyers view all sellers' products as the same. All firms sell their products at the going market price, and buyers will not pay more than that. Thus, this type of market structure gives a marketer no flexibility in setting prices. Farming, as an industry, has some characteristics of perfect competition. Farmers sell their products at the going market price. At times, for example, corn, soybean, and wheat growers have had bumper crops and been forced to sell them at depressed market prices.

◉ Legal and Regulatory Issues

Legal and regulatory issues influence pricing decisions. To curb inflation, the federal government can invoke price controls, freeze prices at certain levels, or determine the rates at which prices may be increased. In some states, regulatory agencies set prices on products such as insurance, dairy products, and liquor.

Many regulations and laws affect pricing decisions and activities. The Sherman Antitrust Act prohibits conspiracies to control prices, and in interpreting the act, courts have ruled that price fixing among firms in an industry is illegal. Marketers must refrain from fixing prices by developing independent pricing policies and setting prices in ways that do not even suggest collusion. Both the Federal Trade Commission Act and the Wheeler-Lea Act prohibit deceptive pricing. In establishing prices, marketers must guard against deceiving customers.

The Robinson-Patman Act has had a strong impact on pricing decisions. For various reasons, marketers may wish to sell the same type of product at different prices. Provisions in the Robinson-Patman Act, as well as those in the Clayton Act, limit the use of such price differentials. The practice of providing price differentials that tend to injure competition by giving one or more buyers a competitive advantage over other buyers is called **price discrimination** and is prohibited by law. However, not all price differentials are discriminatory. A marketer can use price differentials if they do not hinder competition, if they result from differences in the costs of selling or transportation to various customers, or if they arise because the firm has had to cut its price to a particular buyer to meet competitors' prices.

CUSTOMER RELATIONSHIP MANAGEMENT
UNIVERSAL FINE-TUNES CD PRICES

Sales of music CDs have been up and down in recent years—as have prices. One reason for the sales slump is that many consumers perceive CD prices to be disproportionately high, especially in light of the downward trend in DVD movie prices. A second reason is that many people are using the Internet to download and swap music files for free rather than buying new CD releases.

To stimulate sales in a maturing market, Universal Music Group—a major power in manufacturing and wholesaling recorded music around the world—first tried slashing wholesale CD prices by up to 32 percent. It also eliminated cooperative advertising payments to retailers intended to offset some of the costs of advertising CDs locally, reasoning that the money was not always used as designated and that retailers would enjoy higher sales now that wholesale prices were lower.

However, competitors didn't cut prices to the lower levels that Universal expected, nor did retailers that market Universal CDs pass along these lower wholesale costs in the form of lower retail prices. Just as important, the retailers protested the loss of cooperative advertising money. So although Universal reinstated some of the cooperative advertising payments, it also fine-tuned its pricing strategy for higher profits. The company raised the wholesale price of many new CDs by 40 cents (keeping the price below competitors' new CDs prices) while cutting wholesale prices of older CDs even further. Soon CD sales were on the upswing, along with profits.

Addressing wholesale CD prices is only one part of Universal's overall strategy to breathe new life into music sales. Recognizing that legal downloading is gaining in popularity through Apple's iTunes and other online services, Universal is licensing its catalog to Peer Impact and other Web-based music sites. These sites let consumers buy the specific songs they want (for about 99 cents each) rather than paying for an entire album with songs they may not want. Will this help Universal get the desired results from its pricing strategy?[c]

Pricing for Business Markets

Business markets consist of individuals and organizations that purchase products for resale, for use in their own operations, or for producing other products. Establishing prices for this category of buyers sometimes differs from setting prices for consumers. Differences in the size of purchases, geographic factors, and transportation considerations require sellers to adjust prices. In this section, we discuss several issues unique to the pricing of business products, including discounts, geographic pricing, and transfer pricing.

⊙ Price Discounting

Producers commonly provide intermediaries with discounts, or reductions, from list prices. Although there are many types of discounts, they usually fall into one of five

Table 12.3 Discounts Used for Business Markets

Type	Reasons for Use	Examples
Trade (functional)	To attract and keep effective resellers by compensating them for performing certain functions, such as transportation, warehousing, selling, and providing credit	A college bookstore pays about one-third less for a new textbook than the retail price a student pays
Quantity	To encourage customers to buy large quantities when making purchases and, in the case of cumulative discounts, to encourage customer loyalty	Large department store chains purchase some women's apparel at lower prices than do individually owned specialty stores
Cash	To reduce expenses associated with accounts receivable and collection by encouraging prompt payment of accounts	Numerous companies serving business markets allow a 2 percent discount if an account is paid within 10 days
Seasonal	To allow a marketer to use resources more efficiently by stimulating sales during off-peak periods	Florida hotels provide companies holding national and regional sales meetings with deeply discounted accommodations during the summer months
Allowance	In the case of a trade-in allowance, to assist the buyer in making the purchase and potentially earn a profit on the resale of used equipment; in the case of a promotional allowance, to ensure that dealers participate in advertising and sales support programs	A farm equipment dealer takes a farmer's used tractor as a trade-in on a new one Nabisco pays a promotional allowance to a supermarket for setting up and maintaining a large, end-of-aisle display for a two-week period

categories: trade, quantity, cash, seasonal, and allowance. Table 12.3 summarizes some reasons to use each type of discount and provides examples.

● **Trade Discounts.** A reduction off the list price given by a producer to an intermediary for performing certain functions is called a **trade**, or **functional, discount**. A trade discount is usually stated in terms of a percentage or series of percentages off the list price. Intermediaries are given trade discounts as compensation for performing various functions, such as selling, transporting, storing, final processing, and perhaps providing credit services. Although certain trade discounts are often a standard practice within an industry, discounts vary considerably among industries. It is important that a manufacturer provide a trade discount large enough to offset the intermediary's costs, plus a reasonable profit, to entice the reseller to carry the product.

trade discount Also known as functional discount; a reduction off the list price given by a producer to an intermediary for performing certain functions

● **Quantity Discounts.** Deductions from list price that reflect the economies of purchasing in large quantities are called **quantity discounts**. Quantity discounts are used to pass on to the buyer cost savings gained through economies of scale.

Quantity discounts can be either cumulative or noncumulative. **Cumulative discounts** are quantity discounts aggregated over a stated time period. Purchases totaling $10,000 in a three-month period, for example, might entitle the buyer to a 5 percent, or $500, rebate. Such discounts are supposed to reflect economies in selling

quantity discounts Deductions from list price for purchasing large quantities

cumulative discounts Quantity discounts aggregated over a stated period

noncumulative discounts
One-time reductions in price based on specific factors

cash discount   A price reduction given to buyers for prompt payment or cash payment

seasonal discount   A price reduction given to buyers for purchasing goods or services out of season

allowance   A concession in price to achieve a desired goal

geographic pricing   Reductions for transportation and other costs related to the physical distance between buyer and seller

F.O.B. factory   The price of the merchandise at the factory, before shipment

F.O.B. destination   A price indicating the producer is absorbing shipping costs

uniform geographic pricing
Charging all customers the same price, regardless of geographic location

zone pricing   Pricing based on transportation costs within major geographic zones

and to encourage the buyer to purchase from one seller. Noncumulative discounts are one-time reductions in prices based on the number of units purchased, the dollar value of the order, or the product mix purchased. Like cumulative discounts, these discounts should reflect some economies in selling or trade functions.

● **Cash Discounts.**   A cash discount, or price reduction, is given to a buyer for prompt payment or cash payment. Accounts receivable are an expense and a collection problem for many organizations. A policy to encourage prompt payment is a popular practice and sometimes a major concern in setting prices.

Discounts are based on cash payments or cash paid within a stated time. For example, "2/10 net 30" means that a 2 percent discount will be allowed if the account is paid within 10 days. If the buyer does not make payment within the 10-day period, the entire balance is due within 30 days without a discount. If the account is not paid within 30 days, interest may be charged.

● **Seasonal Discounts.**   A price reduction to buyers who purchase goods or services out of season is a seasonal discount. These discounts let the seller maintain steadier production during the year. For example, automobile rental agencies offer seasonal discounts in winter and early spring to encourage firms to use automobiles during the slow months of the automobile rental business.

● **Allowances.**   Another type of reduction from the list price is an allowance, or a concession in price to achieve a desired goal. Trade-in allowances, for example, are price reductions granted for turning in a used item when purchasing a new one. Allowances help make the buyer better able to make the new purchase. This type of discount is popular in the aircraft industry. Another example is a promotional allowance, a price reduction granted to dealers for participating in advertising and sales support programs intended to increase sales of a particular item.

◎ Geographic Pricing

Geographic pricing involves reductions for transportation costs or other costs associated with the physical distance between buyer and seller. Prices may be quoted as F.O.B. (free-on-board) factory or destination. An F.O.B. factory price indicates the price of the merchandise at the factory, before it is loaded onto the carrier, and thus excludes transportation costs. The buyer must pay for shipping. An F.O.B. destination price means the producer absorbs the costs of shipping the merchandise to the customer. This policy may be used to attract distant customers. Although F.O.B. pricing is an easy way to price products, it is sometimes difficult for marketers to administer, especially when a firm has a wide product mix or when customers are widely dispersed. Because customers will want to know about the most economical method of shipping, the seller must be informed about shipping rates.

To avoid the problems involved in charging different prices to each customer, uniform geographic pricing, sometimes called *postage-stamp pricing*, may be used. The same price is charged to all customers regardless of geographic location, and the price is based on average shipping costs for all customers. Gasoline, paper products, and office equipment are often priced on a uniform basis.

Zone pricing sets uniform prices for each of several major geographic zones; as the transportation costs across zones increase, so do the prices. For example, a Florida manufacturer's prices may be higher for buyers on the Pacific Coast and in Canada than for buyers in Georgia.

base-point pricing
Geographic pricing combining factory price and freight charges from the base point nearest the buyer

freight absorption pricing
Absorption of all or part of actual freight costs by the seller

Base-point pricing is a geographic pricing policy that includes the price at the factory, plus freight charges from the base point nearest the buyer. This approach to pricing has virtually been abandoned because of its questionable legal status. The policy resulted in all buyers paying freight charges from one location, such as Detroit or Pittsburgh, regardless of where the product was manufactured.

When the seller absorbs all or part of the actual freight costs, **freight absorption pricing** is being used. The seller might choose this method because it wishes to do business with a particular customer or to get more business; more business will cause the average cost to fall and counterbalance the extra freight cost. This strategy is used to improve market penetration and to retain a hold in an increasingly competitive market.

◉ Transfer Pricing

transfer pricing Prices charged in sales between an organization's units

Transfer pricing occurs when one unit in an organization sells a product to another unit. The price is determined by one of several methods. *Actual full cost* is calculated by dividing all fixed and variable expenses for a period into the number of units produced. *Standard full cost* is computed based on what it would cost to produce the goods at full plant capacity. *Cost plus investment* is full cost, plus the cost of a portion of the selling unit's assets used for internal needs. *Market-based cost* is the market price less a small discount to reflect the lack of sales effort and other expenses. The choice of transfer-pricing method depends on the company's management strategy and the nature of the units' interaction. An organization must also ensure that transfer pricing is fair to all units involved in the purchases.

CHAPTER REVIEW

❶ Understand the role of price.
Price is the value exchanged for products in marketing transactions. Price is not always money paid; barter, the trading of products, is the oldest form of exchange. Price is a key element in the marketing mix because it relates directly to the generation of total revenue. The profit factor can be determined mathematically by multiplying price by quantity sold to get total revenue and then subtracting total costs. Price is the marketing mix variable that usually can be adjusted quickly and easily to respond to changes in the external environment.

❷ Identify the characteristics of price and nonprice competition.
Price competition emphasizes price as the major product differential. Prices fluctuate frequently, and price competition among sellers is aggressive. Nonprice competition emphasizes product differentia-

tion through distinctive features, services, product quality, or other factors. Establishing brand loyalty by using nonprice competition works best when the product can be physically differentiated and the customer can recognize these differences.

❸ Be familiar with demand curves and the price elasticity of demand.
The classic demand curve is a graph of the quantity of products expected to be sold at various prices if other factors hold constant. It illustrates that as price falls, the quantity demanded usually increases. For prestige products, however, there is a direct positive relationship between price and quantity demanded; demand increases as price increases. Price elasticity of demand—the percentage change in quantity demanded relative to a given percentage change in price—must be determined. If demand is elastic, a change in price causes an opposite change in total

revenue. Inelastic demand results in a parallel change in total revenue when a product's price is changed.

4 Understand the relationships among demand, costs, and profits.

Analysis of demand, cost, and profit relationships can be accomplished through marginal analysis or breakeven analysis. Marginal analysis examines what happens to a firm's costs and revenues when production (or sales volume) is changed by one unit. Marginal analysis combines the demand curve with the firm's costs to develop a price that yields maximum profit. Fixed costs do not vary with changes in the number of units produced or sold; average fixed cost is the fixed cost per unit produced. Variable costs vary directly with changes in the number of units produced or sold. Average variable cost is the variable cost per unit produced. Total cost is the sum of average fixed cost and average variable costs times the quantity produced. The optimal price is the point at which marginal cost (the cost associated with producing one more unit of the product) equals marginal revenue (the change in total revenue that occurs when one additional unit of the product is sold).

Breakeven analysis—determining the number of units that must be sold to break even—is important in setting prices. The point at which the cost of production equals the revenue from selling the product is the breakeven point. To use breakeven analysis effectively, a marketer should determine the breakeven point for each of several alternative prices. This determination makes it possible to compare the effects on total revenue, total costs, and the breakeven point for each price under consideration.

5 Describe key factors that may influence marketers' pricing decisions.

Eight factors affect price decision making: organizational and marketing objectives, pricing objectives, costs, other marketing mix variables, channel member expectations, customer interpretation and response, competition, and legal and regulatory issues. When setting prices, marketers should make decisions consistent with the organization's goals and mission. Pricing objectives heavily influence price-setting decisions. Most marketers view a product's cost as the floor below which a product cannot be priced. Because of the interrelation among the marketing mix variables, price can affect product, promotion, and distribution decisions. The revenue that channel members expect for their functions should also be considered when making price decisions. Buyers' perceptions of price vary. Some consumer segments are sensitive to price, but others may not be. Knowledge of the prices charged for competing brands is essential so that the firm can adjust its prices relative to competitors. Government regulations and legislation influence pricing decisions.

6 Be familiar with the major issues that affect the pricing of products for business markets.

The categories of discounts offered to business customers include trade, quantity, cash, seasonal, and allowance. A trade discount is a price reduction for performing functions such as storing, transporting, final processing, or providing credit services. If an intermediary purchases in large enough quantities, the producer gives a quantity discount, which can be either cumulative or noncumulative. A cash discount is a price reduction for prompt payment or payment in cash. Buyers who purchase goods or services out of season may be granted a seasonal discount. A final type of reduction from the list price is an allowance, such as a trade-in allowance.

Geographic pricing involves reductions for transportation costs or other costs associated with the physical distance between buyer and seller. A price quoted as F.O.B. factory means the buyer pays for shipping from the factory. An F.O.B. destination price means the producer pays for shipping; this is the easiest way to price products, but it is difficult for marketers to administer. When the seller charges a fixed average cost for transportation, it is using uniform geographic pricing. Zone prices are uniform within major geographic zones; they increase by zone as the transportation costs increase. With base-point pricing, prices are adjusted for shipping expenses incurred by the seller from the base point nearest the buyer. Freight absorption pricing occurs when a seller absorbs all or part of the freight costs.

Transfer pricing occurs when a unit in an organization sells products to another unit in the same organization. Methods used for transfer pricing include actual full cost, standard full cost, cost plus investment, and market-based cost.

Please visit the student website at www.prideferrell.com for ACE Self-Test questions that will help you prepare for **ACE** exams.

KEY CONCEPTS

price	total cost	price discrimination	F.O.B. destination
barter	average total cost	trade discount	uniform geographic
price competition	marginal cost (MC)	quantity discounts	pricing
nonprice competition	marginal revenue (MR)	cumulative discounts	zone pricing
demand curve	breakeven point	noncumulative discounts	base-point pricing
price elasticity of demand	internal reference price	cash discount	freight absorption pricing
fixed costs	external reference price	seasonal discount	transfer pricing
average fixed cost	value conscious	allowance	
variable costs	price conscious	geographic pricing	
average variable cost	prestige sensitive	F.O.B. factory	

ISSUES FOR DISCUSSION AND REVIEW

1. Why are pricing decisions important to an organization?

2. Compare and contrast price and nonprice competition. Describe the conditions under which each form works best.

3. Why do most demand curves demonstrate an inverse relationship between price and quantity?

4. List the characteristics of products that have inelastic demand, and give several examples of such products.

5. Explain why optimal profits should occur when marginal cost equals marginal revenue.

6. Chambers Company has just gathered estimates for conducting a breakeven analysis for a new product. Variable costs are $7 a unit. The additional plant will cost $48,000. The new product will be charged $18,000 a year for its share of general overhead.

Advertising expenditures will be $80,000, and $55,000 will be spent on distribution. If the product sells for $12, what is the breakeven point in units? What is the breakeven point in dollar sales volume?

7. In what ways do other marketing mix variables affect pricing decisions?

8. What types of expectations may channel members have about producers' prices? How might these expectations affect pricing decisions?

9. How do legal and regulatory forces influence pricing decisions?

10. Compare and contrast a trade discount and a quantity discount.

11. What is the reason for using the term *F.O.B.?*

12. What are the major methods used for transfer pricing?

MARKETING APPLICATIONS

1. Price competition is intense in the fast-food, air travel, and personal computer industries. Discuss a recent situation in which companies had to meet or beat a competitor's price in a price-competitive industry. Did you benefit from this situation? Did it change your perception of the companies and/or their products?

2. Customers' interpretations and responses regarding a product and its price are an important influence on marketers' pricing decisions. Perceptions of price are affected by the degree to which customers are value conscious, price conscious, or prestige sensitive. Discuss how these factors influence the buying decision process for the following products:

a. A new house
b. Weekly groceries for a family of five
c. An airline ticket
d. A soft drink from a vending machine

ONLINE EXERCISE

3. Autosite offers car buyers a free, comprehensive website to find the invoice prices for almost all car models. The browser can also access a listing of all the latest new-car rebates and incentives. Visit this site at **www.autosite.com.**

a. Which Lexus dealer is closest to you? Find the lowest-priced Lexus available today, and examine its features.
b. If you wanted to purchase this Lexus, what are the lowest monthly payments you could make over the longest time period?
c. Is this free site more credible than a "pay" site? Why or why not?

VIDEO CASE

Low-Fare JetBlue Competes on More Than Price

Can JetBlue Airways stay in the black over the long term? Founded by David Neeleman, a savvy entrepreneur who sold his regional airline to Southwest Airlines in 1994, Jet-Blue sent its first flight into the skies in 2000. The airline quickly attained profitability and built a loyal customer base on the winning combination of customer-friendly service and low airfares. In recent years, however, JetBlue's high-flying profitability has lost a little altitude due to high fuel costs and sagging revenues.

CEO Neeleman knows that price is one of the top considerations for travelers. Major carriers typically quote dozens of fares between two locations, depending on time of day and other factors. By comparison, JetBlue's every-day pricing structure is far simpler and avoids complicated requirements such as Saturday-night stayovers. The CEO says that the fares are based on demand and that Jet-Blue uses pricing to equalize the loads on the flights so that no jet takes off empty while another is completely full. Thus, fares for Sunday-night flights tend to be higher because of higher demand, whereas Tuesday-night flights may be priced lower due to lower demand. Still, Jet-Blue's highest fare generally undercuts the lowest fare of its competitors. Pro-motional fares are even lower, such as the unusually low one-way price of $79 for nonstop flights from New York to California.

Price is not the only way that JetBlue sets itself apart from competitors. Whereas many new carriers buy used jets, JetBlue flies new Airbus A320 and Embraer 190 jets with seat-back video screens showing satellite television programming. Rather than squeeze in the maximum 180 seats that A320s can hold, JetBlue flies with only 156, giving passengers more legroom. In addition, the jets are outfitted with roomier leather seats, which cost twice as much as ordinary seats but last twice as long and make passengers feel pampered.

Another advantage of new jets is higher fuel efficiency. A320s can operate on 60 percent of the amount of fuel burned by an equivalent jet built decades before. Even so, JetBlue's profit margin was squeezed as fuel costs skyrocketed from 81 cents per gallon to more than $1.50, pushing annual operating costs above $2.5 million. Nonetheless, the airline's total costs of 6.5 cents per mile remain well below the per-mile costs of most major competitors. In part, this is because JetBlue's technicians work on only two types of jets, which means they gain proficiency at maintenance tasks and therefore save the airline time and money. Also, new jets come with a five-year warranty, so Jet-Blue need not budget for major repairs.

Why base a low-fare airline in New York City? CEO Neeleman made this decision for two main reasons.

First, he knew that New York travelers departing from nearby LaGuardia Airport faced crowds and delays unless they were willing to venture eight miles farther to fly from John F. Kennedy International Airport. Second, unlike some metropolitan airports, JFK was not a regional hub for major airlines or for low-fare carriers such as Southwest. Seizing an opportunity to trade off a slightly less convenient location for lower competition and better on-time performance, Neeleman secured more than 70 takeoff and landing slots at JFK Airport, enough to accommodate JetBlue's growth for years to come.

From its first day of operation, JetBlue has relied on Internet bookings to minimize sales costs. Travelers who buy tickets directly through the company's website (**www.jetblue.com**) get a special discount and are also eligible for online specials such as "Get It Together" fares designed for two people traveling together. JetBlue books about half of its fares on the Web and saves about $5 in transaction costs for each ticket booked online.

The CEO's flight plan is to have JetBlue flying nearly 300 jets by 2010, transforming what was once a tiny start-up into one of the largest airlines in the United States. The biggest question mark in JetBlue's future is the effect of competition. Not only does the airline compete with low-cost carriers such as Southwest and AirTran, but it also must deal with low-fare airline brands established by United and Delta. An airfare price war in Atlanta became so intense not long ago that JetBlue pulled out of the market to concentrate on expanding into western states. Now, as Neeleman adds one new jet every three weeks and hires 1,700 new employees per year, he must keep Jet-Blue's prices competitive without grounding profits.[25]

QUESTIONS FOR DISCUSSION

1. In an industry in which pricing has driven many firms out of business or into bankruptcy protection, why does JetBlue compete so successfully on the basis of price?
2. How does JetBlue use pricing to deal with demand fluctuations?
3. Is a businessperson's demand for air travel likely to be relatively elastic or inelastic? Is a vacationer's demand for air travel likely to be relatively elastic or inelastic?
4. What other factors related to pricing are most important to JetBlue's management when making pricing decisions?

Pricing Management

▶ Can General Motors Keep Riding on Rebates?

When General Motors introduced aggressive cash rebates and 0 percent financing to boost sales after the attacks of September 11, 2001, the company never expected to keep riding on rebates for more than three years. Management's goal was to stimulate sales, preserve market share, and keep GM's factories running. The latter is important because GM's labor costs are relatively fixed under its contract with the United Auto Workers. Thus, even if the company were to cut production, its labor costs would remain about the same. This is why GM chose price incentives to equalize sales and production rather than reducing production to meet demand.

Automakers have been using price incentives to attract customers since 1912, when Henry Ford gave rebate checks to Model T buyers. However, after GM started offering rebates in 2001, domestic and foreign competitors jumped in with a variety of rebates, free upgrades, low financing rates, and other financial incentives. Soon, no automaker could retreat from the rebate war without risking loss of sales and share.

Competitive pressure is not the only problem with price incentives. Another major problem is that rebates and lower financing rates erode automakers' profit margins. Moreover, companies may not achieve the intended objective of protecting market share. Even as GM touted sizable rebates to attract car buyers, Japanese automakers increased their U.S. market share by nearly 10 percent in recent years without offering giant rebates. In the end, GM actually lost market share and posted losses in North America.

Now GM is trying to wean car buyers from their addiction to incentives. As a start, the company recently slashed rebates by an average of $400 per vehicle. The result was a sales drop of nearly 17 percent, compared with healthy sales gains for Japanese rivals Toyota and Nissan during the same month. GM also implemented "Lock 'n' Roll," a deal allowing customers who buy a GM model with low or 0 percent financing to get the same financing arrangement if they buy another GM car before the end of the loan period. Despite the deal's uniqueness, GM dealers initially reported tepid customer response.

While working to reduce incentives, GM is also redesigning 90 percent of its passenger car lineup and introducing new trucks and SUVs to change the competitive focus from price to nonprice

OBJECTIVES

1. Understand the six major stages of the process used to establish prices.
2. Know the issues that are related to developing pricing objectives.
3. Understand the importance of identifying the target market's evaluation of price.
4. Describe how marketers analyze competitive prices.
5. Be familiar with the bases used for setting prices.
6. Explain the different types of pricing strategies.
7. Understand how a final, specific price is determined.

attributes. A cost-cutting program will help GM's bottom line as well. The challenge for GM and all its competitors is to effectively communicate the benefits and value of their products to customers who still remember the years when rebates and cheap financing were the norm.[1]   ◄

Figure 13.1
Stages for Establishing Prices

General Motors, like other automakers, uses rebates as one of its pricing strategies. Selecting pricing strategies is one of the fundamental steps in the process of setting prices. In this chapter, we examine six stages of a process marketers can use when setting prices. Figure 13.1 illustrates these stages. Stage 1 is the development of a pricing objective that is compatible with the organization's overall objectives and its marketing objectives. Stage 2 entails assessing the target market's evaluation of price. Stage 3 involves evaluating competitors' prices, which helps determine the role of price in the marketing strategy. Stage 4 involves choosing a basis for setting prices. Stage 5 is the selection of a pricing strategy, or the guidelines for using price in the marketing mix. Stage 6, determining the final price, depends on environmental forces and marketers' understanding and use of a systematic approach to establishing prices. These stages are not rigid steps that all marketers must follow; rather, they are guidelines that provide a logical sequence for establishing prices.

Development of Pricing Objectives

pricing objectives Goals that describe what a firm wants to achieve through pricing

Pricing objectives are goals that describe what a firm wants to achieve through pricing. Developing pricing objectives is an important task because pricing objectives form the basis for decisions about other stages of pricing. Thus, pricing objectives must be stated explicitly, and the statement should include the time frame for accomplishing them.

Marketers must make sure the pricing objectives are consistent with the organization's marketing objectives and with its overall objectives because pricing objectives influence decisions in many functional areas, including finance, accounting, and production. A marketer can use both short- and long-term pricing objectives and can employ one or multiple pricing objectives. For instance, a firm may wish to increase market share by 18 percent over the next three years, achieve a 15 percent return on investment, and promote an image of quality in the marketplace. In this section, we examine some of the pricing objectives that companies might set for themselves.

◎ Survival

A fundamental pricing objective is survival. Most organizations will tolerate difficulties such as short-run losses and internal upheaval if necessary for survival. Because price is a flexible variable, it is sometimes used to keep a company afloat by increasing sales volume to levels that match expenses. For example, a women's apparel retailer may run a three-day, 60-percent-off sale to generate enough cash to pay creditors, employees, and rent.

MARKETING LEADERS

PRICING NEW MUSIC FOR PROFIT

How can musical groups and independent artists, who haven't yet made it to the big time, make money on new albums? Traditionally, bands that sign with a major music label are entitled to royalties of 10 to 12 percent of the CD price—but they don't receive a dollar until all costs are covered. These include studio and engineering costs ($300 per hour), equipment rental fees ($1,000 and up), packaging and manufacturing costs ($20,000 or more), plus advertising, distribution, and other marketing expenses.

In general, the big labels have to sell about 500,000 copies to profit from a new music CD. Jazz composer Maria Schneider notes that "there are so many pieces of the pie to slice up—for the record company, the distributor, the record stores—that there's nothing left for the person who did all the work: me." Now the Internet is changing the new music pricing and profit equation.

Schneider was the first artist to sign with ArtistShare, a company that markets CDs online (at **www.artistshare. com**). Schneider paid $87,000 to produce her *Concert in the Garden* CD and paid ArtistShare $5,000 for Web services. Thanks to word of mouth communication among fans, the CD rang up prerelease orders of nearly $34,000. ArtistShare deducted 15 percent for its services and Schneider got the rest. "I may even get to the point of making a living entirely off my recordings," she says.

The independent Team Love label is also using the Internet to deal with the challenge of pricing new music for profit. Fans can download artists' songs and music videos for free before they buy CDs, building buzz at minimal expense. In addition, the label bypasses broadcast media in favor of interaction between fans and artists on personalized webpages.

Not only can Team Love break even on sales of 10,000 CDs, it gives up-and-coming artists access to new audiences. "The Internet changes the dynamic," co-founder Conor Oberst says. "It takes away the marketing advantage that the big labels have and gives people a chance to listen to music they couldn't hear on the radio or get in a Wal-Mart."[a]

◉ Profit — Ganancias o Utilidad

Although a business may claim its objective is to maximize profits for its owners, the objective of profit maximization is rarely operational because its achievement is difficult to measure. Because of this difficulty, profit objectives tend to be set at levels that the owners and top-level decision makers view as satisfactory. Specific profit objectives may be stated in terms of actual dollar amounts or in terms of a percentage of sales revenues. For example, the main pricing objective for Shoebuy.com, an online shoe retailer, is to return an overall 30 percent profit. To achieve this objective, the company minimizes costs by having a small work force and holding no inventory. Manufacturers ship directly to customers.[2]

◉ Return on Investment

Pricing to attain a specified rate of return on the company's investment is a profit-related pricing objective. Most pricing objectives based on return on investment (ROI) are achieved by trial and error because not all cost and revenue data needed to project the return on investment are available when prices are set. General Motors uses ROI pricing objectives.

DON'T BOTHER
GETTING TO
THE POINT

TALK AS MUCH AS YOU WANT, WHENEVER YOU WANT WITH VERIZON FREEDOM™.

Philosophize. Talk about the weather. Or just ramble on about your dog. Regardless of what you choose to discuss, take your time. There's no need to rush.

With Verizon Freedom, you get unlimited local and long distance calling for one low monthly price. So you can call anyone, anytime, across town or across the country — even to Canada. You'll also get great services including Caller ID, Home Voice Mail, Three-Way Calling, Call Waiting and Speed Dialing. And it all comes together on one convenient bill that could save you over $240 a year. Of course, standard taxes and surcharges also apply.

Plus, if you add Verizon Online DSL with MSN® Premium and Verizon Wireless, you can save even more. So sign up for Verizon Freedom today. And you'll never again have to say, "I'll make this quick."

$59⁹⁵ A MONTH

Call today to sign up.
1 800 826-5069
verizon.com/unlimited

verizon
Make progress every day

Market Share Pricing Objective
Verizon is attempting to gain market share and is using a market share pricing objective.

Market Share

Many firms establish pricing objectives to maintain or increase market share, a product's sales in relation to total industry sales. Toyota priced its Prius, a hybrid, at a reasonable price, which allowed consumers to afford this car and, in turn, built a strong market share in the hybrid category.[3] Many firms recognize that high relative market shares often translate into higher profits. The Profit Impact of Market Strategies (PIMS) studies, conducted over the last 30 years, have shown that both market share and product quality heavily influence profitability. Thus, marketers often use an increase in market share as a primary pricing objective.

Maintaining or increasing market share need not depend on growth in industry sales. Remember that an organization can increase its market share even if sales for the total industry are flat or decreasing. On the other hand, an organization's sales volume may increase while its market share decreases if total industry sales are growing.

Cash Flow

Some organizations set prices so they can recover cash as quickly as possible. Financial managers understandably seek to quickly recover capital spent to develop products. This objective may have the support of a marketing manager who anticipates a short product life cycle.

Although it may be acceptable in some situations, the use of cash flow and recovery as an objective oversimplifies the value of price in contributing to profits. If this pricing objective results in high prices, competitors with lower prices may gain a large share of the market.

Status Quo

In some cases, an organization is in a favorable position and, desiring nothing more, may set an objective of status quo. Status quo objectives can focus on several dimensions, such as maintaining a certain market share, meeting (but not beating) competitors' prices, achieving price stability, and maintaining a favorable public image. A status quo pricing objective can reduce a firm's risks by helping to stabilize demand for its products. The use of status quo pricing objectives sometimes minimizes pricing as a competitive tool, leading to a climate of nonprice competition in an industry.

Product Quality

A company may have the objective of leading its industry in product quality. This goal normally dictates a high price to cover the high product quality and, in some instances, the high cost of research and development. For example, Mercedes-Benz cars are priced to reflect and emphasize high product quality. As previously mentioned, the PIMS studies have shown that both product quality and market share are good indicators of profitability. The products and brands that customers perceive to be of high quality are more likely to survive in a competitive marketplace. High qual-

Product Quality Pricing Objective
BMW produces high-quality vehicles that are priced to communicate this level of quality.

ity usually enables a marketer to charge higher prices for the product. For example, by setting the price of the MACH3 razor at approximately 35 percent above the Sensor price, Gillette clearly communicates that the MACH3 is a high-quality product. Also, Bentley Motors uses premium prices to help signal the quality of its hand-made cars, which can cost from $190,000 to well over $300,000 depending on accessories and options.[4]

Assessment of the Target Market's Evaluation of Price

Despite the general assumption that price is a major issue for buyers, the importance of price depends on the type of product, the type of target market, and the purchase situation. For example, buyers are probably more sensitive to gasoline prices than to luggage prices. With respect to the type of target market, adults may have to pay more than children for certain products. The purchase situation also affects the buyer's view of price. In other situations, most moviegoers would never pay the prices charged for soft drinks, popcorn, and candy at movie concession stands. By assessing the target market's evaluation of price, a marketer is in a better position to know how much emphasis to put on price. Information about the target market's price evaluation may also help a marketer determine how far above the competition the firm can set its prices.

Because some consumers today are seeking less expensive products and shopping more selectively, some manufacturers and retailers are focusing on the value of their products. Value combines a product's price and quality attributes, which customers use to differentiate among competing brands. Consumers are looking for good deals on products that provide better value for their money. Companies that offer both low prices and high quality, such as Target and Best Buy, have altered consumers' expectations about how much quality they must sacrifice for low prices.[5] Even retail atmospherics can influence consumers' perceptions of price: the use of soft lights and colors has been found to have a positive influence on perception of price fairness.[6] Understanding the importance of a product to customers, as well as their expectations about quality and value, helps marketers correctly assess the target market's evaluation of price.

 ## Evaluation of Competitors' Prices

In most cases, marketers are in a better position to establish prices when they know the prices charged for competing brands. Learning competitors' prices may be a regular function of marketing research. Some grocery and department stores, for example, have full-time comparative shoppers who systematically collect data on prices. However, finding out what prices competitors are charging is not always easy, especially in producer and reseller markets. Competitors' price lists are often closely guarded. Even if a marketer has access to competitors' price lists, these lists may not reflect the actual prices at which competitive products are sold because those prices may be established through negotiation.

Knowing the prices of competing brands can be very important for a marketer. Competitors' prices and the marketing mix variables they emphasize partly determine how important price will be to customers. A marketer in an industry in which price competition prevails needs competitive price information to ensure its prices are the same as, or lower than, competitors' prices. Large retailers like Barnes and Noble and Home Depot have acquired significant market shares through highly competitive pricing.[7] In some instances, an organization's prices are designed to be slightly above competitors' prices to give its products an exclusive image.

Selection of a Basis for Pricing

The three major dimensions on which prices can be based are cost, demand, and competition. The selection of the basis to use is affected by the type of product, the market structure of the industry, the brand's market share position relative to competing brands, and customer characteristics. In this section, we discuss each basis separately. When setting prices, however, an organization generally considers two or all three of these dimensions, even though one may be the primary dimension on which it bases prices. For example, if an organization is using cost as a basis for setting prices, marketers in that organization are also aware of and concerned about competitors' prices. If a company is using demand as a basis for pricing, those making pricing decisions still must consider costs and competitors' prices. In setting prices for its 44,000 products, Fairchild Semiconductor uses software to assess all three dimensions, as well as buying behavior, manufacturing capacity, inventories, and product life cycles.[8]

◎ Cost-Based Pricing

cost-based pricing Adding a dollar amount or percentage to the cost of the product

With cost-based pricing, a dollar amount or percentage is added to the cost of the product. This approach thus involves calculations of desired profit margins. Cost-based pricing does not necessarily take into account the economic aspects of supply and demand, nor must it relate to just one pricing strategy or pricing objective. Cost-based pricing is straightforward and easy to implement. Two common forms of cost-based pricing are cost-plus and markup pricing.

cost-plus pricing Adding a specified dollar amount or percentage to the seller's cost

● **Cost-Plus Pricing.**   In cost-plus pricing, the seller's costs are determined (usually during a project or after a project is completed), and then a specified dollar amount or percentage of the cost is added to the seller's cost to establish the price. When production costs are difficult to predict, cost-plus pricing is appropriate. Projects involving custom-made equipment and commercial construction are often priced by this technique. The government frequently uses such cost-based pricing in granting defense contracts. One pitfall for the buyer is that the seller may increase costs to establish a larger profit base. Furthermore, some costs, such as overhead, may be difficult to determine. In periods of rapid inflation, cost-plus pricing is popular, especially when the producer must use raw materials that are fluctuating in price.

markup pricing Adding to the cost of the product a predetermined percentage of that cost

● **Markup Pricing.**   A common pricing approach among retailers is markup pricing, in which a product's price is derived by adding a predetermined percentage of the cost, called *markup*, to the cost of the product. Although the percentage markup in a retail store varies from one category of goods to another—35 percent of cost for hardware items and 100 percent of cost for greeting cards, for example—the same percentage often is used to determine the price on items within a single product category, and the percentage markup may be largely standardized across an industry at the retail level. Using a standard percentage markup for a specific product category reduces pricing to a routine task that can be performed quickly. This is one of the major reasons that many retailers use markup pricing.

Markup can be stated as a percentage of the cost or as a percentage of the selling price. The following example illustrates how percentage markups are determined and points out the differences in the two methods. Assume that a retailer purchases a can of tuna at 45 cents, adds 15 cents to the cost, and then prices the tuna at 60 cents. Here are the figures:

$$\text{Markup as Percentage of Cost} = \frac{\text{Markup}}{\text{Cost}}$$

$$= \frac{15}{45}$$

$$= 33.3\%$$

$$\text{Markup as a Percentage of Selling Price} = \frac{\text{Markup}}{\text{Selling Price}}$$

$$= \frac{15}{60}$$

$$= 25.0\%$$

Obviously, when discussing a percentage markup, it is important to know whether the markup is based on cost or selling price.

Demand-Based Pricing
Ski resorts use demand-based pricing.

demand-based pricing   Pricing based on the level of demand for the product

competition-based pricing   Pricing influenced primarily by competitors' prices

⊙ Demand-Based Pricing

Marketers sometimes base prices on the level of demand for the product. When **demand-based pricing** is used, customers pay a higher price when demand for the product is strong and a lower price when demand is weak. For example, hotels that otherwise attract numerous travelers often offer reduced rates during lower-demand periods. The Taxi Driver's Association in Berlin arranged to discount cab fares by 50 percent during the early evening, a period of lower demand. If the discount succeeds in attracting more passengers, the taxis will continue to offer it on a regular basis.[9] Some long-distance telephone companies, such as Sprint and Verizon, also use demand-based pricing by charging peak and off-peak rates. To use this pricing basis, a marketer must be able to estimate the amounts of a product consumers will demand at different prices. The marketer then chooses the price that generates the highest total revenue. Obviously, the effectiveness of demand-based pricing depends on the marketer's ability to estimate demand accurately. Compared with cost-based pricing, demand-based pricing places a firm in a better position to reach higher profit levels, assuming buyers value the product at levels sufficiently above the product's cost.

⊙ Competition-Based Pricing

In **competition-based pricing**, an organization considers costs as secondary to competitors' prices. The importance of this method increases when competing products are relatively homogeneous and the organization is serving markets in which price is a key purchase consideration. A firm that uses competition-based pricing may choose to price below competitors' prices, above competitors' prices, or at the same level. Airlines use competition-based pricing, often charging identical fares on the same routes. Also, online travel services such as Orbitz, Expedia, and Travelocity employ competition-based pricing.[10]

Although not all introductory marketing texts have exactly the same price, they do have similar prices. The price the bookstore paid to the publishing company for this textbook was determined on the basis of competitors' prices. Competition-based pricing can help a firm achieve the pricing objective of increasing sales or market share. Competition-based pricing may necessitate frequent price adjustments. For example, for many competitive airline routes, fares are adjusted often.

◎ Selection of a Pricing Strategy

A pricing strategy is an approach or a course of action designed to achieve pricing and marketing objectives. Generally, pricing strategies help marketers solve the practical problems of establishing prices. Table 13.1 lists the most common pricing strategies, which we discuss in this section.

CUSTOMER RELATIONSHIP MANAGEMENT
WIRELESS COMPANIES CALL UP COMPETITIVE PRICING STRATEGIES

Industry consolidation and intense competition among the top three wireless carriers is causing the price of cell phone service to drop across the United States. Verizon Wireless, Cingular Wireless, and Sprint/Nextel often use price to build or defend market share. Some of their campaigns highlight special pricing with limited-period promotional offers to attract new customers or increase revenues from existing customers. The result, according to one study, is that the price of wireless phone service fell more than 7 percent for two consecutive years, and it continues to drop.

The wireless companies price their services based on geographic area, individual or family usage, and volume phone usage, such as 300, 500, or 1,000 calling minutes during a single month. Many of their new-customer campaigns enhance perceived value by increasing the number of monthly minutes without raising rates or offering new cell phones at discounted rates. Customers may be required to sign a one- or two-year service contract and face high fees if they cancel before the contract expires. In addition, carriers sometimes levy an activation fee and may charge for services such as text messaging and call forwarding.

However, the monthly price usually includes valuable extras, such as Verizon's offer of free calls on nights and weekends. Some Cingular plans enable customers who don't use all their calling minutes in one month to roll them over to the next month. Sprint allows the members of one family to share the minutes allotted on a single account among as many as five phones.

Teens and twenty-something customers are a particularly attractive target for the wireless industry. Eyeing this segment, Cingular invites customers to personalize their ring tones by downloading college and university fight songs for 99 cents each. Sprint is turning cell phones into entertainment centers by offering several channels of radio music and streaming video for a monthly fee in addition to the phone service fee. The quest for higher market share in the wireless industry is likely to spawn more creative pricing during the coming years.[b]

◉ Differential Pricing

An important issue in pricing decisions is whether to use a single price or different prices for the same product. Using a single price has several benefits. A primary advantage is simplicity. A single price is easily understood by both employees and customers, and since many salespeople and customers do not like having to negotiate a price, it reduces the chance of an adversarial relationship developing between marketer and customer. The use of a single price does create some challenges, however. If the single price is too high, several potential customers may be unable to afford the product. If it is too low, the organization loses revenue from those customers who would have paid more if the price had been higher.

differential pricing Charging different prices to different buyers for the same quality and quantity of product

Differential pricing means charging different prices to different buyers for the same quality and quantity of product. For differential pricing to be effective, the market must consist of multiple segments with different price sensitivities, and the method should be used in a way that avoids confusing or antagonizing customers.

Table 13.1 Common Pricing Strategies

Differential Pricing	**Psychological Pricing**
Negotiated Pricing	Reference Pricing
Secondary-Market Pricing	Bundle Pricing
Periodic Discounting	Multiple-Unit Pricing
Random Discounting	Everyday Low Prices
	Odd-Even Pricing
New-Product Pricing	Customary Pricing
Price Skimming	Prestige Pricing
Penetration Pricing	
	Professional Pricing
Product-Line Pricing	
Captive Pricing	**Promotional Pricing**
Premium Pricing	Price Leaders
Bait Pricing	Special-Event Pricing
Price Lining	Comparison Discounting

Customers paying the lower prices should not be able to resell the product to the individuals and organizations paying higher prices, unless that is the intention of the seller. Differential pricing can occur in several ways, including negotiated pricing, secondary-market discounting, periodic discounting, and random discounting.

negotiated pricing Establishing a final price through bargaining

● **Negotiated Pricing.** Negotiated pricing occurs when the final price is established through bargaining between seller and customer. Negotiated pricing occurs in numerous industries and at all levels of distribution. Cutler-Hammon/Eaton has streamlined its contract-negotiations process for more than 90,000 products by reducing quote response times and implementing automatic acceptance of offers.[11] Even when there is a predetermined stated price or a price list, manufacturers, wholesalers, and retailers may still negotiate to establish the final sales price. Consumers commonly negotiate prices for houses, cars, and used equipment.

secondary-market pricing Setting one price for the primary target market and a different price for another market

● **Secondary-Market Pricing.** Secondary-market pricing means setting one price for the primary target market and a different price for another market. Often the price charged in the secondary market is lower. However, when the costs of serving a secondary market are higher than normal, secondary-market customers may have to pay a higher price. Examples of secondary markets include a geographically isolated domestic market, a market in a foreign country, and a segment willing to purchase a product during off-peak times. For example, some restaurants offer special "early-bird" prices, during the early evening hours, movie theaters offer senior-citizen discounts, and some textbooks and pharmaceutical products are sold for considerably less in certain foreign countries than in the United States. Secondary markets give an organization an opportunity to use excess capacity and to stabilize the allocation of resources.

periodic discounting Temporary reduction of prices on a patterned or systematic basis

● **Periodic Discounting.** Periodic discounting is the temporary reduction of prices on a patterned or systematic basis. For example, many retailers have annual holiday sales. Automobile dealers regularly discount prices on current models when the next year's models are introduced. From the marketer's point of view, a major problem with periodic discounting is that because the discounts follow a pattern,

Random Discounting
Sears employs "fashion funds" to randomly discount the prices of shoes and apparel for juniors.

random discounting
Temporary reduction of prices on an unsystematic basis

price skimming   Charging the highest possible price that buyers who most desire the product will pay

customers can predict when the reductions will occur and may delay their purchases until they can take advantage of the lower prices.

● **Random Discounting.**   To alleviate the problem of customers knowing when discounting will occur, some organizations employ random discounting; that is, they temporarily reduce their prices on an unsystematic basis. When price reductions of a product occur randomly, current users of that brand are likely to be unable to predict when the reductions will occur and so will not delay their purchases. In the automobile industry, with the increasing reliance on sales, rebates, and incentives such as 0 percent financing, random discounting has become nearly continuous discounting, and some analysts have expressed concern that automakers will find it difficult to "wean" consumers off the generous incentives as the economy improves.[12] Marketers also use random discounting to attract new customers.

Regardless of whether periodic discounting or random discounting is used, retailers often employ tensile pricing when putting products on sale. *Tensile pricing* refers to a broad statement about price reductions as opposed to detailing specific price discounts. Examples of tensile pricing would be statements such as "20 to 50% off," "up to 75% off," and "save 10% or more." Generally, using and advertising the tensile price that mentions only the maximum reduction (such as "up to 50% off") generates the highest customer response.[13]

◉ New-Product Pricing

Setting the base price for a new product is a necessary part of formulating a marketing strategy. The base price is easily adjusted (in the absence of government price controls), and its establishment is one of the most fundamental decisions in the marketing mix. When a marketer sets base prices, it also considers how quickly competitors will enter the market, whether they will mount a strong campaign on entry, and what effect their entry will have on the development of primary demand. Two strategies used in new-product pricing are price skimming and penetration pricing.

● **Price Skimming.**   Price skimming is charging the highest possible price that buyers who most desire the product will pay. The Porsche Cayenne, for example, has a starting price of $56,000, considerably higher than that of other sport-utility vehicles.[14] This approach provides the most flexible introductory base price. Price skimming can provide several benefits, especially when a product is in the introductory stage of its life cycle. A skimming policy can generate much-needed initial cash flows to help offset sizable developmental costs. When introducing a new model of camera, Polaroid initially uses a skimming price to defray large research and development costs. Price skimming protects the marketer from problems that arise when the price is set too low to cover costs. When a firm introduces a product, its production capacity may be limited. A skimming price can help keep demand consistent with

penetration pricing Setting prices below those of competing brands to penetrate a market and gain a significant market share quickly

product-line pricing Establishing and adjusting prices of multiple products within a product line

captive pricing Pricing the basic product in a produce line low while pricing related items at a higher level

premium pricing Pricing the highest-quality or most versatile products higher than other models in the product line

the firm's production capabilities. The use of a skimming price may attract competition into an industry because the high price makes that type of business appear to be quite lucrative.

● **Penetration Pricing.** In penetration pricing, prices are set below those of competing brands to penetrate a market and gain a large market share quickly. In South America, for example, when Industrias Añaños introduced Kola Real to capitalize on limited supplies of Coca-Cola and Pepsi-Cola in Peru, it set an ultra-low penetration price to appeal to the low-income consumers who represent a significant proportion of the population in the region. Kola Real quickly secured one-fifth of the Peruvian market and has made significant gains in Ecuador, Venezuela, and Mexico, forcing larger soft-drink marketers to cut prices.[15] This approach is less flexible for a marketer than price skimming because it is more difficult to raise a penetration price than to lower or discount a skimming price. It is not unusual for a firm to use a penetration price after having skimmed the market with a higher price.

Penetration pricing can be especially beneficial when a marketer suspects that competitors could enter the market easily. If penetration pricing allows the marketer to gain a large market share quickly, competitors may be discouraged from entering the market. In addition, entering a market may be less attractive to competitors when penetration pricing is used because the lower per-unit price results in lower per-unit profit; this may cause competitors to view the market as not being especially lucrative.

◉ Product-Line Pricing

Rather than considering products on an item-by-item basis when determining pricing strategies, some marketers employ product-line pricing. Product-line pricing means establishing and adjusting the prices of multiple products within a product line. When marketers use product-line pricing, their goal is to maximize profits for an entire product line rather than focusing on the profitability of an individual product. Product-line pricing can provide marketers with flexibility in price setting. For example, marketers can set prices so that one product is quite profitable while another increases market share by virtue of having a lower price than competing products. When marketers employ product-line pricing, they have several strategies from which to choose, including captive pricing, premium pricing, bait pricing, and price lining.

● **Captive Pricing.** With captive pricing, the basic product in a product line is priced low, while the price on the items required to operate or enhance it may be higher. For example, a manufacturer of cameras and film may set the price of the cameras at a level low enough to attract customers but set the film price relatively high because to use the cameras, customers must continue to purchase film.

● **Premium Pricing.** Premium pricing is often used when a product line contains several versions of the same product; the highest-quality products or those with the most versatility are given the highest prices. Other products in the line are priced to appeal to price-sensitive shoppers or to those who seek product-specific features. Marketers who use a premium strategy often realize a significant portion of their profits from premium-priced products. Examples of product categories that commonly use premium pricing are small kitchen appliances, beer, ice cream, and cable television service.

● **Bait Pricing.** To attract customers, marketers may put a low price on one item in the product line with the intention of selling a higher-priced item in the line; this

bait pricing Pricing an item in the product line low with the intention of selling a higher-priced item in the line

strategy is known as **bait pricing**. For example, a computer retailer might advertise its lowest-priced computer model, hoping that when customers come to the store they will purchase a higher-priced one. This strategy can facilitate sales of a line's higher-priced products. As long as a retailer has sufficient quantities of the advertised low-priced model available for sale, this strategy is considered acceptable. However, *bait and switch* is an activity in which retailers have no intention of selling the bait product; they use the low price merely to entice customers into the store to sell them higher-priced products. Bait and switch is considered unethical, and in some states it is illegal as well.

price lining Setting a limited number of prices for selected groups or lines of merchandise

● **Price Lining.** When an organization sets a limited number of prices for selected groups or lines of merchandise, it is using **price lining**. A retailer may have various styles and brands of similar-quality men's shirts that sell for $15 and another line of higher-quality shirts that sell for $22. Price lining simplifies customers' decision making by holding constant one key variable in the final selection of style and brand within a line.

The basic assumption in price lining is that the demand for various groups or sets of products is inelastic. If the prices are attractive, customers will concentrate their purchases without responding to slight changes in price. Thus, a women's dress shop that carries dresses priced at $85, $55, and $35 may not attract many more sales with a drop to, say, $83, $53, and $33. The "space" between the price of $85 and $55, however, can stir changes in consumer response.

psychological pricing Pricing that attempts to influence a customer's perception of price to make a product's price more attractive

reference pricing Pricing a product at a moderate level and positioning it next to a more expensive model or brand

◉ Psychological Pricing

Learning the price of a product is not always a pleasant experience for customers. It can sometimes be surprising (as at a movie concession stand) and sometimes downright horrifying. Most of us have been afflicted with "sticker shock." **Psychological pricing** attempts to influence a customer's perception of price to make a product's price more attractive. In this section, we consider several forms of psychological pricing: reference pricing, bundle pricing, multiple-unit pricing, everyday low prices (EDLP), odd-even pricing, customary pricing, and prestige pricing.

MARKETING ENTREPRENEURS

Rich Stachowski

HIS BUSINESS: Water Talkies

FOUNDED AT AGE: 10

SUCCESS: Sold his business for $1 million plus

While snorkeling on a family vacation in Hawaii, Stachowski could hardly mask his elation when he spotted a giant sea turtle. Unfortunately, he was unable to share this experience with his family when he couldn't catch their attention underwater. Determined to remedy this problem, he designed a device using a soccer cone, a snorkel, and duct tape, which enabled him to project his voice in water. He called his invention the Water Talkie, and the idea took off when Toys 'R' Us bought over 50,000 units. He sold his company to a toy manufacturer for over $1 million.[c]

● **Reference Pricing.** **Reference pricing** means pricing a product at a moderate level and positioning it next to a more expensive model or brand in the hope that the customer will use the higher price as an external reference price (i.e., a comparison price). Because of the comparison, the customer is expected to view the moderate price favorably. Reference pricing is based on the "isolation effect," meaning an alternative is less attractive when viewed by itself than when compared with other alternatives. When you go to Sears to buy a DVD player, a moderately priced DVD player may appear especially attractive because it offers most of the important attributes of the more expensive alternatives on display and at a lower price. It is not unusual for an organization's moderately priced private brands to be positioned alongside more expensive, better-known manufacturer brands. On the other hand, some retailers of private store brands are raising prices to improve the image of these products.[16]

● **Bundle Pricing.**   Bundle pricing is packaging together two or more products, usually complementary ones, to be sold for a single price. Cox Communications, for example, bundles local telephone service, high-speed Internet access, and digital cable television for one monthly fee.[17] To attract customers, the single price is usually considerably less than the sum of the prices of the individual products. Some marketing studies suggest that marketers can develop bundles of products with optimal prices for different market segments.[18] Bundle pricing not only helps increase customer satisfaction, but by bundling slow-moving products with ones with higher turnover, an organization can stimulate sales and increase its revenues. It may also help build customer loyalty and reduce "churn," that is, losing dissatisfied customers to rivals.[19] Selling products as a package rather than individually may also result in cost savings. Bundle pricing is commonly used for banking and travel services, computers, and automobiles with option packages.

Some organizations, however, are unbundling in favor of a more itemized approach sometimes called a la carte pricing. This provides customers with the opportunity to pick and choose the products they want without having to purchase bundles that may not be the right mix for their purposes.[20] For example, some television viewers would prefer to subscribe only to their favorite channels rather than a predetermined package of channels.[21] Furthermore, with the help of the Internet, comparison shopping has become more convenient than ever, allowing customers to price items and create their own mixes. Nevertheless, bundle pricing continues to appeal to customers who prefer the convenience of a package.[22]

● **Multiple-Unit Pricing.**   Multiple-unit pricing occurs when two or more identical products are packaged together and sold for a single price. This normally results in a lower per-unit price than the one regularly charged. Multiple-unit pricing is commonly used for twin packs of potato chips, four-packs of light bulbs, and six- and twelve-packs of soft drinks. Customers benefit from the cost saving and convenience this pricing strategy affords. A company may use multiple-unit pricing to attract new customers to its brand and, in some instances, to increase consumption of its brands. When customers buy in larger quantities, their consumption of the product may increase. For example, multiple-unit pricing may encourage a customer to buy larger quantities of snacks, which are likely to be consumed in higher volume at the point of consumption simply because they are available. However, this is not true for all products. For instance, greater availability at the point of consumption of light bulbs, bar soap, and table salt is not likely to increase usage.

Discount stores and especially warehouse clubs, such as Sam's Club, are major users of multiple-unit pricing. For certain products in these stores, customers receive significant per-unit price reductions when they buy packages containing multiple units of the same product, such as an eight-pack of canned tuna fish.

● **Everyday Low Prices (EDLP).**   To reduce or eliminate the use of frequent short-term price reductions, some organizations use an approach referred to as everyday low prices (EDLP). With EDLP, a marketer sets a low price for its products on a consistent basis rather than setting higher prices and frequently discounting them. Everyday low prices, though not deeply discounted, are set far enough below competitors' prices to make customers feel confident they are receiving a fair price. EDLP is employed by retailers like Wal-Mart. In Victoria, Canada, even the Famous Players

SIX ATTRACTIONS INCLUDED!

BOSTON CityPass

ADMIT ONE   ADMIT ONE

VISIT **six** BOSTON ATTRACTIONS

FOR JUST $**36**⁷⁵
a $73⁵⁰ value

AVOID MOST TICKET LINES

Bundle Pricing
Travel- and tour-related products are sometimes priced using bundle pricing.

bundle pricing Packaging together two or more complementary products and selling them for a single price

multiple-unit pricing
Packaging together two or more identical products and selling them for a single price

everyday low prices (EDLP)
Setting a low price for products on a consistent basis

movie theater chain introduced an Everyday Value Price Plan: all tickets cost the same price at any time and for every type of customer. Previously, the theaters charged different prices for adults and children, and for daytime and evening showings.[23] A company that uses EDLP benefits from reduced losses from frequent markdowns, greater stability in sales, and reduced promotional costs. For example, Family Dollar Stores changed its pricing strategy to EDLP. Just prior to the change, Family Dollar was printing and distributing 22 promotional price circulars a year. Now it prints and distributes only three promotional circulars a year, significantly reducing its promotion costs.[24]

A major problem with EDLP is that customers have mixed responses to it. Over the last several years, many marketers have "trained" customers to seek and to expect deeply discounted prices. In some product categories, such as apparel, finding the deepest discount has become almost a national consumer sport. Thus, failure to provide deep discounts can be a problem for certain marketers. In some instances, customers simply don't believe that everyday low prices are what marketers claim they are but are instead a marketing gimmick.

odd-even pricing Ending the price with certain numbers to influence buyers' perceptions of the price or product

● **Odd-Even Pricing.** Through odd-even pricing—ending the price with certain numbers—marketers try to influence buyers' perceptions of the price or the product. Odd pricing assumes that more of a product will be sold at $99.95 than at $100. Supposedly, customers will think, or at least tell friends, that the product is a bargain—not $100, but $99 and change. Also, customers will supposedly think the store could have charged $100 but instead cut the price to the last cent, to $99.95. Some claim, too, that certain types of customers are more attracted by odd prices than by even ones. Research has found a higher-than-expected demand associated with prices ending in 9 in print advertisements.[25] Odd prices are far more common today than even prices.

Even prices are often used to give a product an exclusive or upscale image. An even price supposedly will influence a customer to view the product as being a high-quality, premium brand. A shirtmaker, for example, may print on a premium shirt package a suggested retail price of $42.00 instead of $41.95; the even price of the shirt is used to enhance its upscale image.

customary pricing Pricing on the basis of tradition

● **Customary Pricing.** In customary pricing, certain goods are priced primarily on the basis of tradition. Recent economic uncertainties have made most prices fluctuate fairly widely, but the classic example of the customary, or traditional, price is the price of a candy bar. For years, a candy bar cost 5 cents. A new candy bar would have had to be something very special to sell for more than a nickel. This price was so sacred that rather than change it, manufacturers increased or decreased the size of the candy bar itself as chocolate prices fluctuated. Today, of course, the nickel candy bar has disappeared. Yet most candy bars still sell at a consistent, but obviously higher, price. Thus, customary pricing remains the standard for this market.

prestige pricing Setting prices at an artificially high level to convey prestige or a quality image

● **Prestige Pricing.** In prestige pricing, prices are set at an artificially high level to convey prestige or a quality image. Prestige pricing is used especially when buyers associate a higher price with higher quality. Pharmacists report that some consumers complain when a prescription does not cost enough; apparently some consumers associate a drug's price with its potency. Typical product categories in which selected products are prestige priced include perfumes, liquor, jewelry, and cars. Although traditionally appliances have not been prestige priced, upscale appliances have appeared in recent years to capitalize on the willingness of some consumer segments to "trade up" for high-quality products. These consumers do not mind paying extra for a Subzero refrigerator, a Viking commercial range, or a Whirlpool Duet washer and dryer because these products offer high quality as well as a level of prestige. The Whirlpool Duet washer and dryer, for example, are priced at $2,300 per pair—about $1,500 more than conventional washers and dryers—but offer high performance, large loads, gentle cleaning, and energy efficiency.[26] If producers who use prestige pricing lowered their prices dramatically, the new prices would be inconsistent with the perceived high-quality images of their products.

◉ Professional Pricing

professional pricing Fees set by people with great skill or experience in a particular field

Professional pricing is used by people who have great skill or experience in a particular field. Professionals often believe their fees (prices) should not relate directly to the time and effort spent in specific cases; rather, a standard fee is charged regardless of the problems involved in performing the job. Some doctors' and lawyers' fees are prime examples: $55 for a checkup, $1,500 for an appendectomy, and $399 for a divorce. Other professionals set prices in other ways. Like other marketers, professionals have costs associated with facilities, labor, insurance, equipment, and supplies. Certainly, costs are considered when setting professional prices.

The concept of professional pricing carries the idea that professionals have an ethical responsibility not to overcharge customers. In some situations, a seller can charge customers a high price and continue to sell many units of the product. If a diabetic requires one insulin treatment per day to survive, the individual will buy that treatment whether its price is $1 or $10. In fact, the patient surely would purchase the treatment even if the price went higher. In these situations, sellers could charge exorbitant fees.

price leaders Product priced below the usual markup, near cost, or below cost

◉ Promotional Pricing

As an ingredient in the marketing mix, price is often coordinated with promotion. The two variables sometimes are so interrelated that the pricing policy is promotion oriented. Types of promotional pricing include price leaders, special-event pricing, and comparison discounting.

● **Price Leaders.**   Sometimes a firm prices a few products below the usual markup, near cost, or below cost, which results in prices known as **price leaders**. This type of pricing is used most often in supermarkets and restaurants to attract customers by giving them especially low prices on a few items. In the United Kingdom, for example, the dis-

Special-Event Pricing
A number of marketers, such as Stride Rite, create special events and employ special-event pricing.

Starts Today!

TOTAL SAVINGS OF
44%-78%
LADIES & MEN'S
LEATHER
JACKETS

FROM LEADING MAKERS
GREAT ASSORTMENT,
SELECTION INCLUDES:
•ZIP FRONT•BUTTON FRONT
•BLAZERS•3/4 LENGTHS•BELTED

$**99**⁹⁹

COMPARE AT $179-$450

FILENE'S
BASEMENT

Downtown Boston•Newton•Dedham
Arsenal Mall•North Shore Mall•Hyannis
South Shore Plaza•Square One Mall
Selection Varies By Store

Comparison Discounting
Filene's Basement compares its $99.99
leather jackets with comparable $179–$450
leather jackets sold by competitors.

count store chain ASDA uses packaged food and beverage price leaders to compete more effectively with supermarket chains like Sainsbury and Tesco.[27] Management hopes that sales of regularly priced products will more than offset the reduced revenues from the price leaders.

● **Special-Event Pricing.** To increase sales volume, many organizations coordinate price with advertising or sales promotions for seasonal or special situations. **Special-event pricing** involves advertised sales or price cutting linked to a holiday, season, or event. If the pricing objective is survival, special sales events may be designed to generate the necessary operating capital. Special-event pricing entails coordination of production, scheduling, storage, and physical distribution. Whenever a sales lag occurs, special-event pricing is an alternative that marketers should consider.

● **Comparison Discounting.** **Comparison discounting** sets the price of a product at a specific level and simultaneously compares it with a higher price. The higher price may be the product's previous price, the price of a competing brand, the product's price at another retail outlet, or a manufacturer's suggested retail price. Customers may find comparative discounting informative, and it can have a significant impact on their purchases. However, overuse of comparison pricing may reduce customers' internal reference prices, meaning they no longer believe the higher price is the regular or normal price.[28]

Because this pricing strategy has on occasion led to deceptive pricing practices, the Federal Trade Commission has established guidelines for comparison discounting. If the higher price against which the comparison is made is the price formerly charged for the product, the seller must have made the previous price available to customers for a reasonable period of time. If the seller presents the higher price as the one charged by other retailers in the same trade area, it must be able to demonstrate that this claim is true. When the seller presents the higher price as the manufacturer's suggested retail price, the higher price must be similar to the price at which a reasonable proportion of the product was sold. Some manufacturers' suggested retail prices are so high that very few products are actually sold at those prices. In such cases, comparison discounting would be deceptive.

special-event pricing Advertised sales or price cutting linked to a holiday, season, or event

comparison discounting Setting a price at a specific level and comparing it with a higher price

◉ Determination of a Specific Price

A pricing strategy will yield a certain price. However, this price may need refinement to make it consistent with pricing practices in a particular market or industry.

Pricing strategies should help in setting a final price. If they are to do so, it is important for marketers to establish pricing objectives; have considerable knowledge about target market customers; and determine demand, price elasticity, costs, and competitive factors. Also, the way pricing is used in the marketing mix will affect the final price.

In the absence of government price controls, pricing remains a flexible and convenient way to adjust the marketing mix. The online brokerage arm of American Express (Amex), for example, sets prices on a sliding scale, depending on how much service support each customer uses. Customers who conduct all their securities trades without going through Amex employees pay lower prices than those who work with the firm's financial advisers to complete trades. As a result, American Express can provide the exact services each customer requires at an appropriate price.[29] In many situations, prices can be adjusted quickly—in a matter of minutes or over a few days. Such flexibility is unique to this component of the marketing mix.

CHAPTER REVIEW

① Understand the six major stages of the process used to establish prices.

The six stages in the process of setting prices are (1) developing pricing objectives, (2) assessing the target market's evaluation of price, (3) evaluating competitors' prices, (4) choosing a basis for pricing, (5) selecting a pricing strategy, and (6) determining a specific price.

② Know the issues that are related to developing pricing objectives.

Setting pricing objectives is critical because pricing objectives form a foundation on which the decisions of subsequent stages are based. Organizations may use numerous pricing objectives, including short-term and long-term ones, and different ones for different products and market segments. Pricing objectives are overall goals that describe the role of price in a firm's long-range plans. There are several major types of pricing objectives. The most fundamental pricing objective is the organization's survival. Price usually can be easily adjusted to increase sales volume or combat competition to help the organiza-

tion stay alive. Profit objectives, which are usually stated in terms of sales dollar volume or percentage change, are normally set at a satisfactory level rather than at a level designed for profit maximization. A sales growth objective focuses on increasing the profit base by increasing sales volume. Pricing for return on investment (ROI) has a specified profit as its objective. A pricing objective to maintain or increase market share implies that market position is linked to success. Other types of pricing objectives include cash flow, status quo, and product quality.

③ Understand the importance of identifying the target market's evaluation of price.

Assessing the target market's evaluation of price tells the marketer how much emphasis to place on price and may help determine how far above the competition the firm can set its prices. Understanding how important a product is to customers relative to other products, as well as customers' expectations of quality, helps marketers correctly assess the target market's evaluation of price.

④ Describe how marketers analyze competitive prices.

A marketer needs to be aware of the prices charged for competing brands. This allows the firm to keep its prices in line with competitors' prices when nonprice competition is used. If a company uses price as a competitive tool, it can price its brand below competing brands.

⑤ Be familiar with the bases used for setting prices.

The three major dimensions on which prices can be based are cost, demand, and competition. When using cost-based pricing, the firm determines price by adding a dollar amount or percentage to the cost of the product. Two common cost-based pricing methods are cost-plus and markup pricing. Demand-based pricing is based on the level of demand for the product. To use this method, a marketer must be able to estimate the amounts of a product that buyers will demand at different prices. Demand-based pricing results in a high price when demand for a product is strong and a low price when demand is weak. In the case of competition-based pricing, costs and revenues are secondary to competitors' prices.

⑥ Explain the different types of pricing strategies.

A pricing strategy is an approach or a course of action designed to achieve pricing and marketing objectives. The major categories of pricing strategies are differential pricing, new-product pricing, product-line pricing, psychological pricing, professional pricing, and promotional pricing. When marketers employ differential pricing, they charge different buyers different prices for the same quality and quantity of products. Negotiated pricing, secondary-market discounting, periodic discounting, and random discounting are forms of differential pricing. Two strategies used in new-product pricing are price skimming and penetration pricing. With price skimming, the organization charges the highest price that buyers who most desire the product will pay. A penetration price is a low price designed to penetrate a market and gain a significant market share quickly.

Product-line pricing establishes and adjusts the prices of multiple products within a product line. This category of strategies includes captive pricing, premium pricing, bait pricing, and price lining. Psychological pricing attempts to influence customer's perceptions of price to make a product's price more attractive. Psychological pricing strategies include reference pricing, bundle pricing, multiple-unit pricing, everyday low prices, odd-even pricing, customary pricing, and prestige pricing. Professional pricing is used by people who have great skill or experience in a particular field, therefore allowing them to set the price. This concept carries the idea that professionals have an ethical responsibility not to overcharge customers. As an ingredient in the marketing mix, price is often coordinated with promotion. The two variables are sometimes so interrelated that the pricing policy is promotion oriented. Promotional pricing includes price leaders, special-event pricing, and comparison discounting. Price leaders are products that are priced below the usual markup, near cost, or below cost. Special-event pricing involves advertised sales or price-cutting linked to a holiday, season, or event. Marketers who use a comparison discounting strategy price a product at a specific level and compare it with a higher price.

⑦ Understand how a final, specific price is determined.

Once a price is determined by using one or more pricing strategies, it will need to be refined to a final price consistent with the pricing practices in a particular market or industry. Using pricing strategies helps in setting a final price. The way that pricing is used in the marketing mix affects the final price. Because pricing is flexible, it is a convenient way to adjust the marketing mix.

Please visit the student website at www.prideferrell.com for ACE Self-Test questions that will help you prepare for exams.

KEY CONCEPTS

pricing objectives
cost-based pricing
cost-plus pricing
markup pricing
demand-based pricing
competition-based pricing
differential pricing
negotiated pricing

secondary-market pricing
periodic discounting
random discounting
price skimming
penetration pricing
product-line pricing
captive pricing
premium pricing

bait pricing
price lining
psychological pricing
reference pricing
bundle pricing
multiple-unit pricing
everyday low prices (EDLP)
odd-even pricing

customary pricing
prestige pricing
professional pricing
price leaders
special-event pricing
comparison discounting

ISSUES FOR DISCUSSION AND REVIEW

1. Identify the six stages involved in the process of establishing prices.

2. How does a return on investment pricing objective differ from an objective of increasing market share?

3. Why must marketing objectives and pricing objectives be considered when making pricing decisions?

4. Why should a marketer be aware of competitors' prices?

5. What are the benefits of cost-based pricing?

6. Under what conditions is cost-plus pricing most appropriate?

7. A retailer purchases a can of soup for 24 cents and sells it for 36 cents. Calculate the markup as a percentage of cost and as a percentage of selling price.

8. What is differential pricing? In what ways can it be achieved?

9. For what type of products would price skimming be most appropriate? For what type of products would penetration pricing be more effective?

10. Describe bundle pricing and give three examples using different industries.

11. What are the advantages and disadvantages of using everyday low prices?

12. Why do customers associate price with quality? When should prestige pricing be used?

13. Are price leaders a realistic approach to pricing? Explain your answer.

MARKETING APPLICATIONS

1. Which strategy—price skimming or penetration pricing—is more appropriate for the following products? Explain.
   a. Short airline flights between cities in Florida
   b. A DVD player
   c. A backpack or book bag with a lifetime warranty
   d. Season tickets for a newly franchised NBA team

2. Visit a few local retail stores to find examples of price lining. For what types of products and stores is this practice most common? For what products and stores is price lining not typical or usable?

3. Find examples (advertisements, personal contacts) that reflect a professional-pricing policy. How is the price established? Are there any restrictions on the services performed at that price?

4. Locate an organization that uses several pricing objectives, and discuss how this approach influences the company's marketing mix decisions. Are some objectives oriented toward the short term and others toward the long term? How does the marketing environment influence these objectives?

ONLINE EXERCISE

5. T-Mobile has attempted to position itself as a low-cost cell phone service provider. A person can purchase a calling plan, a cellular phone, and phone accessories at its website. Visit the T-Mobile website at **www.t-mobile.com.**
   a. Determine the various nationwide rates available in Houston, Texas.
   b. How many different calling plans are available in the Houston area?
   c. What type of pricing strategy is T-Mobile using on its Houston rate plans?

VIDEO CASE

How New Balance Runs Its Pricing Strategy

When marketers at New Balance race to develop a new product, they have a particular price in mind from the start. New Balance makes high-quality, high-performance athletic shoes. The brand is, as company ads proclaim, "endorsed by no one," yet New Balance regularly racks up $1 billion in annual sales and currently trails only Nike and Reebok in the U.S. market.

Major competitors keep labor costs down by manufacturing their shoes outside the United States, mainly in the Far East. In contrast, New Balance produces 25 percent of its shoes in five company-owned New England factories: one in Boston; one in Lawrence, Massachusetts; and three in Maine. How can New Balance remain competitive while balancing "made in America" and "the price is right"?

New Balance marketers strive to satisfy customers in a variety of segments by designing, making, and marketing shoes that fit properly, perform properly, and look good. They begin by studying customer needs in a specific category—for instance, running—and ask questions such as: For what type of runner will the shoe be designed? How many miles is that person likely to run every day or week? What is the runner's body makeup?

Although costs and prices are not the key factors in marketing athletic shoes, they are very important. In the first stage of development, New Balance hires an outside firm to prepare a marketing brief. This gives marketers detailed information about the target customer, outlines the special features that the shoe should have, and identifies the target price that will yield adequate profits.

Members of New Balance's design, development, and marketing teams consider costs an integral part of the marketing strategy. They look at material costs, labor costs, and overhead costs, as well as any special treatments the shoe design may include, such as specially molded pieces, labels, or embroidery. As product development progresses, the teams create a rough cost estimate that will be a major factor in the retail price.

Material costs are a key factor in any athletic shoe product. Upscale high-performance shoes may contain more expensive materials and technology and thus sell for higher prices. Lower-end products may employ less technology and use different materials that perform at a different level. By varying both materials and technology, New Balance can offer a variety of products at different price points for various segments in each sports category, such as running shoes or basketball sneakers. Still, most New Balance shoes are priced at $60 and above, reinforcing the brand's high-performance positioning.

Competitors' prices are also an important part of New Balance's pricing strategy. When New Balance is developing an $80 cushioning shoe, for example, its marketers examine $80 cushioning shoes from competitors, comparing features as well as appearance and color. They often purchase competing shoes to see what else is on the market and how New Balance products match up to the competition.

After designing a new shoe, New Balance will either make a prototype in New England or, if the shoe is to be manufactured abroad, have one of the overseas factories make a prototype. This part of the process gives marketers a more realistic picture of material costs, labor costs, and the costs of any extras needed in actually making the product. Then New Balance makes final adjustments to materials, manufacturing, and design in line with the new product's expected price and costs.

New Balance's decision to maintain production facilities in the United States is a smart competitive move for two reasons. First, the company has modernized and reorganized its U.S. factories to cut the production cycle from eight days to just eight hours. This means it can get by with much less inventory. More importantly, it can start production immediately when retailers order merchandise. Second, New Balance has the manufacturing flexibility to fill special orders for unusual sizes and widths quickly, which strengthens its relationships with retail partners.

Other pressures also affect the way New Balance runs its pricing strategy. Retailers continue to use bargain prices to attract shoppers, a trend that is pushing down the average price of athletic shoes at the cash register. In addition, New Balance must consider how fluctuations in the value of the U.S. dollar against the value of foreign currencies affect its costs and export pricing. Every day brings new challenges and opportunities for New Balance to refine its pricing strategy even more.[30]

QUESTIONS FOR DISCUSSION

1. What pricing objectives does New Balance seem to employ?
2. What type of pricing strategy is New Balance using?
3. What other pricing tools does New Balance employ?

Distribution Decisions

Developing products that satisfy customers is important, but it is not enough to guarantee successful marketing strategies. Products must also be available in adequate quantities in accessible locations at the times when customers desire them. Part 7 deals with the distribution of products and the marketing channels and institutions that help make products available. Chapter 14 discusses the structure and functions of marketing channels, as well as the decisions and activities associated with the physical distribution of products, such as order processing, materials handling, warehousing, inventory management, and transportation. Chapter 15 explores retailing and wholesaling, including types of retailers and wholesalers, direct marketing and selling, and strategic retailing issues.

14 Marketing Channels and Supply-Chain Management

OBJECTIVES

1 Describe the nature and functions of marketing channels.

2 Identify the types of marketing channels.

3 Explore the concepts of leadership, cooperation, and conflict in channel relationships.

4 Recognize common strategies for integrating marketing channels.

5 Examine the major levels of marketing coverage.

6 Recognize the importance of the role of physical distribution activities in supply-chain management and overall marketing strategies.

7 Examine the major physical distribution functions of order processing, inventory management, materials handling, warehousing, and transportation.

▶ **Grainger Wires the Business Supply Chain**

W.W. Grainger invites businesses to "call, click, or stop by" to purchase any of the 82,000 products in its extensive inventory. Grainger is an industrial distributor offering virtually one-stop shopping for producer, government, and institutional markets seeking to buy a wide range of maintenance, repair, and operating (MRO) supplies. With more than 575 distribution branches spread across North America, the company can time shipments to arrive quickly when business customers place orders.

William W. Grainger founded the Illinois-based company in the 1920s as a wholesaler of electric motors. In less than a decade, the firm was operating 15 U.S. sales branches and serving business customers from coast to coast. By 1949, the branch network had expanded to 30 states. Today, Grainger rings up more than $4 billion in sales and prints 1.5 million copies of its red-cover catalog every year.

The company puts a high priority on using technology to streamline the supply chain. In the early 1990s, it put a satellite dish on the roof of every branch to communicate with headquarters about sales and orders, inventory levels, and other operational details. In 1995, it launched Grainger.com as a comprehensive catalog site for businesses seeking the convenience of browsing and buying online. Since then, the company has continued to refine its Internet presence by adding live-chat customer assistance, a virtual tour of the site for new customers, special international services, and Web-only price promotions to bring customers back again and again. Now Grainger.com sells $500 million worth of merchandise every year and is on track to keep sales growth in double digits.

Despite its success with online distribution, Grainger is not abandoning its branch system. It is closing less productive branches, opening larger branches near major metropolitan centers, and hiring more sales staff. The company has also opened convenient on-site branches for two big customers, Florida State University and Langley Air Force Base. "Our customers are trying to keep a business running," notes Grainger's vice president of branch services. "It's imperative that we have products and services available when and where the customer needs them."

To prepare for future growth, Grainger is opening nine additional automated distribution centers and implementing a new logistics network. These steps have cut the company's inventory investment by $100 million and strengthened its ability to serve a larger customer base. Grainger is also showing major customers such as the U.S. Postal Service how to better manage their supply chains and cut costs throughout the procurement process. More efficiencies are ahead as the company, already the largest industrial distributor in North America, aggressively pursues higher market share and higher profits.[1] ◀

distribution   The activities that make products available to customers when and where they want to purchase them

Marketers at W. W. Grainger are making decisions regarding the **distribution** component of the marketing mix, which focuses on the decisions and actions involved in making products available to customers when and where they want to purchase them. Choosing marketing channels and managing supply chains are major issues in the development of competitive marketing strategies.

In this chapter, we focus on marketing channels and supply-chain management. First, we discuss the nature of marketing channels and supply-chain management, including the need for intermediaries. Next, we outline the types of marketing channels and consider supply-chain management, including behavioral patterns within marketing channels. We also explore ways to integrate marketing channels and how marketers determine the appropriate intensity of market coverage for a product. Finally, we look at the role of physical distribution within the supply chain, including its objectives and basic functions.

◉)) Marketing Channels and Supply-Chain Management

marketing channel   A group of individuals and organizations directing products from producers to customers

A **marketing channel** (also called a *channel of distribution* or *distribution channel*) is a group of individuals and organizations that directs the flow of products from producers to customers. The major role of marketing channels is to make products available at the right time, at the right place, in the right quantities. Providing customer satisfaction should be the driving force behind marketing channel decisions. Buyers' needs and behavior are therefore important concerns of channel members.

marketing intermediary   A middleman linking producers to other middlemen or ultimate consumers through contractual arrangements or through the purchase and resale of products

Some marketing channels are direct, meaning that the product goes direct from the producer to customer. For example, when a customer orders a computer from Dell, this product is sent from the manufacturer to the customer.[2] A **marketing intermediary** (or *middleman*) links producers to other intermediaries or to ultimate consumers through contractual arrangements or through the purchase and reselling of products. Marketing intermediaries can perform most marketing activities. They also play key roles in customer relationship management, not only through their distribution activities but also by maintaining databases and information systems to help all members of the marketing channel maintain effective customer relationships. For example, eBay serves as a marketing intermediary between Internet sellers and buyers. eBay not only provides a forum for these exchanges, it also keeps an extensive database of members' rankings to facilitate relationships among eBay channel members.[3]

supply-chain management   Long-term partnerships among marketing channel members that reduce inefficiencies, costs, and redundancies and develop innovative approaches to satisfy customers

An important function of the marketing channel is the joint effort of all channel members to create a supply chain, a total distribution system that serves customers and creates a competitive advantage. **Supply-chain management** refers to long-term partnerships among marketing channel members that reduce inefficiencies, costs, and redundancies in the marketing channel and develop innovative approaches to satisfy customers. Worldwide spending on supply-chain management systems is about $20 billion.[4]

Technology Facilities Supply-Chain Management Logistics assists companies in managing their supply chain with efficient software applications.

Supply-chain management involves manufacturing, research, sales, advertising, shipping, and, most of all, cooperation and understanding of tradeoffs throughout the whole channel to achieve the optimal level of efficiency and service. Table 14.1 outlines the key tasks involved in supply-chain management. Whereas traditional marketing channels tend to focus on producers, wholesalers, retailers, and customers, the supply chain is a broader concept that includes facilitating agencies such as shipping companies, communication companies, and other organizations that indirectly take part in marketing exchanges. Thus, the supply chain includes all entities that facilitate product distribution and benefit from cooperative efforts. Toyota, for example, had long relied on a hand-picked group of 213 suppliers to provide low-cost parts and components. Under the pressure of increased global competition, the automaker began encouraging some of its suppliers to work more closely by combining manufacturing operations, attracting more orders to improve economies of scale, and cooperating to create less expensive but high-quality standardized parts.[5]

Supply-chain management is helping more firms realize that optimizing supply chain costs through partnerships will improve all members' profits. All parties should focus on cooperating to reduce the costs of all affected channel members. Supply chains start with the customer and require the cooperation of channel members to satisfy customer requirements. When the buyer, the seller, marketing intermediaries, and facilitating agencies work together, the cooperative relationship results in compromise and adjustments that meet customers' needs regarding delivery, scheduling, packaging, or other requirements.

Technology has dramatically improved the capability of supply-chain management on a global basis. Information technology, in particular, has created an almost seamless distribution process for matching inventory needs to customers' requirements. With integrated information sharing among channel members, costs can be

Table 14.1	Key Tasks in Supply-Chain Management
Planning	Organizational and systemwide coordination of marketing channel partnerships to meet customers' product needs.
Sourcing	Purchasing of necessary resources, goods, and services from suppliers to support all supply-chain members.
Facilitating Delivery	All activities designed to move the product through the marketing channel to the end user.
Building Relationships	All marketing activities related to sales, service, and the development of long-term customer relationships.

reduced, service can be improved, and value provided to the customer can be enhanced. Indeed, information is crucial in operating global supply chains efficiently and effectively. Each marketing channel member requires information from other channel members. For example, suppliers need order and forecast information from the manufacturer; they may also need availability information from their own suppliers. Companies must be able to identify changes in the supply chain, assess their potential impact, and respond to these changes rapidly.[6] Customer relationship management (CRM) systems exploit the information from supply-chain partners' database and information systems to help all channel members make marketing strategy decisions that develop and sustain desirable customer relationships. Thus, managing relationships with supply-chain partners is crucial to satisfying customers. CRM is gaining popularity with big companies like Hewlett-Packard and Amazon.com spending large sums of money on implementation and support for data mining and CRM analytical applications. By 2008, companies that supply CRM technology, such as Siebel, SAS, and NetIQ, are expected to bring in over $11 billion in revenues.[7]

◉ The Importance of Marketing Channels

Although distribution decisions need not precede other marketing decisions, they are a powerful influence on the rest of the marketing mix. Channel decisions are critical because they determine a product's market presence and buyers' accessibility to the product. For example, because small businesses are more likely to purchase computers from office supply stores like Office Depot or warehouse clubs like Sam's, computer companies may be at a disadvantage without distribution through these outlets. Channel decisions have additional strategic significance because they entail long-term commitments. Thus, it is usually easier to change prices or promotional strategies than to change marketing channels.

Marketing channels serve many functions, including creating utility and facilitating exchange efficiencies. Although some of these functions may be performed by a single channel member, most functions are accomplished through both independent and joint efforts of channel members. When managed effectively, the relationships among channel members can also form supply chains that benefit all members of the channel, including the ultimate consumer.

● **Marketing Channels Create Utility.** Marketing channels create three types of utility: time, place, and possession. *Time utility* is having products available when the customer wants them. *Place utility* is created by making products available in locations where customers wish to purchase them. *Possession utility* means the customer has access to the product to use or to store for future use. Possession utility can occur through ownership or through arrangements that give the customer the right to use the product, such as a lease or rental agreement. Channel members sometimes create *form utility* by assembling, preparing, or otherwise refining the product to suit individual customer needs.

● **Marketing Channels Facilitate Exchange Efficiencies.** Marketing intermediaries can reduce the costs of exchanges by efficiently performing certain services or functions. Even if producers and buyers are located in the same city, there are costs associated with exchanges. As Figure 14.1 shows, when four buyers seek products from four producers, 16 transactions are possible. If one intermediary serves both producers and buyers, the number of transactions can be reduced to eight. Intermediaries are specialists in facilitating exchanges. They provide valuable assistance because of their access to and control over important resources used in the proper functioning of marketing channels.

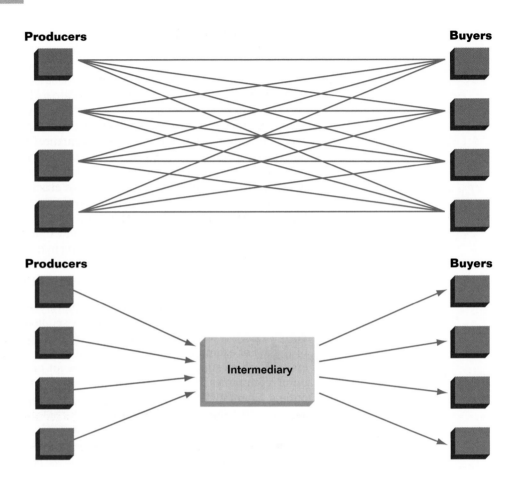

Nevertheless, the press, consumers, public officials, and other marketers freely criticize intermediaries, especially wholesalers. Critics accuse wholesalers of being inefficient and parasitic. Buyers often wish to make the distribution channel as short as possible, assuming the fewer the intermediaries, the lower the price will be. Because suggestions to eliminate them come from both ends of the marketing channel, wholesalers must be careful to perform only those marketing activities that are truly desired. To survive, they must be more efficient and more customer focused than other marketing institutions.

Critics who suggest that eliminating wholesalers would lower customer prices do not recognize that this would not eliminate the need for services that wholesalers provide. Although wholesalers can be eliminated, the functions they perform cannot. Other channel members would have to perform those functions, and customers would still have to pay for them. In addition, all producers would have to deal directly with retailers or customers, meaning every producer would have to keep voluminous records and hire enough personnel to deal with a multitude of customers. Customers might end up paying a great deal more for products because prices would reflect the costs of less efficient channel members.

◉ Types of Marketing Channels

Because marketing channels appropriate for one product may be less suitable for others, many different distribution paths have been developed. The various marketing channels can be classified generally as channels for consumer products and channels for business products.

● **Channels for Consumer Products.**   Figure 14.2 illustrates several channels used in the distribution of consumer products. Channel A depicts the direct movement of goods from producer to consumers. Producers that sell goods directly from their factories to end users are using direct marketing channels, as are companies that sell their own products over the Internet, such as Dell Computer. In fact, with Internet purchases projected to increase significantly over the next several years, direct channels via the Internet are likely to become important components of many companies' distribution strategies. Although direct marketing channels are the simplest, they are not necessarily the most effective distribution method. Faced with the strategic choice of going directly to the customer or using intermediaries, a firm must evaluate the benefits to customers of going direct versus the transaction costs involved in using intermediaries.

Channel B, which moves goods from the producer to a retailer and then to customers, is a frequent choice of large retailers because it allows them to buy in quantity from manufacturers. Retailers like Target and Wal-Mart sell clothing, stereos, and many other items purchased directly from producers. New automobiles and new college textbooks are also sold through this type of marketing channel. Primarily nonstore retailers, such as L.L. Bean and J. Crew, also use this type of channel.

A long-standing distribution channel, especially for consumer products, channel C takes goods from the producer to a wholesaler, then to a retailer, and finally to consumers. It is a practical option for producers that sell to hundreds of thousands of customers through thousands of retailers. A single producer finds it hard to do business directly with thousands of retailers. Consider the number of retailers marketing Wrigley's chewing gum. It would be extremely difficult, if not impossible, for Wrigley to deal directly with each retailer that sells its brand of gum. Manufacturers of tobacco products, some home appliances, hardware, and many convenience goods sell their

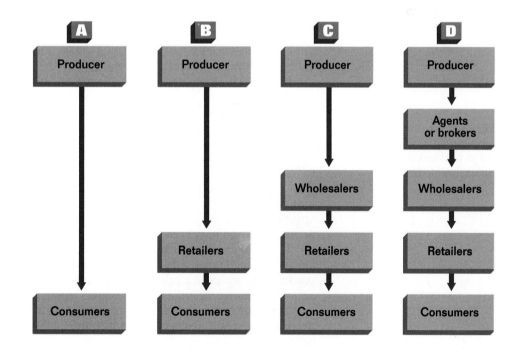

Figure 14.2
Typical Marketing Channels for Consumer Products

Geared for Performance!

BALDOR GEAR PRODUCTS PLAY THEIR PARTS WELL.

One of Baldor's top performers is our complete line of gear products including gearmotors, right angle and "high efficiency" in-line gearboxes. Baldor gearmotors are available in AC or DC voltages with the broadest torque and speed ranges available. Incorporated into the gearmotor is Baldor's exclusive internal expansion bladder, allowing mounting in any direction without the need to add and remove breather plugs.

Baldor's right angle and in-line gearboxes provide the high quality you expect with hundreds of stock variations, including our NEW stainless-steel gearbox! You have speed and torque challenges... Baldor is geared with solutions! Call the nearest Baldor distributor or log on today for more information.

BALDOR
MOTORS, DRIVES & GENERATORS
The Value of Solutions.

1-800-828-4920 • www.baldor.com

Made in the U.S.A.

©2008 Baldor Electric Company
Form No. AR-410

Printed in the U.S.A
3/03 DIV 2500

Industrial Distributor
Baldor is an industrial distributor.

industrial distributor An independent business that takes title to business products and carries inventories

products to wholesalers, which then sell to retailers, which in turn do business with individual consumers.

Channel D, through which goods pass from producer to agents to wholesalers to retailers and then to consumers, is frequently used for products intended for mass distribution, such as processed foods. For example, to place its cracker line in specific retail outlets, a food processor may hire an agent (or a food broker) to sell the crackers to wholesalers. Wholesalers then sell the crackers to supermarkets, vending machine operators, and other retail outlets.

Contrary to popular opinion, a long channel may be the most efficient distribution channel for some consumer goods. When several channel intermediaries perform specialized functions, costs may be lower than when one channel member tries to perform them all.

● **Channels for Business Products.** Figure 14.3 shows four of the most common channels for business products. As with consumer products, manufacturers of business products sometimes work with more than one level of wholesalers.

Channel E illustrates the direct channel for business products. In contrast to consumer goods, more than half of all business products, especially expensive equipment, are sold through direct channels. Business customers like to communicate directly with producers, especially when expensive or technically complex products are involved. For this reason, business buyers prefer to purchase expensive and highly complex mainframe computers directly from IBM, Cray, and other mainframe producers. Intel has established direct-marketing channels for selling its microprocessor chips to computer manufacturers. In these circumstances, a customer wants the technical assistance and personal assurances that only a producer can provide.

In the second business products channel, channel F, an industrial distributor facilitates exchanges between the producer and the customer. An **industrial distributor** is an independent business that takes title to products and carries inventories. Industrial distributors usually sell standardized items such as maintenance supplies, production tools, and small operating equipment. Some industrial distributors carry a wide variety of product lines. Others specialize in one or a small number of lines. Industrial distributors are carrying an increasing percentage of business products. Due to mergers and acquisitions, they have become larger and more powerful.[8] Industrial distributors can be most effectively used when a product has broad market appeal, is easily stocked and serviced, is sold in small quantities, and is needed on demand to avoid high losses.

The third channel for business products, channel G, employs a manufacturers' agent, an independent businessperson who sells complementary products of several producers in assigned territories and is compensated through commissions. Unlike an industrial distributor, a manufacturers' agent does not acquire title to the products and usually does not take possession. Acting as a salesperson on behalf of the producers, a manufacturers' agent has little or no latitude in negotiating prices or sales terms.

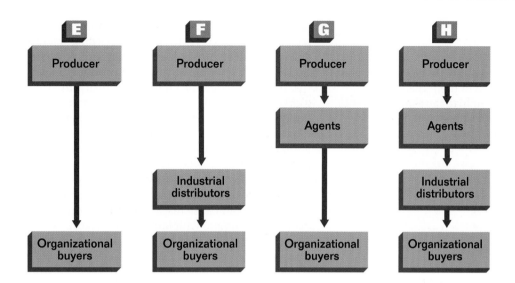

Figure 14.3
Typical Marketing Channels for Business Products

Finally, channel H includes both a manufacturers' agent and an industrial distributor. This channel may be appropriate when the producer wishes to cover a large geographic area but maintains no sales force because of highly seasonal demand or because it cannot afford a sales force. This type of channel can also be useful for a business marketer that wants to enter a new geographic market without expanding its existing sales force.

● **Multiple Marketing Channels and Channel Alliances.** To reach diverse target markets, manufacturers may use several marketing channels simultaneously, with each channel involving a different group of intermediaries. For example, a manufacturer uses multiple channels when the same product is directed to both consumers

Using Multiple Marketing Channels
Coca-Cola Company distributes Dasani Purified Water through different marketing channels simultaneously.

dual distribution   The use of two or more channels to distribute the same product to the same target market

and business customers. When Del Monte markets ketchup for household use, it is sold to supermarkets through grocery wholesalers, or, in some cases, directly to retailers, whereas ketchup going to restaurants or institutions follows a different distribution channel. In some instances, a producer may prefer **dual distribution**, the use of two or more marketing channels to distribute the same products to the same target market. An example of dual distribution is a firm that sells products through retail outlets and its own mail-order catalog or website. For example, the upscale cosmetics manufacturer Estée Lauder is diversifying its marketing channels to fuel growth. In addition to selling through department stores, the company is selling through online retailers such as Gloss.com and selling its Aveda, MAC, and Origins products through single-brand cosmetics stores and websites.[9] Kellogg sells its cereals directly to large retail grocery chains and to food wholesalers that, in turn, sell them to retailers. Dual distribution can cause dissatisfaction among wholesalers and smaller retailers when they must compete with large retail grocery chains that make direct purchases from manufacturers like Kellogg. The practice of dual distribution has been challenged as being anticompetitive.

strategic channel alliance   An agreement whereby the products of one organization are distributed through the marketing channels of another

A **strategic channel alliance** exists when the products of one organization are distributed through the marketing channels of another. The products of the two firms are often similar with respect to target markets or uses, but they are not direct competitors. For example, a brand of bottled water might be distributed through a marketing channel for soft drinks, or a domestic cereal producer might form a strategic channel alliance with a European food processor. Alliances can provide benefits for both the organization that owns the marketing channel and the company whose brand is being distributed through the channel.

◉ Channel Leadership, Cooperation, and Conflict

Each channel member performs a different role in the system and agrees (implicitly or explicitly) to accept certain rights, responsibilities, rewards, and sanctions for nonconformity. Each channel member also holds certain expectations of other channel members. Retailers, for instance, expect wholesalers to maintain adequate inventories and deliver goods on time. Wholesalers expect retailers to honor payment agreements and keep them informed of inventory needs.

Channel partnerships facilitate effective supply-chain management when partners agree on objectives, policies, and procedures for physical distribution efforts associated with the supplier's products. Such partnerships eliminate redundancies and reassign tasks for maximum sys-

"Benjamin Moore calls new Regal® *Matte Finish* their most beautiful, *washable* paint yet. I couldn't *agree* more."

Benjamin Moore Paints

We make it simple. You make it beautiful.™

For a retailer near you call 1-800-6-PAINT-6 or visit www.benjaminmoore.com

Channel Leadership
The manufacturer of Benjamin Moore Paints provides channel leadership in the distribution channels for its products.

channel power   The ability of one channel member to influence another member's goal achievement

temwide efficiency. One of the best-known partnerships is that between Wal-Mart and Procter & Gamble. Procter & Gamble locates some of its staff near Wal-Mart's purchasing department in Bentonville, Arkansas, to establish and maintain the supply chain. Sharing information through a cooperative computer system, Procter & Gamble monitors Wal-Mart's inventory and additional data to determine production and distribution plans for its products. The results are increased efficiency, decreased inventory costs, and greater satisfaction for the customers of both companies. Wal-Mart believes these efforts provide it with a significant competitive advantage.[10] At this point, many suppliers have been unwilling or unable to make this level of commitment. In this section, we discuss channel member behavior, including leadership, cooperation, and conflict, that marketers must understand to make effective channel decisions.

Many marketing channel decisions are determined by consensus. Producers and intermediaries coordinate efforts for mutual benefit. Some marketing channels, however, are organized and controlled by a single leader, or *channel captain*. The channel captain may be a producer, wholesaler, or retailer. Channel captains may establish channel policies and coordinate development of the marketing mix. Wal-Mart, for example, dominates the supply chain for its retail stores by virtue of the magnitude of its resources (especially information management) and strong, nationwide customer base. To become a captain, a channel member must want to influence overall channel performance. To attain desired objectives, the captain must possess **channel power**, the ability to influence another channel member's goal achievement. The member that becomes the channel captain will accept the responsibilities and exercise the power associated with this role.

Channel cooperation is vital if each member is to gain something from other members. By cooperating, retailers, wholesalers, and suppliers can speed up inventory replenishment, improve customer service, and cut the costs of bringing products to the consumer.[11] Without cooperation, neither overall channel goals nor member goals can be realized. All channel members must recognize and understand that the success of one firm in the channel depends, in part, on other member firms. Thus, marketing channel members should make a coordinated effort to satisfy market requirements. Channel cooperation leads to greater trust among channel members and improves the overall functioning of the channel. It also leads to more satisfying relationships among channel members.

Although all channel members work toward the same general goal—distributing products profitably and efficiently—members may sometimes disagree about the best methods for attaining this goal. However, if self-interest creates misunderstanding about role expectations, the end result is frustration and conflict for the whole channel. For individual organizations to function together, each channel member must clearly communicate and understand role expectations. Communication difficulties are a potential form of channel conflict because ineffective communication leads to frustration, misunderstandings, and ill-coordinated strategies, jeopardizing further coordination.

The increased use of multiple channels of distribution, driven partly by new technology, has increased the potential for conflict between manufacturers and intermediaries. For example, Hewlett-Packard makes products available directly to consumers through its website (**www.hewlett-packard.com**), thereby directly competing with existing distributors and retailers.[12] Channel conflicts also arise when intermediaries overemphasize competing products or diversify into product lines traditionally handled by other intermediaries. Sometimes conflict develops because producers strive to increase efficiency by circumventing intermediaries. Such conflict is occurring in marketing channels for computer software. A number of software-only stores are establishing direct relationships with software producers, bypassing whole-sale distributors altogether.

There are several ways to improve channel cooperation. If a marketing channel is viewed as a unified supply chain competing with other systems, individual members will be less likely to take actions that create disadvantages for other members. Similarly, channel members should agree to direct efforts toward common objectives so channel roles can be structured for maximum marketing effectiveness, which in turn can help members achieve individual objectives. Heineken, for example, was having difficulty with its 450 distributors; at one point, the time between order and delivery reached 12 weeks. A cooperative system of supply-chain management, with Internet-based communications, decreased the lead time from order to delivery to four weeks, and Heineken's sales increased 24 percent.[13] A critical component in cooperation is a precise definition of each channel member's tasks. A precise definition provides a basis for reviewing the intermediaries' performance and helps reduce conflicts because each channel member knows exactly what is expected of it.

◉ Channel Integration

Channel members can either combine and control most activities or pass them on to another channel member. Channel functions may be transferred between intermediaries and to producers and even customers. However, a channel member cannot eliminate functions; unless buyers themselves perform the functions, they must pay for the labor and resources needed to perform the functions.

Various channel stages may be combined under the management of a channel captain either horizontally or vertically. Such integration may stabilize supply, reduce costs, and increase coordination of channel members.

vertical channel integration
Combining two or more stages of the marketing channel under one management

● **Vertical Channel Integration.**   Vertical channel integration combines two or more stages of the channel under one management. This may occur when one member of a marketing channel purchases the operations of another member or simply performs the functions of another member, eliminating the need for that intermediary. Unlike conventional channel systems, participants in vertical channel integration coordinate efforts to reach a desired target market. In this more progressive approach to distribution, channel members regard other members as extensions of their own operations. Vertically integrated channels are often more effective against competition because of increased bargaining power and the sharing of information and responsibilities. At one end of a vertically integrated channel, a manufacturer might provide advertising and training assistance, and the retailer at the other end might buy the manufacturer's products in large quantities and actively promote them.

vertical marketing systems (VMSs)   A marketing channel managed by a single channel member

Integration has been successfully institutionalized in marketing channels called vertical marketing systems (VMSs), in which a single channel member coordinates or manages channel activities to achieve efficient, low-cost distribution aimed at satisfying target market customers. Vertical integration brings most or all stages of the marketing channel under common control or ownership. The Limited, a retail clothing chain, uses a wholly owned subsidiary, Mast Industries, as its primary supply source. Radio Shack operates as a VMS, encompassing both wholesale and retail functions. Because efforts of individual channel members are combined in a VMS, marketing activities can be coordinated for maximum effectiveness and economy, without duplication of services. VMSs are competitive, accounting for a share of retail sales in consumer goods.

MARKETING ENTREPRENEURS

Dineh Mohajer

HER BUSINESS: Hard Candy Cosmetics

FOUNDED AT AGE: 22

SUCCESS: Over 60 colors of nail polish are available nationwide

Unable to find nail polish to match her baby blue sandals, Dineh mixed some of her old nail polish colors together and created a new color she called "Sky." Dineh received so many compliments on the unusual color that she decided to sell her creation. Fred Segal, a prestigious boutique in Los Angeles, was the first to introduce her Hard Candy Cosmetics samples. An instant success, many boutiques began placing large orders. Eventually, Dineh rented a warehouse and hired a full-time staff to help her meet the demand. Hard Candy Cosmetics now operates out of three offices (California, Maryland, and Florida), offers over 60 shades of nail polish, makes a full line of other cosmetics, and is available at boutiques throughout the country.[a]

Most VMSs take one of three forms: corporate, administered, or contractual. A *corporate VMS* combines all stages of the marketing channel, from producers to consumers, under a single owner. Supermarket chains that own food-processing plants and large retailers that purchase wholesaling and production facilities are examples of corporate VMSs. In an *administered VMS*, channel members are independent, but a high level of interorganizational management is achieved through informal coordination. Although individual channel members maintain autonomy, as in conventional marketing channels, one channel member (such as a producer or large retailer) dominates the administered VMS so that distribution decisions take the whole system into account. Under a *contractual VMS*, the most popular type of VMS, channel members are linked by legal agreements spelling out each member's rights and obligations. Franchise organizations, such as McDonald's and KFC, are contractual VMSs. Other contractual VMSs include wholesaler-sponsored groups, such as IGA (Independent Grocers' Alliance) stores, and retailer-sponsored cooperatives, which own and operate their own wholesalers.

horizontal channel integration
Combining organizations at the same level of operation under one management

● **Horizontal Channel Integration.** Combining organizations at the same level of operation under one management constitutes horizontal channel integration. An organization may integrate horizontally by merging with other organizations at the same level in the marketing channel. The owner of a dry cleaning firm, for example, might buy and combine several other existing dry cleaning establishments. Horizontal integration may enable a firm to generate sufficient sales revenue to integrate vertically as well.

Although horizontal integration permits efficiencies and economies of scale in purchasing, marketing research, advertising, and specialized personnel, it is not always the most effective method of improving distribution. Problems of size often follow, resulting in decreased flexibility, difficulties in coordination, and the need for additional marketing research and large-scale planning. Unless distribution functions for the various units can be performed more efficiently under unified management than under the previously separate managements, horizontal integration will neither reduce costs nor improve the competitive position of the integrating firm.

◉ Intensity of Market Coverage

In addition to deciding how to organize marketing channels for distributing a product, marketers must determine the intensity of coverage that a product should get, that is, the number and kinds of outlets in which it will be sold. This decision depends on the characteristics of the product and the target market. To achieve the desired

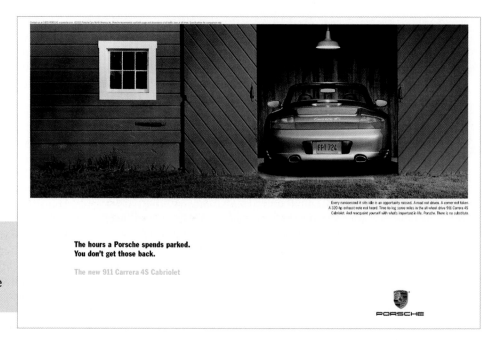

The hours a Porsche spends parked.
You don't get those back.

The new 911 Carrera 4S Cabriolet

PORSCHE

Selective Distribution
Porsches, sold through Porsche dealers, are distributed through selective distribution.

intensity of market coverage, distribution must correspond to behavior patterns of buyers. In considering products for purchase, consumers take into account replacement rate, product adjustment (services), duration of consumption, time required to find the product, and similar factors.[14] These variables directly affect the intensity of market coverage. Three major levels of market coverage are intensive, selective, and exclusive distribution.

Intensive distribution uses all available outlets for distributing a product. Intensive distribution is appropriate for convenience products like bread, chewing gum, soft drinks, and newspapers. Convenience products have a high replacement rate and require almost no service. To meet these demands, intensive distribution is necessary, and multiple channels may be used to sell through all possible outlets. For example, soft drinks, snacks, laundry detergent, and aspirin are available at convenience stores, service stations, supermarkets, discount stores, and other types of retailers. To consumers, availability means a store is located nearby and minimum time is necessary to search for the product at the store. Sales may have a direct relationship to product availability.

Selective distribution uses only some available outlets in an area to distribute a product. Selective distribution is appropriate for shopping products; durable goods like televisions and stereos usually fall into this category. These products are more expensive than convenience goods, and consumers are willing to spend more time visiting several retail outlets to compare prices, designs, styles, and other features. For example, Hermes Parfums is launching Eau des Merveilles, an exclusive new scent, and related products, only to selected high-end retailers. It expects to generate more than $25 million in retail volume in its first year.[15] Selective distribution is desirable when a special effort, such as customer service from a channel member, is important. Shopping products require differentiation at the point of purchase. Many business products are sold on a selective basis to maintain some control over the distribution process.

intensive distribution   Using all available outlets to distribute a product

selective distribution   Using only some available outlets to distribute a product

exclusive distribution   Using a single outlet in a fairly large geographic area to distribute a product

Exclusive distribution uses only one outlet in a relatively large geographic area. Exclusive distribution is suitable for products purchased infrequently, consumed over a long period of time, or requiring service or information to fit them to buyers' needs. It is also used for expensive, high-quality products, such as Porsche automobiles. It is not appropriate for convenience products and many shopping products.

Physical Distribution in Supply-Chain Management

physical distribution   Activities used to move products from producers to consumers and other end users

outsourcing   The contracting of physical distribution tasks to third parties who do not have managerial authority within the marketing channel

Physical distribution, also known as *logistics,* refers to the activities used to move products from producers to consumers and other end users. These activities include order processing, inventory management, materials handling, warehousing, and transportation. Physical distribution systems must meet the needs of both the supply chain and customers. Distribution activities are thus an important part of supply-chain planning and require the cooperation of all partners. Often one channel member manages physical distribution for all channel members.

Within the marketing channel, physical distribution activities may be performed by a producer, a wholesaler, or a retailer, or they may be outsourced. In the context of distribution, **outsourcing** is the contracting of physical distribution tasks to third parties who do not have managerial authority within the marketing channel. Most physical distribution activities can be outsourced to third-party firms that have special expertise in areas such as warehousing, transportation, and information technology. Cooperative relationships with third-party organizations, such as trucking companies, warehouses, and data-service providers, can help reduce marketing channel costs and boost service and customer satisfaction for all supply-chain partners. For example, several e-businesses as well as some traditional brick-and-mortar ones have outsourced physical distribution activities, including shipping and warehousing, to build a supply chain of strategic partners to maximize customer service. Such relationships are increasingly being integrated in the supply chain to achieve physical distribution objectives. When choosing companies through which to outsource, marketers must be cautious and use efficient firms that help the outsourcing company provide excellent customer service.

Planning an efficient physical distribution system is crucial to developing an effective marketing strategy because it can decrease costs and increase customer satisfaction. Speed of delivery, service, and dependability are often as important to customers as costs. Companies that have the right goods in the right place, at the right time, in the right quantity, and with the right support services, are able to sell more than competitors that do not. A construction equipment dealer with a low inventory of replacement parts requires fast, dependable service from component suppliers when it needs parts not in stock. Even when the demand for products is unpredictable, suppliers must be able to respond quickly to inventory needs. In such cases, physical distribution costs may be a minor consideration when compared with service, dependability, and timeliness.

As mentioned earlier, customer relationship management (CRM) systems exploit the information from supply-chain partners' database and information systems to facilitate marketing strategy decisions. This information can help logistics managers identify and root out inefficiencies in the supply chain for the benefit of all marketing channel members—from the producer to the ultimate consumer. Technology is playing a larger and larger role in physical distribution within marketing channels. The Web, in particular, has transformed physical distribution by facilitating

E-MARKETING AND TECHNOLOGY

TECHNOLOGY KEEPS THE HARD ROCK CAFÉ ROCKING

Hard Rock Café International has been serving up casual American meals and rock-and-roll merchandise since opening its first restaurants in 1971. Today the company operates 119 restaurants in 42 countries, as well as hotels, casinos, and a website (**www.hardrock.com**). In all, Hard Rock businesses ring up $360 million in yearly sales.

Along with burgers and beer, Hard Rock Cafés offer branded merchandise, live and recorded music, and rock music memorabilia. Arranging for branded merchandise to be shipped to every café in the right quantities and at the right times is a complex undertaking. Therefore, the company has hired outside experts to help with supplier contacts, inventory management, transportation, and storage. As a result, it needs 44 percent less warehouse space in the United States, has cut operational costs by 20 percent, and has boosted service to restaurants by 22 percent.

The company also rotates its $32 million collection of rock music artifacts between restaurants to draw repeat business. Each restaurant's design reflects the local rock scene, enhanced by the ever-changing memorabilia. On the stage of the Detroit café, for example, a garage door stands as a tribute to garage-band music. The original London café has showcased guitars from Eric Clapton and Pete Townsend, among other British rock artists. Other cafés display costumes, instruments, posters, and photos of Eminem, Elvis Presley, Madonna, John Lennon, Jimi Hendrix, the Goo Goo Dolls, and hundreds of other stars.

Many customers are tourists who eat at a Hard Rock Café and then buy T-shirts or other items as sou-venirs. Some branded, city-specific items can be purchased only in person, which encourages customers to visit other Hard Rock Cafés when they travel. In all, the cost of outfitting a new café can exceed $3 million, not including the cost of food and merchandise available on opening day. By making its distribution system more efficient, the company can rock on with continued expansion and added profits.[b]

just-in-time delivery, precise inventory visibility, and instant shipment tracking capabilities, which help companies avoid expensive mistakes, reduce costs, and even generate revenues.[16] Web-based information technology brings visibility to the supply chain by allowing marketing channel members to see exactly what is moving through the supply chain, when and where.[17] For example, Landstar Logistics, which provides transportation services throughout North America, introduced a new Web-based tracking service that enables customers to track the status of their shipments at any time through their office or laptop computers, or their cell phones or pagers.[18]

Although physical distribution managers try to minimize the costs associated with order processing, inventory management, materials handling, warehousing, and transportation, decreasing the costs in one area often raises them in another. Figure 14.4 shows the percentage of total costs that physical distribution functions represent. A total-cost approach to physical distribution enables managers to view

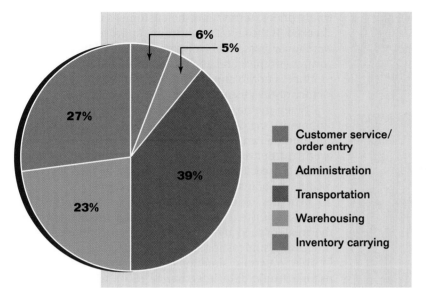

Figure 14.4
Proportional Cost of Each Physical Distribution Function as a Percentage of Total Distribution Costs

Source: From Logistics Cost and Service, 2004, Copyright © 2004, Herbert W. Davis and Company/Establish, Inc.
Source: Herbert W. Davis and Company/Establish, Inc., Ft. Lee, NJ, www.establishinc.com. Reprinted by permission of Herbert W. Davis and Company/Establish, Inc.

cycle time   The time needed to complete a process

order processing   The receipt and transmission of sales order information

physical distribution as a system rather than a collection of unrelated activities. This approach shifts the emphasis from lowering the separate costs of individual activities to minimizing overall distribution costs.

Physical distribution managers must be sensitive to the issue of cost tradeoffs. Higher costs in one functional area of a distribution system may be necessary to achieve lower costs in another. Tradeoffs are strategic decisions to combine (and recombine) resources for greatest cost-effectiveness. When distribution managers regard the system as a network of integrated functions, tradeoffs become useful tools in implementing a unified, cost-effective distribution strategy.

Another important goal of physical distribution involves reducing **cycle time**, the time needed to complete a process. Doing so can reduce costs and/or increase customer service. Many companies, particularly overnight delivery firms, major news media, and publishers of books of current interest, are using cycle-time reduction to gain a competitive advantage. FedEx believes so strongly in this concept that, in the interest of being the fastest provider of overnight delivery, it conducts research on reducing cycle time and identifying new management techniques and procedures for its employees. Seattle's Boeing Company is considering the construction of a plant to be run by two major suppliers and built next to Boeing's proposed 7E7 assembly plant. The plant would assemble about 75 percent of the 7E7's fuselage and deliver it to Boeing's final assembly plant next door. Not only would this arrangement reduce cycle time, but it would also save transportation costs on large pieces.[19]

In the rest of this section, we take a closer look at physical distribution activities, which include order processing, inventory management, materials handling, warehousing, and transportation.

◉ Order Processing

Order processing is the receipt and transmission of sales order information. Although management sometimes overlooks the importance of these activities, efficient order processing facilitates product flow. Computerized order processing provides a database for all supply-chain members to increase their productivity. When carried out quickly and accurately, order processing contributes to customer satisfaction, decreased costs and cycle time, and increased profits.

Order processing entails three main tasks: order entry, order handling, and order delivery. Order entry begins when customers or salespeople place purchase orders via telephone, mail, e-mail, or website. Electronic ordering is less time consuming than a manual, paper-based ordering system, and reduces costs. In some companies, sales representatives receive and enter orders personally, and also handle complaints, prepare progress reports, and forward sales order information.

Order handling involves several tasks. Once an order is entered, it is transmitted to a warehouse, where product availability is verified, and to the credit department,

Order accuracy: up
Fulfillment time: down
"Voice directed picking combined with a smart conveying and sorting network speeds up the fulfillment process and dramatically increases order accuracy."
Tim Beauchamp, Senior Vice President of Distribution Operations for Corporate Express
When Corporate Express needed a high productivity order fulfillment system, Siemens provided an integrated solution consisting of a conveying and sorting system, powerful zone routing software and voice directed picking. The system allows Corporate Express to ship 100,000 orders overnight with greater than 99.95% accuracy.
One Source system solutions:
• Supply Chain Management Services
• WMS, WCS and Material Flow Software
• RFID Integration
• Voice and Light directed Order Fulfillment
• Package Conveyor and Sortation
• Pallet Conveyor and Robotic Palletizing
• AS/RS and AGVS
• Assembly Conveyor
• 24/7 Technical Support
Siemens
Logistics and Assembly Systems
1-877-725-7500
www.usa.siemens-dematic.com
SIEMENS

Improving Order Processing
A number of organizations provide both hardware and software to improve order processing by making it more accurate and efficient.

electronic data interchange (EDI) A computerized means of integrating order processing with production, inventory, accounting, and transportation

inventory management Developing and maintaining adequate assortments of products to meet customers' needs

where prices, terms, and the customer's credit rating are checked. If the credit department approves the purchase, warehouse personnel (sometimes assisted by automated equipment) pick and assemble the order. If the requested product is not in stock, a production order is sent to the factory or the customer is offered a substitute.

When the order has been assembled and packed for shipment, the warehouse schedules delivery with an appropriate carrier. If the customer pays for rush service, overnight delivery by FedEx, UPS, or another overnight carrier is used. The customer is sent an invoice, inventory records are adjusted, and the order is delivered.

Whether to use a manual or an electronic order-processing system depends on which method provides the greater speed and accuracy within cost limits. Manual processing suffices for small-volume orders and is more flexible in certain situations. Most companies, however, use **electronic data interchange (EDI)**, which uses computer technology to integrate order processing with production, inventory, accounting, and transportation. Within the supply chain, EDI functions as an information system that links marketing channel members and outsourcing firms together. It reduces paperwork for all members of the supply chain and allows them to share information on invoices, orders, payments, inquiries, and scheduling. Consequently many companies have pushed their suppliers toward EDI to reduce distribution costs and cycle times. For example, FedEx is a major user of EDI systems. It uses EDI to develop innovative solutions to resolve some of its complex business problems. In addition, a large proportion of its major business customers carry out transactions via EDI.[20]

Inventory Management

Inventory management involves developing and maintaining adequate assortments of products to meet customers' needs. Because a firm's investment in inventory usually represents a significant portion of its total assets, inventory decisions have a major impact on physical distribution costs and the level of customer service provided. When too few products are carried in inventory, the result is *stockouts,* or shortages of products, which in turn result in brand switching, lower sales, and loss of customers. When too many products (or too many slow-moving products) are carried, costs increase, as do risks of product obsolescence, pilferage, and damage. The objective of inventory management is to minimize inventory costs while maintaining an adequate supply of goods to satisfy customers. To achieve this objective, marketers focus on two major issues: when to order and how much to order.

To determine when to order, a marketer calculates the *reorder point,* the inventory level that signals the need to place a new order. To calculate the reorder point, the marketer must know the order lead time, the usage rate, and the amount of safety stock required. The *order lead time* refers to the average time lapse between placing the order and receiving it. The *usage rate* is the rate at which a product's inventory is used or sold during a specific time period. *Safety stock* is the amount of extra inventory a firm keeps to guard against stockouts resulting from above-average usage rates and/or longer-than-expected lead times. The reorder point can be calculated using the following formula:

$$\text{Reorder Point} = (\text{Order Lead Time} \times \text{Usage Rate}) + \text{Safety Stock}$$

Thus, if order lead time is 10 days, usage rate is 3 units per day, and safety stock is 20 units, the reorder point is 50 units.

just-in-time (JIT)   An inventory management approach in which supplies arrive just when needed for production or resale

Efficient inventory management with accurate reorder points is crucial for firms that use a **just-in-time (JIT)** approach, in which supplies arrive just as they are needed for use in production or for resale. When using JIT, companies maintain low inventory levels and purchase products and materials in small quantities whenever they need them. Usually there is no safety stock, and suppliers are expected to provide consistently high-quality products. Just-in-time inventory management requires a high level of coordination between producers and suppliers, but it eliminates waste and reduces inventory costs significantly. This approach has been used successfully by many well-known firms, including DaimlerChrysler, Harley-Davidson, and Dell Computer, to reduce costs and boost customer satisfaction. When a JIT approach is used in a supply chain, suppliers often move close to their customers.

◉ Materials Handling

materials handling   Physical handling of products

Materials handling, the physical handling of products, is an important factor in warehouse operations, as well as in transportation from points of production to points of consumption. Efficient procedures and techniques for materials handling minimize inventory management costs, reduce the number of times a good is handled, improve customer service, and increase customer satisfaction. Systems for packaging, labeling, loading, and movement must be coordinated to maximize cost reduction and customer satisfaction.

Product characteristics often determine handling. For example, the characteristics of bulk liquids and gases determine how they can be moved and stored. Internal packaging is also an important consideration in materials handling; goods must be packaged correctly to prevent damage or breakage during handling and transportation. Most companies employ packaging consultants to help them decide which packaging materials and methods will result in the most efficient handling.

Unit loading and containerization are two common methods used in materials handling. With *unit loading,* one or more boxes are placed on a pallet or skid; these units can then be efficiently loaded by mechanical means such as forklifts, trucks, or conveyer systems. *Containerization* is the consolidation of many items into a single large container, which is sealed at its point of origin and opened at its destination. Containers are usually 8 feet wide, 8 feet high, and 10 to 40 feet long. They can be conveniently stacked and shipped via train, barge, or ship. Once containers reach their destinations, wheel assemblies can be added to make them suitable for ground transportation. Because individual items are not handled in transit, containerization greatly increases efficiency and security in shipping.

◉ Warehousing

warehousing   The design and operation of facilities for storing and moving goods

Warehousing, the design and operation of facilities for storing and moving goods, is another important physical distribution function. Warehousing provides time utility by enabling firms to compensate for dissimilar production and consumption rates. When mass production creates a greater stock of goods than can be sold immediately,

Warehousing
Specialized information technology is helping managers to operate warehouses more efficiently.

private warehouses
Company-operated facilities for storing and shipping products

public warehouses Businesses that lease storage space and related physical distribution facilities to other firms

companies may warehouse the surplus until customers are ready to buy. Warehousing also helps stabilize prices and availability of seasonal items.

The choice of warehouse facilities is an important strategic consideration. The right type of warehouse allows a company to reduce transportation and inventory costs or improve service to customers. The wrong type of warehouse may drain company resources. Beyond deciding how many facilities to operate and where to locate them, a company must determine which type of warehouse is most appropriate. Warehouses fall into two general categories: private and public. In many cases, a combination of private and public facilities provides the most flexible warehousing approach.

Companies operate **private warehouses** for shipping and storing their own products. A firm usually leases or purchases a private warehouse when its warehousing needs in a given geographic market are substantial and stable enough to warrant a long-term commitment to a fixed facility. Private warehouses are also appropriate for firms that require special handling and storage and that want control of warehouse design and operation. Retailers like Sears, Radio Shack, and Kmart find it economical to integrate private warehousing with purchasing and distribution for their retail outlets. When sales volumes are fairly stable, ownership and control of a private warehouse may provide benefits such as property appreciation. Private warehouses, however, face fixed costs such as insurance, taxes, maintenance, and debt expense. They also limit flexibility when firms wish to move inventories to more strategic locations. Many private warehouses are being eliminated by direct links between producers and customers, reduced cycle times, and outsourcing to public warehouses.

Public warehouses lease storage space and related physical distribution facilities as an outsource service to other companies. They sometimes provide distribution services such as receiving, unloading, inspecting, and reshipping products; filling orders; providing financing; displaying products; and coordinating shipments. United Facilities, Inc., for example, offers a wide range of services, including mixing inventory received from different places to consolidate shipments to customers, as well as packaging, filling, painting, assembly, and in-store setup, and corporate services such as purchasing, programming, writing, and order fulfillment.[21] Public warehouses are especially useful to firms that have seasonal production or low-volume storage needs, have inventories that must be maintained in many locations, are testing or entering new markets, or own private warehouses but occasionally require additional storage space. Public warehouses also serve as collection points during product recall programs. Whereas private warehouses have fixed costs, public warehouses offer variable (and often lower) costs because users rent space and purchase warehousing services only as needed.

Many public warehouses furnish security for products being used as collateral for loans, a service provided at either the warehouse or the site of the owner's inventory. *Field public warehouses* are established by public warehouses at the owner's inventory location. The warehouser becomes custodian of the products and issues a receipt that can be used as collateral for a loan. Public warehouses also provide *bonded storage,* a warehousing arrangement in which imported or taxable products are not released until the products' owners pay U.S. customs duties, taxes, or other fees. Bonded warehouses enable firms to defer tax payments on such items until they are delivered to customers.

distribution centers Large, centralized warehouses that focus on moving rather than storing goods

Distribution centers are large, centralized warehouses that receive goods from factories and suppliers, regroup them into orders, and ship them to customers quickly, the focus being on movement of goods rather than storage.[22] Distribution centers are specially designed for rapid flow of products. They are usually one-story buildings (to eliminate elevators) with access to transportation networks such as major highways or railway lines. Many distribution centers are highly automated, with computer-directed robots, forklifts, and hoists that collect and move products to loading docks. W. W. Grainger, Inc., which supplies electric motors and other maintenance, repair, and operating parts, operates nine distribution centers that employ radio frequency technology, bin modules, and takeaway conveyors. The firm projects that all these features will boost productivity by 55 percent.[23] Although some public warehouses offer such specialized services, most distribution centers are privately owned. They serve customers in regional markets and, in some cases, function as consolidation points for a company's branch warehouses.

⊙ Transportation

transportation The movement of products from where they are made to where they are used

Transportation, the movement of products from where they are made to where they are used, is the most expensive physical distribution function. Because product availability and timely deliveries depend on transportation functions, transportation decisions directly affect customer service. A firm may even build its distribution and marketing strategy around a unique transportation system if that system can ensure on-time deliveries and thereby give the firm a competitive edge. Companies may build their own transportation fleets (private carriers) or outsource the transportation function to a common or contract carrier.

● Transportation Modes. There are five basic transportation modes for moving physical goods: railroads, trucks, waterways, airways, and pipelines. Each mode offers distinct advantages. Many companies adopt physical handling procedures that facilitate the use of two or more modes in combination. Figure 14.5 indicates the percentage of intercity freight carried by each transportation mode.

Railroads like Union Pacific and Canadian National carry heavy, bulky freight that must be shipped long distances over land. Railroads commonly haul minerals, sand, lumber, chemicals, and farm products, as well as low-value manufactured goods and an increasing number of automobiles. They are especially efficient for transporting full carloads, which can be shipped at lower rates than smaller quantities because they require less handling. Many companies locate factories or warehouses near rail lines for convenient loading and unloading.

Trucks provide the most flexible schedules and routes of all major transportation modes because they can go almost anywhere. Because trucks have a unique ability to move goods

Figure 14.5
Proportion of Intercity Freight Carried by Various Transportation Modes
Source: U.S. Bureau of the Census, *Statistical Abstract of the United States,* 2004-2005, p. 675.

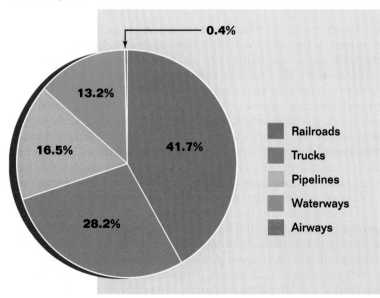

MARKETING AROUND THE WORLD

OSHKOSH B'GOSH CHANGES COURSE ON TRANSPORTATION

OshKosh B'Gosh has been known for making sturdy bib overalls since 1895. Employees originally cut and assembled the overalls (and other clothing) in the company's hometown of Oshkosh, Wisconsin. In recent years, however, OshKosh B'Gosh, like many U.S.-based apparel firms, has shifted much of its production to overseas factories. As a result, the company needed to rethink its transportation arrangements.

When OshKosh B'Gosh first began importing, it had clothing packed into containers, loaded onto ships, and sent to U.S. ports. An outside logistics firm ushered the sealed containers through customs and put them on trucks bound for the company's distribution centers. Between crowded ports and weekday-only working hours, containers that arrived by ship on a Thursday might sit untouched until Monday. Yet OshKosh B'Gosh needed stock replenished as quickly as possible. Even a few days' delay in getting clothing to distribution centers

and into the store network could be costly in terms of sales and profits.

As its volume of imports increased, the company hired a logistics specialist to speed shipments from the ports to the distribution centers. The specialist learned that shipping lines had crews available to offload containers on nights and weekends, although this after-hours service wasn't publicized. Soon OshKosh B'Gosh's containers were being offloaded on a Thursday-to-Sunday schedule at ports in California, Mississippi, and South Carolina. The contents were then sorted into separate trailers for each distribution center and sent on by truck.

Now OshKosh B'Gosh receives its imports up to ten days sooner and pays less for water transportation because the containers remain at the port. Moreover, it can check the status of every container immediately to find out which are still at sea, which have arrived at the port, which have been cleared through customs, and which have been emptied. Changing course on transportation has helped OshKosh B'Gosh keep costs down, keep racks stocked at its company-owned stores, and keep merchandise flowing to other retail customers.[c]

---

directly from factory or warehouse to customer, they are often used in conjunction with other forms of transport that cannot provide door-to-door deliveries. Although trucks usually travel much faster than trains, they are more expensive and somewhat more vulnerable to bad weather. They are also subject to size and weight restrictions on the products they carry. Trucks are sometimes criticized for high levels of loss and damage to freight and for delays caused by the rehandling of small shipments. In response, the trucking industry has turned to computerized tracking of shipments and the development of new equipment to speed loading and unloading. Marten Transport Ltd. in Wisconsin charges its customers for the time drivers have to wait and rewards clients that help keep things moving. Using a satellite-tracking system, the company can track when a driver arrives at a site and how long it takes to load and unload freight. The data are shared with customers, and Marten and its customers work together to eliminate wasteful practices. Marten has lost customers but has also reduced rates to others who have expedited loading and unloading.[24]

Waterways are the cheapest method of shipping heavy, low-value, nonperishable goods such as ore, coal, grain, and petroleum products. Water carriers offer considerable capacity. Powered by tugboats and towboats, barges that travel along intercoastal canals, inland rivers, and navigation systems can haul at least ten times the weight of one rail car, and ocean-going vessels can haul thousands of containers. More than 95 percent of international cargo is transported by water.[25] However, many markets are inaccessible by water transportation unless supplemented by rail or truck. Droughts and floods may also create difficulties for users of inland waterway transportation. Nevertheless, the extreme fuel efficiency of water transportation and the continuing globalization of marketing will likely increase its use in the future.

Air transportation is the fastest but most expensive form of shipping. It is used most often for perishable goods; for high-value, low-bulk items; and for products requiring quick delivery over long distances, such as emergency shipments. Some air carriers transport combinations of passengers, freight, and mail. Despite its expense, air transit can reduce warehousing and packaging costs and losses from theft and damage, thus helping to lower total costs (but truck transportation needed for pickup and final delivery adds to cost and transit time). Although air transport accounts for less than 1 percent of total ton-miles carried, its importance as a mode of transportation is growing. In fact, the success of many businesses is now based on the availability of overnight air delivery service provided by organizations such as UPS, FedEx, DHL, RPS Air, and the U.S. Postal Service. Amazon.com, for example, ships many products ordered online via UPS within a day of order. In addition, a number of companies are turning to air freight because they are ordering smaller quantities more frequently and requiring high-speed transportation in an effort to reduce inventory costs.[26]

Pipelines, the most automated transportation mode, usually belong to the shipper and carry the shipper's products. Most pipelines carry petroleum products or chemicals. The Trans-Alaska Pipeline, owned and operated by a consortium of oil companies that includes ExxonMobil and BP-Amoco, transports crude oil from remote oil-drilling sites in central Alaska to shipping terminals on the coast. Slurry pipelines carry pulverized coal, grain, or wood chips suspended in water. Pipelines move products slowly but continuously and at relatively low cost. They are dependable and minimize the problems of product damage and theft. However, contents are subject to as much as 1 percent shrinkage, usually from evaporation. Pipelines have also been a concern to environmentalists, who fear installation and leaks could harm plants and animals.

● **Choosing Transportation Modes.**   Logistics managers select a transportation mode based on the combination of cost, speed, dependability, load flexibility, accessibility, and frequency that is most appropriate for their products and generates the desired level of customer service. Table 14.2 shows relative ratings of each transportation mode by these selection criteria.

Marketers compare alternative transportation modes to determine whether benefits from a more expensive mode are worth higher costs. Companies such as Accuship can assist marketers in analyzing various transportation options. This Internet firm's software gives corporate users, like Coca-Cola and the Home Shopping Network, information about the speed and cost of different transportation modes and allows them to order shipping and then track shipments online. Accuship processes almost a million shipments every day.[27]

● **Coordinating Transportation.**   To take advantage of the benefits offered by various transportation modes and compensate for deficiencies, marketers often combine and coordinate two or more modes. In recent years, intermodal transportation, as this integrated approach is sometimes called, has become easier because of new developments within the transportation industry.

Several kinds of intermodal shipping are available. All combine the flexibility of trucking with the low cost or speed of other forms of transport. Containerization

intermodal transportation
Two or more transportation modes used in combination

Table 14.2	**Relative Ratings of Transportation Modes by Selection Criteria**					
Mode	**Cost**	**Speed**	**Dependability**	**Load Flexibility**	**Accessibility**	**Frequency**
Railroads	Moderate	Average	Average	High	High	Low
Trucks	High	Fast	High	Average	Very high	High
Waterways	Very low	Very slow	Average	Very high	Limited	Very low
Airways	Very high	Very fast	High	Low	Average	Average
Pipelines	Low	Slow	High	Very low	Very limited	Very high

facilitates intermodal transportation by consolidating shipments into sealed containers for transport by *piggyback* (shipping that uses both truck trailers and railway flatcars), *fishyback* (truck trailers and water carriers), and *birdyback* (truck trailers and air carriers). As transportation costs have increased, intermodal shipping has gained popularity.

Specialized outsource agencies provide other forms of transport coordination. Known as **freight forwarders**, these firms combine shipments from several organizations into efficient lot sizes. Small loads (less than 500 pounds) are much more expensive to ship than full carloads or truckloads, which frequently require consolidation. Freight forwarders take small loads from various marketers, buy transport space from carriers, and arrange for goods to be delivered to buyers. Freight forwarders' profits come from the margin between the higher, less-than-carload rates they charge each marketer and the lower carload rates they themselves pay. Because large shipments require less handling, use of freight forwarders can speed delivery. Freight forwarders can also determine the most efficient carriers and routes and are useful for shipping goods to foreign markets. Some companies prefer to outsource their shipping to freight forwarders because the latter provide door-to-door service.

Another transportation innovation is the development of **megacarriers**, freight transportation companies that offer several shipment methods, including rail, truck, and air service. CSX, for example, has trains, barges, container ships, trucks, and pipelines, thus offering a multitude of transportation services. In addition, air carriers have increased their ground transportation services. As they expand the range of transportation alternatives, carriers too put greater stress on customer service.

freight forwarders Organizations that consolidate shipments from several firms into efficient lot sizes

megacarriers Freight transportation firms that provide several modes of shipment

CHAPTER REVIEW

1 Describe the nature and functions of marketing channels.

A marketing channel, or channel of distribution, is a group of individuals and organizations that directs the flow of products from producers to customers. The major role of marketing channels is to make products available at the right time, at the right place, and in the right amounts. In most channels of distribution, producers and consumers are linked by marketing intermediaries, usually wholesalers and/or retailers. Marketing channels also form a supply chain, which refers to long-term partnerships among channel members working together to reduce inefficiencies, costs, and redundancies. Marketing channels create time, place, and possession utility by making products available when and where customers want them and providing customers with access to product use through sale or rental. Marketing intermediaries facilitate exchange efficiencies, by reducing the total number of transactions that otherwise would be required to move products from producer to ultimate users.

2 **Identify the types of marketing channels.**
Marketing channels are broadly classified as channels for consumer products and channels for business products. Although consumer goods can move directly from producer to consumers, consumer product channels that include wholesalers and retailers are usually more economical and efficient. For business products, direct distribution channels are common. Business channels often include industrial distributors, manufacturers' agents, or a combination of agents and distributors. Most producers employ multiple or dual channels so that they can adapt the distribution system for various target markets.

3 **Explore the concepts of leadership, cooperation, and conflict in channel relationships.**
Each channel member performs a different role in the supply chain and agrees to accept certain rights, responsibilities, and rewards, as well as sanctions for nonconformance. Although marketing channels may be determined by consensus, many are organized and controlled by a single leader, or channel captain. A channel leader may be a producer, wholesaler, or retailer. Channels function most effectively when members cooperate; when they deviate from their roles, channel conflict can arise.

4 **Recognize common strategies for integrating marketing channels.**
Vertical integration combines two or more stages of the marketing channel under one management. The vertical marketing system (VMS) is managed centrally for the mutual benefit of all channel members. Vertical marketing systems may be corporate, administered, or contractual. Horizontal integration combines institutions at the same level of channel operation under a single management.

5 **Examine the major levels of marketing coverage.**
A marketing channel is managed so that products receive appropriate market coverage. Intensive distri-

bution makes a product available to all possible dealers. In selective distribution, only some outlets in an area are chosen to distribute a product. Exclusive distribution usually gives one dealer exclusive right to sell a product in a large geographic area.

6 **Recognize the importance of the role of physical distribution activities in supply-chain management and overall marketing strategies.**
Physical distribution, or logistics, refers to the activities used to move products from producers to customers and other end users. These activities include order processing, inventory management, materials handling, warehousing, and transportation. An efficient physical distribution system is an important component of an overall marketing strategy because it can decrease costs and increase customer satisfaction. Within the marketing channel, physical distribution activities are often performed by a wholesaler, but they may also be performed by a producer or retailer or outsourced to a third party. Efficient physical distribution systems can decrease costs and transit time while increasing customer service.

7 **Examine the major physical distribution functions of order processing, inventory management, materials handling, warehousing, and transportation.**
Order processing is the receipt and transmission of sales order information. It consists of three main tasks—order entry, order handling, and order delivery—which may be done manually but are more often handled through electronic data interchange systems. Inventory management involves developing and maintaining adequate assortments of products to meet customers' needs. Logistics managers must strive to find the optimal level of inventory to satisfy customer needs while keeping costs down. Materials handling, the physical handling of products, is a crucial element in warehousing and transporting products. Warehousing involves the design and operation of facilities for storing and moving goods; such facilities may be privately owned or public. Transportation, the movement of products from where they are made to where they are purchased and used, is the most expensive physical distribution function. The basic modes of transporting goods include railroads, trucks, waterways, airways, and pipelines.

Please visit the student website at www.prideferrell.com for ACE Self-Test questions that will help you prepare for exams.

KEY CONCEPTS

distribution	vertical marketing systems (VMSs)	cycle time	private warehouses
marketing channel		order processing	public warehouses
marketing intermediary	horizontal channel integration	electronic data interchange (EDI)	distribution centers
supply-chain management			transportation
industrial distributor	intensive distribution	inventory management	intermodal transportation
dual distribution	selective distribution	just-in-time (JIT)	freight forwarders
strategic channel alliance	exclusive distribution	materials handling	megacarriers
channel power	physical distribution	warehousing	
vertical channel integration	outsourcing		

ISSUES FOR DISCUSSION AND REVIEW

1. Describe the major functions of marketing channels. Why are these functions better accomplished through the combined efforts of channel members?

2. Compare and contrast the four major types of marketing channels for consumer products. Through which type of channel is each of the following products most likely to be distributed?
   a. New automobiles
   b. Saltine crackers
   c. Cut-your-own Christmas trees
   d. New textbooks
   e. Sofas
   f. Soft drinks

3. Outline the four most common channels for business products. Describe the products or situations that lead marketers to choose each channel.

4. "Channel cooperation requires that members support the overall channel goals to achieve individual goals." Comment on this statement.

5. Explain the major characteristics of each of the three types of vertical marketing systems: corporate, administered, and contractual.

6. Explain the differences among intensive, selective, and exclusive methods of distribution.

7. Discuss the cost and service tradeoffs involved in developing a physical distribution system.

8. What are the main tasks involved in order processing?

9. Explain the tradeoffs inventory managers face when reordering products or supplies. How is the reorder point computed?

10. Explain the major differences between private and public warehouses. How do they differ from a distribution center?

11. Compare and contrast the five major transportation modes in terms of cost, speed, and dependability.

MARKETING APPLICATIONS

1. Select one of the following companies and explain how supply-chain management could increase marketing productivity.
   a. Dell Computer
   b. FedEx
   c. Nike
   d. Taco Bell

2. Find an article in a newspaper or on the Internet that describes a strategic channel alliance. Briefly summarize the article and indicate the benefits each organization expects to gain.

3. Indicate the intensity level—intensive, selective, or exclusive—best suited for the following products, and explain why it is appropriate.
   a. Personal computer
   b. Deodorant
   c. Collector baseball autographed by Mark McGwire
   d. Windows XP computer software

4. Assume that you are responsible for the physical distribution of computers at a mail-order company. What would you do to ensure product availability, timely delivery, and quality service for your customers?

ONLINE EXERCISE

5. FedEx has become a critical link in the distribution network of both small and large firms. With its efficient and strategically located superhub in Memphis, FedEx has truly revolutionized the shipping industry. View the company's website at **www.fedex.com.**
   a. Comment on how the website's overall design reflects the services the site promotes.
   b. Why does FedEx so prominently display a "News" area on its website?
   c. Does FedEx differentiate between small and large customers on its website? Why or why not?

VIDEO CASE

SmarterKids Uses Smarter Channel Management

No store? No problem for Excelligence Learning Corporation, which rings up $115 million in annual sales through online retailing, catalogs, and direct sales to institutional customers. Its Early Childhood division includes the award-winning SmarterKids website, a channel to reach parents who want to buy quality educational toys. Other Excelligence divisions develop new educational toys, market supplies and furniture to schools through printed catalogs, and offer products for schools to buy for resale during fundraising drives.

Excelligence maintains a sales force of 51 representatives who visit schools and child-care facilities to sell the full array of company products. In addition, it publishes a magazine and maintains a website for educators who work with preschool and elementary school students. Because Excelligence has so many businesses focused on children and education, it is in a unique position to effectively manage the flow of products to each of its target markets.

Consider the SmarterKids site (**www.smarterkids.com**), which features products made by the parent company as well as by outside manufacturers. Many toy retailers try to compete with industry giants such as Toys 'R' Us by stocking a huge number of products. SmarterKids, however, narrows the choices by having a team of teachers individually test each product. The teachers even watch every video and play every computer game being considered for the website. Then they rate the products using hundreds of criteria, including ease of use, creativity, educational approach, and durability. The result is a smaller but much more focused selection of approximately 4,000 products that meet SmarterKids' extremely demanding criteria for advancing children's development and education.

SmarterKids' marketers know that parents have limited time and do not want to wander endlessly through cavernous stores looking at a dizzying array of toys that may or may not be right for their children. Ideally parents want to buy products that their children—newborns to teenagers—will enjoy for more than a few days. And they want to buy products that will help children develop their skills and build their knowledge. Customers may well be impressed by the number of toys a retailer stocks. However, many will find more value in buying from SmarterKids because it helps narrow the choices to a manageable subset of toys, games, movies, and books that make sense for a particular child.

When customers log onto the colorful SmarterKids website,

they can search for toys in four ways. First, they can search according to age categories (such as birth to one year or preschool). Second, they can choose a particular toy category (such as music or arts and crafts). Third, they can search by developmental area (such as language arts). Fourth, they can enter a keyword (such as a brand name or type of toy). In addition, the homepage highlights toys that are sold exclusively by SmarterKids, toys that are best sellers in their category, and discounted toys featured in the site's clearance section. Then, instead of pushing a shopping cart through endless miles of cramped aisles, customers simply point and click to browse and buy. Thus, SmarterKids makes the online shopping experience more efficient and more productive for its time-pressured customers.

Parents can also access special sections of the SmarterKids site to learn more about six child developmental areas. The site explains why each area of development is important and posts a number of fun, easy activities for home use. No SmarterKids toys are needed. Instead, the activities are designed to bring parents and children together for a few minutes of educational playtime involving simple household items such as pots and pans or sponges. These sections represent an evolution from the detailed, personalized assessments that SmarterKids once offered on the site.

SmarterKids has found through research that customers who take full advantage of the site's information and activities wind up purchasing twice as much as those who don't. More data means the retailer can do a better job of buying the most appropriate toys and planning e-mail newsletters and other targeted promotions. The idea is to establish and strengthen connections with customers by showing that SmarterKids is dedicated to satisfying their needs and the needs of their children. Big stores may have bigger inventories, but SmarterKids believes its retailing strategy is smarter for long-term customer loyalty. "If you are able to develop a trusting relationship with consumers, they're going to come back time and time again," says the CEO.[28]

QUESTIONS FOR DISCUSSION

1. What is Excelligence's approach to channel integration?
2. Some toys are sold to parents through the direct selling "party plan." Should SmarterKids use this channel in addition to online retailing? Explain.
3. Under what conditions would a toy manufacturer be as interested in marketing its products through SmarterKids as it would through Toys 'R' Us?

Retailing, Direct Marketing, and Wholesaling

▶ **Mercantile Stores Serve Small-Town USA**

Is cooperative retailing the future for shoppers in small-town USA? It is for residents of three towns in Wyoming and Nevada where community-owned Mercantile stores have given local retailing a much-needed boost.

The Mercantile success story starts in 2001, when the Stage department store in Powell, Wyoming, closed. With a population of 5,500 and an isolated location, the town could not attract any large retailers. Many storefronts in Powell's three-block business district sat empty, the victims of local economic woes and competition from nearby malls and discount stores including a giant Wal-Mart 23 miles away in Cody.

Unwilling to let the town wither, Powell's leaders organized a movement to start a community-owned clothing store by selling shares in the "Merc" (short for "Mercantile") for $500 a piece. The Merc raised $400,000 by selling 800 shares to farmers, teachers, college students, and other residents. A board of directors was elected by the shareholders to oversee store operations, a store manager was hired, and residents were surveyed about the types of clothing they wanted the store to carry.

The Merc opened for business in August 2002, in a 7,500-square-foot space in downtown Powell. First-year sales topped $522,000—well ahead of the $500,000 goal—and second-year sales shot up by 9 percent to $571,000. Building on this success, the Merc opened a 2,500-square-foot annex selling children's clothes in 2004. Not only is the Merc thriving, it's bringing more traffic to other downtown businesses as well.

Now other towns are following Powell's example and opening community-supported stores. After Worland, Wyoming, lost its Stage department store, residents sold stock to finance the Washakie Wear store in 2003. When JCPenney closed its store in the mining town of Ely, Nevada, the nearest department store was more than 100 miles away. A group of Ely's residents decided to look for alternatives. They found out about the Merc in Powell, traveled there to learn more, presented their findings to the town, and soon started selling shares in a new retail cooperative.

OBJECTIVES

1 Understand the purpose and function of retailers in the marketing channel.

2 Identify the major types of retailers.

3 Explore strategic issues in retailing.

4 Recognize the various forms of direct marketing and selling.

5 Understand the nature and functions of wholesalers.

6 Understand how wholesalers are classified.

The Ely Renaissance Society repainted the JCPenney store while other volunteers set up fixtures and stocked shelves. By the time the Garnet Merc opened in late 2004, during the town's annual holiday festival, it had 880 shareholders and a staff of nine. It was mobbed by shoppers even before all the inventory was on display. Can the Merc fill the business void left by the departing JCPenney? So far, the answer is yes: "We're making 20 percent more than JCPenney did a year ago," says the general manager.[1]   ◄

Retailers like the Mercantile are the most visible and accessible marketing channel members to consumers. They are an important link in the marketing channel because they are both marketers for and customers of producers and wholesalers. They perform many supply-chain functions, such as buying, selling, grading, risk taking, and developing and maintaining information databases about customers. Retailers are in a strategic position to develop relationships with consumers and partnerships with producers and intermediaries in the marketing channel.

In this chapter, we examine the nature of retailing, direct marketing, and wholesaling and their importance in supplying consumers with goods and services. First, we explore the major types of retail stores and consider strategic issues in retailing: location, retail positioning, store image, scrambled merchandising, and the wheel of retailing. Next, we discuss direct marketing, including catalog marketing, direct response marketing, telemarketing, television home shopping, online retailing, and direct selling. Finally, we examine the importance of wholesalers in marketing channels, including their functions and classifications.

Retailing

retailing   Transactions in which the ultimate consumers are the buyers

retailer   An organization that purchases products for the purpose of reselling them to ultimate consumers

Retailing includes all transactions in which the buyer intends to consume the product through personal, family, or household use. Buyers in retail transactions are therefore the ultimate consumers. A **retailer** is an organization that purchases products for the purpose of reselling them to ultimate consumers. Although most retailers' sales are made directly to the consumer, nonretail transactions occasionally occur when retailers sell products to other businesses. Retailing often takes place in stores or service establishments, but it also occurs through direct selling, direct marketing, and vending machines outside stores.

Retailing is important to the national economy. Approximately 1.1 million retailers operate in the United States.[2] This number has remained relatively constant for the past 25 years, but sales volume has increased more than fourfold. Most personal income is spent in retail stores, and nearly one out of every seven people employed in the United States works in a retail operation.

Retailers add value, provide services, and assist in making product selections. They can enhance the value of products by making buyers' shopping experiences more convenient, as in home shopping. Through their locations, retailers can facilitate comparison shopping; for example, car dealerships often cluster in the same general vicinity. Product value is also enhanced when retailers offer services, such as technical advice, delivery, credit, and repair. Finally, retail sales personnel can demonstrate to customers how products can satisfy their needs or solve problems.

The value added by retailers is significant for both producers and ultimate consumers. Retailers are the critical link between producers and ultimate consumers because they provide the environment in which exchanges with ultimate consumers occur. Ultimate consumers benefit through retailers' performance of marketing functions that result in the availability of broader arrays of products. Retailers play a major role in creating time, place, and possession utility and, in some cases, form utility.

Leading retailers such as Wal-Mart, Home Depot, Macy's, and Toys 'R' Us offer consumers a place to browse and compare merchandise to find just what they need. However, such traditional retailing is being challenged by direct marketing channels that provide home shopping through catalogs, television, and the Internet. Traditional retailers are responding to this change in the retail environment in various ways. Wal-Mart has joined forces with fast-food giants like McDonald's and KFC to attract consumers and offer them the added convenience of eating where they shop. In response to competition from Amazon.com, Barnes & Noble developed a website to sell books over the Internet.

New store formats and advances in information technology are making the retail environment highly dynamic and competitive. Instant-messaging technology is helping online retailers converse with customers so they don't click away to another site. Rather than e-mail a retail site and wait for a response, shoppers on the Lands' End website simply click to chat, via keyboard, directly with a customer service representative about sizes, colors, or other product details.[3] This technology has helped the company triple its online sales in just three years. The key to success in retailing is to have a strong customer focus with a retail strategy that provides the level of service, product quality, and innovation that consumers desire. Partnerships among noncompeting retailers and other marketing channel members are providing new opportunities for retailers. For example, airports are leasing space to retailers such as Sharper Image, McDonald's, Sunglass Hut, and The Body Shop. Kroger and Nordstrom have developed joint co-branded credit cards that offer rebates to customers at participating stores.

Retailers are also finding global opportunities. For example, Gap Inc. is now opening more international stores than domestic ones, a trend that is likely to continue for the foreseeable future. Starbucks has opened hundreds of stores in Japan and Southeast Asia. McDonald's is growing faster outside the United States than domestically.

◉ Major Types of Retail Stores

Many types of retail stores exist. One way to classify them is by the breadth of products offered. Two general categories include general merchandise retailers and specialty retailers.

● General Merchandise Retailers.   A retail establishment that offers a variety of product lines stocked in considerable depth is referred to as a **general merchandise retailer**. The types of product offerings, mixes of customer services, and operating styles of retailers in this category vary considerably. The primary types of general merchandise retailers are department stores, discount stores, supermarkets, superstores, hypermarkets, warehouse clubs, and warehouse and catalog showrooms (see Table 15.1).

general merchandise retailer
A retail establishment that offers a variety of product lines that are stocked in depth

Department Stores.   **Department stores** are large retail organizations characterized by wide product mixes and employing at least 25 people. To facilitate marketing efforts and internal management in these stores, related product lines are organized into separate departments, such as cosmetics, housewares, apparel, home furnishings, and appliances. Often each department functions as a self-contained business, and buyers for individual departments are fairly autonomous. Typical department stores, such as Macy's, Sears, Marshall Field's, Dillard's, and Neiman Marcus, obtain a

department stores   Large retail organizations characterized by wide product mixes and organized into separate departments to facilitate marketing efforts and internal management

Table 15.1 General Merchandise Retailers

Type of Retailer	Description	Examples
Department Store	Large organization offering wide product mix and organized into separate departments	**Macy's, Sears, JCPenney**
Discount Store	Self-service, general merchandise store offering brand name and private brand products at low prices	**Wal-Mart, Target, Kmart**
Supermarket	Self-service store offering complete line of food products and some nonfood products	**Kroger, Albertson's, Winn-Dixie**
Superstore	Giant outlet offering all food and nonfood products found in supermarkets, as well as most routinely purchased products	**Wal-Mart Supercenters**
Hypermarket	Combination supermarket and discount store; larger than a superstore	**Carrefour**
Warehouse Club	Large-scale, members-only establishments combining cash-and-carry wholesaling with discount retailing	**Sam's Club, Costco**
Warehouse Showroom	Facility in a large, low-cost building with large on-premises inventories and minimal service	**IKEA**
Catalog Showroom	Type of warehouse showroom where consumers shop from a catalog and products are stored out of buyers' reach and provided in the manufacturer's carton	**Service Merchandise**

large proportion of sales from apparel, accessories, and cosmetics. Other products that these stores carry include gift items, luggage, electronics, home accessories, and sports equipment. Some department stores offer services such as automobile insurance, hair care, income tax preparation, and travel and optical services. In some cases, space for these specialized services is leased out, with proprietors managing their own operations and paying rent to department stores. Many department stores also sell products through their websites.

Department stores are somewhat service oriented. Their total product may include credit, delivery, personal assistance, merchandise returns, and a pleasant atmosphere. Although some so-called department stores are actually large, departmentalized specialty stores, most department stores are shopping stores. Consumers can compare price, quality, and service at one store with those at competing stores. Along with large discount stores, department stores are often considered retailing leaders in a community and are found in most places with populations of more than 50,000.

Discount Stores. In recent years, department stores have been losing market share to discount stores.[4] **Discount stores** are self-service, general merchandise outlets that regularly offer brand name and private brand products at low prices. Discounters accept lower margins than conventional retailers in exchange for high sales volume. To keep inventory turnover high, they carry a wide but carefully selected assortment of products, from appliances to housewares and clothing. Major discount establishments also offer food products, toys, automotive services, garden supplies, and sports equipment. Wal-Mart and Target are the two largest discount

discount stores Self-service, general merchandise stores offering brand name and private brand products at low prices

Department Stores
Large retail organizations, such as JCPenney, carry wide product mixes and are organized into separate departments to facilitate marketing efforts and internal management.

stores. Wal-Mart has grown to 4,800 stores worldwide and brings in more than $256 billion in sales annually.[5] When Kmart Holding Corporation agreed to buy Sears, Roebuck and Company, they decided that they would introduce a smaller version of the Sears Grand department store to compete with Target, Kohl's, and Wal-Mart. Recently, 25 new Sears Essentials stores were opened.[6] Some discounters such as Meijer, Inc., are regional organizations. Most operate in large (50,000 to 80,000 square feet), no-frills facilities. Discount stores usually offer everyday low prices rather than relying on sales events.

supermarkets Large, self-service stores that carry a complete line of food products, along with some nonfood products

Supermarkets. Supermarkets are large, self-service stores that carry a complete line of food products, as well as some nonfood products such as cosmetics and non-prescription drugs. Supermarkets are arranged in departments for maximum efficiency in stocking and handling products but have central checkout facilities. They offer lower prices than smaller neighborhood grocery stores, usually provide free parking, and may also cash checks. Today consumers make more than three-quarters of all grocery purchases in supermarkets. Even so, supermarkets' total share of the food market is declining because consumers now have widely varying food preferences and buying habits, and in many communities shoppers can choose from several convenience stores, discount stores, and specialty food stores, as well as a wide variety of restaurants. Wal-Mart, for example, expects to generate in its "supermarket-type" sales more in revenues than the top three U.S. supermarket chains—Kroger, Albertson's, and Safeway—combined. To attract more customers, Albertson's plans to make grocery shopping quick and easy with new technology that will eliminate checkout lines.[7]

superstores Giant retail outlets that carry food and nonfood products found in supermarkets, as well as most routinely purchased consumer products

Superstores. Superstores, which originated in Europe, are giant retail outlets that carry not only food and nonfood products ordinarily found in supermarkets but also routinely purchased consumer products. Superstores combine features of discount

Discount Stores
Discount stores, such as Target, are self-service, general-merchandise retailers that offer manufacturer and private brands, low prices, and low margins.

stores and supermarkets. Examples include Wal-Mart Supercenters and some Kroger stores. Besides a complete food line, superstores sell housewares, hardware, small appliances, clothing, personal-care products, garden products, and tires—about four times as many items as supermarkets. Services available at superstores include dry cleaning, automotive repair, check cashing, bill paying, and snack bars. To cut handling and inventory costs, they use sophisticated operating techniques and often have tall shelving that displays entire assortments of products. Superstores can have an area of as much as 200,000 square feet (compared with 20,000 square feet in traditional supermarkets). Sales volume is two to three times that of supermarkets, partly because locations near good transportation networks help generate the in-store traffic needed for profitability.

hypermarkets Stores that combine supermarket and discount store shopping in one location

Hypermarkets. Hypermarkets combine supermarket and discount store shopping in one location. Larger than superstores, they range from 225,000 to 325,000 square feet and offer 45,000 to 60,000 different types of low-priced products. They commonly allocate 40 to 50 percent of their space to grocery products and the remainder to general merchandise, including athletic shoes, designer jeans, and other apparel; refrigerators, televisions, and other appliances; housewares; cameras; toys; jewelry; hardware; and automotive supplies. Many lease space to noncompeting businesses such as banks, optical shops, and fast-food restaurants. All hypermarkets focus on low prices and vast selections. Although Kmart, Wal-Mart, and Carrefour (a French retailer) have operated hypermarkets in the United States, most of these stores have been unsuccessful and have closed. Such stores may be too big for time-constrained U.S. shoppers. However, hypermarkets are more successful in Europe, South America, and Mexico. For example, the hypermarket has become such a success in Mexico that the leading chains are currently waging a retail war. Wal-Mart de Mexico is leading the battle with annual sales of $11.7 billion, but competitors such as Soriana, with annual sales of $3.2 billion, are taking risks and fighting back.[8]

warehouse clubs Large-scale, members-only establishments that combine features of cash-and-carry wholesaling with discount retailing

Warehouse Clubs. Warehouse clubs, a rapidly growing form of mass merchandising, are large-scale, members-only selling operations combining cash-and-carry wholesaling with discount retailing. Sometimes called *buying clubs,* warehouse clubs offer the same types of products as discount stores, but in a limited range of sizes and styles. Whereas most discount stores carry around 40,000 items, a warehouse club handles only 3,500 to 5,000 products, usually acknowledged brand leaders. Sam's Club stores, for example, stock about 4,000 items, with 1,400 available most of the time and the rest being one-time buys. Costco leads the warehouse club industry with sales of $48.1 billion. Sam's Club is second with $34.5 billion in store sales. A third company, BJ's Wholesale Club, which operates in the Northeast and Florida, has a much smaller market.[9] All these establishments offer a broad product mix, including food, beverages, books, appliances, housewares, automotive parts, hardware, and furniture.

warehouse showrooms Retail facilities in large, low-cost buildings with large on-premises inventories and minimal services

To keep prices lower than those of supermarkets and discount stores, warehouse clubs provide few services. They generally do not advertise, except through direct mail. Their facilities, often located in industrial areas, have concrete floors and aisles wide enough for forklifts. Merchandise is stacked on pallets or displayed on pipe racks. Customers must transport purchases themselves. Warehouse clubs appeal to many price-conscious consumers and small retailers unable to obtain wholesaling services from large distributors. The average warehouse club shopper has more education, a higher income, and a larger household than the average supermarket shopper.

Warehouse and Catalog Showrooms. Warehouse showrooms are retail facilities with five basic characteristics: large, low-cost buildings; warehouse materials handling technology; vertical merchandise

Warehouse Showroom
IKEA is an example of a warehouse showroom.

displays; large on-premises inventories; and minimal services. IKEA, a Swedish company, sells furniture, household goods, and kitchen accessories in warehouse showrooms and through catalogs around the world, including China and Russia. These high-volume, low-overhead operations stress fewer personnel and services. Lower costs are possible because some marketing functions have been shifted to consumers, who must transport, finance, and perhaps store larger quantites of products. Most consumers carry away purchases in the manufacturer's carton, although stores will deliver for a fee.

catalog showrooms A form of warehouse showroom where consumers shop from a catalog and products are stored out of buyers' reach

In **catalog showrooms**, one item of each product is displayed, often in a locked case, with remaining inventory stored out of the buyer's reach. Using catalogs that have been mailed to their homes or are on store counters, customers order products by phone or in person. Clerks fill orders from the warehouse area, and products are presented in the manufacturer's carton. In contrast to traditional catalog retailers, which offer no discounts and require that customers wait for delivery, catalog showrooms regularly sell below list price and often provide goods immediately. Catalog showrooms usually sell jewelry, luggage, photographic equipment, toys, small appliances and housewares, sporting goods, and power tools. They advertise extensively and carry established brands and models that are not likely to be discontinued. Because catalog showrooms have higher product turnover, fewer losses through shoplifting, and lower labor costs than department stores, they can feature lower prices. They offer minimal services, however. Customers may have to stand in line to examine items or place orders. Recently, some high-end retailers such as Neiman Marcus are toying with the concept by implementing showrooms in two of their main markets: Plano, Texas, and Chicago, Illinois.[10]

● **Specialty Retailers.** In contrast to general merchandise retailers with their broad product mixes, specialty retailers emphasize narrow and deep assortments. Despite their name, specialty retailers do not sell specialty items (except when specialty goods complement the overall product mix). Instead, they offer substantial

Specialty Retailers
Banana Republic is an example of a traditional specialty store.

assortments in a few product lines. We examine three types of specialty retailers: traditional specialty retailers, category killers, and off-price retailers.

traditional specialty retailers
Stores that carry a narrow product mix with deep product lines

Traditional specialty retailers are stores that carry a narrow product mix with deep product lines. Sometimes called *limited-line retailers,* they may be referred to as *single-line retailers* if they carry unusual depth in one main product category. Traditional specialty retailers commonly sell shopping products such as apparel, jewelry, sporting goods, fabrics, computers, toys, and pet supplies. The Limited, Radio Shack, Hickory Farms, Gap, and Foot Locker are examples of retailers offering limited product lines but great depth within those lines.

Because they are usually small, specialty stores may have high costs in proportion to sales, and satisfying customers may require carrying some products with low turnover rates. However, these stores sometimes obtain lower prices from suppliers by purchasing limited lines of merchandise in large quantities. Successful traditional specialty stores understand their customer types and know what products to carry, thus reducing the risk of unsold merchandise. Traditional specialty stores usually offer better selections and more sales expertise than department stores, their main competitors. By capitalizing on fashion, service, personnel, atmosphere, and location, these retailers position themselves strategically to attract customers in specific market segments. For example, customers seeking fashion jeans likely would shop at traditional specialty stores. About 21 percent of U.S. jean purchases are made in traditional specialty stores.[11]

category killer   A very large specialty store concentrating on a major product category and competing on the basis of low prices and product availability

Over the last 15 years, a new breed of specialty retailer, the category killer, has evolved. A category killer is a very large specialty store that concentrates on a major product category and competes on the basis of low prices and enormous product availability. These stores are referred to as category killers because they expand rapidly and gain sizable market shares, taking business away from smaller, high-cost retail outlets. Examples of category killers include Home Depot and Lowe's (home improvement chains); Staples, Office Depot, and OfficeMax (office supply chains); Borders and Barnes & Noble (booksellers); Petco and Petsmart (pet supply chains); and Best Buy (consumer electronics).

off-price retailers   Stores that buy manufacturers' seconds, overruns, returns, and off-season merchandise for resale to consumers at deep discounts

Off-price retailers are stores that buy manufacturers' seconds, overruns, returns, and off-season production runs at below-wholesale prices for resale to consumers at deep discounts. Unlike true discount stores, which pay regular wholesale prices for goods and usually carry second-line brand names, off-price retailers offer limited lines of national-brand and designer merchandise, usually clothing, shoes, or housewares. The number of off-price retailers has grown since the mid-1980s. Ross is an off-price clothing retailer that appeals to customers who want to "dress for less." Frequently found near other off-price retailers such as T.J. Maxx, Marshalls, Stein Mart, and Burlington Coat Factory, Ross targets customers with an annual household income of $50,000 to $60,000. To appeal to a lower income customer with their deeply discounted name-brand merchandise, Ross recently opened DD's Discounts in a number of small neighborhood shopping centers in California.[12] Another form of off-price retailer is the manufacturer's outlet mall, which makes available manufacturer overstocks and unsold merchandise from other retail outlets. Prices are low, and diverse manufacturers are represented in these malls.

Off-price stores charge 20 to 50 percent less than do department stores for comparable merchandise, but offer few customer services. They often feature community dressing rooms and central checkout counters. Some of these stores do not take returns or allow exchanges. Off-price stores may or may not sell goods with the original labels intact. They turn over their inventory nine to twelve times a year, three times as often as traditional specialty stores. They compete with department stores for the same customers: price-conscious customers who are knowledgeable about brand names.

⊚ Strategic Issues in Retailing

Whereas most business purchases are based on economic planning and necessity, consumer purchases may result from social and psychological influences. Because consumers shop for various reasons—to search for specific items, escape boredom, or learn about something new—retailers must do more than simply fill space with merchandise. They must make desired products available, create stimulating shopping environments, and develop marketing strategies that increase store patronage. In this section, we discuss how store location, retail positioning, store image, scrambled merchandising, and the wheel of retailing affect retailing objectives.

● **Location, Location, Location.**   Location, the least flexible of the strategic retailing issues, is one of the most important because location dictates the limited geographic trading area from which a store draws its customers. Retailers consider various factors when evaluating potential locations, including location of the firm's target market within the trading area, kinds of products being sold, availability of public transportation, customer characteristics, and competitors' locations.

In choosing a location, a retailer evaluates the relative ease of movement to and from the site, including factors such as pedestrian and vehicular traffic, parking, and transportation. Retailers also evaluate the characteristics of the site itself: types of stores in the area; size, shape, and visibility of the lot or building under consideration; and rental, leasing, or ownership terms. Retailers look for compatibility with nearby retailers because stores that complement one another draw more customers for everyone.

Many retailers choose to locate in downtown central business districts, while others prefer sites within various types of planned shopping centers. Some retailers, including Toys 'R' Us, Wal-Mart, Home Depot, and many fast-food restaurants, opt for freestanding structures that are not connected to other buildings, but many chain stores are found in planned shopping centers and malls. Although shopping centers

Free-Standing Stores
There are many fast food restaurants in free-standing locations.

have been very popular over the last three decades, today's time-challenged consumers are increasingly turning to freestanding specialty and discount stores where they can park nearby, grab exactly what they want, and check out quickly.[13]

Planned shopping centers include neighborhood, community, and regional shopping centers. **Neighborhood shopping centers** usually consist of several small convenience and specialty stores, such as small grocery stores, gas stations, and fast-food restaurants. Many of these retailers consider their target markets to be consumers who live within two to three miles of their stores, or ten minutes' driving time. Because most purchases are based on convenience or personal contact, there is usually little coordination of selling efforts within a neighborhood shopping center. Generally product mixes consist of essential products, and depth of the product lines is limited.

Community shopping centers include one or two department stores and some specialty stores, as well as convenience stores. They draw consumers looking for shopping and specialty products not available in neighborhood shopping centers. Because these centers serve larger geographic areas, consumers must drive longer distances to community shopping centers than to neighborhood centers. Community shopping centers are planned and coordinated to attract shoppers. Special events, such as art exhibits, automobile shows, and sidewalk sales, stimulate traffic. Managers of community shopping centers look for tenants that complement the centers' total assortment of products. Such centers have wide product mixes and deep product lines.

Regional shopping centers usually have the largest department stores, the widest product mixes, and the deepest product lines of all shopping centers. Many shopping malls are regional shopping centers, although some are community shopping centers. With 150,000 or more consumers in their target market, regional shopping centers must have well-coordinated management and marketing activities. Target markets may include consumers traveling from a distance to find products and prices not available in their hometowns. Because of the expense of leasing space in regional shopping centers, tenants are more likely to be national chains than small, independent stores. Large centers usually advertise, have special events, furnish transportation to some consumer groups, maintain their own security forces, and carefully select the mix of stores.

Several new types of shopping centers have emerged that differ significantly from traditional shopping centers. Factory outlet malls feature discount and factory outlet stores carrying traditional manufacturer brands, such as Van Heusen, Levi Strauss, HealthTex, and Wrangler. Manufacturers own these stores and make a special effort to avoid competing with traditional retailers of their products. Miniwarehouse malls are loosely planned centers that sell space to retailers, who operate what are essentially retail stores out of warehouse bays. Some miniwarehouses are located in high-traffic areas and provide ample customer parking, as well as display windows visible from the street. Home improvement materials, specialty foods, pet supplies, and garden and yard supplies are often sold in these malls. A third type of emerging shopping center is one that does not include a

neighborhood shopping centers Shopping centers usually consisting of several small convenience and specialty stores

community shopping centers Shopping centers with one or two department stores, some specialty stores, and convenience stores

regional shopping center A type of shopping center with the largest department stores, the widest product mix, and the deepest product lines of all shopping centers

MARKETING ENTREPRENEURS

Joseph Tantillo

HIS BUSINESS: GreekGear.com

FOUNDED AT AGE: 31

SUCCESS: Revenues of $1.9 million a year

Joseph Tantillo wanted a job that would enable him to work from home. His membership in a fraternity during his college years inspired him to launch GreekGear.com, a website that sells personalized apparel to Greek organizations across the country. In its second month, the site served just three customers. In only a few years, that number had grown to 9,700.[a]

traditional anchor department store. Shopping center developers are combining off-price stores with category killers in "power center" formats. Off-price centers are growing, resulting in a variety of formats vying for the same retail dollar.

● **Retail Positioning.**   The emergence of new types of stores and the expansion of product offerings by traditional stores have intensified retailing competition. Retail positioning is therefore an important consideration. Retail positioning involves identifying an unserved or underserved market segment, and serving it through a strategy that distinguishes the retailer from others in the minds of those customers. For example, Hot Topic, a specialty store chain, has carved out a unique retail position by stocking alternative merchandise, such as glow-in-the-dark tongue rings, hair dye, gothic boots, and other apparel and accessories that appeal to those suburban teens who dislike trendy stores such as Gap, Abercrombie & Fitch, and Wet Seal.[14] Many discount and specialty store chains are positioning themselves to appeal to time- and cash-strapped consumers with convenient locations and layouts as well as low prices. This strategy has helped discount and specialty stores gain market share at the expense of large department stores.[15]

retail positioning   Identifying an unserved or underserved market segment and serving it through a strategy that distinguishes the retailer from others in the minds of consumers in that segment

● **Store Image.**   To attract customers, a retail store must project an image—a functional and psychological picture in the consumer's mind—that appeals to its target

MARKETING AROUND THE WORLD
GAS, COFFEE, AND CONVENIENCE IN THAILAND

Motorists all over Thailand can drive into Jet Stations owned by Conoco (Thailand) Ltd., fill their tanks, and grab a cup of coffee—or two. Jet is the country's fastest-growing retail gasoline brand and has the highest fuel sales per service station. Each of the 139 Jet Stations contains a Jiffy convenience store as well as a franchised Ban Rai Coffee House bar. Jiffy's sales have been growing at an even faster rate than those of Jet fuel since Conoco opened the first convenience store inside its Thai service stations in 1993. A survey by ACNielsen (Thailand) found that 56 percent of new Jet customers became regular customers. One reason for this high customer retention rate is the convenience of having a Ban Rai Coffee House bar inside every Jiffy store.

Plantation and Farm Design Company, Ltd., owns the franchise to operate Ban Rai Coffee Houses at Jet Stations. The founder noticed that many Thai drivers like to drink coffee to stay alert. To satisfy this market, Ban Rai brews freshly roasted, strong Thai coffee on-site for takeout at each convenience store. At a time

when "buy Thai" sentiments are growing, Ban Rai's emphasis on supporting products from local communities, such as coffee and cookies, is proving quite effective. Also, Ban Rai serves coffee in reusable clay cups instead of paper cups to bring out the flavor and differentiate its brand, another reason why customers are willing to pay premium prices for its coffee. By placing franchised outlets in Conoco's Jet Stations, Ban Rai has been able to expand distribution to cover most highways throughout Thailand.

In the past year, the Black Canyon restaurant chain has begun opening branches in some Jet Stations around Bangkok and other Thai cities. Black Canyon's managing director says that having two food outlets in one gas station will not be a competitive problem for either. "The target group for Black Canyon and Ban Rai might overlap, but our restaurants and coffee styles are different," he observes. In the end, more food choices could make Jet Stations an even more welcome sight to Thai drivers on the road.[b]

market. Store environment, merchandise quality, and service quality are key determinants of store image.

atmospherics The physical elements in a store's design that appeal to consumers' emotions and encourage buying

Atmospherics, the physical elements in a store's design that appeal to consumers' emotions and encourage buying, help to create an image and position a retailer. McDonald's, for example, is opening McCafés within existing McDonald's restaurants, complete with special café decor and menu items such as gourmet coffee and desserts. McDonald's has about 300 McCafés in 17 countries and plans to open several in the United States soon.[16] Other McDonald's outlets feature distinctly different atmospherics and menu items, such as the diner-style concept being tested in Indiana.[17]

Exterior atmospheric elements include the appearance of the storefront, display windows, store entrances, and degree of traffic congestion. Exterior atmospherics are particularly important to new customers, who tend to judge an unfamiliar store by its outside appearance and may not enter if they feel intimidated by the building or inconvenienced by the parking lot. Interior atmospheric elements include aesthetic considerations such as lighting, wall and floor coverings, dressing facilities, and store fixtures. Interior sensory elements contribute significantly to atmosphere. Color can attract shoppers to a retail display. Many fast-food restaurants use bright colors, such as red and yellow, because these have been shown to make customers feel hungrier and eat faster, which increases turnover. Sound is another important sensory component of atmosphere and may range from silence to subdued background music. One study indicated that retail customers shop for a longer period when exposed to unfamiliar music than they do when exposed to familiar music.[18]

scrambled merchandising The addition of unrelated products and product lines to an existing product mix, particularly fast-moving items that can be sold in volume

● **Scrambled Merchandising.** When retailers add unrelated products and product lines—particularly fast-moving items that can be sold in volume—to an existing product mix, they are practicing scrambled merchandising. Retailers adopting this strategy hope to accomplish one or more of the following: (1) convert stores into one-stop shopping centers, (2) generate more traffic, (3) realize higher profit margins, and (4) increase impulse purchases. In scrambled merchandising, retailers must deal with diverse marketing channels. Scrambled merchandising can also blur a store's image in consumers' minds, making it more difficult for a retailer to succeed in today's highly competitive, saturated markets. Finally, scrambled merchandising intensifies competition among traditionally distinct types of stores and forces suppliers to adjust distribution systems to accommodate new channel members.

wheel of retailing A hypothesis holding that new retailers usually enter the market as low-status, low-margin, low-price operators but eventually evolve into high-cost, high-price merchants

● **The Wheel of Retailing.** As new types of retail businesses come into being, they strive to fill niches in a dynamic retailing environment. One hypothesis regarding the evolution and development of new types of retail stores is the wheel of retailing. According to this theory, new retailers enter the marketplace with low prices, margins, and status. Their low prices are usually the result of innovative cost-cutting procedures and soon attract imitators. Gradually, as these businesses attempt to broaden their customer base and increase sales, their operations and facilities become more elaborate and more expensive. They may move to more desirable locations, begin to carry higher-quality merchandise, or add services. Eventually, they emerge at the high end of the price, cost, and service scales, competing with newer discount retailers following the same evolutionary process.[19]

Consider the evolution of department stores, discount stores, warehouse clubs, category killers, and online retailers, shown in Figure 15.1. Department stores like Sears started out as high-volume, low-cost merchants competing with general stores and other small retailers. Discount stores developed later in response to rising expenses of services in department stores. Many discount outlets now appear to be

Figure 15.1
The Wheel of Retailing
If the "wheel" is considered to be turning slowly in the direction of the arrows, then the department stores around 1900 and the discounters that came later can be viewed as coming on the scene at the low end of the wheel. As it turns slowly, they move with it, becoming higher-price operations and leaving room for lower-price firms to gain entry at the low end of the wheel.

Source: Adapted from Robert F. Hartley, *Retailing: Challenge and Opportunity,* 3rd ed., p. 42. Copyright © 1984 by Houghton Mifflin Company. Reprinted by permission of the author.

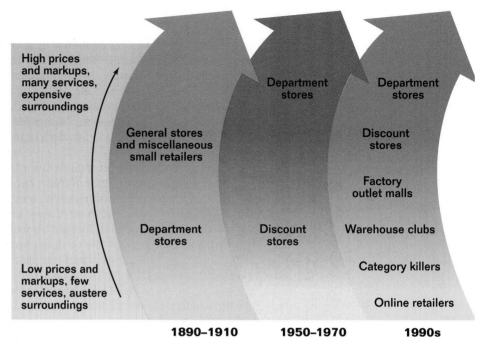

following the wheel of retailing by offering more services, better locations, quality inventories, and therefore higher prices. Some discount stores, such as Kohl's, are almost indistinguishable from department stores. In response have emerged category killers, such as Petsmart and Office Depot, which concentrate on a major product category and offer enormous product depth, in many cases at lower prices than discount stores. Yet even these retailers seem to be following the wheel. Lowe's, a home improvement retailer, has added big-ticket items and more upscale brands, such as Laura Ashley. Consumers have less time to shop and greater access to more sophisticated technology, so retailing venues like catalog retailing, television home shopping, and online retailing will take on greater importance. New retailers will evolve to capitalize on these opportunities, while those that cannot adapt will not survive.

Direct Marketing and Direct Selling

Although retailers are the most visible members of the supply chain, many products are sold outside the confines of a retail store. Direct selling and direct marketing account for an increasing percentage of product sales. Products may also be sold in automatic vending machines, but these account for less than 2 percent of all retail sales.

Direct Marketing

direct marketing The use of telecommunications and nonpersonal media to introduce products to consumers, who then can purchase them via mail, telephone, or the Internet

Direct marketing is the use of telecommunications and nonpersonal media to communicate product and organizational information to customers, who then can purchase products via mail, telephone, or the Internet. Direct marketing can occur through catalog marketing, direct response marketing, telemarketing, television home shopping, and online retailing.

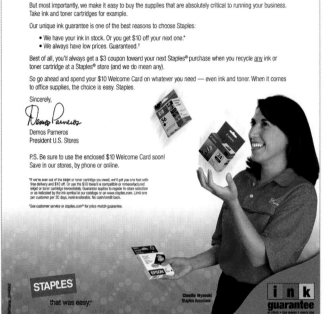

Direct Marketing
In addition to its retail stores, Staples employs direct marketing, offering its products online and through catalogs.

catalog marketing   A type of marketing in which an organization provides a catalog from which customers make selections and place orders by mail, telephone, or the Internet

direct-response marketing
A type of marketing that occurs when a retailer advertises a product and makes it available through mail or telephone orders

telemarketing   The performance of marketing-related activities by telephone

● **Catalog Marketing.**   In catalog marketing, an organization provides a catalog from which customers make selections and place orders by mail, telephone, or the Internet. Catalog marketing began in 1872, when Montgomery Ward issued its first catalog to rural families. Today there are more than 7,000 catalog marketing companies in the United States, as well as several retail stores, such as JCPenney, that engage in catalog marketing. Some organizations, including Spiegel and JCPenney, offer a broad array of products spread over multiple product lines. Catalog companies like Lands' End, Pottery Barn, and J. Crew offer considerable depth in one major line of products. Still other catalog companies specialize in only a few products within a single line. Some catalog retailers—for instance, Crate and Barrel and The Sharper Image—have stores in major metropolitan areas. When Sears, Roebuck and Company acquired Lands' End, it continued to operate both entities separately, but found ways to incorporate Lands' End into Sears by opening mini-Lands' End stores within Sears stores.[20]

The advantages of catalog retailing include efficiency and convenience for customers. The retailer benefits by being able to locate in remote, low-cost areas; save on expensive store fixtures; and reduce both personal selling and store operating expenses. On the other hand, catalog retailing is inflexible, provides limited service, and is most effective for a selected set of products.

Catalog sales are about $132 billion annually and are expected to grow to $177 billion by 2008.[21] Even though the cost of mailing catalogs continues to rise, catalog sales are growing at double the rate of in-store retailing. Williams-Sonoma, for example, sells kitchenware and home and garden products through five catalogs, including Pottery Barn and Gardeners' Eden.

● **Direct Response Marketing.**   Direct response marketing occurs when a retailer advertises a product and makes it available through mail or telephone orders. Generally a purchaser may use a credit card, but other forms of payment are acceptable. Examples of direct response marketing include a television commercial offering a recording artist's musical collection available through a toll-free number, a newspaper or magazine advertisement for a series of children's books available by filling out the form in the ad or calling a toll-free number, and even a billboard promoting floral services available by calling 1-800-Flowers. Direct response marketing is also conducted by sending letters, samples, brochures, or booklets to prospects on a mailing list and asking that they order the advertised products by mail or telephone. In general, products must be priced above $20 to justify the advertising and distribution costs associated with direct response marketing.

● **Telemarketing.**   A number of organizations use the telephone to strengthen the effectiveness of traditional marketing methods. Telemarketing is the performance of marketing-related activities by telephone. Some organizations use a prescreened list of prospective clients. Telemarketing can help generate sales leads, improve customer service, speed up payments on past-due accounts, raise funds for nonprofit organizations, and gather marketing data.

Currently the laws and regulations regarding telemarketing, while in a state of flux, are becoming more restrictive. Several states have established do-not-call lists of customers who do not want to receive telemarketing calls from companies operating in their state. On October 1, 2003, the U.S. Congress implemented the national do-not-call registry for consumers who do not wish to receive telemarketing calls. By the end of 2003, more than 54 million phone numbers were listed on the registry, nearly one-third of the 166 million residential phone numbers in the United States. Companies are subject to a fine of up to $12,000 for each call made to a consumer listed on the national do-not-call registry.[22] The national registry is enforced by the Federal Trade Commission and the Federal Communications Commission.[23] Certain exceptions apply to do-not-call lists. A company can still use telemarketing to communicate with existing customers. In addition, charitable, political, and telephone survey organizations are not restricted by the national registry.

television home shopping
A form of selling in which products are presented to television viewers, who can buy them by calling a toll-free number and paying with a credit card

● **Television Home Shopping.** Television home shopping presents products to television viewers, encouraging them to order through toll-free numbers and pay with credit cards. Home Shopping Network in Florida originated and popularized this format. The most popular products sold through television home shopping are jewelry (40 percent of total sales), clothing, housewares, and electronics. Home shopping channels have grown so rapidly in recent years that more than 60 percent of U.S. households have access to home shopping programs. Home Shopping Network and QVC are two of the largest home shopping networks. Approximately 60 percent of home shopping sales revenues come from repeat purchasers.

The television home shopping format offers several benefits. Products can be demonstrated easily, and an adequate amount of time can be spent showing the product so that viewers are well informed. The length of time a product is shown depends not only on the time required for doing demonstrations but also on whether the product is selling. Once the calls peak and begin to decline, a new product is shown. Other benefits are that customers can shop at their convenience and from the comfort of their homes.

online retailing Retailing that makes products available to buyers through computer connections

● **Online Retailing.** Online retailing makes products available to buyers through computer connections. The phenomenal growth of Internet use and online information services such as AOL has created new retailing opportunities. Many retailers have set up websites to disseminate information about their companies and products. Although most retailers with websites use them primarily to promote products, a number of companies, including Barnes & Noble, REI, Lands' End, and OfficeMax, sell goods online. Consumers can purchase hard-to-find items, such as Pez candy dispensers and Elvis memorabilia, on eBay. They can buy upscale items for their dogs at SitStay.com, a Web retailer specializing in high-end dog supplies that carries a carefully screened selection of 1,500 products. "We don't have 10,000 products," explains co-founder Kent Krueger. "We have the best of the best."[24] Banks and brokerage firms have established websites to give customers direct access to manage their accounts and enable them to trade online. With advances in computer technology continuing and consumers ever more pressed for time, online retailing will continue to escalate.

Although online retailing represents a major retailing venue, security remains an issue. In a recent survey conducted by the Business Software Alliance, about 75 percent of Internet users expressed concerns about shopping online. The major issues are identity theft and credit card theft.

CUSTOMER RELATIONSHIP MANAGEMENT

DIRECT MARKETING KEEPS PROFITS FLOWING FOR DELL

Catalogs may seem old-fashioned in this era of online marketing, but not to Dell. The company was a pioneer in marketing personal computers (PCs) directly to customers rather than through traditional distribution channels for such products. Today Dell maintains an extensive Web presence where customers can buy built-to-order PCs and other electronics, but its main vehicle for reaching business customers is the catalog. "We mail several different versions each month and touch the entire small and medium-sized business universe," says Mark Thompson, a Dell marketing executive.

In addition to catalogs, Dell uses direct response marketing to bring in customer inquiries from e-mail, television and radio commercials, and inserts in local newspapers. The company has learned that customers who see or hear one of these direct marketing messages may wind up ordering through a different response mode. "People might see the television ad and dial the number on the back of the catalog," Thompson explains. "In the past, we might have attributed it to the catalog and missed the link from television."

Dell's use of direct marketing allows the company to keep costs low and profits at an acceptable level. Parts arrive precisely when needed, so the company can maintain ultra-low inventory levels and minimize warehousing costs. The build-to-order business model eliminates excess inventory, which in the highly dynamic computer industry can become obsolete overnight. In contrast, competitors that market through retailers must assemble PCs in advance, ship them to stores, and have inventory on hand to fill reorders quickly. Moreover, Dell's control over its marketing channel gives it more flexibility to test new marketing ideas.

Dell's efficient and effective direct marketing strategy has paid off handsomely. In many cases, Dell can book an order, build the PC, and receive payment before it must pay suppliers for the components in that product. When PC sales are slow, Dell's low costs allow it to compete on price and increase its market share. When PC sales are strong, Dell can introduce new models at attractive prices to keep the orders—and the profits—rolling in.[c]

Online Retailing
Amazon.com is an online retailer of a wide array of products, such as books.

◉ Direct Selling

direct selling   The marketing of products to ultimate consumers through face-to-face sales presentations at home or in the workplace

Direct selling is the marketing of products to ultimate consumers through face-to-face sales presentations at home or in the workplace. Traditionally called *door-to-door selling,* direct selling in the United States began with peddlers more than a century ago and has since grown into a sizable industry of several hundred firms. Although direct sellers historically used a cold-canvass, door-to-door approach for finding prospects, many companies today, such as Kirby, Amway, Mary Kay, and Avon, use other approaches. They initially identify customers through the mail, telephone, Internet, or shopping mall intercepts and then set up appointments.

While the majority of direct selling takes place on an individual, or person-to-person, basis, it sometimes also includes the use of a group, or "party," plan. With a party plan, a consumer acts as a host and invites friends and associates to view merchandise in a group setting, where a salesperson demonstrates products. The congenial party atmosphere helps to overcome customers' reluctance and encourages them to buy. Tupperware and Mary Kay were the pioneers of this selling technique, paving the way for companies like the Pampered Chef to grow from a basement business into a corporation that brings in over $700 million in revenues annually.[25]

Direct selling has both benefits and limitations. It gives the marketer an opportunity to demonstrate the product in an environment—usually customers' homes—where it would most likely be used. The door-to-door seller can give the customer personal attention, and the product can be presented to the customer at a convenient time and location. Personal attention to the customer is the foundation on which some direct sellers, such as Mary Kay, have built their businesses. Because commissions for salespeople are so high, ranging from 30 to 50 percent of the sales price, and great effort is required to isolate promising prospects, overall costs of direct selling make it the most expensive form of retailing. Furthermore, some customers view direct selling negatively, owing to unscrupulous and fraudulent practices used by some direct sellers in the past. Some communities even have local ordinances that control or, in some cases, prohibit direct selling. Despite these negative views held by some individuals, direct selling is still alive and well, bringing in revenues of over $29 billion a year.[26]

 # Wholesaling

wholesaling   Transactions in which products are bought for resale, for making other products, or for general business operations

wholesaler   An individual or organization that facilitates and expedites wholesale transactions

Wholesaling refers to all transactions in which products are bought for resale, for making other products, or for general business operations. It does not include exchanges with ultimate consumers. A **wholesaler** is an individual or organization that facilitates and expedites exchanges that are primarily wholesale transactions. In other words, wholesalers buy products and resell them to reseller, government, and institutional users. For example, SYSCO, the nation's number 1 food-service distributor, supplies restaurants, hotels, schools, industrial caterers, and hospitals with everything from frozen and fresh food and paper products to medical and cleaning supplies. Wholesaling activities are not limited to goods; service companies, such as financial institutions, also use active wholesale networks. For example, some banks buy loans in bulk from other financial institutions as well as making loans to their own retail customers. There are approximately 438,000 wholesaling establishments in the United States,[27] and more than half of all products sold in this country pass through these firms.

Wholesalers may engage in many supply-chain management activities, including warehousing, shipping and product handling, inventory control, information system management and data processing, risk taking, financing, budgeting, and even marketing research and promotion. Regardless of whether there is a wholesaling firm involved in the supply chain, all product distribution requires the performance of these activities. In addition to bearing the primary responsibility for the physical distribution of products from manufacturers to retailers, wholesalers may establish information systems that help producers and retailers better manage the supply chain from producer to customer. Many wholesalers are using information technology and the Internet to allow their employees, customers, and suppliers to share information between intermediaries and facilitating agencies such as trucking companies and warehouse firms. Other firms are making their databases and marketing information systems available to their supply-chain partners to facilitate order processing, shipping, and product development and to share information about changing market conditions and customer desires. As a result, some wholesalers play a key role in supply-chain management decisions.

◉ Services Provided by Wholesalers

Wholesalers provide essential services to both producers and retailers. By initiating sales contacts with a producer and selling diverse products to retailers, wholesalers serve as an extension of the producer's sales force. Wholesalers also provide financial assistance. They often pay for transporting goods; they reduce a producer's warehousing expenses and inventory investment by holding goods in inventory; they extend credit and assume losses from buyers who turn out to be poor credit risks; and when they buy a producer's entire output and pay promptly or in cash, they are a source of working capital. Wholesalers also serve as conduits for information within the marketing channel, keeping producers up to date on market developments and passing along the manufacturers' promotional plans to other intermediaries. Using wholesalers therefore gives producers a distinct advantage because the specialized services wholesalers perform allow producers to concentrate on developing and manufacturing products that match customers' needs and wants.

Wholesalers support retailers by assisting with marketing strategy, especially the distribution component. Wholesalers also help retailers select inventory. They are often specialists on market conditions and experts at negotiating final purchases. In industries in which obtaining supplies is important, skilled buying is indispensable. For example, Atlanta-based Genuine Parts Company (GPC), the nation's top automotive parts wholesaler, has more than 70 years of experience in the auto parts business. This experience helps it serve its customers effectively. GPC supplies more than 300,000 replacement parts (from 150 different suppliers) to 6,000 NAPA Auto Parts stores.[28] Effective wholesalers make an effort to understand the businesses of their customers. They can reduce a retailer's burden of looking for and coordinating supply sources. If the wholesaler purchases for several different buyers, expenses can be shared by all customers. Furthermore, whereas a manufacturer's salesperson offers retailers only a few products at a time, independent wholesalers always have a wide range of products available. Thus, through partnerships, wholesalers and retailers can forge successful relationships for the benefit of customers.

The distinction between services performed by wholesalers and those provided by other businesses has blurred in recent years. Changes in the competitive nature of business, especially the growth of strong retail chains like Wal-Mart, Home Depot, and Best Buy, are changing supply-chain relationships. In many product categories, such as electronics, furniture, and even food products, retailers have discovered that they can deal directly with producers, performing wholesaling activities themselves at a lower cost. An increasing number of retailers are relying on computer technology to expedite ordering, delivery, and handling of goods. Technology is thus allowing retailers to take over many wholesaling functions. However, when a wholesaler is eliminated from a marketing channel, wholesaling activities still have to be performed by a member of the supply chain, whether a producer, retailer, or facilitating agency. These wholesaling activities are critical components of supply-chain management.

◉ Types of Wholesalers

Wholesalers are classified according to several criteria. Whether a wholesaler is independently owned or owned by a producer influences how it is classified. Wholesalers can also be grouped according to whether they take title to (own) the products they handle. The range of services provided is another criterion used for classification. Finally, wholesalers are classified according to the breadth and depth of their product lines. Using these criteria, we discuss three general types of wholesaling establishments: merchant wholesalers, agents and brokers, and manufacturers' sales branches and offices.

merchant wholesalers
Independently owned businesses that take title to goods, assume ownership risks, and buy and resell products to other wholesalers, business customers, or retailers

● **Merchant Wholesalers.**   Merchant wholesalers are independently owned businesses that take title to goods, assume risks associated with ownership, and generally buy and resell products to other wholesalers, business customers, or retailers. A producer is likely to rely on merchant wholesalers when selling directly to customers would be economically unfeasible. Merchant wholesalers are also useful for providing market coverage, making sales contacts, storing inventory, handling orders, collecting market information, and furnishing customer support. Some merchant wholesalers are even involved in packaging and developing private brands to help retail customers be competitive. Merchant wholesalers go by various names, including *wholesaler, jobber, distributor, assembler, exporter,* and *importer.* They fall into one of two broad categories: full-service and limited-service (see Figure 15.2).

full-service wholesalers
Merchant wholesalers that perform the widest range of wholesaling functions

Full-service wholesalers perform the widest possible range of wholesaling functions. Customers rely on them for product availability, suitable assortments, breaking large quantities into smaller ones, financial assistance, and technical advice and service. Universal Corporation, the world's largest buyer and processor of leaf tobacco, is an example of a full-service wholesaler. Based in Richmond, Virginia, the firm buys, resells, packs, and ships tobacco, and provides financing for its customers, which include cigarette manufacturers like Philip Morris (which accounts for a significant portion of Universal's sales). Universal is also involved in sales of lumber, rubber, tea, nuts, dried fruit, and other products and has operations in 40 countries.[29] Full-service

Figure 15.2
Types of Merchant Wholesalers

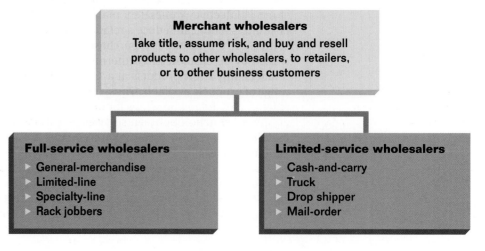

Merchant wholesalers
Take title, assume risk, and buy and resell products to other wholesalers, to retailers, or to other business customers

Full-service wholesalers
▸ General-merchandise
▸ Limited-line
▸ Specialty-line
▸ Rack jobbers

Limited-service wholesalers
▸ Cash-and-carry
▸ Truck
▸ Drop shipper
▸ Mail-order

wholesalers handle either consumer or business products and provide numerous marketing services to their customers. Many large grocery wholesalers help retailers with store design, site selection, personnel training, financing, merchandising, advertising, coupon redemption, and scanning. Although full-service wholesalers often earn higher gross margins than other wholesalers, their operating expenses are also higher because they perform a wider range of functions.

Full-service wholesalers are categorized as general merchandise, limited-line, and specialty-line wholesalers, and as rack jobbers. General merchandise wholesalers carry a wide product mix but offer limited depth within product lines. They deal in products such as drugs, nonperishable foods, cosmetics, detergents, and tobacco. Limited-line wholesalers carry only a few product lines, such as groceries, lighting fixtures, or oil-well drilling equipment, but offer an extensive assortment of products within those lines. Bergen Brunswig Corporation, for example, is a limited-line wholesaler of pharmaceuticals and health and beauty aids. Limited-line wholesalers provide a range of services similar to those of general merchandise wholesalers. Specialty-line wholesalers offer the narrowest range of products, usually a single product line or a few items within a product line. Red River Commodities, Inc., for example, is the leading importer (specialty-line wholesaler) of nuts, seeds, and dried fruits in the United States.[30] Rack jobbers are full-service, specialty-line wholesalers that own and maintain display racks in supermarkets, drugstores, and discount and variety stores. They set up displays, mark merchandise, stock shelves, and keep billing and inventory records; retailers need furnish only space. Rack jobbers specialize in nonfood items with high profit margins, such as health and beauty aids, books, magazines, hosiery, and greeting cards.

Limited-service wholesalers provide fewer marketing services than do full-service wholesalers and specialize in just a few functions. Producers perform the remaining functions or pass them on to customers or to other intermediaries. Limited-service wholesalers take title to merchandise but often do not deliver merchandise, grant credit, provide marketing information, store inventory, or plan ahead for customers' future needs. Because they offer restricted services, limited-service wholesalers are compensated with lower rates and have smaller profit margins than full-service wholesalers. The decision about whether to use a limited-service or a full-service wholesaler depends on the structure of the marketing channel and the need to manage the supply chain to provide competitive advantage. Although certain types of limited-service wholesalers are few in number, they are important in the distribution of products such as specialty foods, perishable items, construction materials, and coal. Table 15.2 summarizes the services provided by four typical limited-service wholesalers: cash-and-carry wholesalers, truck wholesalers, drop shippers, and mail-order wholesalers.

Cash-and-carry wholesalers are intermediaries whose customers—usually small businesses—pay cash and furnish transportation. Cash-and-carry wholesalers usually handle a limited line of products with a high turnover rate, such as groceries, building materials, and electrical or office supplies. Many small retailers whose accounts are refused by other wholesalers survive because of cash-and-carry wholesalers. Truck wholesalers, sometimes called *truck jobbers,* transport a limited line of products directly to customers for on-the-spot inspection and selection. They are often small operators who own and drive their own trucks. They usually have regular routes, calling on retailers and other institutions to determine their needs. Drop shippers, also known as *desk jobbers,* take title to goods and negotiate sales but never take actual possession of products. They forward orders from retailers, business buyers, or other wholesalers to manufacturers and arrange for carload shipments of items to be delivered directly from producers to these customers. They assume responsibility for products during the entire transaction, including the

general merchandise wholesalers   Full-service wholesalers with a wide product mix but limited depth within product lines

limited-line wholesalers   Full-service wholesalers that carry only a few product lines but many products within those lines

specialty-line wholesalers   Full-service wholesalers that carry only a single product line or a few items within a product line

rack jobbers   Full-service, specialty-line wholesalers that own and maintain display racks in stores

limited-service wholesalers   Merchant wholesalers that provide some services and specialize in a few functions

cash-and-carry wholesalers   Limited-service wholesalers whose customers pay cash and furnish transportation

truck wholesalers   Limited-service wholesalers that transport products directly to customers for inspection and selection

drop shippers   Limited-service wholesalers that take title to products and negotiate sales but never take actual possession of products

Table 15.2   Services That Limited-Service Wholesalers Provide

	Cash-and-Carry	Truck	Drop Shipper	Mail-Order
Physical Possession of Merchandise	Yes	Yes	No	Yes
Personal Sales Calls on Customers	No	Yes	No	No
Information about Market Conditions	No	Some	Yes	Yes
Advice to Customers	No	Some	Yes	No
Stocking and Maintenance of Merchandise in Customers' Stores	No	No	No	No
Credit to Customers	No	No	Yes	Some
Delivery of Merchandise to Customers	No	Yes	No	No

mail-order wholesalers Limited-service wholesalers that sell products through catalogs

costs of any unsold goods. **Mail-order wholesalers** use catalogs instead of sales forces to sell products to retail and business buyers. Wholesale mail-order houses generally feature cosmetics, specialty foods, sporting goods, office supplies, and automotive parts. Mail-order wholesaling enables buyers to choose and order particular catalog items for delivery through United Parcel Service, the U.S. Postal Service, or other carriers. This is a convenient and effective method of selling small items to customers in remote areas that other wholesalers might find unprofitable to serve. The Internet has provided an opportunity for mail-order wholesalers to sell products over their own websites and have the products shipped by the manufacturers.

● **Agents and Brokers.**   Agents and brokers negotiate purchases and expedite sales but do not take title to products (see Figure 15.3). Sometimes called *functional middlemen,* they perform a limited number of services in exchange for a commission, which is generally based on the product's selling price. **Agents** represent either buyers or sellers on a permanent basis, whereas **brokers** are intermediaries that buyers or sellers employ temporarily.

agents Intermediaries that represent either buyers or sellers on a permanent basis

brokers Intermediaries that bring buyers and sellers together temporarily

Although agents and brokers perform even fewer functions than limited-service wholesalers, they are usually specialists in particular products or types of customers and can provide valuable sales expertise. They know their markets well and often form long-lasting associations with customers. Agents and brokers enable manufacturers to expand sales when resources are limited, to benefit from the services of a trained sales force, and to hold down personal selling costs. Table 15.3 summarizes the services provided by agents and brokers.

manufacturers' agents Independent intermediaries that represent more than one seller and offer complete product lines

Manufacturers' agents, which account for more than half of all agent wholesalers, are independent intermediaries that represent two or more sellers and usually offer customers complete product lines. They sell and take orders year-round, much as a manufacturer's sales force does. Restricted to a particular territory, a manufacturers' agent handles noncompeting and complementary products. The relationship

Figure 15.3
Types of Agents and Brokers

between the agent and the manufacturer is governed by written contracts that outline territories, selling price, order handling, and terms of sale relating to delivery, service, and warranties. Manufacturers' agents have little or no control over producers' pricing and marketing policies. They do not extend credit and may be unable to provide technical advice. Manufacturers' agents are commonly used in sales of apparel, machinery and equipment, steel, furniture, automotive products, electrical goods, and certain food items.

selling agents Intermediaries that market a whole product line or a manufacturer's entire output

Selling agents market either all of a specified product line or a manufacturer's entire output. They perform every wholesaling activity except taking title to products. Selling agents usually assume the sales function for several producers simultaneously and are often used in place of marketing departments. In fact, selling agents are used most often by small producers or by manufacturers that have difficulty maintaining a marketing department because of seasonal production or other factors. In contrast to manufacturers' agents, selling agents generally have no territorial limits and have complete authority over prices, promotion, and distribution. To avoid conflicts of interest, selling agents represent noncompeting product lines. They play a key role in advertising, marketing research, and credit policies of the sellers they represent, at times even advising on product development and packaging.

Table 15.3 Services That Agents and Brokers Provide

	Manufacturers' Agents	Selling Agents	Commission Merchants	Brokers
Physical Possession of Merchandise	Some	Some	Yes	No
Long-Term Relationship with Buyers or Sellers	Yes	Yes	Yes	No
Representation of Competing Product Lines	No	No	Yes	Yes
Limited Geographic Territory	Yes	No	No	No
Credit to Customers	No	Yes	Some	No
Delivery of Merchandise to Customers	Some	Yes	Yes	No

commission merchants
Agents that receive goods on consignment and negotiate sales in large, central markets

Commission merchants receive goods on consignment from local sellers and negotiate sales in large, central markets. Sometimes called *factor merchants,* these agents have broad powers regarding prices and terms of sale. They specialize in obtaining the best price possible under market conditions. Most often found in agricultural marketing, commission merchants take possession of truckloads of commodities, arrange for necessary grading or storage, and transport the commodities to auction or markets where they are sold. When sales are completed, the agents deduct commission and the expense of making the sale, and then turn over profits to the producer. Commission merchants also offer planning assistance and sometimes extend credit, but usually do not provide promotional support.

A broker's primary purpose is to bring buyers and sellers together. Thus, brokers perform fewer functions than other intermediaries. They are not involved in financing or physical possession, have no authority to set prices, and assume almost no risks. Instead, they offer customers specialized knowledge of a particular commodity and a network of established contacts. Brokers are especially useful to sellers of certain types of products, such as supermarket products and real estate. Food brokers, for example, sell food and general merchandise to retailer-owned and merchant wholesalers, grocery chains, food processors, and business buyers.

● **Manufacturers' Sales Branches and Offices.** Sometimes called *manufacturers' wholesalers,* manufacturers' sales branches and offices resemble merchant wholesalers' operations.

sales branches Manufacturer-owned intermediaries that sell products and provide support services to the manufacturer's sales force

Sales branches are manufacturer-owned intermediaries that sell products and provide support services to the manufacturer's sales force. Situated away from the manufacturing plant, they are usually located where large customers are concentrated and demand is high. They offer credit, deliver goods, give promotional assistance, and furnish other services. Customers include retailers, business buyers, and other wholesalers. Manufacturers of electrical supplies, such as Westinghouse Electric, and of plumbing supplies, such as American Standard, often have branch operations. They are also common in the lumber and automotive parts industries.

sales offices Manufacturer-owned operations that provide services normally associated with agents

Sales offices are manufacturer-owned operations that provide services normally associated with agents. Like sales branches, they are located away from manufacturing plants, but unlike branches, they carry no inventory. A manufacturer's sales office (or branch) may sell products that enhance the manufacturer's own product line.

Manufacturers may set up these branches or offices to reach their customers more effectively by performing wholesaling functions themselves. A manufacturer may also set up such a facility when specialized wholesaling services are not available through existing intermediaries. A manufacturer's performance of wholesaling and physical distribution activities through its sales branch or office may strengthen supply-chain efficiency. In some situations, though, a manufacturer may bypass its sales office or branches entirely—for example, if the producer decides to serve large retailer customers directly.

CHAPTER REVIEW

❶ Understand the purpose and function of retailers in the marketing channel.
Retailing includes all transactions in which buyers intend to consume products through personal, family, or household use. Retailers, organizations that sell products primarily to ultimate consumers, are important links in the marketing channel because they are both marketers for and customers of wholesalers and producers. They add value, provide services, and assist in making product selections.

❷ Identify the major types of retailers.

Retail stores can be classified according to the breadth of products offered. Two broad categories are general merchandise retailers and specialty retailers. The primary types of general merchandise retailers include department stores, which are large retail organizations organized by departments and characterized by wide product mixes in considerable depth; discount stores, which are self-service, low-price, general merchandise outlets; supermarkets, which are large, self-service food stores that carry some nonfood products; superstores, which are giant retail outlets carrying all the products found in supermarkets and most consumer products purchased on a routine basis; hypermarkets, which offer supermarket and discount store shopping at one location; warehouse clubs, which are large-scale, members-only discount operations; and warehouse and catalog showrooms, which are low-cost operations characterized by warehouse methods of materials handling and display, large inventories, and minimal services. Specialty retailers offer substantial assortments in a few product lines. They include traditional specialty retailers, which carry narrow product mixes with deep product lines; category killers, large specialty stores that concentrate on a major product category and compete on the basis of low prices and enormous product availability; and off-price retailers, which sell brand name manufacturers' seconds and product overruns at deep discounts.

❸ Explore strategic issues in retailing.

Location, the least flexible of the strategic retailing issues, determines the trading area from which a store draws its customers and therefore should be evaluated carefully. When evaluating potential sites, retailers take into account various factors, including the location of the firm's target market within the trading area, customer characteristics, kinds of products sold, availability of public transportation and/or parking, and competitors' locations. Retailers can choose among several types of locations, including freestanding structures, traditional business districts, traditional planned shopping centers, or nontraditional shopping centers.

Retail positioning involves identifying an unserved or underserved market segment and serving it through a strategy that distinguishes the retailer from others in those customers' minds. Store image, which should facilitate positioning, derives not only from atmosphere but also from location, products offered, customer services, prices, promotion, and the store's overall reputation. Atmospherics refers to the physical elements of a store's design that can be adjusted to appeal to consumers' emotions and thus induce them to buy. Scrambled merchandising adds unrelated product lines to an existing product mix and is being used by a growing number of stores to generate sales.

The wheel-of-retailing theory holds that new retail institutions start as low-status, low-margin, and low-price operations. As they develop, they increase service and raise prices and eventually become vulnerable to newer institutions, which enter the market and repeat the cycle.

❹ Recognize the various forms of direct marketing and selling.

Direct marketing is the use of telecommunications and nonpersonal media to communicate product and organizational information to consumers, who then can purchase products by mail, telephone, or Internet. Such communication may occur through a catalog (catalog marketing), advertising (direct response marketing), telephone (telemarketing), television (television home shopping), or online (online retailing). Direct selling markets products to ultimate consumers through face-to-face sales presentations at home or in the workplace.

❺ Understand the nature and functions of wholesalers.

Wholesaling consists of all transactions in which products are bought for resale, for making other products, or for general business operations. Wholesalers are individuals or organizations that facilitate and expedite exchanges that are primarily wholesale transactions. For producers, wholesalers are a source of financial assistance and information; by performing specialized accumulation and allocation functions, they allow producers to concentrate on manufacturing products. Wholesalers provide retailers with buying expertise, wide product lines, efficient distribution, and warehousing and storage.

❻ Understand how wholesalers are classified.

Merchant wholesalers are independently owned businesses that take title to goods and assume ownership risks. They are either full-service wholesalers, offering the widest possible range of wholesaling functions, or limited-service wholesalers, providing only some marketing services and specializing in a few functions. Full-service merchant wholesalers include general merchandise wholesalers, which offer a wide but relatively shallow product mix;

limited-line wholesalers, which offer extensive assortments within a few product lines; specialty-line wholesalers, which carry only a single product line or a few items within a line; and rack jobbers, which own and service display racks in supermarkets and other stores. Limited-service merchant wholesalers include cash-and-carry wholesalers, which sell to small businesses, require payment in cash, and do not deliver; truck wholesalers, which sell a limited line of products from their own trucks directly to customers; drop shippers, which own goods and negotiate sales but never take possession of products; and mail-order wholesalers, which sell to retail and business buyers through direct mail catalogs.

Agents and brokers negotiate purchases and expedite sales in exchange for a commission, but they do not take title to products. Whereas agents represent buyers or sellers on a permanent basis, brokers are intermediaries employed by buyers and sellers on a temporary basis to negotiate exchanges. Manufacturers' agents market the complete product lines of two or more sellers. Selling agents market a complete product line or a producer's entire output and perform every wholesaling function except taking title to products. Commission merchants are agents that receive goods on consignment from local sellers and negotiate sales in large, central markets.

Manufacturers' sales branches and offices are owned by manufacturers. Sales branches sell products and provide support services for the manufacturer's sales force in a given location. Sales offices carry no inventory and function much as agents do.

Please visit the student website at www.prideferrell.com for ACE Self-Test questions that will help you prepare for exams.

KEY CONCEPTS

retailing	category killer	telemarketing	cash-and-carry
retailer	off-price retailers	television home shopping	wholesalers
general merchandise	neighborhood shopping	online retailing	truck wholesalers
retailer	centers	direct selling	drop shippers
department stores	community shopping	wholesaling	mail-order wholesalers
discount stores	centers	wholesaler	agents
supermarkets	regional shopping center	merchant wholesalers	brokers
superstores	retail positioning	full-service wholesalers	manufacturers' agents
hypermarkets	atmospherics	general merchandise	selling agents
warehouse clubs	scrambled merchandising	wholesalers	commission merchants
warehouse showrooms	wheel of retailing	limited-line wholesalers	sales branches
catalog showrooms	direct marketing	specialty-line wholesalers	sales offices
traditional specialty	catalog marketing	rack jobbers	
retailers	direct-response marketing	limited-service wholesalers	

ISSUES FOR DISCUSSION AND REVIEW

1. What value is added to the product by retailers? What value is added by retailers for producers and for ultimate consumers?

2. What are the major differences between discount stores and department stores?

3. In what ways are traditional specialty stores and off-price retailers similar? How do they differ?

4. What major issues should be considered when determining a retail site location?

5. Describe the three major types of traditional shopping centers. Give an example of each type in your area.

6. Discuss the major factors that help determine a retail store's image. How does atmosphere add value to products sold in a store?

7. In what ways does the use of scrambled merchandising affect a store's image?

8. How is door-to-door selling a form of retailing? Some consumers believe direct response orders bypass the retailer. Is this true?

9. What services do wholesalers provide to producers and retailers?

10. What is the difference between a full-service merchant wholesaler and a limited-service merchant wholesaler?

11. Drop shippers take title to products but do not accept physical possession of them, whereas commission merchants take physical possession of products but do not accept title. Defend the logic of classifying drop shippers as wholesale merchants and commission merchants as agents.

12. Why are manufacturers' sales offices and branches classified as wholesalers? Which independent wholesalers are replaced by manufacturers' sales branches? By sales offices?

MARKETING APPLICATIONS

1. Juanita wants to open a small retail store that specializes in high-quality, high-priced children's clothing. What types of competitors should she be concerned about in this competitive retail environment? Why?

2. Location of retail outlets is an issue in strategic planning. What initial steps would you recommend to Juanita (see Marketing Application 1) when she considers a location for her store?

3. Visit a retail store you shop in regularly or one in which you would like to shop. Identify the store and describe its atmospherics. Be specific about both exterior and interior elements, and indicate how the store is being positioned through its use of atmospherics.

4. Contact a local retailer you patronize and ask the store manager to describe the store's relationship with one of its wholesalers. Using your text as a guide, identify the distribution activities performed by the wholesaler. Are any of these activities shared by both the retailer and the wholesaler? How do these activities benefit the retailer? How do they benefit you as a consumer?

ONLINE EXERCISE

5. Wal-Mart provides a website from which customers can shop for products, search for a nearby store, and even preorder new products. The website lets customers browse what's on sale and view company information. Access Wal-Mart's website at **www.walmart.com.**
   a. How does Wal-Mart attempt to position itself on its website?
   b. Compare the atmospherics of Wal-Mart's website to the atmospherics of a traditional Wal-Mart store. Are they consistent? If not, should they be?
   c. Find Wal-Mart's history on the website. Relate the firm's history to the wheel-of-retailing concept.

VIDEO CASE

Adventures in Retailing at REI

Few retailers allow customers to test-ride mountain bikes on special indoor trails or let them pour water through different filtration devices before they decide which model to purchase. An open invitation to "try it before you buy it" is just one reason Recreational Equipment Inc. (REI) stands out in the world of retailing.

REI was founded in 1938 by 25 mountain climbers who pooled their buying power to get a better deal on ice axes and other climbing gear. From the start, REI was a consumer cooperative: a retail business that shares some of its profits with members. Today the retailer sells a vast array of outdoor sporting goods and apparel through

71 stores in 24 states, a printed catalog, two websites, and telephone sales. It also operates REI Adventures, a travel service for those who want to paddle, climb, cycle, ski, hike, or enjoy a combination of outdoor activities while on vacation.

REI's store atmospherics are unique, making the shopping experience an adventure in itself. Every store contains a two-story climbing wall that customers are invited to scale when trying out gear before buying. For example, the store in Sandy, Utah, features a 22-foot-high climbing wall modeled after the granite walls of a local canyon. Like other stores in the chain, the Sandy store has demonstration areas devoted to camp stoves, water filter testing, and hiking boots. Surrounding these special areas are acres and acres of items that one employee calls "grown-up toys," from kayaks and canteens to snow shoes and sleeping bags.

Store employees are enthusiastic about the merchandise they sell because they share their customers' love of the active life. "A passion for the outdoors comes first throughout REI and is a natural bond between employees and customers," observes REI's vice president of direct sales. "That passion and commitment to quality are reflected whether you're in an REI store, shopping online, or placing a catalog order on the phone." Employees are trained to determine their customers' needs, demonstrate appropriate products, and help customers make informed buying decisions.

REI's two retail websites feature page after page of product details, product comparisons, and how-to articles about outdoor sports and equipment. These sites are accessible from Internet kiosks set up in each REI store so customers can order any of 45,000 products for home delivery. If they prefer, customers can eliminate shipping fees by having online orders sent to any REI store for pickup—an option chosen by more than 30 percent of REI-Outlet.com's customers.

Customers can become members of the REI cooperative by paying a one-time fee of $15. They are then eligible for refund vouchers of up to 10 percent on their total annual purchases from REI stores, catalogs, and websites. They also pay lower prices for equipment rented or repaired in REI stores and for travel packages arranged through REI Adventures.

One of REI's core values is its ongoing commitment to protecting the natural environment by donating to nature centers, open-space projects, youth recreation programs, land conservation, and related activities in local communities. Moreover, as REI's president notes, store employees invest a great deal of "sweat equity" in the local community by volunteering their time to maintain hiking trails, clean up rivers, and preserve the environment in many other ways.

The market for outdoor sporting goods and apparel is increasingly competitive. Bass Pro Shops, headquartered in Missouri, targets customers who like fishing, hunting, and boating. Its 27 U.S. stores offer demonstration areas for fishing and other sports, creating a focal point for customers. Eastern Mountain Sports (EMS), headquartered in New Hampshire, operates 100 stores in eastern and midwestern states. In addition, REI competes with many independent stores and chain retailers that carry clothing and gear for the active lifestyle.

Today, REI generates more than $840 million in revenue and serves 2 million customers yearly. Its stores range in size from 10,000 to 95,000 square feet, so no two stores carry exactly the same merchandise. "Even though we don't have a lot of stores, we have a lot of variety in our stores," says REI's inventory planning manager, "and that creates merchandising challenges for us." REI's solution: analyze the profitability and sales per square foot of each product category in each store, and then eliminate the weakest categories to make room for the strongest. This helps the retailer manage inventory more efficiently and choose the most profitable assortment for each store.[31]

QUESTIONS FOR DISCUSSION

1. Why would REI locate many of its stores in freestanding structures rather than in shopping centers?
2. What is the likely effect of REI's consumer cooperative structure on the retailer's ability to build customer relationships?
3. What is REI's retail positioning, and why is it appropriate for the target market?

Promotion Decisions

P art 8 focuses on communication with target market members and, at times, other groups. A specific marketing mix cannot satisfy people in a particular target market unless they are aware of the product and know where to find it. Some promotion decisions relate to a specific marketing mix whereas others are geared toward promoting the entire organization. Chapter 16 discusses integrated marketing communications. It describes the communication process and the major promotional methods that can be included in promotion mixes. Chapter 17 analyzes the major steps in developing an advertising campaign. It also explains what public relations is and how it can be used. Chapter 18 deals with the management of personal selling and the role it can play in a firm's promotional efforts. It also explores the general characteristics of sales promotion and describes sales promotion techniques.

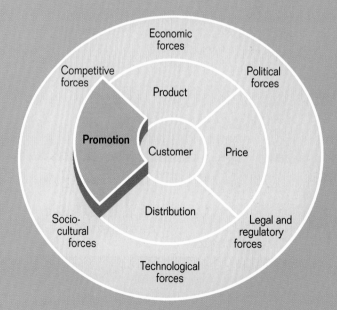

16 Integrated Marketing Communications

OBJECTIVES

1 Discuss the nature of integrated marketing communications.

2 Understand the role of promotion in the marketing mix.

3 Describe the process of communication.

4 Explain the objectives of promotion.

5 Understand the major elements of the promotion mix.

6 Describe the factors that affect the choice of promotion mix elements.

7 Understand the criticisms and defenses of promotion.

Apple's iPOD Shines with Promotion

Credit Steve Jobs with making Apple a brand name that once again turns heads—but this time in the music business. Apple, a pioneer in the computer industry in the 1980s, has long concentrated on developing innovative products that people will want tomorrow and beyond. How did Apple regain its shine? Thank the cutting-edge iPod portable digital music player, which runs on both the Macintosh and Microsoft Windows platforms. Indeed, Jobs has been acknowledged as the key person responsible for getting the music business moving in the right direction again.

With more than 10 million units sold, Apple's iPod dominates the portable digital music player segment with 60 percent of the market. The company continues to introduce new versions of the player, including the $99, 512-megabyte Shuffle, in 2005. Although the company faces new competition from Wal-Mart, Microsoft, and other companies eager to cash in on the rising trend, Apple executives are optimistic that their product can maintain a leadership position. Apple has already sold more than half a billion songs through its iTunes Music Store at 99 cents each. Each downloaded song nets Apple just 10 cents in profits, but it helps sell iPods.

Promotion for the iPod has been more strategic than sizable. The company spent just $10 million advertising iTunes and $9 million for iPods in the first eight months of 2003, a fraction of the $69 million Apple spent on promotions. However, Apple has leveraged its youthful brand image by entering into cooperative arrangements with Volkswagen and PepsiCo, and a joint venture with McDonald's is in the works.

A great deal of Apple's rationale behind a more thoughtful, strategic approach to paid media is likely the result of the company's successful public relations campaign. Tens of thousands of articles have been written about the iPod and the iTunes service, enabling the company's advertising dollars to reinforce the highly successful publicity and buzz marketing campaigns. Apple has excelled at generating publicity for its products.

The Apple brand has become so desirable that noncompeting firms are asking to link their products and brands with the Apple image. As Apple continues to craft its brand and image, it will likely continue to partner strategically with firms that can leverage their smaller advertising budgets while remaining sensitive to firms that "fit" with Apple's much-valued brand name.[1] ◀

Organizations like Apple employ various promotional methods to communicate with their target markets. Providing information to customers is vital to initiating and developing long-term customer relationships. In this chapter, we look at the general dimensions of promotion. First, we discuss the nature of integrated marketing communications. We then define and examine the role of promotion. Next, we analyze the meaning and process of communication and explore some of the reasons promotion is used. After that, we consider major promotional methods and the factors that influence marketers' decisions to use particular methods. Finally, we examine criticisms and defenses of promotion.

What Is Integrated Marketing Communications?

integrated marketing communications (IMC) Coordination of promotional efforts for maximum informational and persuasive impact

Integrated marketing communications (IMC) refer to the coordination of promotional efforts to ensure maximum informational and persuasive impact on customers. Coordinating multiple marketing tools to produce this synergistic effect requires a marketer to employ a broad perspective. A major goal of integrated marketing communications is to send a consistent message to customers. Masterfoods USA, for example, has attempted to integrate its well-known M&Ms brand with iconic consumer events such as the Academy Awards to help reinforce the fact that M&Ms are the number 1 snack food at the movies. In addition to humorous appearances by its "Red" and "Yellow" spokescharacters at pre-Oscar events, print ads for M&Ms featured a bingo game that consumers could play along with the awards ceremony, while television commercials offered tips for using M&Ms to host an Oscar party.[2]

Because various units both inside and outside most companies have traditionally planned and implemented promotional efforts, customers have not always received consistent messages. Integrated marketing communications provide a firm with a way to coordinate and manage its promotional efforts to ensure that customers receive consistent messages. This approach fosters not only long-term customer relationships but also the efficient use of promotional resources.

The concept of integrated marketing communications has been increasingly accepted for several reasons. Advertising to a mass audience, a very popular promotional method in the past, is used less today because of its high cost and unpredictable audience size. Marketers can now take advantage of more precisely targeted promotional tools such as cable TV, direct mail, the Internet, special-interest magazines, CDs and DVDs, and even cell phones. Database marketing is also allowing marketers to target individual customers more precisely. Until recently, suppliers of marketing communications were specialists. Advertising agencies developed advertising campaigns, sales promotion companies provided sales promotion activities and materials, and public relations firms engaged in publicity efforts. Today several promotion-related companies provide one-stop shopping to the client seeking advertising, sales promotion, and public relations, thus reducing coordination problems for the sponsoring company. Because the overall cost of marketing communications has risen significantly, upper management demands systematic evaluations of communication efforts and a reasonable return on investment.

The specific communication vehicles employed and the precision with which they are used are changing as both information technology and customer interests become increasingly dynamic. Frito-Lay, for example, used radio and outdoor ads, a website, and text messaging to target 16- to 24-year-olds to promote its new Black Pepper Jack Doritos. The ads asked consumers to send a text message and guess what they thought the phrase "inNw?" meant in order to gain an opportunity to win free music and video downloads and other prizes through the website.[3] Today, marketers and customers have almost unlimited access to data about each other. Integrating and customizing marketing communications while protecting customer privacy has become a major challenge. Through the Internet, companies can provide product information and services that are coordinated with traditional promotional activities. Communication relationships with customers can actually determine the nature of the product. Reflect.com, an online cosmetics firm, mixes makeup for different skin types based on information exchanges with customers. Thus, consumers may be willing to exchange personal information for customized products.[4] The sharing of information and use of technology to facilitate communication between buyers and sellers is necessary for successful customer relationship management.

The Role of Promotion

promotion Communication to build and maintain relationships by informing and persuading one or more audiences

Promotion is communication that builds and maintains favorable relationships by informing and persuading one or more audiences to view an organization more positively and to accept its products. While a company may pursue several promotional objectives (discussed later in this chapter), the overall role of promotion is to stimulate product demand. Toward this end, many organizations spend considerable resources on promotion to build and enhance relationships with current and potential customers. For example, the lumber ("Be Constructive"), pork ("Pork: The Other White Meat"), and milk ("Got Milk?") industries promote the use of these products to stimulate demand.[5] Marketers also indirectly facilitate favorable relationships by focusing information about company activities and products on interest groups (such as environmental and consumer groups), current and potential investors, regulatory agencies, and society in general. For example, some organizations promote responsible use of products criticized by society such as tobacco, alcohol, and violent movies. Companies sometimes promote programs that help selected groups. Yoplait, for instance, supports the Susan G. Komen Breast Cancer Research Foundation with its "Save Lids to Save Lives" campaign, which contributes 10 cents to the charity for every pink yogurt lid sent in by consumers.[6] Such *cause-related marketing* efforts link the purchase of products to philanthropic efforts for one or more causes. By contributing to causes that its target markets support, cause-related marketing can help marketers boost sales and generate goodwill. Marketers also sponsor special events, often leading to news coverage and positive promotion of organizations and their brands. Reebok, for example, held a star-studded party in Manhattan to promote Allen Iverson's Answer 7 and 50 Cents' G6 footwear. The event's highlight was a 6,000-pound half-court basketball court that floated down from the ceiling at midnight.[7]

Role of Promotion
The 3-A-Day of Dairy campaign promotes the health benefits of multiple dairy products.

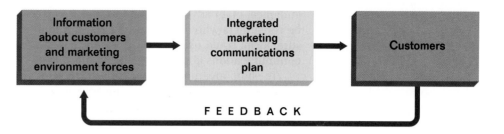

Figure 16.1
Information Flows Are Important in Integrated Marketing Communications

For maximum benefit from promotional efforts, marketers strive for proper planning, implementation, coordination, and control of communications. Effective management of integrated marketing communications is based on information about and feedback from customers and the marketing environment, often obtained from an organization's marketing information system (see Figure 16.1). How successfully marketers use promotion to maintain positive relationships depends largely on the quantity and quality of information the organization receives. Because customers derive information and opinions from many different sources, integrated marketing communications planning also takes into account informal methods of communication such as word of mouth and independent information sources on the Internet. Because promotion is communication that can be managed, we now analyze what communication is and how the communication process works.

Promotion and the Communication Process

Communication is essentially the transmission of information. For communication to take place, both the sender and receiver of information must share some common ground. They must have a common understanding of the symbols, words, and pictures used to transmit information. Thus, we define **communication** as a sharing of meaning.[8] Implicit in this definition is the notion of transmission of information because sharing necessitates transmission.

As Figure 16.2 shows, communication begins with a source. A **source** is a person, group, or organization with a meaning it attempts to share with an audience. A source could be a salesperson wishing to communicate a sales message or an organization wanting to send a message to thousands of customers through an advertisement. Developing a strategy can enhance the effectiveness of the source's communication. A **receiver** is the individual, group, or organization that decodes a coded message, and an *audience* is two or more receivers. The intended receivers, or

communication A sharing of meaning

source A person, group, or organization with a meaning it tries to share

receiver The individual, group, or organization that decodes a coded message

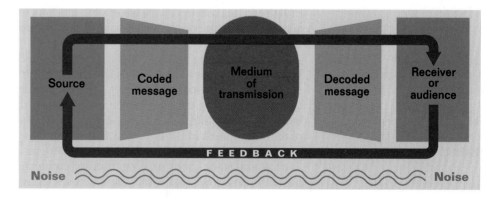

Figure 16.2
The Communication Process

audience, of an advertisement for Kashi's Heart to Heart cereal, for example, might be consumers who are concerned about reducing their cholesterol and blood pressure. Kashi could use this information to target receivers with integrated marketing communications about its products.

coding process Converting meaning into a series of signs or symbols

To share meaning, a source must convert the meaning into a series of signs or symbols representing ideas or concepts. This is called the **coding process** or *encoding*. When coding meaning into a message, the source must consider certain characteristics of the receiver or audience. To share meaning, the source should use signs or symbols familiar to the receiver or audience. Research has shown that persuasive messages from a source are more effective when the appeal matches an individual's personality.[9] Marketers who understand this realize the importance of knowing their target market and ensuring that an advertisement, for example, uses language the target market understands. Thus, when General Mills advertises Cheerios, it does not mention in its advertising all the ingredients used to make the cereal because some ingredients would have little meaning to consumers. Some notable problems have occurred in translating English advertisements into other languages to communicate with customers in global markets. For example, Budweiser has been advertised in Spain as the "Queen of Beers," and the Chinese have been encouraged to "eat their fingers off" when receiving KFC's slogan "Finger-Lickin' Good."[10] Clearly it is important that people understand the language used in promotion.

When coding a meaning, a source needs to use signs or symbols that the receiver or audience uses for referring to the concepts the source intends to convey. Instead of technical jargon, explanatory language that helps consumers understand is more likely to result in positive attitudes and purchase intentions.[11] Marketers try to avoid signs or symbols that may have several meanings for an audience. For example, *soda* as a general term for soft drinks might not work well in national advertisements. Although in some parts of the United States the word means "soft drink," in other regions it may connote bicarbonate of soda, an ice cream drink, or something one mixes with Scotch whiskey.

medium of transmission The means of carrying the coded message from the source to the receiver or audience

To share a coded meaning with the receiver or audience, a source selects and uses a medium of transmission. A **medium of transmission** carries the coded message from the source to the receiver or audience. Transmission media include ink on paper, air wave vibrations produced by vocal cords, chalk marks on a chalkboard, and electronically produced vibrations of air waves (in radio and television signals, for example).

When a source chooses an inappropriate medium of transmission, several problems may arise. The coded message may reach some receivers, but the wrong ones. Coded messages may also reach intended receivers in incomplete form because the intensity of the transmission is weak. For example, radio and broadcast television signals are received effectively only over a limited range, which varies depending on climatic conditions. Members of the target audience living on the fringe of the broadcast area may receive a weak signal; others well within the broadcast area may also receive an incomplete message if, for example, they listen to the radio while driving or studying.

decoding process Converting signs or symbols into concepts and ideas

In the **decoding process**, signs or symbols are converted into concepts and ideas. When a receiver finds that a message runs counter to his or her own attitudes, the source may influence the decoding process.[12] Seldom does a receiver decode exactly the same meaning that the source coded. When the result of decoding differs from what was coded, noise exists. **Noise** is anything that reduces the clarity and accuracy of the communication; it has many sources and may affect any or all parts of the communication process. Noise sometimes arises within the medium of transmission itself. Radio static, poor or slow Internet connections, and laryngitis are sources of noise. Noise also occurs when a source uses signs or symbols that are unfamiliar to

noise Anything that reduces a communication's clarity and accuracy

the receiver or have a different meaning from the one intended. Noise may also originate in the receiver; a receiver may be unaware of a coded message when perceptual processes block it out.

feedback   The receiver's response to a message

The receiver's response to a message is **feedback** to the source. The source usually expects and normally receives feedback, although perhaps not immediately. During feedback, the receiver or audience is the source of a message directed toward the original source, which then becomes a receiver. Feedback is coded, sent through a medium of transmission, and decoded by the receiver, the source of the original communication. Thus, communication is a circular process, as indicated in Figure 16.2.

During face-to-face communication, such as occurs in personal selling and product sampling, verbal and nonverbal feedback can be immediate. Instant feedback lets communicators adjust messages quickly to improve the effectiveness of their communication. For example, when a salesperson realizes through feedback that a customer does not understand a sales presentation, the salesperson adapts the presentation to make it more meaningful to the customer. This may be why face-to-face sales presentations create higher behavioral intentions to purchase services than do telemarketing sales contacts.[13] In interpersonal communication, feedback occurs through talking, touching, smiling, nodding, eye movements, and other body movements and postures.

When mass communication such as advertising is used, feedback is often slow and difficult to recognize. For example, Nickelodeon, a cable television network, is trying to expand its market by targeting "tweens," children ages 9 to 14, with advertising between programs and commercial-free Nick Jr. programs on CBS on Saturday mornings.[14] It may be several years, however, before the effects of this promotion will be known. Feedback does exist for mass communication in the form of measures of changes in sales volume or in consumers' attitudes and awareness levels.

channel capacity   The limit on the volume of information a communication channel can handle effectively

Each communication channel has a limit on the volume of information it can handle effectively. This limit, called **channel capacity**, is determined by the least efficient component of the communication process. Consider communications that depend on speech. An individual source can speak only so fast, and there is a limit to how much an individual receiver can take in aurally. Beyond that point, additional messages cannot be decoded; thus, meaning cannot be shared. Although a radio announcer can read several hundred words a minute, a one-minute advertising message should not exceed about 150 words because most announcers cannot articulate words into understandable messages at a rate beyond 150 words per minute.

Objectives of Promotion

Promotional objectives vary considerably from one organization to another and within organizations over time. Large firms with multiple promotional programs operating simultaneously may have quite varied promotional objectives. For the purpose of analysis, we focus on eight promotional objectives. Although this set of possible promotional objectives is not exhaustive, one or more of these objectives underlie many promotional programs.

◎ Create Awareness

A considerable amount of promotion focuses on creating awareness. For an organization introducing a new product or a line extension, making customers aware of the product is crucial to initiating the product adoption process. A marketer that has invested heavily in product development strives to create product awareness quickly to generate revenues to offset the high costs of product development and

Creating Awareness
Chick-fil-A creates awareness of the health benefits of consuming chicken.

Over 30 years ago, the folks at Chick-fil-A® invented the original reason to eat more chicken. Namely, the world's first chicken sandwich. Ever since then, they've been responsible for one tasty chicken creation after another. And because chicken's the healthier choice, one thing's for sure: You'll have no beef with us.

introduction. To create awareness of its new Crest Pro-Health mouthwash, for example, Procter & Gamble ran print and television ads and passed out samples in dentists' and doctors' offices and health clubs.[15]

Creating awareness is important for existing products, too. Promotional efforts may aim to increase awareness of brands, product features, image-related issues (such as organizational size or socially responsive behavior), or operational characteristics (such as store hours, locations, and credit availability). Some promotional programs are unsuccessful because marketers fail to generate awareness of critical issues among a significant portion of target market members or because the programs do not target the right audience.

◉ Stimulate Demand

primary demand Demand for a product category rather than for a specific brand

pioneer promotion Promotion that informs consumers about a new product

When an organization is the first to introduce an innovative product, it tries to stimulate **primary demand**—demand for a product category rather than for a specific brand of product—through pioneer promotion. **Pioneer promotion** informs potential customers about the product: what it is, what it does, how it can be used, and where it can be purchased. Because pioneer promotion is used in the introductory stage of the product life cycle, which means there are no competing brands, it neither emphasizes brand names nor compares brands. The first company to introduce the digital video recorder, for instance, initially attempted to stimulate primary demand by emphasizing the benefits of digital video recorders in general rather than the benefit of its specific brand. Primary-demand stimulation is not just for new products. At times an industry trade association rather than a single firm uses promotional efforts to stimulate primary demand. Major League Baseball, for example, spent $250 million to get more consumers to watch major league baseball games.[16]

selective demand Demand for a specific brand

To build **selective demand**, demand for a specific brand, a marketer employs promotional efforts that point out the strengths and benefits of a specific brand. Building selective demand also requires singling out attributes important to potential buyers. Selective demand can be stimulated by differentiating the product from competing

Stimulating Primary Demand
The Almond Board of California promotes almonds to stimulate primary demand.

brands in the minds of potential buyers. Microsoft, for example, spent $50 million to lure AOL subscribers to its MSN Internet service after AOL raised its price for Internet service, promising them that Microsoft would not raise MSN's already lower rate.[17] It can also be stimulated by increasing the number of product uses and promoting them through advertising campaigns, as well as through price discounts, free samples, coupons, consumer contests and games, and sweepstakes. Promotions for large package sizes or multiple-product packages are directed at increasing consumption, which in turn can stimulate demand. In addition, selective demand can be stimulated by encouraging existing customers to use more of the product.

Encourage Product Trial

When attempting to move customers through the product adoption process, a marketer may successfully create awareness and interest, but customers may stall during the evaluation stage. In this case, certain types of promotion, such as free samples, coupons, test drives or limited free-use offers, contests, and games, are employed to encourage product trial. Silk, for example, gave out coupons and samples to promote its new Silk live! Smoothie product.[18] Whether a marketer's product is the first of a new product category, a new brand in an existing category, or simply an existing brand seeking customers, trial-inducing promotional efforts aim to make product trial convenient and low risk for potential customers.

Identify Prospects

Certain types of promotional efforts are directed at identifying customers who are interested in the firm's product and are most likely to buy it. A marketer may use a magazine advertisement with a direct-response information form, requesting the reader to complete and mail the form to receive additional information. Some advertisements have toll-free numbers to facilitate direct customer response. Customers who fill out information blanks or call the organization usually have higher interest in

Encouraging Product Trial
Eastland Park Hotel in Portland, Maine, encourages trial by offering a second meal at half price.

the product, which makes them likely sales prospects. The organization can respond with phone calls, follow-up letters, or personal contact by salespeople. Dun & Bradstreet, for example, offered a free article on customer relationship management to businesspeople who mailed in a card or called a toll-free number. This helped the consulting firm identify prospects to sell data used to develop and maintain customer relationships.

◉ Retain Loyal Customers

Clearly, maintaining long-term customer relationships is a major goal of most marketers. Such relationships are quite valuable. For example, the lifetime value of a Taco Bell customer amounts to $12,000.[19] Promotional efforts directed at customer retention can help an organization control its costs because the costs of retaining customers are usually considerably lower than those of acquiring new ones. Frequent-user programs, such as those sponsored by airlines, car rental agencies, and hotels, seek to reward loyal customers and encourage them to remain loyal. Some organizations employ special offers that only their existing customers can use. To retain loyal customers, marketers not only advertise loyalty programs but also use reinforcement advertising, which assures current users they have made the right brand choice and tells them how to get the most satisfaction from the product.

◉ Facilitate Reseller Support

Reseller support is a two-way street. Producers generally want to provide support to resellers to maintain sound working relationships, and in turn they expect resellers to support their products. When a manufacturer advertises a product to consumers, resellers should view this promotion as a form of strong manufacturer support. In some instances, a producer agrees to pay a certain proportion of retailers' advertising expenses for promoting its products. When a manufacturer is introducing a new consumer brand in a highly competitive product category, it may be difficult to persuade supermarket managers to carry this brand. However, if the manufacturer promotes the new brand with free samples and coupon distribution in the retailer's area, a supermarket manager views these actions as strong support and is much more likely to handle the product. To encourage wholesalers and retailers to market their products more aggressively, a manufacturer may provide them with special offers, buying allowances, and contests. In certain industries, a producer's salesperson may provide support to a wholesaler by working with the wholesaler's customers (retailers) in the presentation and promotion of the products. Strong relationships with resellers are important to a firm's ability to maintain a sustainable competitive advantage. The use of various promotional methods can help an organization achieve this goal.

◉ Combat Competitive Promotional Efforts

At times a marketer's objective in using promotion is to offset or lessen the effect of a competitor's promotional program. This type of promotional activity does not necessarily increase the organization's sales or market share, but it may prevent a sales or market share loss. A combative promotional objective is used most often by firms in extremely competitive consumer markets, such as the fast-food and automobile industries. When some automakers began advertising their automobiles' ability to withstand collisions, as determined by crash tests conducted by various federal and private agencies, Volkswagen, BMW, Saturn, Mercedes-Benz, Toyota, and other firms quickly followed suit to combat their competitors' advertising. Although these ads were trying to promote safety records, the companies were also trying to prevent market share loss in a very competitive market.[20]

◉ Reduce Sales Fluctuations

Demand for many products varies from one month to another because of factors such as climate, holidays, and seasons. A business, however, cannot operate at peak efficiency when sales fluctuate rapidly. Changes in sales volume translate into changes in production, inventory levels, personnel needs, and financial resources. When promotional techniques reduce fluctuations by generating sales during slow periods, a firm can use its resources more efficiently.

Promotional techniques are often designed to stimulate sales during sales slumps. For example, advertisements promoting price reduction of lawn care equipment can increase sales during fall and winter months. During peak periods, a marketer may refrain from advertising to prevent stimulating sales to the point where the firm cannot handle all the demand. On occasion, an organization advertises that customers can be better served by coming in on certain days. A pizza outlet, for example, might distribute coupons that are valid only Monday through Thursday because on Friday through Sunday the restaurant is extremely busy.

To achieve the major objectives of promotion discussed here, companies must develop appropriate promotional programs. In the next section, we consider the basic components of such programs, referred to as the promotion mix elements.

◉))) The Promotion Mix

Several promotional methods can be used to communicate with individuals, groups, and organizations. When an organization combines specific methods to manage the integrated marketing communications for a particular product, that combination constitutes the promotion mix for that product. The four possible elements of a **promotion mix** are advertising, personal selling, public relations, and sales promotion (see Figure 16.3). For some products, firms use all four ingredients; for others, they use only two or three.

promotion mix   A combination of promotional methods used to promote a specific product

◉ Advertising

Advertising is a paid nonpersonal communication about an organization and its products transmitted to a target audience through mass media, including television, radio, the Internet, newspapers, magazines, direct mail, outdoor displays, and signs on mass transit vehicles. Individuals and organizations use advertising to promote goods, services, ideas, issues, and people. Being highly flexible, advertising can reach an extremely large target audience or focus on a small, precisely defined segment. For instance, Burger King's advertising focuses on a large audience of potential fast-food customers, ranging from children to adults, whereas advertising for Gulfstream jets aims at a much smaller and more specialized target market.

Advertising offers several benefits. It is extremely cost efficient when it reaches a vast number of people at a low cost per person. For example, the cost of a four-color, one-page advertisement in *Time* magazine is $234,000. Because the magazine reaches more than 4 million subscribers, the cost of reaching 1,000 subscribers is only about $59.[21] Advertising also lets the source repeat the message several times. Levi Strauss, for example, advertises on television, in magazines, and in outdoor displays. Furthermore, advertising a product a certain way can add to its value, and the visibility an organization gains from advertising can enhance its image. At

Figure 16.3
The Four Possible Elements of a Promotion Mix

TECHNOLOGY IN ACTION

It's nice to know your loved ones are safe at home. Wherever you are, you can monitor your home – even remotely control home appliances, temperatures and security devices. And in the ubiquitous networked society of the near future, you'll be connected to everyone and everything, anytime and anyplace. Even your cat. From broadband access networks, data storage solutions and hard disk drive technologies, to information devices like plasma displays and PDAs, Hitachi's technological expertise and services are making this a reality. Just one more example of technology not for its own sake but for the benefit of all. As an innovative global solutions company, Hitachi touches your life in many ways. Visit us on the Web and see technology in action.

HITACHI
Inspire the Next

www.hitachi.com/inspire/

Advertising
Hitachi uses the visual aspects of advertising to promote its efforts to use technology to address environmental issues.

times a firm tries to enhance its own or its product's image by including celebrity endorsers in advertisements. For example, the National Fluid Milk Processor Promotion Board's "milk moustache" campaign has featured Pete Sampras, the Back Street Boys, Britney Spears, and Elton John, as well as animated "celebrities" such as Garfield, the Rugrats, and Blue of *Blue's Clues*.[22]

Advertising has disadvantages as well. Even though the cost per person reached may be low, the absolute dollar outlay can be extremely high, especially for commercials during popular television shows. High costs can limit, and sometimes prevent, use of advertising in a promotion mix. Advertising rarely provides rapid feedback. Measuring its effect on sales is difficult, and it is ordinarily less persuasive than personal selling. In most instances, the time available to communicate a message to customers is limited to seconds, since people look at a print advertisement for only a few seconds and most broadcast commercials are 30 seconds or less. Of course, the use of infomercials can increase exposure time for viewers.

◉ Personal Selling

Personal selling is a paid personal communication that seeks to inform customers and persuade them to purchase products in an exchange situation. The phrase *purchase products* is interpreted broadly to encompass acceptance of ideas and issues. Telemarketing, direct selling over the telephone, relies heavily on personal selling.

Personal selling has both advantages and limitations when compared with advertising. Advertising is general communication aimed at a relatively large target audience, whereas personal selling involves more specific communication directed at one or several persons. Reaching one person through personal selling costs considerably more than through advertising, but personal selling efforts often have greater impact on customers. Personal selling also provides immediate feedback, allowing marketers to adjust their messages to improve communication. It helps them determine and respond to customers' information needs.

When a salesperson and a customer meet face to face, they use several types of interpersonal communication. The predominant communication form is language, both spoken and written. A salesperson and customer frequently use **kinesic communication**, or communication through the movement of head, eyes, arms, hands, legs, or torso. Winking, head nodding, hand gestures, and arm motions are forms of kinesic communication. A good salesperson often can evaluate a prospect's interest in a product or presentation by noting eye contact and head nodding. **Proxemic communication**, a less obvious form of communication used in personal selling situa-

kinesic communication
Communicating through the movement of head, eyes, arms, hands, legs, or torso

proxemic communication
Communicating by varying the physical distance in face-to-face interactions

CUSTOMER RELATIONSHIP MANAGEMENT
THE PERILS OF CELEBRITY ADVERTISING

When DaimlerChrysler signed a three-year, $14 million deal with recording artist Céline Dion to promote its automobiles, managers thought they were on to a good thing. The popular French-Canadian diva, who has recorded a number of best-selling albums and singles, is adored by millions of fans around the world for her powerful vocals and unabashedly sentimental tunes. To Chrysler managers, she offered a sophisticated image, which seemed the perfect vehicle to steer the company on its "path to premium."

But just a year after signing the deal, Dion's image and voice were conspicuously absent from the company's advertising. Although Dion's partnership with Chrysler helped increase record sales for Dion, it failed to sell cars for Chrysler. Unhappy dealers grumbled that the advertising campaign did more to sell the vocalist than cars.

How could such a seemingly brilliant match have failed to ignite sales? Sources suggest the Chrysler's advertising agency had advised Chrysler *against* signing the deal on the grounds that Dion's devoted audience was older than the buyers Chrysler sought to target. Despite this counsel, Chrysler arranged for Dion to star in a number of extravagant commercials and events as part of its "Drive & Love" campaign. The company even

sponsored her highly touted Las Vegas show called "A New Day."

Dion's failure to appeal to car buyers underscores some of the pitfalls of using celebrities to endorse products. First, managers impressed by star power may be all too eager to sign deals, even when market research suggests that a particular celebrity may not be the best match for a particular product or target market. Moreover, a celebrity with Dion's superstar power can easily eclipse a brand.

Another stumbling block is the possibility that a spokesperson might engage in scandalous or illegal behavior—as in the case of Indiana Pacer Ron Artest, who was suspended for a season after a brawl during a basketball game with the Detroit Pistons. The scandal threatened Artest's endorsement deals with LA Gear and D-Apparel. Baseball's seven-time Most Valuable Player Barry Bonds likewise caused a scandal after admitting to using steroids; the admission threatened endorsement deals for Bonds and created a public relations issue for Major League Baseball. Other problems may arise if celebrities become overexposed by being linked with too many products, or if they become unable to perform and lose their status in the field.[a]

tions, occurs when either person varies the physical distance separating them. When a customer backs away from a salesperson, for example, he or she may be displaying a lack of interest in the product or expressing dislike for the salesperson. Touching, or **tactile communication**, is also a form of communication, although less popular in the United States than in many other countries. Handshaking is a common form of tactile communication both in the United States and elsewhere.

tactile communication
Communicating through touching

◉ Public Relations

While many promotional activities are focused on a firm's customers, other stakeholders—suppliers, employees, stockholders, the media, educators, potential investors, government officials, and society in general—are important to an organization as well. To communicate with customers and stakeholders, a company employs public relations. Public relations is a broad set of communication efforts used to create and maintain favorable relationships between an organization and its stakeholders. Maintaining a positive relationship with one or more stakeholders can affect a firm's current sales and profits, as well as its long-term survival.

Public relations uses various tools, including annual reports, brochures, event sponsorship, and sponsorship of socially responsible programs aimed at protecting the environment or helping disadvantaged individuals. Nintendo, for example, is seeking to target older game players by hosting Super Bowl parties with men's magazines *Maxim* and *FHM,* as well as Spring Break parties and music tours, and it sponsored the Burton snowboarding championships.[23] Merrill Lynch sponsored a "Women of the World" art exhibit, which featured art by women artists from around the world, to help the financial services firm achieve its goal of targeting more affluent women.[24]

Other tools arise from the use of publicity, which is a component of public relations. Publicity is nonpersonal communication in news story form about an organization or its products, or both, transmitted through a mass medium at no charge. A few examples of publicity-based public relations tools are news releases, press conferences, and feature articles. Ordinarily, public relations efforts are planned and implemented to be consistent with and support other elements of the promotion mix. Public relations efforts may be the responsibility of an individual or of a department within the organization, or the organization may hire an independent public relations agency.

Unpleasant situations and negative events such as product tampering or an environmental disaster may provoke unfavorable public relations for an organization. To minimize the damaging effects of unfavorable coverage, effective marketers have policies and procedures in place to help manage any public relations problems. For example, after Wal-Mart suffered negative publicity due to news stories and lawsuits related to its hiring practices, union management, and aggressive expansion policies, the company ran a full-page newspaper ad in more than 100 newspapers promoting its job creation, employee diversity, and employee-benefit packages.[25]

Public relations should not be viewed as a set of tools to be used only during crises. To get the most from public relations, an organization should have someone responsible for public relations either internally or externally and should have an ongoing public relations program.

◉ Sales Promotion

Sales promotion is an activity or material that acts as a direct inducement, offering added value or incentive for the product, to resellers, salespeople, or consumers.[26] Examples include free samples, games, rebates, displays, sweepstakes, contests, premiums, and coupons. For example, Trimspa sponsored a "Million Dollar Makeover Challenge," asking users of its weight-loss product to submit before and after photos of themselves to compete to win $1 million in prizes.[27] *Sales promotion* should not be confused with *promotion;* sales promotion is just one part of the comprehensive area of promotion. Marketers spend more on sales promotion than on advertising, and sales promotion appears to be a faster-growing area than advertising.

Sales Promotion
Expedia promotes the use of a coffee gift card as a sales promotion incentive.

MARKETING LEADERS
JONES SODA BENEFITS FROM PUBLICITY

Seattle-based Jones Soda Company markets premium soft drinks known for creative flavors, labels, and promotions that clearly differentiate them from mass-market offerings by Coca-Cola and PepsiCo. The 55-person company continuously promotes its premium brand and regularly changes flavors and labels, which may include photos sent in by customers. Customers can even suggest new flavors to Jones on the company's website or customize their own soda labels.

Despite its reputation for curious flavors, Jones's management was surprised by the deluge of publicity generated by the release of a turkey-and-gravy-flavored soft drink around Thanksgiving. The company produced just a few thousand bottles of the seasonal flavor to draw attention to its 15 other soft drinks. Turkey & Gravy Soda sold out in a matter of hours, perhaps because it seemed fun, unique, and timely. Although product developers at Jones characterized the product as a sipping soda rather than a thirst-satisfying one, the timing of its holiday release helped fuel its success.

One thing is clear about Turkey & Gravy Soda: people loved talking about the soft drink that was purported to taste like "microwaved Thanksgiving leftovers." In the three weeks following its introduction, the company's president, Peter Van Stolk, was contacted more than 500 times by the media, resulting in nearly 100 radio interviews. Even *Business Week* acknowledged the product. Jones was particularly pleased by Turkey & Gravy Soda because the company's target market is teenagers, who are known to be devoted radio listeners. Van Stolk further maximized the public relations impact by mentioning in every radio interview that the company planned to donate all profits from Turkey & Gravy Soda to the Toys for Tots charity. It is doubtful that paid advertising could have generated nearly as much interest in the curiously flavored soft drink as this buzz marketing approach did. Indeed, Turkey & Gravy Soda has been Jones's most successful promotion to date, exceeding the impact of previous promotions associated with flavors such as Ham and Fish-Taco.

Such publicity has been beneficial for a small firm that does very little advertising. Much of the firm's promotion budget is spent on sponsorships of "passionate young people" like skateboarder Tony Hawk, as well as a website that allows nearly 500 unsigned bands to post their music for download. Such creativity in marketing certainly seems to have paid off for Jones Soda: its sales have doubled over the last four years, to more than $20 million.[b]

Generally, when companies employ advertising or personal selling, they depend on them continuously or cyclically. However, a marketer's use of sales promotion tends to be irregular. Many products are seasonal. A company like Toro may offer more sales promotions in August than in the peak selling season of April or May, when more people buy tractors, lawn mowers, and other gardening equipment. Marketers frequently rely on sales promotion to improve the effectiveness of other promotion mix ingredients, especially advertising and personal selling. Decisions to cut sales promotion can have significant negative effects on a company. For example, Clorox decided to cut the promotion budget for Glad branded products two years in a row, in part to compensate for rising plastic resin prices. When competitors did not decrease their promotional budgets, Glad lost significant market share in trash bags (down 10.3 percent), food storage bags (down 10.6 percent), and lawn and leaf bags (down 23.2 percent).[28]

Selecting Promotion Mix Elements

Marketers vary the composition of promotion mixes for many reasons. Although a promotion mix can include all four elements, frequently a marketer selects fewer than four. Many firms that market multiple product lines use several promotion mixes simultaneously.

An effective promotion mix requires the right combination of components. To see how such a mix is created, we now examine the factors and conditions affecting the selection of promotion mix elements that an organization uses for a specific promotion mix.

Customer Involvement

When making decisions about the composition of promotion mixes, marketers should recognize that commercial messages, whether from advertising, personal selling, sales promotion, or public relations, are limited in the extent to which they can inform and persuade customers and move them closer to making purchases. Depending on the type of customers and the products involved, buyers to some extent rely on word-of-mouth communication from personal sources such as family members and friends. Most consumers seek information from friends and family members when buying medical, legal, and auto repair services. Word-of-mouth communication is also very important when people are selecting restaurants and entertainment, and automotive, banking, and personal services like hair care. Effective marketers who understand the importance of word-of-mouth communication attempt to identify advice givers and to encourage them to try their products in the hope they will spread favorable word about them.

An approach called *buzz marketing* is an attempt to create a trend or acceptance of a product through word-of-mouth communications. Toyota, for example, parked its new Scions outside of raves and hip cafés, coffee shops, and clothing stores, where shoppers could take informal test drives in order to get the "buzz" going about the new marque.[29] The idea behind buzz marketing is that an accepted member of a social group will always be more credible than any other form of paid communication.[30] Related to buzz marketing is the notion of *viral marketing*, a strategy to get Internet users to

MARKETING ENTREPRENEURS

Mike Gellman

THE BUSINESS: SpireMedia

FOUNDED: 1998

SUCCESS: More than $3 million in annual revenue

Mike Gellman founded SpireMedia in 1998, with just two computers, a fax machine, and one client (eBags). The firm is now Denver's biggest web-development firm with 25 employees, 200 clients, and around $3.5 million in annual revenue. SpireMedia provides web strategy, information architecture, and business analysis services. The key to Gellman's success has been producing quality work for his clients without a penny of outside financing and with word-of-mouth communication as his biggest promotion outlet. He maintains an open-book policy with his employees so that they are aware of how the business is doing and how they affect productivity. By growing slowly and acquiring clients from big competitors that went under in the 1990s, SpireMedia has become a successful company with clients such as Western Union, Qwest, Jeppessen, and even David Letterman.[c]

share ads and promotions with their friends. Burger King, for example, created the "Subservient Chicken" website, where web surfers seem to be able to control a person in a chicken suit by typing in commands. Viral communications resulted in nearly 14 million visitors to the website in less than a year.[31] In any case, marketers should not underestimate the importance of word-of-mouth communications and personal influence, nor should they have unrealistic expectations about the performance of commercial messages.

A growing technique for reaching consumers is the selective placement of products within the context of television programs viewed by the target market. Nielsen Media estimates that 15 percent of product appearances in television programming are paid product placements representing an approximate market ad value of $9 billion. Perhaps the biggest commitment to a program was the eleven minutes purchased by the National Football League in the TV comedy, "According to Jim." The advertising value of that time was calculated at $9.9 million for the NFL.[32] Such product placement has become more important due to the increasing fragmentation of television viewers who have ever-expanding viewing options and technology that can screen advertisements (e.g., digital video recorders such as TiVo). Research indicates that 60 to 80 percent of digital video recorder users skip the commercials when replaying programming.[33] In-program product placements have been successful in reaching consumers as they are being entertained rather than in the competitive commercial break time periods. Table 16.1 identifies some of the top ten brands in product placement. After Oprah Winfrey gave 276 audience members new Pontiac G6s, it generated tremendous publicity for both *Oprah* and Pontiac, with more than 600 media outlets commenting on the giveway in the days following the show. The sales of the G6 are higher than its closest competitor by 20 percent.[34] Reality programming in particular has been a natural fit for product placements because of the close interchange between the participants and the product (e.g., Sears and *Extreme Makeover Home Edition;* Levi's, Burger King, Marquis Jet, and Dove and *The Apprentice;* Coca-Cola and *American Idol*). When Genworth Financial was evaluating this advertising tactic, it found that its target market aligned well with the viewership of *The Apprentice,* which is among the wealthiest and highest educated for network television. Genworth Financial was featured in the last episode of season 2 and was exposed to 30.4 million *Apprentice* viewers. As a new company, Genworth did not have the prior brand recognition of competitors such as MetLife, Prudential, or Allstate.[35]

Table 16.1	Top Ten Brands in Product Placement	
	Brand	**Occurrences**
1.	Coca-Cola Classic	2,245
2.	Pepsi Cola	1,109
3.	Nike	1,030
4.	NetZero ISP	907
5.	Boston Red Sox	804
6.	Golden Nugget Hotel/Casino	523
7.	Ford	413
8.	Moosehead beer	391
9.	Chicago Bears	364
10.	AT&T Wireless	359

Source: Nielsen Media Research for January through September 2004, in Lynna Goch, "The Place to Be," *Best's Review,* February 2005, pp. 64–65.

◉ Promotional Resources, Objectives, and Policies

The size of an organization's promotional budget affects the number and relative intensity of promotional methods included in a promotion mix. If a company's promotional budget is extremely limited, the firm is likely to rely on personal selling because it is easier to measure a salesperson's contribution to sales than to measure the sales effectiveness of advertising. Organizations with extensive promotional resources generally include more elements in their promotion mixes, but having more promotional dollars to spend does not necessarily mean using more promotional methods.

An organization's promotional objectives and policies also influence the types of promotion selected. If a company's objective is to create mass awareness of a new convenience good, such as a breakfast cereal, its promotion mix probably leans heavily toward advertising, sales promotion, and possibly public relations. If a company hopes to educate customers about the features of a durable good, such as a home appliance, its promotion mix may combine a moderate amount of advertising, possibly some sales promotion designed to attract customers to retail stores, and a great deal of personal selling because this method is an excellent way to inform customers about such products.

◉ Characteristics of the Target Market

Size, geographic distribution, and demographic characteristics of a firm's target market help dictate the methods to include in a product's promotion mix. To some degree, market size determines composition of the mix. If the size is limited, the promotion mix will probably emphasize personal selling, which can be very effective for reaching small numbers of people. Firms selling to business markets and firms marketing products through only a few wholesalers frequently make personal selling the major component of their promotion mixes. When a product's market consists of millions of customers, businesses rely on advertising and sales promotion because these methods reach masses of people at a low cost per person.

Geographic distribution of a firm's customers also affects the choice of promotional methods. Personal selling is more feasible if a company's customers are concentrated in a small area than if they are dispersed across a vast region. When the company's customers are numerous and dispersed, advertising may be more practical. Distribution of a target market's demographic characteristics, such as age, income, or education, may affect the types of promotional techniques a marketer selects, as well as the messages and images employed.

◉ Characteristics of the Product

Generally promotion mixes for business products concentrate on personal selling, whereas advertising plays a major role in promoting consumer goods. This generalization should be treated cautiously, though. Marketers of business products use some advertising to promote products. Personal selling is used extensively for consumer durables, such as home appliances, automobiles, and houses, whereas consumer convenience items are promoted mainly through advertising and sales promotion. Public relations appears in promotion mixes for both business and consumer products. Marketers of highly seasonal products often emphasize advertising, and sometimes sales promotion as well, because off-season sales generally will not support an extensive year-round sales force. Although most toy producers have sales forces to sell to resellers, many of these companies depend chiefly on advertising to promote their products.

A product's price also influences the composition of the promotion mix. High-priced products call for personal selling because consumers associate greater risk with the purchase of such products and usually want information from a salesperson. Few people, for example, are willing to purchase a refrigerator from a self-service establishment. For low-priced convenience items, marketers use advertising rather than personal selling. When products are marketed through intensive distribution, firms depend strongly on advertising and sales promotion. Many convenience products, such as lotions, cereals, and coffee, are promoted through samples, coupons, and money refunds. When marketers choose selective distribution, promotion mixes vary considerably. Items handled through exclusive distribution, such as expensive watches, furs, and high-quality furniture, typically require a significant amount of personal selling. Manufacturers of highly personal products, such as laxatives, non-prescription contraceptives, and feminine hygiene products, depend on advertising because many customers do not want to talk with salespeople about these products.

◉ Costs and Availability of Promotional Methods

Costs of promotional methods are major factors to analyze when developing a promotion mix. National advertising and sales promotion require large expenditures. If these efforts succeed in reaching extremely large audiences, however, the cost per individual reached may be quite small, possibly a few pennies. For instance, Diageo estimated that the cost of reaching 1,000 people when advertising its José Cuervo

tequila on network television would be $15. Instead, the firm opted to use public relations. By leasing a small Caribbean island and using publicity efforts such as petitioning to join the United Nations, the cost of reaching 1,000 people dropped to 15 cents.[36] Some forms of advertising are relatively inexpensive. Many small, local businesses advertise goods and services through local newspapers, radio and television stations, outdoor displays, and signs on mass transit vehicles.

Another consideration that marketers explore when formulating a promotion mix is availability of promotional techniques. Despite the tremendous number of media vehicles in the United States, a firm may find that no available advertising medium effectively reaches a certain target market. The problem of media availability becomes more pronounced when marketers advertise in some foreign countries. Some media, such as television, simply may not be available, or it may be illegal to advertise on television. In China, the State Administration for Radio, Film, and Television banned a Nike commercial that featured basketball star LeBron James besting a kung fu master and a pair of dragons in a video game. In recent years, the agency has cracked down on U.S. and

Pull Channel Policy
Kelloggs uses a pull strategy to create awareness of its new cereal.

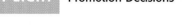

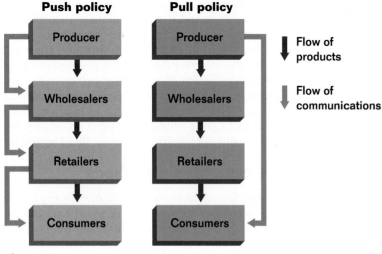

Figure 16.4
Comparison of Push and Pull Promotional Strategies

Japanese advertisements that fail to "uphold national dignity and interest, and respect the motherland's culture" of China.[37] Available media may not be open to certain types of advertisements. In some countries, advertisers are forbidden to make brand comparisons on television.

◉ Push and Pull Channel Policies

Another element marketers consider when planning a promotion mix is whether to use a push policy or a pull policy. With a push policy, the producer promotes the product only to the next institution down the marketing channel. In a marketing channel with wholesalers and retailers, the producer promotes to the wholesaler because in this case the wholesaler is the channel member just below the producer (see Figure 16.4). Each channel member in turn promotes to the next channel member. A push policy normally stresses personal selling. Sometimes sales promotion and advertising are used in conjunction with personal selling to push the products down through the channel.

As Figure 16.4 shows, a firm using a pull policy promotes directly to consumers to develop strong consumer demand for its products. It does so primarily through advertising and sales promotion. Because consumers are persuaded to seek the products in retail stores, retailers in turn go to wholesalers or the producers to buy the products. This policy is intended to pull the goods down through the channel by creating demand at the consumer level. Consumers are told that if the stores don't have it, ask them to get it. Push and pull policies are not mutually exclusive. At times an organization uses both simultaneously.

push policy Promoting a product only to the next institution down the marketing channel

pull policy Promoting a product directly to consumers to develop strong consumer demand that pulls products through the marketing channel

◉)) Criticisms and Defenses of Promotion

Even though promotional activities can help customers make informed purchasing decisions, social scientists, consumer groups, government agencies, and members of society in general have long criticized promotion. There are two main reasons for such criticism: promotion does have some flaws, and it is a highly visible business activity that pervades our daily lives. Although people almost universally complain that there is simply too much promotional activity, several more specific issues have been raised. Promotional efforts have been called deceptive. Promotion has been blamed for increasing prices. Other criticisms of promotion are that it manipulates

Table 16.2 Criticisms and Defenses of Promotion

Issue	Discussion
Is promotion deceptive?	Although no longer widespread, some deceptive promotion still occurs; laws, government regulations, and industry self-regulation have helped to decrease intentionally deceptive promotion; customers may be unintentionally misled because some words have diverse meanings.
Does promotion increase prices?	When promotion stimulates demand, higher production levels may result in lower per-unit production costs, which keeps prices lower; when demand is not stimulated, however, prices increase due to the added costs of promotion. Promotion fuels price competition, which helps to keep prices lower.
Does promotion create needs?	Many marketers capitalize on people's needs by basing their promotional appeals on these needs; however, marketers do not actually create these needs. If there were no promotion, people would still have basic needs like those suggested by Maslow.
Does promotion encourage materialism?	Because promotion creates awareness and visibility for products, it may contribute to materialism in the same way that movies, sports, theater, art, and literature may contribute to materialism. If there were no promotion, it is likely that there would still be materialism among some groups as evidenced by the existence of materialism among some ancient groups of people.
Does promotion help customers without costing too much?	Customers learn about products and services through promotion, allowing them to make more intelligent buying decisions.
Should potentially harmful products be advertised?	Some critics suggest that the promotion of possibly unhealthy products should not be allowed at all; others argue that as long as it is legal to sell such products, promoting those products should be allowed.

consumers into buying products they do not need, that it leads to a more materialistic society, that customers do not benefit sufficiently from promotion to justify its high costs, and that promotion is used to market potentially harmful products. These issues are discussed in Table 16.2.

CHAPTER REVIEW

1 **Discuss the nature of integrated marketing communications.**

Integrated marketing communications is the coordination of promotion and other marketing efforts to ensure the maximum informational and persuasive impact on customers. Sending consistent messages to customers is a major goal of integrated marketing communications. As both information technology and customer interests become increasingly dynamic, the specific communication vehicles employed and the precision with which they are used are changing.

2 **Understand the role of promotion in the marketing mix.**

Promotion is communication to build and maintain relationships by informing and persuading one or more audiences. The overall role of promotion is to stimulate product demand, although a company might pursue several promotional objectives. Cause-related marketing efforts link the purchase of products to philanthropic efforts for one or more causes. Marketers strive for proper planning, implementation, coordination, and control of communications for maximum benefit from promotional efforts. Integrated marketing communications planning takes into account informal methods of communication because customers derive information and opinions from many different sources.

3 **Describe the process of communication.**

Communication is a sharing of meaning. The communication process involves several steps. First, the source translates meaning into code, a process known as coding or encoding. The source should employ signs or symbols familiar to the receiver or audience. The coded message is sent through a medium of transmission to the receiver or audience. The receiver or audience then decodes the message and usually supplies feedback to the source. When the decoded message differs from the encoded one, a condition called noise exists.

4 **Explain the objectives of promotion.**

Eight primary objectives underlie many promotional programs. Promotion aims to create awareness of a new product, new brand, or existing product; to stimulate primary and selective demand; to encourage product trial through the use of free samples, coupons, limited free-use offers, contests, and games; to identify prospects; to retain loyal customers; to facilitate reseller support; to combat competitive promotional efforts; and to reduce sales fluctuations.

5 **Understand the major elements of the promotion mix.**

The promotion mix for a product may include four major promotional methods: advertising, personal selling, public relations, and sales promotion. Advertising is paid nonpersonal communication about an organization and its products transmitted to a target audience through a mass medium. Personal selling is paid personal communication that attempts to inform customers and persuade them to purchase products in an exchange situation. Public relations is a broad set of communication efforts used to create and maintain favorable relationships between an organization and its stakeholders. Sales promotion is an activity or material that acts as a direct inducement, offering added value or incentive for the product, to resellers, salespeople, or consumers.

6 **Describe the factors that affect the choice of promotion mix elements.**

Major determinants of which promotional methods to include in a product's promotion mix are the organization's promotional resources, objectives, and policies; characteristics of the target market; characteristics of the product; and cost and availability of promotional methods. Marketers also consider whether to use a push policy or a pull policy. With a push policy, the producer promotes the product only to the next institution down the marketing channel. Normally, a push policy stresses personal selling.

Firms that use a pull policy promote directly to consumers, with the intention of developing strong consumer demand for the products. Once consumers are persuaded to seek the products in retail stores, retailers go to wholesalers or the producer to buy the products.

7 Understand the criticisms and defenses of promotion.

Promotional activities can help consumers make informed purchasing decisions, but they have also evoked many criticisms. Promotion has been accused of deception. Although some deceiving or misleading promotions do exist, laws, government regulation, and industry self-regulation minimize deceptive promotion. Promotion has been blamed for increasing prices, but it usually tends to lower them. When demand is high, production and marketing costs decrease, which can result in lower prices. Promotion also helps keep prices lower by facilitating price competition. Other criticisms of promotional activity are that it manipulates consumers into buying products they do not need, that it leads to a more materialistic society, and that consumers do not benefit sufficiently from promotional activity to justify its high cost. Finally, some critics of promotion suggest that potentially harmful products, especially those associated with violence, sex, and unhealthy activities, should not be promoted at all.

Please visit the student website at **www.prideferrell.com** for ACE Self-Test questions that will help you prepare for exams.

KEY CONCEPTS

integrated marketing
   communications
promotion
communication
source
receiver

coding process
medium of transmission
decoding process
noise
feedback
channel capacity

primary demand
pioneer promotion
selective demand
promotion mix
kinesic communication
proxemic communication

tactile communication
push policy
pull policy

ISSUES FOR DISCUSSION AND REVIEW

1. What does *integrated marketing communications* mean?

2. What is the major task of promotion? Do firms ever use promotion to accomplish this task and fail? If so, give several examples.

3. What is communication? Describe the communication process. Is it possible to communicate without using all the elements in the communication process? If so, which ones can be omitted?

4. Identify several causes of noise. How can a source reduce noise?

5. Describe the possible objectives of promotion and discuss the circumstances under which each objective might be used.

6. Identify and briefly describe the four promotional methods an organization can use in its promotion mix.

7. What forms of interpersonal communication besides language can be used in personal selling?

8. How do target market characteristics determine which promotional methods to include in a promotion mix? Assume a company is planning to promote a cereal to both adults and children. Along what major dimensions would these two promotional efforts have to differ from each other?

9. How can a product's characteristics affect the composition of its promotion mix?

10. Evaluate the following statement: "Appropriate advertising media are always available if a company can afford them."

11. Explain the difference between a pull policy and a push policy. Under what conditions should each policy be used?

12. Which criticisms of promotion do you believe are the most valid? Why?

13. Should organizations be allowed to promote offensive, violent, sexual, or unhealthy products that can be legally sold and purchased? Support your answer.

MARKETING APPLICATIONS

1. Identify two television commercials, one aimed at stimulating primary demand and one aimed at stimulating selective demand. Describe each commercial and discuss how each attempts to achieve its objective.

2. Which of the four promotional methods—advertising, personal selling, public relations, or sales promotion—would you emphasize if you were developing the promotion mix for the following products? Explain your answers.
   a. Washing machine
   b. Cereal
   c. Halloween candy
   d. Compact disc

3. Suppose marketers at Falcon International Corporation have come to you for recommendations on how they should promote their products. They want to develop a comprehensive promotional campaign and have a generous budget with which to implement their plans. What questions would you

ask them, and what would you suggest they consider before developing a promotional program?

4. Identify two products for which marketers should use a push policy and a pull policy, and a third product that might best be promoted using a mix of the two policies. Explain your answers.

ONLINE EXERCISE

5. As you will probably discover in a few years, university alumni associations are themselves marketing organizations. Thanks in large part to a popular course related to Internet marketing taught at the University of Iowa and to the Iowa City Chamber of Commerce, a local bank, and a bookstore, the University of Iowa Alumni Association is now online. Visit its website at **www.iowalum.com.**
   a. Who are the target markets for the alumni association's Internet marketing efforts?
   b. What is being promoted to these individuals?
   c. What are the promotional objectives of the website?

VIDEO CASE

Jordan's Furniture

Samuel Tatelman began selling furniture out of the back of his truck in Waltham, Massachusetts, in 1918. Today his great-grandsons, Eliot and Barry, sell more furniture per square foot at Jordan's Furniture than any other furniture retailer in the country and attract record numbers of visitors each week. With just 4 stores, Jordan's Furniture has grown from 15 employees 25 years ago to more than 1,200 employees today. The company has broken just about all industry standards: inventory in stores turns over at a rate of 13 times a year (versus 1 to 2 times a year in average furniture stores); advertising and marketing expenditures are 2 percent (the industry average is 7 percent); and sales per square foot are $950 (most furniture stores average $150 per square foot). The company was purchased by Berkshire Hathaway Inc., Warren Buffet's holding company, in 1999.

The differences between Jordan's Furniture and its competitors strike consumers the moment they pull into the parking lot. The stores in Avon and Natick, Massachusetts, have 650 parking spaces and host more than 4,000 visitors on an average weekend. Inside the store, customers are greeted with a welcome map, although they can see clear, bright signs from the entry directing to points of interest. All furniture in the store is tagged with a full product description, including the manufacturer, construction details, warranty information, product care, and physical dimensions. Although salespeople are present and attentive, they are not aggressive. In the bedding department, salespeople known as "Sleep Technicians" even wear white lab coats to reinforce their image. Unlike more "sales-oriented" furniture stores, Jordan's offers "underprices" and never has "sales."

At Jordan's Furniture, the sale is certainly important, but it is the follow-up after the sale that often determines whether customers will return. No matter the size or price of the purchase, customers are asked about their entire experience from entering the store to checking out, from delivery to product setup. Results from these follow-up contacts are collected as part of the "Daily Report Card," which is sent directly to Barry and Eliot Tatelman. This gives them the opportunity both to correct any problems quickly and praise personnel who have done their jobs well. Barry Tatelman views such after-sale service as vital because everyone needs furniture, and "one satisfied customer can give you $300,000 worth of furniture over a lifetime."

With a slimmer advertising budget than its competitors, Jordan's employs "quirky" ads to gain consumers' attention in a saturated television market. The company has also sought ways to generate publicity, from supporting local and national causes, communicating about its employees and customers, or creating a unique retail experience. Jordan's Natick store features a 6-story, 262-seat, 3D IMAX Theater, a commercial venture run by AT&T. To enter the theater, patrons must walk through the furniture store. Riding the escalator to the theater gives customers the feeling of being a celebrity among the strobe lights, paparazzi murals, and crowd videos. David Grain, senior vice president for AT&T Broadband states, "This partnership unites two companies that truly appreciate the value of entertainment for the American family." The company has also benefited from a three-year BlueCross BlueShield of Massachusetts ad campaign that spotlights some of its endorsers, including Eliot and Barry Tatelman.

Jordan's also gains publicity from its support of local causes. Among the recipients of its largesse are Project Bread, which supports hungry people throughout Massachusetts; Furniture Bank, to which it donates 50 pieces of furniture a week to the MA Coalition for the Homeless; and M.O.M., a program that contributes to a group of charities including the AIDS Action Committee, American Cancer Society, American Red Cross, Arthritis Foundation,

Children's Happiness Foundation, March of Dimes, and Muscular Dystrophy Association. Proceeds from Streetcar Named Dessert go to children's charities, as well as many others.

For its strong ethical and socially responsible business practices, Jordan's Furniture was recognized by the Better Business Bureau in 1997 with the National Torch Award for Marketplace Ethics and by Ernst & Young with the Entrepreneur of the Year/Social Responsibility award. The company was named "Retailer of the Year" by the National Home Furnishing Association and the GERS Retail System, and voted "The Most Unusual Furniture Store in the World" by *Home Furnishings Daily* and *Furniture Today.* Jordan's has also won Telly awards for many of its advertisements, as well as many other noteworthy awards.[38]

QUESTIONS FOR DISCUSSION
1. Describe the marketing mix of Jordan's Furniture.
2. How do the promotional efforts of Jordan's Furniture rise above the "noise" of regular furniture store promotions?
3. How does Jordan's promotional strategy illustrate integrated marketing communications?

Advertising and Public Relations

▶ **"Livestrong" Wristbands Raise Funds for Cancer Survivors**

Many athletes and celebrities, including Senator John Kerry (himself a cancer survivor), Robin Williams, Jay Leno, Angelina Jolie, Matt Damon, and Serena Williams, have been seen sporting yellow rubber wristbands. Sold by the Lance Armstrong Foundation to raise funds for cancer survivor initiatives, the wristbands are imprinted with the simple phrase "LIVESTRONG." Although most people have purchased the $1 bands to support the cause, many have chosen to wear them to symbolize their own fight with cancer or to honor friends and family members who have endured cancer. In any case, the wristbands quickly became a must-have fashion accessory, in part due to the excitement surrounding Armstrong's sixth and seventh wins of the renowned Tour de France cycling championship. In addition, hundreds of articles have appeared in publications around the world about the foundation's "Wear Yellow" campaign. More than 30 million of the wristbands have been sold to date, boosting the foundation's 2004 fundraising total to about $45 million. Nike agreed to produce the wristbands for the foundation and also donated $1 million to the campaign.

Armstrong started the foundation in 1997 after surviving testicular cancer and going on to win seven consecutive Tour de France competitions. Prior to the foundation's "Wear Yellow" campaign, the foundation had never brought in more than $10 million a year.

A common adage holds that imitation is the sincerest form of flattery, and the yellow wristband campaign quickly spawned a host of imitators in support of other causes. The Campaign for Tobacco Free Kids issued red wristbands to highlight awareness of the number of smoking-related deaths every year. The Breast Cancer Research Foundation sold pink wristbands at Target.

Funds from the sale of the yellow wristbands, a Ride for the Roses cycling event, and other efforts will help the 10 million survivors of cancer living in the United States. The foundation used a portion of the funds to sponsor a survey of cancer survivors to identify the most pressing issues they face, such as loss of income during treatment and finding support to help them address the emotional needs associated with fighting cancer. The foundation is now involved in four core programs to help address these needs, including education, advocacy, public health, and research.[1] ◀

OBJECTIVES

1. Describe the nature and types of advertising.
2. Explain the major steps in developing an advertising campaign.
3. Identify who is responsible for developing advertising campaigns.
4. Recognize the tools used in public relations.
5. Understand how public relations is used and evaluated.

Many organizations, both for profit and nonprofit, use advertising and public relations tools to stimulate demand, launch new products, promote current brands, improve organizational images, or boost awareness of public issues. In this chapter, we explore several dimensions of advertising and public relations. First, we focus on the nature and types of advertising. Next, we examine the major steps in developing an advertising campaign and describe who is responsible for developing such campaigns. We then discuss the nature of public relations and how public relations is used. We examine various public relations tools and ways to evaluate the effectiveness of public relations. Finally, we focus on how companies deal with unfavorable public relations.

The Nature and Types of Advertising

advertising   Paid nonpersonal communication about an organization and its products transmitted to a target audience through mass media

Advertising permeates our daily lives. At times, we may view it positively; at other times, we avoid it. Some advertising informs, persuades, or entertains us; some bores and even offends us.

As mentioned in Chapter 16, **advertising** is a paid form of nonpersonal communication transmitted through mass media, such as television, radio, the Internet, newspapers, magazines, direct mail, outdoor displays, and signs on mass transit vehicles. In Boston, for example, some taxicabs are sporting a cup of Starbucks coffee magnetically attached to their roofs.[2] Organizations use advertising to reach different audiences ranging from small, specific groups, such as stamp collectors in Idaho, to extremely large groups, such as all athletic-shoe purchasers in the United States.

When asked to name major advertisers, most people immediately mention business organizations. However, many nonbusiness types of organizations, including governments, churches, universities, and charitable organizations, take advantage of advertising. For example, a number of states attorneys general pooled their resources to run television advertisements to persuade young men that roll-over-prone sport utility vehicles should be driven more carefully.[3] In 2003, the U.S. government was the twenty-eighth largest advertiser in the country, spending more than $1 billion on advertising.[4] Although we analyze advertising in the context of business organizations here, much of the material applies to all types of organizations.

institutional advertising
Promotes organizational images, ideas, and political issues

advocacy advertising
Promotes a company's position on a public issue

product advertising   Promotes products' uses, features, and benefits

pioneer advertising   Tries to stimulate demand for a product category rather than a specific brand by informing potential buyers about the product

Advertising is used to promote goods, services, ideas, images, issues, people, and anything else that advertisers want to publicize or foster. Depending on what is being promoted, advertising can be classified as institutional or product advertising. **Institutional advertising** promotes organizational images, ideas, and political issues. It can be used to create or maintain an organizational image. Institutional advertisements may deal with broad image issues, such as organizational strength or the friendliness of employees. They may also aim to create a more favorable view of the organization in the eyes of stakeholders such as shareholders, consumer advocacy groups, potential stockholders, or the general public. When a company promotes its position on a public issue—for instance, a tax increase, abortion, gun control, or international trade coalitions—institutional advertising is referred to as **advocacy advertising**. Institutional advertising may be used to promote socially approved behavior like recycling and moderation in consuming alcoholic beverages. Philip Morris, for example, has run television advertisements urging parents to talk to their children about not smoking. This type of advertising not only has societal benefits but also helps build an organization's image.

Product advertising promotes the uses, features, and benefits of products. There are two types of product advertising: pioneer and competitive. **Pioneer advertising** focuses on stimulating demand for a product category (rather than a specific brand) by informing potential customers about the product's features, uses, and benefits.

competitive advertising
Points out a brand's special features, uses, and advantages relative to competing brands

comparative advertising
Compares two or more brands on the basis of one or more product characteristics

reminder advertising
Reminds consumers about an established brand's uses, characteristics, and benefits

reinforcement advertising
Assures users they chose the right brand and tells them how to get the most satisfaction from it

This type of advertising is employed when the product is in the introductory stage of the product life cycle. **Competitive advertising** attempts to stimulate demand for a specific brand by promoting the brand's features, uses, and advantages, sometimes through indirect or direct comparisons with competing brands. To make direct product comparisons, marketers use a form of competitive advertising called **comparative advertising**, which compares two or more brands on the basis of one or more product characteristics. Gillette, for example, is using comparative advertising to promote the performance of its Duracell alkaline batteries as compared to less expensive heavy-duty batteries from Energizer.[5] Often the brands promoted through comparative advertisements have low market shares and are compared with competitors that have the highest market shares in the product category. Product categories that commonly use comparative advertising include soft drinks, toothpaste, pain relievers, foods, tires, automobiles, and detergents. Under the provisions of the 1988 Trademark Law Revision Act, marketers using comparative advertisements must not misrepresent the qualities or characteristics of competing products. Other forms of competitive advertising include reminder and reinforcement advertising. **Reminder advertising** tells customers that an established brand is still around and still offers certain characteristics, uses, and advantages. **Reinforcement advertising** assures current users they have made the right brand choice and tells them how to get the most satisfaction from that brand.

Developing an Advertising Campaign

An **advertising campaign** (see definition on p. 418) involves designing a series of advertisements and placing them in various advertising media to reach a particular target audience. As Figure 17.1 indicates, the major steps in creating an advertising campaign are (1) identifying and analyzing the target audience, (2) defining the advertising objectives, (3) creating the advertising platform, (4) determining the advertising appropriation, (5) developing the media plan, (6) creating the advertising message, (7) executing the campaign, and (8) evaluating advertising effectiveness. The number of steps and the exact order in which they are carried out may vary according to an organization's resources, the nature of its product, and the type of target audience to be reached. Nevertheless, these general guidelines for developing an advertising campaign are appropriate for all types of organizations.

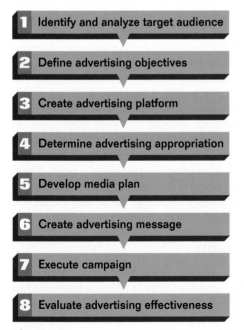

1. Identify and analyze target audience
2. Define advertising objectives
3. Create advertising platform
4. Determine advertising appropriation
5. Develop media plan
6. Create advertising message
7. Execute campaign
8. Evaluate advertising effectiveness

Figure 17.1
General Steps in Developing and Implementing an Advertising Campaign

Identifying and Analyzing the Target Audience

The **target audience** (see definition on p. 418) is the group of people at whom advertisements are aimed. Advertisements for Barbie cereal are targeted toward young girls who play with Barbie dolls, whereas those for Special K cereal are directed at health-conscious adults. Identifying and analyzing the target audience are critical actions. The information yielded helps determine other steps in developing the campaign. The target audience may include everyone in the firm's target market. Marketers may, however, direct a campaign at only a portion of the target market. For example, Handspring has started targeting women with ads in *Martha Stewart Living, Country Home,* and *Wired* to position its Visor handheld computing device as a chic fashion accessory.[6]

Advertisers research and analyze advertising targets to establish an information base for a campaign. Information commonly needed includes location and geographic distribution of the target group; the distribution of demographic factors, such as age, income, race, sex, and education; lifestyle information; and consumer attitudes regarding purchase and use of both the advertiser's products and competing products. The exact kind of information an organization finds useful depends on the type of product being advertised, the characteristics of the target audience, and the type and amount of competition. Generally, the more an advertiser knows about the target audience, the more likely the firm is to develop an effective advertising campaign. When the advertising target is not precisely identified and properly analyzed, the campaign may fail.

◉ Defining the Advertising Objectives

The advertiser's next step is to determine what the firm hopes to accomplish with the campaign. Because advertising objectives guide campaign development, advertisers should define objectives carefully. Advertising objectives should be stated clearly, precisely, and in measurable terms. Precision and measurability allow advertisers to evaluate advertising success at the end of the campaign in terms of whether or not objectives have been met. To provide precision and measurability, advertising objectives should contain benchmarks and indicate how far the advertiser wishes to move from these standards. If the goal is to increase sales, the advertiser should state the current sales level (the benchmark) and the amount of sales increase sought through advertising. An advertising objective should also specify a time frame so that advertisers know exactly how long they have to accomplish the objective. An advertiser with average monthly sales of $450,000 (the benchmark) might set the following objective: "Our primary advertising objective is to increase average monthly sales from $450,000 to $540,000 within 12 months."

If an advertiser defines objectives on the basis of sales, the objectives focus on increasing absolute dollar sales, or unit sales; increasing sales by a certain percentage; or increasing the firm's market share. Even though an advertiser's long-run goal is to increase sales, not all campaigns are designed to produce immediate sales. Some campaigns are designed to increase product or brand awareness, make consumers' attitudes more favorable, or increase consumers' knowledge of product features. These types of objectives are stated in terms of communication.

◉ Creating the Advertising Platform

Before launching a political campaign, party leaders develop a political platform stating the major issues that are the basis of the campaign. Like a political platform, an **advertising platform** consists of the basic issues or selling points that an advertiser wishes to include in the advertising campaign. New Balance, for example, launched a campaign that mocks professional athletes while reminding its 25- to 49-year-old tar-

advertising campaign Designing a series of advertisements and placing them in various advertising media to reach a particular target audience

target audience The group of people at whom advertisements are aimed

advertising platform Basic issues or selling points to be included in the advertising campaign

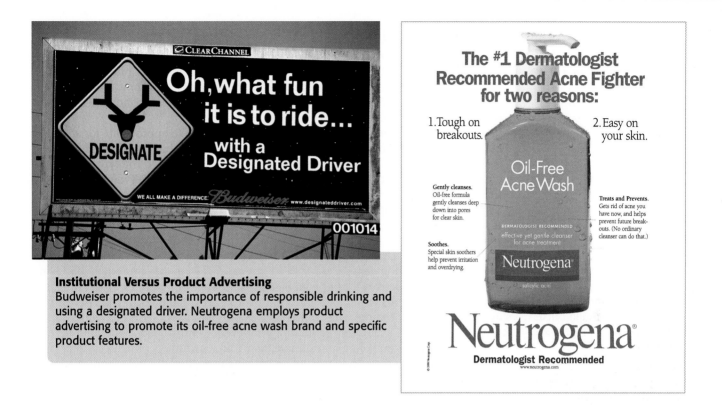

Institutional Versus Product Advertising
Budweiser promotes the importance of responsible drinking and using a designated driver. Neutrogena employs product advertising to promote its oil-free acne wash brand and specific product features.

get market about the joys of competing for fun and the love of sports.[7] A single advertisement in an advertising campaign may contain one or several issues from the platform. Although the platform sets forth the basic issues, it does not indicate how to present them.

An advertising platform should consist of issues important to customers. One of the best ways to determine those issues is to survey customers about what they consider most important in the selection and use of the product involved. Selling features must not only be important to customers, they should also be strongly competitive features of the advertised brand. For example, New Balance's "Love or Money" campaign stemmed in part from Internet research that found that many people have become disturbed by the behavior of well-known professional athletes, some of whom receive millions of dollars a year in endorsements from New Balance's competitors.[8]

Although research is the most effective method for determining what issues to include in an advertising platform, it is expensive. Therefore, an advertising platform is most commonly based on opinions of personnel within the firm and of individuals in the advertising agency, if an agency is used. This trial-and-error approach generally leads to some successes and some failures.

Because the advertising platform is a base on which to build the advertising message, marketers should analyze this stage carefully. A campaign can be perfect in terms of selection and analysis of its target audience, statement of its objectives, its media strategy, and the form of its message. But the campaign will ultimately fail if the advertisements communicate information that consumers do not deem important when selecting and using the product.

◉ Determining the Advertising Appropriation

advertising appropriation
Advertising budget for a specified period

The **advertising appropriation** is the total amount of money a marketer allocates for advertising for a specific time period. New Balance, for example, planned to spend $21 million on its "Love or Money" campaign.[9] It is hard to decide how much to spend on advertising for a specific period because the potential effects of advertising are so difficult to measure precisely.

Many factors affect a firm's decision about how much to appropriate for advertising. Geographic size of the market and the distribution of buyers within the market have a great bearing on this decision. As Table 17.1 shows, both the type of product advertised and the firm's sales volume relative to competitors' sales volumes also play their respective parts in determining what proportion of revenue to spend on advertising. Advertising appropriations for business products are usually quite small relative to product sales, whereas consumer convenience items, such as soft drinks, soaps, and cosmetics, generally have large advertising expenditures relative to sales.

objective-and-task approach
Budgeting for an advertising campaign by first determining its objectives and then calculating the cost of all the tasks needed to attain them

Of the many techniques used to determine the advertising appropriation, one of the most logical is the **objective-and-task approach**. Using this approach, marketers determine the objectives a campaign is to achieve and then attempt to list the tasks required to accomplish them. The costs of the tasks are calculated and added to arrive at the total appropriation. This approach has one main problem: marketers sometimes have trouble accurately estimating the level of effort needed to attain certain objectives. A coffee marketer, for example, may find it extremely difficult to determine how much of an increase in television advertising is needed to raise a brand's market share from 8 to 10 percent.

percent-of-sales approach
Budgeting for an advertising campaign by multiplying the firm's past or expected sales by a standard percentage

In the more widely used **percent-of-sales approach**, marketers simply multiply the firm's past sales, plus a factor for planned sales growth or decline, by a standard percentage based on what the firm traditionally spends on advertising and perhaps

Table 17.1	Top Ten Leading National Advertisers		
Organization	Advertising Expenditures ($ millions)	U.S. Sales ($ millions)	Advertising Expenditures as Percentage of Sales
1. General Motors	3,430	133,897	2.6
2. Procter & Gamble	3,323	21,853	15.2
3. Time Warner	3,097	32,123	9.6
4. Pfizer	2,839	26,844	10.6
5. DaimlerChrysler	2,318	72,814	3.2
6. Ford Motor	2,234	103,435	2.2
7. Walt Disney	2,129	22,124	9.6
8. Johnson & Johnson	1,996	25,274	7.9
9. Sony	1,815	20,727	8.8
10. Toyota Motor	1,683	52,323	3.2

Source: *Advertising Age,* June 28, 2004, pp. S-4, S-10.

on the industry average. This approach is flawed because it is based on the incorrect assumption that sales create advertising rather than the reverse. A marketer using this approach during declining sales will reduce the amount spent on advertising, but such a reduction may further diminish sales. Though illogical, this technique has been widely used because it is easy to implement.

competition-matching approach Determining an advertising budget by trying to match competitors' ad outlays

Another way to determine the advertising appropriation is the **competition-matching approach**. Marketers following this approach try to match their major competitors' appropriations in absolute dollars or to allocate the same percentage of sales for advertising that their competitors do. Although a marketer should be aware of what competitors spend on advertising, this technique should not be used alone because the firm's competitors probably have different advertising objectives and different resources available for advertising. Many companies and advertising agencies review competitive spending on a quarterly basis, comparing competitors' dollar expenditures on print, radio, and television with their own spending levels.

arbitrary approach Budgeting for an advertising campaign as specified by a high-level executive in the firm

At times marketers use the **arbitrary approach**, which usually means a high-level executive in the firm states how much to spend on advertising for a certain period. The arbitrary approach often leads to underspending or overspending. Although hardly a scientific budgeting technique, it is expedient.

Advertising is particularly important during economic downturns. Instead of cutting back on advertising, management should maintain or even increase the budget. For instance, the online broker E*Trade tore up its IMC budget after seeing revenues drop for six months during a downturn. The company actually increased its promotional spending—and attracted 17 percent more new customers than it had during the previous 12 months.[10]

◉ Developing the Media Plan

As Table 17.2 shows, advertisers spend tremendous amounts on advertising media. These amounts have grown rapidly during the past two decades. To derive maximum results from media expenditures, marketers must develop effective media plans. A

Media Plan
Automobile manufacturers know the importance of reaching their target market through auto magazines such as *Hot Rod*.

Table 17.2 **Total Advertising Expenditures**		
	2003	
	Total Dollar Amount (in millions of dollars)	**Percentage of Total**
Television	60,746	24.7
Direct Mail	48,370	19.7
Newspapers	44,843	18.3
Miscellaneous	31,990	13.0
Radio	19,100	7.8
Yellow Pages	13,896	5.7
Magazines	11,435	4.7
Internet	5,650	2.3
Outdoor	5,443	2.2
Business Press	4,004	1.6
TOTAL	243,680	100.0%

Source: Robert J. Coen, "U.S. Advertising Volume, 2000–2004," Universal McCann, www.universalmccann.com/coen_report.html (accessed January 17, 2005).

media plan Specifies media vehicles and schedule for running the advertisements

media plan sets forth the exact media vehicles to be used (specific magazines, television stations, newspapers, and so forth) and the dates and times the advertisements will appear. The plan focuses on how many people in the target audience will be exposed to a message and the frequency of exposure. It also determines, to some degree, the effects of the message on those individuals. Media planning is a complex task requiring thorough analysis of the target audience. Sophisticated computer models have been developed to attempt to maximize the effectiveness of media plans.

To formulate a media plan, the planners select the media for the campaign and prepare a time schedule for each medium. The media planner's primary goal is to reach the largest number of people in the advertising target that the budget will allow. A secondary goal is to achieve the appropriate message reach and frequency for the target audience while staying within budget. *Reach* refers to the percentage of consumers in the target audience actually exposed to a particular advertisement in a stated period. *Frequency* is the number of times these targeted consumers are exposed to the advertisement.

Media planners begin with broad decisions but eventually make very specific ones. They first decide which kinds of media to use: radio, television, the Internet, newspapers, magazines, direct mail, outdoor displays, or signs on mass transit vehicles. Internet advertising in particular is growing, with companies spending $4 billion in 2004 to run ads alongside Internet searches in sites like Google and Yahoo![11] Media planners assess different formats and approaches to determine which are the most effective. Some media plans are quite focused and use just one medium. The media plans of manufacturers of consumer packaged goods can be quite complex and dynamic.

Media planners take many factors into account when devising a media plan. They analyze location and the demographic characteristics of people in the target audience because people's tastes in media differ according to demographic groups and locations. There are radio stations especially for teenagers, magazines for men ages 18 to 34, and television cable channels aimed at women in various age groups. Media planners also consider the sizes and types of audiences that specific media reach. Dillard's, for example, cut back on newspaper advertising because that medium reaches fewer target customers for its department stores.[12] Several data services collect and periodically provide information about circulations and audiences of various media.

The content of the message sometimes affects media choice. Print media can be used more effectively than broadcast media to present complex issues or numerous details in single advertisements. If an advertiser wants to promote beautiful colors, patterns, or textures, media offering high-quality color reproduction—magazines or television—should be used instead of newspapers. For example, food can be effectively promoted in full-color magazine advertisements but far less effectively in black and white.

cost comparison indicator
A means of comparing the cost of vehicles in a specific medium in relation to the number of people reached

The cost of media is an important but troublesome consideration. Planners try to obtain the best coverage possible for each dollar spent. But there is no accurate way to compare the cost and impact of a television commercial with the cost and impact of a newspaper advertisement. A cost comparison indicator lets an advertiser compare the costs of several vehicles within a specific medium (such as two magazines) in relation to the number of people each vehicle reaches. The "cost per thousand" (CPM) is the cost comparison indicator for magazines; it shows the cost of exposing a thousand people to a one-page advertisement. Table 17.2 shows that the extent to which each medium is used varies. Media are selected by weighing the various characteristics, advantages, and disadvantages of each (see Table 17.3).

Like media selection decisions, media scheduling decisions are affected by numerous factors, such as target audience characteristics, product attributes, product seasonality, customer media behavior, and size of the advertising budget. There are three general types of media schedules: continuous, flighting, and pulsing. When a *continuous* schedule is used, advertising runs at a constant level with little variation throughout the campaign period. With a *flighting* schedule, advertisements run for set periods of time, alternating with periods in which no ads run. For example, an advertising campaign might have an ad run for two weeks, then suspend it for two weeks, and then run it again for two weeks. A *pulsing* schedule combines continuous and flighting schedules. During the entire campaign, a certain portion of advertising runs continuously, and during specific time periods of the campaign, additional advertising is used to intensify the level of communication with the target audience.

◉ Creating the Advertising Message

The basic content and form of an advertising message are functions of several factors. A product's features, uses, and benefits affect the content of the message. Characteristics of the people in the target audience—gender, age, education, race, income, occupation, lifestyle, and other attributes—influence both content and form. When Procter & Gamble promotes Crest toothpaste to children, the company emphasizes daily brushing and cavity control. When Crest is marketed to adults, tartar and plaque control are emphasized. To communicate effectively, advertisers use words, symbols, and illustrations that are meaningful, familiar, and attractive to people in the target audience.

An advertising campaign's objectives and platform also affect the content and form of its messages. If a firm's advertising objectives involve large sales increases, the

Table 17.3 **Characteristics, Advantages, and Disadvantages of Major Advertising Media**

Medium	Types	Unit of Sale	Factors Affecting Rates
Newspaper	Morning Evening Sunday Sunday supplement Weekly Special	Agate lines Column inches Counted words Printed lines	Volume and frequency discounts Number of colors Position charges for preferred and guaranteed positions Circulation level Ad size
Magazine	Consumer Business Farm Regional	Pages Partial pages Column inches	Circulation level Cost of publishing Type of audience Volume discounts Frequency discounts Size of advertisement Position of advertisement (covers) Number of colors Regional issues
Direct mail	Letters; catalogs; price lists; calendars; brochures; coupons; circulars; newsletters; postcards; booklets; broadsides; samplers	Not applicable	Cost of mailing lists Postage Production costs
Radio	AM FM	Programs: sole sponsor, co-sponsor, participative sponsor Spots: 5, 10, 20, 30, 60 seconds	Time of day Audience size Length of spot or program Volume and frequency discounts
Television	Network Local Cable	Programs: sole sponsor, co-sponsor, participative sponsor Spots: 5, 10, 15, 30, 60 seconds	Time of day Length of program Length of spot Volume and frequency discounts Audience size
Internet	Websites Banners Buttons Sponsorships Pop-ups Interstitials Classified ads	Not applicable	Length of time Complexity Type of audience Keywords Continuity
Inside transit	Buses Subways	Full, half, and quarter showings sold on monthly basis	Number of riders Multiple-month discounts Production costs Position
Outside transit	Buses Taxicabs	Full, half, and quarter showings; space also rented on per-unit basis	Number of advertisements Position Size
Outdoor	Papered posters Painted displays Spectaculars	Papered posters: sold on monthly basis in multiples called "showings" Painted displays and spectaculars: sold on per-unit basis	Length of time purchased Land rental Cost of production Intensity of traffic Frequency and continuity discounts Location

Source: Information from William F. Arens, *Contemporary Advertising* (Burr Ridge, IL: Irwin/McGraw-Hill, 2002); George E. Belch and Michael Belch, *Advertising and Promotion* (Burr Ridge, IL: Irwin/McGraw-Hill, 2001).

Cost Comparison Indicator	Advantages	Disadvantages
Milline rate = (cost per agate line × 1,000,000) divided by circulation	Reaches large audience; purchased to be read; national geographic flexibility; short lead time; frequent publication; favorable for cooperative advertising; merchandising services	Not selective for socioeconomic groups; short life; limited reproduction capabilities; large advertising volume limits exposure to any one advertisement
Cost per thousand (CPM) = (cost per page × 1,000) divided by circulation	Demographic selectivity; good reproduction; long life; prestige; geographic selectivity when regional issues are available; read in leisurely manner	High absolute dollar cost; long lead time
Cost per contact	Little wasted circulation; highly selective; circulation controlled by advertiser; few distractions; personal; stimulates actions; use of novelty; relatively easy to measure perfor- mance; hidden from competitors	Expensive; no editorial matter to attract readers; considered junk mail by many; criticized as invasion of privacy
Cost per thousand (CPM) = (cost per minute × 1,000) divided by audience size	Reaches 95% of consumers age 12 and older; highly mobile; low-cost broadcast medium; message can be quickly changed; geographic selectivity; demographic selectivity	Provides only audio message; short life of message; listeners' attention limited because of other activities while listening
Cost per thousand (CPM) = (cost per minute × 1,000) × divided by audience size	Reaches large audience; low cost per exposure; uses audio and video; highly visible; high prestige; geographic and demographic selectivity	High dollar costs; highly perishable message; size of audience not guaranteed; amount of prime time limited
Cost per thousand or by the number of click-throughs	Immediate response; potential to reach a precisely targeted audience; ability to track customers and build databases; very interactive medium	Costs of precise targeting are high; inappropriate ad placement; effects difficult to measure; concerns about security and privacy
Cost per thousand riders	Low cost; "captive" audience; geographic selectivity	Does not reach many professional persons; does not secure quick results
Cost per thousand exposures	Low cost; geographic selectivity; reaches broad, diverse audience	Lacks demographic selectivity; does not have high impact on readers
No standard indicator	Allows for repetition; low cost; message can be placed close to point of sale; geographic selectivity; operable 24 hours a day	Message must be short and simple; no demographic selectivity; seldom attracts readers' full attention; criticized as traffic hazard and blight on countryside

message may include hard-hitting, high-impact language and symbols. When campaign objectives aim at increasing brand awareness, the message may use much repetition of the brand name and words and illustrations associated with it.

Choice of media obviously influences the content and form of the message. Effective outdoor displays and short broadcast spot announcements require concise, simple messages. Magazine and newspaper advertisements can include considerable detail and long explanations. Because several kinds of media offer geographic selectivity, a precise message can be tailored to a particular geographic section of the target audience. Some magazine publishers produce regional issues, in which advertisements and editorial content of copies appearing in one geographic area differ from those appearing in other areas. For example, *Time* magazine publishes eight regional issues. A company advertising in *Time* might decide to use one message in the New England region and another in the rest of the nation. A company may also choose to advertise in only one region. Such geographic selectivity lets a firm use the same message in different regions at different times.

regional issues Versions of a magazine that differ across geographic regions

copy The verbal portion of advertisements

● **Copy.** Copy is the verbal portion of an advertisement and may include headlines, subheadlines, body copy, and signature (see Figure 17.2). Not all advertising contains all of these copy elements. Even handwritten notes on direct-mail advertising that say, "Try this. It works!" seem to increase requests for free samples.[13] The headline is critical because often it is the only part of the copy that people read. It should attract readers' attention and create enough interest to make them want to read the body copy. The subheadline, if there is one, links the headline to the body copy and sometimes is used to explain the headline.

Body copy for most advertisements consists of an introductory statement or paragraph, several explanatory paragraphs, and a closing paragraph. Some copywriters have adopted guidelines for developing body copy systematically: (1) identify a specific desire or problem, (2) recommend the product as the best way to satisfy that desire or solve that problem, (3) state product benefits and indicate why the product is best for the buyer's particular situation, (4) substantiate advertising claims, and (5) ask the buyer to take action. When substantiating claims, it is important to present the substantiation in a credible manner. The proof of claims should help strengthen the image of the product and company integrity. Typeface selection can help advertisers create a desired impressions by using fonts that are engaging, reassuring, or very prominent.[14]

The signature identifies the advertisement's sponsor. It may contain several elements, including the firm's trademark, logo, name, and address. The signature should be attractive, legible, distinctive, and easy to identify in a variety of sizes.

Because radio listeners often are not fully "tuned in" mentally, radio copy should be informal and conversational to attract listeners' attention, resulting in greater impact. Radio messages are highly perishable and should consist of short, familiar terms. The length should not require a rate of speech exceeding approximately two and one-half words per second.

In television copy, the audio material must not overpower the visual material, and vice versa. However, a television message should make optimal use of its visual portion, which can be very effective for product demonstrations. Copy for a television commercial is sometimes initially written in parallel script form. Video is described in the left column and audio in the right. When the parallel script is approved, the copywriter and artist combine copy with visual material by using a storyboard, which depicts a series of miniature television screens showing the sequence of major scenes in the commercial. Beneath each screen is a description of the audio portion to be used with that video segment. Technical personnel use the storyboard as a blueprint when producing the commercial.

storyboard A mockup combining copy and visual material to show the sequence of major scenes in a commercial

Figure 17.2
Components of a Print Advertisement
This advertisement includes all the major components of a print advertisement.

artwork An ad's illustrations and layout

illustrations Photos, drawings, graphs, charts, and tables used to spark audience interest

● **Artwork** Artwork consists of an advertisement's illustrations and layout. Although **illustrations** are often photographs, they can also be drawings, graphs, charts, and tables. Illustrations can be more important in capturing attention than text or brand elements, independent of size.[15] They are used to attract attention, encourage audiences to read or listen to the copy, communicate an idea quickly, or communicate ideas that are difficult to put into words.[16] Advertisers use various illustration techniques. They may show the product alone, in a setting, or in use, or they may show the results of its use. Illustrations can also be in the form of comparisons, contrasts, and diagrams.

Internet advertisers can take advantage of new technology to create more creative artwork. The advertising agency for Wells Fargo Bank, for example, came up with a 10-second ad that changed shape and content as it moved across the screen, ending up as a banner ad inviting viewers to click for more information. This unusual ad drew four times as many responses as the bank's traditional banner ads.[17]

layout The physical arrangement of an ad's illustration and copy

The **layout** of an advertisement is the physical arrangement of the illustration and the copy—headline, subheadline, body copy, and signature. These elements can be arranged in many ways. The final layout is the result of several stages of layout preparation. As it moves through these stages, the layout promotes an exchange of ideas among people developing the advertising campaign and provides instructions for production personnel.

◎ Executing the Campaign

Execution of an advertising campaign requires extensive planning and coordination because many tasks must be completed on time and many people and firms are involved. Production companies, research organizations, media firms, printers,

E-MARKETING AND TECHNOLOGY
THINK TECHNOLOGY LETS YOU AVOID ALL THOSE COMMERCIALS?

Think again. Although viewers can now avoid commercials by videotaping or digitally recording television programs and then zapping the advertisements, or simply using the remote control to channel surf during commercial breaks, advertisers are fighting back. Surveys show that 39 percent of U.S. viewers often change channels when commercials come on, and another 19 percent either mute or lower the volume. Faced with widespread avoidance of traditional commercials, many advertisers are adopting an in-your-face approach, using a blend of technology and sponsorship to integrate their products directly into programming.

Princeton Video Image, a New Jersey–based company, digitally inserts products and signage into televised shows and sports events. Cable network ESPN uses this technology to place advertisers' logos, brands, and signs around the playing field during baseball games and other televised events. The fans in the stands don't see these virtual advertisements, but the ads are clearly visible to viewers at home.

INNX, a television production firm, invites advertisers to sponsor "news-adjacent targeted advertising." When INNX produces a news segment about a flu epidemic or another health-related development, it attaches a 12-second commercial at the end, including a web address for more information. Procter & Gamble recently contracted to feature NyQuil, Crest, and other P&G brands in commercials tacked onto the ends of INNX segments. Distributed to 200 NBC stations and viewed by 9 million people every day, these segments are giving P&G access to a sizable audience.

Even TiVo, the pioneer of commercial-avoiding digital video recorders, has unveiled a program that will present static images, such as corporate logos, as TV viewers fast-forward through commercials. Many companies are also using low-tech product placement to reach television audiences. Product placements are prominent on *Survivor,* for example, where contestants gaze hungrily at a bag of Doritos and vie for merchandise from Target and cars from Pontiac. Although advertisers like having their products featured in zap-proof programming, such placements "destroy the advertising-entertainment line," complains Gary Ruskin, director of Commercial Alert. On the other hand, as *Survivor's* executive producer notes, "Marketers have to get a benefit for their dollars. As long as you do it in a tasteful way and don't lie to the audience, it's fine."[a]

photoengravers, and commercial artists are just a few of the people and firms contributing to a campaign.

Implementation requires detailed schedules to ensure that various phases of the work are done on time. Advertising management personnel must evaluate the quality of the work and take corrective action when necessary. In some instances, changes are made during the campaign so it meets objectives more effectively. Sometimes, one firm develops a campaign and another executes it.

⊙ Evaluating Advertising Effectiveness

pretest Evaluation of ads performed before a campaign begins

consumer jury A panel of a product's actual or potential buyers who pretest ads

Advertising can be evaluated before, during, and after the campaign. An evaluation performed before the campaign begins is called a **pretest**. A pretest usually attempts to evaluate the effectiveness of one or more elements of the message. To pretest advertisements, marketers sometimes use a **consumer jury**, a panel of actual or potential buyers of the advertised product. Jurors judge one or several dimensions of

Pre-Testing Advertisements
Decision Analyst, through the use of online qualitative research, pretests print and broadcast advertisements.

two or more advertisements. Such tests are based on the belief that consumers are more likely than advertising experts to know what influences them.

To measure advertising effectiveness during a campaign, marketers sometimes use "inquiries." In a campaign's initial stages, an advertiser may use several advertisements simultaneously, each containing a coupon, form, or toll-free phone number through which potential customers can request information. The advertiser records the number of inquiries returned from each type of advertisement. If an advertiser receives 78,528 inquiries from advertisement A, 37,072 from advertisement B, and 47,932 from advertisement C, advertisement A is judged superior to advertisements B and C.

Evaluation of advertising effectiveness after the campaign is called a **posttest**. Advertising objectives often determine what kind of posttest is appropriate. If the objectives focus on communication—to increase awareness of product features or brands or to create more favorable customer attitudes—the posttest should measure changes in these dimensions. Advertisers sometimes use consumer surveys or experiments to evaluate a campaign based on communication objectives.

For campaign objectives stated in terms of sales, advertisers should determine the change in sales or market share attributable to the campaign. However, changes in sales or market share brought about by advertising cannot be measured precisely. Many factors independent of advertisements affect a firm's sales and market share. Competitors' actions, government actions, and changes in economic conditions, consumer preferences, and weather are only a few factors that might enhance or diminish a company's sales or market share. By using data about past and current sales and advertising expenditures, advertisers can make gross estimates of the effects of a campaign on sales or market share.

Because it is difficult to determine the direct effects of advertising on sales, some advertisers evaluate print advertisements according to how well consumers can remember them. Posttest methods based on memory include recognition and recall tests. Such tests are usually performed by research organizations through surveys. In a **recognition test**, respondents are shown the actual advertisement and asked whether they recognize it. If they do, the interviewer asks additional questions to determine how much of the advertisement each respondent read. When recall is evaluated, the respondents are not shown the actual advertisement but instead are asked about what they have seen or heard recently. Recall can be measured through either unaided or aided recall methods. In an **unaided recall test**, respondents identify advertisements they have seen recently but are not shown any clues to help them remember. A similar procedure is used with an **aided recall test**, but respondents are shown a list of products, brands, company names, or trademarks to jog

posttest Evaluation of advertising effectiveness after the campaign

recognition test A posttest in which individuals are shown the actual ad and asked if they recognize it

unaided recall test A posttest in which respondents identify ads they have recently seen but are given no recall clues

aided recall test A posttest that asks respondents to identify recent ads and provides clues to jog their memories

their memories. Several research organizations, such as Daniel Starch, provide research services that test recognition and recall of advertisements. The major justification for using recognition and recall methods is that people are more likely to buy a product if they can remember an advertisement about it than if they cannot. Researchers also use sophisticated techniques based on *single-source data* to help evaluate advertisements. With this technique, individuals' behaviors are tracked from televisions to checkout counters. Monitors are placed in preselected homes, and computers record when the television is on and which station is being viewed. At the supermarket checkout, the individual in the sample household presents an identification card. Checkers then record the purchases by scanner, and data are sent to the research facility. Some single-source data companies provide sample households with scanning equipment for use at home to record purchases after returning from shopping trips. Single-source data provide information that links exposure to advertisements with purchase behavior.

Who Develops the Advertising Campaign?

An advertising campaign may be handled by an individual or by a few persons within a firm, by a firm's own advertising department, or by an advertising agency.

In very small firms, one or two individuals are responsible for advertising (and for many other activities as well). Usually these individuals depend heavily on personnel at local newspapers and broadcast stations for copywriting, artwork, and advice about scheduling media.

In certain large businesses—especially large retail organizations—advertising departments create and implement advertising campaigns. Depending on the size of the advertising program, an advertising department may consist of a few multiskilled persons or a sizable number of specialists, such as copywriters, artists, media buyers, and technical production coordinators. Advertising departments sometimes obtain

Who Develops the Advertising Campaign? Brand Vista develops advertising for international clients such as GM's Buick.

MARKETING ENTREPRENEURS

Cathey Finlon

THE BUSINESS: McClain Finlon Advertising

FOUNDED: 1982

SUCCESS: $129.8 million in billings

In 1982 Cathey Finlon started her first ad agency with only $250 cash, a typewriter, and some art pads. Now, McClain Finlon Advertising is the highest earning, independently owned ad agency in Denver. The secret of Finlon's success comes from cutting-edge tactics that use a different language to market to a new generation of consumers. One example was a controversial 2002 Breckenridge Ski Resort ad campaign that employed words such as "bitch" to target young men. Although the ads were heavily criticized and caused an uproar among Denver locals, they earned several advertising awards for creativity from the Denver Advertising Federation and went on to compete nationally. Some McClain Finlon clients include Xcel Energy, Sun Microsystems, and the Denver Zoo.[b]

the services of independent research organizations and hire freelance specialists when a particular project requires it.

Many firms employ an advertising agency to develop advertising campaigns. New Belgium Brewing, for example, contracted with Amalgamated, a New York agency, to create its first $10 million advertising campaign.[18] When an organization uses an advertising agency, the firm and the agency usually develop the advertising campaign jointly. Advertising agencies assist businesses in several ways. An agency, especially a large one, can supply the services of highly skilled specialists—not only copywriters, artists, and production coordinators, but also media experts, researchers, and legal advisers. Agency personnel often have broad advertising experience and are usually more objective than a firm's employees about the organization's products. Because an agency traditionally receives most of its compensation from a 15 percent commission paid by the media from which it makes purchases, firms can obtain some agency services at low or moderate costs. If an agency contracts for $400,000 of television time for a firm, it receives a commission of $60,000 from the television station. Although the traditional compensation method for agencies is changing and now includes other factors, media commissions still offset some costs of using an agency.

 # Public Relations

public relations Communication efforts used to create and maintain favorable relations between an organization and its stakeholders

Public relations is a broad set of communication efforts used to create and maintain favorable relationships between an organization and its stakeholders. An organization communicates with various stakeholders, both internal and external, and public relations efforts can be directed toward any and all of these. A firm's stakeholders can include customers, suppliers, employees, stockholders, the media, educators, potential investors, government officials, and society in general.

Public relations can be used to promote people, places, ideas, activities, and even countries. It focuses on enhancing the image of the total organization. Assessing public attitudes and creating a favorable image are no less important than direct promotion of the organization's products. Because the public's attitudes toward a firm are likely to affect the sales of its products, it is very important for firms to maintain positive public perceptions. In addition, employee morale is strengthened if the public perceives the firm positively.[19] Although public relations can make people aware of a company's products, brands, or activities, it can also create specific company images, such as innovativeness or dependability. Companies like Ben & Jerry's, Patagonia, Sustainable Harvest, and Honest Tea have reputations for being socially responsible not only because they engage in socially responsive behavior but because their actions are reported through news stories and other public relations efforts.[20] By getting the

Contact: Rick Stockwood
(617) 426-6500, ext. 213
Stockwood@BostonKids.org

NEW EXHIBIT HELPS CREATE POSITIVE AWARENESS OF PEOPLE LIVING WITH DISABILITIES

Boston Children's Museum to open access/Ability June 17, 2004

(Boston, MA) May 19, 2004…Boston Children's Museum will open *access/Ability June 17, 2004.* This exhibition is a highly interactive, yet sensitive disability awareness exhibit that delivers the message to children, parents and educators that as human beings, we are more alike than different.

This unique exhibit presents people living with disabilities as participants in the world and features fun and engaging activities that show the similarities and differences in how each of us, with or without disabilities, go places, communicate, have fun, and learn. Visitors will have a chance to learn phrases in American Sign Language, type their name in Braille, try a hand-pedaled bike and take part in a multi-sensory City Walk.

Throughout the exhibit, My Way kiosks introduce individuals living with disabilities who talk about themselves, their accomplishments, and how they overcome challenges in their lives. A resource area provides a quiet space where visitors can learn more about disabilities through books and computer resources.

This exhibition was created by the Boston Children's Museum and was funded in part by Lead Local Sponsor Liberty Mutual and with additional support provided by the Mitsubishi Electric America Foundation.

About Boston Children's Museum
Boston Children's Museum exists to help children understand and enjoy the world in which they live. It is a private, non-profit, educational institution that is recognized internationally as a research and development center and pacesetter for children's exhibitions, educational programs and curriculum. The Children's Museum focuses on three key areas of expertise: visitor programs, teacher resources and early childhood education. More information about The Children's Museum can be found at http://www.bostonkids.org.

Hours and Admission
The Museum is open daily from 10:00 a.m. – 5:00 p.m. and Fridays until 9:00 p.m. Children (2-15) and senior citizens, $7; other adults $9; one year olds, $2; Fridays 5:00pm – 9:00pm, all visitors $1. Infants under one and Museum members are always free. Special rates available for school and community groups; reservations required, call (617) 426-8433.

-end-

Example of a News Release
The Boston Children's Museum issued this information release to publicize an exhibit on positive awareness of people living with physical challenges.

media to report on a firm's accomplishments, public relations helps the company maintain positive public visibility.

◉ Public Relations Tools

Companies use various public relations tools to convey messages and create images. Public relations professionals prepare written materials, such as brochures, newsletters, company magazines, news releases, and annual reports, that reach and influence their various stakeholders.

Public relations personnel also create corporate identity materials, such as logos, business cards, stationery, and signs, that make firms immediately recognizable. Speeches are another public relations tool. Because what a company executive says publicly at meetings or to the media can affect the organization's image, his or her speech must convey the desired message clearly.

Event sponsorship, in which a company pays for part or all of a special event, such as a benefit concert or a tennis tournament, is another public relations tool. Examples are Home Depot's sponsorship of NASCAR and the U.S. Olympic team. Sponsoring special events can be an effective means of increasing company or brand recognition with relatively minimal expenditures. Event sponsorship can gain companies considerable amounts of free media coverage. For example, corporate sponsors of professional beach volleyball, such as McDonald's, Nissan, and Budweiser, benefited from more than 1 billion media impressions during the 2004 season.[21] An organization tries to make sure its product and the sponsored event target a similar audience and that the two are easily associated in customers' minds. Public relations personnel also organize unique events to "create news" about the company. These may include grand openings with celebrities, prizes, hot-air balloon rides, and other attractions that appeal to a firm's publics.

publicity   A news story type of communication transmitted through a mass medium at no charge

Publicity is part of public relations. **Publicity** is communication in news story form about the organization, its products, or both, transmitted through a mass medium at no charge. Although public relations has a larger, more comprehensive communication function than publicity, publicity is a very important aspect of public relations. Publicity can be used to provide information about goods or services; to announce expansions, acquisitions, research, or new-product launches; or to enhance a company's image.

news release   A short piece of copy publicizing an event or a product

The most common publicity-based public relations tool is the **news release**, sometimes called a *press release*, which is usually a single page of typewritten copy contain-

MARKETING LEADERS

UNC'S MONFORT COLLEGE EXCELS AT PUBLIC RELATIONS AS MALCOLM BALDRIGE WINNER

Although public relations can help an organization maintain favorable relationships with its stakeholders, there must first be a demonstrated media-worthy event to achieve publicity. When the University of Northern Colorado's Monfort College of Business was awarded the prestigious 2004 Malcolm Baldrige National Quality Award, it gained an opportunity for national publicity as well as increased recognition and visibility among key stakeholders. As *USA Today* reported, "Business schools preach quality, but Harvard wasn't the first Baldrige winner for practicing what it preaches." In fact, Monfort College was the first business school in the nation to receive the Baldrige award.

The Malcolm Baldrige National Quality Award is given annually to business, educational, and health-care organizations judged to be outstanding in seven key areas related to quality. The University of Northern Colorado is only the second college or university to win the honor since the award's inception in 1987, and it was chosen over 60 other applicants nationwide. Monfort College has one of the country's few accredited undergraduate-only

business programs. This highest government-sponsored award for quality was given to the dean, Joe Alexander, and other University of Northern Colorado representatives in a ceremony hosted by Vice President Dick Cheney. President George W. Bush sent a congratulatory message stating that the college was selected based on its "exemplifying the qualities of excellence and ethics," adding that "through their efforts, they help make America better and stronger."

With the award, Monfort College's reputation and visibility will improve, according to Dean Alexander. He also stated that financial donations and student applications will likely soar. In addition, other colleges and universities will visit Monfort College to learn how the school won the award and why the school ranks among the nation's best in student satisfaction. Not only does Monfort College rank high in quality, its tuition for in-state students is 45 percent below the national average. The mass media and business education publications provided the publicity that made the achievement extremely valuable to the long-term success of the college.[c]

---

feature article A manuscript of up to 3,000 words prepared for a specific publication

captioned photograph A photo with a brief description of its contents

press conference A meeting used to announce major news events

ing fewer than 300 words and describing a company event or product. A news release gives the firm's or agency's name, address, phone number, and contact person. News releases can tackle a multitude of specific issues. A **feature article** is a manuscript of up to 3,000 words prepared for a specific publication. A **captioned photograph** is a photograph with a brief description explaining the picture's content. Captioned photographs are effective for illustrating new or improved products with highly visible features.

There are several other kinds of publicity-based public relations tools. A **press conference** is a meeting called to announce major news events. Media personnel are invited to a press conference and are usually supplied with written materials and photographs. Letters to the editor and editorials are sometimes prepared and sent to newspapers and magazines. Videos and audiotapes may be distributed to broadcast stations in the hope that they will be aired.

Publicity-based public relations tools offer several advantages, including credibility, news value, significant word-of-mouth communications, and a perception of being endorsed by the media. The public may consider news coverage more truthful and credible than an advertisement because the media are not paid to provide the information. In addition, stories regarding a new-product introduction or a new environmentally responsible company policy, for example, are handled as news items and are likely to receive notice. Finally, the cost of publicity is low compared with the cost of advertising.[22]

Publicity-based public relations tools have some limitations. Media personnel must judge company messages to be newsworthy if the messages are to be published or broadcast at all. Consequently, messages must be timely, interesting, accurate, and in the public interest. Many communications do not qualify. It may take a great deal of time and effort to convince media personnel of the news value of publicity releases. Although public relations personnel usually encourage the media to air publicity releases at certain times, they control neither the content nor the timing of the communication. Media personnel alter length and content of publicity releases to fit publishers' or broadcasters' requirements and may even delete the parts of messages that company personnel view as most important. Furthermore, media personnel use publicity releases in time slots or positions most convenient for them. Thus, messages sometimes appear in locations or at times that may not reach the firm's target audiences. Although these limitations can be frustrating, properly managed publicity-based public relations tools offer an organization substantial benefits.

◉ Evaluating Public Relations Effectiveness

Because of the potential benefits of good public relations, it is essential that organizations evaluate the effectiveness of their public relations campaigns. Research can be conducted to determine how well a firm is communicating its messages or image to its target audiences. *Environmental monitoring* identifies changes in public opinion affecting an organization. A *public relations audit* is used to assess an organization's image among the public or to evaluate the effect of a specific public relations program. A communications audit may include a content analysis of messages, a readability study, or a readership survey. If an organization wants to measure the extent to which stakeholders view it as being socially responsible, it can conduct a *social audit.*

One approach to measuring the effectiveness of publicity-based public relations is to count the number of exposures in the media. To determine which releases are published in print media and how often, an organization can hire a clipping service, a firm that clips and sends news releases to client companies. To measure the effectiveness of television coverage, a firm can enclose a card with its publicity releases, requesting that the television station record its name and the dates when the news item is broadcast (although station personnel do not always comply). Though some television and radio tracking services exist, they are extremely costly.

Counting the number of media exposures does not reveal how many people have actually read or heard the company's message or what they thought about the message afterward. However, measuring changes in product awareness, knowledge, and attitudes resulting from the publicity campaign does. To assess these changes, companies must measure these levels before and after public relations campaigns. Although precise measures are difficult to obtain, a firm's marketers should attempt to assess the impact of public relations efforts on the organization's sales.

◉ Dealing with Unfavorable Public Relations

We have thus far discussed public relations as a planned element of the promotion mix. However, companies may have to deal with unexpected and unfavorable public relations resulting from an unsafe product, an accident, controversial actions of employees, or some other negative event or situation. For example, an airline that experiences a plane crash faces a very tragic and distressing situation. Unfavorable coverage can have quick and dramatic effects. After Martha Stewart was convicted on securities fraud charges, the stock of her firm, Martha Stewart Living Omnimedia, plummeted, advertisers abandoned her self-titled magazine, and her show was

e-site

Domestic and international corporate press releases are available at PR Newswire (www.prnewswire.com). Special subject areas highlight market segments, investor interests, and current news.

dumped.[23] A single negative event that produces public relations can wipe out a company's favorable image and destroy positive customer attitudes established through years of expensive advertising campaigns and other promotional efforts. Today's mass media, including online services and the Internet, disseminate information faster than ever before, and bad news generally receives considerable media attention.

To protect its image, an organization needs to prevent unfavorable public relations or at least lessen its effect if it occurs. First and foremost, the organization should try to prevent negative incidents and events through safety programs, inspections, and effective quality control procedures. However, because negative events can befall even the most cautious firms, an organization should have predetermined plans in place to handle them when they do occur. Firms need to establish policies and procedures for reducing the adverse impact of news coverage of a crisis or controversy. In most cases, organizations should expedite news coverage of negative events rather than trying to discourage or block them. If news coverage is suppressed, rumors and other misinformation may replace facts and be passed along anyway. An unfavorable event can easily balloon into serious problems or public issues and become quite damaging. By being forthright with the press and public and taking prompt action, firms may be able to convince the public of their honest attempts to deal with the situation, and news personnel may be more willing to help explain complex issues to the public. Dealing effectively with a negative event allows an organization to lessen the unfavorable impact on its image. Consider that after Martha Stewart went to prison even while appealing her conviction, public sympathy for her situation helped quadruple her firm's stock, and she had two new television shows waiting for her when she left prison in 2005.[24]

CHAPTER REVIEW

1 Describe the nature and types of advertising.

Advertising is a paid form of nonpersonal communication transmitted to consumers through mass media such as television, radio, the Internet, newspapers, magazines, direct mail, outdoor displays, and signs on mass transit vehicles. Both nonbusiness and business organizations use advertising. Institutional advertising promotes organizational images, ideas, and political issues. When a company promotes its position on a public issue like taxation, institutional advertising is referred to as advocacy advertising. Product advertising promotes uses, features, and benefits of products. The two types of product advertising are pioneer advertising, which focuses on stimulating demand for a product category rather than a specific brand, and competitive advertising, which attempts to stimulate demand for a specific brand by indicating the brand's features, uses, and advantages. To make direct product comparisons, marketers use comparative advertising, in which two or more brands are compared. Two other forms of competitive advertising are reminder advertising, which tells customers that an established brand is still around, and reinforcement advertising, which assures current users they have made the right brand choice.

2 Explain the major steps in developing an advertising campaign.

Although marketers may vary in how they develop advertising campaigns, they should follow a general pattern. First, they must identify and analyze the target audience, the group of people at whom advertisements are aimed. Second, they should establish what they want the campaign to accomplish by defining advertising objectives. Objectives should be clear, precise, and presented in measurable terms. Third, marketers must create the advertising platform, which contains basic issues to be presented in the campaign. Advertising platforms should consist of issues important to consumers. Fourth, advertisers must decide how much money to spend on the campaign; they arrive at this decision through the objective-and-task approach, percent-of-sales approach, competition-matching approach, or arbitrary approach.

Advertisers must then develop a media plan by selecting and scheduling media to use in the campaign. Some of the factors affecting the media plan are location and demographic characteristics of the target audience, content of the message, and cost of the various media. The basic content and form of the advertising message are affected by product features, uses, and benefits; characteristics of the people in the target audience; the campaign's objectives and platform; and the choice of media. Advertisers use copy and artwork to create the message. The execution of an advertising campaign requires extensive planning and coordination.

Finally, advertisers must devise one or more methods for evaluating advertisement effectiveness. Evaluations performed before the campaign begins are called pretests; those conducted after the campaign are called posttests. Two types of posttests are a recognition test, in which respondents are shown the actual advertisement and asked whether they recognize it, and a recall test. In aided recall tests, respondents are shown a list of products, brands, company names, or trademarks to jog their memories. In unaided tests, no clues are given.

3 Identify who is responsible for developing advertising campaigns.

Advertising campaigns can be developed by personnel within the firm or in conjunction with advertising agencies. When a campaign is created by the firm's personnel, it may be developed by one or more individuals or by an advertising department within the firm. Use of an advertising agency may be advantageous because an agency provides highly skilled, objective specialists with broad experience in advertising at low to moderate costs to the firm.

4 Recognize the tools used in public relations.

Public relations is a broad set of communication efforts used to create and maintain favorable relationships between an organization and its stakeholders. Public relations can be used to promote people, places, ideas, activities, and countries and to create and maintain a positive company image. Public relations tools include written materials, such as brochures, newsletters, and annual reports; corporate identity materials, such as business cards and signs; speeches; event sponsorships; and special events. Publicity is communication in news story form about an organization, its products, or both, transmitted through a mass medium at no charge. Publicity-based public relations tools include news releases, feature articles, captioned photographs, and press conferences. Problems that organizations confront in using publicity-based public relations include reluctance of media personnel to print or air releases and lack of control over timing and content of messages.

5 Understand how public relations is used and evaluated.

To evaluate the effectiveness of their public relations programs, companies conduct research to determine how well their messages are reaching their audiences. Environmental monitoring, public relations audits, and counting the number of media exposures are all means of evaluating public relations effectiveness. Organizations should avoid negative public relations by taking steps to prevent negative events that result in unfavorable publicity. To diminish the impact of unfavorable public relations, organizations should institute policies and procedures for dealing with news personnel and the public when negative events occur.

Please visit the student website at www.prideferrell.com for ACE Self-Test questions that will help you prepare for exams.

KEY CONCEPTS

advertising
institutional advertising
advocacy advertising
product advertising
pioneer advertising
competitive advertising
comparative advertising
reminder advertising
reinforcement advertising
advertising campaign

target audience
advertising platform
advertising appropriation
objective-and-task
   approach
percent-of-sales approach
competition-matching
   approach
arbitrary approach
media plan

cost comparison indicator
regional issues
copy
storyboard
artwork
illustrations
layout
pretest
consumer jury
posttest

recognition test
unaided recall test
aided recall test
public relations
publicity
news release
feature article
captioned photograph
press conference

ISSUES FOR DISCUSSION AND REVIEW

1. What is the difference between institutional and product advertising?

2. What is the difference between competitive advertising and comparative advertising?

3. What are the major steps in creating an advertising campaign?

4. What is a target audience? How does a marketer analyze the target audience after identifying it?

5. Why is it necessary to define advertising objectives?

6. What is an advertising platform, and how is it used?

7. What factors affect the size of an advertising budget? What techniques are used to determine an advertising budget?

8. Describe the steps in developing a media plan.

9. What is the function of copy in an advertising message?

10. Discuss several ways to posttest the effectiveness of advertising.

11. What role does an advertising agency play in developing an advertising campaign?

12. What is public relations? Who can an organization reach through public relations?

13. How do organizations use public relations tools? Give several examples that you have observed recently.

14. Explain the problems and limitations associated with publicity-based public relations.

15. In what ways is the effectiveness of public relations evaluated?

16. What are some sources of negative public relations? How should an organization deal with unfavorable public relations?

MARKETING APPLICATIONS

1. Which of the following advertising objectives would be most useful for a company, and why?
   a. The organization will spend $1 million to move from second in market share to market leader.
   b. The organization wants to increase sales from $1.2 million to $1.5 million this year to gain the lead in market share.
   c. The advertising objective is to gain as much market share as possible within the next 12 months.
   d. The advertising objective is to increase sales by 15 percent.

2. Select a print ad and identify how it (1) identifies a specific problem, (2) recommends the product as the best solution to the problem, (3) states the product's advantages and benefits, (4) substantiates the ad's claims, and (5) asks the reader to take action.

3. Look through several recent newspapers and magazines, and identify a news release, a feature article, and a captioned photograph used to publicize a product. Describe the type of product.

4. Identify a company that recently was the target of negative public relations. Describe the situation and discuss the company's response. What did marketers at this company do well? What, if anything, would you recommend that they change about their response?

ONLINE EXERCISE

5. The LEGO company has been making toys since 1932 and has become one of the most recognized brand names in the toy industry. With the company motto "Only the best is good enough," it is no surprise that the LEGO company has developed such an exciting and interactive website. See how the company promotes the LEGO products as well as encourages consumer involvement with the brand by visiting **www.lego.com**.
   a. Which type of advertising is LEGO using on its website?
   b. What target audience is the LEGO company intending to reach?
   c. Identify the advertising objectives that the LEGO company is attempting to achieve through this website.

VIDEO CASE

Vail Resorts Uses Public Relations to Put Out a Fire

Vail Resorts, Inc., is one of the leading resort operators in North America. The company operates four ski resorts in Colorado, including Vail, Keystone, Beaver Creek, and Breckenridge, as well as one in Lake Tahoe. Vail Mountain has become the most popular ski destination in the United States, with 1.6 million skier visits in the 2003–2004 season. *SKI* magazine has ranked Vail as the number 1 ski resort in North America 13 times since 1988.

Despite its success, the company experienced a very challenging year in 1998. In October of that year, just two weeks before the beginning of the ski season, the Vail Mountain resort suffered the largest "ecoterrorist" event in U.S. history. Several structures, including Patrol Headquarters, the Two Elk restaurant, and Camp One, were burned to the ground, and four chair lift operator buildings were damaged. Total damages exceeded $12 million. The deliberately and strategically set fires disabled three central lifts and the biggest restaurant and guest service center on the mountain.

Shortly after the fires, the Earth Liberation Front (ELF), a radical environmental organization, claimed responsibility. In an e-mail, ELF, which splintered off the better-known Earth First! organization, claimed to have set the fires to protest a planned expansion of the resort, which, the group argued, would threaten habitat needed to reintroduce the Canada lynx, an endangered wild cat. In the e-mail, ELF said, "Putting profits ahead of Colorado's wildlife will not be tolerated." ELF's communiqué also warned skiers to stay away from the resort "for your safety and convenience." However, Earth First! and many other environmental groups, which had protested Vail's controversial plans to expand into lynx habitat, were quick to condemn ELF's firebombing at Vail.

As with most disasters, the mass media quickly swarmed the scene at Vail Mountain, and the resulting stories published around the country were not always beneficial to Vail Mountain and nearby Vail, Colorado—or accurate. Some newspapers reported that all ski lifts had been destroyed and that the resort would be unable to open for the season. A few reported that the nearby town of Vail was on fire, including hotels.

Vail Resorts responded to the misinformation by launching a direct-mail campaign to communicate with everyone who had made reservations for ski vacations through Vail Central Reservations, as well as to travel agents and individual hotels in town. The company reassured skiers that the resort would indeed open and would be a safe place for their families to vacation. Vail Resorts managed to salvage the season and make it successful, despite the havoc wreaked by the fires.

Vail Resorts, like many firms, had a generic crisis plan in place at the time of the incident. However, some analysts contend that the degree to which the company followed that plan was questionable. In hindsight, Vail management has stated that things might have gone more smoothly in the first 48 hours after the crisis if they had adhered more closely to that plan. For example, managers now recognize that they did not utilize their staff as effectively as possible. Instead of clearly defining responsibilities up front, staff members were called up somewhat randomly, adding to the confusion surrounding the event. The plan also failed to address communication with employees. Resort management quickly decided that keeping employees fully informed was a top priority because they were the best ambassadors to the public.

Crisis management has been defined as preparation for low-probability or unexpected events that could threaten an organization's viability, reputation, or profitability. It has traditionally been viewed as "damage control," with little preplanning taking place. However, with the changing global political climate, events such as terrorist attacks and workplace violence have become more common, increasing the need for crisis management and disaster recovery planning for businesses. Even small companies are beginning to recognize the need to plan for the unexpected.

Crisis management and disaster recovery are critical for most organizations that deal with large numbers of customers, especially in the recreation and entertainment industries. The negative publicity resulting from a crisis can be potentially more devastating than a natural disaster such as an earthquake or a technological disruption such as a major power failure. The disruption of routine operations and paralysis of employees and customers in the face of crisis can reduce productivity, destroy long-established reputations, and erode public confidence in a company. Crisis planning can arm a company with tools and procedures to manage a crisis, protect a company's image, and reduce unfavorable publicity. By being forthright with the press and the public and taking prompt action, companies may be able to convince the public of their honest attempts to resolve the situation, and news media may be more willing to help explain complex issues to the public. Effectively dealing with a negative event allows an organization to reduce the unfavorable impact on its image.

In the case of Vail Resorts, managers believe they could have followed their previously established crisis management plan more closely. During the two days immediately following the fires, management was disorganized and employees and Vail residents were confused about the future of the resort. Ultimately Vail chose to be honest and open with the media and its employees, which helped the resort weather the crisis with its image intact. The company's direct-mail campaign to vacationers also helped preserve public trust in the company.

To prepare for unexpected events, all firms should develop a crisis management program, which includes four basic steps: conducting a crisis audit, making contingency plans, assigning a crisis management team, and practicing the plan. Conducting a crisis audit involves assessing the potential impacts of different events, such as the death of an executive or a natural disaster. *Contingency planning* refers to the development of back-up plans for emergencies that specify actions to be taken and their expected consequences. Crisis management teams should also be designated so that key areas are covered in case of emergency, such as media relations and legal affairs. Finally, companies should practice the crisis management plan and update it as necessary on a regular basis so that all employees are familiar with the plan.[25]

QUESTIONS FOR DISCUSSION

1. What tools did Vail Resorts use to respond to the crisis?

2. Evaluate Vail Resorts' response to the crisis. What did the firm do right? What else could it have done to relieve public concerns about the safety of the resort as well as its controversial expansion?

3. How can creating a crisis management and disaster recovery plan help a company protect its reputation, customer relationships, and profits?

Personal Selling and Sales Promotion

▶ **Frequent-Flyer Programs Encourage Customer Loyalty**

Customer sales promotion methods attempt to develop loyalty and repeat purchases. One sales promotion method that has been extremely effective in developing loyalty and repeat purchases is frequent-user incentives in the airline industry. Customers get incentives or rewards for engaging in repeat purchases in the form of frequent-flyer miles that can be redeemed for future flights. Ultra-high-mileage fliers, such as those who accumulate 1 million flight miles, receive benefits such as 100 percent frequent-flier mileage bonuses, class upgrades, and additional check-in and boarding privileges. At United Airlines, for example, million-mile fliers earn lifetime "premier executive" status. Ultra-high-mileage customers at America West earn lifetime "gold elite" status as well as tickets to a major league baseball game and a professional golf tournament.

Despite the success of these programs, the major airlines continue to suffer huge losses, and, as a result, many have cut back food service and other amenities. In order to compete with the rising popularity of low-cost carriers such as Southwest, the major airlines have been reducing their first-class and business fares for both domestic and international flights. Although lower fares may seem beneficial for everyone, some frequent fliers with elite status have experienced negative consequences. Lower first-class fares mean that more travelers are willing to pay for first-class seats, leaving fewer first-class seats available for upgrades for elite-status fliers. In years past, elite status was highly valued; some business travelers would even make unnecessary or complicated year-end trips just to meet the annual mileage requirements, often around 100,000 miles per year. But fewer travelers are seeing the value of maintaining elite status anymore. Often, there are twice as many elite members waiting for an upgrade than there are first-class seats available on any given flight.

Of the 120 million frequent-flier club members of the world's airlines, about 307,000 have earned more than a million miles in at least one airline's program. Airline executives believe that it makes sense to continue these programs to maintain loyal relationships and rewards for their best customers. While these benefits may apply to a small number of customers, these customers represent the most lucrative for the airline industry. Moreover, customer loyalty in the airline industry is under pressure due to Internet booking of reservations, poor service, and availability of low-cost providers such as Southwest Airlines, AirTran, Frontier, and JetBlue. Airlines such as Delta, American, and Northwest will have to balance their benefits to provide not only frequent flier incentives, but also service and prices that are competitive.[1] ◀

OBJECTIVES

1 Define personal selling and understand its purpose.

2 Describe the basic steps in the personal-selling process.

3 Identify the types of sales force personnel.

4 Understand sales management decisions and activities.

5 Explain what sales promotion activities are and how they are used.

6 Recognize specific consumer and trade sales promotion methods.

For many organizations, programs that reward frequent customers play a major role in maintaining long-term, satisfying customer relationships, which in turn contribute to the company's success. As we saw in Chapter 16, personal selling and sales promotion are two possible elements in a promotion mix. Sales promotion is sometimes a company's sole promotional tool, although it is generally used in conjunction with other promotion mix elements. It is playing an increasingly important role in marketing strategies. Personal selling is becoming more professional and sophisticated, with sales personnel acting more as consultants and advisers.

In this chapter, we focus on personal selling and sales promotion. We first consider the purposes of personal selling and then its basic steps. Next, we look at types of salespeople and how they are selected. We then discuss major sales force management decisions, including setting objectives for the sales force and determining its size; recruiting, selecting, training, compensating, and motivating salespeople; managing sales territories; and controlling and evaluating sales force performance. Then we examine several characteristics of sales promotion, reasons for using sales promotion, and sales promotion methods available for use in a promotion mix.

What Is Personal Selling?

personal selling Paid personal communication that informs customers and persuades them to buy products

Personal selling is paid personal communication that attempts to inform customers and persuade them to purchase products in an exchange situation. For example, a salesperson describing the benefits of a Kenmore dryer to a customer in a Sears store is engaging in personal selling. Personal selling goals vary from one firm to another. However, they usually involve finding prospects, persuading prospects to buy, and keeping customers satisfied. Although the public may harbor negative perceptions of personal selling, unfavorable stereotypes of salespeople are changing thanks to the efforts of major corporations, professional sales associations, and academic institutions. Research indicates that personal selling will continue to gain respect as professional sales associations develop and enforce ethical codes of conduct.[2]

Personal selling gives marketers the greatest freedom to adjust a message so that it will satisfy customers' information needs. Compared with other promotion methods, personal selling is the most precise, enabling marketers to focus on the most promising sales prospects. Other promotion mix elements are aimed at groups of people, some of whom may not be prospective customers. However, personal selling is generally the most expensive element in the promotion mix. The average cost of a business sales call is about $170.[3]

Salespeople must be aware of their competitors. They must monitor the development of new products and know about competitors' sales efforts in their sales territories, how often and when the competition calls on their accounts, and what the competition is saying about their product in relation to its own. For example, at Power TV, a California firm that makes software and operating systems for digital cable television boxes, salespeople routinely collect information about competitors' activities and send it to the marketing department for posting on the firm's intranet. This steady flow allows all 240 employees to stay abreast of competitive developments so the company can respond quickly.[4] Salespeople must emphasize the benefits that their products provide, especially when competitors' products do not offer those specific benefits.

Few businesses survive solely on profits from one-time customers. For long-run survival, most marketers depend on repeat sales and therefore strive to keep their customers satisfied. Satisfied customers provide favorable word-of-mouth communications, attracting new customers. Even though the whole organization is responsible

MARKETING ENTREPRENEURS

Lara Merriken

THE BUSINESS: Larabars

FOUNDED: 2000

SUCCESS: 11 employees and a reputation for quality

Lara Merriken, an avid hiker and founder of Humm Foods, wanted an alternative to the sugar and junk-filled energy bars that were available on the market, so she started experimenting with recipes using a simple food processor. The result was the Larabar, a snack bar made with no preservatives, no refined sugar, and all-natural quality ingredients. She finished her first order of 500 bars by hand in her home kitchen. As demand increased, so did the size of her operation, but not much. Lara initially got her product into stores by presenting them to her former employer, Whole Foods. Her ability to personally sell the product made the difference. She now has 11 employees (two of which are her dogs) and distributes Larabars to local natural foods stores throughout Colorado, as well as to some grocers in California and even in Canada. Larabars now retail at around $1.99 each or $29.99 for a case of 16. A super-high-quality product and good marketing created success.[a]

for achieving customer satisfaction, much of the burden falls on salespeople because they are almost always closer to customers than anyone else in the company and often provide buyers with information and service after the sale. Such contact gives salespeople an opportunity to generate additional sales and offers them a good vantage point for evaluating the strengths and weaknesses of the company's products and other marketing mix components. Their observations help develop and maintain a marketing mix that better satisfies both customers and the firm. Thus, marketing managers want salespeople to know as much as possible about the firm's marketing strategy and the customers' perceived value in the products they sell.[5]

The Personal Selling Process

The specific activities involved in the selling process vary among salespeople and selling situations. No two salespeople use exactly the same selling methods. Nonetheless, many salespeople move through a general selling process as they sell products. This process consists of seven steps, outlined in Figure 18.1: prospecting, preapproach, approach, making the presentation, overcoming objections, closing the sale, and following up.

● **Prospecting for Customers.** Developing a list of potential customers is called **prospecting** (see definition on p. 444). Salespeople seek names of prospects from company sales records, trade shows, commercial databases, newspaper announcements (of marriages, births, deaths, and so on), public records, telephone directories, trade association directories, and many other sources. Sales personnel also use responses to advertisements that encourage interested persons to send in information request forms. Seminars and meetings targeted at particular types of clients, such as attorneys or accountants, may also produce leads.

Many salespeople prefer to use referrals—recommendations from current customers—to find prospects. Obtaining referrals requires that the salesperson have a good relationship with the current customer and so must have performed well before asking the customer for help. Research shows that one referral is as valuable as 12 cold calls. Also, 80 percent of clients are willing to give referrals, but only 20 percent are ever asked. Sales experts indicate that the advantages of using referrals are that the resulting sales leads are highly qualified, the sales rates are higher, initial transactions are larger, and the sales cycle is shorter.[6]

Consistent activity is critical to successful prospecting. Salespeople must actively search the customer base for qualified prospects who fit the target market profile. After developing the prospect list, a salesperson evaluates whether each prospect is able, willing, and authorized to buy the product. Based on this evaluation, prospects are ranked according to desirability or potential.

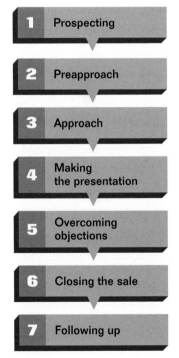

1 Prospecting

2 Preapproach

3 Approach

4 Making the presentation

5 Overcoming objections

6 Closing the sale

7 Following up

Figure 18.1
General Steps in the Personal Selling Process

Identifying Prospects
IdEXEC helps companies connect with the right potential business customers.

prospecting   Developing a list of potential customers

approach   The manner in which a salesperson contacts a potential customer

● **Evaluating Prospects.**   Before contacting acceptable prospects, a salesperson finds and analyzes information about each prospect's specific product needs, current use of brands, feelings about available brands, and personal characteristics. In short, salespeople need to know what potential buyers and decision makers consider most important and why they need a specific product.[7] The most successful salespeople are thorough in their evaluation of prospects. This *preapproach* step involves identifying key decision makers, reviewing account histories and problems, contacting other clients for information, assessing credit histories, preparing sales presentations, and identifying product needs. Many companies employ information technology and customer relationship management systems to scour their databases and thus identify the most profitable products and customers. These systems can also help sales departments manage leads, track customers, develop sales forecasts, and measure performance.[8] A salesperson with a lot of information about a prospect is better equipped to develop a presentation that communicates precisely with the prospect.

● **Approaching the Customer.**   The **approach**, the manner in which a salesperson contacts a potential customer, is a critical step in the sales process. In more than 80 percent of initial sales calls, the purpose is to gather information about the buyer's needs and objectives. Creating a favorable impression and building rapport with prospective clients are important tasks in the approach. During the initial contact, the salesperson strives to develop a relationship rather than just push a product. The salesperson may have to call on a prospect several times before the product is considered. The approach must be designed to deliver value to targeted customers. If the sales approach is inappropriate, the salesperson's efforts are likely to have poor results.

As mentioned earlier, one type of approach is based on referrals: the salesperson approaches the prospect and explains that an acquaintance, associate, or relative suggested the call. Another type of approach is the "cold canvass," in which a salesperson calls on potential customers without prior consent. The exact type of approach depends on the salesperson's preferences, the product being sold, the firm's resources, and the prospect's characteristics.

● **Making the Presentation.**   During the sales presentation, the salesperson must attract and hold the prospect's attention, stimulate interest, and spark a desire for the product. The salesperson should have the prospect touch, hold, or use the product. If possible, the salesperson should demonstrate the product. Audiovisual equipment and software may also enhance the presentation.

During the presentation, the salesperson must not only talk but also listen. The sales presentation gives the salesperson the greatest opportunity to determine the prospect's specific needs by listening to questions and comments and observing responses. Even though the salesperson plans the presentation in advance, she or he must be able to adjust the message to meet the prospect's informational needs.

ADAM
SALES MANAGER
WEBEX FANATIC

webex

event center

meeting center

Put your foot in hundreds of doors at once.   sales center

support center

training center

Enhancing Sales Presentations
Many sales teams are using WebEx technology for sales presentations.

● **Overcoming Objections.** An effective salesperson usually seeks out a prospect's objections so that he or she can address them. If they are not apparent, the salesperson cannot deal with them, and the prospect may not buy. One of the best ways to overcome objections is to anticipate and counter them before the prospect raises them. However, this approach can be risky because the salesperson may mention objections that the prospect would not have raised. If possible, the salesperson should handle objections as they arise. They can also be addressed at the end of the presentation.

closing The stage in the selling process when the salesperson asks the prospect to buy the product

● **Closing the Sale.** Closing is the stage of the selling process when the salesperson asks the prospect to buy the product. During the presentation, the salesperson may use a "trial close" by asking questions that assume the prospect will buy the product. The salesperson might ask the potential customer about financial terms, desired colors or sizes, or delivery arrangements. One questioning approach uses broad questions (*what, how, why*) to probe or gather information and focused questions (*who, when, where*) to clarify and close the sale. Reactions to such questions usually indicate how close the prospect is to buying. A trial close allows prospects to indicate indirectly that they will buy the product without having to say those sometimes difficult words, "I'll take it."

A salesperson should try to close at several points during the presentation because the prospect may be ready to buy. One closing strategy involves asking the potential customer to place a low-risk tryout order. An attempt to close the sale may result in objections. Thus, closing can uncover hidden objections, which the salesperson can then address.

● **Following Up.** After a successful closing, the salesperson must follow up the sale. In the follow-up stage, the salesperson determines whether the order was delivered on time and installed properly, if installation was required. He or she should contact the customer to learn if any problems or questions regarding the product have arisen. The follow-up stage is also used to determine customers' future product needs.

◉ Types of Salespeople

To develop a sales force, a marketing manager decides what kind of salesperson will sell the firm's products most effectively. Most organizations use several different kinds of sales personnel. Based on the functions performed, salespeople can be classified into three groups: order getters, order takers, and support personnel. One salesperson can, and often does, perform all three functions.

order getter   The salesperson who sells to new customers and increases sales to current ones

● **Order Getters.**   To obtain orders, a salesperson informs prospects and persuades them to buy the product. The role of the **order getter** is to increase sales by selling to new customers and increasing sales to current customers. This task sometimes is called *creative selling.* It requires that salespeople recognize potential buyers' needs and give them necessary information. Order getting is sometimes divided into two categories: current-customer sales and new-business sales.

order takers   Salespersons who primarily seek repeat sales

● **Order Takers.**   Salespeople take orders to perpetuate long-lasting, satisfying customer relationships. **Order takers** seek repeat sales. They generate the bulk of many organizations' total sales. One major objective is to be certain customers have sufficient product quantities where and when needed. Most order takers handle orders for standardized products purchased routinely and not requiring extensive sales efforts. The role of order takers is evolving, however. In the future, they will probably serve more as identifiers and problem solvers to meet the needs of their customers. There are two groups of order takers: inside order takers and field order takers.

In many businesses, *inside order takers,* who work in sales offices, receive orders by mail, telephone, and the Internet. Certain producers, wholesalers, and retailers have sales personnel who sell from within the firm rather than in the field. This does not mean that inside order takers never communicate with customers face to face. For example, retail salespeople are classified as inside order takers. As more orders are placed through the Internet, the role of the inside order taker will continue to change.

Salespeople who travel to customers are *outside,* or *field, order takers.* Often customers and field order takers develop interdependent relationships. The buyer relies on the salesperson to take orders periodically (and sometimes to deliver them), and the salesperson counts on the buyer to purchase a certain quantity of products periodically. Use of notebook and handheld computers has improved the field order taker's inventory and order tracking capabilities.

support personnel   Sales staff members who facilitate selling but usually are not involved solely with making sales

● **Support Personnel.**   **Support personnel** facilitate selling but usually are not involved solely with making sales. They are engaged primarily in marketing industrial products, locating prospects, educating customers, building goodwill, and providing service after the sale. There are many kinds of sales support personnel; the three most common are missionary, trade, and technical salespeople.

missionary salespeople   Support salespersons who assist the producer's customers in selling to their own customers

Missionary salespeople, usually employed by manufacturers, assist the producer's customers in selling to their own customers. Missionary salespeople may call on retailers to inform and persuade them to buy the manufacturer's products. When they succeed, retailers purchase products from wholesalers, who are the producer's customers. Manufacturers of medical supplies and pharmaceuticals often use missionary salespeople, called *detail reps,* to promote their products to physicians, hospitals, and retail druggists.

trade salespeople Salespersons involved mainly in helping a producer's customers promote a product

technical salespeople Support salespersons who give technical assistance to a firm's current customers

Trade salespeople are not strictly support personnel because they usually take orders as well. However, they direct much effort toward helping customers, especially retail stores, promote the product. They are likely to restock shelves, obtain more shelf space, set up displays, provide in-store demonstrations, and distribute samples to store customers. Food producers and processors commonly employ trade salespeople.

Technical salespeople give technical assistance to the organization's current customers, advising them on product characteristics and applications, system designs, and installation procedures. Because this job is often highly technical, the salesperson usually has formal training in one of the physical sciences or in engineering. Technical sales personnel often sell technical industrial products, such as computers, heavy equipment, and steel.

When hiring sales personnel, marketers seldom restrict themselves to a single category because most firms require different types of salespeople. Several factors dictate how many of each type a particular company should have. Product use, characteristics, complexity, and price influence the kind of sales personnel used, as do the number and characteristics of customers. The types of marketing channels and the intensity and type of advertising also affect the composition of a sales force.

Sales and Marketing Management magazine has a website (www.salesandmarketing.com) that focuses on weekly news and trends in the areas of personal selling and sales management. This site contains sales training tips, suggestions about what to read, and other content of interest to those in the field of sales management.

⊚ Managing the Sales Force

The sales force is directly responsible for generating one of an organization's primary inputs—sales revenue. Without adequate sales revenue, businesses cannot survive. In addition, a firm's reputation is often determined by the ethical conduct of its sales force. The morale and ultimately the success of a firm's sales force depend in large part on adequate compensation, room for advancement, adequate training, and management support—all key areas of sales management. Salespeople who are not satisfied with these elements may leave. Evaluating the input of salespeople is an important part of sales force management because of its strong bearing on a firm's success.

We explore eight general areas of sales management: establishing sales force objectives, determining sales force size, recruiting and selecting salespeople, training sales personnel, compensating salespeople, motivating salespeople, managing sales territories, and controlling and evaluating sales force performance.

● **Establishing Sales Force Objectives.**   To manage a sales force effectively, sales managers must develop sales objectives. Sales objectives tell salespeople what they are expected to accomplish during a specified time period. They give the sales force direction and purpose, and serve as standards for evaluating and controlling the performance of sales personnel. Research indicates that a focus on sales performance increases efforts to achieve sales objectives.[9] Sales objectives should be stated in precise, measurable terms and should specify the time period and geographic areas involved.

Sales objectives are usually developed for both the total sales force and each salesperson. Objectives for the entire force are normally stated in terms of sales volume, market share, or profit. Volume objectives refer to dollar or unit sales. For example, the objective for an electric drill producer's sales force might be to sell $18 million worth of drills, or 600,000 drills, annually. When sales goals are stated in terms of market share, they usually call for an increase in the proportion of the firm's sales relative to the total number of products sold by all businesses in that industry. When sales objectives are based on profit, they are generally stated in terms of dollar amounts or return on investment.

Sales objectives, or quotas, for individual salespeople are commonly stated in terms of dollar or unit sales volume. Other bases used for individual sales objectives

ETHICS AND SOCIAL ISSUES

RESPONSIBLE SELLING IMPROVES CUSTOMER RELATIONSHIPS

Salespeople are trained about the products they sell so they can serve their customers and maximize sales revenues. Sometimes, however, it is not what a salesperson does but what he or she doesn't do that makes or breaks customer relationships. The six "deadly sins" for salespeople are (1) not being adequately prepared, (2) being overbearing or pushy, (3) going over a buyer's head to find a higher-ranking decision maker, (4) failing to follow up on a sale, (5) being rude, and (6) misleading customers about their products. Another increasingly frequent issue is offering extravagant gifts, bribes, and even kickbacks. During a slow economy, salespeople may resort to less than ethical tactics to close a deal, even back-stabbing their own colleagues. Such transgressions can result in inappropriate or unethical behavior, which can jeopardize relationships with customers.

For example, most customers prefer a salesperson who is confident but not pushy. Responsive salespeople can earn customers' trust, but pushy sales reps are often viewed as overly aggressive and even obnoxious. Salespeople also need to give a customer enough space so she or he doesn't feel pressured. Although giving a customer more time to make a decision may allow a competing salesperson time to make a presentation, it may help foster real customer loyalty. A salesperson should also focus on the individual who has the authority to make a purchase decision; if the salesperson chooses to go above that person to someone at a higher rank in the company, he or she risks insulting the decision maker and losing a sale. Another fine line sales reps must decide on is how much information to provide about their products. A customer who has been burned by a misleading or deceptive sales pitch most likely will refuse to do business with that salesperson or company again.

Research indicates that 60 percent of firms fail to follow up on prospective customers within 60 days, a trend attributed to increasing reliance on the Internet and other sales-related technologies instead of face-to-face contact between salespeople and customers. Salespeople who follow up on delivery, installation, warranty interpretation, product performance, and related customer service issues tend to have better performance. Word-of-mouth promotion is very important in sales, and a salesperson known for honesty and integrity will get many referrals.

Avoiding these "deadly sins" of personal selling can lead to a positive attitude toward sales presentations as well as long-term and lucrative customer relationships.[b]

---

include average order size, average number of calls per time period, and ratio of orders to calls.

● **Determining Sales Force Size.**   Sales force size is important because it influences the company's ability to generate sales and profits. The size of the sales force affects the compensation methods used, salespeople's morale, and overall sales force management. Sales force size must be adjusted periodically because a firm's marketing plans change along with markets and forces in the marketing environment. One danger in cutting back the size of the sales force to increase profits is that the sales organization may lose strength, preventing it from rebounding when growth occurs or better market conditions prevail.

Several analytical methods can help determine optimal sales force size. One method involves determining how many sales calls per year are necessary for the organization to serve customers effectively and then dividing this total by the average

Recruiting
Many sales organizations use Hotjobs.com to find and recruit for sales positions.

number of sales calls a salesperson makes annually. A second method is based on marginal analysis, whereby additional salespeople are added to the sales force until the cost of an additional salesperson equals the additional sales generated by that person. Although marketing managers may use one or several analytical methods, they normally temper decisions with subjective judgments.

● **Recruiting and Selecting Salespeople.** To create and maintain an effective sales force, sales managers must recruit the right type of salespeople. Effective recruiting efforts are a vital part of implementing the strategic sales-force plan and can help assure successful organizational performance.[10] In recruiting, the sales manager develops a list of qualified applicants for sales positions. To ensure the recruiting process results in a pool of qualified salespeople from which to hire, a sales manager establishes a set of qualifications before beginning to recruit. Two activities help establish this set of required attributes. First, the sales manager should prepare a job description listing specific tasks salespeople are to perform. Second, the manager should analyze characteristics of the firm's successful salespeople, as well as those of ineffective sales personnel. From the job description and analysis of traits, the sales manager should be able to develop a set of specific requirements and be aware of potential weaknesses that could lead to failure.

A sales manager generally recruits applicants from several sources: departments within the firm, other firms, employment agencies, educational institutions, respondents to advertisements, and individuals recommended by current employees. The specific sources depend on the type of salesperson required and the manager's experiences with particular sources.

The process of recruiting and selecting salespeople varies considerably from one company to another. Companies intent on reducing sales force turnover are likely to have strict recruiting and selection procedures. Some organizations use the specialized services of other companies to hire sales personnel. Recruitment should not be sporadic. It should be a continuous activity aimed at reaching the best applicants. The selection process should systematically and effectively match applicants' characteristics and needs with the requirements of specific selling tasks. Finally, the selection process should ensure that new sales personnel are available where and when needed.

● **Training Sales Personnel.** Many organizations have formal training programs; others depend on informal, on-the-job training. Some systematic training programs are quite extensive, whereas others are rather short and rudimentary. Whether the training program is complex or simple, developers must consider what to teach, whom to train, and how to train them.

A sales training program can concentrate on the company, its products, or selling methods. Training programs often cover all three. Such programs can be aimed at newly hired salespeople, experienced salespeople, or both. Training for experienced company salespeople usually emphasizes product information, although salespeople must also be informed about new selling techniques and changes in company plans, policies, and procedures. Ordinarily, new sales personnel require comprehensive training, whereas experienced personnel need both refresher courses on established products and training regarding new-product information.

Sales training may be done in the field, at educational institutions, in company facilities, and/or online using Web-based technology. For many companies, online training saves time and money and helps salespeople learn about new products quickly.[11] Some firms train new employees before assigning them to a specific sales position. Others put them into the field immediately, providing formal training only after they have gained some experience. Training programs for new personnel can be

MARKETING LEADERS
THE PAMPERED CHEF

Doris Christopher is a former home economics teacher and stay-at-home mom. Her own experiences helped her recognize a need for kitchen tools and techniques that make cooking faster and easier, and a place to turn for advice on how to solve kitchen problems. Inspired to help others preserve the tradition of family mealtimes, she founded The Pampered Chef out of the basement of her Chicago home in 1980.

Christopher did not set out to found a national company with $700 million in annual sales. She really wanted to start a part-time business that would allow her to do activities she enjoyed without interfering with the time she wanted to spend with her family. She came up with the idea of giving home demonstration parties, which were essentially sales presentations where she would show people how to use the proper kitchen tools with real food—a kind of show-and-tell that gave customers a "try-before-you-buy" experience. She sold about $175 worth of kitchenware at her first in-home show at a friend's home in October 1980. Christopher expanded her direct-selling organization by following the personal selling process with the in-home presentation as the heart of the sales process.

Christopher founded her business with just $3,000 in capital borrowed on a life insurance policy—the only cash the firm has ever borrowed. She identified roughly 30 products that she felt were indispensable in any kitchen,

and she set off to find them in the wholesale showrooms at Chicago's Merchandise Mart. While many suppliers were initially amused by Christopher's business plan, they began to take her more seriously after a few orders and even extended her credit. The business quickly grew to the point that Christopher had to ship her customers' orders by UPS, instead of hand delivering them as she had in the beginning.

At first, Christopher handled all of the in-home demonstrations herself, but in 1981 she took on her first outside "kitchen consultant" or salesperson. By the end of that year, she had a dozen sales consultants and had established a commission incentive for selling the products. She also began holding sales meetings in her home, training her sales consultants on running effective presentations, demonstrating recipes, and introducing new products.

With the help of her husband, Jay Christopher, a business executive with 30 years of experience, she built a fast-growing company that now has more than 70,000 Pampered Chef Kitchen Consultants selling more than 150 products. Long ago outgrowing her family's home, the firm's inventory now takes up more than 660,000 square feet of warehouse space, and thousands of orders fill an average of nine UPS trucks per day. Christopher's approach to personal selling, inspired by her dedication to family and home, helped to create a successful privately held company.[c]

as short as several days or as long as three years; some are even longer. Because experienced salespeople usually need periodic retraining, a firm's sales management must determine the frequency, sequencing, and duration of these efforts.

Materials for sales training programs range from videos, texts, online materials, manuals, and cases to programmed learning devices and audio- and videocassettes. Lectures, demonstrations, simulation exercises, and on-the-job training can all be effective teaching methods. Choice of methods and materials for a particular sales training program depends on type and number of trainees, program content and complexity, length and location, size of the training budget, number of teachers, and teacher preferences.

● **Compensating Salespeople.** To develop and maintain a highly productive sales force, a business must formulate and administer a compensation plan that attracts, motivates, and retains the most effective individuals. The plan should give sales management the desired level of control and provide sales personnel with acceptable levels of income, freedom, and incentive. It should be flexible, equitable, easy to administer, and easy to understand. Good compensation programs facilitate and encourage proper treatment of customers. Obviously it is quite difficult to incorporate all of these requirements into a single program.

Developers of compensation programs must determine the general level of compensation required and the most desirable method of calculating it. In analyzing the required compensation level, sales management must ascertain a salesperson's value to the company on the basis of the tasks and responsibilities associated with the sales position. Sales managers may consider a number of factors, including salaries of other types of personnel in the firm, competitors' compensation plans, costs of sales force turnover, and nonsalary selling expenses. The average low-level salesperson earns about $64,000 annually (including commissions and bonuses), whereas a high-level, high-performing salesperson can make as much as $153,000 a year.[12] Table 18.1 lists average salaries for sales personnel.

Sales compensation programs usually reimburse salespeople for selling expenses, provide some fringe benefits, and deliver the required compensation level. To achieve this, a firm may use one or more of three basic compensation methods: straight salary, straight commission, or a combination of salary and commission. In a **straight salary compensation plan**, salespeople are paid a specified amount per time

straight salary compensation plan Paying salespeople a specific amount per time period

Table 18.1	Average Salaries for Sales Representatives and Executives		
	Base Salary	**Bonus + Commissions**	**Total Compensation**
Executives	$95,170	$49,483	$144,653
Top performers	$87,342	$66,075	$153,417
Mid-level reps	$58,546	$33,791	$ 92,337
Low-level reps	$44,289	$19,486	$ 63,775
Average	**$70,588**	**$40,547**	**$111,135**

Source: From Christine Galea, "2004 Salary Survey," *Sales and Marketing Management,* May 2004, p. 29.
©2004 VNU Business Media, Inc. Reprinted with permission from Sales and Marketing Management.

straight commission compensation plan Paying salespeople according to the amount of their sales in a given time period

combination compensation plan Paying salespeople a fixed salary plus a commission based on sales volume

period. This sum remains the same until they receive a pay increase or decrease. In a **straight commission compensation plan**, salespeople's compensation is determined solely by sales for a given period. A commission may be based on a single percentage of sales or on a sliding scale involving several sales levels and percentage rates. In a **combination compensation plan**, salespeople receive a fixed salary plus a commission based on sales volume. Some combination programs require that a salesperson exceed a certain sales level before earning a commission; others offer commissions for any level of sales. Table 18.2 lists the pros and cons of each compensation method. Research suggests that sales managers may be moving away from individual performance-based commissions and toward salary and team-based compensation methods.[13] For example, the Container Store, which markets do-it-yourself organizing and storage products, prefers to pay its sales staff salaries that are 50 to 100 percent higher than that offered by rivals, instead of paying salespeople according to commission plans.[14]

● **Motivating Salespeople.** Although financial compensation is an important incentive, additional programs are necessary for motivating sales personnel. A sales manager should develop a systematic approach for motivating salespeople to be

Table 18.2 Characteristics of Sales Force Compensation Methods

Compensation Method	Frequency of Use (%)*	When Especially Useful	Advantages	Disadvantages
Straight Salary	17.5	Compensating new salespersons; firm moves into new sales territories that require developmental work; sales requiring lengthy presale and postsale services	Gives salesperson security; gives sales manager control over salespersons; easy to administer; yields more predictable selling expenses	Provides no incentive; necessitates closer supervision of salespersons; during sales declines, selling expenses remain constant
Straight Commission	14.0	Highly aggressive selling is required; nonselling tasks are minimized; company uses contractors and part-timers	Provides maximum amount of incentive; by increasing commission rate, sales managers can encourage salespersons to sell certain items; selling expenses relate directly to sales resources	Salespersons have little financial security; sales manager has minimum control over sales force; may cause salespeople to give inadequate service to smaller accounts; selling costs less predictable
Combination	68.5	Sales territories have relatively similar sales potential; firm wishes to provide incentive but still control sales force activities	Provides certain level of financial security; provides some incentive; can move sales force efforts in profitable direction	Selling expenses less predictable; may be difficult to administer

*The figures are computed from *Dartnell's 30th Sales Force Compensation Survey,* Dartnell Corporation, Chicago, 1999.

Source: Charles Futrell, *Sales Management* (Ft. Worth: Dryden, 2001), pp. 307–316.

Compensating and Motivating Salespeople
Omaha Steaks provides sales incentives programs to companies to assist salespeople in achieving their goals.

productive. Effective sales force motivation is achieved through an organized set of activities performed continuously by the company's sales management.

Sales personnel, like other people, join organizations to satisfy personal needs and achieve personal goals. Sales managers must identify these needs and goals and strive to create an organizational climate that allows each salesperson to fulfill them. Enjoyable working conditions, power and authority, job security, and opportunity to excel are effective motivators, as are company efforts to make sales jobs more productive and efficient. At the Container Store, for example, sales personnel receive hundreds of hours of training every year about the company's products so that they can help customers solve their organization and storage problems.[15] Sales contests and other incentive programs can also be effective motivators. Sales contests can motivate salespeople to increase sales or add new accounts, promote special items, achieve greater volume per sales call, and cover territories more thoroughly. However, companies need to understand salespersons' preferences when designing contests in order to make them effective in increasing sales.[16] Some companies find such contests powerful tools for motivating sales personnel to achieve company goals.

Properly designed incentive programs pay for themselves many times over, and sales managers are relying on incentives more than ever. Recognition programs that acknowledge outstanding performance with symbolic awards, such as plaques, can be very effective when carried out in a peer setting. Other common awards include travel, merchandise, and cash. Travel reward programs can confer a high-profile honor, provide a unique experience that makes recipients feel special, and build camaraderie among award-winning salespeople. However, some recipients of travel awards may feel they already travel too much on the job. Cash rewards are easy to administer, are always appreciated by recipients, and appeal to all demographic groups. However, cash has no visible "trophy" value and provides few "bragging rights." The benefits of awarding merchandise are that the items have visible trophy value, recipients who are allowed to select the merchandise feel more control, and merchandise awards can help build momentum for the sales force. The disadvantages of using merchandise include administrative complications and problems with perceived value on the part of recipients.[17] Some companies outsource their incentive programs to expert companies such as O. C. Tanner, which manufactures custom medals and jewelry for employee-recognition programs and administers corporate-recognition programs.[18]

● **Managing Sales Territories.**   The effectiveness of a sales force that must travel to customers is somewhat influenced by management's decisions regarding sales territories. When deciding on territories, sales managers must consider size, shape, routing, and scheduling.

Several factors enter into the design of a sales territory's size and shape. First, sales managers must construct territories so that sales potential can be measured. Sales territories often consist of several geographic units, such as census tracts, cities, counties, or states, for which market data are obtainable. Sales managers usually try to create territories with similar sales potential or requiring about the same amount

Managing Sales Territories
Dell workstations provide mobile technology support for sales managers on the road.

of work. If territories have equal sales potential, they will almost always be unequal in geographic size. Salespeople with larger territories have to work longer and harder to generate a certain sales volume. Conversely, if sales territories requiring equal amounts of work are created, sales potential for those territories will often vary. At times sales managers use commercial programs to help them balance sales territories. Although a sales manager seeks equity when developing and maintaining sales territories, some inequities always prevail. A territory's size and shape should also help the sales force provide the best possible customer coverage and should minimize selling costs. Customer density and distribution are important factors.

The geographic size and shape of a sales territory are the most important factors affecting the routing and scheduling of sales calls. Next in importance are the number and distribution of customers within the territory, followed by sales call frequency and duration. In some firms, salespeople plan their own routes and schedules with little or no assistance from the sales manager; in other organizations, the sales manager draws up the routes and schedules. No matter who plans the routing and scheduling, the major goals should be to minimize salespeople's nonselling time (time spent traveling and waiting) and maximize their selling time. Planners should try to achieve these goals so that a salesperson's travel and lodging costs are held to a minimum.

● **Controlling and Evaluating Sales Force Performance.** To control and evaluate sales force performance properly, sales managers need information. A sales manager can use call reports, customer feedback, and invoices. Call reports identify the customers called on and present detailed information about interaction with those clients. In addition, sales managers can keep abreast of a salesperson's activities through Web-enabled mobile phones and personal digital assistants.[19] Data about a salesperson's interactions with customers and prospects can be included in the company's customer relationship management system. This information provides insights about the salesperson's performance.

Dimensions used to measure a salesperson's performance are determined largely by sales objectives, normally set by the sales manager. If an individual's sales objective is stated in terms of sales volume, that person should be evaluated on the basis of sales volume generated. Sales managers often evaluate many performance indicators, including average number of calls per day, average sales per customer, actual sales relative to sales potential, number of new-customer orders, average cost per call, and average gross profit per customer.

To evaluate a salesperson, a sales manager may compare one or more of these dimensions with predetermined performance standards. However, sales managers commonly compare a salesperson's performance with that of other employees operating under similar selling conditions or the salesperson's current performance with past performance. Sometimes management judges factors that have less direct bearing on sales performance, such as personal appearance and product knowledge. The positive relationship between organizational commitment and job performance is stronger for sales personnel than for nonsales employees.[20]

After evaluating salespeople, sales managers take any needed corrective action to improve sales force performance. They may adjust performance standards, provide additional training, or try other motivational methods. Corrective action may demand comprehensive changes in the sales force.

What Is Sales Promotion?

sales promotion An activity and/or material meant to induce resellers or salespeople to sell a product or consumers to buy it

Sales promotion is an activity or material, or both, that acts as a direct inducement, offering added value or incentive for the product, to resellers, salespeople, or consumers. It encompasses all promotional activities and materials other than personal selling, advertising, and public relations. In competitive markets, where products are very similar, sales promotion provides additional inducements that encourage product trial and purchase.

Marketers often use sales promotion to facilitate personal selling, advertising, or both. Companies also employ advertising and personal selling to support sales promotion activities. For example, marketers frequently use advertising to promote contests, free samples, and premiums. The most effective sales promotion efforts are highly interrelated with other promotional activities. Decisions regarding sales promotion often affect advertising and personal selling decisions, and vice versa.

Sales promotion can increase sales by providing extra purchasing incentives. Many opportunities exist to motivate consumers, resellers, and salespeople to take desired actions. Some kinds of sales promotion are designed specifically to stimulate resellers' demand and effectiveness, some are directed at increasing consumer demand, and some focus on both consumers and resellers. Regardless of the purpose, marketers must ensure that sales promotion objectives are consistent with the organization's overall objectives, as well as with its marketing and promotion objectives.

When deciding which sales promotion methods to use, marketers must consider several factors, particularly product characteristics (size, weight, costs, durability, uses, features, and hazards) and target market characteristics (age, gender, income, location, density, usage rate, and shopping patterns). How products are distributed and the number and types of resellers may determine the type of method used. The competitive and legal environment may also influence the choice.

The use of sales promotion has increased dramatically over the last twenty years, primarily at the expense of advertising. This shift in how promotional dollars are used has occurred for several reasons. Heightened concerns about value have made customers more responsive to promotional offers, especially price discounts and point-of-purchase displays. Thanks to their size and access to checkout scanner data, retailers have gained considerable power in the supply chain and are demanding greater promotional efforts from manufacturers to boost retail profits. Declines in brand loyalty have produced an environment in which sales promotions aimed at persuading customers to switch brands are more effective. Finally, the stronger emphasis placed on improving short-term performance results calls for greater use of sales promotion methods that yield quick (albeit perhaps short-lived) sales increases.[21]

In the remainder of this chapter, we examine several consumer and trade sales promotion methods, including what they entail and what goals they can help marketers achieve.

⦿ Consumer Sales Promotion Methods

consumer sales promotion methods Ways of encouraging consumers to patronize specific stores or try particular products

Consumer sales promotion methods encourage or stimulate consumers to patronize specific retail stores or try particular products. These methods initiated by retailers often aim to attract customers to specific locations, whereas those used by manufacturers generally introduce new products or promote established brands. In this section we discuss coupons, cents-off offers, money refunds and rebates, frequent-user incentives, demonstrations, point-of-purchase displays, free samples, premiums, consumer contests and games, and consumer sweepstakes.

coupons Written price reductions used to encourage consumers to buy a specific product

● **Coupons and Cents-Off Offers.** **Coupons** reduce a product's price and are used to prompt customers to try new or established products, increase sales volume quickly, attract repeat purchasers, or introduce new package sizes or features. Savings may be deducted from the purchase price or offered as cash. Research indicates that coupons are most effective when a small face-value coupon is used in conjunction with a lower product price available for all consumers.[22] Coupons are the most widely used consumer sales promotion technique. In 2003, consumer packaged goods manufacturers distributed 258 billion coupons, of which 3.6 billion were redeemed, saving consumers an estimated $3 billion. Nearly 80 percent of all consumers use coupons.[23] Table 18.3 shows the product categories with the greatest distribution of coupons.

For best results, the coupons should be easy to recognize and state the offer clearly. The nature of the product (seasonal demand for it, life cycle stage, frequency of purchase) is the prime consideration in setting up a coupon promotion. Paper coupons are distributed on and in packages, through freestanding inserts (FSIs), in print advertising, and through direct mail. Electronic coupons are distributed online, via in-store kiosks, through shelf dispensers in stores, and at checkout counters. When deciding on the distribution method for coupons, marketers should consider strategies and objectives, redemption rates, availability, circulation, and exclusivity. The coupon distribution and redemption arena has become

Coupons
Coupons should be easily recognized and should state the offer clearly as in this Crayola advertisement.

Table 18.3

Product Categories with the Greatest Distribution of Coupons

1. Household cleaners
2. Medications, remedies, health aids
3. Paper products
4. Detergents
5. Condiments, gravies, sauces

Source: Natalie Schwartz, "Clipping Path," *Promo,* April 1, 2004, http://promomagazine.com/mag/marketing_clipping_path.

very competitive. To draw customers to their stores, some grocers double and sometimes even triple the value of customers' coupons.

Coupons offer several advantages. Print advertisements with coupons are often more effective at generating brand awareness than are print ads without coupons. In China, research has found that coupons positively influence consumer attitudes toward a brand.[24] Generally, the larger the coupon's cash offer, the better the recognition generated. Coupons reward present product users, win back former users, and encourage purchases in larger quantities. Because they are returned, coupons also let a manufacturer determine whether it reached the intended target market. The advantages of using electronic coupons over paper coupons include lower cost per redemption, greater targeting ability, improved data-gathering capabilities, and improved experimentation capabilities to determine optimal face values and expiration cycles.[25] On the other hand, motivated consumers are likely to consider information in a print coupon more carefully than in an online coupon.[26]

Drawbacks of coupon use include fraud and misredemption, which can be expensive for manufacturers. The Coupon Information Council estimates that coupon fraud—including counterfeit Internet coupons as well as coupons cashed in under false retailer names—amounts to $500 million a year in the United States.[27] Another disadvantage, according to some experts, is that coupons are losing their value; because so many manufacturers offer them, consumers have learned not to buy without some incentive, whether it is a coupon, rebate, or refund. Furthermore, brand loyalty among heavy coupon users has diminished, and many consumers redeem coupons only for products they normally buy. It is believed that about three-fourths of coupons are redeemed by people already using the brand on the coupon. Thus, coupons have questionable success as an incentive for consumers to try a new brand or product. An additional problem with coupons is that stores often do not have enough of the coupon item in stock. This situation generates ill will toward both the store and the product.

cents-off offer   A promotion that lets buyers pay less than the regular price to encourage purchase

With a **cents-off offer**, buyers pay a certain amount less than the regular price shown on the label or package. Similar to coupons, this method can be a strong incentive for trying products. It can stimulate product sales, yield short-lived sales increases, and promote products in off-seasons. It is an easy method to control and is often used for specific purposes. If used on an ongoing basis, however, cents-off offers reduce the price for customers who would buy at the regular price and may also cheapen a product's image. In addition, the method often requires special handling by retailers.

money refunds   A sales promotion technique offering consumers money when they mail in a proof of purchase, usually for multiple product purchases

● **Refunds and Rebates.**   With **money refunds**, consumers submit proof of purchase and are mailed a specific amount of money. Usually manufacturers demand multiple product purchases before consumers qualify for refunds. With **rebates**, the customer is sent a specified amount of money for making a single purchase. Money refunds, used primarily to promote trial use of a product, are relatively low in cost, but because they sometimes generate a low response rate, they have limited impact on sales.

rebates   A sales promotion technique whereby a customer is sent a specific amount of money for purchasing a single product

One problem with money refunds and rebates is that many people perceive the redemption process as too complicated. Only about half of individuals who purchase rebated products actually apply for the rebates.[28] Consumers may also have negative perceptions of manufacturers' reasons for offering rebates. They may believe the products are new, are untested, or haven't sold well. If these perceptions are not changed, rebate offers may actually degrade the image and desirability of the products.

point-of-purchase (P-O-P) materials   Signs, window displays, display racks, and similar means used to attract customers

demonstrations   A sales promotion method manufacturers use temporarily to encourage trial use and purchase of a product or to show how a product works

free samples   Samples of a product given out to encourage trial and purchase

● **Frequent-User Incentives.**   Do you have a "Sub Club Card" from Subway? Many firms develop incentive programs to reward customers who engage in repeat (frequent) purchases. As mentioned earlier, most major airlines offer frequent-flier programs that reward customers who have flown a specified number of miles with free tickets for additional travel. Frequent-user incentives foster customer loyalty to a specific company or group of cooperating companies. They are favored by service businesses, such as airlines, auto rental agencies, hotels, and restaurants. Hilton hotels, for example, uses its Hilton Honors program to reward travelers who stay at its hotels with points redeemable for stays at Hilton hotels and travel adventures such as African safaris. To encourage members to try its Hampton Inn chain, the company created a special program awarding 1 million Hilton Honors points to one Hampton Inn guest every month.[29]

● **Point-of-Purchase Materials and Demonstrations.**   **Point-of-purchase (P-O-P) materials** include outdoor signs, window displays, counter pieces, display racks, and self-service cartons. Innovations in P-O-P displays include sniff-teasers, which give off a product's aroma in the store as consumers walk within a radius of four feet, and computerized interactive displays. These items, often supplied by producers, attract attention, inform customers, and encourage retailers to carry particular products. A retailer is likely to use P-O-P materials if they are attractive, informative, well constructed, and in harmony with the store's image.

Demonstrations are excellent attention getters. Manufacturers offer them temporarily to encourage trial use and purchase of a product or to show how a product works. Because labor costs can be extremely high, demonstrations are not used widely. They can be highly effective for promoting certain types of products, such as appliances, cosmetics, and cleaning supplies. Cosmetics marketers, such as Merle Norman and Clinique, sometimes offer potential customers "makeovers" to demonstrate product benefits and proper application.

● **Free Samples and Premiums.**   Marketers use **free samples** to stimulate trial of a product, increase sales volume in the early stages of a product's life cycle, and obtain desirable distribution. Sampling is the most expensive sales promotion method because production and distribution—at local events, by mail or door-to-door delivery, online, in stores, and on packages—entail high costs. Nivea, for example, distributed more than 3 million samples of its Nivea Soft moisturizer, as well as coupons, at events, festivals, and carnivals across the nation.[30] Many consumers prefer to get their samples by mail. In designing a free sample, marketers should consider factors such as seasonal demand for the product, market

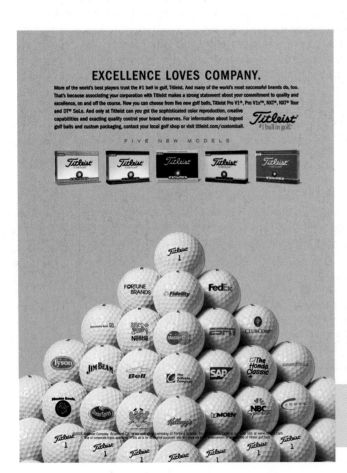

Premiums
Titleist provides logoed golf balls for firms that want to provide loyalty to a brand name.

characteristics, and prior advertising. Free samples usually are not appropriate for slow-turnover products. Despite high costs, use of sampling is increasing. In a given year, almost three-fourths of consumer product companies may use sampling. Distribution of free samples through websites such as StartSampling.com and FreeSamples.com is growing.

premiums Items offered free or at a minimal cost as a bonus for purchasing a product

Premiums are items offered free or at minimal cost as a bonus for purchasing a product. They are used to attract competitors' customers, introduce different sizes of established products, add variety to other promotional efforts, and stimulate consumer loyalty. Creativity is essential when using premiums; to stand out and achieve a significant number of redemptions, the premium must match both the target audience and the brand's image. Premiums must also be easily recognizable and desirable. Premiums are placed on or in packages and can also be distributed by retailers or through the mail. Examples include a service station giving a free carwash with a fill-up, a free toothbrush available with a tube of toothpaste, and a free plastic storage box given with the purchase of Kraft Cheese Singles.

consumer contests and games Sales promotion methods in which individuals compete for prizes based on analytical or creative skills

consumer sweepstakes A sales promotion in which entrants submit their names for inclusion in a drawing for prizes

● **Consumer Games, Contests, and Sweepstakes.**   In consumer contests and games, individuals compete for prizes based on analytical or creative skills. Entrants in a consumer sweepstakes submit their names for inclusion in a drawing for prizes. The Campbell Soup Company, for example, sponsored a "Taste and Live the Best of Life" sweepstakes, with a $50,000 kitchen makeover as the grand prize, to promote its soups and other products.[31] Sweepstakes are employed more often than consumer contests and tend to attract a greater number of participants. However, contestants are usually more involved in consumer contests and games than in sweepstakes, even though total participation may be lower. Contests, games, and sweepstakes may be used in conjunction with other sales promotion methods, such as coupons. It is important to know regulations and laws for contests and sweepstakes because some state laws may view some types of events as forms of gambling or lotteries.[32]

◉ Trade Sales Promotion Methods

trade sales promotion methods Ways of persuading wholesalers and retailers to carry a producer's products and market them aggressively

To encourage resellers, especially retailers, to carry their products and to promote them effectively, producers use sales promotion methods. Trade sales promotion methods stimulate wholesalers and retailers to carry a producer's products and market those products more aggressively. These methods include buying allowances, buy-back allowances, scan-back allowances, merchandise allowances, cooperative advertising, dealer listings, free merchandise, dealer loaders, premium or push money, and sales contests.

buying allowance A temporary price reduction to resellers for purchasing specified quantities of a product

● **Trade Allowances.**   Many manufacturers offer trade allowances to encourage resellers to carry a product or stock more of it. One such trade allowance is a buying allowance, which is a temporary price reduction offered to resellers for purchasing specified quantities of a product. A soap producer, for example, might give retailers $1 for each case of soap purchased. Such offers provide an incentive for resellers to handle new products, achieve temporary price reductions, or stimulate purchase of items in larger than normal quantities. The buying allowance, which takes the form of money, yields profits to resellers and is simple and straightforward. There are no restrictions on how resellers use the money, which increases the method's effectiveness. One drawback of buying allowances is that customers may buy "forward," meaning that they buy large amounts that keep them supplied for many months. Another problem is that competitors may match (or beat) the reduced price, which can lower profits for all sellers.

buy-back allowance   A sum of money given to a reseller for each unit bought after an initial promotion deal is over

scan-back allowance
A manufacturer's reward to retailers based on the number of pieces scanned

merchandise allowance
A manufacturer's agreement to pay resellers certain amounts of money for providing special promotional efforts

cooperative advertising   An arrangement in which a manufacturer agrees to pay a certain amount of a retailer's media costs for advertising the manufacturer's products.

dealer listing   An advertisement that promotes a product and identifies the names of participating retailers that sell the product

free merchandise   A manufacturer's reward given to resellers for purchasing a stated quantity of products

dealer loader   A gift, often part of a display, given to a retailer purchasing a specified quantity of merchandise

premium money (or **push money**)   Also called push money; extra compensation to salespeople for pushing a line of goods

A **buy-back allowance** is a sum of money that a producer gives to a reseller for each unit the reseller buys after an initial promotional deal is over. This method is a secondary incentive in which the total amount of money that resellers receive is proportional to their purchases during an initial consumer promotion, such as a coupon offer. Buy-back allowances foster cooperation during an initial sales promotion effort and stimulate repurchase afterward. The main disadvantage of this method is expense.

A **scan-back allowance** is a manufacturer's reward to retailers based on the number of pieces moved through the retailers' scanners during a specific time period. To participate in scan-back programs, retailers are usually expected to pass along savings to consumers through special pricing. Scan-backs are becoming widely used by manufacturers because they link trade spending directly to product movement at the retail level.

A **merchandise allowance** is a manufacturer's agreement to pay resellers certain amounts of money for providing promotional efforts such as advertising or P-O-P displays. This method is best suited to high-volume, high-profit, easily handled products. A drawback is that some retailers perform activities at a minimally acceptable level simply to obtain allowances. Before paying retailers, manufacturers usually verify their performance. Manufacturers hope that retailers' additional promotional efforts will yield substantial sales increases.

● **Cooperative Advertising and Dealer Listings.**   **Cooperative advertising** is an arrangement whereby a manufacturer agrees to pay a certain amount of a retailer's media costs for advertising the manufacturer's products. The amount allowed is usually based on the quantities purchased. As with merchandise allowances, a retailer must show proof that advertisements did appear before the manufacturer pays the agreed-upon portion of the advertising costs. These payments give retailers additional funds for advertising. Some retailers exploit cooperative-advertising agreements by crowding too many products into one advertisement. Not all available cooperative-advertising dollars are used. Some retailers cannot afford to advertise, while others can afford it but do not want to advertise. A large proportion of all cooperative-advertising dollars are spent on newspaper advertisements.

Dealer listings are advertisements promoting a product and identifying participating retailers that sell the product. Dealer listings can influence retailers to carry the product, build traffic at the retail level, and encourage consumers to buy the product at participating dealers.

● **Free Merchandise and Gifts.**   Manufacturers sometimes offer **free merchandise** to resellers that purchase a stated quantity of products. Occasionally, free merchandise is used as payment for allowances provided through other sales promotion methods. To avoid handling and bookkeeping problems, the "free" merchandise usually takes the form of a reduced invoice.

A **dealer loader** is a gift to a retailer who purchases a specified quantity of merchandise. Dealer loaders are often used to obtain special display efforts from retailers by offering essential display parts as premiums. For example, a manufacturer might design a display that includes a sterling silver tray as a major component and give the tray to the retailer. Marketers use dealer loaders to obtain new distributors and to push larger quantities of goods.

● **Premium (Push) Money.**   **Premium money** (or **push money**) is additional compensation to salespeople offered by the manufacturer as an incentive to push a line of goods. This method is appropriate when personal selling is an important part of the marketing effort; it is not effective for promoting products sold through self-service. The method often helps manufacturers obtain a commitment from the sales force, but it can be very expensive.

sales contest A promotion method used to motivate distributors, retailers, and sales personnel through recognition of outstanding achievements

● **Sales Contests.** A **sales contest** is designed to motivate distributors, retailers, and sales personnel by recognizing outstanding achievements. To be effective, this method must be equitable for all persons involved. One advantage is that it can achieve participation at all distribution levels. Positive effects may be temporary, however, and prizes are usually expensive.

CHAPTER REVIEW

① Define personal selling and understand its purpose.
Personal selling is paid personal communication that attempts to inform customers and persuade them to purchase products in an exchange situation. Three general purposes of personal selling are finding prospects, persuading them to buy, and keeping customers satisfied.

② Describe the basic steps in the personal-selling process.
Many salespeople move through a general selling process when they sell products. In prospecting, the salesperson develops a list of potential customers. Before contacting prospects, the salesperson conducts a preapproach that involves finding and analyzing information about prospects and their needs. The approach is the way in which a salesperson contacts potential customers. During the sales presentation, the salesperson must attract and hold the prospect's attention to stimulate interest in and desire for the product. If possible, the salesperson should handle objections as they arise. During the closing, the salesperson asks the prospect to buy the product or products. After a successful closing, the salesperson must follow up the sale.

③ Identify the types of sales force personnel.
In developing a sales force, marketing managers consider which types of salespeople will sell the firm's products most effectively. The three classifications of salespeople are order getters, order takers, and support personnel. Order getters inform both current customers and new prospects and persuade them to buy. Order takers seek repeat sales and fall into two categories: inside order takers and field order takers.

Sales support personnel facilitate selling but their duties usually extend beyond making sales. The three types of support personnel are missionary, trade, and technical salespeople.

④ Understand sales management decisions and activities.
Sales force management is an important determinant of a firm's success because the sales force is directly responsible for generating the organization's sales revenue. Major decision areas and activities include establishing sales force objectives; determining sales force size; recruiting, selecting, training, compensating, and motivating salespeople; managing sales territories; and controlling and evaluating sales force performance.

⑤ Explain what sales promotion activities are and how they are used.
Sales promotion is an activity or a material (or both) that acts as a direct inducement, offering added value or incentive for the product to resellers, salespeople, or consumers. Marketers use sales promotion to identify and attract new customers, introduce new products, and increase reseller inventories.

⑥ Recognize specific consumer and trade sales promotion methods.
Sales promotion techniques fall into two general categories: consumer and trade. Consumer sales promotion methods encourage consumers to trade at specific stores or try a specific product. These sales promotion methods include coupons, cents-off offers, money refunds and rebates, frequent-user incentives, point-of-purchase displays, demonstrations, free samples, premiums, and consumer

contests, games, and sweepstakes. Trade sales promotion techniques can motivate resellers to handle a manufacturer's products and market those products aggressively. These sales promotion techniques include buying allowances, buy-back allowances, scan-back allowances, merchandise allowances, cooperative advertising, dealer listings, free merchandise, dealer loaders, premium (or push) money, and sales contests.

Please visit the student website at www.prideferrell.com for ACE Self-Test questions that will help you prepare for exams.

KEY CONCEPTS

personal selling
prospecting
approach
closing
order getter
order takers
support personnel
missionary salespeople
trade salespeople
technical salespeople
straight salary
   compensation plan

straight commission
   compensation plan
combination
   compensation plan
sales promotion
consumer sales promotion
   methods
coupons
cents-off offer
money refunds
rebates

point-of-purchase (P-O-P)
   materials
demonstrations
free samples
premiums
consumer contests and
   games
consumer sweepstakes
trade sales promotion
   methods
buying allowance

buy-back allowance
scan-back allowance
merchandise allowance
cooperative advertising
dealer listing
free merchandise
dealer loader
premium money
sales contest

ISSUES FOR DISCUSSION AND REVIEW

1. What is personal selling? How does personal selling relate to other types of promotional activities?

2. Identify the elements of the personal selling process. Must a salesperson include all these elements when selling a product to a customer? Why or why not?

3. How does a salesperson find and evaluate prospects? Do you consider any of these methods to be ethically questionable? Explain.

4. Are order getters more aggressive or creative than order takers? Why or why not?

5. How should a sales manager establish criteria for selecting sales personnel? What do you think are the general characteristics of a good salesperson?

6. What major issues or questions should management consider when developing a training program for the sales force?

7. Explain the major advantages and disadvantages of the three basic methods of compensating salespeople. In general, which method would you prefer? Why?

8. How does a sales manager, who cannot be with each salesperson in the field on a daily basis, control the performance of sales personnel?

9. What is sales promotion? Why is it used?

10. For each of the following, identify and describe three techniques, and give several examples: (a) consumer sales promotion methods and (b) trade sales promotion methods.

MARKETING APPLICATIONS

1. Briefly describe an experience you have had with a salesperson at a clothing store or an automobile dealership. Describe the steps used by the salesperson. Did the salesperson skip any steps? What did the salesperson do well? Not so well?

2. Refer to your answer to Marketing Application 1. Would you describe the salesperson as an order getter, an order taker, or a support salesperson? Why? Did the salesperson perform more than one of these functions?

3. Identify a familiar type of retail store or product. Recommend at least three sales promotion methods that should be used to promote the store or product. Explain why you would use these methods.

4. Identify which method or methods of sales promotion a producer might use in the following situations, and explain why the method would be appropriate.
   a. A golf ball manufacturer wants to encourage retailers to add a new type of golf ball to current product offerings.
   b. A life insurance company wants to increase sales of its universal life products, which have been lagging recently (the company has little control over sales activities).
   c. A light bulb manufacturer with an overproduction of 100-watt bulbs wants to encourage its grocery store chain resellers to increase their bulb inventories.

ONLINE EXERCISE

5. TerrAlign offers consulting services and software products designed to help a firm maximize control and deployment of its field sales representatives. Review its website at **www.terralign.com.**
   a. Identify three features of TerrAlign software that are likely to benefit salespeople.
   b. Identify three features of TerrAlign software that are likely to benefit sales managers.
   c. Why might field sales professionals object to the use of software from TerrAlign?

VIDEO CASE

Selling Bicycles and More at Wheelworks

From tricycles to tandems, Wheelworks sells just about every kind of bicycle. Founded in the 1970s, this three-store chain in suburban Boston has been named one of the top ten in the United States for more than a decade. The chain currently markets more than 10,000 bicycles and brings in $10.5 million in sales revenue every year, with a staff of 45 full-time employees plus 55 additional employees to handle seasonal sales spikes.

Wheelworks' salespeople are cycling enthusiasts who are extremely knowledgeable about the company's products and enjoy sharing what they know with customers. Some were recruited through referrals and personal contacts with store staff, who often participate in local cycling groups. Others were hired after replying to job openings posted on the Wheelworks website. New salespeople hired for the main store go through a formal training program. At the two branch stores, experienced salespeople act as mentors to new hires in an informal buddy system that supplements on-the-job training. All of the firm's salespeople have the opportunity to gain more product knowledge and ask questions when manufacturers' representatives visit. In addition, they can take classes to become certified in technical skills such as fitting bicycles.

Wheelworks doesn't believe in scripted sales pitches. Instead its salespeople focus on building relationships by asking questions, providing information, and making suggestions to match the right product to the right customer. Kurt Begemann, a competitive racer who sells at Wheelworks, says that "it's better to be seen as a teacher than to be seen as a salesperson." To keep their product knowledge updated, salespeople attend three to five in-store training clinics every month, each focusing on a particular product, product category, or manufacturer. From time to time, the sales manager appeals to his team's competitive spirit to spur higher closing rates as salespeople strive to match or exceed their colleagues' sales accomplishments.

Just as the salespeople work hard to match the right product to the right customer, Doug Shoemaker, the sales manager, works hard to match the right salesperson to the right customer. When a new Wheelworks customer begins browsing the sales floor, Shoemaker makes the initial approach, quickly sizes up the customer's needs and interests, and then brings in the salesperson he believes will work best with that customer. Even language poses no barrier, because staff members speak French, Italian, Spanish, and Chinese.

After a sale is closed, sales personnel add that customer's name and address to the firm's mailing list to receive announcements of upcoming special events and sales. The store also invites customers to bring their new bicycles back for a free tune-up after 30 days. This allows salespeople to follow up by checking on customer satisfaction and making any necessary adjustments.

Wheelworks sales personnel receive competitive retail wages and benefits such as health insurance coverage, vacation and sick pay, profit sharing, and store discounts. They are also rewarded with seasonal bonuses tied to the company's sales achievements rather than to individual sales records. Sales manager Shoemaker stresses that this compensation method gives his salespeople the freedom to sell the right product for each customer's needs rather than trying to earn a special incentive by selling an item that's not right for the customer. The salespeople also prefer this compensation method. Salesperson Juliana Popper says that Wheelworks customers "don't feel preyed upon" because they know the salespeople aren't trying to make more money by selling higher-priced bicycles.

Each salesperson sets goals for personal development as well as for store sales contributions. Store managers formally evaluate the performance of new salespeople six months after the salespeople are hired, and then on an annual basis. But sales personnel don't have to wait months to find out how they are doing. Because Wheelworks is not a huge organization, managers and peers constantly provide informal feedback and support. And salespeople who turn out to be stronger or more interested in nonsales activities can easily transfer, because at Wheelworks everybody, from the repair technicians to the graphic designer, has an important role to play in the personal selling process.[33]

QUESTIONS FOR DISCUSSION

1. Which of the three types of sales force compensation methods does Wheelworks use? Should Wheelworks change to another method? Why?
2. How does Wheelworks motivate sales personnel?
3. What type of salesperson is Kurt Begemann? Explain.

Appendix: Careers in Marketing

 ## Changes in the Workplace

Between one-fourth and one-third of the civilian work force in the United States is employed in marketing-related jobs. Although the field offers a multitude of diverse career opportunities, the number of positions in each area varies. For example, millions of workers are employed in many facets of sales, but relatively few people work in public relations and marketing research.

Many nonbusiness organizations now recognize that they perform marketing activities. For that reason, the number of marketing positions in government agencies, hospitals, charitable and religious groups, educational institutions, and similar organizations is increasing. Today's nonprofit organizations are competitive and better managed, with job growth rates often matching those of private-sector firms. Another area ripe with opportunities is online. With so many businesses setting up websites, demand will rise for people who have the skills to develop and design marketing strategies for the Web.

Many workers outplaced from large corporations are choosing an entrepreneurial path, creating still more new opportunities for first-time job seekers. Even some of those who have secure managerial positions are leaving corporations and heading to smaller companies, toward greater responsibility and autonomy. The traditional career path used to be graduation from college, then a job with a large corporation, and a climb up the ladder to management. This pattern has changed, however. Today people are more likely to experience a career path of sideways "gigs" rather than sequential steps up a corporate ladder.

Career Choices Are Major Life Choices

Many people think career planning begins with an up-to-date résumé and a job interview.[1] In reality, it begins long before you prepare your résumé. It starts with *you* and what you want to become. In some ways, you have been preparing for a career ever since you started school. Everything you have experienced during your lifetime you can use as a resource to help you define your career goals. Since you will likely spend more time at work than at any other single place during your lifetime, it makes sense to spend that time doing something you enjoy. Some people just work at a *job* because they need money to survive. Other people choose a *career* because of their interests and talents or commitment to a particular profession. Whether you are looking for a job or a career, you should examine your priorities.

◉ Personal Factors Influencing Career Choices

Before choosing a career, you need to consider what motivates you and what skills you can offer an employer. The following questions may help you define what you consider important in life.

1. *What types of activities do you enjoy?* Although most people know what they enjoy in a general way, a number of interest inventories exist. By helping you determine specific interests and activities, these inventories can help you land a job that will

lead to a satisfying career. In some cases, it may be sufficient just to list the activities you enjoy, along with those you dislike. Watch for patterns that may influence your career choices.

2. *What do you do best?* All jobs and all careers require employees to be able to "do something." It is extremely important to assess what you do best. Be honest with yourself about your ability to succeed in a specific job. It may help to make a list of your strongest job-related skills. Also, try looking at your skills from an employer's perspective: What can you do that an employer would be willing to pay for?

3. *What kind of education will you need?* The amount of education you need is determined by the type of career you choose. In some careers, it is impossible to get an entry-level position without at least a college degree. In other careers, technical or hands-on skills may also be important. Generally, more education increases your potential earning power.

4. *Where do you want to live?* Initially some college graduates will want to move to a different part of the country before entering the job market, whereas others may prefer to reside close to home, friends, and relatives. In reality, successful job applicants must be willing to go where the jobs are. The location of an entry-level job may be influenced by the type of marketing career selected. For example, some of the largest advertising agencies are in New York, Chicago, and Los Angeles. Likewise, large marketing research organizations are based in metropolitan areas. On the other hand, sales positions and retail management jobs are available in medium-size as well as large cities.

Job Search Activities

When people begin to search for a job, they often first go online or turn to the classified ads in their local newspaper. Those ads are an important source of information about jobs in a particular area, but they are only one source. Many other sources can lead to employment and a satisfying career. Because there is a wealth of information about career planning, you should be selective in both the type and the amount of information you use to guide your job search.

In recent years the library, a traditional job-hunting tool, has been joined by the Internet. Both the library and the Internet are sources of everything from classified newspaper ads and government job listings to detailed information on individual companies and industries. You can use either resource to research an area of employment or a particular company that interests you. In addition, the Internet allows you to check electronic bulletin boards for current job information, exchange ideas with other job seekers through online discussion groups or e-mail, and get career advice from professional counselors. You can also create your own webpage to inform prospective employers of your qualifications. You may even have a job interview online. Many companies use their websites to post job openings, accept applications, and interview candidates.

As you start your job search, you may find the following websites helpful. (Addresses of additional career-related websites can be accessed through the Student Career Center at www.prideferrell.com.)

America's Job Bank: www.ajb.dni.us
This massive site contains information on nearly 250,000 jobs. Listings come from 1,800 state employment offices around the country and represent every

line of work, from professional and technical to blue-collar, and from entry level on up.

CareerBuilder: www.careerbuilder.com
This site is one of the largest on the Internet, with more than 900,000 jobs to view. The site allows a job seeker to find jobs, post résumés, get advice and career resources, and obtain information on career fairs.

Hoover's Online: www.hoovers.com
Hoover's offers a variety of job search tools, including information on potential employers and links to sites that post job openings.

Monster: www.monster.com
Monster carries hundreds of pages of job listings and offers links to related sites, such as company homepages and a site with information about job fairs.

Federal jobs: www.fedworld.gov/jobs/jobsearch.html
If you are interested in working for a government agency, this site lists positions across the country. You can limit your search to specific states or do a general cross-country search for job openings.

Other web addresses for job seekers include:

www.careers-in-marketing.com

www.marketingjobs.com

www.careermag.com

www.salary.com

In addition to the library and the Internet, the following sources can be of great help when trying to find the "perfect job":

1. *Campus placement offices.* Colleges and universities have placement offices staffed by trained personnel specialists. In most cases, these offices serve as clearinghouses for career information. The staff may also be able to guide you in creating a résumé and preparing for a job interview.

2. *Professional sources and networks.* A network is a group of people—friends, relatives, and professionals—who are in a position to exchange information, including information about job openings. According to many job applicants, networking is one of the best sources of career information and job leads. Start with as many people as you can think of to establish your network. (The Internet can be very useful in this regard.) Contact these people and ask specific questions about job opportunities they may be aware of. Also, ask each individual to introduce or refer you to someone else who may be able to help you in your job search.

3. *Private employment agencies.* Private employment agencies charge a fee for helping people find jobs. Typical fees can be as high as 15 to 20 percent of an employee's first-year salary. The fee may be paid by the employer or the employee. Like campus placement offices, private employment agencies provide career counseling, help create résumés, and provide preparation for job interviews. Before you use a private employment agency, be sure you understand the terms of any contract or agreement you sign. Above all, make sure you know who is responsible for paying the agency's fee.

4. *State employment agencies.* The local office of your state employment agency is a source of information about job openings in your immediate area. Some job applicants are reluctant to use state agencies because most jobs available through them are for semiskilled or unskilled workers. From a practical standpoint, though, it can't hurt to consult state employment agencies. They will have

information about some professional and managerial positions available in your area, and you will not be charged a fee if you obtain a job through one of these agencies.

Many graduates want a job immediately and are discouraged at the thought that an occupational search can take months. But people seeking entry-level jobs should expect their job search to take considerable time. Of course, the state of the economy and whether or not employers are hiring can shorten or extend a job search.

During a job search, you should use the same work habits that effective employees use on the job. Resist the temptation to "take the day off" from job hunting. Instead, make a master list of the activities you want to accomplish each day. If necessary, force yourself to make contacts, do job research, or schedule interviews that might lead to job opportunities. (In fact, many job applicants look at the job hunt as their actual job and "work" full time at it until they find the job they want.) Above all, realize that an occupational search requires patience and perseverance. According to many successful applicants, perseverance may be the job hunter's most valuable trait.

Planning and Preparation

The key to landing the job you want is planning and preparation—and planning begins with goals. In particular, it is important to determine your *personal* goals, decide on the role your career will play in reaching those goals, and then develop your *career* goals. Once you know where you are going, you can devise a feasible plan for getting there.

The time to begin planning is as early as possible. You must, of course, satisfy the educational requirements for the occupational area you desire. Early planning will give you the opportunity to do so. However, some of the people who will compete with you for the better jobs will also be fully prepared. Can you do more? Company recruiters say the following factors give job candidates a definite advantage:

- *Work experience.* You can get valuable work experience in cooperative work/school programs, during summer vacations, or in part-time jobs during the school year. Experience in your chosen occupational area carries the most weight, but even unrelated work experience is useful.

- *The ability to communicate well.* Verbal and written communications skills are increasingly important in all aspects of business. Yours will be tested in your letters to recruiters, in your résumé, and in interviews. You will use these same communication skills throughout your career.

- *Clear and realistic job and career goals.* Recruiters feel most comfortable with candidates who know where they are headed and why they are applying for a specific job.

Again, starting early will allow you to establish well-defined goals, sharpen your communication skills (through elective courses, if necessary), and obtain solid work experience. To develop your own personal career plan, go to the www.prideferrell. com student site and access the Student Career Center. There you will find personal career plan worksheets.

The Résumé

An effective résumé is one of the keys to being considered for a good job. Because your résumé states your qualifications, experiences, education, and career goals, a potential employer can use it to assess your compatibility with the job requirements. The résumé should be accurate and current.

In preparing a résumé, it helps to think of it as an advertisement. Envision yourself as a product and the company, particularly the person or persons doing the hiring, as your customer. To interest the customer in buying the product—hiring you—your résumé must communicate information about your qualities and indicate how you can satisfy the customer's needs—that is, how you can help the company achieve its objectives. The information in the résumé should persuade the organization to take a closer look at you by calling you in for an interview.

To be effective, the résumé should be targeted at a specific position, as Figure A.1 shows. This document is only one example of an acceptable résumé. The job target section is specific and leads directly to the applicant's qualifications for the job. The qualifications section details capabilities—what the applicant can do—and also shows that the applicant has an understanding of the job's requirements. Skills and strengths that relate to the specific job should be emphasized. The achievement section ("Experiences" in Figure A.1) indicates success at accomplishing tasks or goals on the job and at school. The work experience section in Figure A.1 includes an unusual listing, which might pique the interest of an interviewer: "helped operate relative's blueberry farm in Michigan for three summers." That is something that could help launch an interview discussion. It tends to inspire, rather than satisfy curiosity, thus inviting further inquiry.

Another type of résumé is the chronological résumé, which lists work experience and educational history in order by date. This type of résumé is useful for those just entering the job market because it helps highlight education and work experience. In some cases, education is more important than unrelated work experience because it indicates the career direction you desire despite the work experience you have acquired thus far.

Common suggestions for improving résumés include: use a clear and easily read (not elaborate) format, delete outdated information, improve organization, use high-quality paper and printer, ensure correct grammar and spelling, and provide a detailed description of work experiences. Keep in mind that the person who will look at your résumé may have to sift through hundreds in the course of the day in addition to handling other duties. Consequently it is important to keep your résumé short (one page is best, never more than two), concise, and neat. Moreover, you want your résumé to be distinctive so it will stand out from all the others.

In addition to having the proper format and content, a résumé should be easy to read. It is best to use only one or two kinds of type, and plain white paper. When sending a résumé to a large company, several copies may be made and distributed. Textured, gray, or colored paper may make a good impression on the first person who sees the résumé, but it will not reproduce well for the others, who will see only a poor copy. You should also proofread your résumé with care. Typos and misspellings will grab attention—the wrong kind.

Along with the résumé itself, always submit a cover letter. In the letter, you can include somewhat more information than in your résumé and convey a message that expresses your interest and enthusiasm about the organization and the job.

LORRAINE MILLER
2212 WEST WILLOW
PHOENIX, AZ 12345
(416) 862-9169

EDUCATION: B.A. Arizona State University, 2005, Marketing, achieved a 3.4 on a 4.0 scale throughout college

POSITION DESIRED: Product manager with an international firm providing future career development at the executive level

QUALIFICATIONS:

- Communicates well with individuals to achieve a common goal
- Handles tasks efficiently and in a timely manner
- Understands advertising sales, management, marketing research, packaging, pricing, distribution, and warehousing
- Coordinates many activities at one time
- Receives and carries out assigned tasks or directives
- Writes complete status or research reports

EXPERIENCES:

- Assistant Editor of college paper
- Treasurer of the American Marketing Association (student chapter)
- Internship with 3-Cs Advertising, Berkeley, CA
- Student Assistantship with Dr. Steve Green, Professor of Marketing, Arizona State University
- Solo cross-Canada canoe trek, summer 2003

WORK RECORD:

2004–Present	Blythe and Company Advertising	
	—Assistant Account Executive	
2002–2003	Student Assistant for Dr. Steve Green	
	—Research Assistant	
2000–2001	The Men	
	—Retail sales and consumer relations	
1998–1999	Farmer	
	—Helped operate relative's blueberry farm in Michigan for three summers	

Figure A.1
A Résumé Targeted at a Specific Position

◉ The Job Interview

In essence, your résumé and cover letter are an introduction. The deciding factor in the hiring process is the interview (or several interviews) with representatives of the firm. It is through the interview that the firm gets to know you and your qualifications. At the same time, the interview gives you a chance to learn about the firm.

Here again, preparation is the key to success. Research the firm before your first interview. Learn all you can about its products, its subsidiaries, the markets in which it operates, its history, the locations of its facilities, and so on. If possible, obtain and

Table A.1   Interview Questions Job Applicants Often Find Difficult to Answer

1. Tell me about yourself.
2. What do you know about our organization?
3. What can you do for us? Why should we hire you?
4. What qualifications do you have that make you feel you will be successful in your field?
5. What have you learned from the jobs you've held?
6. If you could write your own ticket, what would be your ideal job?
7. What are your special skills, and where did you acquire them?
8. Have you had any special accomplishments in your lifetime that you are particularly proud of?
9. Why did you leave your most recent job?
10. How do you spend your spare time? What are your hobbies?
11. What are your strengths and weaknesses?
12. Discuss five major accomplishments.
13. What kind of boss would you like? Why?
14. If you could spend a day with someone you've known or known of, who would it be?
15. What personality characteristics seem to rub you the wrong way?
16. How do you show your anger? What type of things make you angry?
17. With what type of person do you spend the majority of your time?

Source: Adapted from *The Ultimate Job Hunter's Guidebook.* 4th ed., Susan D. Greene and Melanie C. L. Martel. Copyright © 2004 by Houghton Mifflin Company.

read the firm's most recent annual report. Be prepared to ask questions about the firm and the opportunities it offers. Interviewers welcome such questions. They expect you to be interested enough to spend some time thinking about your potential relationship with their organization.

Also, prepare to respond to questions the interviewer may ask. Table A.1 lists typical interview questions that job applicants often find difficult to answer. But don't expect interviewers to stick to the list given in the table or to the items appearing in your résumé. They will be interested in anything that helps them decide what kind of person and worker you are.

Make sure you are on time for your interview and are dressed and groomed in a businesslike manner. Interviewers take note of punctuality and appearance just as they do of other personal qualities. Bring a copy of your résumé, even if you already sent one to the firm. You may also want to bring a copy of your course transcript and letters of recommendation. If you plan to furnish interviewers with the names and addresses of references rather than with letters of recommendation, make sure you have your references' permission to do so.

Consider the interview itself as a two-way conversation rather than a question-and-answer session. Volunteer any information that is relevant to the interviewer's questions. If an important point is skipped in the discussion, don't hesitate to bring it up. Be yourself, but emphasize your strengths. Good eye contact and posture are also important; they should come naturally if you take an active part in the interview. At the conclusion of the interview, thank the recruiter for taking the time to see you.

In most cases, the first interview is used to *screen* applicants, or choose those who are best qualified. These applicants are then given a second interview, and perhaps a third, usually with one or more department heads. If the job requires relocation to a different area, applicants may be invited there for these later interviews. After the interviewing process is complete, applicants are told when to expect a hiring decision.

◉ After the Interview

Attention to common courtesy is important as a follow-up to your interview. You should send a brief note of thanks to the interviewer and give it as much care as you did your résumé and cover letter. A short, typewritten letter is preferred to a hand-written note or card, or an e-mail. Avoid not only typos but also overconfident statements such as "I look forward to helping you make Universal Industries successful over the next decade." Even in the thank-you letter, it is important to show team spirit and professionalism, as well as convey proper enthusiasm. Everything you say and do reflects on you as a candidate.

◉ After the Hire

Clearly, performing well in a job has always been a crucial factor in keeping a position. In a tight economy and job market, however, a person's attitude, as well as his or her performance, counts greatly. People in their first jobs can commit costly political blunders by being insensitive to their environments. Politics in the business world includes how you react to your boss, how you react to your coworkers, and your general demeanor. Here are a few rules to live by:

1. *Don't bypass your boss.* One major blunder an employee can make is to go over the boss's head to resolve a problem. This is especially hazardous in a bureaucratic organization. You should become aware of the generally accepted chain of command, and when problems occur, follow that protocol, beginning with your immediate superior. No boss likes to look incompetent, and making him or her appear so is sure to hamper or even crush your budding career. However, there may be exceptions to this rule in emergency situations. It is wise to discuss with your supervisor what to do in an emergency, before an emergency occurs.

2. *Don't criticize your boss.* Adhering to the old adage, "praise in public and criticize in private," will keep you out of the line of retaliatory fire. A more sensible and productive alternative is to present the critical commentary to your boss in a diplomatic way during a private session.

3. *Don't show disloyalty.* If dissatisfied with the position, a new employee may start a fresh job search, within or outside the organization. However, it is not advisable to begin a publicized search within the company for another position unless you have held your current job for some time. Careful attention to the political climate in the organization should help you determine how soon to start a new job campaign and how public to make it. In any case, it is not a good idea to publicize that you are looking outside the company for a new position.

4. *Don't be a naysayer.* Employees are expected to become part of the organizational team and to work together with others. Behaviors to avoid, especially if you are a new employee, include being critical of others; refusing to support others' projects; always playing devil's advocate; refusing to help others when a crisis occurs; and complaining all the time, even about such matters as the poor quality of the food in the cafeteria, the crowded parking lot, or the temperature in the office.

5. *Learn to correct mistakes appropriately.* No one likes to admit having made a mistake, but one of the most important political skills you can acquire is minimizing

the impact of a blunder. It is usually advantageous to correct the damage as soon as possible to avoid further problems. Some suggestions: be the first to break the bad news to your boss; avoid being defensive; stay poised and don't panic; and have solutions ready for fixing the blunder.[2]

Types of Marketing Careers

In considering marketing as a career, the first step is to evaluate broad categories of career opportunities in the areas of marketing research, sales, industrial buying, public relations, distribution management, product management, advertising, retail management, direct marketing, and e-marketing and customer relationship management. Keep in mind that the categories described here are not all-inclusive and that each encompasses hundreds of marketing jobs.

Marketing Research

Clearly, marketing research and information systems are vital aspects of marketing decisionmaking. Marketing researchers survey customers to determine their habits, preferences, and aspirations. The information about buyers and environmental forces that research and information systems provide improves a marketer's ability to understand the dynamics of the marketplace and therefore make effective decisions.

Marketing research firms are usually employed by a client organization such as a provider of goods or services, a nonbusiness organization, a research consulting firm, or an advertising agency. The activities performed include concept testing, product testing, package testing, advertising testing, test-market research, and new-product research.

Marketing researchers gather and analyze data relating to specific problems. A researcher may be involved in one or several stages of research depending on the size of the project, the organization of the research unit, and the researcher's experience. Marketing research trainees in large organizations usually perform a considerable amount of clerical work, such as compiling secondary data from the firm's accounting and sales records and from periodicals, government publications, syndicated data services, the Internet, and unpublished sources. A junior analyst may edit and code questionnaires or tabulate survey results. Trainees may also participate in gathering primary data through mail and telephone surveys, personal interviews, and observation. As a marketing researcher gains experience, he or she may become involved in defining problems and developing research questions; designing research procedures; and analyzing, interpreting, and reporting findings. Exceptional personnel may assume responsibility for entire research projects.

Although most employers consider a bachelor's degree sufficient qualification for a marketing research trainee, many specialized positions require a graduate degree in business administration, statistics, or other related fields. Today trainees are more likely to have a marketing or statistics degree than a liberal arts degree. Courses in statistics, information technology, psychology, sociology, communications, economics, and technical writing are valuable preparation for a career in marketing research.

The Bureau of Labor Statistics indicates that marketing research provides abundant employment opportunities, especially for applicants with graduate training in marketing research, statistics, economics, and the social sciences. Generally, the value of information gathered by marketing information and research systems rises as competition increases, thus expanding opportunities for prospective marketing research personnel.

The major career paths in marketing research are with independent marketing research agencies/data suppliers and marketing research departments in advertising agencies and other businesses. In a company in which marketing research plays a key role, the researcher is often a member of the marketing strategy team. Surveying or interviewing customers is the heart of the marketing research firm's activities. A statistician selects the sample to be surveyed, analysts design the questionnaire and synthesize the gathered data into a final report, data processors tabulate the data, and the research director controls and coordinates all these activities so each project is completed to the client's satisfaction.

Salaries in marketing research depend on the type, size, and location of the firm, as well as the nature of the position. Generally, starting salaries are somewhat higher and promotions somewhat slower than in other occupations requiring similar training. The typical salary for a market analyst is $38,000 to $48,000; a marketing research director can earn $62,000 to $92,000.[3]

◉ Sales

Millions of people earn a living through personal selling. Chapter 18 defined personal selling as paid personal communication that attempts to inform customers and persuade them to purchase products in an exchange situation. Although this definition describes the general nature of sales positions, individual selling jobs vary enormously with respect to the types of businesses and products involved, the educational background and skills required, and the specific activities sales personnel perform. Because the work is so varied, it offers numerous career opportunities for people with a wide range of qualifications, interests, and goals. The two types of career opportunities we discuss relate to business-to-business sales.

● **Sales Positions in Wholesaling** Wholesalers buy products intended for resale, for use in making other products, and for general business operations and sell them directly to business markets. Wholesalers thus provide services to both retailers and producers. They can help match producers' products to retailers' needs and provide services that save producers time, money, and resources. Some activities a sales representative for a wholesaling firm is likely to perform include planning and negotiating transactions; assisting customers with sales, advertising, sales promotion, and publicity; facilitating transportation and storage; providing customers with inventory control and data processing assistance; establishing prices; and giving customers technical, managerial, and merchandising assistance.

The background needed by wholesale personnel depends on the nature of the product handled. A sales representative for a drug wholesaler, for example, needs extensive technical training and product knowledge, and may have a degree in chemistry, biology, or pharmacology. A wholesaler of standard office supplies, on the other hand, may find it more important that its sales staff be familiar with various brands, suppliers, and prices than have technical knowledge about the products. A person just entering the wholesaling field may begin as a sales trainee or hold a nonselling job that provides experience with inventory, prices, discounts, and the firm's customers. A college graduate usually enters a wholesaler's sales force directly. Competent salespeople also transfer from manufacturer and retail sales positions.

The number of sales positions in wholesaling is expected to grow about as rapidly as the average for all occupations. Earnings for wholesale personnel vary widely because commissions often make up a large proportion of their incomes.

● **Sales Positions in Manufacturing**   A manufacturer's sales personnel sell the firm's products to wholesalers, retailers, and industrial buyers; they thus perform many of the same activities as a wholesaler's representatives. As in wholesaling, educational requirements for a sales position depend largely on the type and complexity of the products and markets. Manufacturers of nontechnical products usually hire college graduates who have a liberal arts or business degree and train them so they become knowledgeable about the firm's products, prices, and customers. Manufacturers of highly technical products generally prefer applicants who have degrees in fields associated with the particular industry and market.

Sales positions in manufacturing are expected to increase at an average rate. Manufacturers' sales personnel are well compensated and earn above-average salaries; most are paid a combination of salary and commission. Commissions vary according to the salesperson's efforts, abilities, and sales territory, as well as the type of products sold. Annual salary and/or commission for sales positions range from $84,000 to $112,000 for a sales manager and $44,000 to $62,000 for a field salesperson. A sales trainee would start at about $38,000 in business sales positions.[4]

◉ Industrial Buying

Industrial buyers, or purchasing agents, are responsible for maintaining an adequate supply of the goods and services an organization requires for its operations. In general, industrial buyers purchase all items needed for direct use in producing other products and for use in day-to-day operations. Industrial buyers in large firms often specialize in purchasing a single, specific class of products—for example, all petroleum-based lubricants. In smaller organizations, buyers may be responsible for many different categories of purchases, including raw materials, component parts, office supplies, and operating services.

An industrial buyer's main job is to select suppliers that offer the best quality, service, and price. When the products to be purchased are standardized, buyers may base their purchasing decisions on suppliers' descriptions of their offerings in catalogs and trade journals. Buyers who purchase highly homogeneous products often meet with salespeople to examine samples and observe demonstrations. Sometimes buyers must inspect the actual product before purchasing it; in other cases, they invite suppliers to bid on large orders. Buyers who purchase equipment made to specifications often deal directly with manufacturers. After choosing a supplier and placing an order, an industrial buyer usually must trace the shipment to ensure on-time delivery. Sometimes the buyer is also responsible for receiving and inspecting an order and authorizing payment to the shipper.

Training requirements for a career in industrial buying relate to the needs of the firm and the types of products purchased. A manufacturer of heavy machinery may prefer an applicant who has a background in engineering. A service company, on the other hand, may recruit liberal arts majors. Although not generally required, a college degree is becoming increasingly important for industrial buyers who wish to advance to management positions.

Employment prospects for industrial buyers are expected to increase faster than average. Opportunities will be excellent for individuals with a master's degree in business administration or a bachelor's degree in engineering, science, or business administration. Companies that manufacture heavy equipment, computer equipment, and communications equipment will need buyers with technical backgrounds.

◉ Public Relations

Public relations encompasses a broad set of communication activities designed to create and maintain favorable relationships between an organization and its stakeholders—customers, employees, stockholders, government officials, and society in general. Public relations specialists help clients create the image, issue, or message they wish to present and communicate it to the appropriate audience. According to the Public Relations Society of America, about 120,000 people work in public relations in the United States. Half the billings of the nation's 4,000 public relations agencies and firms come from Chicago and New York. The highest starting salaries are also found there. Communication is basic to all public relations programs. To communicate effectively, public relations practitioners must first gather data about the firm's stakeholders to assess their needs, identify problems, formulate recommendations, implement new plans, and evaluate current activities.

Public relations personnel disseminate large amounts of information to the organization's stakeholders. Written communication is the most versatile tool of public relations; thus, good writing skills are essential. Public relations practitioners must be adept at writing for a variety of media and audiences. It is not unusual for a person in public relations to prepare reports, news releases, speeches, broadcast scripts, technical manuals, employee publications, shareholder reports, and other communications aimed at both organizational personnel and external groups. In addition, a public relations practitioner needs a thorough knowledge of the production techniques used in preparing various communications. Public relations personnel also establish distribution channels for the organization's publicity. They must have a thorough understanding of the various media, their areas of specialization, the characteristics of their target audiences, and their policies regarding publicity. Anyone who hopes to succeed in public relations must develop close working relationships with numerous media personnel to enlist their interest in disseminating clients' communications.

A college education combined with writing or media-related experience is the best preparation for a career in public relations. Most beginners have a college degree in journalism, communications, or public relations, but some employers prefer a business background. Courses in journalism, business administration, marketing, creative writing, psychology, sociology, political science, economics, advertising, English, and public speaking are recommended. Some employers ask applicants to present a portfolio of published articles, scripts written for television or radio programs, slide presentations, and other work samples. Other agencies require written tests that include such tasks as writing sample press releases. Manufacturing firms, public utilities, transportation and insurance companies, and trade and professional associations are the largest employers of public relations personnel. In addition, sizable numbers of public relations personnel work for health-related organizations, government agencies, educational institutions, museums, and religious and service groups.

Although some larger companies provide extensive formal training for new personnel, most new public relations employees learn on the job. Beginners usually perform routine tasks such as maintaining files about company activities and searching secondary data sources for information to be used in publicity materials. More experienced employees write press releases, speeches, and articles and help plan public relations campaigns.

Employment opportunities in public relations are expected to increase faster than the average for all occupations. One caveat is in order, however: competition for beginning jobs is keen. The prospects are best for applicants who have solid academic preparation and some media experience. Abilities that differentiate candidates, such as an understanding of information technology, are becoming increasingly important. Public relations specialists can earn from $35,000 to $44,000. Public relations agency managers earn in the $68,000 to $92,000 range.[5]

◉ Distribution Management

A distribution manager arranges for transportation of goods within firms and through marketing channels. Transportation is an essential distribution activity that permits a firm to create time and place utility for its products. It is the distribution manager's job to analyze various transportation modes and select the combination that minimizes cost and transit time while providing acceptable levels of reliability, capability, accessibility, and security.

To accomplish this task, a distribution manager performs many activities. First, the individual must choose one or a combination of transportation modes from the five major modes available: railroads, trucks, waterways, airways, and pipelines. The distribution manager must then select the specific routes the goods will travel and the particular carriers to be used, weighing such factors as freight classifications and regulations, freight charges, time schedules, shipment sizes, and loss and damage ratios. In addition, this person may be responsible for preparing shipping documents, tracing shipments, handling loss and damage claims, keeping records of freight rates, and monitoring changes in government regulations and transportation technology.

Distribution management employs relatively few people and is expected to grow about as fast as the average for all occupations in the near future. Manufacturing firms are the largest employers of distribution managers, although some distribution managers work for wholesalers, retail stores, and consulting firms. Salaries of experienced distribution managers vary, but generally are much higher than the average for all nonsupervisory personnel. Entry-level positions are diverse, ranging from inventory control and traffic scheduling to operations or distribution management. Inventory management is an area of great opportunity because of increasing global competition. While salaries in the distribution field vary depending on the position and information technology skill requirements, entry salaries are in the $35,000 to $45,000 range.[6]

Most employers of distribution managers prefer to hire graduates of technical programs or people who have completed courses in transportation, logistics, distribution management, economics, statistics, computer science, management, marketing, and commercial law. A successful distribution manager is adept at handling technical data and is able to interpret and communicate highly technical information.

◉ Product Management

The product manager occupies a staff position and is responsible for the success or failure of a product line. Product managers coordinate most of the activities required to market a product. However, because they hold a staff position, they have relatively little actual authority over marketing personnel. Nevertheless, they take on a large amount of responsibility and typically are paid quite well relative to other marketing

What jobs pay today

Median salaries for entry-level positions in the U.S.:

PAY TO:	
Customer Service Rep	$28,381
Sales Assistant	$30,991
Advertising Assistant	$35,002
Public Relations Assistant	$39,221
Assistant Merchandise Buyer	$40,042

Source: Data from Monster Salary Center, http://salary.monster.com (accessed June 24, 2005).

employees. Being a product manager can be rewarding both financially and psychologically, but it can also be frustrating because of the disparity between responsibility and authority.

A product manager should have a general knowledge of advertising, transportation modes, inventory control, selling and sales management, sales promotion, marketing research, packaging, pricing, and warehousing. The individual must be knowledgeable enough to communicate effectively with personnel in these functional areas and to make suggestions and help assess alternatives when major decisions are being made.

Product managers usually need college training in an area of business administration. A master's degree is helpful, although a person usually does not become a product manager directly out of school. Frequently, several years of selling and sales management experience are prerequisites for a product management position, which often is a major step in the career path of top-level marketing executives. Product managers can earn $102,000 to $146,000, while an assistant product manager starts at about $46,000.[7]

◉ Advertising

Advertising pervades our daily lives. Business and nonbusiness organizations use advertising in many ways and for many reasons. Advertising clearly needs individuals with diverse skills to fill a variety of jobs. Creativity, imagination, artistic talent, and expertise in expression and persuasion are important for copywriters, artists, and account executives. Sales and managerial abilities are vital to the success of advertising managers, media buyers, and production managers. Research directors must have a solid understanding of research techniques and human behavior. A related occupation is an advertising salesperson, who sells newspaper, television, radio, or magazine advertising to advertisers.

Advertising professionals disagree on the most beneficial educational background for a career in advertising. Most employers prefer college graduates. Some employers seek individuals with degrees in advertising, journalism, or business; others prefer graduates with broad liberal arts backgrounds. Still other employers rank relevant work experience above educational background.

"Advertisers look for generalists," says a staff executive of the American Association of Advertising Agencies. "Thus, there are just as many economics or general liberal arts majors as M.B.A.'s." Common entry-level positions in an advertising agency are found in the traffic department, account service (account coordinator), or the media department (media assistant). Starting salaries in these positions are often quite low, but to gain experience in the advertising industry, employees must work their way up in the system. Assistant account executives start at $28,000 to $43,000, while a typical account executive earns $54,000 to $72,000. Copywriters earn $33,000 to $42,000 a year.[8]

A variety of organizations employ advertising personnel. Although advertising agencies are perhaps the most visible and glamorous employers, many manufacturing firms, retail stores, banks, utility companies, and professional and trade associations maintain advertising departments. Advertising jobs are also available with television and radio stations, newspapers, and magazines. Other businesses that employ advertising personnel include printers, art studios, letter shops, and package design firms. Specific advertising jobs include advertising manager, account executive, research director, copywriter, media specialist, and production manager.

About 59 percent of advertising employees are between 25 and 44 years of age compared to 51 percent of all workers in the U.S. economy. Employment opportunities in advertising are expected to increase much faster than the average of all occupations through 2008.[9]

◉ Retail Management

Although a career in retailing may begin in sales, there is more to retailing than simply selling. Many retail personnel occupy management positions. Besides managing the sales force, they focus on selecting and ordering merchandise, promotional activities, inventory control, customer credit operations, accounting, personnel, and store security.

Organization of retail stores varies. In many large department stores, retail management personnel rarely engage in actual selling to customers; these duties are performed by retail salespeople. Other types of retail organizations may require management personnel to perform selling activities from time to time.

Large retail stores offer a variety of management positions, including assistant buyers, buyers, department managers, section managers, store managers, division managers, regional managers, and vice president of merchandising. The following list describes the general duties of four of these positions; the precise nature of these duties may vary from one retail organization to another.

> A section manager coordinates inventory and promotions and interacts with buyers, salespeople, and ultimate consumers. The manager performs merchandising, labor relations, and managerial activities, and usually works more than a 40-hour workweek.

> The buyer's task is more focused. This fast-paced occupation involves much travel and pressure, and the need to be open-minded with respect to new, potentially successful items.

> The regional manager coordinates the activities of several stores within a given area, usually monitoring and supporting sales, promotions, and general procedures.

> The vice president of merchandising has a broad scope of managerial responsibility and reports to the organization's president.

Most retail organizations hire college graduates, put them through management training programs, and then place them directly in management positions. They frequently hire candidates with backgrounds in liberal arts or business administration. Sales positions and retail management positions offer the greatest employment opportunities for marketing students.

Retail management positions can be exciting and challenging. Competent, ambitious individuals often assume a great deal of responsibility very quickly and advance rapidly. However, a retail manager's job is physically demanding and sometimes entails long working hours. In addition, managers employed by large chain stores may be required to move frequently during their early years with the company. Nonetheless, positions in retail management often offer the chance to excel and gain promotion. Growth in retailing, which is expected to accompany the growth in population, is likely to create substantial opportunities during the next ten years. While a trainee may start in the $39,000 to $48,000 range, a store manager may earn an excess of $100,000 depending on the size of the store.[10]

◉ Direct Marketing

One of the most dynamic areas in marketing is direct marketing, in which the seller uses one or more direct media (telephone, online, mail, print, or television) to solicit a response. The telephone is a major vehicle for selling many consumer products. Telemarketing is direct selling to customers using a variety of technological improvements in telecommunications. Direct mail catalogs appeal to such market segments as working women and people who find going to retail stores difficult or inconvenient. Newspapers and magazines offer great opportunity, particularly in special market segments. *Golf Digest*, for example, is obviously a good medium for selling golfing equipment. Cable television provides many opportunities for selling directly to consumers. Home shopping channels, for instance, have been very successful. The Internet offers numerous direct marketing opportunities.

The most important asset in direct marketing is experience. Employers often look to other industries to locate experienced professionals. This preference means that if you can get an entry-level position in direct marketing, you will have an advantage in developing a career.

Jobs in direct marketing include buyers, such as department store buyers, who select goods for catalog, telephone, or direct mail sales. Catalog managers develop marketing strategies for each new catalog that goes into the mail. Research/mail-list management involves developing lists of products that will sell in direct marketing and lists of names of consumers who are likely to respond to a direct mail effort. Order fulfillment managers direct the shipment of products once they are sold. The effectiveness of direct marketing is enhanced by periodic analysis of advertising and communications at all phases of contact with the consumer. Direct marketing involves all aspects of marketing decisionmaking. Most positions in direct marketing involve planning and market analysis. Some direct marketing jobs involve the use of databases that include customer information, sales history, and other tracking data. A direct marketing representative might receive a salary of $42,000 to $61,000. A direct marketing director in business-to-business sales could receive a salary of $80,000 to $100,000.[11]

◉ E-Marketing and Customer Relationship Management

Today only about 1.5 percent of all retail sales are conducted on the Internet. Currently, approximately one-half of all businesses order online. One characteristic of firms engaged in e-marketing is a renewed focus on relationship marketing by building customer loyalty and retaining customers—in other words, on customer relationship management (CRM). This focus on CRM is possible because of e-marketers' ability to target individual customers. This effort is enhanced over time as the customer invests more time and effort in "teaching" the firms what he or she wants.

Opportunities abound to combine information technology expertise with marketing knowledge. By providing an integrated communication system of websites, fax and telephone numbers, and personal contacts, marketers can personalize customer relationships. Careers exist for individuals who can integrate the Internet as a touch point with customers as part of effective CRM. Many Internet-only companies ("dot-coms") failed because they focused too heavily on brand awareness and did not understand an integrated marketing strategy.

The use of laptops, cellular phones, e-mail, voice mail, and other devices is necessary to maintain customer relationships and allow purchases on the Internet. A variety of jobs exist for marketers who have integrated technology into their work and job skills. Job titles include e-marketing manager, customer relationship manager, and e-services manager, as well as jobs in dot-coms.

Salaries in this rapidly growing area depend on technical expertise and experience. For example, CRM customer service manager receives a salary in the $55,000 to $72,000 range. Database managers receive higher salaries of approximately $65,000 to $90,000. With five years of experience in e-marketing, individuals who are responsible for online product offerings can earn from $63,000 to $106,000.[12]

Glossary

accessibility The ability to obtain information available on the Internet

accessory equipment Equipment used in production or office activities

addressability A marketer's ability to identify customers before they make a purchase

advertising Paid nonpersonal communication about an organization and its products transmitted to a target audience through mass media

advertising appropriation Advertising budget for a specified period

advertising campaign Designing a series of advertisements and placing them in various advertising media to reach a particular target audience

advertising platform Basic issues or selling points to be included in the advertising campaign

advocacy advertising Promotes a company's position on a public issue

aesthetic modifications Changes to the sensory appeal of a product

agents Intermediaries that represent either buyers or sellers on a permanent basis

aided recall test A posttest that asks respondents to identify recent ads and provides clues to jog their memories

allowance A concession in price to achieve a desired goal

approach The manner in which a salesperson contacts a potential customer

arbitrary approach Budgeting for an advertising campaign as specified by a high-level executive in the firm

artwork An ad's illustration and layout

Asia-Pacific Economic Cooperation (APEC) An alliance that promotes open trade and economic and technical cooperation among member nations throughout the world

atmospherics The physical elements in a store's design that appeal to consumers' emotions and encourage buying

attitude An individual's enduring evaluation of, feelings about, and behavioral tendencies toward an object or idea

attitude scale Means of measuring consumer attitudes by gauging the intensity of individuals' reactions to adjectives, phrases, or sentences about an object

average fixed cost The fixed cost per unit produced

average total cost The sum of the average fixed cost and the average variable cost

average variable cost The variable cost per unit produced

bait pricing Pricing an item in the product line low with the intention of selling a higher-priced item in the line

balance of trade The difference in value between a nation's exports and its imports

barter The trading of products

base-point pricing Geographic pricing combining factory price and freight charges from the base point nearest the buyer

benchmarking Comparing the quality of the firm's goods, services, or processes with that of the best-performing competitors

benefit segmentation The division of a market according to benefits that customers want from the product

Better Business Bureau A local, nongovernmental regulatory agency, supported by local businesses, that helps settle problems between customers and specific business firms

blogs Web-based journals in which writers editorialize and interact with other Internet users

brand An identifying name, term, design, or symbol

brand equity The marketing and financial value associated with a brand's strength in a market

brand extension Using an existing brand to brand a new product in a different product category

brand insistence The degree of brand loyalty in which a customer strongly prefers a specific brand and will accept no substitute

brand licensing An agreement whereby a company permits another organization to use its brand on other products for a licensing fee

brand loyalty A customer's favorable attitude toward a specific brand

brand manager The person responsible for a single brand

brand mark The part of a brand not made up of words

brand name The part of a brand that can be spoken

brand preference The degree of brand loyalty in which a customer prefers one brand over competitive offerings

brand recognition A customer's awareness that a brand exists and is an alternative purchase

breakdown approach Measuring company sales potential based on a general economic forecast for a specific period and the market potential derived from it

breakeven point The point at which the costs of producing a product equal the revenue made from selling the product

brokers Intermediaries that bring buyers and sellers together temporarily

buildup approach Measuring company sales potential by estimating how much of a product a potential buyer in a specific geographic area will purchase in a given period, multiplying the estimate by the number of potential buyers, and adding the totals of all the geographic areas considered

bundle pricing Packaging together two or more complementary products and selling them for a single price

business analysis Assessing the potential of a product idea for the firm's sales, costs, and profits

business (organizational) buying behavior The purchase behavior of producers, government units, institutions, and resellers

business cycle A pattern of economic fluctuations that has four stages: prosperity, recession, depression, and recovery

business market Individuals or groups that purchase a specific kind of product for resale, direct use in producing other products, or use in general daily operations

business products Products bought to use in an organization's operations, to resell, or to make other products

business services The intangible products that many organizations use in their operations

buy-back allowance A sum of money given to a reseller for each unit bought after an initial promotion deal is over

buying allowance A temporary price reduction to resellers for purchasing specified quantities of a product

buying behavior The decision processes and acts of people involved in buying and using products.

buying center The people within an organization, including users, influencers, buyers, deciders, and gatekeepers, who make business purchase decisions

buying power Resources, such as money, goods, and services, that can be traded in an exchange

captioned photograph A photo with a brief description of its contents

captive pricing Pricing the basic product in a product line low while

pricing related items at a higher level

cash-and-carry wholesalers Limited-service wholesalers whose customers pay cash and furnish transportation

cash discount A price reduction given to buyers for prompt payment or cash payment

catalog marketing A type of marketing in which an organization provides a catalog from which customers make selections and place orders by mail, telephone, or the Internet

catalog showrooms A form of warehouse showroom where consumers shop from a catalog and products are stored out of buyers' reach

category killer A very large specialty store concentrating on a major product category and competing on the basis of low prices and product availability

causal research Research in which it is assumed that a particular variable X causes a variable Y

cause-related marketing The practice of linking products to a particular social cause on an ongoing or short-term basis

centralized organization A structure in which top management delegates little authority to levels below it

cents-off offer A promotion that lets buyers pay less than the regular price to encourage purchase

channel capacity The limit on the volume of information a communication channel can handle effectively

channel power The ability of one channel member to influence another member's goal achievement

client-based relationships Interactions that result in satisfied customers who use a service repeatedly over time

closing The stage in the selling process when the salesperson asks the prospect to buy the product

co-branding Using two or more brands on one product

codes of conduct Formalized rules and standards that describe what the company expects of its employees

coding process Converting meaning into a series of signs or symbols

cognitive dissonance A buyer's doubts shortly after a purchase about whether the decision was the right one

combination compensation plan Paying salespeople a fixed salary plus a commission based on sales volume

commercialization Deciding on full-scale manufacturing and marketing plans and preparing budgets

commission merchants Agents that receive goods on consignment and negotiate sales in large, central markets

Common Market of the Southern Cone (MERCOSUR) An alliance that promotes the free circulation of goods, services, and production factors, and has a common external tariff and commercial policy among member nations in South America

communication A sharing of meaning

community A sense of group membership or feeling of belonging

community shopping centers Shopping centers with one or two department stores, some specialty stores, and convenience stores

company sales potential The maximum percentage of market potential that an individual firm can expect to obtain for a specific product

comparative advertising Compares two or more brands on the basis of one or more product characteristics

comparison discounting Setting a price at a specific level and comparing it with a higher price

competition-based pricing Pricing influenced primarily by competitors' prices

competition-matching approach Determining an advertising budget by trying to match competitors' ad outlays

competitive advantage The result of a company's matching a core competency to opportunities in the marketplace

competitive advertising Points out a brand's special features, uses, and advantages relative to competing brands

component parts Items that become part of the physical product and are either finished items ready for assembly or items that need little processing before assembly

concentrated targeting strategy A strategy in which an organization targets a single market segment using one marketing mix

concept testing Seeking potential buyers' responses to a product idea

consideration set A group of brands that a buyer views as alternatives for possible purchase

consistency of quality The degree to which a product has the same level of quality over time

consumer buying behavior Buying behavior of people who purchase products for personal or household use and not for business purposes

consumer buying decision process A five-stage purchase decision process that includes problem recognition, information search, evaluation of alternatives, purchase, and post-purchase evaluation

consumer contests and games Sales promotion methods in which individuals compete for prizes based on analytical or creative skills

consumer jury A panel of a product's actual or potential buyers who pretest ads

consumer market Purchasers and household members who intend to consume or benefit from the purchased products and do not buy products to make profits

consumer products Products purchased to satisfy personal and family needs

consumer sales promotion methods Ways of encouraging consumers to patronize specific stores or try particular products

consumer socialization The process through which a person acquires the knowledge and skills to function as a consumer

consumer sweepstakes A sales promotion in which entrants submit their names for inclusion in a drawing for prizes

consumerism Organized efforts by individuals, groups, and organizations to protect consumers' rights

contract manufacturing The practice of hiring a foreign firm to produce a designated volume of product to specification

control Customers' ability to regulate the information they view and the rate and sequence of their exposure to that information

convenience products Relatively inexpensive, frequently purchased items for which buyers exert minimal purchasing effort

cookie An identifying string of text stored on a website visitor's computer

cooperative advertising An arrangement in which a manufacturer agrees to pay a certain amount of a retailer's media costs for advertising the manufacturer's products

copy The verbal portion of advertisements

core competencies Things a firm does extremely well, which sometimes give it an advantage over its competition

corporate strategy A strategy that determines the means for utilizing resources in the various functional areas to reach the organization's goals

cost comparison indicator A means of comparing the cost of vehicles in a specific medium in relation to the number of people reached

cost-based pricing Adding a dollar amount or percentage to the cost of the product

cost-plus pricing Adding a specified dollar amount or percentage to the seller's cost

coupons Written price reductions used to encourage consumers to buy a specific product

culture The values, knowledge, beliefs, customs, objects, and concepts of a society

cumulative discounts Quantity discounts aggregated over a stated period

customary pricing Pricing on the basis of tradition

customer contact The level of interaction between provider and customer needed to deliver the service

customer forecasting survey A survey of customers regarding the types and quantities of products they intend to buy during a specific period

customer relationship management (CRM) Using information about customers to create marketing strategies that develop and sustain desirable customer relationships

customer services Human or mechanical efforts or activities that add value to a product

customers The purchasers of organizations' products; the focal point of all marketing activities

cycle analysis An analysis of sales figures for a period of three to five years to ascertain whether sales fluctuate in a consistent, periodic manner

cycle time The time needed to complete a process

database A collection of information arranged for easy access and retrieval

dealer listing An advertisement that promotes a product and identifies the names of participating retailers that sell the product

dealer loader A gift, often part of a display, given to a retailer purchasing a specified quantity of merchandise

decentralized organization A structure in which decision-making authority is delegated as far down the chain of command as possible

decline stage The stage of a product's life cycle when sales fall rapidly

decoding process Converting signs or symbols into concepts and ideas

Delphi technique A procedure in which experts create initial forecasts, submit them to the company for averaging, and then refine the forecasts

demand curve A graph of the quantity of products expected to be sold at various prices if other factors remain constant

demand-based pricing Pricing based on the level of demand for the product

demonstrations A sales promotion method manufacturers use temporarily to encourage trial use and purchase of a product or to show how a product works

department stores Large retail organizations characterized by wide product mixes and organized into separate departments to facilitate marketing efforts and internal management

depth of product mix The average number of different product items offered in each product line

derived demand Demand for industrial products that stems from demand for consumer products

descriptive research Research conducted to clarify the characteristics of certain phenomena and thus solve a particular problem

differential pricing Charging different prices to different buyers for the same quality and quantity of product

differentiated targeting strategy A strategy in which an organization targets two or more segments by developing a marketing mix for each

digitalization The ability to represent a product, or at least some of its benefits, as digital bits of information

direct marketing The use of telecommunications and nonpersonal media to introduce products to consumers, who then can purchase them via mail, telephone, or the Internet

direct ownership A situation in which a company owns subsidiaries or other facilities overseas

direct response marketing A type of marketing that occurs when a retailer advertises a product and makes it available through mail or telephone orders

direct selling The marketing of products to ultimate consumers through face-to-face sales presentations at home or in the workplace

discount stores Self-service, general merchandise stores offering brand name and private brand products at low prices

discretionary income Disposable income available for spending and saving after an individual has purchased the basic necessities of food, clothing, and shelter

disposable income After-tax income

distribution The activities that make products available to customers when and where they want to purchase them

distribution centers Large, centralized warehouses that focus on moving rather than storing goods

drop shippers Limited-service wholesalers that take title to products and negotiate sales but never take actual possession of products

dual distribution The use of two or more channels to distribute the same product to the same target market

dumping Selling products at unfairly low prices

early adopters Careful choosers of new products

early majority Those adopting new products just before the average person

electronic commerce (e-commerce) "Sharing . . . business information, maintaining business relationships, and conducting business transactions by means of telecommunications networks"

electronic data interchange (EDI) A computerized means of integrating order processing with production, inventory, accounting, and transportation

electronic marketing (e-marketing) The strategic process of creating, distributing, promoting, and pricing products for targeted customers in the virtual environment of the Internet

embargo A government's suspension of trade in a particular product or with a given country

empowerment Giving customer-contact employees authority and responsibility to make marketing decisions on their own

environmental analysis The process of assessing and interpreting the information gathered through environmental scanning

environmental scanning The process of collecting information about forces in the marketing environment

ethical issue An identifiable problem, situation, or opportunity requiring a choice among several actions that must be evaluated as right or wrong, ethical or unethical

European Union (EU) An alliance that promotes trade among its member countries in Europe

evaluative criteria Objective and subjective characteristics that are important to a buyer

everyday low prices (EDLP) Setting a low price for products on a consistent basis

exchange controls Government restrictions on the amount of a particular currency that can be bought or sold

exchanges The provision or transfer of goods, services, or ideas in return for something of value

exclusive distribution Using a single outlet in a fairly large geographic area to distribute a product

executive judgment Sales forecasting based on the intuition of one or more executives

experiment A research method that attempts to maintain certain variables while measuring the effects of experimental variables

expert forecasting survey Sales forecasts prepared by experts such as economists, management consultants, advertising executives, college professors, or other persons outside the firm

exploratory research Research conducted to gather more information about a problem or to make a tentative hypothesis more specific

exporting The sale of products to foreign markets

extended problem solving A type of consumer problem-solving process employed when purchasing unfamiliar, expensive, or infrequently bought products

external customers Individuals who patronize a business

external reference price A comparison price provided by others

external search An information search in which buyers seek information from outside sources

F.O.B. destination A price indicating the producer is absorbing shipping costs

F.O.B. factory The price of the merchandise at the factory, before shipment

family branding Branding all of a firm's products with the same name

family packaging Using similar packaging for all of a firm's products or packaging that has one common design element

feature article A manuscript of up to 3,000 words prepared for a specific publication

Federal Trade Commission (FTC) An agency that regulates a variety of business practices and curbs false advertising, misleading pricing, and deceptive packaging and labeling

feedback The receiver's response to a message

fixed costs Costs that do not vary with changes in the number of units produced or sold

focus-group interview A research method involving observation of group interaction when members are exposed to an idea or a concept

franchising A form of licensing in which a franchiser, in exchange for a financial commitment, grants a franchisee the right to market its product in accordance with the franchiser's standards

free merchandise A manufacturer's reward given to resellers for purchasing a stated quantity of products

free samples Samples of a product given out to encourage trial and purchase

freight absorption pricing Absorption of all or part of actual freight costs by the seller

freight forwarders Organizations that consolidate shipments from several firms into efficient lot sizes

full-service wholesalers Merchant wholesalers that perform the widest range of wholesaling functions

functional modifications Changes affecting a product's versatility, effectiveness, convenience, or safety

General Agreement on Tariffs and Trade (GATT) An agreement among nations to reduce worldwide tariffs and increase international trade

general merchandise retailer A retail establishment that offers a variety of product lines that are stocked in depth

general merchandise wholesalers Full-service wholesalers with a wide product mix but limited depth within product lines

generic brands Brands indicating only the product category

geodemographic segmentation Marketing segmentation that clusters people in zip code areas and smaller neighborhood units based on lifestyle and demographic information

geographic pricing Reductions for transportation and other costs related to the physical distance between buyer and seller

globalization The development of marketing strategies that treat the entire world (or its major regions) as a single entity

good A tangible physical entity

government markets Federal, state, county, and local governments that buy goods and services to support their internal operations and provide products to their constituencies

green marketing The specific development, pricing, promotion, and distribution of products that do not harm the natural environment

gross domestic product (GDP) The market value of a nation's total output of goods and services for a given period; an overall measure of economic standing

growth stage The stage of a product's life cycle when sales rise rapidly and profits reach a peak and then start to decline

heterogeneity Variation in quality

heterogeneous markets Markets made up of individuals or organizations with diverse needs for products in a specific product class

homogeneous market A market in which a large proportion of customers have similar needs for a product

horizontal channel integration Combining organizations at the same level of operation under one management

hypermarkets Stores that combine supermarket and discount shopping in one location

hypothesis An informed guess or assumption about a certain problem or set of circumstances

idea A concept, philosophy, image, or issue

idea generation Seeking product ideas to achieve objectives

illustrations Photos, drawings, graphs, charts, and tables used to spark audience interest

import tariff A duty levied by a nation on goods bought outside its borders and brought in

importing The purchase of products from a foreign source

impulse buying An unplanned buying behavior resulting from a powerful urge to buy something immediately

individual branding A policy of naming each product differently

industrial distributor An independent business that takes title to business products and carries inventories

inelastic demand Demand that is not significantly altered by a price increase or decrease

information inputs Sensations received through the sense organs

in-home (door-to-door) interview A personal interview that takes place in the respondent's home

innovators First adopters of new products

inseparability Being produced and consumed at the same time

installations Facilities and nonportable major equipment

institutional advertising Promotes organizational images, ideas, and political issues

institutional markets Organizations with charitable, educational, community, or other nonbusiness goals

intangibility A service that is not physical and cannot be touched

integrated marketing communications Coordination of promotional efforts for maximum informational and persuasive impact

intended strategy The strategy the company decides on during the planning phase

intensive distribution Using all available outlets to distribute a product

interactivity The ability to allow customers to express their needs and wants directly to the firm in response to the firm's marketing communications

intermodal transportation Two or more transportation modes used in combination

internal customers A company's employees

internal marketing Coordinating internal exchanges between the firm and its employees to achieve successful external exchanges between the firm and its customers

internal reference price A price developed in the buyer's mind through experience with the product

internal search An information search in which buyers search their memories for information about products that might solve their problem

international marketing Developing and performing marketing activities across national boundaries

introduction stage The initial stage of a product's life cycle—its first appearance in the marketplace— when sales start at zero and profits are negative

inventory management Developing and maintaining adequate assortments of products to meet customers' needs

joint demand Demand involving the use of two or more items in combination to produce a product

joint venture A partnership between a domestic firm and a foreign firm or government

just-in-time (JIT) An inventory management approach in which supplies arrive just when needed for production or resale

kinesic communication Communicating through the movement of head, eyes, arms, hands, legs, or torso

labeling Providing identifying, promotional, or other information on product labels

laggards The last adopters, who distrust new products

late majority Skeptics who adopt new products when they feel it is necessary

layout The physical arrangement of an ad's illustration and copy

learning Changes in an individual's thought processes and behavior caused by information and experience

level of involvement An individual's intensity of interest in a product and the importance of the product for that person

level of quality The amount of quality a product possesses

licensing An alternative to direct investment requiring a licensee to pay commissions or royalties on sales or supplies used in manufacturing

lifestyle An individual's pattern of living expressed through activities, interests, and opinions

limited problem solving A type of consumer problem-solving process that buyers use when purchasing products occasionally or when they need information about an unfamiliar brand in a familiar product category

limited-line wholesalers Full-service wholesalers that carry only a few product lines but many products within those lines

limited-service wholesalers Merchant wholesalers that provide some services and specialize in a few functions

line extension Development of a product that is closely related to existing products in the line but meets different customer needs

mail survey A research method in which respondents answer a questionnaire sent through the mail

mail-order wholesalers Limited-service wholesalers that sell products through catalogs

manufacturer brands Brands initiated by producers

manufacturers' agents Independent intermediaries that represent more than one seller and offer complete product lines

marginal cost (MC) The extra cost a firm incurs by producing one more unit of a product

marginal revenue (MR) The change in total revenue resulting from the sale of an additional unit of a product

market A group of individuals and/or organizations that have needs for products in a product class and have the ability, willingness, and authority to purchase those products

market density The number of potential customers within a unit of land area

market manager The person responsible for managing the marketing activities that serve a particular group of customers

market opportunity A combination of circumstances and timing that permits an organization to take action to reach a target market

market potential The total amount of a product that customers will purchase within a specified period at a specific level of industrywide marketing activity

market segment Individuals, groups, or organizations with one or more similar characteristics that cause them to have similar product needs

market segmentation The process of dividing a total market into groups with relatively similar product needs to design a marketing mix that matches those needs

market share The percentage of a market that actually buys a specific product from a particular company

market test Making a product available to buyers in one or more test areas and measuring purchases and consumer responses

market-growth/market-share matrix A strategic planning tool based on the philosophy that a product's market growth rate and market share are important in determining marketing strategy

marketing The process of creating, distributing, promoting, and pricing goods, services, and ideas to facilitate satisfying exchanges with customers and develop and maintain favorable relationships with stakeholders in a dynamic environment

marketing channel A group of individuals and organizations directing products from producers to customers

marketing citizenship The adoption of a strategic focus for fulfilling the economic, legal, ethical, and philanthropic social responsibilities expected by stakeholders

marketing concept A managerial philosophy that an organization should try to satisfy customers' needs through a coordinated set of activities that also allows the organization to achieve its goals

marketing control process Establishing performance standards and trying to match actual performance to those standards

marketing decision support system (MDSS) Customized computer software that aids marketing managers in decision making

marketing environment The competitive, economic, political, legal and regulatory, technological, and sociocultural forces that surround the customer and affect the marketing mix

marketing ethics Principles and standards that define acceptable marketing conduct as determined by various stakeholders

marketing implementation The process of putting marketing strategies into action

marketing information system (MIS) A framework for the management and structuring of information gathered regularly from sources inside and outside an organization

marketing intermediary A middleman linking producers to other middlemen or ultimate consumers through contractual arrangements or through the purchase and resale of products

marketing management The process of planning, organizing, implementing, and controlling marketing activities to facilitate exchanges effectively and efficiently

marketing mix Four marketing activities—product, pricing, distribution, and promotion—that a firm can control to meet the needs of customers within its target market

marketing objective A statement of what is to be accomplished through marketing activities

marketing orientation An organizationwide commitment to researching and responding to customer needs

marketing plan A written document that specifies the activities to be performed to implement and control an organization's marketing activities

marketing planning The process of assessing opportunities and resources, determining objectives, defining strategies, and establishing guidelines for implementation and control of the marketing program

marketing research The systematic design, collection, interpretation, and reporting of information to help marketers solve specific marketing problems or take advantage of marketing opportunities

marketing strategy A plan of action for identifying and analyzing a target market and developing a marketing mix to meet the needs of that market

markup pricing Adding to the cost of the product a predetermined percentage of that cost

Maslow's hierarchy of needs The five levels of needs that humans seek to satisfy, from most to least important

materials handling Physical handling of products

maturity stage The stage of a product's life cycle when the sales curve peaks and starts to decline as profits continue to fall

media plan Specifies media vehicles and schedule for running the advertisements

medium of transmission The means of carrying the coded message from the source to the receiver

megacarriers Freight transportation firms that provide several modes of shipment

memory The ability to access databases or data warehouses containing individual customer profiles and past purchase histories and to use these data in real time to customize a marketing offer

merchandise allowance A manufacturer's agreement to pay resellers certain amounts of money for providing special promotional efforts

merchant wholesalers Independently owned businesses that take title to goods, assume ownership risks, and buy and resell products to other wholesalers, business customers, or retailers

micromarketing An approach to market segmentation in which organizations focus precise marketing efforts on very small geographic markets

mission statement A long-term view of what the organization wants to become

missionary salespeople Support sales-persons who assist the producer's customers in selling to their own customers

modified rebuy purchase A new-task purchase that is changed on subse-quent orders or when the require-ments of a straight rebuy purchase are modified

money refunds A sales promotion technique offering consumers money when they mail in a proof of purchase, usually for multiple product purchases

motive An internal energizing force that directs a person's behavior toward satisfying needs or achieving goals

MRO supplies Maintenance, repair, and operating items that facilitate production and operations but do not become part of the finished product

multinational enterprise A firm that has operations or subsidiaries in many countries

multiple sourcing An organiza-tion's decision to use several suppliers

multiple-unit pricing Packaging together two or more identical products and selling them for a single price

National Advertising Review Board (NARB) A self-regulatory unit that considers challenges to issues raised by the National Advertising Division (an arm of the Council of Better Business Bureaus) about an advertisement

negotiated pricing Establishing a final price through bargaining

neighborhood shopping centers Shopping centers usually consisting of several small convenience and specialty stores

new-product development process A seven-phase process for introducing products

news release A short piece of copy publicizing an event or a product

new-task purchase An initial purchase by an organization of an item to be used to perform a new job or solve a new problem

noise Anything that reduces a communication's clarity and accuracy

noncumulative discounts One-time reductions in price based on specific factors

nonprice competition Emphasizing factors other than price to distin-guish a product from competing brands

nonprobability sampling A sampling technique in which there is no way to calculate the likelihood that a specific element of the population being studied will be chosen

North American Free Trade Agreement (NAFTA) An alliance that merges Canada, Mexico, and the United States into a single market

North American Industry Classifica-tion System (NAICS) An industry classification system that will generate comparable statistics among the United States, Canada, and Mexico

objective-and-task approach Budgeting for an advertising campaign by first determining its objectives and then calculating the cost of all the tasks needed to attain them

odd-even pricing Ending the price with certain numbers to influence buyers' perceptions of the price or product

off-price retailers Stores that buy manufacturers' seconds, overruns, returns, and off-season merchandise for resale to consumers at deep discounts

online retailing Retailing that makes products available to buyers through computer connections

online survey A research method in which respondents answer a ques-tionnaire via e-mail or on a website

opinion leader A reference group member who provides information about a specific sphere that interests reference group participants

order getter The salesperson who sells to new customers and increases sales to current ones

order processing The receipt and transmission of sales order information

order takers Salespersons who primarily seek repeat sales

outsourcing The contracting of physical distribution tasks to third parties who do not have managerial authority within the marketing channel

patronage motives Motives that influence where a person purchases products on a regular basis

penetration pricing Setting prices below those of competing brands to penetrate a market and gain a signif-icant market share quickly

percent-of-sales approach Budgeting for an advertising campaign by multiplying the firm's past or expected sales by a standard percentage

perception The process of selecting, organizing, and interpreting information inputs to produce meaning

performance standard An expected level of performance

periodic discounting Temporary reduction of prices on a patterned or systematic basis

perishability The inability of unused service capacity to be stored for future use

personal interview survey A research method in which participants respond to survey questions face to face

personal selling Paid personal communication that informs customers and persuades them to buy products

personality A set of internal traits and distinct behavioral tendencies that result in consistent patterns of behavior

physical distribution Activities used to move products from producers to consumers and other end users

pioneer advertising Tries to stimulate demand for a product category rather than a specific brand by informing potential buyers about the product

pioneer promotion Promotion that informs consumers about a new product

point-of-purchase (P-O-P) materials Signs, window displays, display racks, and similar means used to attract customers

population All the elements, units, or individuals of interest to researchers for a specific study

portal A multiservice website that serves as a gateway to other websites

posttest Evaluation of advertising effectiveness after the campaign

premium money Also called push money; extra compensation to salespeople for pushing a line of goods

premium pricing Pricing the highest-quality or most versatile products higher than other models in the product line

premiums Items offered free or at a minimal cost as a bonus for purchasing a product

press conference A meeting used to announce major news events

prestige pricing Setting prices at an artificially high level to convey prestige or a quality image

prestige sensitive Drawn to products that signify prominence and status

pretest Evaluation of ads performed before a campaign begins

price Value exchanged for products in a marketing transaction

price competition Emphasizing price and matching or beating competitors' prices

price conscious Striving to pay low prices

price discrimination Providing price differentials that injure competition by giving one or more buyers a competitive advantage

price elasticity of demand A measure of the sensitivity of demand to changes in price

price leaders Products priced below the usual markup, near cost, or below cost

price lining Setting a limited number of prices for selected groups or lines of merchandise

price skimming Charging the highest possible price that buyers who most desire the product will pay

pricing objectives Goals that describe what a firm wants to achieve through pricing

primary data Data observed and recorded or collected directly from respondents

primary demand Demand for a product category rather than for a specific brand

private distributor brands Brands initiated and owned by resellers

private warehouses Company-operated facilities for storing and shipping products

probability sampling A sampling technique in which every element in the population being studied has a known chance of being selected for study

process materials Materials that are used directly in the production of other products but are not readily identifiable

producer markets Individuals and business organizations that purchase products to make profits by using them to produce other products or using them in their operations

product A good, a service, or an idea

product adoption process The stages buyers go through in accepting a product

product advertising Promotes products' uses, features, and benefits

product deletion Eliminating a product from the product mix

product design How a product is conceived, planned, and produced

product development Determining if producing a product is feasible and cost effective

product differentiation Creating and designing products so that customers perceive them as different from competing products

product features Specific design characteristics that allow a product to perform certain tasks

product item A specific version of a product

product life cycle The progression of a product through four stages: introduction, growth, maturity, and decline

product line A group of closely related product items viewed as a unit because of marketing, technical, or end-use considerations

product manager The person within an organization responsible for a product, a product line, or several distinct products that make up a group

product mix The total group of products that an organization makes available to customers

product modification Change in one or more characteristics of a product

product positioning Creating and maintaining a certain concept of a product in customers' minds

product-line pricing Establishing and adjusting prices of multiple products within a product line

professional pricing Fees set by people with great skill or experience in a particular field

promotion Communication to build and maintain relationships by informing and persuading one or more audiences

promotion mix A combination of promotional methods used to promote a specific product

prospecting Developing a list of potential customers

proxemic communication Communicating by varying the physical distance in face-to-face interactions

psychological influences Factors that partly determine people's general behavior, thus influencing their behavior as consumers

psychological pricing Pricing that attempts to influence a customer's perception of price to make a product's price more attractive

public relations Communications efforts used to create and maintain favorable relations between an organization and its stakeholders

public warehouses Businesses that lease storage space and related physical distribution facilities to other firms

publicity A news story type of communication transmitted through a mass medium at no charge

pull policy Promoting a product directly to consumers to develop strong consumer demand that pulls products through the marketing channel

push policy Promoting a product only to the next institution down the marketing channel

quality The overall characteristics of a product that allow it to perform as expected in satisfying customer needs

quality modifications Changes relating to a product's dependability and durability

quantity discounts Deductions from list price for purchasing large quantities

quota A limit on the amount of goods an importing country will accept for certain product categories in a specific time period

quota sampling A nonprobability sampling technique in which researchers divide the population into groups and then arbitrarily choose participants from each group

rack jobbers Full-service, specialty-line wholesalers that own and maintain display racks in stores

random discounting Temporary reduction of prices on an unsystematic basis

random factor analysis An analysis attempting to attribute erratic sales variation to random, nonrecurrent events

random sampling A type of probability sampling in which all units in a population have an equal chance of appearing in a sample

raw materials Basic natural materials that become part of a physical product

realized strategy The strategy that actually takes place

rebates A sales promotion technique whereby a customer is sent a specific amount of money for purchasing a single product

receiver The individual, group, or organization that decodes a coded message

reciprocity An arrangement unique to business marketing in which two organizations agree to buy from each other

recognition test A posttest in which individuals are shown the actual ad and asked if they recognize it

reference group Any group that positively or negatively affects a person's values, attitudes, or behavior

reference pricing Pricing a product at a moderate level and positioning it next to a more expensive model or brand

regional issues Versions of a magazine that differ across geographic regions

regional shopping center A type of shopping center with the largest department stores, the widest product mix, and the deepest product lines of all shopping centers

regression analysis A method of predicting sales based on finding a relationship between past sales and one or more variables, such as population or income

reinforcement advertising Assures users they chose the right brand and tells them how to get the most satisfaction from it

relationship marketing Establishing long-term, mutually satisfying buyer-seller relationships

reliability A condition existing when a research technique produces almost identical results in repeated trials

reminder advertising Reminds consumers about an established brand's uses, characteristics, and benefits

research design An overall plan for obtaining the information needed to address a research problem or issue

reseller markets Intermediaries who buy finished goods and resell them for profit

retail positioning Identifying an unserved or underserved market segment and serving it through a strategy that distinguishes the retailer from others in the minds of consumers in that segment

retailer An organization that purchases products for the purpose of reselling them to ultimate consumers

retailing Transactions in which ultimate consumers are the buyers

role Actions and activities that a person in a particular position is supposed to perform based on expectations of the individual and surrounding persons

routinized response behavior A type of consumer problem-solving process used when buying frequently purchased, low-cost items that require very little search-and-decision effort

sales branches Manufacturer-owned intermediaries that sell products and provide support services to the manufacturer's sales force

sales contest A promotion method used to motivate distributors, retailers, and sales personnel through recognition of outstanding achievements

sales force forecasting survey A survey of a firm's sales force regarding anticipated sales in their territories for a specified period

sales forecast The amount of a product a company expects to sell during a specific period at a specified level of marketing activities

sales offices Manufacturer-owned operations that provide services normally associated with agents

sales promotion An activity and/or material meant to induce resellers or salespeople to sell a product or consumers to buy it

sample A limited number of units chosen to represent the characteristics of the population

sampling The process of selecting representative units from a total population

scan-back allowance A manufacturer's reward to retailers based on the number of pieces scanned

scrambled merchandising The addition of unrelated products and product lines to an existing product mix, particularly fast-moving items that can be sold in volume

screening Choosing the most promising ideas for further review

seasonal analysis An analysis of daily, weekly, or monthly sales figures to evaluate the degree to which seasonal factors influence sales

seasonal discount A price reduction given to buyers for purchasing goods or services out of season

secondary data Data compiled both inside and outside the organization for some purpose other than the current investigation

secondary-market pricing Setting one price for the primary target market and a different price for another market

segmentation variables Characteristics of individuals, groups, or organizations used to divide a market into segments

selective demand Demand for a specific brand

selective distortion An individual's changing or twisting of information when it is inconsistent with personal feelings or beliefs

selective distribution Using only some available outlets to distribute a product

selective exposure The process of selecting inputs to be exposed to our awareness while ignoring others

selective retention Remembering information inputs that support personal feelings and beliefs and forgetting inputs that do not

self-concept Perception or view of oneself

selling agents Intermediaries that market a whole product line or a manufacturer's entire output

service An intangible product involving a deed, performance, or effort that cannot be physically possessed

shopping mall intercept interview A research method that involves interviewing a percentage of persons passing by "intercept" points in a mall

shopping products Items for which buyers are willing to expend considerable effort in planning and making purchases

single-source data Information provided by a single marketing research firm

situational influences Influences resulting from circumstances, time, and location that affect the consumer buying decision process

social class An open group of individuals with similar social rank

social influences The forces other people exert on one's buying behavior

social responsibility An organization's obligation to maximize its positive impact and minimize its negative impact on society

sociocultural forces The influences in a society and its culture(s) that change people's attitudes, beliefs, norms, customs, and lifestyles

sole sourcing An organization's decision to use only one supplier

source A person, group, or organization with a meaning it tries to share with an audience

spam Unsolicited commercial e-mail

special-event pricing Advertised sales or price cutting linked to a holiday, season, or event

specialty products Items with unique characteristics that buyers are willing to expend considerable effort to obtain

specialty-line wholesalers Full-service wholesalers that carry only a single product line or a few items within a product line

stakeholders Constituents who have a "stake" or claim in some aspect of a company's products, operations, markets, industry, and outcomes

Standard Industrial Classification (SIC) System The federal government system for classifying selected economic characteristics of industrial, commercial, financial, and service organizations

statistical interpretation Analysis of what is typical or what deviates from the average

storyboard A mockup combining copy and visual material to show the sequence of major scenes in a commercial

straight commission compensation plan Paying salespeople according to the amount of their sales in a given time period

straight rebuy purchase A routine purchase of the same products by a business buyer

straight salary compensation plan Paying salespeople a specific amount per time period

strategic alliances Partnerships formed to create a competitive advantage on a worldwide basis

strategic business unit (SBU) A division, product line, or other profit center within a parent company

strategic channel alliance An agreement whereby the products of one organization are distributed through the marketing channels of another

strategic philanthropy The synergistic use of organizational core competencies and resources to address key stakeholders' interests and achieve both organizational and social benefits

strategic planning The process of establishing an organizational mission and formulating goals, corporate strategy, marketing objectives, marketing strategy, and a marketing plan

strategic windows Temporary periods of optimal fit between the key requirements of a market and a firm's capabilities

stratified sampling A type of probability sampling in which the population is divided into groups according to a common attribute and a random sample is then chosen within each group

styling The physical appearance of a product

subculture A group of individuals whose characteristic values and behavior patterns are similar and differ from those of the surrounding culture

supermarkets Large, self-service stores that carry a complete line of food products, along with some nonfood products

superstores Giant retail outlets that carry food and nonfood products found in supermarkets, as well as most routinely purchased consumer products

supply-chain management Long-term partnerships among marketing channel members that reduce inefficiencies, costs, and redundancies and develop innovative approaches to satisfy customers

support personnel Sales staff members who facilitate selling but usually are not involved solely with making sales

sustainable competitive advantage An advantage that the competition cannot copy

SWOT analysis A tool that marketers use to assess an organization's strengths, weaknesses, opportunities, and threats

tactile communication Communicating through touching

target audience The group of people at whom advertisements are aimed

target market A specific group of customers on whom an organization focuses its marketing efforts

technical salespeople Support salespersons who give technical assistance to a firm's current customers

technology The application of knowledge and tools to solve problems and perform tasks more efficiently

telemarketing The performance of marketing-related activities by telephone

telephone depth interview An interview that combines the traditional focus group's ability to probe with the confidentiality provided by telephone surveys

telephone survey A research method in which respondents' answers to a questionnaire are recorded by interviewers on the phone

television home shopping A form of selling in which products are presented to television viewers, who can buy them by calling a toll-free number and paying with a credit card

test marketing Introducing a product on a limited basis to measure the extent to which potential customers will actually buy it

time series analysis A forecasting method that uses historical sales data to discover patterns in the firm's sales over time and generally involves trend, cycle, seasonal, and random factor analyses

total cost The sum of average fixed and average variable costs times the quantity produced

total quality management (TQM) A philosophy that uniform commitment to quality in all areas of the organization will promote a culture that meets customers' perceptions of quality

trade discount Also known as functional discount; a reduction off the list price given by a producer to an intermediary for performing certain functions

trade name Full legal name of an organization

trade sales promotion methods Ways of persuading wholesalers and retailers to carry a producer's products and market them aggressively

trade salespeople Salespersons involved mainly in helping a producer's customers promote a product

trademark A legal designation of exclusive use of a brand

traditional specialty retailers Stores that carry a narrow product mix with deep product lines

transfer pricing Prices charged in sales between an organization's units

transportation The movement of products from where they are made to where they are used

trend analysis An analysis that focuses on aggregate sales data over a period of many years to determine general trends in annual sales

truck wholesalers Limited-service wholesalers that transport products directly to customers for inspection and selection

unaided recall test A posttest in which respondents identify ads they have recently seen but are given no recall clues

undifferentiated targeting strategy A strategy in which an organization defines an entire market for a particular product as its target market, designs a single marketing mix, and directs it at that market

uniform geographic pricing Charging all customers the same price, regardless of geographic location

unsought products Products purchased to solve a sudden problem, products of which customers are unaware, and products that people do not necessarily think about buying

validity A condition existing when a research method measures what it is supposed to measure

value A customer's subjective assessment of benefits relative to costs in determining the worth of a product

value analysis An evaluation of each component of a potential purchase

value conscious Concerned about price and quality of a product

variable costs Costs that vary directly with changes in the number of units produced or sold

vendor analysis A formal, systematic evaluation of current and potential vendors

venture team A cross-functional group that creates entirely new products that may be aimed at new markets

vertical channel integration Combining two or more stages of the marketing channel under one management

vertical marketing system (VMS) A marketing channel managed by a single channel member

warehouse clubs Large-scale, members-only establishments that combine features of cash-and-carry wholesaling with discount retailing

warehouse showrooms Retail facilities in large, low-cost buildings with large on-premises inventories and minimal services

warehousing The design and operation of facilities for storing and moving goods

wheel of retailing A hypothesis holding that new retailers usually enter the market as low-status, low-margin, low-price operators but eventually evolve into high-cost, high-price merchants

wholesaler An individual or organization that facilitates and expedites wholesale transactions

wholesaling Transactions in which products are bought for resale, for making other products, or for general business operations

width of product mix The number of product lines a company offers

willingness to spend An inclination to buy because of expected satisfaction from a product, influenced by the ability to buy and numerous psychological and social forces

World Trade Organization (WTO) An entity that promotes free trade among member nations

zone pricing Pricing based on transportation costs within major geographic zones

Notes

CHAPTER 1

1. "1st: Chevrolet Corvette Coupe," *Road and Track,* March 2004, pp. 74–76; Csaba Csere, "Simply the Fastest-Ever Production Vette," *Car and Driver,* February 2005, p. 74; James R. Healey, "Hot, Fun, and Even Functional," *USA Today,* November 26, 2004, p. 10D; "Mattel Joins with GM to Roll Out Hot Wheels Corvette C6," Mattel, press release, January 13, 2004, http://collectibles.about.com/cs/automobiliaracing/a/blPRmattel11404.htm; Ron Perry, "Chevrolet Corvette vs. Porsche 911 Carrera S: Classic Warfare," *Road and Track,* December 2004, p. 87–96; Rachel Sams, "PRS Guitars Signs Pact with Corvette," *Baltimore Business Journal,* January 15, 2005, http://baltimore.bizjournals.com/baltimore/stories/2005/01/17/daily2.html.
2. *Marketing News,* September 15, 2004, p. 1.
3. Michael J. Weiss, "To Be About to Be," *American Demographics,* September 2003, pp. 29–36.
4. Tom Lowry, "Wow! Yao!" *Business Week,* October 25, 2004, pp. 86–90.
5. "A New Way to Dial Up the Net," *Time,* November 24, 2003, p. 84.
6. Shelly K. Schwartz, "Do Big Boxes Stack Up?" CNN, May 3, 2001, www.cnn.com.
7. Lorrie Grant, "Scrimping to Splurge," *USA Today,* January 28, 2005, p. 1B.
8. Grainger David, "Can McDonald's Cook Again," *Fortune,* April 14, 2003, p. 122; "McDonald's Worldwide Corporate Site," McDonald's, www.mcdonalds.com/corp/about.html (accessed January 25, 2005).
9. Great Southern Sauce Company, www.greatsauce.com (accessed January 25, 2005).
10. James Tenser, "Endorser Qualities Count More Than Ever," *Advertising Age,* November 8, 2004, pp. S-2, S-4.
11. Dan McDonough, Jr., "Newgen Customizes CRM for Ford, Mercury Dealers," CRMDaily.com, December 11, 2001, www.crmdaily.com/perl/story/?id=15236.
12. Steven Gray, "Pressure Mounts on Fast-Food Chains to Remove Trans Fats," *The Wall Street Journal,* December 14, 2004, p. D1, http://online.wsj.com.
13. Ajay K. Kohli and Bernard J. Jaworski, "Market Orientation: The Construct, Research Propositions, and Managerial Implications," *Journal of Marketing,* April 1990, pp. 1–18.
14. Eugene W. Anderson, Claes Fornell, and Sanal K. Mazvancheryl, "Customer Satisfaction and Shareholder Value," *Journal of Marketing,* October 2004, pp. 172–185.
15. Kohli and Jaworski, "Market Orientation: The Construct, Research Propositions, and Managerial Implications."
16. Sunil Gupta, Donald R. Lehmann, and Jennifer Ames Stuart, "Valuing Customers," *Journal of Marketing Research,* February 2004, pp. 7–18.
17. Jacquelyn S. Thomas, Robert C. Blattberg, and Edward J. Fox, "Recapturing Lost Customers," *Journal of Marketing Research,* February 2004, pp. 31–45.
18. Alan Grant and Leonard Schlesinger, "Realize Your Customers' Full Profit Potential," *Harvard Business Review,* September/October 1995, p. 59.
19. Jagdish N. Sheth and Rajendras Sisodia, "More Than Ever Before, Marketing Is Under Fire to Account for What It Spends," *Marketing Management,* Fall 1995, pp. 13–14.
20. Lynette Ryals and Adrian Payne, "Customer Relationship Management in Financial Services: Towards Information-Enabled Relationship Marketing," *Journal of Strategic Marketing,* March 2001, p. 3.

21. O. C. Ferrell and Michael Hartline *Marketing Strategy* (Mason, OH: South-Western, 2005), p. 114.
22. Werner J. Reinartz and V. Kumar, "On the Profitability of Long-Life Customers in a Noncontractual Setting: An Empirical Investigation and Implications for Marketing," *Journal of Marketing,* October 2000, pp. 17–35.
23. Libby Estell, "This Call Center Accelerates Sales," *Sales & Marketing Management,* February 1999, p. 72.
24. Roland T. Rust, Katherine N. Lemon, and Valarie A. Zeithaml, "Return on Marketing: Using Customer Equity to Focus Marketing Strategy," *Journal of Marketing,* January 2004, pp. 109–127.
25. Rajkumar Venkatesan and V. Kumar, "A Customer Lifetime Value Framework for Customer Selection and Resource Allocation Strategy," *Journal of Marketing,* October 2004, pp. 106–125.
26. Alan Brown, "How Amazon.com Sells," *eCompany,* June 2001, p. 114.
27. Ferrell and Hartline, *Marketing Strategy,* p. 108.
28. Keith Regan, "Yahoo! Inks Web Development Deal with Cigna Health," *E-Commerce Times,* January 9, 2002, www.ecommerce-times.com/perl/story/?id=15697.
29. Gordon T. Anderson, "Lights! Camera! The New $20," CNN/Money, September 18, 2003, http://money.cnn.com/2003/09/16/pf/banking/marketing_new_money/.
30. "Americans Give $241 Billion to Charity," American Association of Fundraising Counsel, press release, June 21, 2004, www.aafrc.org/press_releases/trustreleases/index.html.
31. Steve Lohr, "Is IBM's Lenovo Proposal a Threat to National Security?" *The New York Times,* January 31, 2005, www.nytimes.com.
32. Keith Regan, "Report: Online Sales Top $100 Billion," *E-Commerce Times,* June 1, 2004, www.ecommercetimes.com/story/34148.html.
33. Susan Berfield, with Diane Brady and Tom Lowry, "The CEO of Hip Hop," *Business Week,* October 27, 2003, pp. 90–98.
34. Donna Hood Crecca, "Higher Calling," *Chain Leader,* December 2002, p. 14; "Finagle Sees a Return to More Normal Business Mode," *Foodservice East,* Fall 2002, pp. 1, 17; interview with Laura B. Trust and Alan Litchman, February 25, 2003; "The One to Top," Finagle A Bagel, www.finagleabagel.com/index2.htm (accessed January 25, 2005); "Sloan Grads Bet Their Money on Bagels," *Providence Business News,* October 25, 1999, p. 14; "State Fare: Finagle A Bagel, Boston," *Restaurants and Institutions,* October 1, 2002, www.rimag.com/1902/sr.htm.
a. David Gaffen, "Gillette Sparkles on Merger," *The Wall Street Journal,* January 28, 2005, http://online.wsj.com; Atifa Hargrave-Silk, "P&G Broadening China Sweet Spot," *Media Asia,* January 16, 2004, p. 3, accessed via Business Source Premier; Cliff Peale, "P&G in Deal to Buy Gillette," *USA Today,* January 28, 2005, p. 1B; Procter & Gamble Annual Report, 2004.
b. Lambert's Café History, distributed by Lambert's Café, 2515 E. Malone, Sikeston, MO 63801, 2005, pp. 1, 80; Lambert's Café, www.throwedrolls.com/ (accessed February 9, 2005).
c. Ford Motor Company, www.ford.com (accessed January 26, 2005); John S. McClenahen, "Ford's Formidable Challenge," *Industry Week,* February 1, 2003, www.industryweek.com/currentArticles/asp/articles.asp?ArticleID=1379; Joann Muller, "Lean Green Machine," *Forbes,* February 3, 2003, www.forbes.com/global/2003/0203023_print.html; Chuck Salter, "Ford's Escape Route," *Fast Company,* October 2004, pp. 106+.

CHAPTER 2

1. Cynthia Crossen and Kortney Stringer, "A Merchant's Evolution," *The Wall Street Journal,* November 18, 2004, pp. B1–B2; David Lieberman, "Retailing Giants Team Up," *USA Today,* November 18, 2004, p. 1A; Amy Merrick and Dennis Berman, "Kmart to Buy Sears for $11.5 Billion," *The Wall Street Journal,* November 18, 2004, pp. A1, A8; David Runk, "The Mind Behind the Merger," *The [Fort Collins] Coloradoan,* November 18, 2004, pp. D8, D7.
2. O. C. Ferrell and Michael Hartline, *Marketing Strategy* (Mason, OH: South-Western, 2005), p. 10.
3. Christian Homburg, Karley Krohmer, and John P. Workman, Jr., "A Strategy Implementation Perspective of Market Orientation," *Journal of Business Research* 57 (2004): 1331–1340.
4. Ferrell and Hartline, *Marketing Strategy,* p. 10.
5. Ibid, p. 51.
6. Graham J. Hooley, Gordon E. Greenley, John W. Cadogan, and John Fahy, "The Performance Impact of Marketing Resources," *Journal of Business Research* 58 (2005): 18–27.
7. Steven Gray, "Wendy's Stumbles with Baja Fresh," *The Wall Street Journal,* January 4, 2005, p. B7, http://online.wsj.com.
8. Derek F. Abell, "Strategic Windows," *Journal of Marketing,* July 1978, p. 21.
9. Michael Krauss, "EBay 'Bids' on Small-Biz Firms to Sustain Growth," *Marketing News,* December 8, 2003, p. 6.
10. Catherine Yang with Jay Green, "You've Got Mail—But Not Enough Ads," *Business Week,* October 25, 2004, p. 48.
11. Ibid.
12. Michael McCarthy, "CD Prices Hit Sour Note with Retailers, Buyers," *USA Today,* December 8, 2003, pp. 1B, 2B.
13. Ibid.
14. Douglas Bowman and Hubert Gatignon, "Determinants of Competitor Response Time to a New Product Introduction," *Journal of Marketing Research,* February 1995, pp. 42–53.
15. Chuck Salter, "Ford's Escape Route," *Fast Company,* October 2004, www.fastcompany.com/magazine/87/ford.html.
16. "Our Mission," Celestial Seasonings, www.celestialseasonings.com/whoweare/corporatehistory/mission.jhtml (accessed January 28, 2005).
17. Steven Gray, "Starbucks Brews Broader Menu," *The Wall Street Journal,* February 9, 2005, p. B9.
18. Thomas Ritter and Hans Georg Gemünden, "The Impact of a Company's Business Strategy on Its Technological Competence, Network Competence and Innovation Success," *Journal of Business Research* 57 (2004): 548–556.
19. Robert McMillan, "Mozilla Gains on IE," *PCWorld,* June 9, 2004, www.pcworld.com/news/article/0,aid,116848,00.asp.
20. Robert D. Buzzell, "The PIMS Program of Strategy Research: A Retrospective Appraisal," *Journal of Business Research* 57 (2004): 478–483.
21. Joseph P. Guiltinan and Gordon W. Paul, *Marketing Management: Strategies and Programs* (New York: McGraw-Hill, 1991), p. 43.
22. George S. Day, "Diagnosing the Product Portfolio," *Journal of Marketing,* April 1977, pp. 30–31.
23. G. Tomas, M. Hult, David W. Cravens, and Jagdish Sheth, "Competitive Advantage in the Global Marketplace: A Focus on Marketing Strategy," *Journal of Business Research,* January 2001, pp. 1–3.
24. Kwaku Atuahene-Gima and Janet Y. Murray, "Antecedents and Outcomes of Marketing Strategy Comprehensiveness," *Journal of Marketing,* October 2004, pp. 33–46.
25. "The Echo Boomers," 60 Minutes, October 3, 2004, CBSNews.com; Michael J. Weiss, "To Be About to Be," *American Demographics,* September 2003, pp. 28–36.
26. Nancy Einhart, "How the New T-Bird Went Off Course," *Business 2.0,* November 2003, pp. 74–76.
27. Christian Homburg, John P. Workman, and Ove Jensen, "Fundamental Changes in Marketing Organization: The Movement Toward a Customer-Focused Organizational Structure," *Journal of the Academy of Marketing Science,* Fall 2000, pp. 459–478.
28. Weiss, "To Be About to Be."
29. Rajdeep Grewal and Patriya Tansuhaj, "The Chain of Effects from Brand Trust and Brand Affect to Brand Performance: The Role of Brand Loyalty," *Journal of Marketing,* April 2001, pp. 67–80.
30. Steve Watkins, "Marketing Basics: The Four P's Are as Relevant Today as Ever," *Investor's Business Daily,* February 4, 2002, p. A1.
31. Bent Dreyer and Kjell Grønhaug, "Uncertainty, Flexibility, and Sustained Competitive Advantage," *Journal of Business Research* 57 (2004): 484–494.
32. Hemant C. Sashittat and Avan R. Jassawalla, "Marketing Implementation in Smaller Organizations: Definition, Framework, and Propositional Inventory," *Journal of the Academy of Marketing Science,* Winter 2001, pp. 50–69.
33. Ferrell and Hartline, *Marketing Strategy,* p. 257.
34. Weiss, "To Be About to Be," pp. 28–36.
35. Adapted from Nigel F. Piercy, *Market-Led Strategic Change* (Newton, MA: Butterworth-Heinemann, 1992), pp. 374–385.
36. Ian N. Lings, "Internal Market Orientation: Construct and Consequences," *Journal of Business Research* 57 (2004): 405–413.
37. Sybil F. Stershic, "Internal Marketing Campaign Reinforces Service Goals," *Marketing News,* July 31, 1998, p. 11.
38. Wuthichai Sittimalakorn and Susan Hart, "Market Orientation Versus Quality Orientation: Sources of Superior Business Performance," *Journal of Strategic Marketing,* December 2004, pp. 243–253.
39. Philip B. Crosby, *Quality Is Free: The Art of Making Quality Certain* (New York: McGraw-Hill, 1979), pp. 9–10.
40. Piercy, *Market-Led Strategic Change.*
41. Douglas W. Vorhies and Neil A. Morgan, "Benchmarketing Marketing Capabilities for Sustainable Competitive Advantage," *Journal of Marketing,* January 2005, pp. 80–94.
42. Kenneth W. Thomas and Betty A. Velthouse, "Cognitive Elements of Empowerment: An 'Interpretive' Model of Intrinsic Task Motivation," *Academy of Management Review,* October 1990, pp. 666–681.
43. Ferrell and Hartline, *Marketing Strategy.*
44. Rohit Deshpande and Frederick E. Webster, Jr., "Organizational Culture and Marketing: Defining the Research Agenda," *Journal of Marketing,* January 1989, pp. 3–15.
45. REI, www.rei.com (accessed January 31, 2005).
46. Kathleen Cholewka, "CRM: Lose the Hype and Strategize," *Sales & Marketing Management,* June 2001, pp. 27–28.
47. Bernard J. Jaworski, "Toward a Theory of Marketing Control: Environmental Context, Control Types, and Consequences," *Journal of Marketing,* July 1988, pp. 23–39.
48. James R. Healey, "Hot, Fun, and Even Functional," *USA Today,* November 26, 2004, p. 10D.
49. "Lincoln Ranks Highest in Customer Satisfaction with Dealer Service, Setting New CSI Record," J. D. Powers & Associates press release, July 20, 2004, www.jdpa.com/news/releases/pressrelease.asp?ID=2004065.
50. Brian Steinberg and Ann Zimmerman, "Lesson Learned, Wal-Mart Touts Lower Prices," *The Wall Street Journal,* December 3, 2004, http://online.wsj.com.
51. "About Jared," Subway, www.subway.com/subwayroot/MenuNutrition/Jared/jaredStats.aspx (accessed January 31, 2005); Jessica Bujol, "Subway Restaurants Passes McDonald's in the U.S.," Subway press release, February 1, 2002, www.subway.com/subwayroot/AboutSubway/mckyd.aspx; Houghton Mifflin video, *Global Growth: The Subway Story;* "Franchise Opportunities," Subway, www.subway.com/subwayroot/Development/ (accessed January 31, 2005); "Jared, the Subway Guy:

Superstar," CNN, November 17, 2003, www.cnn.com/2003/ SHOWBIZ/TV/11/17/subway.guy.ap/; "Man Loses 245 Pounds Eating Nothing But SUBWAY® Sandwiches," Subway, December 2000, www.subway.com/society/public_rel/pcr_press/ 011101pr.htm; "Subway® Restaurants Announces Opening of First Location in Croatia," Subway, June 2001, www.subway.com/society/ public_rel/pcr_press/062501.htm; "Subway® Restaurants Announces Opening of First Location in France," Subway, July 2001, www.subway.com/society/public_rel/pcr_press/070301.htm; "Subway® Restaurants Announces Opening of First Location in Oman," Subway, February 2001, www.subway.com/society/ public_rel/pcr_press/020701.htm; "Subway Student and Educator and Resource Guide," Subway, November 25, 2003, www.subway. com/StudentGuide/.

a. "Case Study: AllDorm," *ecommstats,* www.ecommstats.com/case_ alldorm.jsp (accessed February 9, 2005); Rachel Metz, "Setting Up the Dorm Remotely" *Wired,* August, 18, 2004, www.wired.com/ new/school/0%2c1383%2c64601%2c00.html; Erin Ryan, "Classmates click as Business Partners," *Santa Clara Magazine,* Fall 2003, www.scu.edu/scm/fall2003/bp-alldorm.cfm.

b. Ben Dobbin, "Kodak Gains on Sony in U.S. Digital Camera Market," *The [Fort Collins] Coloradoan,* November 20, 2004, p. D12; Jerry Gleeson, "Digital Revolution Shakes Kodak," *The Coloradoan,* November 1, 2004, p. E1; Alexandra Jardine, "Is This a Kodak Moment?" *Marketing,* October 13, 2004, p. 28, accessed via LexisNexis Academic Database; Robyn Meredith, "Middle Kingdom, Middle Class," *Forbes,* November 15, 2004, pp. 188–192.

c. Joann Louiglio, "Totally Cereal-ous: All-Cereal Restaurant," *The Coloradoan,* December 2004, pp. E1, E2; Cereality, www.cereality. com (accessed January 28, 2005); "A Cereal Store for Cereal (Seriously)," *Business 2.0,* October 2004, p. 42; "Carb Appeal," *Fortune Small Business,* October 2004, p. 28.

CHAPTER 3

1. Michael Barbaro, "A Model Lawsuit: Local Train Maker Wins $40.8 Million Judgment Against Lionel," *The Washington Post,* June 9, 2004, p. E01, via Lexis-Nexis Academic Database; "About Us," MTH Electric Trains, www.mth-railking.com/us/history.asp (accessed February 3, 2005); Joseph Pereira and Ethan Smith, "Bumpy Ride for Bankrupt Lionel Trains," *The [Fort Collins] Coloradoan,* November 21, 2004, pp. E1–E2.

2. P. Varadarajan, Terry Clark, and William M. Pride, "Controlling the Uncontrollable: Managing Your Market Environment," *Sloan Management Review,* Winter 1992, pp. 39–47.

3. "U.S. Soft Drink Sales Flat in 2003, Beverage Marketing Corporation Reports," Beverage Marketing Corporation, press release, March 4, 2004, www.beveragemarketing.com/news2oo.htm.

4. O. C. Ferrell and Michael D. Hartline, *Marketing Strategy* (Mason, OH: South-Western, 2005), p. 58.

5. Rodolfo Vazquez, Maria Leticia Santos, and Luis Ignacio Álvarez, "Market Orientation, Innovation and Competitive Strategies in Industrial Firms," *Journal of Strategic Marketing,* March 2001, pp. 69–90.

6. Lorrie Grant, "Scrimping to Splurge," *USA Today,* January 28, 2005, p. 1B.

7. Patrick Barta and Anne Marie Chaker, "Consumers Voice Rising Dissatisfaction with Companies," *The Wall Street Journal,* May 21, 2001, p. A2.

8. Paula Lyon Andruss, "Staying in the Game: Turning an Economic Dip into Opportunity," *Marketing News,* May 7, 2001, pp. 1, 9.

9. Debbie Thorne McAlister, O.C. Ferrell, and Linda Ferrell, *Business and Society: A Strategic Approach to Corporate Citizenship* (Boston: Houghton Mifflin, 2005); Don Corney, Amy Borrus, and Jay Greene, "Microsoft's All Out Counterattack," *Business Week,* May 15, 2000, pp. 103–106.

10. "FTC: Skin Patches Do Not Cause Weight Loss," Federal Trade Commission, press release, December 15, 2004, www.ftc.gov/opa/2004/12/transdermal.htm.

11. "NAD Refers Advertising Claims by Aventis to the Government," National Advertising Division, press release, October 4, 2004, www.nadreview.org.

12. Chris Woodward, "Some Offices Opt for Cellphones Only," *USA Today,* January 25, 2005, p. B1.

13. McAlister, Ferrell, and Ferrell, *Business and Society.*

14. Ibid.

15. Ibid.

16. Nicholas Negroponte, "Will Everything Be Digital?" *Time,* June 19, 2000.

17. U.S. Bureau of the Census, *Statistical Abstract of the United States,* 2003 (Washington DC: Government Printing Office, 2004), p. 14.

18. Ibid., p. 15.

19. Ibid., p. 18.

20. Rebecca Gardyn, "What's Cookin," *American Demographics,* March 2002, pp. 29–31.

21. Isabelle Maignan and O. C. Ferrell, "Corporate Social Responsibility and Marketing: An Integrative Framework," *Journal of the Academy of Marketing Science,* January 2004, pp. 3–19.

22. "Report: Merck Aware of Vioxx Problems," *The Austin American-Statesman,* November 2, 2004, http://statesman.com.

23. "The Avon Breast Cancer Crusade," Avon, www.avoncompany.com/ women/avoncrusade/ (accessed February 3, 2005).

24. McAlister, Ferrell, and Ferrell, *Business and Society.*

25. O. C. Ferrell, "Business Ethics and Customer Stakeholders," *Academy of Management Executive,* May 2004, pp. 126–129.

26. "Corporate Citizenship Report 2003–2004," Ford Motor Company, www.ford.com/en/company/about/corporateCitizenship/report/ (accessed February 4, 2005).

27. Archie Carroll, "The Pyramid of Corporate Social Responsibility: Toward the Moral Management of Organizational Stakeholders," *Business Horizons,* July/August 1991, p. 42.

28. William T. Neese, Linda Ferrell, and O. C. Ferrell, "An Analysis of Federal Mail and Wire Fraud Cases Related to Marketing," *Journal of Business Research* 58 (2005): 910–918.

29. Devon Leonard, "The Curse of Pooh," *Fortune,* January 20, 2003, pp. 85–92; "Pooh Suit Against Disney Dismissed," CNN, March 29, 2004, www.cnn.com.

30. *Business Ethics,* January/February 1995, p. 13.

31. "Arthur Andersen: Questionable Accounting Practices," in O. C. Ferrell, John Fraedrich, and Linda Ferrell, *Business Ethics: Ethical Decision Making and Cases,* 6th ed. (Boston: Houghton Mifflin, 2005), pp. 281–289.

32. Andrew Backover and Matt Kranz, "Global Crossing Expects 'Significant' Loss, Delays Report," *USA Today,* March 11, 2002, p. 1B.

33. Tim Barnett and Sean Valentine, "Issue Contingencies and Marketers' Recognition of Ethical Issues, Ethical Judgments and Behavioral Intentions," *Journal of Business Research* 57 (2004): 338–346.

34. "2003 Contributions," Giving USA Foundation—AAFRC Trust for Philanthropy/Giving USA 2004, chart, www.aafrc.org/about_aafrc/ bysourceof66.html (accessed February 3, 2005).

35. Jessica Stannard-Friel, "Tsunami Relief Update: A Compilation of Current Corporate Commitments," *onPhilanthropy,* January 12, 2005, www.onphilanthropy.com/onthescene/os2005-01-12.html.

36. "American Express Launches Nationwide Campaign to Help Raise Awareness and Funds for St. Jude Children's Research Hospital," American Express, press release, November 17, 2004, www. findarticles.com/p/articles/mi_m0EIN/is_2004_Nov_17/ ai_n6363419.

37. McAlister, Ferrell, and Ferrell, *Business and Society.*

38. Alan K. Reichert, Marlon S. Webb, and Edward G. Thomas, "Corporate Support for Ethical and Environmental Policies: A Financial Management Perspective," *Journal of Business Ethics* 25 (2000): 53–64.

39. Keith Naughton, with Patrick Crowley, "Green," *Newsweek,* November 22, 2004, pp. 50–56.

40. McAlister, Ferrell, and Ferrell, *Business and Society.*

41. Isabelle Maignan and Debbie Thorne McAlister, "Socially Responsible Organizational Buying: How Can Stakeholders Dictate Purchasing Policies?" *Journal of Macromarketing,* December 2003, pp. 78–89.

42. Stephanie Thompson, "Aveda Pressures Mags to Go Green," *Advertising Age,* November 29, 2004, p. 19.

43. Jill Gabrielle Klein, N. Craig Smith, and Andrew John, "Why We Boycott: Consumer Motivations for Boycott Participation," *Journal of Marketing,* July 2004, pp. 92–109.

44. Bruce R. Gaumnitz and John C. Lere, "Contents of Codes of Ethics of Professional Business Organizations in the United States," *Journal of Business Ethics* 35 (2002): 35–49.

45. Ferrell and Hartline, *Marketing Strategy.*

46. Isabelle Maignan, "Antecedents and Benefits of Corporate Citizenship: A Comparison of U.S. and French Businesses" (Ph.D. dissertation, University of Memphis, 1997).

47. Dale Kurschner, "5 Ways Ethical Busine$$ Creates Fatter Profit$," *Business Ethics,* March/April 1996, pp. 20–23.

48. Margaret A. Stroup, Ralph L. Newbert, and Jerry W. Anderson, Jr., "Doing Good, Doing Better: Two Views of Social Responsibility," *Business Horizons,* March/April 1987, p. 23.

49. Peter Asmus, "Goodbye Coal, Hello Wind," *Business Ethics,* July/August 1999, pp. 10–11; Robert Baun, "New Belgium Hits Top 5 Among U.S. Specialty Brewers," *The Coloradoan,* February 21, 2002, p. 09; Robert Baun, "What's in a Name? Ask the Makers of Fat Tire," *The Coloradoan,* October 8, 2000, pp. E1, E3; Rachel Brand, "Colorado Breweries Bring Home 12 Medals in Festival," *Rocky Mountain [Denver] News,* www.insidedenver.com/news/1008beer6. shtml (accessed November 6, 2000); Stevi Deter, "Fat Tire Amber Ale," *The Net Net,* www.thenetnet.com/reviews/fat.html (accessed February 3, 2005); DirtWorld.com, www.dirtworld.com/races/Colorado_race745.htm (accessed November 6, 2000); Robert F. Dwyer and John F. Tanner, Jr., *Business Marketing* (Burr Ridge, IL: Irwin McGraw-Hill, 1999), p. 104; "Fat Tire Amber Ale," Achwiegut (The Guide to Austrian Beer), www.austrianbeer.com/beer/b000688.shtml (accessed March 5, 2001); Del I. Hawkins, Roger J. Best, and Kenneth A. Coney, *Consumer Behavior: Building Marketing Strategy,* 8th ed. (Burr Ridge, IL: Irwin McGraw-Hill, 2001); David Kemp, Tour Connoisseur, New Belgium Brewing Company, personal interview by Nikole Haiar, November 21, 2000; New Belgium Brewing Company, Ft. Collins, CO, www.newbelgium. com (accessed February 5, 2005); New Belgium Brewing Company Tour by Nikole Haiar, November 20, 2000; Dan Rabin, "New Belgium Pours It on for Bike Riders," *Celebrator Beer News,* 1998, www. celebrator.com/9808/rabin.html; Lisa Sanders, "This Beer Will Reduce Your Anxiety," *Advertising Age,* January 17, 2005, p. 25. This case was prepared by Nikole Haiar for classroom discussion rather than to illustrate either effective or ineffective handling of administrative, ethical or legal decision by management.

a. "The Able Jo Waldron," WomenOf, www.womenof.com/Articles/cb_3_29_04.asp (accessed February 10, 2005); "Now Hear This," ColoradoBiz, August 2003, p. 14; Christine Turner, "Inventing Technology That Matters," Colorado Company, January/February 2004, www.coloradocompany.biz/jan_feb/inventing_technology. shtml.

b. Anthony Bianco and Wendy Zellner, "Is Wal-Mart Too Powerful?" *Business Week,* October 6, 2003, pp. 102–110; Cora Daniels, "Women vs. Wal-Mart," *Fortune,* July 21, 2003, pp. 79–82; Charles Fishman, "The Wal-Mart You Don't Know: Why Low Prices Have a High Cost,"

Fast Company, December 2003, pp. 70–80; Daren Fonda, "Will Wal-Mart Steal Christmas?" *Time,* December 8, 2003, pp. 54–56.

c. Anne D'Innocenzio, "Charges Imperil Stewart Company," *The [Fort Collins] Coloradoan,* June 5, 2003, pp. D1, D7; Constance L. Hays, "As Martha Stewart Does Time, Flush Times for Her Company," *The New York Times,* January 20, 2005, www.nytimes.com; "Martha Stewart: Insider-Trading Scandal," in O. C. Ferrell, John Fraedrich, and Linda Ferrell, *Business Ethics: Ethical Decision Making and Cases,* 6th ed. (Boston: Houghton Mifflin, 2005), pp. 300–306; Sarah Rush, "Kmart Suing Stewart's Company," *The Coloradoan,* February 14, 2004, p. D10; Kara Scannell and Matthew Rose, "Stewart Lawyer Says the Case Wasn't Proved," *The Wall Street Journal,* March 3, 2004, http://online.wsj.com; "Stewart Convicted on All Charges," CNN/Money, March 5, 2004, http://money.cnn.com/2004/03/05/news/companies/martha_verdict/.

CHAPTER 4

1. "Amazon.com Announces 76% Free Cash Flow Growth and 29% Sales Growth—Expects Record Holiday Season with Expanded Selection, Lower Prices, and Free Shipping," Amazon.com, press release, October 21, 2004, http://phx.corporate-ir.net/phoenix. zhtml?c=97664&p=IROL-NewsText&t=Regular&id=634252&; "Amazon Seeing Growth in Apparel Store," *Puget Sound Business Journal,* March 9, 2004, http://seattle.bizjournals.com/seattle/stores/2004/03/08/daily13.html; Allison Linn, "Amazon.com Aims for Post-Boom Success," *Contra Costa Times,* March 23, 2004, www.contracostatimes.com/mld/cctimes/8254499.htm; David Stires, "Amazon's Secret," *Fortune,* April 19, 2004, p. 144.

2. Vladimir Zwass, "Electronic Commerce: Structures and Issues," *International Journal of Electronic Commerce,* Fall 1996, pp. 3–23.

3. Stan Crock, "Lockheed Martin," *Business Week,* November 24, 2003, p. 85.

4. Ruby P. Lee and Rajdeep Grewal, "Strategic Responses to New Technology and Their Impact on Performance," *Journal of Marketing,* October 2004, pp. 157–171.

5. Michael Totty, "The Researcher," *The Wall Street Journal,* July 16, 2001, p. R20.

6. "Shop Around the Clock," *American Demographics,* September 2003, p. 18.

7. David W. Stewart and Qin Zhao, "Internet Marketing, Business Models, and Public Policy," *Journal of Public Policy & Marketing,* Fall 2000, pp. 287–296.

8. Jon Mark Giese, "Place Without Space, Identity Without Body: The Role of Cooperative Narrative in Community and Identity Formation in a Text-Based Electronic Community," unpublished dissertation, Pennsylvania State University, 1996.

9. Robert D. Hof, with Seanna Browder and Peter Elstrom, "Internet Communities," *Business Week,* May 5, 1997, pp. 64–80.

10. David Kirkpatrick and Daniel Roth, "Why There's No Escaping the Blog," *Fortune,* January 10, 2005, pp. 44–50.

11. Robyn Greenspan, "Europe, U.S. on Different Sides of Gender Divide," ClickZ, October 21, 2003, www.clickz.com/stats/sectors/demographics/article.php/5901_3095681.

12. "U.S. Internet Population Continues to Grow," ClickZ, February 6, 2002, www.clickz.com/stats/sectors/geographics/article.php/5911_969541.

13. Rob McGann, "People Aged 55 and Up Drive U.S. Web Growth," ClickZ, December 10, 2004, www.clickz.com/stats/sectors/traffic_patterns/article.php/3446641.

14. Richard Karpinski, "Behavioral Targeting," *Intelligence,* Spring 2004, pp. 14–17.

15. "Daily Internet Activities," Pew Internet & American Life Project, chart, June 30, 2004, www.pewinternet.org/trends/Daily_Activities_4.23.04.htm.

16. Rob McGann, "Online Banking Increased 47 Percent Since 2002," ClickZ, February 9, 2005, www.clickz.com/stats/sectors/

demographics/article.php/3481976; "More Work, Less Play for American Internet Users," ClickZ, March 4, 2002, www.clickz.com/stats/sectors/demographics/article.php/5901_984721.

17. Rob McGann, "Broadband: High Speed, High Spend," ClickZ, January 24, 2005, www.clickz.com/stats/sectors/broadband/article.php/3463191.

18. "Key Facts: Dell," *The Wall Street Journal,* http://online.wsj.com (accessed February 16, 2005).

19. "Southwest Airlines Fact Sheet," Southwest Airlines, www.iflyswa.com/about_swa/press/factsheet.html (accessed February 16, 2005).

20. Andrew Park, "Imperial Sugar," *Business Week,* November 24, 2003, p. 98.

21. "Connecting Buyers and Suppliers," *Inbound Logistics,* November 2004, p. 24.

22. Carrie A. Johnson, "Commentary: Watching E-Commerce Grow," Forrester Research, reported in c|net News, April 11, 2004, http://news.com.com/Commentary+Watching+e-commerce+grow/2030-1069_3-5305945.html.

23. "Amazon.com Announces 76% Free Cash Flow Growth and 29% Sales Growth."

24. "Small Businesses Use Net for Customer Service, Communications," ClickZ, November 12, 2001, www.clickz.com/stats/sectors/small_enterprises/article.php/10098_921821.

25. Nat Ives, "Entertaining Web Sites Promote Products Subtly," *The New York Times,* December 22, 2004, www.nytimes.com.

26. "Valpak.com Success, Growth Based on Offering Local Coupons, Commitment to Value and Strong Backing," *Business Wire,* September 24, 2001, via www.findarticles.com.

27. Franceca Sotgiu and Fabio Ancarani, "Exploiting the Opportunities of Internet and Multi-Channel Pricing: An Exploratory Research," *Journal of Product and Brand Management* 13 (2004): 125–136.

28. Stephanie Stahl and John Soat, "Feeding the Pipeline: Procter & Gamble Uses IT to Nurture New Product Ideas," *Information Week,* February 24, 2003, www.informationweek.com/.

29. Werner Reinartz, Jacquelyn S. Thomas, and V. Kumar, "Balancing Acquisition and Retention Resources to Maximize Customer Profitability," *Journal of Marketing,* January 2005, pp. 63–79.

30. O. C. Ferrell and Michael D. Hartline, *Marketing Strategy* (Mason, OH: South-Western, 2005), p. 72.

31. Ruby Roy Dholakia and Nikhilesh Dholakia, "Mobility and Markets: Emerging Outlines of M-Commerce," *Journal of Business Research* 57 (2004): 1391–1396.

32. J. Bonasia, "Eyeing Growth in Customer Relationship Management Software," *Investors Business Daily,* January 8, 2002, p. 7.

33. "Better Relationships, Better Business," *Business Week,* Special Advertising Section, April 29, 2002.

34. Edward Prewitt, "How to Build Customer Loyalty in an Internet World," *CIO,* January 1, 2002, www.cio.com/archive/010102/loyalty_content.html.

35. Michael Pastore, "CRM Takes Priority Among IT Investments," ClickZ, February 25, 2002, www.clickz.com/stats/sectors/software/article.php/1301_980111.

36. Michael Krauss, "At Many Firms, Technology Obscures CRM," *Marketing News,* March 18, 2002, p. 5.

37. Prewitt, "How to Build Customer Loyalty in an Internet World."

38. Ibid.

39. Itamar Simonson, "Determinants of Customers' Responses to Customized Offers: Conceptual Framework and Research Propositions," *Journal of Marketing,* January 2005, pp. 32–45.

40. David Pottruck and Terry Peace, "Listening to Customers in the Electronic Age," *Fortune,* May 2000, www.business2.com/articles/mag/0,1640,7700,00.html.

41. Stephenie Steitzer, "Commercial Web Sites Cut Back On Collections of Personal Data," *The Wall Street Journal,* March 28, 2002, http://online.wsj.com/public/us.

42. Ibid.

43. "BBBOnLine Privacy Seal," BBBOnLine, www.BBBOnLine.org/privacy/index.asp (accessed February 16, 2005).

44. "European Union Directive on Privacy," E-Center for Business Ethics, www.e-businessethics.com/privacy.eud.htm (accessed February 16, 2005).

45. "Study: Spam Costing Companies $22 Billion a Year," CNN, February 4, 2005, www.cnn.com.

46. Tim Hanrahan and Jason Fry, "Spammers, Human Mind Do Battle Over Spelling," *The Wall Street Journal,* February 9, 2004, http://online.wsj.com; Tom Zeller, "Law Barring Junk E-Mail Allows a Flood Instead," *The New York Times,* February 1, 2005, www.nytimes.com.

47. Douglas Heingartner, "Software Piracy Is in Resurgence" New York Times News Service, *Naples Daily News,* January 20, 2004, www.naplesnews.com/npdn/business/article/0,2071,NPDN_14901_2588425,00.html.

48. William T. Neese and Charles R. McManis, "Summary Brief: Law, Ethnics and the Internet: How Recent Federal Trademark Law Prohibits a Remedy Against Cyber-squatters," Proceedings from the Society of Marketing Advances, November 4–7, 1998.

49. Computers4SURE.com, www.computers4sure.com (accessed February 16, 2005); "Computers4SURE.com Awarded Three Prominent Industry Web Site Awards," PRNewswire, October 25, 1999, via www.findarticles.com; "Engage Enabling Technologies: Ad Management Solutions with AdBureau and AdManager," Engage, Inc., case study, www.engage.com/au/solutions/cs_solutions_shop4sure.cfm (accessed September 19, 2001); David Jastrow, "Attacking the B2B Market," *Computer Reseller News,* www.ern.com/sections/special/estars/estars.asp?ArticleID=15761 (accessed September 20, 2001); "Office Depot Announces Acquisition or Computers4Sure.com and Solutions4Sure.com," 4SURE.com, press release, July 9, 2001, www.computers4sure.com/static/releaseOfficeDepot.asp; "Shopping4SURE.com," BATV, video, www.batv.com (accessed September 20, 2001); "Shopping4SURE.com, the Award Winning On-line Retailer, Chooses ICC's B2B Fulfillment Solution," Internet Commerce Corporation, press release, December 15, 1999, www.icc.net/aboutICC/ICCnews/pressReleases/1215299.html; Solutions4SURE.com, www.solutions4sure.com (accessed April 2, 2002).

a. Matt Drudge, "Anyone with a Modem Can Report on the World," Liberty Round Table: Essays, www.libertyroundtable.org/library/essay.drudge.html (accessed February 16, 2005); Rich Ord, "Drudge Report Is Third Most Searched for News Source," WebProNews, December 2, 2004, www.webpronews.com/news/ebusinessnews/wpn-45-20041202DrudgeReportIsThirdMostSearchedForNewsSource.html; Camille Paglia, "Drudge Match," Radar Magazine, June 2003, www.radarmagazine.com/features/issue_02/drudge.html; "The Secrets of Drudge Inc.," Business 2.0, April 2003, p. 56.

b. "About Us," ING Direct, http://home.ingdirect.com/about/corporate_content.html (accessed June 8, 2004); "ING Direct Bank Does One Thing Noticeably Well," ING Direct, news release, March 7, 2004, http://home.ingdirect.com/about/aboutus_news.html#03072004; Lisa Sanders, "ING Café: Coffee, Tea or Mortgage," *Advertising Age,* June 14, 2004, p. 8; Matthew Sibel, "Where Money Doesn't Talk," *Forbes,* May 24, 2004, p. 176.

c. "E-Channels," Yellow Freight, www.myyellow.com/dynamic/services/content/ecommerce/echannels/index.jsp (accessed July 21, 2005; "E-Commerce Tools," Yellow Freight, www.myyellow.com/dynamic/services/content/ecommerce/etools/index.jsp (accessed July 21, 2005; "File Transfer Protocol (FTP) FAQ," Yellow Freight, www.myyellow.com/dynamic/services/content/ecommerce/edi/ftp.jsp (accessed July 21, 2005); "The First Internet-Based Live Voice Ecommerce Service in the Transportation Industry," Yellow Freight, press release, September 18, 2000, www.yellowfreight.com/aboutyellow/newsroom/pressreleases/pr_archive/pr_091900.html; "Yellow," Moore Store, www.themoorestore.com/yf (accessed February 16, 2005); Yellow Freight, www.yellowfreight.com (accessed February 16, 2005).

CHAPTER 5

1. "Cola Wars," *inBusiness South Australia,* July/August 2004, www.in-business.com.au/issue_17/export/cola_wars.php; Janet Guyon, "Brand America," *Fortune,* October 27, 2003, pp. 179–82; David Luhnow and Chad Terhune, "Latin Pop: A Low-Budget Cola Shakes Up Markets South of the Border," *The Wall Street Journal,* October 27, 2003, pp. A1, A18; Paula M. Miller, "Wahaha: The Chinese Beverage Company's Expansion Is No Laughing Matter," *The China Business Review,* September-October 2004, pp. 59–62; Arundhati Parmar, "Drink Politics," *Marketing News,* February 15, 2004, pp. 1, 11.

2. David Bauder, "MTV to Reach Milestone with 100 Affiliated Networks around the World," *The [McAllen, Texas] Monitor,* December 25, 2004, p. 2D.

3. Amy Guthrie, "Mexico's Snack Stores Are Expanding," *The Wall Street Journal,* February 2, 2005, http://online.wsj.com.

4. "Product Pitfalls Proliferate in Global Cultural Maze," *The Wall Street Journal,* May 14, 2001, p. B11.

5. Anton Piësch, "Speaking in Tongues," *Inc.,* June 2003, p. 50.

6. "Product Pitfalls Proliferate in Global Cultural Maze."

7. George Balabanis and Adamantios Diamantopoulos, "Domestic Country Bias, Country-or-Origin Effects, and Consumer Ethnocentrism: A Multidimensional Unfolding Approach," *Journal of the Academy of Marketing Science,* January 2004, pp. 80–95.

8. Zeynep Gürhan-Canli and Durairaj Maheswaran, "Cultural Variations in Country of Origin Effects," *Journal of Marketing Research,* August 2000, pp. 309–317.

9. Ming-Huei Hsieh, Shan-Ling Pan, and Rudy Setiono, "Product-, Corporate-, and Country-Image Dimensions and Purchase Behavior: A Multicountry Analysis," *Journal of the Academy of Marketing Science,* July 2004, pp. 251–270.

10. Jay Solomon, "Amid Anti-American Protests, Mr. Bambang Invokes Allah to Sell Big Macs in Indonesia," *The Wall Street Journal,* October 26, 2001, http://online.wsj.com.

11. U.S. Bureau of the Census, *Statistical Abstract of the United States,* 2004 (Washington, DC: Government Printing Office, 2005), pp. 841–843, 853.

12. Paul Blustein, "2004 Trade Deficit Hits All-Time High," *The Washington Post,* February 10, 2005 www.washingtonpost.com/wp-dyn/articles/A13474-2005Feb10.html.

13. Charles R. Taylor, George R. Franke, and Michael L. Maynard, "Attitudes Toward Direct Marketing and Its Regulation: A Comparison of the United States and Japan," *Journal of Public Policy & Marketing,* Fall 2000, pp. 228–237.

14. Frederik Balfour, "Fakes!," *Business Week,* February 7, 2005, pp. 54–64.

15. Charles Hutzler, "Chinese Car's Design Is Pirated, U.S. Says," *The Asian Wall Street Journal,* January 14–16, 2005, pp. A1, A8.

16. Dave Izraeli and Mark S. Schwartz, "What We Can Learn from the Federal Sentencing Guidelines for Organizational Ethics," *Journal of Business Ethics,* July 1998, pp. 9–10.

17. Michael Pastore, "European Consumers Getting Comfortable with Online Channel," ClickZ, July 6, 2001, www.clickz.com/stats/sectors/geographics/article.php/5911_794321.

18. "Population Explosion," ClickZ, February 8, 2005, www.clickz.com/stats/sectors/geographics/article.php/151151.

19. "Report: Mobile Phone Users Double Since 2000," CNN, December 9, 2004, www.cnn.com.

20. Elisa Batista, "Telcos Duke It Out over Iraq," Wired News, June 27, 2003, www.wired.com/news/politics/0,1283,59410,00.html.

21. U.S. Bureau of the Census, *Statistical Abstract,* pp. 841–843, 854; "NAFTA: A Decade of Strengthening a Dynamic Relationship," U.S. Department of Commerce, pamphlet, 2003, available at www.ustr.gov.

22. U.S. Bureau of the Census, *Statistical Abstract,* pp. 841, 853.

23. "Trade with Canada: 2004," U.S. Bureau of the Census, www.census.gov/foreign-trade/balance/c1220.html (accessed February 22, 2005).

24. William C. Symonds, "Meanwhile, to the North, NAFTA Is a Smash," *Business Week,* February 27, 1995, p. 66.

25. U.S. Bureau of the Census, *Statistical Abstract,* pp. 798, 816, 842, 853; "NAFTA: A Decade of Strengthening a Dynamic Relationship."

26. Geri Smith and Cristina Lindblad, "Mexico: Was NAFTA Worth It?" *Business Week,* December 22, 2003, pp. 66–72; Cheryl Farr Leas, "The Big Boom," *Continental,* April 2001, pp. 85–94.

27. "The European Union at a Glance," Europa (European Union online), http://europa.eu.int/abc/index_en.htm# (accessed February 21, 2005).

28. "The European Union at a Glance"; T. R. Reid, "The New Europe," *National Geographic,* January 2002, pp. 32–47.

29. Stanley Reid, with Ariane Sains, David Fairlamb, and Carol Matlack, "The Euro: How Damaging a Hit?" *Business Week,* September 29, 2003, p. 63; "The Single Currency," CNN, www.cnn.com/SPECIALS/2000/eurounion/story/currency/ (accessed February 21, 2005).

30. Reid, "The New Europe."

31. "Common Market of the South (MERCOSUR): Agri-Food Regional Profile Statistical Overview," Agriculture and Agrifood Canada, October 2002, http://atn-riae.agr.ca/latin/e3431.htm; "Mercosur," Export Virginia, www.exportvirginia.org/FastFacts_2004/FF%20Issues%20Mercosur.pdf (accessed February 21, 2005).

32. "About APEC," Asia-Pacific Economic Cooperation, www.apecsec.org.sg/apec/about_apec.html, (accessed February 21, 2005).

33. "South Korean Auto Exports to U.S. Hit Record High in 2001," *Inbound Logistics,* March 2002, p. 26.

34. David Goetz, "Yum Keeps China Focus," *The [Louisville] Courier-Journal,* February 3, 2005, www.courier-journal.com/apps/pbcs.dll/article?AID=/20050203/BUSINESS/502030359.

35. "What Is the WTO?," World Trade Organization, www.wto.org/ (accessed February 21, 2005).

36. George Chryssochoidis and Vasilis Theoharakis, "Attainment of Competitive Advantage by the Exporter-Importer Dyad: The Role of Export Offering and Import Objectives," *Journal of Business Research,* April 2004, pp. 329–337.

37. Gerry Khermouch, " 'Whoa, Cool Shirt.' 'Yeah, It's a Pepsi,' " *Business Week,* September 10, 2001, p. 84.

38. Farok J. Contractor and Sumit K. Kundu. "Franchising versus Company-Run Operations: Model Choice in the Global Hotel Sector," *Journal of International Marketing,* November 1997, pp. 28–53.

39. Solomon, "Amid Anti-American Protests."

40. Andrew Kupfer, "How to Be a Global Manager," *Fortune,* March 14, 1988, pp. 52–58.

41. Kathryn Rudie Harrigan, "Joint Ventures and Competitive Advantage," *Strategic Management Journal,* May 1988, pp. 141–158.

42. "What We're About," NUMMI, www.nummi.com/co_info.html (accessed February 21, 2005).

43. Romesh Ratnesar, "Fresh from the Border," *Time,* March 5, 2003, www.time.com/time/insidebiz/article/0,9171,1101030310-428051,00.html.

44. Jagdish N. Sheth, "From International to Integrated Marketing," *Journal of Business Research,* January 2001, pp. 5–9.

45. Ronald Paul Hill and Kanwalroop Kathy Dhanda, "Globalization and Technological Advancement: Implications for Macromarketing and the Digital Divide," *Journal of Macromarketing,* December 2004, pp. 147–155.

46. Deborah Owens, Timothy Wilkinson, and Bruce Kellor, "A Comparison of Product Attributes in a Cross-Cultural/Cross-National Context," *Marketing Management Journal,* Fall/Winter 2000, pp. 1–11.

47. William E. Kilbourne, "Globalization and Development: An Expanded Macromarketing View," *Journal of Macromarketing,* December 2004, pp. 122–135.
48. Anil K. Gupta and Vijay Govindarajan, "Converting Global Presence into Global Competitive Advantage," *Academy of Management Executive,* May 2001, pp. 45–58.
49. "About BMW Group," BMW, www.bmwusa.com/about/group.htm (accessed February 21, 2005); "About BMW North America-Manufacturing," BMW, www.bmwusa.com/About/manufacturing.htm (accessed February 21, 2005); Neal E. Boudette, "BMW's CEO Just Says 'No' to Protect Brand," *The Wall Street Journal,* November 26, 2003, http://online.wsj.com; Neil E. Boudette, "BMW's Push to Broaden Line Hits Some Bumps in the Road," *The Wall Street Journal,* January 10, 2005, p. A1; "Excerpt from 'Trading Up'," *USA Today,* December 14, 2003, www.usatoday.com/money/books/reviews/2003-12-14-trading-up-excerpt_x.thm; "Frequently Asked Questions—Corporate Goals and Strategies," BMW, www.bmwgroup.com/e/nav/?/0_0_www_bmwgroup_com/homepage/index.jsp?1_0 (accessed April 8, 2004); "The Psychology of Luxury," *USA Today,* December 15, 2003, www.usatoday.com/money/books/reviews/2003-12-15-trade-book_x.htm; Joseph B. White, "DaimlerChrysler Will Launch Smart Mini Car Brand in U.S," *The Wall Street Journal,* December 9, 2003, http://online.wsj.com.
a. "I Am Focusing on God, Family, and Domino's Pizza," American Dreams, www.usdreams.com/Monaghan7677.html (accessed February 23, 2005); "Domino's Pizza," Franchise Business, www.franchisebusiness.co.uk/dominos/ (accessed February 23, 2005); Tom Monaghan, "Tom Monaghan: Domino's Pizza," Fortune Small Business, September 13, 2003, www.fortune.com/fortune/smallbusiness/articles/0%2C15114%2C475582%2C00.html; Amy Zuber, "Tom Monaghan, Nation's Restaurant News," September 13, 1999, www.findarticles.com/p/articles/mi_m3190/is_37_33/ai_55821088.
b. Clay Chandler, "Inside the New China," *Fortune,* October 4, 2004, pp. 84–98; Pete Engardio and Dexter Roberts, "The China Price," *Business Week,* December 6, 2004, pp. 102–112; Ted C. Fishman, "How China Will Change Your Business," *Inc.,* March 2005, pp. 70–84; April Terreri, "The Dragon Awakens," *Inbound Logistics,* October 2004, pp. 79–90.
c. Barbara Labarbara, "The Point Rider," *Angus Journal,* June/July 1997; Sarah Scott, personal communications with Skylar Houston, October 2004. This case was prepared by Sarah Scott, under the supervision of Dr. O. C. Ferrell.

CHAPTER 6

1. Bruce Horovitz, "Boston Market Attempts Ambitious Rebound," *The [Fort Collins] Coloradoan,* May 23, 2004, p. E4; Julie Jargon, "McDonald's Lounge?" *Crain's Chicago Business,* July 19, 2004, p. 3, accessed via Lexis-Nexis Academic Database; Bob Mook, "Not-So-Fast Food: Quick Eateries Going Upscale Hoping Diners Stick Around," *The Coloradoan,* September 13, 2004, p. E1; Kim Severson, "Is the Bay Area Ready for Its Morning McLatte?" *The San Francisco Chronicle,* November 30, 2003, p. A1, accessed via Lexis-Nexis Academic Database.
2. Anne L. Souchon, John W. Cadogan, David B. Procter, and Belinda Dewsnap, "Marketing Information Use and Organisational Performance: The Mediating Role of Responsiveness," *Journal of Strategic Marketing,* December 2004, pp. 231–242.
3. Suzanne Vranica, "McDonald's Tries for 'Viral' Buzz," *The Wall Street Journal,* February 8, 2005, http://online.wsj.com.
4. Ellen Byron, "New Penney: Chain Goes for 'Missing Middle,' " *The Wall Street Journal,* February 14, 2005, http://online.wsj.com.
5. Catherine Arnold, "Self-Examination: Researchers Reveal State of MR in Survey," *Marketing News,* February 1, 2005, pp. 55, 56.
6. Mark Jewell, "Dunkin' Donuts Eyes Turn Westward: Chain Evolves from No Frills," *The Coloradoan,* January 17, 2005, p. E1.
7. Aaron Bernstein, with Christopher Palmeri and Roger O. Crockett, "An Inner-City Renaissance," *Business Week,* October 27, 2003, pp. 64–68.
8. Vikas Mittal and Wagner A. Kamakura, "Satisfaction, Repurchase Intent, and Repurchase Behavior: Investigating the Moderating Effects of Customer Characteristics," *Journal of Marketing Research,* February 2001, pp. 131–142.
9. "Internal Secondary Market Research," CCH Business Owner's Toolkit, www.toolkit.cch.com/text/P03_3020.asp (accessed January 7, 2005).
10. Haya El Nasser, "Census Bureau No Longer Waiting 10 Years for Data," *The Coloradoan,* January 17, 2005, p. A2.
11. "Information Resources, Inc.," *Marketing News,* June 15, 2004, pp. H10, H12.
12. "External Secondary Market Research," CCH Business Owner's Toolkit, www.toolkit.cch.com/text/P03_3011.asp (accessed January 7, 2005).
13. Arnold, "Self-Examination."
14. Maria Grubbs Hoy and Avery M. Abernethy, "Nonresponse Assessment in Marketing Research: Current Practice and Suggested Improvements," in Marketing Theory and Applications, American Marketing Association Winter Educators' Conference proceedings, 2002.
15. David Jobber, John Saunders, Vince-Wayne Mitchell, "Prepaid Monetary Incentive Effects on Mail Survey Response," *Journal of Business Research,* January 2004, pp. 347–350.
16. John Harwood and Shirley Leung, "Hang-Ups: Why Some Pollsters Got It So Wrong This Election Day," *The Wall Street Journal,* November 8, 2003, pp. A1, A6.
17. Ibid.
18. Robert V. Kozinets, "The Field Behind the Screen: Using Netnography for Marketing Research in Online Communities," *Journal of Marketing Research,* February 2002, pp. 61–72.
19. Glen L. Urban and John R. Hauser, " 'Listening In' to Find and Explore New Combinations of Customer Needs," *Journal of Marketing,* April 2004, pp. 72–87.
20. Leonardo Felson, "Netting Limitations: Online Researchers' New Tactics for Tough Audiences," *Marketing News,* February 26, 2001, www.ama.org/pubs/.
21. Alissa Quart, "Ol' College Pry," *Business 2.0,* April 3, 2001.
22. "Focus Groups in Nebraska Help Market Tourism," *Marketing News,* January 6, 2003, p. 5.
23. Peter DePaulo, "Sample Size for Qualitative Research," *Quirk's Marketing Research Review,* December 2000, www.quirks.com.
24. Theodore T. Allen and Kristen M. Maybin, "Using Focus Group Data to Set New Product Prices," *Journal of Product and Brand Management,* January 2004, pp. 15–24.
25. Barbara Allan, "The Benefits of Telephone Depth Sessions," *Quirk's Marketing Research Review,* December 2000, www.quirks.com.
26. Alison Stein Wellner, "Research on a Shoestring," *American Demographics,* April 2001, www.americandemographics.com.
27. Doug Tsuruoka, "How to Lower Marketing Costs—and Eliminate the Guesswork," *Investor's Business Daily,* November 21, 2001, p. A1.
28. Judy Strauss and Donna J. Hill, "Consumer Complaints by E-mail: An Exploratory Investigation of Corporate Responses and Customer Reactions," *Journal of Interactive Marketing,* Winter 2001, pp. 63–73.
29. Kevin Kelleher, "66,207,986 Bottles of Beer on the Wall," *Business 2.0,* via CNN, February 25, 2004, www.cnn.com.
30. "Group Warns of Grocery Grab for Data," *Marketing News,* April 15, 2002.
31. Noah Rubin Brier, John McManus, David Myron, and Christopher Reynolds, " 'Zero-In' Heroes," *American Demographics,* October 2004, pp. 36–45.
32. Laurence N. Goal, "High Technology Data Collection for Measurement and Testing," *Marketing Research,* March 1992, pp. 29–38.

33. Kathleen Cholewka, "Tiered CRM: Serving Pip-Squeaks to VIPs," *Sales & Marketing Management,* April 2001, pp. 25–26.
34. Amy Merrick, "New Population Data Will Help Marketers Pitch Their Products," *The Wall Street Journal,* February 14, 2001, http://online.wsj.com.
35. Carlos Denton, "Time Differentiates Latino Focus Groups," *Marketing News,* March 15, 2004, p. 52.
36. Jack Honomichl, "Top 50 U.S. Research Organizations," *Marketing News,* June 15, 2004.
37. Lambeth Hochwald, "Are You Smart Enough to Sell Globally?" *Sales & Marketing Management,* July 1998, pp. 52–56.
38. Ibid.
39. "Company Overview," Information Resources, Inc., www.infores.com/public/us/about/default.htm (accessed January 10, 2005); "Information Resources, Inc.," *Marketing News,* June 15, 2004, pp. H10, H11; "Information Resources, Inc.," *Marketing News,* June 9, 2003, pp. H10, H11; "Key Facts," *The Wall Street Journal,* http://online.wsj.com (accessed January 2, 2004); "On-Line Purchases of Consumer Packaged Goods on the Rise" (study by Information Resources, Inc.), *DSN Retailing Today,* June 4, 2001, www.findarticles.com/cf_0/m0FNP/11_40/75452753/p1/article.jhtml?term=%22Information+Resources%22.
a. Sarah Moore, "On Your Markets," *Working Woman,* February 2001, p. 26; "Quest for Cool," *Time,* September 2003, via www.look-look.com/looklook/html/Test_Drive_Press_Time.html; "Who We Are," Look-Look.com, www.look-look.com/dynamic/looklook/jsp/What_We_Do.jsp (accessed January 7, 2005); "Who We Are," Look-Look.com, www.look-look.com/looklook/html/Test_Drive_Who_We_Are.html (accessed January 7, 2005).
b. Jordan Robertson, "Toe the Line Between Corporate and Cool," *Business 2.0,* November 2004; "Marc Ecko Fashion Collections," First View, www.firstview.com/alldesigners/MarcEcko.html#Anchor3 (accessed March 1, 2005); Samantha Critchell, "Designer Marc Ecko's Building a Fashion Empire," *The [Massachusetts] Standard-Times,* May 12, 2004, p. B1, www.southcoasttoday.com/daily/05-04/05-12-04/b01li040.htm.
c. Constance L. Hays, "What Wal-Mart Knows About Customers' Habits," *The New York Times,* November 14, 2004, www.nytimes.com; "Wal-Mart Expands Its Teradata® Warehouse to Optimize Decision Support Capabilities 10/13/04," Teradata, press release, October 13, 2004, www.teradata.com/t/page/128640/index.html.

CHAPTER 7

1. Jane Kitchen, "Ashley Campaign Stars Nickelodeon Brands," *Home Textiles Today,* January 3, 2005, p. 21; "Nickelodeon Grows Beyond TV-Based Products," *Los Angeles Times,* October 12, 2004, p. C3; Dawn Wilensky, "Nick Unveils EverGirl," *License,* January 2004, p. 14; Joe Flint, "Testing Limits of Licensing," *The Wall Street Journal,* October 9, 2003, p. B1; Diane Brady and Gerry Khermouch, "How to Tickle a Child," *Business Week,* July 7, 2003, pp. 48–50.
2. Mark Rechtin, "Hyundai Targets Sedan Superstars," *Automotive News,* January 17, 2005, pp. 14–15.
3. Dan Higgins, "Pens, A Fountain of Inspiration," *The [Albany] Times Union,* November 5, 2004, p. E1.
4. Laura Mazur, "Life Stages Hold Key to Improving Customer Bonds," *Marketing,* August 16, 2001, p. 16.
5. Service Corporation International, www.hoovers.com (accessed January 26, 2005).
6. "Disney Hopes Virtual Park Delivers Real-World Results," *Advertising Age,* January 3, 2005, p. 4.
7. U.S. Bureau of the Census, *Statistical Abstract of the United States,* 2004–2005, p. 12.
8. J. D. Mosley-Matchett, "Marketers: There's a Feminine Side to the Web," *Marketing News,* February 16, 1998, p. 6.
9. Traci Carl, "Mexico Businesses Vie for Hot U.S. Hispanic Market," *The [Fort Collins] Coloradoan,* January 27, 2002, p. E4.
10. *The Food Institute Report,* March 15, 2004, p. 5.
11. Laura Heller, "Sears Targets Ethnic Customers with New Lines, Bilingual Associates," *DSN Retailing Today,* October 25, 2004, p. 69.
12. Jason Fields, "America's Families and Living Arrangements: 2003," *Current Population Reports* (Washington, DC: U.S. Census Bureau, November 2003), pp. 1–20.
13. "Clients and Case Studies," MicroMarketing, Inc., www.micromarketing.com/clients/index.html (accessed February 1, 2005).
14. "Yum, Bally Fitness Team Up for Promo," *Advertising Age,* January 3, 2005, p. 2.
15. Joseph T. Plummer, "The Concept and Application of Life Style Segmentation," *Journal of Marketing,* January 1974, p. 33
16. "Catching Up With the Next Generation: They're Not Slackers Anymore," *PR Newswire,* October 26, 2004.
17. Rebecca Piirto Heath, "You Can Buy A Thrill: Chasing the Ultimate Rush," *American Demographics,* June 1997, pp. 47–51.
18. Beverage World, "Beverage Market Index 2003," June 15, 2003, VNU Business Media.
19. Philip Kotler, *Marketing Management: Analysis, Planning, Implementation, and Control,* 7th ed. (Englewood Cliffs, NJ: Prentice Hall, 2003), p. 144.
20. "Analysis: Huge Cardiovascular Market Potential in Aging Baby Boomers," *Heart Disease Weekly,* via NewsRX.com and NewsRX.net, April 11, 2004, p. 92.
21. Charles W. Chase, Jr., "Selecting the Appropriate Forecasting Method," *Journal of Business Forecasting,* Fall 1997, pp. 2, 23, 28–29.
22. Kristen Bremner, "Albany Ranked No. 1," *Acxiom,* May 24, 2004.
23. Daniel Fisher, "Gone Flat," *Forbes,* October 15, 2001, www.forbes.com.
24. Tricia Duryee, "Bellevue, Wash.-based Online Brokerage ShareBuilder Rare Dot-Com Survivor," *Seattle Times,* September 6, 2004, www.seattletimes.com; Terri Cullen, "As Schwab Returns to Its Discount Roots, Small Investors Face Shifting Choices," *The Wall Street Journal,* August 4, 2004, p. D1; "Fahnestock Viner Holdings Completes Acquisition of BuyandHold," BuyandHold.com, press release, March 12, 2002, www.buyandhold.com/bh/en/about/news43.html; Eve Epstein, "Dot-Com Brokerage Exploits a Market Niche, *InfoWorld,* January 8, 2001, pp. 34+; "BuyandHold.com First to Introduce the Virtual Direct Stock Purchase Plan," *PR Newswire,* April 25, 2000, www.prnewswire.com; John P. Mello, Jr., "Going Direct," *CFO,* October 2000, p. 22; BuyandHold.com, www.buyandhold.com (accessed June 26, 2005).
a. Brendan I. Koerner, "A Salute to the Stray Sock," *The New York Times,* October 3, 2004, sec. 3, p. 2; Emily Holt, "A Pair of Odd Socks," *Women's Wear Daily,* August 9, 2004; "The Sock of the New," *Boston Globe,* October 14, 2004.
b. *Linda Koco, "Targeting Seniors? Talk to Senior Helpers,"* National Underwriter Life, June 7, 2004, p. 42; "Magic Johnson Again Stars in Y&R's Lincoln-Mercury Ads," *Adweek,* February 2, 2004, p. 4; Robert Strauss, "Appealing to Youth, Selling to the Not-So-Young," *The New York Times,* October 22, 2003, p. G37; Ann D. Middleman, "The New Mature Market: How Mature Is It?" *Marketing News,* May 1, 2003, www.ientry.com; Arundhati Parmar, "Knowledge of Mature Market Pays Reward," *Marketing News,* April 28, 2003, pp. 5–6.
c. Geoff Keighley, "The Onion Is No Joke," *Business 2.0,* September 2003, p. 88; Seth Porges, "'The Onion' Rolls On," Editor & Publisher, November 26, 2003.

CHAPTER 8

1. Arlena Sawyers, "AutoTrader Signs Up Again for NFL Ads," *Automotive News,* September 13, 2004, p. 41; Lisa Kalis and Dana White, "Kicking the Tires, from Afar and Online," *The New York Times,* August 13, 2004, p. F10; "AutoTrader.com," *Automotive News,* May 10, 2004, p. 33; Gregory Jordan, "Online, Used Car Lots That Cover the Nation," *The New York Times,* October 22, 2003, pp. G13+; Steve Jarvis, "Pedal to the Cyber-Metal," *Marketing News,* January 21, 2002, pp. 6–7.

2. "First Source for Car Shoppers in Online Households," *USA Today Snapshot,* November 16, 2001, www.usatoday.com/snapshot.

3. Russell W. Belk, "Situational Variables and Consumer Behavior," *Journal of Consumer Research,* December 1975, pp. 157–164.

4. "Sorry Cupid, Santa's the One Handing Out Engagement Rings This Year—and He's Buying Them Online," *PR Newswire,* December 6, 2004.

5. Kim Ann Zimmermann, "Safeway Enters Online Grocery Turnstile," *E-Commerce Times,* January 16, 2002, www.ecommercetimes.com/perl/story/?id=15809.

6. Margaret Sheridan, "Made to Measure: Patient Satisfaction Surveys Provide Hospitals with Paths to Improvement," *Restaurants & Institutions,* November 1, 2003, p. 69.

7. Laura Q. Hughes and Alice Z. Cuneo, "Lowe's Retools Image in Push Toward Women," *Advertising Age,* February 26, 2001, www.adage.com/news_and_features/features/20010226/article7.html.

8. Gigi Suhanic, "What's Green and Purple and Grows in the Fridge?," *Financial Post,* August 23, 2004, p. FP4.

9. Julie Cook, "Making the Grade: Markets Set Their Sites on Luring Savvy, On-the-Go Teens to Dairy Products," *Dairy Field,* April 2002, p.50.

10. U.S. Bureau of the Census, "2002 American Community Survey Profile," www.census.gov (accessed January 26, 2005).

11. Jeffrey M. Humphreys, *Georgia Business and Economic Conditions* 63, no. 2 (2003): 4.

12. Ibid.

13. Stuart Elliott, "Campaigns for Black Consumers," *The New York Times,* June 13, 2003, www.nytimes.com.

14. Ibid.

15. Ibid.

16. Daimler Chrysler Corporation, press release, www.csrwire.com (accessed May 20, 2004).

17. "Hawaiian Punch Announces 2003 Black History Contest," www.blackvoices.com (accessed May 20, 2004).

18. "2002 American Community Survey Profile."

19. "Ethnic Analysis," www.databankusa.com (accessed January 25, 2005).

20. Ibid.

21. "Minority Buying Power to Triple," *Dallas Morning News,* August 15, 2003, www.dallas.news.

22. Elliott, "Campaigns for Black Consumers."

23. Noel C. Paul, "Advertisers Slip into Spanish," *The Christian Science Monitor,* June 2, 2003, www.csmonitor.com/2003/0602/p16s01-wmcn.html.

24. Ibid.

25. "2002 American Community Survey Profile."

26. "Kmart Marketing: Urban/Ethnic Strategy Remains Pillar of Competitive Advantage," *DSN Retailing Today,* March 5, 2001, pp. 44–46.

27. Greta Guest, "Analysts Commend New Kmart Ads; Campaign to Capitalize on Store's Strengths," *Detroit Free Press,* October 17, 2003, www.freep.com/index.htm.

28. Christina Hoag, "Asian-Americans Are Fastest Growing Group," *Miami Herald,* April 7, 2003, www.miami.com/mld/miamiherald/.

29. Ibid.

30. Phuong Ly, "Immigrants Find a Taste of Home; Foreign Food Shops Expand to U.S. to Serve Old Customers—and New," *Washington Post,* January 22, 2002, p. B1.

31. "Build-A-Bear Translates Concept to Dolls," *Home Textiles Today,* January 3, 2005, p. A24; Mary Jo Feldstein, "St. Louis Toy Retailer Build-A-Bear Claws Its Way to Profitable IPO," *St. Louis Post-Dispatch,* October 29, 2004, www.stltoday.com; Doug Desjardins, "Build-A-Bear Workshops Going Public," *DSNRetailing Today,* September 20, 2004, p. 24; Alyson Grala, "'Bear'ing It All," *License!,* May 2004, pp. 22–24; Allison Fass, "Bear Market," *Forbes,* March 1, 2004, p. 88; Sharon Nelton, "Building an Empire One Smile at a Time," *Success,* September 2000, pp. 34+; Brad Petten, "Teddy Bear Bonanza Run by Sweetheart of a System," *Washington Business Journal,* February 4, 2000, p. 53; Marilyn Vise, "Corporate Culture: Build-A-Bear Workshop," *St. Louis Business Journal,* May 7, 2001, http://stlouis.bcentral.com/stlouis/stories/2001/05/07/focus11.html.

a. "Give Your Kids the Biz—Of Their Own That Is," YoungBiz.com, 2003, http://www.youngbiz.com/aspindex.asp?fileName5family_biz/give_your_kids_the_biz.htm; "Entrepreneur of the Year Finalists Revealed," Bob Mook, *Denver Business Journal,* April 28, 1997.

b. Mae Anderson, "On the Crest of the Wave," *Adweek,* September 13, 2004, www.adweek.com; Matt DeMazza, "Teen Magnets," *Footwear News,* November 17, 2003, p. 15; Lev Grossman, "The Quest for Cool," *Time,* September 8, 2003, pp. 48–54; Irma Zandl, "B-T-S: Anything Hot?" Marketing Insight from the Zandl Group, August 2003 (n.p.), via www.refresher.com/!tzg.html; Barbara White-Sax, "Teens Become Price Savvy in Search for What's Cool," *Drug Store News,* March 23, 2003, pp. 17+.

c. William F. Gloede, "The Art of Cultural Correctness," *American Demographics,* November 1, 2004, pp. 9+; Eliot Tiegel, "Multicultural Focus for McDonald's," *Television Week,* September 8, 2003, p. 20; Tammy Mastroberte, "Shell Unveils Multicultural Marketing Campaign," *Convenience Store News,* August 25, 2003, p. 10; Laurel Wentz, "Pepsi Puts Interests Before Ethnicity," *Advertising Age,* July 7, 2003, p. S4; "Advertisers Use Their Census," *Crain's New York Business,* June 9, 2003, p. 22.

CHAPTER 9

1. "3M Net Rises 16% Despite Slow Optical-Film Sales," *The New York Times,* January 19, 2005, p. B5; John S. McClenahen, "New World Leader: 3M Co.'s James McNerney, CEO of the Year," *Industry Week,* January 2004, pp. 36+; Jennifer Bjorhus, "3M Unveils Drastic Shakeup of Research and Development Division," *Saint Paul Pioneer Press,* September 27, 2003, www.twincities.com/mld/pioneerpress; Robert Westervelt, "3M Reorganizes R&D Effort," *Chemical Week,* October 5, 2003, p. 11; Tim Studt, "3M-Where Innovation Rules," *R&D,* April 2003, pp. 20+; Rita Shor, "Managed Innovation: 3M's Latest Model for New Products," *Manufacturing and Technology News,* (n.d.), www.manufacturingnews.com/news/editorials/shor.html.

2. U.S. Bureau of the Census, *Statistical Abstract of the United States,* 2004–2005 (Washington, DC: Government Printing Office, 2005), pp. 654–656.

3. Ibid.

4. Ibid., pp. 308–309.

5. Ibid., p. 262.

6. "Identix Wins the U.S. Department of State Facial Recognition Solicitation," *Business Wire,* September 29, 2004.

7. "Adina Genn, "E-Deals Even Small-Biz Playing Field," *Long Island Business News,* July 9, 2004.

8. Michael A. Verespej, "Sitting Pretty," *Industry Week,* March 5, 2001, www.industryweek.com.

9. Das Narayandas and V. Kasturi Rangan, "Building and Sustaining Buyer-Seller Relationships in Mature Industrial Markets," *Journal of Marketing,* July 2004, p. 63.

10. "Dell Expands Global Services Capabilities with European Command Center," *Business Wire,* December 1, 2004.

11. Moin Uddin, "Loyalty Programs: The Ultimate Gift," *DSN Retailing Today,* March 5, 2001, p. 12.

12. Frederick E. Webster, Jr., and Yoram Wind, "A General Model for Understanding Organizational Buyer Behavior," *Marketing Management,* Winter/Spring 1996, pp. 52–57.

13. Robert D. McWilliams, Earl Naumann, and Stan Scott, "Determining Buying Center Size," *Industrial Marketing Management* 21 (1992): 43–49.

14. Doug Bartholomew, "CEO of the Year-The King of Customer," *Industry Week,* February 1, 2002, www.industryweek.com/CurrentArticles/Asp/articles.asp?ArticleId=1180.

15. Laura Heller, *DSN Retailing Today*, January 10, 2005, pp. 13–14.
16. Suzanne Sabrosk, "NAICS Codes: A New Classification System for a New Economy," *Technology Information*, November 2000, p. 18.
17. Rod Kurtz, "Firms Turn to Perks in Lieu of Bonus Checks," *Inc.*, December 2004, p. 26; Toddi Gutner, "A Dot-Com's Survival Story," *Business Week*, May 13, 2002, p. 122; Maria Bruno, "Winning Customers: Concierge Services," *Bank Technology News*, July 2001, www.electronicbanker.com/btn/articles/btnjul01-6.shtml#top; "VIPdesk Expands Web-Based Personal Assistant Service to Wireless Devices," VIPdesk news release, June 25, 2001, www.vipdesk.com; VIPdesk homepage, www.vipdesk.com (accessed June 28, 2005).
a. "When You Can't Beat Them, Ambush Them," *Industry*, October 1, 2004, www.businesswire.com; "Building the Brighton Business," *Brighton View*, 2003, pp. 1–22; Brighton homepage, www.brighton.com (accessed June 28, 2005); interview with a Bryan, Texas, Brighton retailer, December 18, 2003.
b. Desiree J. Hanford, "eBay Will Test Its Pricing Power Via Fee Increase," *The Wall Street Journal*, January 13, 2005, p. B5; Molly Strzelecki, "Behind the Bidding: Yay or Nay?" *Private Label Buyer*, August 2004, pp. 18+; Anne Kadet, "Sold on eBay," *SmartMoney*, January 2004, pp. 92–98; "Buy or Sell in Bulk on eBay," *HardwareCentral*, September 8, 2003, (n.p.); Jane Salodof MacNeil, "Beyond eBay," *Inc.*, March 2002, p. 124; Peralte C. Paul, "Atlanta-Based Online Auction Equipment Maker Sees Surge in Big-Name Customers," *Atlanta Journal-Constitution*, January 2, 2002, www.ajc.com.
c. "GlobalTek Solutions: Small, Successful, and Led by a 15-year-old CEO," *Web Services Journal*, 2004, www.sys-con.com/webservices/article.cfm?id=199; Nichole L. Torres, "Generation Next," Entrepreneur.com, July 2004, www.entrepreneur.com/article/0,4621,299288-2,00.html; Afshan Khoja, "Executive Watch," NewsLine, September 2004, www.newsline.com.pk/NewsSep2004/executivesep.htm.

CHAPTER 10

1. Gary McWilliams, "Dell Ousts H-P as Top PC Seller in the 4th Period," *The Wall Street Journal*, January 19, 2005, p. B3; Cathy Booth Thomas, "Dell Wants Your Home," *Time*, October 6, 2003, pp. 48–50; Bolaji Ojo, "Equipped with Hard Drive," *EBN*, October 27, 2003, p. 2; Cynthia L. Webb, "Battle of the Consumer Electronics Giants," Washingtonpost.com, September 26, 2003, www.washingtonpost.com.
2. James Champy, "New Products or New Processes?" *Sales & Marketing Management*, May 2001, pp. 30–32.
3. Debbie Howell, "New HEB Concept Store Puts the Super Back in Market," *DSN Retailing Today*, July 19, 2004, p. 4.
4. Earle Eldridge, "Bentley Gets Buyers' Hearts Racing," *USA Today*, May 21, 2001, p. 3B.
5. Karen Richardson, "First Service's Odd Mix Works," *The Wall Street Journal*, December 22, 2004, p. C4.
6. *Businessline*, February 6, 2005, www.pg.com/common/sitemap/jhtml.
7. "Drink Up," *Prepared Foods*, September 2004, p. 27.
8. "Who Is Dr. Gadget?" The Dettman Group, 2005, www.doctorgadget.com/Who_Is_Dr._Gadget.html.
9. Peter Lewis, "Play That Funky Music, White Toy," *Fortune*, February 7, 2005, pp. 38–39.
10. Micheline Maynard, "Navigation Aids No Longer Just for Luxury Cars," *The New York Times*, January 27, 2002, sec. 3, p. 10.
11. O. C. Ferrell, and Michael Hartline, *Marketing Strategy* (Mason, OH: South-Western, 2005), pp. 172–173.
12. Matthew Swibel, "Spin Cycle," *Forbes*, April 2, 2001, p. 118.
13. Adapted from Everett M. Rogers, *Diffusion of Innovations* (New York: Macmillan, 1962), pp. 81–86.
14. Ibid., pp. 247–250.
15. Peter D. Bennett, ed., *Dictionary of Marketing Terms* (Chicago: American Marketing Association, 1995), p. 27.

16. U.S. Bureau of the Census, *Statistical Abstract of the United States, 2004–2005* (Washington, DC: Government Printing Office, 2005), p. 500.
17. David A. Aaker, *Managing Brand Equity: Capitalizing on the Value of a Brand Name* (New York: Free Press, 1991), pp. 16–17.
18. Private Label Manufacturers Association, *PLMA's 2003 Private Label Yearbook*, p. 8.
19. Mike Beirne, "Philip Morris to Put New Name, Altria, Aloft," *Brandweek*, December 16, 2002, p. 4.
20. Dorothy Cohen, "Trademark Strategy," *Journal of Marketing*, January 1986, p. 63.
21. Chiranjev Kohli and Rajheesh Suri, "Brand Names That Work: A Study of the Effectiveness of Different Brand Names," *Marketing Management Journal*, Fall/Winter 2000, pp. 112–120.
22. U.S. Trademark Association, "Trademark Stylesheet," no. 1A, n.d.
23. Dorothy Cohen, "Trademark Strategy Revisited," *Journal of Marketing*, July 1991, pp. 46–59.
24. Suzanne Bidlake, "Unilever's Leaner Lineup to Get $1.6 Bil Spending Boost," *Advertising Age*, February 2000; "Unilever Unveils 'Big Hit' Innovations, Brand Cull Progress," *Advertising Age*, February 9, 2001, www.adage.com.
25. Vicki R. Lane, "The Impact of Ad Repetition and Ad Content on Consumer Perceptions of Incongruent Extensions," *Journal of Marketing*, April 2000, pp. 80–91.
26. Christopher Palmeri, "Mattel: Up the Hill Minus Jill," *Business Week*, April 9, 2001, pp. 53–54.
27. Thomas J. Madden, Kelly Hewett, and Martin S. Roth, "Managing Images in Different Cultures: A Cross-National Study of Color Meanings and Preferences," *Journal of International Marketing*, Winter 2000, p. 90.
28. Gary Grossman, "Put Some Pizzazz in Your Packaging," *Brandweek*, January 17, 2005, p. 17.
29. Stephanie Thompson, "Nestlé Gives Mate Update in New Package, Ad Effort," *Advertising Age*, September 18, 2000, p. 8.
30. Valerie Folkes and Shashi Matta, "The Effect of Package Shape on Consumers' Judgment of Product Volume: Attention as a Mental Contaminant," *Journal of Consumer Research*, September 2004, p. 390.
31. "FDA Proposed New Rules for GM Foods," *Chemical Market Reporter*, January 29, 2001, p. 7.
32. Yuri Kageyama, "Sony Admits Losing Out on Gadgets," *Washington Post*, January 21, 2005, p. E5; "What If Xbox Never Had Halo?" *Electronic Gaming Monthly*, December 15, 2004, n.p.; Phred Dvorack, "Nintendo Girds for New Hand-Held Game Player from Sony," *The Wall Street Journal*, November 8, 2004, pp. B1+; Steven Levy, "Sony Gets Personal," *Newsweek*, October 25, 2004, pp. 78–88; "Technology Briefing Hardware: PlayStation 2 Sales Surpass 70 Million," *The New York Times*, January 15, 2004, p. C21; "Sony Corp.: Scaled-Back PSX Machine to Debut in Japan Saturday," *The Wall Street Journal*, December 9, 2003, p. 1; "Changing the Game," *The Economist*, December 6, 2003, p. 16; Byron Acohido, "Microsoft Bets on Xbox Success, but Some Skeptical," *USA Today*, April 24, 2001, p. 6B; "Sony Ships 60th Million PlayStation 2," *Online Reporter*, September 13, 2003, www.onlinereporter.com/.
a. "Nokia to Cut Jobs in Plan to Reduce Research Spending," *The Wall Street Journal*, January 12, 2005, p. 1; Japy Solomon, "Nokia Plans Factory in India," *The Wall Street Journal*, December 2, 2004, p. B5; Heather Timmons, "Technology Briefing Telecommunications: Nokia Gains Market Share," *The New York Times*, December 2, 2004, p. C6; David Pringle, "Cell Division," *The Wall Street Journal*, November 12, 2004, p. A1; "Nokia Ships One Millionth N-Gage Game Deck," *Telecomworldwire*, September 1, 2004, n.p.; Andy Reinhardt, "Nokia's Big Leap," *Business Week*, October 13, 2003, pp. 50–52.
b. "Harley-Davidson Inc.: Net Income Grows by 15% But Competition Damps Sales," *The Wall Street Journal*, January 21, 2005, p. 1; Dale Buss, "Can Harley Ride the New Wave?" *Brandweek*, October 25,

2004, pp. 20+; James D. Speros, "Why the Harley Brand's So Hot," *Advertising Age*, March 15, 2004, p. 26; Mark Yost, "Harley Davidson Centenary Bash Brings Out Armchair 'Rebels,' " *The Wall Street Journal*, September 3, 2003, p. D4; Monica Davey, "Harley at 100," *The New York Times*, September 1, 2003, p. A1; Harley-Davidson, www.harley-davidson.com.

   c. "Teen Titans," *People*, November 8, 2004, p. 129; "Teen of the Month," iParenting.com, February 2004, http://teenagerstoday.com/tom/0204.htm; Devlin Smith, "Generation Next," Entrepreneur.com, July 2004, www.entrepreneur.com/article/0,4621,299288-11,00.html.

CHAPTER 11

1. Bill Breen, "Written in the Stars," *Fast Company*, February 2005, pp. 54–59; Chris Walsh, "Pure Radio Satellite Providers Cut Out Commercials, Playlists," *Rocky Mountain News*, November 15, 2004, p. 1B; Tom Lowry, "Satellite Radio Shoots the Moon," *Business Week*, November 8, 2004, p. 52; Brad Stone, "Greetings, Earthlings: Satellite Radio for Cars Is Taking Off and Adding New Features-Now Broadcasters Are Starting to Fight Back," *Newsweek*, January 26, 2003, p. 55; Stephen Holden, "High-Tech Quirkiness Restores Radio's Magic," *The New York Times*, December 26, 2003, pp. E1+; David Pogue, "Satellite Radio Extends Its Orbit," *The New York Times*, December 18, 2003, p. G1.
2. Kate MacArthur, "Drink Your Fruits, Veggies: Water's the New Fitness Fad," *Advertising Age*, January 3, 2005, p. 4.
3. Ibid.
4. Warren Brown, "Nuts & Bolts; 2005 Ford Mustang GT Convertible," *The Washington Post*, January 16, 2001, p. G1.
5. Robert M. McMath, "Kellogg's Cereal Mates: 'It's Not for Breakfast Anymore,' " *Failure Magazine*, December 2003, www.failuremag.com/arch_mcmath_kelloggs.html.
6. Lee G. Cooper. "Strategic Marketing Planning for Radically New Products," *Journal of Marketing*, January 2000, pp. 1–16.
7. Lisa C. Troy, David M. Szymanski, and P. Rajan Varadarajan, "Generating New Product Ideas: An Initial Investigation of the Role of Market Information and Organizational Characteristics," *Journal of the Academy of Marketing Science*, January 2001, pp. 89–101.
8. Mark Roberti, "Space-Age Electric Parka? Sir, Yes, Sir!" *Business 2.0*, March 2002, pp. 28–29.
9. John Grossman, "The Idea Guru," *Inc.*, May 2001, pp. 32–41.
10. Aric Rindfleisch and Christine Moorman, "The Acquisition and Utilization of Information in New Product Alliances: A Strength-of-Ties Perspective," *Journal of Marketing*, April 2001, pp. 1–18.
11. "P&G Ends Test of Impress Plastic Wrap," *Advertising Age*, www.adage.com.
12. "P&G to Launch Hair Care for Men," *Advertising Age*, www.adage.com.
13. Faye Rice, "How to Deal with Tougher Customers," *Fortune*, December 3, 1990, pp. 39–48.
14. Adapted from Michael Levy and Barton A. Weitz, *Retailing Management* (Burr Ridge, IL: Irwin/McGraw-Hill, 2001), p. 585.
15. Sara Schaefer Munoz, "Food Group Joins Sugar Producers Critical of Splenda," *The Wall Street Journal*, February 15, 2005, p. D4; Marian Burros, "Splenda's 'Sugar' Claim Unites Odd Couple of Nutrition Wars," *The New York Times*, February 15, 2005, p. A12.
16. Jerry Morris, "Farewell to Olds, A Venerable Nameplate," *Boston Globe*, February 18, 2001, p. K41.
17. Jack Neff, "White Clouds Could Bring Rain on P&G," *Advertising Age*, July 2, 2001, p. 4.
18. Leonard L. Berry and A. Parasuraman, *Marketing Services: Competing through Quality* (New York: Free Press, 1991), p. 5.
19. The information in this section is based on K. Douglas Hoffman and John E. G. Bateson, *Essentials of Services Marketing* (Mason, OH: South-Western, 2001); and Valarie A. Zeithaml, A. Parasuraman, and Leonard L. Berry, *Delivering Quality Service: Balancing Customer Perceptions and Expectations* (New York: Free Press, 1990).

20. J. Paul Peter and James H. Donnelly, *A Preface to Marketing Management* (Burr Ridge, IL: Irwin/McGraw-Hill, 2003), p. 212.
21. Michael D. Hartline and O. C. Ferrell, "Service Quality Implementation: The Effects of Organizational Socialization and Managerial Actions of Customer Contact Employee Behavior," *Marketing Science Institute Report*, no. 93–122 (Cambridge, MA: Marketing Science Institute, 1993).
22. "Starbucks Corporation Fact Sheet," *Hoover's Online*, March 3, 2005, www.hoovers.com/starbucks/—ID__15745—/free-co-factsheet.xhtml.
23. Sam Schechner, "Testing Out Airline Web Sites," *The Wall Street Journal*, February 15, 2005, p. D5.
24. International Smart Tan Network, www.smarttan.com/beta/page.php?pid=4 (accessed February 1, 2005).
25. Julie Cantwell, "GM Redefines Role of Brand Managers," *Automotive News*, January 14, 2002, p. 3.
26. Rajesh Sethi, "New Product Quality and Product Development Teams," *Journal of Marketing*, April 2000, pp. 1–14.
27. "Snippets: Giftables . . . Spa with a Name . . . Brushing Up," *WWD*, August 20, 2004, p. 9; "The WWD List," *WWD*, December 8, 2003, p. 34S; Patricia Van Arnum, "The Two Faces of the Global Cosmetics/Personal Care Market," *Chemical Market Reporter*, December 1, 2003, pp. FR3+; "An Ancient Italian Recipe for Success," *European Cosmetic Markets*, November 2002, p. 397; Jean Patteson, "Olive Oil, Essences Are Being Poured into Beauty Products," *The Morning Call*, August 3, 2001, www.mcall.comhtml/news/am_mag/d_pg001oliveoil.htm; Pamela Sauer, "A Makeover for Personal Care and Cosmetics," *Chemical Market Reporter*, May 14, 2001, www.findarticles.com.

   a. "World: Since Acquiring Demeter Fragrances in 2002, the Freedom Marketing Group Has Been Working Overtime," *Cosmetics International Cosmetic Products Report*, June 2004, p. 3; "Beauty Diary: Demeter Fragrances," Sephora website, n.d., www.sephora.com (accessed June 30, 2005); Matthew W. Evans, "Demeter to Launch Two New Brands," *WWD*, February 25, 2004, p. 35; Cassandra Chiacchio, "Dirt Has Been Sold," *WWD*, July 5, 2002, p. 1.

   b. Lee Hawkins, Jr., "GM's 'Car Guy' Faces Test with New Pontiac, Buick Sedans," *The Wall Street Journal*, January 11, 2005, p. B1; Jim Mateja, "Low Sales Bring Much-Criticized SUV Pontiac Aztek to Stop," *Chicago Tribune*, October 28, 2004, www.chicagotribune.com; Douglas Kalajian, "Oldsmobile Marque Drives into History," *The (Kitchener-Waterloo, Ontario) Record*, July 2, 2004, p. E2; "Chevrolet's Cavalier Continues to Deliver Strong Sales, GM Reports," *Vindicator (Youngstown, OH)*, December 3, 2003, www.vindy.com; Dave Guilford, "As Olds Folds, GM Fights to Keep Owners," *Automotive News*, August 11, 2003, p. 6.

   c. "World Acclaim for Young Business Achiever" Ercan Baysal, *Zaman Daily Online*, December 3, 2004, www.zaman.com/?bl=national&alt=&trh=20041203&hn=14389; Alternative Camp, "What Is Alternative Camp?" www.alternativecamp.org/web/eng/index.asp?menu=can (accessed June 30, 2005); Ashoka, "Ashoka Fellows—Turkey," www.ashoka.org/global/aw_ce_turkey.cfm (accessed June 30, 2005).

CHAPTER 12

1. "Napster Reports 50% Rise in Subscribers," *The New York Times*, January 14, 2005, p. C6; Jay Greene, "Whistling a Different iTune," *Business Week*, November 8, 2004, p. 148; Stephen F. Nathans, "Sonic Acquires Roxio Software," *EMedia*, October 2004, pp. 7+; Ben Fritz and Gordon Masson, "Napster Racing iTunes to Europe," *Daily Variety*, March 4, 2004, p. 6; Sean O'Neill and Elizabeth Kountze, "Music for a Song," *Kiplinger's Personal Finance*, January 2004, p. 102; "Napster, But in Name Only," *Wired News*, July 28, 2003, www.wired.com/news/digiwood/0,1412,59789,00.html; Stephen Hinkle, "RIAA, Surrender Now!" Dmusic.com, http://news.dmusic.com/print/5026.

2. Rajneesh Suri and Kent B. Monroe, "The Effects of Time Constraints on Consumers' Judgments of Prices and Products," *Journal of Consumer Research,* June 2003, pp. 92+.

3. "Hewlett-Packard," Professional Pricing Society, case study, www.pricingsociety.com/casestudiesdetails3.asp (accessed February 3, 2005).

4. "Broadcast of New Vision Gets Mixed Reception from the Street," *DSN Retailing Today,* January 2001, p. 16.

5. Jon Swartz, "Price War Looms for High-Speed Net Access," *USA Today,* November 14, 2003, p. 1B.

6. Akshay R. Rao, Mark E. Bergen, and Scott Davis, "How to Fight a Price War," *Harvard Business Review,* March/April 2000, pp. 107–116.

7. Matt Richtel and Ken Bilson, "Reshaping Telecommunications: The Overview; Phone Mergers May Curb Price Wars," *The New York Times,* February 15, 2005, p. C1.

8. David Aaker and Erich Joachimsthaler, "An Alternative to Price Competition," *American Demographics.* September 2000, p. 11.

9. Frank Byrt, "Vermont Pure Seeks to Deliver Higher Margins by Shifting Focus," *The Wall Street Journal,* February 16, 2005, p. 1.

10. Cliff Edwards, "Intel Inside the War Room," *Business Week,* April 30, 2001, p. 40.

11. Peter D. Bennett, *Dictionary of Marketing Terms* (Chicago: American Marketing Association, 1995), p. 79.

12. "Want a Cheaper Flat-Panel TV?" *CNNMoney,* December 4, 2003, http://money.cnn.com/.

13. Bennett, *Dictionary of Marketing Terms,* p. 215.

14. Carleen Hawn, "The Global Razor's Edge," *Fast Company,* February 2004, pp. 27–28.

15. Donald Lichtenstein, Nancy M. Ridgway, and Richard G. Netemeyer, "Price Perceptions and Consumer Shopping Behavior: A Field Study," *Journal of Marketing Research,* May 1993, pp. 234–245.

16. "Sony Ericsson to Offer Luxury Cell Phones," *EuropeMedia,* February 5, 2002, www.vandusseldorp.com.

17. Robert Guy Matthews, "A Surge in Ocean-Shipping Rates Could Increase Consumer Prices," *The Wall Street Journal,* November 4, 2003, http://online.wsj.com/public/us.

18. Carolyn Shapiro, "Verizon Tries Out New Pricing for Quick Pay-Phone Calls in Norfolk, Va., Area," *Daily [Hampton Roads, VA] Press,* January 30, 2002, www.dailypress.com.

19. Bruce L. Alford and Brian T. Engelland, "Advertised Reference Price Effects on Consumer Price Estimates, Value Perception, and Search Intention," *Journal of Business Research,* May 2000, pp. 93–100.

20. Wayne Niemi, "H Marks the Spot: The New Affordable-Luxe Brand Is Finding Success by Appealing to a Price-Conscious, Upscale Customer," *Footwear News,* December 6, 2004, p. 34.

21. Peter Burrows, "Apple's Down Market Gamble; By Launching a Much Cheaper Mac and iPod, Steve Jobs Is Appealing to Hordes of Price-Conscious Consumers," *Business Week Online,* January 12, 2005, www.businessweek.com.

22. Lichtenstein, Ridgway, and Netemeyer, "Price Perceptions."

23. Gail Edmundson, "This SUV Can Tow an Entire Carmaker," *Business Week,* January 19, 2004, pp. 40–41.

24. Linda Tischler, "The Price Is Right," *Fast Company,* November 2003, pp. 83+.

25. Alexandra Marks, "New Fare War Adds to Pressure on Airlines," *Christian Science Monitor,* January 10, 2005, p. 2; Jeremy W. Peters, "Rougher Times Amid Higher Costs at JetBlue," *The New York Times,* November 11, 2004, pp. C1+; Chuck Salter, "And Now the Hard Part," *Fast Company,* May 2004, pp. 66+; Amy Goldwasser, "Something Stylish, Something Blue," *Business 2.0,* February 2002, pp. 94–95; "Blue Skies: Is JetBlue the Next Great Airline-Or Just a Little Too Good to Be True?" *Time,* July 30, 2001, pp. 24+; Darren Shannon, "Three of a Kind," *Travel Agent,* July 23, 2001, pp. 60+; JetBlue, www.jetblue.com (accessed June 30, 2005).

a. Pui-Wing Tam, "H-P Gains Applause as It Cedes PC Market Share to Dell," *The Wall Street Journal,* January 18, 2005, p. C1; William M. Bulkeley and Evan Ramstad, "IBM Veteran Sees an Opportunity with Lenovo," *The Wall Street Journal,* December 9, 2004, p. B3; Andrew Park, "Dell Outfoxes Its Rivals," *Business Week,* September 6, 2004, p. 54; John G. Spooner, "Study: PC Prices Rocking to the Bottom," C-Net, April 4, 2003, http://zdnet.com.com.2100-1103-995560.html; Cynthia L. Webb, "The 1 Percent Recovery?" Washingtonpost.com, February 20, 2004, www.washingtonpost.com.

b. "Teen Tech Wizard," YoungBiz.com, 2004, www.youngbiz.com; "Pankaj Arora Software's Tumi Cursor Powerpack," www.paware.com/pastcp/ (accessed June 1, 2005); "What Is Success?" Amy Fennell Christian, Entrepreneur.com, January 2004, www.entrepreneur.com/tsu/article/0,5788,312524,00.html.

c. Bob Tedeschi, "Cheaper Than It Seems," *The New York Times,* January 10, 2005, p. C9; Ethan Smith, "Music Labels Back Online Service," *The Wall Street Journal,* November 26, 2004, p. B3; Tom Lowry, "Extended Play for Universal's Music Man," *Business Week Online,* September 23, 2004, www.businessweekonline.com; John Chesto, "Universal Spins Hike in CD Prices," Boston Herald, *April 17, 2004, p. 21; Tyler Hamilton, "What's Music Worth?"* Toronto Star, January 13, 2004, www.thestar.com; Kevin C. Johnson, "On a Not So Sour Note . . . CD Sales in 2003 Dropped," *St. Louis Post-Dispatch,* January 9, 2004, www.stltoday.com; Ethan Smith, "Universal Slashes Its CD Prices in Bid to Revive Music Industry," *The Wall Street Journal,* September 4, 2003, http://online.wsj.com/public/us.

CHAPTER 13

1. "A Jump Start at GM," *Business Week,* January 17, 2005, p. 40; Joseph B. White and Lee Hawkins, Jr., "GM's Sales Drop as Discounts Fade," *The Wall Street Journal,* December 2, 2004, p. A3; Shannon McMahon, "Big Three Automakers Being Made to Pay for Car Deals Consumers Can't Refuse," *San Diego Union-Tribune,* November 28, 2004, www.uniontrib.com; Danny Hakim, "Buy a G.M. Car at 0% Now, Get the Same Deal in 5 Years," *The New York Times,* November 10, 2004, p. C4; David Welch, "A Dangerous Skid," *Business Week,* November 1, 2004, pp. 40+.

2. Christopher Caggiano, "E-tailing by the Numbers," *Inc. Tech 2001,* March 15, 2001, pp. 46–49.

3. Kevin Schweitzer, "Hybrid Potential Limited Only by Price," *Chicago Tribune,* February 11, 2005, p. 10.

4. "New Bentley Pricing," Automotive.com, 2005, www.automotive.com/new-cars/pricing/01/bentley/index.html.

5. Robert J. Frank, Jeffrey P. George, and Laxman Narasimhan, "When Your Competitor Delivers More for Less," *McKinsey Quarterly,* www.mckinseyquarterly.com.

6. Barry J. Babin, David M. Hardesty, and Tracy A. Suter, "Color and Shopping Intentions: The Intervening Effect of Price Fairness and Perceived Affect," *Journal of Business Research,* July 2003, pp. 541–551.

7. David Moin, "Category Killers' Concerns: Overgrowth and Extinction," *WWD,* January 6, 2005, p. 17.

8. "Fairchild Dynamic Pricing Team," Professional Pricing Society, case study, www.pricingsociety.com/casestudiesdetails.asp (accessed February 4, 2005).

9. Allan Hall, "Berlin Taxis Offer Half-Price 'Happy-Hours,' " *Evening Standard,* February 22, 2002, www.thisislondon.co.uk.

10. Melanie Trottman, "Scoring Travel Discounts Gets Easier," *The Wall Street Journal,* November 4, 2003, http://online.wsj.com/public/us.

11. "Cutler-Hammon/Eaton Corporation," Professional Pricing Society, case study, www.pricingsociety.com/casestudiesdetails1.asp (accessed February 4, 2004).

12. "Can Detroit Break the Rebate Habit?" *Business Week,* January 12, 2004, p. 110; Joann Muller, "Outpsyching the Car Buyer," *Forbes,* February 17, 2003, p. 52.

13. Marla Royne Stafford and Thomas F. Stafford, "The Effectiveness of Tensile Pricing Tactics in the Advertising of Services," *The Journal of Advertising,* Summer 2000, pp. 45–56.

14. Gail Edmundson, "This SUV Can Tow an Entire Carmaker," *Business Week,* January 19, 2004, pp. 40–41.

15. David Lunhow and Chad Terhume, "Latin Pop: A Low-Budget Cola Shakes Up Markets South of the Border," *The Wall Street Journal,* October 27, 2003, pp. A1, A18.

16. Daniel A. Sheinin and Janet Wagner, "Pricing Store Brands Across Categories and Retailers," *Journal of Product & Brand Management* 12, no. 4 (2003): 201–220.

17. Keith Damsell, "Telecom Bundling Seen Luring Customers," *The Globe and Mail,* September 29, 2003, p. B8, www.globetechnology.com.

18. Jaihak Chung and Vithala R. Rao, "A General Choice Model for Bundles with Multiple-Category Products: Application to Market Segmentation and Optimal Pricing for Bundles," *Journal of Marketing Research,* May 2003, pp. 115–130.

19. Damsell, "Telecom Bundling Seen Luring Customers."

20. George Mannes, "The Urge to Unbundle," *Fast Company,* February 2005, pp. 23–25.

21. Doug Halonen, "Watchdog Sets Sights on a la Carte," *TelevisionWeek,* January 10, 2005, p. 8.

22. Mannes, "The Urge to Unbundle."

23. "Famous Players to Introduce Everyday Value Price Plan at Its Victoria Theaters," *Canadian Corporate News,* February 28, 2002, www.comtextnews.com.

24. Adulla Cellini Linecker, "Family Dollar Store Uses 'Hardline' Stance to Get a Leg Up in Discount Battles," *Investor's Daily Business,* May 23, 2001, p. A1.

25. Keith S. Coulter, "The Influence of Print Advertisement Organization on Odd-Ending Price Image Effects," *Journal of Product & Brand Management* 11, no. 4 (2002): 319+.

26. Linda Tischler, "The Price Is Right," *Fast Company,* November 2003, pp. 83+.

27. "Price Promotions Give ASDA a Lift and Multibuys Boost Sainsbury," *Grocer,* February 2, 2002, p. 30.

28. Bruce L. Alford and Brian T. Engelland, "Advertised Reference Price Effects on Consumer Price Estimates, Value Perception, and Search Intention," *Journal of Business Research,* May 2000, pp. 93–100.

29. Nigel Cox, "Amex Charges Ahead," *Smart Business,* April 2001, pp. 123–128.

30. Kathy Lally, "Marketers in Full Bloom: As the Biggest Generation Passes 50, Retailers Refit Their Appeal," *Washington Post,* January 9, 2005, p. F6; Daren Fonda, "Sole Survivor," *Time,* November 8, 2004, p. 48; Thomas J. Ryan, "The Price Is Right," *Footwear Business,* February 2004, n.p.; interviews with Jim Sciabarrasi, Christine Epplett, and Paul Heffernan of New Balance, video, Houghton Mifflin Company, 2003.

a. Heather Green, "Kissing Off the Big Labels," *Business Week,* September 6, 2004, pp. 90–92; Fred Kaplan, "D.I.Y. Meets N.R.L.," *The New York Times,* July 4, 2004, sec. 2, p. 23.

b. Gary Forsee, "Sprint," *Business Week,* January 10, 2005, p. 60; Matt Richtel, "Sprint Will Offer a Radio Service That Plays Music over Cell Phones," *The New York Times,* December 20, 2004, p. C3; Jesse Drucker, Almar Latour, and Dennis K. Berman, "Cut Loose," *The Wall Street Journal,* December 16, 2004, p. A1; Jesse Drucker and Anne Marie Sequeo, "Cellular Merger to Alter Service for Millions," *The Wall Street Journal,* October 26, 2004, p. D1.

c. "Teen Titans," *People,* November 8, 2004, p. 129; Jacky Johnson, "Young and Inventive," *St. Petersburg Times Online,* March 3, 2003, www.sptimes.com/2003/03/03/Xpress/Young_and_inventive.shtml; "Kid Inventor," Wild Planet Kid Inventor Challenge, www.kidinventorchallenge.com/rich_stachowski.php.

CHAPTER 14

1. "W. W. Grainger Arm to Buy Direct Auto Products Marketer," *America's Intelligence Wire,* January 10, 2005, n.p.; Jim Lucy, "The Super Influentials," *Electrical Wholesaling,* April 1, 2004; Susan Avery, "Grainger Eases Access to Products for MRO Buyers," *Purchasing,* June 3, 2004, pp. 48+.

2. "Standards," Dell.com, www1.us.dell.com/content/topics/global.aspx/corp/standards/en/index?c=us&l=en&s=corp#mastheadtop (accessed March 22, 2005).

3. "eBay: The World's Online Marketplace," eBay.com, http://pages.ebay.com/aboutebay/thecompany/companyoverview.html (accessed March 22, 2005).

4. "When Complexity Pays Off," *CFO, The Magazine for Financial Executives,* Winter 2003, p. 14.

5. Chester Dawson, "Machete Time," *Business Week,* April 9, 2001, pp. 42–44.

6. "From Planning to Control: Improving the High-Tech Supply Chain," Valdero Corporation, white paper, January 4, 2002, accessible via www.manufacturing.net.

7. "Trendspotting," *Intelligent Enterprises,* March 2005, p. 17; Doug Henschen, "Content and CRM: Completing the Picture Intelligent Enterprise," *Intelligent Enterprises,* March 2005, pp. 34+.

8. Lester E. Goodman and Paul A. Dion, "The Determinants of Commitment in the Distributor-Manufacturer Relationship," *Industrial Marketing Management,* April 2001, pp. 287–300.

9. "Estée Lauder Sees Dept. Stores as Smaller Portion of Its Business," *Forbes,* February 28, 2001, www.forbes.com/newswire/2001/02/28/rtri94332.html.

10. Tony Seideman, "Get with the Program," *Inbound Logistics,* September 1998, p. 29.

11. Wroe Alderson, *Dynamic Marketing Behavior* (Homewood, IL: Irwin, 1965), p. 239.

12. Jonathan D. Hibbard, Nirmalya Kumar, and Louis W. Stern, "Examining the Impact of Destructive Acts in Marketing Channel Relationships," *Journal of Marketing Research,* February 2001, pp. 45–61.

13. Seideman, "Get with the Program," p. 31.

14. Leo Aspinwall, "The Marketing Characteristics of Goods," *Four Marketing Theories* (Boulder: University of Colorado Press, 1961), pp. 27–32.

15. Jennifer Weil and Brid Costello, "Hermes Planning to Launch a Wonder," *WWD,* December 12, 2003, p. 10.

16. Lee Pender, "The Basic Links of SCM," Supply Chain Management Research Center, www.cio.com/research/scm/edit/020501_basic.html (accessed January 22, 2002).

17. William Atkinson, "Gaining Supply Chain Visibility," *Supply Chain Management Review,* November 15, 2001, www.manufacturing.net.

18. William Atkinson, "E-Logistics and E-Procurement: Here to Stay," *Supply Chain Management Review,* November 15, 2001, www.manufacturing.net.

19. Dominic Gates, "Boeing 7E7 Site Winner Will Get Second Plant Bonus," *Seattle Times,* November 19, 2003.

20. Margaret L. Williams and Mark N. Frolick, "The Evolution of EDI for Competitive Advantage: The FedEx Case," *Information Systems Management,* Spring 2001, pp. 47–53.

21. "Manufacturing Your Way into the Warehouse Business," *Inbound Logistics,* January 2002, pp. 106–108.

22. Anne T. Coughlan, Erin Anderson, Louis W. Stern, and Adel I. El-Ansary, *Marketing Channels* (Upper Saddle River, NJ: Prentice Hall, 2001), p. 510.

23. "The 75-Year-Old Supply Chain," *Inbound Logistics,* January 2002, pp. 96–104.

24. Daniel Machalaba, "Trucker Rewards Customers for Good Behavior," *The Wall Street Journal,* September 9, 2003, http://online.wsj.com/article/0,,SB106306613229256300,00.html.

25. "Ports Bridge the Great Global Divide," *Inbound Logistics,* November 2001, p. 52.

26. "Low Inventory, High Expectations," *Inbound Logistics,* June 2000, pp. 36–42.

27. Anne Stuart, "Express Delivery," *Inc. Tech 2001,* March 15, 2001, pp. 54–56.

28. "Excelligence Learning Posts Q3 Net of $4.1 M," *Investor's Business Daily,* November 8, 2004, www.investors.com; "Excelligence Learning Releases Third Quarter 2003 Results," *Business Wire,* November 5, 2003, www.businesswire.com; Nichole Cipriani, "Testing Your Child—Online," *Parenting,* May 2001, p. 21; Susan Holly, "Get Smarter," *PC Magazine,* October 17, 2000, pp. 19+; SmarterKids, www.smarterkids.com (accessed July 13, 2005); Excelligence Learning Corporation, www.excelligencelearning.com (accessed July 13, 2005).

a. Hard Candy, "Company History," http://www.hardcandy.com/cs/aboutUs.cfm (accessed July 5, 2005); "Candy Girl," YoungBiz.com, 2003, www.youngbiz.com/aspindex.asp?fileName=career_gears/Turning%20 Pro/candy_girl.htm; Jeffrey Zaslow, "Strait Talk," *USA Weekend Magazine,* June 26, 1998.

b. Donna Hood Crecca, "School of Rock," *Chain Leader,* November 2004, pp. 61+; "Avicon Leads Hard Rock Café's Successful Transition to Outsourced Logistics, Fulfillment, and Distribution," Business Wire, December 1, 2003, www.businesswire.com; "Hard Rock Café Selects Kuehne & Nagel Subsidiary," Business Wire, November 24, 2003, www.businesswire.com; Ben Worthen, "Hard Rock Goes IT," *CIO,* May 1, 2001, www.itworld.com; Hard Rock Café, "History: The Hard Rock Café Story," n.d., www.hardrock.com/corporate/history (accessed July 5, 2005).

c. "It's APL Logistics, B'Gosh," *Traffic World,* July 5, 2004, p. 16; David Moin, "OshKosh B'Gosh Grows Up," *WWD,* April 28, 2004, p. 3; Doris Hajewski, "OshKosh B'Gosh to Close Two Factories," *Milwaukee Journal Sentinel,* December 13, 2003, p. 3D; Rachel Gecker, "An Overall Inbound Success," *Inbound Logistics,* November 2003, pp. 56–58.

CHAPTER 15

1. Kevin Savetz, "Dell.Com, Direct PC Vendors," *Computer Shopper,* January 2005, p. 161. Emily Kumler, "Ely, Nev., Community-Based Store Prepares to Open to Public," *Las Vegas Review-Journal,* December 1, 2004, www.lvrj.com; Emily Kumler, "New Retailer Cooperative Restores Shopping in Ely, Nev.," *Las Vegas Review-Journal,* November 9, 2004, www.lvrj.com; Becky Bohrer, "Rural Towns Turn to Mercantiles," *Desert Morning News,* March 6, 2004, http://desertnews.com; Michelle Nijhuis, "For Sale by Owners," *Smithsonian Magazine,* October 2004, pp. 30–32; Penelope Patsuris, "Wal-Mart's Next Victims," Forbes.com, www.forbes.com/2004/11/10/cx_pp_1109wmt_print.html; Mike Stark, "Success Story: Community-Owned Wyoming Mercantiles Lead the Way," *Billings Gazette,* December 21, 2003, www.billingsgazette.com/index.php?id=1&display=rednews/2003/12/21/build/business/30-oops.inc.

2. U.S. Bureau of the Census, *Statistical Abstract of the United States,* 2004–2005 (Washington, DC: Government Printing Office, 2005), p. 654.

3. Roger O. Crockett, "Chat Me Up . . . Please," *Business Week,* March 19, 2001, p. EB10.

4. Amy Merrick, Jeffrey A. Trachtenberg, and Ann Zimmerman, "Department Stores Fight to Save a Model That May Be Outdated," *The Wall Street Journal,* March 12, 2002, http://online.wsj.com/public/us.

5. Wal-Mart Fact Sheet, Hoover's Online, www.hoovers.com/free (accessed March 21, 2005).

6. "A Different Type of Sears Store," *The New York Times,* February 9, 2005, p. C5.

7. Stanley Holmes, "The Jack Welch of the Meat Aisle; Former GE Exec Larry Johnston Brings High-Tech to Troubled Albertson's," *Business Week,* January 24, 2005, p. 60.

8. Richard C. Morais, "One Hot Tamale," *Forbes,* December 27, 2004, p. 137.

9. Sam's Club Fact Sheet and Costco Wholesale Corporation Fact Sheet, Hoover's Online, *www.hoovers.com/free* (accessed February 7, 2005).

10. Paul Miller, "Neiman Marcus Tests Catalog Showrooms," *Catalog Age,* May 14, 2004, http://bg.catalogagemag.com/ar/marketing_neiman_marcus_tests.

11. Jeffrey Arlan, "Retailers Jockeyed for $180 Billion in 2000 Sales: Who Are the Winners?" *DSN Retailing Today,* February 5, 2001, pp. A6–A8.

12. Jenny Strasburg, "High Hopes for Low Prices; Ross Appeals to Bargain Hunters with DD's Discounts," *San Francisco Chronicle,* August 14, 2004, p. C1.

13. Merrick, Trachtenberg, and Zimmerman, "Department Stores Fight to Save a Model That May Be Outdated."

14. Maureen Tkacik, " 'Alternative' Teens Are Hip to Hot Topic's Mall Stores," *The Wall Street Journal,* February 12, 2002, http://interactive.wsj.com.

15. Merrick, Trachtenberg, and Zimmerman, "Department Stores Fight to Save a Model That May Be Outdated."

16. "McDonald's Corp. Plans to Test Market a String of Coffee Bars Called *McCafés,*" *The Food Institute Report,* September 15, 2003, p. 6.

17. "McDonald's New McCafé," CNNfn.com, March 23, 2001, http://cnnfn.cnn.com/2001/03/23/companies/wires/mcdonaldswg/.

18. Richard F. Yalch and Eric R. Spangenberg, "The Effects of Music in a Retail Setting on Real and Perceived Shopping Times," *Journal of Business Research,* August 2000, pp. 139–147.

19. Stephen Brown, "The Wheel of Retailing: Past and Future," *Journal of Retailing,* Summer 1990, pp. 143–149.

20. Patrick Seitz, "After a Failure, Reinvent Yourself," *Investor's Business Daily,* December 8, 2003, p. A08.

21. Pete Barlas, "Rising Security Fears Will Result in Less Shopping Online: Survey," *Investor's Business Daily,* November 21, 2003.

22. Scott Frey, "Complying with Do-Not-Call," *National Underwriter Life & Health — Financial Services Edition,* December 8, 2003, p. 17.

23. Frequently Asked Questions, www.donotcall.gov/FAQ (accessed January 18, 2004).

24. Jill Hecht Maxwell, "Sit! Stay! Make Money! Good Company," *Inc. Tech 2001,* March 15, 2001, pp. 42–44.

25. Lucinda Hahn, "Pampered Life," *Chicago Tribune,* January 18, 2005, p. 1.

26. "Fact Sheet: 2004 Direct Selling Growth & Outlook Survey," *Direct Selling Association, www.dsa.org* (accessed February 11, 2005).

27. U.S. Bureau of the Census, *Statistical Abstract of the United States,* 2004–2005, p. 654.

28. Genuine Parts Company Fact Sheet, Hoover's Online, www.hoovers.com/free (accessed March 21, 2005).

29. Universal Corporation Fact Sheet, Hoover's Online, www.hoovers.com/free (accessed March 21, 2005).

30. Red River Commodities Inc. Fact Sheet, Hoover's Online, www.hoovers.com/free (accessed February 7, 2005); Red River Commodities Inc., www.redriv.com (accessed February 7, 2005).

31. "REI Named to *Fortune's* 100 Best Companies List," *Business Wire,* January 10, 2005, www.businesswire.com; Ken Clark, "REI Scales New Heights," *Chain Store Age,* July 2004, pp. 26A+; "REI Climbs to New Heights Online," *Chain Store Age,* October 2003, pp. 72+; Recreational Equipment, Inc., www.rei.com; Mike Gorrell, "New REI Store Opens in Salt Lake City Area," *Salt Lake Tribune,* March 28, 2003, www.sltrib.com.

a. "On a Shoestring," Entrepreneur, November 1, 2004, www.entrepreneur.com; Will Buss, "Magazine to Feature Freeburg, Illinois, Design Business," *Belleville News-Democrat,* September 29, 2004.

b. "More Black Canyons on Way at Jet Service Stations," *America's Intelligence Wire.* April 9, 2004, n.p.; Boonsong Kositchitethana, "Conoco Boosts Presence While Rivals Close Service Stations: 160 Service Stations Planned by 2003," *Bangkok Post.* March 30, 2001, www.siamfuture.com/thainews/thnewstxt.asp?tid=579; Sutthinee Sattarugawong, "Ban Rai Coffee House," *Masters in Marketing*

Program, Competitive Strategies course, Thammasat University, Bangkok, Thailand, Winter 2002; Nareeat Wiriyapong, "Convenience Store: Conoco Set to Invest Bt3bn," *The Nation.* June 5, 2000, www.siamfuture.com/thainews/thnewstxt.asp?tid=169.

c. Kevin Savetz, "Dell.Com, Direct PC Vendors," *Computer Shopper.* January 9, 2005, p. 161; Carol Krol, "Dell Sees Continued Success with DM," *B to B,* October 25, 2004, p. 8; "Repeat Performers," *Business Week,* January 12, 2004, p. 68; Sam Diaz, "Dell Succeeds by Breaking Silicon Valley Rules," *San Jose Mercury News,* December 17, 2003, www.mercurynews.com; Joan Magretta, "The Power of Virtual Integration: An Interview with Dell Computer's Michael Dell," *Harvard Business Review,* March–April 1998, pp. 74–84; "I'm Going Full Blast," *Business Week,* September 24, 2001, www.businessweek.com.

CHAPTER 16

1. Apple, www.apple.com (accessed August 2, 2005); Alice Z. Cuneo, "Marketer of the Year: Apple," *Advertising Age,* December 15, 2003, www.adage.com; Scott Donaton, "A Marketing Tale of the Great and the Desperate," *Advertising Age,* December 15, 2003, www.adage.com; Nick Wingfield, "Apple Tries a New Tack: Lower Prices," *The Wall Street Journal,* January 12, 2005, p. D1.

2. Stephanie Thompson, "Masterfoods Ties M&M's to Movies with Oscar Effort," *Advertising Age,* January 24, 2005, pp. 4, 54.

3. Nat Ives, "Interactive Viral Campaigns Ask Consumers to Spread the Word," *The New York Times,* February 18, 2005, www.nytimes.com; Patricia Odell, "Doritos Targets Texters in Integrated Campaign," *Promo,* March 3, 2005, http://promomagazine.com/news/doritos_campaign_030305/.

4. Rebecca Gardyn, "Swap Meet: Customers Are Willing to Exchange Personal Information for Personalized Products," *American Demographics,* July 2001, pp. 51–55.

5. Chad Terhune, "Wood Folks Hope for 'Got Milk' Success," *The Wall Street Journal,* February 9, 2001, p. B7.

6. "Yoplait Is Committed to Fighting Breast Cancer!" Yoplait, www.youplait.com/breastcancer_commitment.aspx (accessed January 12, 2005).

7. Theresa Howard, "Marketing Parties' Pizazz Pulls Plenty," *USA Today,* November 19, 2003, www.usatoday.com.

8. Terence A. Shimp, Advertising, Promotion, and Supplemented Aspects of Integrated Marketing Communications (Fort Worth: Dryden, 2000), p. 117.

9. Salvador Ruiz and María Sicilia, "The Impact of Cognitive and/or Affective Processing Styles on Consumer Response to Advertising Appeals," *Journal of Business Research* 57 (2004): 657–664.

10. John S. McClenahen, "How Can You Possibly Say That?" *Industry Week,* July 17, 1995, pp. 17–19; Anton Piësch, "Speaking in Tongues," *Inc.,* 25 (June 2003): 50.

11. Samuel D. Bradley III and Robert Meeds, "The Effects of Sentence-Level Context, Prior Word Knowledge, and Need for Cognition on Information Processing of Technical Language in Print Ads," *Journal of Consumer Psychology* 14, no. 3 (2004): 291–302.

12. Zakary L. Tormala and Richard E. Petty, "A Source Credibility and Attitude Certainty: A Metacognitive Analysis of Resistance to Persuasion," *Journal of Consumer Psychology,* 14, no. 4 (2004): 427–442.

13. David M. Szymanski, "Modality and Offering Effects in Sales Presentations for a Good Versus a Service," *Journal of the Academy of Marketing Science* 29, no. 2 (2001): 179–189.

14. Sally Beatty, "Advance Sales of Children's Ads Slacken," *The Wall Street Journal,* May 11, 2001, p. B8.

15. Patricia Odell, "P&G to Debut New Mouthwash in $100 Million Campaign," *Promo,* February 8, 2005, http://promomagazine.com/campaigns/p-g_mouthwash_020805/.

16. Michael McCarthy, "$250M Ad Campaign Aims to Hit Homer," *USA Today,* April 3, 2001, p. 3B.

17. Reshma Kapadia, "AOL Internet Service Members Surpass 30 Million," Reuters Newswire, via AOL, June 25, 2001.

18. Patricia Odell, "Silk Goes Guerilla to Sample New Smoothie," *Promo Magazine,* August 18, 2004, http://promomagazine.com/sampling/silk_goes_guerrilla/.

19. Libby Estell, "This Call Center Accelerates Sales," *Sales & Marketing Management,* February 1999, p. 72.

20. Karen Lundegaard, "Car Crash Ads May Lose Impact," *The Detroit News,* April 15, 2001, p. C1.

21. "2005 Rates and Editions," *Time,* www.time-planner.com/planner/rates/index.html (accessed January 13, 2005).

22. "Got Milk," National Fluid Milk Processor Promotion Board, www.whymilk.com, (accessed January 13, 2005).

23. Beth Snyder Bulik, "Nintendo 'Maximi'-izes to Lure Older Generation of Gamers," *Advertising Age,* February 7, 2005, p. 8.

24. Colleen DeBaise, "To Draw Women Investors, Firms Appeal to Senses," *Marketing News,* February 15, 2005, p. 14.

25. "Wal-Mart on PR Blitz," CNN, January 13, 2005, www.cnn.com.

26. John J. Burnett, *Promotion Management* (Boston: Houghton Mifflin, 1993), p. 5.

27. "Trimspa Sweep Boats $1 Million Prize Pool," *Promo Magazine,* January 4, 2005, http://promomagazine.com/games/trimspa_million_sweeps_010405/.

28. Jack Neff, "Clorox Gives in on Glad, Hikes Trade Promotion," *Advertising Age,* July 19, 2001, www.adage.com.

29. *Business 2.0,* January/February 2005, pp. 67–68; Michael J. Weiss, "To Be About to Be," *American Demographics,* September 2003, pp. 28–36.

30. Gerry Khermouch and Jeff Green, "Buzz Marketing," *Business Week,* July 30, 2001, pp. 50–51.

31. Ives, "Interactive Viral Campaigns Ask Consumers to Spread the Word."

32. Joe Mandese, "How Much Is Product Placement Worth?" *Broadcasting and Cable,* December 13, 2004, p. 18.

33. Lynna Goch, "The Place to Be," *Best's Review,* February 2005, pp. 64–65.

34. Andrew Tilin, "The G6 Does Oprah," *Business 2.0,* January/February 2005, p. 47.

35. Goch, "The Place to Be."

36. Gerry Khermouch, "Booze Ads: There Go the Creative Juices," *Business Week,* January 21, 2002, p. 52.

37. Geoffrey A. Fowler, "China Bans Nike's LeBron Ad as Offensive to Nation's Dignity," *The Wall Street Journal,* December 7, 2004, http://online.wsj.com.

38. "About Us," "History," "Charities," and "News and Events," Jordan's Furniture, www.jordans.com (accessed January 13, 2005); "Berkshire Hathaway Unit to Acquire Jordan's Furniture," *Boston Business Journal,* October 11, 1999, www.bizjournals.com/boston/stories/1999/10/11/daily1.html; "Jordan's Furniture," Hoover's Online, www.hoovers.com/free/co/factsheet.xhtml?COID=99028 (accessed January 13, 2005); Massachusetts General Hospital Hotline, www.mgh.harvard.edu (accessed May 6, 2004); Barry Tatelman and Eliot Tatelman, "Why Are These People Smiling," Blue Cross/Blue Shield of Massachusetts, www.bluecrossma-values.com/barryelliot.php3 (accessed May 6, 2004); "Winners! BBB National Torch Awards: Jordan's Furniture," Better Business Bureau, www.bbb.org/BizEthics/winners/jordans.asp (accessed May 6, 2004).

a. "Chrysler: Drive & Love," DaimlerChrysler, www.chrysler.com/celine/celine.html (accessed January 13, 2005); David Kiley, "Chrysler Bets Big on Dion's Auto Endorsement Deal," *USA Today,* June 8, 2003, http://advertising.about.cm/library/weekly/aa72903a.htm; Jason Stein, "Inside Chrysler's Celine Dion Advertising Disaster: Selling the Celebrity Instead of the Product," *Advertising Age,* November 24, 2003, www.adage.com; Rich Thomaselli, "Marketers Cut Artest But Stand by the NBA," *Advertising Age,* December 6,

2004, pp. 4, 35; Rich Thomaselli, "Steroid Scandal Threatens to End MLB's Zeitgeist," *Advertising Age*, December 6, 2004, pp. 4, 35.

b. "About Jones Soda," Jones Soda, www.jonessoda.com/files_new/about.html (accessed January 12, 2005); "Jones Soda Swamped with Requests for Turkey & Gravy Soda," Jones Soda, press release, November 20, 2003, www.jonessoda.com/stockstuff/pdf_documents/2003/tandg.pdf; Dave Joseph, "Jones Soda Creates a Pop Culture," *South Florida Sun-Sentinel*, October 27, 2004, via www.jonessoda.com/media_archives/2004/041027-jones_soda_creates_pop_culture.pdf; Edward Popper, "Talking Turkey about Pop Culture," *Business Week*, November 25, 2003, www.businessweek.com.

c. Adam Cole, "Mike Gellman of Spire Media," TechDenver Online, May 24, 2004, www.techdenver.com/viewpoint-23864-313.html; Mike Taylor, "Unfunded Spire Outlasts Tech's Early High Fliers," *ColoradoBiz*, September 2003, p. 60.

CHAPTER 17

1. Anuska Asthana, "How a Yellow Wristband Became a Fashion Must," *The [U.K.] Observer*, August 8, 2004, http://overserver.co.uk/uk_news/story/0,6903,1278575,00.html; Suzanne S. Brown, "Millions Banding Together for 'Amazing' Armstrong," *Denver Post*, July 22, 2004, www.denverpost.com; Robert Elder, "Amstrong Foundation Has Record Year," *Austin American-Statesman*, December 2, 2004, www.statesman.com; Robert Elder, "Armstrong Yellow Wristbands Spawn a Host of Copycats," *Austin American-Statesman*, October 25, 2004, www.statesman.com; Lance Armstrong Foundation, www.laf.org (accessed January 14, 2005).

2. "Starbucks Revs Up Advertising with Taxi Rooftop Campaign," *Marketing News*, February 1, 2005, p. 12.

3. Karen Lundegaard, "Safety Campaign Aims to Tame SUVs," *The Wall Street Journal*, January 31, 2005, p. B4.

4. "100 Leading National Advertisers," *Advertising Age*, June 28, 2004, p. S-2.

5. Jack Neff, "Duracell Unleashes Attack in Bare-Knuckle Battery Brawl," *Advertising Age*, November 29, 2004, p. 6.

6. Tobi Elkin, "Handspring Handheld Goes High Fashion," *Advertising Age*, March 16, 2001, www.adage.com/news_and_features/features/20010316/article2.html.

7. Joe Pereira, "New Balance Sneaker Ads Jab at Pro Athletes' Pretentions," *The Wall Street Journal*, March 10, 2005, p. B1.

8. Ibid.

9. Ibid.

10. John Gaffney, "The Buzz Must Go On," *Business 2.0*, February 2002, pp. 49–50.

11. Marcelo Prince, "Red Hot Online Ad Market Boosts Google, Yahoo," *The Wall Street Journal*, February 2, 2005, http://online.wsj.com.

12. Chuck Bartel, "Newspaper Ads No Longer Best Fit for Dillard's," *Marketing News*, September 15, 2003, p. 5.

13. Daniel J. Howard and Roger A. Kerin, "The Effects of Personalized Product Recommendations on Advertisement Response Rates: The 'Try This. It Works!' Technique," *Journal of Consumer Psychology* 14, no. 3 (2004): 271–279.

14. Pamela W. Henderson, Joan L. Giese, and Joseph A. Cote, "Impression Management Using Typeface Design," *Journal of Marketing*, October 2004, pp. 60–72.

15. Rik Pieters and Michel Wedel, "Attention Capture and Transfer in Advertising: Brand, Pictorial, and Text-Size Effects," *Journal of Marketing*, April 2004, pp. 36–50.

16. William F. Arens, *Contemporary Advertising* (Burr Ridge, IL: Irwin McGraw-Hill, 2002), pp. 412–413.

17. Peter Loftus, "What's Shaking?" *The Wall Street Journal*, January 14, 2002, pp. R6–R7.

18. Lisa Sanders, "This Beer Spot Will Reduce Your Anxiety," *Advertising Age*, January 17, 2005, p. 25.

19. George E. Belch and Michael A. Belch, *Advertising and Promotion* (Burr Ridge, IL: Irwin/McGraw-Hill, 2001), pp. 576–577.

20. Thea Singer, "Can Business Still Save the World?" *Inc.*, April 30, 2001, pp. 58–71.

21. Deborah L. Vence, "Serves Them Right," *Marketing News*, February 1, 2005, pp. 13, 16.

22. Belch and Belch, *Advertising and Promotion*, p. 598.

23. Keith Naughton, "Martha Breaks Out," *Newsweek*, March 7, 2005, pp. 36–44.

24. Ibid.

25. Robert S. Boynton, "Powder Burn," *Outside*, January 1999, http://outside.away.com/magazine/0199/9901vail.html; "Destination Vail," Vail Resorts, www.vailresorts.com/ourresorts.cfm?mode=vail (accessed January 18, 2005); "Earth Liberation Front Sets Off Incendiary at Vail Colorado," FactNet, www.factnet.org/cults/earth_liberation_front/vail_fire.html (accessed January 18, 2005); Robert Kreitner, *Management*, 9th ed. (Boston: Houghton Mifflin, 2004), p. 572; Sarah Love, "Investigation into Vail Fires Continues," *Mountain Zone*, November 4, 1998, http://classic.mountainzone.com/news/vail10-21.html.

a. Beth Snyder Bulik, "Who Wants to Use AT&T?" *Business 2.0*, July 10, 2001, pp. 30–31; Becky Ebenkamp, "Return to Peyton Placement," *Brandweek*, June 4, 2001, p. S10; Michael McCarthy, "Digital Ads Show Up in Unexpected Places," *USA Today*, June 19, 2001, www.usatoday.com; "TiVo Pop-Up Ads May Erode Consumer Control," CNN, November 26, 2004, www.cnn.com; Joanne Weintraub, "Products Play Big Roles in Plots—Whether You Know It or Not," *Dallas Morning News*, June 9, 2001, p. 4C.

b. McClain Finlon, www.mcclainfinlon.com/shocked/pageone_sw.html (accessed March 11, 2005); Jane Stebbins, " 'Bitch' Ads Advance to National Competition," *Summit Daily*, April 3, 2003, www.summitdaily.com/article/20030403/news/304030101/0/archives; Mike Taylor, "Image Maker," *ColoradoBiz*, May 2003, www.cobizmag.com/articles.cfm?article_ID=180&archive=1.

c. Del Jones, "Malcolm Baldrige Winners Set and Met Goals," *USA Today*, November 26, 2004, p. 5B; "Malcolm Baldrige National Quality Award, 2004 Award Recipient, Education: Kenneth W. Monfort College of Business," National Institute of Standards and Technology, www.nist.gov/public_affairs/releases/monfort_business.htm (accessed December 1, 2004); Will Shanley, "Quality Award Goes to UNC, First Business School to Win Baldrige," *Denver Post*, November 24, 2004, p. C01.

CHAPTER 18

1. "Don't Get Caught in a Frequent-Flier Fiasco," NBCSandiego.com, February 18, 2005, www.nbcsandiego.com/print/4213801/detail.html; Joe Sharkey, "Frequent Fliers Worry: Is Elite Status Worth It?" *The New York Times*, January 30, 2005, p. 6; Gary Stoller, "Airlines' 'Million Milers' Get Quiet Perks," *USA Today*, February 22, 2005, p. 8B.

2. Jon M. Hawes, Anne K. Rich, and Scott M. Widmier, "Assessing the Development of the Sales Profession," *Journal of Personal Selling & Sales Management*, Winter 2004, pp. 27–37.

3. "What a Sales Call Costs," *Sales & Marketing Management*, September 2000, p. 80.

4. Dan Brekke, "What You Don't Know Can Hurt You," *Smart Business*, March 2001, pp. 64–74.

5. Bob Donath, "Chief Customer Officers Integrate Operations," *Marketing News*, November 1, 2004, p. 5.

6. Sarah Lorge, "The Best Way to Prospect," *Sales & Marketing Management*, January 1998, p. 80.

7. Bob Donath, "Tap Sales 'Hot Buttons' to Stay Competitive," *Marketing News*, March 1, 2005, p. 8.

8. J. Bonasia, "Keep Sales Up by Finding New Customers, Focusing on Strengths," *Investor's Business Daily*, March 25, 2002, p. A4.

9. Eric G. Harris, John C. Mowen, and Tom J. Brown, "Re-examining Salesperson Goal Orientations: Personality, Influencers, Customer Orientation, and Work Satisfaction," *Journal of the Academy of Marketing Science* 33, no. 1 (2005): 19–35.

10. Michael A. Wiles and Rosann L. Spiro, "Research Notes: Attracting Graduates to Sales Positions and the Role of Recruiter Knowledge: A Reexamination," *Journal of Personal Selling & Sales Management,* Winter 2004, pp. 39–48.

11. Mark McMaster, "Express Train," *Sales & Marketing Management,* May 2002, pp. 46–52.

12. Christine Galea, "The 2004 Salary Survey," *Sales & Marketing Management,* May 2004, pp. 28–34.

13. Susan Mudambi, "Salesforce Compensation and the Web: Managing Change in the Information Age," *American Marketing Association,* Winter 2002, p. 489.

14. Kirk Shinkle, "All of Your People Are Salesmen: Do They Know? Are They Ready?" *Investor's Business Daily,* February 6, 2002, p. A1.

15. Ibid.

16. William H. Murphy, Peter A. Dacin, and Neil M. Ford, "Sales Contest Effectiveness: An Examination of Sales Contest Design Preferences of Field Sales Forces," *Journal of the Academy of Marketing Science,* 32, no. 2 (2004): 127–143.

17. Nora Wood, "What Motivates Best?" *Sales & Marketing Management,* September 1998, pp. 71–78.

18. David Drickhamer, "Best Practices—Manufacturer Goes for the Gold," *Industry Week,* February 1, 2002, www.industryweek.com/ CurrentArticles/Asp/articles.asp?ArticleId=1182.

19. Mudambi, "Salesforce Compensation and the Web."

20. Fernando Jaramillo, Jay Prakash Mulki, and Greg W. Marshall, "A Meta-Analysis of the Relationship Between Organizational Commitment and Salesperson Job Performance: 25 Years of Research," *Journal of Business Research* 58 (2005): 705–714.

21. George E. Belch and Michael A. Belch, *Advertising and Promotion* (Burr Ridge, IL: Irwin/McGraw-Hill, 2001), pp. 526–532.

22. Eric T. Anderson and Inseong Song, "Coordinating Price Reductions and Coupon Events," *Journal of Marketing Research,* November 2004, pp. 411–422.

23. "All About Coupons," Coupon Council, www.couponmonth.com/ pages/allabout.htm (accessed January 21, 2005); "September Is National Coupon Month," Coupon Council, press release, August 30, 2004, www.couponmonth.com/pages/news.htm; Natalie Schwartz, "Clipping Path," *Promo,* April 1, 2004, http://promomagazine.com/ mag/marketing_clipping_path/.

24. Michel Laroche, Maria Kalamas, and Qinchao Huang, "Effects of Coupons on Brand Categorization and Choice of Fast Foods in China," *Journal of Business Research,* May 2005, pp. 674–686.

25. Arthur L. Porter, "Direct Mail's Lessons for Electronic Couponers," *Marketing Management Journal,* Spring/Summer 2000, pp. 107–115.

26. Rajneesh Suri, Srinivasan Swaminathan, and Kent B. Monroe, "Price Communications in Online and Print Coupons: An Empirical Investigation," *Journal of Interactive Marketing,* Autumn 2004, pp. 74–86.

27. Karen Holt, "Coupon Crimes," *Promo,* April 1, 2004, http:// promomagazine.com/mag/marketing_coupon_crimes/.

28. Janet Singleton, "Mail-in Rebates Aren't Worth the Trouble for Most Customers," *Denver Post,* May 6, 2001, p. D08.

29. "Hotels Plan Deals to Lure Cost-Conscious Travelers," *Promo,* April 11, 2001, www.marketingclick.com.

30. Patricia Odell, "Nivea Introduces Moisturizing Cream with $1 Million Campaign," *Promo,* August 17, 2004, http://promomagazine. com/mag/marketing_coupon_crimes/.

31. "Campbell Plays Wellness Sweeps," *Promo,* January 11, 2005, http://promomagazine.com/games/campbell_plays_wellness/.

32. Burt A. Lazar, "Agencies Held Liable for Client Ads, Promos," *Marketing News,* February 15, 2005, p. 6.

33. Based on a personal interview with Deborah Bernard of Wheelworks, August 22, 2001; "Motivating the Sales Force at Wheelworks" video; "Wheelworks Top 10 Best Selling Road P&A (Road Rules)," *Bicycle Retailer & Industry News,* February 2004, via www.findarticles.com/p/articles/mi_hb029/is_200402/ai_hibm1G11 13600582; Wheelworks, www.wheelworks.com (accessed January 21, 2005).

a. Mike Taylor, "Startup Junkies Get Monthly Fix," *ColoradoBiz* 30, no. 10 (2003): 52, www.cobizmag.com/columns.cfm?column_ID= 121&columnist_ID=4&archive=1; "Larabars Are Unique Food Bars with No Preservatives, No Refined Sugars: Exclusive Interview with Lara Merriken," NewsTarget.com, www.newstarget.com/002690. html (accessed March 15, 2005); "Larabars Expand in Distribution, Bringing Real Food Bars to Health-Conscious Consumers: Exclusive Interview with Lara Merriken," FoodFactor.org, www.foodfactor.org/002696.html (accessed March 15, 2005).

b. Julia Chang, "Codes of Conduct," *Sales & Marketing Management,* November 2003, p. 22; Betsy Cummings, "Do Customers Hate Salespeople? Only If They Commit One of These Six Deadly Sins of Selling," *Sales & Marketing Management,* June 2001, pp. 44–51; Melinda Ligos, "Gimme! Gimme!" *Sales & Marketing Management,* March 2002, pp. 32–40; "60% of B2B Firms Not Following Up with Prspective Customers," *Direct Marketing,* November 2001, p. 10; Christopher Stewart, "Desperate Measures," *Sales & Marketing Management,* September 2003, pp. 32–36; Anthony J. Urbaniak, "After the Sale—What Really Happens to Customer Service," *American Salesman,* February 2001, pp. 14–17.

c. "About Our Founder: Doris Christopher," The Pampered Chef, www.pamperedchef.com/our_company/doris.html (accessed January 21, 2005); Gregory Ericksen, "A Woman Entrepreneur Tells Her Story: Doris Christopher," available at www.womenof.com/ Articles/cb051799.asp (accessed January 21, 2005); "The Pampered Chef, Ltd.," Hoover's Online, www.hoovers.com/ the-pampered-chef,-ltd./—ID__42750—/free-co-factsheet.xhtml (accessed January 21, 2005).

APPENDIX

1. This section and the three that follow are adapted from William M. Pride, Robert J. Hughes, and Jack R. Kapoor, *Business* (Boston: Houghton Mifflin, 2002), pp. A1–A9.

2. Andrew J. DuBrin, "Deadly Political Sins," *Wall Street Journal's Managing Your Career,* Fall 1993, pp. 11–13.

3. Monster Salary Center, http://salary.monster.com (accessed June 27, 2005).

4. Ibid.

5. Ibid.

6. Ibid.

7. Careers in Marketing, "Product Management: Salaries," www.careers-in-marketing.com/pmsal.htm (accessed July 28, 2005).

8. Monster Salary Center, http://salary.monster.com (accessed June 27, 2005).

9. U.S. Department of Labor, Bureau of Labor Statistics, *Occupational Outlook Handbook,* http://bls.gov/oco/ocos020.htm (accessed June 27, 2005).

10. Monster Salary Center, http://salary.monster.com (accessed June 27, 2005).

11. Ibid.

12. Ibid.

Credits

Chapter 1
Page 2: Bill Pugliano/Getty Images. Page 4: Reprinted with permission of the Kellogg Company. Page 5: Reprinted with permission of The Breast Cancer Research Foundation © 2005. Page 6: Michael Newman/PhotoEdit Inc. Page 9: Courtesy of Starwood Hotels & Resorts Worldwide, Inc. Page 14: Courtesy of Xerox Corporation. Page 17: Photo copyright Jay P. Morgan/Reprinted with permission of Pilot Air Freight. Page 18: © Marc Muench/Courtesy of The Nature Conservancy. Page 19: Lester Lefkowitz/Getty Images. Page 22: Photodisc Green/Getty Images.

Chapter 2
Page 25: Jeff Greenberg/PhotoEdit Inc. Page 26: Courtesy of Prophesy. Page 28: AP/Wide World Photos. Page 31: Courtesy of Wendy's. Page 34: Copyright State Farm Mutual Insurance Company, 2004. Used by permission. Page 35: C Squared Studios/Getty Images. Page 36: © 2005 Eveready Battery Company, Inc. Reprinted with permission. Page 37: Royalty-Free/CORBIS. Page 41: Reprinted with permission of Evans Distribution Systems. Page 44: Reprinted with permission of Accenture. Page 48: Photodisc Collection/Getty Images.

Chapter 3
Page 51: PhotoObjects.net/PictureQuest. Page 53: Use of the Registered Honda trademarks is courtesy of American Honda Motor Co., Inc. Page 54 (top): Courtesy of Wendy's. Page 54 (bottom): 2002 General Motors Corporation. Used with permission of HUMMER and General Motors. Page 57: Courtesy of www.adbusters.org. Page 60: © 2005 Dell, Inc. All Rights Reserved. Page 62: Courtesy of the Kellogg Company. Page 66: Cathy Melloan/PhotoEdit Inc. Page 69: Copyright 2005 Newman's Own, Inc. Page 70: Reprinted with permission from Hitachi America, Ltd. Page 75: Photodisc Green/Getty Images.

Chapter 4
Page 78: Bill Freeman/PhotoEdit Inc. Page 80: Photo courtesy of Roy Zipstein/Ad reprinted with permission of Deutsch Inc. for Expedia.com. Page 82: Reprinted with permission of Iomega Corporation. Page 84: Reprinted with permission of Napster, LLC. Page 85: Reprinted with permission of HKS USA, Inc. Page 87: David Young-Wolff/PhotoEdit Inc. Page 91: Reprinted with permission of Surado Solutions, Inc. Page 93: Reprinted with permission of Steve Killian and SurfControl. Page 94: Tim Boyle/Getty Images. Page 100: PhotoDisc Collection/Getty Images.

Chapter 5
Page 101: Stephen Shaver/Getty Images. Page 104: Reprinted with permission of Martin Williams Advertising and Getty Images. Courtesy of Cargill. Page 105: Reprinted with permission of Ernst & Young LLP. Page 111: Bonnie Kamin/PhotoEdit Inc. Page 112: Royalty-Free/CORBIS. Page 114: Daniel Garcia/Getty Images. Page 117: Reprinted with permission of JPMorgan Chase & Co. Page 118: Reprinted with permission of Tom Wyville and FMI International. Page 122: Sion Touhig/Getty Images.

Chapter 6
Page 124: Bo Zanders/CORBIS. Page 126: Courtesy of Luth Research. Page 129: Reprinted with permission of CfMC Research Software. Page 131: Getty Images. Page 134: Reprinted with permission of Directions Research, Inc. Page 135: Reprinted with permission of Western Watts, Inc. Page 138: Reprinted with permission of Decision Analyst. Page 140: Reprinted with permission of Donnelley Marketing. Page 141: Getty Images. Page 143: Opinion Place is a registered trademark of America Online, Inc. The Opinion Place advertising content © 2005 by America Online, Inc. Used with permission. Page 144: Reprinted with permission of GMI (Global Market Insite, Inc. www.gmi-mr.com). Page 147: Brand X Pictures/Getty Images.

Chapter 7
Page 149: Royalty-Free/CORBIS. Page 151 (left): Bill Aron/PhotoEdit Inc. Page 151 (right): Reprinted with permission of Ricoh Corporation. Page 154: Reprinted with permission of A. T. Cross. Page 157: © 2005 Eveready Battery Company, Inc. Reprinted with permission. Page 159: Rubberball Productions/Getty Images. Page 160: Reprinted with permission of Saab Cars USA, Inc. Page 162: Bill Aron/PhotoEdit Inc. Page 168: Courtesy of MapInfo. Page 173: PhotoDisc/Getty Images.

Chapter 8
Page 176: AP/Wide World Photos. Page 178 (left): Courtesy of Bell-Carter Foods, Inc. Page 178 (right): Courtesy of Walden Kayaks. Page 180: Courtesy of Delta Carbona. Page 181: Reprinted with permission of the Hoover Company. Page 184: M. C. Escher's "Sky and Water I" © 2005 The M. C. Escher Company—Holland. All rights reserved. Page 187: Reprinted with permission of McKee Wallwork Henderson Advertising. Page 189: Bill Aron/PhotoEdit Inc. Page 190: Reprinted with permission of KPMG LLP (U.S.). Page 192: PhotoDisc/Getty Images. Page 195: Courtesy of Procter & Gamble Cosmetics/Noxell Corporation. Page 196: David Young-Wolff/PhotoEdit Inc. Page 200: Brand X Pictures/Getty Images.

Chapter 9
Page 201: Amy etra/PhotoEdit Inc. Page 203: Reprinted with permission of TRI-K Industries, Inc. Page 204: Reprinted with permission of American Valve. Page 205: Courtesy of Morgan Fitzgerald's, Bryan, TX. Page 207: Reprinted with permission of ERB Industries, Inc. Page 210: Reprinted with permission of Liggett-Stashower, Inc. Page 211: AP/Wide World Photos. Page 212: Reprinted with permission of National Peanut Board. Page 214: Reprinted with permission of Altria Corporate Services, Inc. Page 216: Reprinted with permission of Websense, Inc. Page 221: PhotoDisc Green/Getty Images.

Chapter 10
Page 224: Brand X Pictures/Getty Images. Page 226: Reprinted with permission of Hoffman York, Inc. Page 227: AP/Wide World Photos. Page 229 (left): Business Wire/Getty Images. Page 229 (right): Reprinted with permission of Coates Kokes, www.coateskokes.com. Page 231: Reprinted with permission of the Hain Celestial Group. Page 234: Jakc Hollingsworth/CORBIS. Page 236: Jeff Greenberg/PhotoEdit Inc. Page 242: Tony Freeman/PhotoEdit Inc. Page 246: Reprinted with permission of Vitro Packaging Inc. Page 248: Reprinted with permission of The Procter & Gamble Company. Page 253: Eric Fowke/PhotoEdit Inc.

Chapter 11
Page 255: ThinkStock/Getty Images. Page 257: Advertisement provided courtesy of Frito-Lay, Inc. Page 258: Reprinted with permission of Ford Motor Company. Page 259: Eyewire/Getty Images. Page 265: Myrna Suarez/Getty Image. Page 268 (left): Reprinted with permission of Chipotle Mexican Grill. Page 268 (right): Reprinted with permission of Red Bull North America. Page 271: Tim Boyle/Getty Images. Page 273: Photography by Jim Erickson, Reprinted with permission of MGM Grand Hotel & Casino. Page 274: AP/Wide World Photos. Page 275: Reprinted with permission of Devito/Verdi and Mount Sinai Medical Center. Page 284: C Squared Studios/Getty Images.

Chapter 12

Page 286: AP/Wide World Photos. Page 288: Reprinted with permission of The Dial Corporation. Page 289: Bill Aron/PhotoEdit Inc. Page 291: Reprinted with permission of Steuben. Page 298: Reprinted with permission of Wausau Insurance Company. Page 299: Reprinted with permission of Xerox. Page 300: Reprinted with permission of Buy.com & Thinkbig Media. Page 302: Reprinted with permission of AsiaTone, L. L. C. Page 303: Tom Grill/CORBIS. Page 309: AP/Wide World Photos.

Chapter 13

Page 311: Rudi Von Briel/PhotoEdit Inc. Page 313: Getty Images. Page 314: Reprinted with permission of Verizon. Page 315: © 2005 BMW of North America, LLC, used with permission. The BMW name and logo are registered trademarks. Page 318: Reprinted with permission of Ski Butternut-Great Barrington, MA. Page 319: C Squared Studios/Getty Images. Page 321: Reprinted with permission of Sears Roebuck & Co. Page 324: Reprinted with permission of CityPass, Inc. Page 326: Reprinted with permission of Stride Rite. Page 327: Reprinted with permission of Filene's Basement. Page 331: Rubberball Productions/Getty Images.

Chapter 14

Page 334: PhotoDisc Green/Getty Images. Page 336: Reprinted with permission of Allan J. Miner, President, CT Logistics. Page 340: Reprinted with permission of Baldor Electric Company. Page 341: Corbis Images. Page 342: Reprinted with permission of Benjamin Moore & Co. Page 346: PORSCHE, CARRERA, US, the Porsche Crest and the shape of PORSCHE 911 CARRERA 4S are registered trademarks of Dr. Ing. H.c.F.Forsche AG. Used with permission of Porsche Cars North America, Inc. Copyrighted by Porsche Cars North America. Page 348: C Squared Studios/Getty Images. Page 350: Reprinted with permission Siemens L & A, Jonathan Stein. Page 352: Courtesy of PEAK Technologies, Inc. Page 354: Geostock/Getty Images. Page 359: PhotoDisc Green/Getty Images.

Chapter 15

Page 361: Rubberball/Getty Images. Page 365: Reprinted with permission of J. C. Penney Co., Inc. Page 366: Bonnie Kamin/PhotoEdit, Inc.

Page 367 (left): Michael Newman/PhotoEdit Inc. Page 367 (right): AP/Wide World Photos. Page 368: Bill Aron/PhotoEdit Inc. Page 370: John Neuberger/PhotoEdit Inc. Page 372: John A. Rizzo/Getty Images. Page 375: Courtesy of Staples, Inc. Page 377: Justin Sullivan/Getty Images. Page 388: C Squared Studios/Getty Images.

Chapter 16

Page 390: Bill Aron/PhotoEdit Inc. Page 392: Reprinted with permission of American Dairy Association. Page 396: Reprinted with permission of Chicl-fil-A, Inc. Page 397 (top): Reprinted with permission of Sterling-Rice Group, Boulder, Colorado. Page 397 (bottom): Reprinted with permission of Eastland Park Hotel/Magna Hospitality. Page 400: Reprinted with permission of Hitachi, Ltd. Page 402: Reprinted with permission of Expedia Corporate Travel. Page 403: Ron Wurzer/Getty Images. Page 407: Jeff Greenberg/PhotoEdit Inc. Page 413: PhotoDisc Green/Getty Images.

Chapter 17

Page 415: David Young-Wolff/PhotoEdit Inc. Page 418: Reprinted with permission of Unilever and CarbSmart, Inc. Page 419 (left): Bill Aron/PhotoEdit Inc. Page 419 (right): Reprinted with permission of Neutrogena Corp. Page 421: Tony Freeman/PhotoEdit Inc. Page 427: Reprinted with permission of Xerox Corporation. Page 428: AP/Wide World Photos. Page 429: Reprinted with permission of Decision Analyst. Page 430: © James Leynse/Corbis. Page 432: Reprinted with permission of Boston Children's Museum. Page 439: Jonathan Nourak/PhotoEdit Inc.

Chapter 18

Page 441: ThinkStock/Getty Images. Page 444: Reprinted with permission of InfoUSA and Monica Messer. Page 445: Reprinted with permission of WebEx Communications Inc. Page 448: PhotoDisc Green/Getty Images. Page 449: Courtesy of HotJobs.com. Page 450: Ryan McVay/Getty Images. Page 453: Reprinted with permission of Omaha Steaks. Page 454: © Dell Inc. All Rights Reserved. Page 456: © 2005 Binney & Smith, Crayola and chevron design are registered trademarks, smile design is a trademark of Binney & Smith. Page 458: Reprinted with permission of Acushet Company. Page 464: ThinkStock/Getty Images.

Name Index

Aaker, David A., 504–17, 506–8
Abell, Derek F., 496–8
Abernethy, Avery M., 501–14
Acohido, Byron, 504–32
Alderson, Wroe, 507–11
Alexander, Joe, 433
Alford, Bruce L., 506–19, 507–28
Allan, Barbara, 501–25
Allen, Theodore T., 501–24
Álvarez, Luis Ignacio, 497–5
Ancarani, Fabio, 499–27
Anderson, Eric T., 511–22
Anderson, Erin, 507–22
Anderson, Eugene W., 495–14
Anderson, Gordon T., 495–29
Anderson, Jerry W., Jr., 498–48
Anderson, Mae, 503–31b
Andruss, Paula Lyon, 497–8
El -Ansary, Adel I., 507–22
Arens, William F., 510–16
Arlan, Jeffrey, 508–11
Armstrong, Lance, 415
Arnold, Catherine, 501–5, 501–13
Arora, Pankaj, 292
Artest, Ron, 401
Asmus, Peter, 498–49
Aspinwall, Leo, 507–14
Asthana, Anuska, 510–1
Atkinson, William, 507–17–18
Atuahene-Gima, Kwaku, 496–24
Avery, Susan, 507–1

Babin, Barry J., 506–6
Bacher, Rick, 37
Backover, Andrew, 497–32
Back Street Boys, 400
Balabanis, George, 500–7
Balfour, Frederik, 500–14
Barbaro, Michael, 497–1
Barlas, Pete, 508–21
Barnett, Tim, 497–33
Barta, Patrick, 497–7
Bartel, Chuck, 510–12
Bartholomew, Doug, 503–14
Bateson, John E.G., 505–19
Batista, Elisa, 500–20

Bauder, David, 500–2
Baun, Robert, 498–49
Beatty, Sally, 509–14
Begemann, Kurt, 463
Beirne, Mike, 504–19
Belch, George E., 510–19, 510–22, 511–21
Belch, Michael A., 510–19, 510–22, 511–21
Belk, Russell W., 503–3
Bennett, Peter D., 504–15, 506–11, 506–13
Berfield, Susan, 495–33
Bergen, Mark E., 506–6
Berman, Dennis K., 496–1, 507–30b
Bernard, Deborah, 511–33
Bernstein, Aaron, 501–7
Berry, Leonard L., 505–18–19
Best, Roger J., 498–49
Bezos, Jeffrey P., 78, 79–80
Bianco, Anthony, 498–49b
Bidlake, Suzanne, 504–24
Biel, Jessica, 190
Bilson, Ken, 506–7
Bjorhus, Jennifer, 503–1
Blattberg, Robert C., 495–17
Blustein, Paul, 500–12
Bohrer, Becky, 508–1
Bonasia, J., 499–32, 510–8
Bonds, Barry, 401
Borrus, Amy, 497–9
Boudette, Neal E., 501–49
Bowman, Douglas, 496–14
Boynton, Robert S., 510–25
Bradley, Samuel D., III, 509–11
Brady, Diane, 495–33, 502–1
Brand, Rachel, 498–49
Breen, Bill, 505–1
Breen, Peter E., 173
Brekke, Dan, 510–4
Bremner, Kristen, 502–22
Brier, Noah Rubin, 501–31
Browder, Seanna, 498–9
Brown, Alan, 495–26
Brown, Stephen, 508–19
Brown, Suzanne S., 510–1
Brown, Tom J., 511–9
Brown, Warren, 505–4

Bruno, Maria, 504–17
Buck, Peter, 48
Bujol, Jessica, 496–51
Bulik, Beth Snyder, 509–23, 510–25a
Bulkeley, William M., 506–25a
Burleigh, Joan, 61
Burnett, John J., 509–26
Burnett, Mark, 67
Burros, Marian, 505–15
Burrows, Peter, 506–21
Bush, George W., 433
Buss, Dale, 504–32b
Buss, Will, 508–31a
Buzzell, Robert D., 496–20
Byron, Ellen, 501–4
Byrt, Frank, 506–9

Cadogan, John W., 496–6, 501–2
Caggiano, Christopher, 506–2
Cali, Consuelo, 284
Cantwell, Julie, 505–25
Carl, Traci, 502–9
Carroll, Archie, 497–27
Chaker, Anne Marie, 497–7
Champy, James, 504–2
Chandler, Clay, 501–49b
Chang, Julia, 511–33b
Chase, Charles W., Jr., 502–21
Cheney, Dick, 433
Chesto, John, 506–25c
Chiacchio, Cassandra, 505–27a
Cholewka, Kathleen, 496–46, 502–33
Christian, Amy Fennell, 506–25b
Christopher, Doris, 451
Christopher, Jay, 451
Chryssochoidis, George, 500–36
Chuck D, 136
Chung, Jaihak, 507–18
Cipriani, Nichole, 508–28
Clapton, Eric, 348
Clark, Ken, 508–31
Clark, Maxine, 199
Clark, Terry, 497–2

Clinton, Bill, 83
Cohen, Dorothy, 504–20, 504–23
Cole, Adam, 510–38c
Coleman, Richard P., 193
Coney, Kenneth A., 498–49
Conroy, Erin, 192
Contractor, Farok J., 500–38
Cook, Julie, 503–9
Cooper, Lee G., 505–6
Corney, Don, 497–9
Costello, Brid, 507–15
Cote, Joseph A., 510–14
Coughlan, Anne T., 507–22
Coulter, Keith S., 507–25
Couric, Katie, 49
Cox, Nigel, 507–29
Cravens, David W., 496–23
Crecca, Donna Hood, 495–34, 508–28b
Critchell, Samantha, 502–39b
Crock, Stan, 498–3
Crockett, Roger O., 501–7, 508–3
Crosby, Philip B., 496–39
Crossen, Cynthia, 496–1
Crowley, Patrick, 498–39
Csere, Csaba, 495–1
Cullen, Terri, 502–24
Cummings, Betsy, 511–33b
Cuneo, Alice Z., 503–7, 509–1

Dacin, Peter A., 511–16
Damon, Matt, 415
Damsell, Keith, 507–17, 507–19
Daniels, Cora, 498–49b
Davey, Monica, 505–32b
Davis, Scott, 506–6
Dawson, Chester, 507–5
Day, George S., 496–22
DeBaise, Colleen, 509–24
Dell, Michael, 224
DeLuca, Fred, 48
DeMazza, Matt, 503–31b
Denton, Carlos, 502–35
DePaulo, Peter, 501–23
Deshpande, Rohit, 496–44

Desjardins, Doug, 503–31
Deter, Stevi, 498–49
Dettman, Dave, 233
Dewsnap, Belinda, 501–2
Dhanda, Kanwalroop Kathy, 500–45
Dholakia, Nikhilesh, 499–31
Dholakia, Ruby Roy, 499–31
Diamantopoulos, Adamantios, 500–7
Diaz, Sam, 509–31c
Dillman, Linda, 141
D'Innocenzio, Anne, 498–49c
Dion, Céline, 401
Dion, Paul A., 507–8
Dobbin, Ben, 497–51b
Donath, Bob, 510–5, 510–7
Donaton, Scott, 509–1
Donnelly, James H., 505–20
Dreyer, Bent, 496–31
Drickhamer, David, 511–18
Droogan, Mary, 221
Drucker, Jesse, 507–30b
Drudge, Matt, 83, 499–49a
DuBrin, Andrew J., 511–2app.
Duryee, Tricia, 502–24
Dvorack, Phred, 504–32
Dwyer, Robert F., 498–49

Ebenkamp, Becky, 510–25a
Eckstut, Arielle, 155
Edmundson, Gail, 506–23, 507–14
Edwards, Cliff, 506–10
Einhart, Nancy, 496–26
Elder, Robert, 510–1
Eldridge, Earle, 504–4
Elkin, Tobi, 510–6
Elliott, Stuart, 503–13–15, 503–22
Elstrom, Peter, 498–9
Eminem, 348
Engardio, Clay, 501–49b
Engelland, Brian T., 506–19, 507–28
Epplett, Christine, 507–30
Epstein, Eve, 502–24
Ericksen, Gregory, 511–33c
Estell, Libby, 495–23, 509–19
Ethridge, Melissa, 2
Evans, Matthew E., 505–27a

Fahy, John, 496–6
Fairlamb, David, 500–29

Fass, Allison, 503–31
Feldstein, Mary Jo, 503–31
Felson, Leonardo, 501–20
Ferrell, Linda, 497–9, 497–13–15, 497–24, 497–28, 497–31, 497–37, 498–40, 498–49c
Ferrell, O.C., 495–21, 495–27, 496–2, 496–4–5, 496–33, 496–43, 497–4, 497–9, 497–13–15, 497–21, 497–24–25, 497–28, 497–31, 497–37, 498–40, 498–45, 498–49c, 499–30, 504–11, 505–21
Fields, Debbie, 237
Fields, Jason, 502–12
Finlon, Cathey, 431
Finlon, McClain, 510–25b
Fisher, Daniel, 502–23
Fishman, Charles, 498–49b
Fishman, Ted C., 501–49b
Fiske, Neil, 122
Flint, Joe, 502–1
Fogle, Jared S., 48–49
Folkes, Valerie, 504–30
Fonda, Daren, 498–49b, 507–30
Ford, Henry, 311
Ford, Neil M., 511–16
Ford, William Clay, Jr., 19
Fornell, Claes, 495–14
Forsee, Gary, 507–30b
Fowler, Geoffrey A., 509–37
Fox, Edward J., 495–17
Fraedrich, John, 497–31, 498–49c
Frank, Robert J., 506–5
Franke, George R., 500–13
Frey, Scott, 508–22
Fritz, Ben, 505–1
Frolick, Mark N., 507–20
Fry, Jason, 499–46
Fuentes, Daisy, 195

Gable, Christopher, 259
Gaffen, David, 495–34a
Gaffney, John, 510–10
Galea, Christine, 511–12
Gardyn, Rebecca, 497–20, 509–4
Garman, Ryan, 29
Gates, Bill, 53
Gates, Dominic, 507–19

Gatignon, Hubert, 496–14
Gaumnitz, Bruce R., 498–44
Gecker, Rachel, 508–28c
Gellman, Mike, 404
Gemünden, Hans Georg, 496–18
Genn, Adina, 503–7
George, Jeffrey P., 506–5
Giese, Joan L., 510–14
Giese, Jon Mark, 498–8
Gleeson, Jerry, 497–51b
Gloede, William F., 503–31c
Goal, Laurence N., 501–32
Goch, Lynna, 509–33, 509–35
Goetz, David, 500–34
Goldwasser, Amy, 506–25
Gollick, Mallory, 186
Gollick, Melissa, 186
Goodman, Lester E., 507–8
Goo Goo Dolls, 348
Gordon, DeeDee, 131
Gorrell, Mike, 508–31
Govindarajan, Vijay, 501–48
Grain, David, 413
Grainger, David, 495–8
Grainger, William W., 334
Grala, Alyson, 503–31
Grant, Alan, 495–18
Grant, Lorrie, 495–7, 497–6
Gray, Steven, 495–12, 496–7, 496–17
Green, Heather, 507–30a
Green, Jeff, 509–30
Greene, Jay, 496–10–11, 497–9, 505–1
Greenley, Gordon E., 496–6
Greenspan, Robyn, 498–11
Grewal, Rajdeep, 496–29, 498–4
Grønhaug, Kjell, 496–31
Grossman, Gary, 504–28
Grossman, John, 505–9
Grossman, Lev, 503–31b
Guest, Greta, 503–27
Guilford, Dave, 505–27b
Guiltinan, Joseph P., 496–21
Gupta, Anil K., 501–48
Gupta, Sunil, 495–16
Gürhan-Canli, Zeynep, 500–8
Guthrie, Amy, 500–3
Gutner, Toddi, 504–17
Guyon, Janet, 500–1

Hahn, Lucinda, 508–25
Haiar, Nikole, 498–49
Hajewski, Doris, 508–28c
Hakim, Danny, 506–1
Hall, Allan, 506–9
Halonen, Doug, 507–21
Hanford, Desiree J., 504–17b
Hanrahan, Tim, 499–46
Hardesty, David M., 506–6
Hargrave-Silk, Atifa, 495–34a
Harrigan, Kathryn Rudie, 500–41
Harris, Eric G., 511–9
Hart, Susan, 496–38
Hartline, Michael D., 495–21, 495–27, 496–2, 496–4–5, 496–33, 496–43, 497–4, 498–45, 499–30, 504–11, 505–21
Harwood, John, 501–16–17
Hauser, John R., 501–19
Hawes, Jon M., 510–2
Hawk, Tony, 403
Hawkins, Del I., 498–49
Hawkins, Lee, Jr., 505–27b, 506–1
Hawn, Carleen, 506–14
Hays, Constance L., 498–49c, 502–39c
Healey, James R., 495–1, 496–48
Heath, Rebecca Piirto, 502–17
Heffernan, Paul, 507–30
Heingartner, Douglas, 499–47
Heller, Laura, 502–11, 504–15
Henderson, Pamela W., 510–14
Hendrix, Jimi, 348
Henschen, Doug, 507–7
Hernandez, Mirna, 22
Hewett, Kelly, 504–27
Hewitt, Jennifer Love, 190
Hibbard, Jonathan D., 507–12
Higgins, Dan, 502–3
Hilfiger, Tommy, 301
Hill, Donna J., 501–28
Hill, Ronald Paul, 500–45
Hinkle, Stephen, 505–1
Hoag, Christina, 503–28
Hochwald, Lambeth, 502–37
Hof, Robert D., 498–9
Hoffman, K. Douglas, 505–19
Holden, Stephen, 505–1
Holly, Susan, 508–28
Holmes, Stanley, 508–7

Holt, Emily, 502–24a
Holt, Karen, 511–27
Homburg, Christian, 496–3, 496–27
Honomichl, Jack, 502–36
Hooley, Graham J., 496–6
Horovitz, Bruce, 501–1
Houston, Anita, 114
Houston, Ben, 114
Houston, Skylar, 114, 501–49c
Howard, Daniel J., 510–13
Howard, Theresa, 509–7
Howell, Debby, 504–3
Hoy, Maria Grubbs, 501–14
Hsieh, Ming-Huel, 500–9
Huang, Qinchao, 511–24
Hughes, Laura Q., 503–7
Hughes, Robert J., 511–1app.
Hult, M., 496–23
Humphreys, Jeffrey M., 503–11–12
Hutzler, Charles, 500–15

Iverson, Allen, 392
Ives, Nat, 499–25, 509–3, 509–31
Izraeli, Dave, 500–16

James, LeBron, 407
Jaramillo, Fernando, 511–20
Jardine, Alexandra, 497–51b
Jargon, Julie, 501–1
Jarvis, Steve, 502–1
Jassawalla, Avan R., 496–32
Jastrow, David, 499–49
Jaworski, Bernard J., 495–13, 495–15, 496–47
Jensen, Ove, 496–27
Jewell, Mark, 501–6
Joachimsthaler, Erich, 506–8
Jobber, David, 501–15
Jobs, Steve, 390
John, Andrew, 498–43
John, Elton, 400
Johnson, Carrie A., 499–22
Johnson, Chris, 169
Johnson, Earvin "Magic," 159
Johnson, Jacky, 507–30c
Johnson, Kevin C., 506–25c
Jolie, Angelina, 415
Jones, Del, 510–25c
Jones, Nora, 8
Jordan, Gregory, 502–1

Jordan, Kim, 74, 75
Joseph, Dave, 510–38b

Kadet, Anne, 504–17b
Kageyama, Yuri, 504–32
Kalajian, Douglas, 505–27b
Kalamas, Maria, 511–24
Kalis, Lisa, 502–1
Kamakura, Wagner A., 501–8
Kapadia, Reshma, 509–17
Kaplan, Fred, 507–30a
Kapoor, Jack R., 511–1app.
Karpinski, Richard, 498–14
Keck, Tim, 169
Keighley, Geoff, 502–24c
Kelleher, Kevin, 501–29
Keller, Andrew, 192
Kellor, Bruce, 500–46
Kemp, David, 498–49
Kennedy, John F., 71
Kerin, Roger A., 510–13
Kerry, John, 415
Khermouch, Gerry, 500–37, 502–1, 509–30, 509–36
Khoja, Afshan, 504–17c
Kilbourne, William E., 501–47
Kiley, David, 509–38a
Kirkpatrick, David, 498–10
Kitchen, Jane, 502–1
Klein, Jill Gabrielle, 498–43
Knowles, Beyoncé, 196
Koerner, Brendan I., 502–24a
Kohl, Jerry, 205
Kohli, Ajay K., 495–13, 495–15
Kohli, Chiranjev, 504–21
Kositchitethana, Boonsong, 508–31b
Kotler, Philip, 502–19
Kountze, Elizabeth, 505–1
Kozinets, Robert V., 501–18
Kranz, Matt, 497–32
Krauss, Michael, 496–9, 499–36
Kreitner, Robert, 510–25
Krohmer, Karley, 496–3
Krol, Carol, 509–31c
Krueger, Kent, 376
Kumar, Nirmalya, 507–12
Kumar, V., 495–22, 495–25, 499–29
Kumler, Emily, 508–1
Kundu, Sumit K., 500–38
Kupfer, Andrew, 500–40

Kurschner, Dale, 498–47
Kurtz, Rod, 504–17

Labarbara, Barbara, 501–49c
Lacy, Linwood, 100
Lally, Kathy, 507–30
Lambert, Agnes, 10
Lambert, Earl, 10
Lambert, Norman Ray, 10
Lane, Vicki R., 504–25
Laroche, Michel, 511–24
Lasswell, Shirley Slesinger, 65, 66
Latour, Almar, 507–30b
Lazar, Burt A., 511–32
Leas, Cheryl Farr, 500–26
Lebesch, Jeff, 74, 75
Lee, Brett, 265
Lee, Ruby Pui-Wan, 498–4
Lee, Sharon, 131
Lee, Spike, 136
Lehmann, Donald R., 495–16
Lemon, Katherine N., 495–24
Lennon, John, 348
Leno, Jay, 415
Leonard, Devon, 497–29
Lere, John C., 498–44
Letterman, David, 404
Leung, Shirley, 501–16–17
Levy, Michael, 505–14
Levy, Steven, 504–32
Lewinsky, Monica, 83
Lewis, Peter, 504–9
Lichtenstein, Donald, 506–15, 506–22
Lieberman, David, 496–1
Ligos, Melinda, 511–33b
Lindblad, Cristina, 500–26
Linecker, Adulla Cellini, 507–24
Lings, Ian N., 496–36
Linn, Allison, 498–1
Litchman, Alan, 22, 23
Loftus, Peter, 510–17
Lohr, Steve, 495–31
Lorge, Sarah, 510–6
Louiglio, Joann, 497–51c
Love, Sarah, 510–25
Lowry, Tom, 495–4, 495–33, 505–1, 506–25c
Lucas, George H., Jr., 504–11
Lucy, Jim, 507–1
Luhnow, David, 500–1

Lundegaard, Karen, 509–20, 510–3
Lunhow, David, 507–15
Ly, Phuong, 503–30

MacArthur, Kate, 505–2–3
Machalaba, Daniel, 507–24
MacMillan, Elise, 243
MacMillan, Evan, 243
MacNeil, Jane Salodof, 504–17b
Madden, Thomas J., 504–27
Madonna, 348
Magretta, Joan, 509–31c
Maheswaran, Durairaj, 500–8
Maignan, Isabelle, 497–21, 498–41, 498–46
Mandese, Joe, 509–32
Mannes, George, 507–20, 507–22
Marks, Alexandra, 506–25
Marshall, Greg W., 511–20
Martin, Bruce, 100
Maslow, Abraham H., 185
Masson, Gordon, 505–1
Mastroberte, Tammy, 503–31c
Mateja, Jim, 505–27b
Matlack, Carol, 500–29
Matta, Shashi, 504–30
Matthews, Robert Guy, 506–17
Maxwell, Jill Hecht, 508–24
Maybin, Kristen M., 501–24
Maynard, Michael L., 500–13
Maynard, Micheline, 504–10
Mazur, Laura, 502–4
Mazvancheryl, Sanal K., 495–14
McAlister, Debbie Thorne, 497–9, 497–13–15, 497–24, 497–37, 498–40–41
McCarthy, Michael, 496–12–13, 509–16
McClenahen, John S., 495–34c, 503–1, 509–10
McDonough, Dan, Jr., 495–11
McGann, Rob, 498–13, 498–16, 499–17
McMahon, Shannon, 506–1
McManis, Charles R., 499–48
McManus, John, 501–31
McMaster, Mark, 511–11
McMath, Robert M., 505–5
McMillan, Robert, 496–19
McQuade, Shayne, 82

McWilliams, Gary, 504–1
McWilliams, Robert D., 503–13
Meeds, Robert, 509–11
Mello, John P., Jr., 502–24
Meredith, Robyn, 497–51b
Merrick, Amy, 496–1, 502–34, 508–4, 508–15
Merriken, Lara, 511–33a
Metz, Rachel, 497–51a
Middleman, Ann D., 502–24b
Milecofsky, Marc, 136
Miller, Nicole, 126
Miller, Paul, 508–10
Miller, Paula M., 500–1
Milne, A. A., 65
Ming, Yao, 5
Mitchell, Vince-Wayne, 501–15
Mittal, Vikas, 501–8
Mohajer, Dineh, 345
Mohamed, Shazad, 212
Moin, David, 506–7, 508–28c
Monaghan, Tom, 103, 501–49a
Monroe, Kent B., 506–2, 511–26
Mook, Bob, 501–1, 503–31a
Moore, Sarah, 502–39a
Moorman, Christine, 505–10
Morais, Richard C., 508–8
Morgan, Neil A., 496–41
Morris, Jerry, 505–16
Mosley-Matchett, J.D., 502–8
Mowen, John C., 511–9
Mudambi, Susan, 511–13, 511–19
Mulki, Jay Prakash, 511–20
Muller, Joann, 495–34c, 506–12
Munoz, Sara Schaefer, 505–15
Murphy, William H., 511–16
Murray, Janet Y., 496–24
Myron, David, 501–31

Narasimhan, Laxman, 506–5
Narayandas, Das, 503–9
El Nasser, Haya, 501–10
Nathans, Stephen F., 505–1
Naughton, Keith, 498–39, 510–23–24
Naumann, Earl, 503–13
Naylor, Mary, 221–222
Neeleman, David, 309–310
Neese, William T., 497–28, 499–48

Neff, Jack, 505–17, 509–28, 510–5
Negroponte, Nicholas, 497–16
Nelson, Bruce, 100
Nelton, Sharon, 503–31
Netemeyer, Richard G., 506–15, 506–22
Newbert, Ralph L., 498–48
Newman, Paul, 69
Niemi, Wayne, 506–20
Nijhuis, Michelle, 508–1

Oberst, Conor, 313
Odell, Patricia, 509–3, 509–15, 509–18, 511–30
Ojo, Bolaji, 504–1
O'Neill, Sean, 505–1
Ord, Rich, 83, 499–49a
Osbourne, Ozzy, 226
Owens, Deborah, 500–46

Paglia, Camille, 499–49a
Palmeri, Christopher, 501–7, 504–26
Pan, Shan-Ling, 500–9
Parasuraman, A., 505–18–19
Park, Andrew, 499–20, 506–25a
Parmar, Arundhati, 500–1, 502–24b
Pastore, Michael, 499–35, 500–17
Patsuris, Penelope, 508–1
Patteson, Jean, 505–27
Paul, Gordon W., 496–21
Paul, Noel C., 503–23–24
Paul, Peralte C., 504–17b
Payne, Adrian, 495–20
Peace, Terry, 499–40
Peale, Cliff, 495–34a
Pender, Lee, 507–16
Pereira, Joseph, 497–1, 510–7–9
Perry, Chip, 176
Perry, Ron, 495–1
Peter, J. Paul, 505–20
Peters, Jeremy W., 506–25
Petten, Brad, 503–31
Petty, Richard E., 509–12
Piercy, Nigel F., 496–35, 496–40
Piësch, Anton, 500–5, 509–10
Pieters, Rik, 510–15
Plummer, Joseph T., 502–15
Pogue, David, 505–1
Popper, Edward, 510–38b

Popper, Juliana, 464
Porges, Seth, 502–24c
Porter, Arthur L., 511–25
Pottruck, David, 499–40
Presley, Elvis, 348
Prewitt, Edward, 37–38, 499–34
Pride, William M., 497–2, 511–1app.
Prince, Marcelo, 510–11
Pringle, David, 504–32a
Procter, David B., 501–2

Quart, Alissa, 501–21

Rabin, Dan, 498–49
Rachmadi, Bambang, 116
Rainie, Lee, 85
Ramstad, Evan, 506–25a
Rangan, V. Kasturi, 503–9
Rao, Akshay R., 506–6
Rao, Vithala R., 507–18
Ratnesar, Romesh, 500–43
Rechtin, Mark, 502–2
Regan, Keith, 495–28, 495–32
Reichert, Alan K., 498–38
Reid, Stanley, 500–29–30
Reid, T.R., 500–28
Reinartz, Werner J., 495–29, 499–28
Reinhardt, Andy, 504–32a
Reynolds, Christopher, 501–31
Rice, Faye, 505–13
Rich, Anne K., 510–2
Richardson, Karen, 504–5
Richtel, Matt, 506–7, 507–30b
Ridgway, Nancy M., 506–15, 506–22
Rindfleisch, Aric, 505–10
Ritter, Thomas, 496–18
Roberti, Mark, 505–8
Roberts, Dexter, 501–49b
Robertson, Heather, 22, 23
Robertson, Jordan, 502–39b
Rogers, Everett M., 504–13–14
Rose, Matthew, 498–49c
Roth, Daniel, 498–10
Roth, David, 37
Roth, Martin S., 504–27
Rugrats, 400
Ruiz, Salvador, 509–9
Runk, David, 496–1
Rush, Sarah, 498–49c
Ruskin, Gary, 428

Rust, Roland T., 495–24
Ruth, Babe, 228
Ryals, Lynette, 495–20
Ryan, Erin, 497–51a
Ryan, Thomas J., 507–30

Sabrosk, Suzanne, 504–16
Sains, Ariane, 500–29
Salter, Chuck, 495–34c, 496–15, 506–25
Sampras, Pete, 400
Sams, Rachel, 495–1
Sanders, Lisa, 498–49, 499–49b, 510–18
Santana, Carlos, 2
Santos, Maria Leticia, 497–5
Sarnoff, David, 237
Sashittat, Hemant C., 496–32
Sattarugawong, Sutthinee, 508–31b
Sauer, Pamela, 505–27
Saunders, John, 501–15
Savetz, Kevin, 508–1, 509–31c
Sawyers, Arlena, 502–1
Scannell, Kara, 498–49c
Schechner, Sam, 505–23
Schlesinger, Leonard, 495–18
Schneider, Maria, 313
Schwartrz, Natalie, 457, 511–23
Schwartz, Mark S., 500–16
Schwartz, Shelly K., 495–6
Schweitzer, Kevin, 506–3
Sciabarrasi, Jim, 507–30
Scott, Sarah, 501–49c
Scott, Stan, 503–13
Segal, Fred, 345
Seideman, Tony, 507–10, 507–13
Seitz, Patrick, 508–20
Sequeo, Anne Marie, 507–30b
Sethi, Rajesh, 505–26
Setiono, Rudy, 500–9
Severson, Kim, 501–1
Shakira, 195, 196
Shanley, Will, 510–25c
Shannon, Darren, 506–25
Shapiro, Carolyn, 506–18
Sharkey, Joe, 510–1
Sheinin, Daniel A., 507–16
Sheridan, Margaret, 503–6
Sheth, Jagdish N., 495–19, 496–23, 500–44
Shimp, Terence A., 509–8

Shinkle, Kirk, 511–14–15
Shoemaker, Doug, 464
Shor, Rita, 503–1
Sicilia, Maria, 509–9
Silverstein, Michael, 122
Simmons, Russell, 19
Simonson, Itamar, 499–39
Singer, Thea, 510–20
Singleton, Janet, 511–28
Sisodia, Rajendras, 495–19
Sittimalakorn, Withichai, 496–38
Smith, Devlin, 505–32c
Smith, Ethan, 497–1, 506–25c
Smith, Fred, 237
Smith, Geri, 500–26
Smith, N. Craig, 498–43
Soat, John, 499–28
Solomon, Jay, 500–10, 500–39, 504–32a
Song, Inseong, 511–22
Souchon, Anne L., 501–2
Spangenberg, Eric R., 508–18
Spears, Britney, 190, 400
Speros, James D., 505–32b
Spiro, Rosann L., 511–10
Spooner, John G., 506–25a
Stachowski, Rich, 323
Stafford, Marla Royne, 506–13
Stafford, Thomas F., 506–13
Stahl, Stephanie, 499–28
Stannard-Friel, Jessica, 497–35
Stark, Mike, 508–1
Stebbins, Jane, 510–25b
Stein, Jason, 509–38a
Steinberg, Brian, 496–50
Steitzer, Stephenie, 499–41
Stern, Louis W., 507–12, 507–22
Stershic, Sybil F., 496–37
Stewart, Christopher, 511–33b
Stewart, David W., 498–7
Stewart, Martha, 67, 434, 435
Stewart, Tony, 7
Stires, David, 498–1
Stoller, Gary, 510–1
Stone, Brad, 505–1
Stotgiu, Franceca, 499–27
Strasburg, Jenny, 508–12
Strauss, Judy, 501–28

Strauss, Robert, 502–24b
Stringer, Kortney, 496–1
Stroup, Margaret A., 498–48
Strzelecki, Molly, 504–17b
Stuart, Anne, 508–27
Stuart, Jennifer Ames, 495–16
Studt, Tim, 503–1
Suhanic, Gigi, 503–8
Suri, Rajneesh, 504–21, 506–2, 511–26
Suter, Tracy A., 506–6
Swaminathan, Srinivasan, 511–26
Swartz, Jon, 506–5
Swibel, Matthew, 504–12
Symonds, William C., 500–24
Szymanski, David M., 505–7, 509–13

Tam, Pui-Wing, 506–25a
Tanner, John F., Jr., 498–49
Tansuhaj, Patriya, 496–29
Tantillo, Joseph, 371
Tatelman, Barry, 413, 509–38
Tatelman, Elliot, 413, 509–38
Tatelman, Samuel, 413
Taylor, Charles R., 500–13
Taylor, Mike, 510–25b, 510–38c, 511–33a
Tedeschi, Bob, 506–25c
Tenser, James, 495–10
Terhune, Chad, 500–1, 507–15, 509–5
Terreri, April, 501–49b
Theoharakis, Vasilis, 500–36
Thomas, Cathy Booth, 504–1
Thomas, Edward G., 498–38
Thomas, Jacquelyn S., 495–17, 499–29
Thomas, Kenneth W., 496–42
Thomaselli, Rich, 509–38a
Thompson, Mark, 377
Thompson, Stephanie, 498–42, 504–29, 509–2
Tiegel, Eliot, 503–31c
Tilin, Andrew, 509–34
Timmons, Heather, 504–32a
Tischler, Linda, 506–24, 507–26
Tkacik, Maureen, 508–14

Tomas, G., 496–23
Tormala, Zakary L., 509–12
Torres, Nichole L., 504–17c
Totty, Michael, 498–5
Townsend, Pete, 348
Trachtenberg, Jeffrey A., 508–4, 508–13, 508–15
Trottman, Melanie, 506–10
Troy, Lisa C., 505–7
Trust, Laura, 22, 23
Tsuruoka, Doug, 501–27
Turner, Christine, 498–49a
Tutal, Ercan, 278
Twain, Shania, 29

Uddin, Moin, 503–11
Urban, Glen L., 501–19
Urbaniak, Anthony J., 511–33b

Valentine, Sean, 497–33
Van Arnum, Patricia, 505–27
VanFleteren, Bob, 209
Van Stolk, Peter, 403
Varadarajan, P. Rajan, 497–2, 505–7
Vazquez, Rodolfo, 497–5
Velthouse, Betty A., 496–42
Vence, Deborah L., 510–21
Venkatesan, Rajkumar, 495–25
Verespej, Michael A., 503–8
Vise, Marilyn, 503–31
Vorhies, Douglas W., 496–41
Vranica, Suzanne, 501–3

Wagner, Janet, 507–16
Waldron, Jo, 61
Walsh, Chris, 505–1
Warner, H. M., 237
Watkins, Steve, 496–30
Watson, Thomas, 237
Watson, Tom, 240
Webb, Cynthia L., 504–1, 506–25a
Webb, Marion S., 498–38
Webster, Frederick E., Jr., 496–44, 503–12
Wedel, Michel, 510–15
Weil, Jennifer, 507–15
Weintraub, Joanne, 510–25a

Weiss, Michael J., 495–3, 496–25, 496–28, 496–34, 509–29
Weitz, Barton A., 505–14
Welch, David, 506–1
Wellner, Alison Stein, 501–26
Wentz, Laurel, 503–31c
Westervelt, Robert, 503–1
White, Dana, 502–1
White, Joseph B., 501–49, 506–1
White-Sax, Barbara, 503–31b
Widmier, Scott M., 510–2
Wilensky, Dawn, 502–1
Wiles, Michael A., 511–10
Wilkinson, Timothy, 500–46
Williams, Margaret L., 507–20
Williams, Robin, 415
Williams, Serena, 415
Wind, Yoram, 503–12
Winfrey, Oprah, 405
Wingfield, Nick, 509–1
Winnie the Pooh, 65
Wiriyapong, Nareeat, 509–31b
Wood, Nora, 511–17
Woodward, Chris, 497–12
Workman, John P., Jr., 496–3, 496–27
Worthen, Ben, 508–28b

Yalch, Richard F., 508–18
Yang, Catherine, 11, 496–10
Yost, Mark, 505–32b

Zandl, Irma, 192, 503–31b
Zaslow, Jeffrey, 508–28a
Zeithaml, Valarie A., 495–24, 505–19
Zeller, Tom, 499–46
Zellner, Wendy, 498–49b
Zhao, Qin, 498–7
Zimmerman, Ann, 496–50, 508–4, 508–13, 508–15
Zimmermann, Kim Ann, 503–5
Zuber, Amy, 501–49a
Zwass, Vladimir, 498–2

Organization Index

A&W Restaurants, 161
Abbey Ale, 74, 75
Abbey Grand Cru, 74
ABC, 196
Abercrombie & Fitch, 372
Able Planet Inc., 61
About.com, Inc., 305
Accenture, 44
Accuship, 355
ACNielsen Company, 130, 140, 142, 263, 372, 402
Acxiom's Best/Worst, 170
Adidas, 118, 189
Advertising Age, 142
AIDS Action Committee, 414
Airbus A320, 309
AirTran, 310, 441
Ajax dishwashing liquid, 242
Alaska Airlines, 89
Albertson's, 147, 364, 366
AllDorm.com, 29
Allegra, 10, 60
All laundry detergent, 244
Allstate, 196, 227, 279, 405
Almond Board of California, 397
Alternative Camp for Disabled Individuals, 278
Altoid, 227
Altria Group, 214, 242
Always, 6
Amalgamated, 74, 431
Amazing Grace body scrub, 284
Amazon.com, 12, 13, 36, 37, 78–79, 81, 88, 143, 337, 355, 363, 377
American Airlines, 278, 441
American Cancer Society, 414
American Express, 69, 221, 245, 328
American Marketing Association (AMA), 3, 96, 97, 133
American Red Cross, 414
American Standard, 384
American Valve, 204
America Online (AOL), 29, 83, 84, 397
America West, 441
Amoco, 7

AmSouth Bank, 13
Amway, 112, 378
Anheuser-Busch, 139
Animorphs, 149
Answer 7 and 50 Cents' G6 footwear, 392
Applebee's, 63
Apple Computer, 33, 233, 286, 301, 391
Aquafina, 256
Arbitron, 142, 402
Ariel, 6
Aristocrat Angus Ranch, 114
Aristocrat Land and Cattle Company, 114
Arm & Hammer, 7, 235, 244, 247
Arthritis Foundation, 414
Arthur Andersen, 67
ArtistShare, 313
AT&T, 245, 413
AT&T Broadband, 413
AT&T Wireless, 405
Athlete's Foot, 104
Auctionworks, 209
Audi, 255
Audi TT, 35
Autobytel, 85, 90
AutoTrader.com, 176–177
Aveda, 70, 342
Aventis, 60
Avia, 163
Avon Products, 64, 378

Baby Einstein, 150
Baja Fresh Mexican Grill, 28
Baldor, 340
Bali, 244
Ball Park, 244
Bally Total Fitness, 161
Banana Republic, 368
Ban Rai Coffee House bar, 372
Barbie cereal, 417
Barbie dolls, 417
Barnes & Noble, 316, 363, 369, 376
Bass Pro Shops, 388
Bayer, 17
Bayerische Motoren Werke (BMW), 121–122

BBBOnLine (Council of Better Business Bureaus), 3, 95
BBBOnline Reliability Program, 100
Behavior Scan (IRI), 141, 148
Bell South, 195
Benadryl, 60
Benjamin Moore Paints, 342
Ben & Jerry's, 10, 431
Bentley, 154, 228, 315
Bergen Brunswig Corporation, 381
Berkshire Hathaway Inc., 413
Best Buy, 65, 82, 215, 288, 316, 369, 379
Better Business Bureau (BBB), 59, 60, 414
Beverage Market Index, 162
Bibo, 284
Bic pens, 43, 242, 299
Big Boy, 104
Big Cola, 101–102
Big Mac, 196
Bissell, 137
Bizrate.com, 100
BJ's Wholesale Club, 367
Black Canyon, 372
Black Entertainment Television, 196
Black Pepper Jack Doritos, 391
Blockbuster, 142
Bloomberg Report, 142
Blue Cross Blue Shield of Massachusetts, 413
Bluefly, 83
Blue Nile, 183
Blue Paddle Pilsner, 74, 75
Blue's Clues, 149
BMW, 2, 27, 55, 121, 301, 315, 398
BMW Group, 121
BMW Manufacturing Corporation, 121
BMW Motorcycles, 121
BMW (US) Holding Corporation, 121
BMW Z4 Roadster, 35, 242
The Body Shop, 363
Boeing Company, 211, 349
Borders, 369

Boston Children's Museum, 432
Boston Consulting Group (BCG), 33, 46
Boston Market, 63, 125
Boston Red Sox, 405
Bounty paper towels, 6, 33
BP-Amoco, 117, 355
Breast Cancer Awareness Crusade, 64
Breast Cancer Research Foundation, 5, 415
Brighton, 205
Bristol-Myers Squibb, 69
Brown Shoe, 192
BudNet, 139, 140
Budweiser, 75, 394, 419, 432
Buick, 44, 112, 271
Build-A-Bear, 199–200
Bureau of the Census, 142
Burger King, 4, 89, 399, 405
Burlington Coat Factory, 369
Business Software Alliance, 96, 376
Business Week, 130, 142, 403
BuyandHold.com, 173–174
Buy.com, 300

Cadillac, 44
Cadillac Catera, 271
Cadillac Eldorado, 271
Cadillac XLR, 2
Caffeine-Free Coke, 165
Caffeine-Free Diet Coke, 165
Cali Beauty Farm, 284
Cali Cosmetics, 283–284
California Prune Growers, 188
Campaign for Tobacco Free Kids, 415
Campbell's Soup, 157, 246, 459
Canadian National, 353
Canon, 35
Capital Hotel Dubrovnik, 48
Cap'n Crunch, 37
Carbona, 180
CarbSmart ice cream, 418
Cargill, 104
Carrefour, 364, 366
Cartier watches, 243

Cascade dishwasher detergent, 242
Casio, 181, 233
Caterpillar Inc., 208, 257
CBS, 196
CDNow, 81
Celestial Seasonings, 30, 63
Census of Agriculture, 130
Census of Business, 130
Census of Population, 130
Century 21, 86
CEO Express, 33
Cereality: Cereal Bar and Café, 37
CfMC Research Software, 129
Champion, 239, 244
Chaps clothing, 5
Charlie the Tuna, 241
Charmin, 6
Cheer, 242
Cheerios, 394
Cheez Whiz, 269
Cherry Coca-Cola, 165
Chery Automobile Company, 108
Chevrolet, 2, 3, 16
Chevrolet Cavalier, 271
Chevrolet Corvette, 2, 44
Chevrolet Spark, 108
Chevron, 7, 17
Chica Cola, 101
Chicago Bears, 405
Chick-fil-A, 396
Children's Happiness Foundation, 414
Chili's Grill & Bar restaurants, 182
Chipotle Mexican Grill, 268
Chiquita, 249
Chocolatefarm.com, 243
Chrysler, 266, 401
Chrysler Crossfire, 26
Chrysler Group, 195
Chrysler PT Cruiser, 38
Cigna Health, 14
Cingular Wireless, 319
Circ hair coloring, 264
Cisco Systems, 92
Citibank, 221
City Guide, 131
ClickZ Network, 86
Clinique, 458
Clorox, 403
Close-Up, 267

Club Olay, 90
CMN International, 228
CNN, 17, 81
Coach, 7, 55
Coastal Tool & Supply, 80
Coca-Cola Classic, 165, 405
Coca-Cola Company, 5, 55, 69, 101, 102, 151, 170, 225, 256, 257, 268, 290, 322, 341, 355, 403, 405
Cocoa Puffs, 37
Coffee Mate, 248
Coke, 249
Coke Classic, 53, 101–102
Colliers International, 228
Colorado Genetics, Inc., 114
Commercial Alert, 428
Compaq Computer, 100, 241, 289
computers4SURE.com, 100
comScore Networks, 80
Conoco (Thailand), 372
Consumer Product Safety Commission (CPSC), 59
Consumer Reports, 180
Consumerworld.org, 195
Container Store, 453
Cool Whip, 246
Coors, 75, 104
Corn Chex, 37
Corvette, 82
Costco stores, 301, 364, 367
Council of Better Business Bureaus, 60
Country Home, 417
Coupon Information Council, 457
CoverGirl, 190
Cox Communications, 324
CPGNetwork.com, 148
CP+B, 192
Craftsman tools, 25
Crate&Barrel, 375
Cray, 340
Crayola, 456
Cremora coffee creamer, 32
Crest, 6, 267, 423, 428
Crest Pro-Health, 396
Cross Pen Company, 154, 299
CSX, 356
CT Logistics, 336
Curious Buddies, 150
Cutler-Hammer/Eaton, 320

DaimlerChrysler, 26, 117, 122, 351, 401, 420
DaimlerChrysler African American Network, 195
DaimlerChrysler Smart minicar, 122
Daniel Starch, 430
Dannon Natural Spring Water, 18
D-Apparel, 401
Dasani, 256, 341
Dave Matthews Band, 287
De Beers diamonds, 241
Decca Recording Co., 237
Decision Analyst, 138, 429
Dell Axim, 224
Dell Computer, 60, 85, 88, 92, 208, 224–225, 289, 335, 339, 351, 377, 454
Dell Digital Jukebox (DJ), 224
Dell Music Store, 225
Del Monte, 342
Delta Airlines, 310, 441
Demeter Fragrance Library, 259
Denver Advertising Federation, 431
Denver Zoo, 431
Department of State, 142
DFSS—Design for Six Sigma, 202
DHL, 355
Diageo PLC, 407
Dial Corporation, 288
Diehard, 25
Diet Cherry Coca-Cola, 165
Diet Coke, 53, 151, 165
Diet Vanilla Coke, 165
Dillard's, 363, 423
Diner's Club, 221
Directions Research, 134
Discover, 221
Disney World, 3
Doane Pet Care, 209
Dodge Grand Caravan, 242
Dominick's Pizza, 103
Domino's Pizza, 103, 165
Donnelley Marketing Information Services, 140
Dora the Explorer, 149
Doritos, 196, 257, 428
Dove Bar, 405
Downy fabric softner, 6, 270
Dr. Gadget, 233

Dr. Pepper, 241, 242
Drudge Report, 83
Dual, 10
Dun & Bradstreet, 217, 398
Dunkin' Donuts, 127
Duracell battery, 5, 6, 417

Earth First!, 438
Earth Liberation Front (ELF), 438–440
Eastern Mountain Sports (EMS), 388
Eastland Park Hotel, 397
Eastman Kodak Company, 35
EasyShare, 35
Eau des Merveilles, 346
eBags, 78, 404
eBay, 28, 88, 176, 209, 335, 376
E-Channels, 94
Ecko Unlimited, 136
Eddie Bauer, 78
Edmund's, 90
Electronic Data Interchange (EDI), 94
Ely Renaissance Society, 362
Embraer 190, 309
Empire, 10
Energizer batteries, 257, 417
Enron, 67–68
Entrepreneur, 48, 115
ePublicBids, 206
Era laundry detergent, 269
ERB Industries, 207
Ernst & Young, 105, 414
Essence of Vali, 233
Estée Lauder, 283, 342
E-Tools, 94
E*Trade, 80, 421
Eureka Ranch, 260
Evans Distribution Systems, 41
EverGirl, 150
Excelligence Learning Corporation, 359
Excite, 86
Expedia, 80, 318, 402
Extra Strength Tylenol P.M., 244
Exxon, 242
ExxonMobil, 355
Exxon/Mobil, 117
EZ Squirt ketchup, 190

Fairchild Semiconductor, 316–317
Family Dollar Stores, 325
Famous Players movie theaters, 324–325
Fat Tire Amber Ale, 74
Federal Communications Commission (FCC), 376
Federal Trade Commission (FTC), 57–58, 207, 250, 327, 376
FedEx Corporation, 84, 140, 237, 349, 350, 355
FedWorld, 142
Feichang Kele ("Future Cola"), 101
FHM, 402
Fiemex SA's El Gallito, 101
Filene's Basement, 327
Finagle A Bagel, 22–23
First Service, 228
Fleetwood Enterprises, 213
Florida State University, 334
FMI International, 118
Folger's Cafe Latte, 3
Folger's Coffee, 6, 248
Food and Drug Administration (FDA), 59, 249
Foot Locker, 369
Ford Escape SUV, 19, 30, 70
Ford Expedition, 19
Ford F-150, 83, 258
Ford Motor Company, 9, 19, 29, 35–36, 42, 61, 70, 83, 109, 117–118, 136, 142, 238, 405, 420
Ford Mustang, 258
Ford Rouge Center, 19
Ford Thunderbird, 35
Formula 409 cleaner, 242
Forrester Research, 86
Fortune, 70, 142
Foundation for a Smokefree America, 57
4SURE.com, 100
Frambozen beer, 74
Freedom Investments, 173–174
FreeSamples.com, 459
Free Trade Area of the Americas, 109
Frequent Finagler, 23
Frito-Lay, 9, 43, 391
Frontier Airlines, 54, 441

Fruit of the Loom, 155
Fuddruckers, 48
Furniture Bank, 414
Furniture Medic, 228
Furniture Today, 414

Gallup Organization, 128, 142
Gallup poll, 132
GameBoy, 234
The Gap, 116, 363, 369, 372
Gardeners' Eden, 375
Gartner Dataquest, 86
Gateway computers, 88, 289
Gatorade Xtremo, 196
General Electric, 117
General Foods, 279
General Motors Corporation, 2, 17, 31, 33, 42, 44, 82–83, 107–108, 109, 112, 116–117, 154, 243, 245, 255, 270, 280, 311–312, 313, 420
Genuine Parts Company (GPC), 379
Genworth Financial, 405
GERS Retail System, 414
Gigante grocery chain, 116
Gillette Company, 6, 417
Gillette M3 Power Razor, 230, 315
Gillette Sensor razor, 315
Gillette's Personal Care Division, 263
Gingko Acquisition Corporation, 147
Girl Tech, 157
Glad products, 403–404
Global Crossing Ltd., 68
GlobalTek Solutions, 212
Gloss.com, 342
GMC Sierra, 83
GM Daewoo, 108
GMI, 144
GM Smallblock Engine, 82
Golden Arches, 14, 238
Golden Nugget Hotel/Casino, 405
Gomez.com, 100
Goodmark foods, 260
Google, Inc., 29, 86, 422
Gorilla Mobile, 302
Grainger.com, 334
W. W. Grainger, 334–335, 353
Great American Beer Festival, 75

Great Southern Sauce Company, 7
GreekGear.com, 371
Green Giant, 241
Guess?, 78, 239

Habitat for Humanity, 16, 69
Haggle Online, 88
Hain Pure Foods, 231
Halo 2, 253
Hampton Inns, 275
Handspring, 18, 233, 417
Hanes, 244
Hangzhou Wahaha Group Co., 101
Hard Candy Cosmetics, 345
Hard Rock Café, 348
Harley-Davidson, 37, 240, 245, 351
Harley Owners Group, 240
Harry Potter, 245
Hawaiian Punch, 195
Head and Shoulders, 6
HealthTex, 371
Healthy Choice, 245
Hearts and Roses, 283
HEB, 228
HEB Plus, 228
H.E.B.'s Central Market, 63
Heineken, 210, 344
H.J. Heinz, 127, 190, 244, 249
Herman Miller, Inc., 70
Hermes Parfums, 346
Hewlett-Packard, 109, 181, 224–225, 233, 266, 287, 289, 337, 343
H Hilfiger, 301
Hickory Farms, 369
Hilton Hotels, 48–49, 115, 458
Hitachi, 70, 400
HKS, 85
hksusa.com, 85
Holiday Inn, 116
Home Depot, 25, 65, 69, 70, 209, 316, 363, 369–370, 379, 432
Home Furnishings Daily, 414
Home Shopping Network, 355, 376
Honda Motor, 2, 53, 70, 255
Honest Tea, 431
Hoover, 181
Hotjobs.com, 449
Hotline cards, 141

Hot Rod magazine, 421
Hot Topic, 372
Hot Wheels, 2
Hummer, 54
Humm Foods, 443
Hussey Seating, 206
Hyundai Motor America, 111
Hyundai Sonata, 154

Iams, 6, 166
IBM, 16, 109, 242, 289, 340
Identix, 205
IdEXEC, 444
IKEA, 364, 367–368
ImClone Systems, 67
Imperial Sugar, 88
Impress, 263
IMS International, 130
Inc., 142
Independent Grocers' Alliance (IGA), 345
Industrial Marketing, 130
Industrias Añaños, 101, 322
Infiniti, 44
Information Resources, Inc. (IRI), 130, 141–142, 147–148
InfoScan, 147–148
ING Direct, 87
ING Group, 87
INNX, 428
International eRetail Association, 376
Internet Explorer, 33
Iomega, 82
iPod, 33, 225, 233, 269, 390
iPod Mini, 233
iPod Shuffle, 233, 301, 390
The Italian Job, 122
iTunes Music Store, 225, 269, 286–287, 303, 390
Ivory Body Wash, 244
Ivory soap, 7

J. C. Penney's Arizona, 241
J. Crew, 339, 375
JanSport, 266
JCPenney, 125–126, 362, 364, 375
Jeopardy, 16
Jeppessen, 404
JetBlue, 274, 309, 441
Jet Stations, 372
Jiffy store, 372
Jimmy Dean, 244

John Deere, 29, 109, 209
Johnson & Johnson, 420
Jolly Green Giant, 241
Jones Soda Company, 403
Jordan's Furniture, 413–414
José Cuervo tequila, 407
JP Morgan Chase, 117
Jungle Beans, 186
Jupiter Research, 86

Kashi Cereal Company, 62, 394
Kazoo, 29
Kellogg Company, 14, 69, 342
Kellogg's Cereal Mates, 258–259
Kellogg's Corn Flakes, 14, 244
Kellogg's Frosted Flakes, 244
Kellogg's Healthy Choice Cereal, 245
Kellogg's Rice Krispies, 244
Kenmore, 25, 241, 442
KFC, 96, 104, 111, 116, 118, 161, 345, 363, 394
Kia, 111
Kimberly-Clark, 69, 109
Kirby, 378
Klondike, 418
Kmart, 25, 82, 352, 364, 366
Kmart Holding Corporation, 365
Kodak, 35, 242
Kohl's, 150, 365, 374
Kola Real, 101, 322
Kool-Aid Brand Soft Drink Mix, 243
KPMG, 190
Kraft Cheese Singles, 459
Kraft General Foods, 89, 269
Kraft's Lunchables, 245
Krispy Kreme, 127, 231
Kroger's, 147, 363, 364, 366

L. L. Bean, 14, 339
LaFolie beer, 74–75
LA Gear, 401
Lambert's Café, 10
Lance Armstrong Foundation, 415
Landor Associates, 242
Lands' End, 25, 363, 375, 376
Landstar Logistics, 348
Langley Air Force Base, 334
Larabar, 443

Laura Ashley, 374
L'eggs, 244
Lenovo, 17, 289
Lever Bros., 147
Levi's jeans, 5, 118, 241, 405
Levi Strauss, 108, 266, 371, 399
LEXIS-NEXIS, 141
Lexus, 13, 44, 185
Liberty, 259
The Limited, 344, 369
Lincoln automobiles, 44
Lincoln Town Cars, 159
Lindsay olives, 178
Lionel LLC, 51, 52
Little Caesars, 103–104
LittleMissMatched, 155
Lockheed Martin, 79
Long John Silver's, 161
Look-Look.com, 131
L'Oréal, 190, 283
Louis Vuitton, 243
Love Thy Hair, 283
Lowe's Companies, Inc., 188, 369, 374
Lucky Charms, 37
Luth Research, 126
Lycos, 86

MAC, 342
Macintosh, 390
Mac Mini, 301
MA Coalition for the Homeless, 414
Macy's, 363, 364
MADD (Mothers Against Drunk Driving), 226
Major League Baseball, 396, 401
Malcolm Baldrige National Quality Award, 433
Mama Bear's Cold Care, 63
M&M/Mars, 391
Manolo shoes, 82
Map of Music, 287
March of Dimes, 414
Maria's Bakery, 197
Marion General Hospital, 187
Marketing Learning Center, 18
Marketing Research, 130
Marketing Research Association, 143
Marquis Jet, 405
Marriott International, 116
Marshall Field's, 363

Marshalls, 369
Marten Transport Ltd., 354
Martha Stewart Everyday, 25
Martha Stewart Living, 67, 417
Martha Stewart Living Omnimedia Inc., 67, 434–435
Mary Kay, 378
MasterCard, 221, 245
Masterfoods USA, 391
Matahari, 283
Mattel, Inc., 2, 245
Maxim, 66, 402
Maxim coffee, 279
Maxwell House coffee, 279
May Department Stores, 199
Mazda MX-5 Miata, 242
McCafe, 124, 373
McClain Finlon Advertising, 431
McDonald's Corporation, 5, 7, 15–16, 48, 63, 105, 111, 116, 118, 124–125, 127, 137, 195–197, 238, 266, 345, 363, 373, 390, 432
McDonald's Indonesia, 116
MCI, 108
McNeil Consumer Products, 244
Meijer, 366
MelMaps, 186
Mercantile, 361–362
Mercedes-Benz, 2, 239, 398
Mercedes mountain bike, 33
Mercedes SLK, 26
Merchandise Mart, 451
Merck & Company, 10, 64
Mercury, 9
Merle Norman, 458
Merriken, Lara, 443
Merrill Lynch, 80, 173, 402
MetLife, 405
MGM Grandt Hotel & Casino, 273
Michelin tires, 241
Microsoft Corporation, 6, 28, 33, 53, 57, 69, 104, 253, 286, 390, 397
Microsoft Xbox Live, 253
Million Dollar Directory, 217
Mini, 121, 122
Minnesota Mining and Manufacturing, 201
Minute Rice, 242

M.I.S.S. (Marketing Is Simply Smart), 205
Mitsubishi, 244
Moe's Southwest Grill, 28
M.O.M., 414
Moms Online, 157
Monday Night Football, 176
Mont Blanc pens, 7, 154, 228, 243
Montfort College of Business, University of Northern Colorado, 433
Montgomery Ward, 25, 375
Moosehead beer, 405
Mosaic Group, 148
Moschino, 299
Motorola, 108–109, 112, 234
Mountain Dew, 53
Mountain Dew Code Red, 138
Mountain View McDonald's, 124
Mount Sinai, 275
Mozilla's Firefox, 33
MP3, 36, 224, 233–234
Mrs. Fields' Cookies, 237
MSN Internet, 29, 83–84, 397
MSN Music, 286, 287
MTC, 96
MTH Electric Trains, Inc., 51, 52
MTV, 17, 102, 192
Muscular Dystrophy Association, 414
MusicMatch Jukebox, 286
"My Catalog," 83
MyStockFund, 174

Nabisco, 407
NAPA Auto Parts, 379
Napster, 286–287
Napster.com, 84
NASCAR, 432
National Advertising Division (NAD) (Council of Better Business Bureaus), 60
National Advertising Review Board (NARB), 60
National Association of Realtors, 28
National Fluid Milk Processor Promotion Board, 400
National Football League, 405
National Home Furnishing Association, 414

National Peanut Board, 212
National Quality Research Center (University of Michigan), 266, 55
Nation's Restaurant News, 48
Natural Health, 70
The Nature Conservancy, 18
NBC, 196
NCR, 141
Need for Speed, 253
Neiman Marcus, 363, 368
Nestlé, 17, 147, 247–248, 256–257, 290
NetIQ, 337
NetZero ISP, 405
NeuroServer, 142
Neutrogena, 190, 419
New Balance, 265, 331–332, 418–419, 420
New Belgium Brewing Company (NBB), 74–75, 431
Newman's Own, 69
New Mexico Department of Health, 187
Newsweek, 83
New United Motor Manufacturing, Inc. (NUMMI), 116
New York Stock Exchange, 71
Nickelodeon Enterprises, 102, 149, 150, 395
Nick Jr., 395
Nick Zone, 149
Nielsen/Net Ratings, 86
Nielson Media, 405
Nike, 4, 69, 118, 128, 181, 239, 266, 331, 405, 407, 415
Nintendo, 401–402
Nintendo GameBoy, 253
Nintendo GameBoy Advance, 253
Nintendo GameCube, 253
Nissan, 2, 255, 311, 432
Nivea, 458
Noah Knows Best, 149
Nokia, 102, 234
Nokia N-Gage, 234
Nordstrom, 363
Northwest Airlines, 441
NoTobacco.org, 57
NyQuil, 428

Office Depot, 100, 337, 369, 374
OfficeMax, 369, 376
Ofoto, 35

Ogilvy, 430
Oil of Olay, 90
Olay, 6, 90
Oldsmobile, 33, 270–271
Old Spice deodorant, 7, 157
O-live a Little lotion, 284
Olive Garden, 182
Olive Leaf, 284
Omaha Steaks, 453
1-800-Flowers, 375
1554 Black Ale, 74
OneWorld magazine, 19
The Onion, 169
Online Women's Business Center, 157
Opinion Place, 143
Oprah, 49
Oracle, 142
Oral-B, 6
Orbitz, 278, 318
Origins, 342
Oscar Mayer, 245
OshKosh B'Gosh, 78, 354
Oxxo, 103

Palm, 18, 233
PalmPilot, 18, 222, 233
Palm VII, 94
Pampered Chef, 378, 451
Panasonic, 85
Pankaj Arora Software, 292
Pantene, 6
Parker Brothers, 12
Patagonia, 431
paWare, 292
PEAK Technologies, 352
Peanut Butter Creme Oreos, 407
Peer Impact, 303
Pentium, 290
PepsiCo, 5, 9, 101–102, 115, 138, 147, 168, 190, 195–196, 256–257, 268, 290, 322, 390, 403
Pepsi-Cola, 53, 405
Persil, 244
Petco, 301, 369
Pete's Wicked Ale, 75
PETsMART, 369, 374
Pew Internet & American Life Project, 85
Pez candy, 376
Pfizer, 10, 60, 420
Phat Fashions, 19
Philip Morris, 242, 380, 416

Philosophy, 284
Pillsbury Dough Boy, 241
Pilot Air Freight, 17
Pizza Hut, 48, 111, 161, 165
Plantation and Farm Design Company, Ltd., 372
Planter's nuts, 246
PlayStation, 234
Polaroid Corporation, 321
Polo clothing, 5, 239
Pontiac, 428
Pontiac Aztek, 271
Pontiac G6, 405
Pontiac Grand Am, 271
Pontiac Vibe, 116
Pop-Tarts, 141
Porsche, 2, 346
Porsche Cayenne, 301, 321
Portfolio Builder, 174
Post-it Notes, 5, 201, 259, 260
Pottery Barn, 375
PowerTV, 442
Press Ganey Associates, 187
Princeton Video Image, 428
Pringles, 6
PR Newswire, 434
Procter & Gamble Company, 3, 6–7, 33, 43, 90, 112, 147, 157, 178, 195, 230–232, 235, 244, 258, 263–264, 270, 283, 343, 396, 420, 423, 428
Product Development & Management Association (PDMA), 237
Profit Impact of Market Strategies (PIMS), 314
Progress and Freedom Foundation, 93
Project Bread, 414
Prophesy, 40
Prudential Equity Group, 405
Pure Life Splash, 257
Purex, 288
Purina, 166
Pyramid Pale Ale, 75

Qibla-Cola, 101
Quaker Oats Company, 37, 247
Quality Controlled Services, 130
Qwest Communications, 404

Radio Shack, 344, 352, 369
Ragu, 7, 89
Ralph Lauren, 5

RatingWonders.com, 100
ReaLemon juice, 32
Recording Industry Association of America (RIAA), 286
Recreational Equipment, Inc. (REI), 41, 42, 376, 387–388
Red Bull, 268
Red Cross, 69
Red Lobster, 14
Redox Brands, 235
Red River Commodities, Inc., 381
Reebok, 5, 116, 128, 181, 331, 392
Reflect.com, 392
REI-Outlet.com, 388
Rescue Rooter, 228
Restaurants and Institutions (Choice and Chains)Gold Award, 48
Retail Link, 141
Rice-A-Roni, 247
Richland Equipment, 209
Ricoh, 151
Right Guard, 6
Ritz Carlton Hotels, 13, 31, 41
Ritz crackers, 248
Road and Track, 2
Rolex watches, 27, 55, 226, 266
Rolls-Royce, 4, 121
Ross Dress For Less, 369
Roxio, 286
Royal Dutch/Shell, 117
RPS Air, 355
Ruby Tuesday restaurants, 9
Rush Communications, 19
Rush Philanthropic Arts Foundation, 19

Saab, 91–92, 160
Safeway, 186, 366
Safeway.com, 186
Sainsbury, 327
St. Jude's Children's Research Hospital, 23, 69
Sales & Marketing Management magazine, 130, 142
Sam's Club stores, 141, 301, 324, 337, 364, 367
Samsung Electronics, 225, 234
Sara Lee, 109, 244
SAS, 337
Saturn, 44, 398
Saturn Ion, 5
Saturn VUE SUV, 260

Schick Quattro, 36
Schick x-treme 3, 157
Charles Schwab, 80, 90, 173
Scotch-Brite, 201
Scotch Tape, 238
Sears, Roebuck and Company, 25, 321, 323, 352, 363–365, 375, 442
Sears Essentials, 365
Sears Grand, 365
Sears Holdings, 25, 26
Sears World Trade, 114
Securities and Exchange Commission (SEC), 68
Sephora, 259
Service Corporation International (SCI), 157
ServiceMaster, 228
Service Merchandise, 364
Sesame Street, 25
7-Eleven, 103, 170
7Up, 238, 268
ShareBuilder.com, 174
Sharp, 181
Sharper Image, 363, 375
Shiseido, 283
Siebel Systems, 213, 337
Siemens, 350
Sierra Nevada, 75
Silk, 397
Silk live! Smoothie, 397
Simmons-Lathan Media Group, 19
Sirius Satellite Radio, 256
SitStay.com, 376
Six Sigma, 202
Ski Butternut, 318
skyhighairlines.com, 89
Sleepytime, 63
SmarterKids, 359–360
Smartphone, 6
Smart Tan Network, 279
Snickers, 186
Solutions4SURE.com, 100
Sony Electronics, 17, 35, 100, 118, 225, 233, 244, 298, 420
Sony Ericsson, 299
Sony PlayStation, 253
Sorensen Associates, 148
Soriana, 366
Southwest Airlines, 7, 54, 86, 309–310, 441
Special K, 417
Spiegel, 78, 375
SpinBrush, 247

SpireMedia, 404
Splenda, 236, 268
SpongeBob SquarePants, 149
Spray 'n Wash, 242
Sprint, 318
Sprint/Nextel, 319
Sprite, 53
SPSS Inc., 126, 133
Stage department store, 361
Standard & Poor's Register, 217
Stanford Global Supply Chain Management Forum, 343
Staples, 369, 375
Starbucks, 30, 32, 69, 108, 124, 127, 142, 226–227, 275, 301, 363, 416
StartSampling.com, 459
State Administration for Radio, Film, and Television, 407
State Farm Insurance, 34
Statistical Abstract of the United States, 130, 142
Steam Gun, 137
Steam N Clean, 137
Stein Mart, 369
Steuben Hellenic Urn, 291
Streetcar Named Dessert, 414
Stride Rite, 326
Subservient Chicken, 89, 405
Subway Sandwich Shops, 48–49, 115, 458
Sub-Zero, 8, 301, 325
Sunglass Hut, 363
Sun Microsystems, 431
Sunny Delight, 258
Sunshine Wheat, 74
Surado SCMSQL, 91
SurfControl, 93
Survey of Buying Power, 130
Survivor, 67, 428
Susan G. Komen Breast Cancer Research Foundation, 392
Sustainable Harvest, 431
SYSCO, 378

Taco Bell Corp., 13, 15, 63, 96, 111, 118, 161, 398
Tak and the Power of Juju, 150
O. C. Tanner, 453
Target, 25, 55, 130, 147, 316, 339, 364–365, 428
Taxi Driver's Association, 318
Team Love Label, 313

Telemundo, 196
Ten Ren, 197
Teradata, 141
Tesco, 327
Texas Instruments, 181
Thalia Sodi, 25
ThomasNet, 88
Thomas Register of Manufacturers, 217
3-A-Day of Dairy, 392
3M, 5, 69, 201–202, 214
3M Acceleration system, 201
The Thymes, 284
Tide HE, 3
Tide laundry detergent, 6, 178, 270
Tiger Power, 4
Timberland, 163
Time magazine, 399, 426
Time Warner, 420
Timex watches, 259, 266
Titleist, 458
TiVo, 405, 428
T.J. Maxx, 369
Today, 49
Tommy Hilfiger, 239
Toro, 403
Toshiba, 17
Total, 117
Toyota Corolla, 116
Toyota Motors, 17, 36, 70, 83, 116, 117, 311, 398, 420
Toyota Prius, 314
Toyota Scion, 36, 404
Toyota Tacoma, 5, 116
Toyota Tundra, 83
Toyota Voltz, 116
Toys for Tots, 403
Toys 'R' Us, 38, 323, 359, 363, 370
Trading Up, 122
Trans-Alaska Pipeline, 355
Trans America, 279
Transdermal Products International Marketing Corporation, 57
Travelocity, 278, 318
TRI-K Industries, 203
Trimspa, 402
Tripod, 82
Trippel Ale, 74
Tupperware, 378
Turkey & Gravy Soda, 403
Tylenol, 5, 17, 244

Unilever, 244, 283
Union Pacific, 353
United Air Lines, 278, 310, 441
United Facilities, Inc., 352
United Parcel Service (UPS), 215, 350, 355, 382
United Way, 69
Universal Corporation, 380
Universal Music Group, 29–30, 303
Univision, 196
U.S. Army, 16, 185, 260
U.S. Bureau of Labor Statistics, 322
U.S. Census Bureau, 62, 142, 157, 194, 218
U.S. Department of Commerce, 144
U.S. Department of State, 205
U.S. Government Printing Office, 206
U.S. Justice Department, 207
U.S. Olympic Team, 432
U.S. Patent and Trademark Office, 238, 242
U.S. Postal Service (UPS), 335, 355, 382
U.S. Treasury Department, 16
USA Today, 18, 49, 433
Usher, 5

Vail Central Reservations, 439
Vail Resorts, Inc., 438–440
Val-pak, 89
VALS™ Program (SRI Consulting Business Intelligence), 162
Van Heusen, 371
Vanilla Coke, 165
Vanish toilet bowl cleaner, 242
Van Kampen, 221
VeriSign, 100
Verizon, 300, 314, 318
Verizon's Annual Small Business Internet Survey, 89
Verizon Wireless, 301, 302, 319
Vermont Pure, 290
VF Corporation, 109
Viking, 325
Vioxx, 64
VIPdesk, 221–222
Viper, 2
Virgin, 286
Virtual Direct Stock Purchase Plan, 174

Virtual Magic Kingdom, 157
Visa, 5, 221, 245
Visor, 18, 417
Vitro Packaging, Inc., 246
VM Marketing, 205–206
VNU, Inc., 144
Volkswagen, 103, 104, 390, 398

Walden Kayaks, 178
Walgreen's, 147
The Wall Street Journal, 18,
    130, 144
Wal-Mart de Mexico, 366
Wal-Mart Stores, 7, 17, 25, 38,
    45, 55, 65–66, 79, 82, 101,
    117, 141, 160, 214, 270, 324,
    339, 343, 361, 363–366, 370,
    379, 390, 402
Wal-Mart Supercenters, 364,
    366

The Walt Disney Company, 3,
    65, 66, 67, 150, 157, 174,
    233, 243, 420
Warner Brothers, 51, 233, 237,
    243, 245
Waterman pens, 7
Water Talkie, 323
Wausau, 298
WebEx, 445
Websense, 208
Weight Watcher's foods, 246
Wells Fargo Bank, 427
Wendys, 4, 54, 116
Wendy's International, Inc., 31
Western Union, 237, 404
Western Wats, 135
Westinghouse Electric, 384
Westin Hotels & Resorts, 9
Wet Seal, 372
Wheaties, 37

Wheel of Fortune, 16
Wheelworks, 463–464
Whirlpool Duet washer, 325,
    326
White cloud toilet tissue, 270
Whole Foods, 443
*Who Wants to be a Million-
    aire?,* 16
Williams-Sonoma, 375
Windows Media, 286, 390
Winn-Dixie, 364
Wired, 417
Wisk laundry detergent, 242,
    244
Women.com, 157
Woo Lae Oak, 197
World Card, 221
World Customs Organization,
    107
World Fact Book, 109

World Young Business Associ-
    ation, 278
Wrangler, 371
Wrigley, 339

Xcel Energy, 431
Xerox Corporation, 14, 238,
    299, 427
XM Satellite Radio, 255–256

Yahoo!, 14, 29, 79, 83–86, 209,
    422
Yellow Freight, 94
Yellow Live/Voice, 94
Yoplait, 115, 392
Yum!Brands, 111, 161

ZDNet, 292

Subject Index

Accessibility, 83–84
Accessory equipment, 229
Actual full cost, 306
Addressability, 81
Administered vertical marketing system (VMS), 345
Advertising
  appropriation for, 420–421
  careers in, 430–431, 478–479
  cooperative, 460
  expenditures for, 420, 422
  explanation of, 399–400, 416
  feedback from, 395, 400
  Internet, 89
  message transmitted by, 423, 426
  types of, 416–417
Advertising agencies, 431
Advertising campaigns
  creating message for, 423, 426–427
  creating platform for, 418–419
  defining objectives for, 418
  determining appropriation for, 420–421
  developing media plan for, 421–423
  evaluation of, 428–430
  execution of, 427–428
  explanation of, 417
  individuals involved in, 430–431
  target audience for, 417–418
Advertising platform, 418–419
Advocacy advertising, 416
Aesthetic modifications, 258
African American subculture, 194–195
Age, as segmentation variable, 157–159
Agents, 382–384
Aided recall test, 429–430
Allowances, 304, 305
Antitrust Improvements Act, 58
Approach, 444
Arbitrary approach, 421
Argentina, 86
Artwork, 427
Asian American subculture, 196–197
Asia-Pacific Economic Cooperation (APEC), 110–111
Atmospherics, 373
Attitudes, 187–188
Attitude scale, 187–188
Australia, 86
Autonomic decision making, 190
Average fixed costs, 293
Average total costs, 293

Average variable costs, 293
Awareness, product, 17–18, 395–396

Baby boomers, 36, 62, 162
Bait pricing, 322–323
Balance of trade, 107
Banner ads, 89
Barter, 287
Base-point pricing, 306
Behavioristic variables, 162–163
Benchmarking, 41
Benefit segmentation, 163
Better Business Bureau, 59–60, 93
Birdyback, 356
Bonded storage, 352–353
Boston Consulting Group (BCG) approach, 33
Brand equity, 239–241
Brand extensions, 244
Brand licensing, 245
Brand managers, 279–280
Brand name, 242
Brands
  co-, 244–245
  explanation of, 238
  family, 244
  generic, 241
  individual, 243–244
  licensing of, 245
  manufacturer, 241
  policies regarding, 243–244
  private distributor, 241
  protection of, 242–243
  types of, 241
  value of, 239
Breakdown approach, 166
Breakeven analysis, 296
Breakeven point, 296
Brokers, 382–384
Buildup approach, 166
Bundle pricing, 324
Business analysis, 261–262
Business buying
  explanation of, 208
  methods of, 208–209
  purchase types and, 209–210
Business buying behavior
  buying center and, 212–213
  decision process stages and, 213–215
  explanation of, 212
  influences on, 215–216
Business customers
  attributes of, 207

  characteristics of transactions with, 206–207
  primary concerns of, 207–208
  purchase methods of, 208–209
Business cycle, 56
Business markets
  explanation of, 151, 202
  government, 204–206
  industrial classification systems and, 216–218
  institutional, 206
  marketing to business customers in, 206–212
  pricing for, 303–306
  producer, 203–204
  reseller, 204
  segmentation variables for, 164
Business press advertising, 422
Business products
  demand for, 210–212
  explanation of, 227–229
  marketing channels for, 340–341
  types of, 209–210, 229–230
Business purchases
  methods of, 208–209
  types of, 209–210
Business services, 230
Business-to-business (B2B) auctions, 209
Business-to-business (B2B) markets, 151, 202. See also Business markets
Business-to-consumer (B2C) markets, 150. See also Consumer markets
Business-unit strategy, 32–34
Button ads, 89
Buy-back allowance, 460
Buying allowance, 459
Buying behavior, 177
Buying center, 212–213
Buying clubs. See Warehouse clubs
Buying decision process
  business, 212–218
  consumer, 177–197
Buying power, 54–55
Buzz marketing, 404

Campus placement offices, 467
Canada
  economic conditions in, 105, 106, 109
  Internet use in, 86
  NAFTA and, 109
Captioned photographs, 433

Captive pricing, 322
Careers. *See* Marketing careers
Cash-and-carry wholesalers, 381
Cash discounts, 304, 305
Cash flow, 314
Catalog marketing, 375
Catalog showrooms, 368
Category-consistent packaging, 248
Category killer, 369
Causal research, 128
Cause-related marketing, 69, 392
Celler-Kafauver Act, 58
Centralized organizations, 42
Cents-off offers, 457
Chain of distribution. *See* Marketing
    channels
Channel capacity, 395
Channel captains, 343
Channel member expectations, 299
Channel power, 343
Children's Online Privacy Protection
    Act, 58
Chile, 86
China
    coupon use in, 457
    digital market in, 35
    as economic powerhouse, 112
    international property standards in,
        107
    Internet use in, 86
    marketing research in, 145
    media availability in, 407–408
Clayton Act, 302, digdig58
Client-based relationships, 274, 276
Clients, 274. *See also* Customers
Closing, 445
Closure, 184–185
Co-branding, 244–245
Code of ethics
    e-marketing, 96, 97
    explanation of, 72–73
Code of Ethics for Marketing on the
    Internet (American Marketing
    Association), 96–97
Coding process, 394
Cold canvass, 444
Combination compensation plan,
    450–452
Commercialization, 263–265
Commission merchants, 384
Common Market of the Southern Cone
    (MERCOSUR), 110
Communication
    explanation of, 393
    face-to-face, 395
    kinetic, 400

process of, 393–395
    proxemic, 400–401
    tactile, 401
Communications audit, 434
Community, 82
Community shopping centers, 371
Company sales potential, 165–166
Comparative advertising, 417
Comparison discounting, 327
Competition
    monitoring your, 54
    nonprice, 289–290
    positioning to avoid, 268–269
    price and, 288–289, 301–302
Competition-based pricing, 318
Competition-matching approach, 421
Competitive advantage
    example of, 36
    explanation of, 28–29
Competitive advertising, 417
Competitive forces, 53–54
Competitive promotional efforts, 398
Component parts, 230
Computers, prevalence of, 61
Concentrated targeting strategy
    explanation of, 152, 154
    market segmentation and, 154
Concept testing, 261
Consideration set, 181
Consistency of quality, 266
Consumer buying behavior
    explanation of, 177
    level of involvement and problem-
        solving processes of, 177–179
Consumer buying decision process
    evaluation of alternatives and, 181
    explanation of, 179
    information search and, 180–181
    postpurchase evaluation and, 182
    problem recognition and, 180
    psychological influences on, 183–185
    purchase and, 181
    situational influences on, 182–183
Consumer buying decisions
    attitudes and, 187–188
    culture and subcultures and, 194–197
    family influences on, 190–191
    learning and, 186
    motives and, 185–187
    personality and self-concept and,
        188–189
    reference groups and opinion leaders
        and, 191–192
    social classes and, 192–194
    social influences on, 189–197
Consumer contests and games, 459

Consumer Goods Pricing Act, 58
Consumerism, 70–71
Consumer jury, 428–429
Consumer markets
    behavioristic variables for, 162–163
    demographic variables for, 156–159
    explanation of, 150
    geographic variables for, 159–160
    psychographic variables for, 160–162
Consumer products
    explanation of, 227–228
    marketing channels for, 339–340
Consumer Product Safety Act, 58
Consumer Product Safety Commission
    (CPSC), 59
Consumers. *See also* Business
    customers
    buying power and willingness to
        spend by, 54–55
    as focus of marketing, 3–4
Consumer sales promotion methods
    explanation of, 456
    types of, 456–459
Consumer socialization, 190
Consumer sweepstakes, 459
Contract manufacturing, 116
Contracts, purchases by negotiated,
    209, 210
Contractual vertical marketing system
    (VMS), 345
Control, e-marketing, 83
Controlling the Assault of Non-
    Solicited Pornography and
    Marketing (CAN-SPAM), 95
Controlling the Assault of Non-
    Solicited Pornography and
    Marketing (CAN-SPAM) Law, 95–96
Convenience products, 227, 407
Cookies, 81
Cooperative advertising, 460
Copy, 426
Copyrights, 96
Core competencies, 28
Corporate strategies, 32
Corporate vertical marketing system
    (VMS), 345
Cost-based pricing, 317
Cost comparison indicator, 423
Cost plus investment, 306
Cost-plus pricing, 317
Costs
    analysis of, 292–293
    as pricing consideration, 293–294,
        298
Coupons, 456–457
Creative selling, 446

Credit, 55
Cultural differences, 103–105
Cultural forces. *See* Sociocultural forces
Culture, 194
Cumulative discounts, 304–305
Customary pricing, 325
Customer contact, 275–276
Customer relationship management
   (CRM)
  application of, 303
  careers in, 480–481
  customer satisfaction as goal of,
    92–93
  explanation of, 13, 90–91
  software for, 92
  supply-chain partners and, 337, 347
  surveys and, 92
  technology and, 42, 91–92
Customers. *See also* Business
   customers; Consumers
  explanation of, 3–4
  external, 40
  organizing by types of, 43
  prestige-sensitive, 301
  price-conscious, 299–301
  prospecting for, 443–444
  retaining loyal, 398
  value-conscious, 301
Customer services, 267
Cycle analysis, 169
Cycle time, 349

Data
  primary, 129, 132–138, 144–145
  secondary, 129–131, 144
  single-source, 141, 430
  technology use to gather and
    analyze, 139–141
  types of, 129
Databases
  explanation of, 82
  marketing information on, 140–141
Database technology, 140–141
Data warehouse, 141
Dealer listings, 460
Dealer loader, 460
Decentralized organizations, 42
Decline stage of product life cycle,
  235–236
Decoding process, 394
Delphi technique, 169
Demand
  analysis of, 290–292
  derived, 210
  fluctuating, 212, 291
  inelastic, 210–211

price elasticity of, 291–292
  primary, 396
  selective, 396–397
Demand-based pricing, 318
Demand curve, 290–291
Demographic change, effects of, 62
Demonstrations, 458
Department stores, 363–364
Depression, 56
Derived demand, 210
Description, 208
Descriptive research, 128
Detail reps, 446
Dichotomous questions, 137
Differential pricing, 319–321
Differentiated targeting strategy, 153,
  155
Differentiation. *See* Product differentia-
  tion
Digitalization, 84
Digital Millennium Copyright Act
  (DMCA), 96
Direct mail advertising, 422, 424–425
Direct marketing
  careers in, 480
  explanation of, 374
  types of, 375–377
Direct ownership, 116–117
Direct-response marketing, 375
Direct selling, 378
Discounts, business market, 303–305
Discount stores, 364–365
Discretionary income, 55
Disposable income, 55
Distribution
  dual, 342
  e-marketing and, 87–88
  exclusive, 347
  explanation of, 7, 335
  intensive, 346
  marketing mix and, 7
  selective, 346–347
  of services, 278
Distribution centers, 353
Distribution channels. *See* Marketing
  channels
Distribution management, 477
Do Not Call Implementation Act, 58
Do-not-call lists, 376
Door-to-door interviews. *See* In-home
  interviews
Door-to-door selling. *See* Direct selling
Dot-coms, 80
Drop shippers, 381–382
Dual distribution, 342
Dumping, 111

Early adopters, 237–238
Early majority, 238
E-commerce, 79
Economic forces
  in international marketing, 105–106
  in marketing environment, 54–57
Economic responsibilities, 64–65
Economy, state of, 56
Education and training
  Internet and, 86–87
  for sales force, 449–450
Electronic commerce. *See* E-commerce
Electronic data interchange (EDI), 350
Electronic mail. *See* E-mail
Electronic marketing. *See* E-marketing;
  E-marketing strategies
E-mail
  unsolicited, 95–96
  use of, 80
E-marketing
  accessibility and, 83–84
  addressability of, 81
  careers in, 480–481
  control and, 83
  customer relationship management
    and, 90–93
  digitalization and, 84
  explanation of, 79–80
  impact of, 80
  interactivity of, 81–82
  legal and ethical issues in, 93–97
  memory and, 81–83
  pricing and, 90
E-marketing strategies
  distribution considerations and,
    87–88
  pricing considerations and, 90
  product considerations and, 85–87
  promotion considerations and,
    88–90
  target markets and, 84–85
Embargo, 106
Employment agencies, 467
Empowerment, 41
Encoding, 394
Enduring involvement, 177
Environmental analysis, 39, 52
Environmental monitoring, 434
Environmental scanning, 52
Esteem needs, 185
Ethical issues. *See also* Marketing ethics
  e-marketing and, 93–97
  environment and, 19
  explanation of, 67, 68
  in international marketing, 107–108
  in marketing research, 143

marketing standards and, 67–68
powerful businesses and, 66
in promotion, 408–409
in sales, 448
strategic planning and, 71–72
Ethics codes, 71–72
Ethnicity, as segmentation variable, 157
European Union Directive on Data
    Protection, 95
European Union (EU), 109–110
Everyday low prices (EDLP), 324–325
Evoked set, 181
Exchange controls, 106
Exchanges, 8, 338
Exclusive distribution, 347
Executive judgment, 168
Experiments, 138
Expert forecasting survey, 169
Exploratory research, 128
Exporting, 113–114
Extended problem solving, 178–179
External customers, 40
External reference price, 300
External search, 180

Fair Credit Reporting Act of 1971, 94
Fair Packaging and Labeling Act, 58
Family, as consumer buying decision
    influence, 190–191
Family branding, 244
Family life cycle
    purchasing decisions and, 191
    as segmentation variable, 158–159
Family packaging, 246
Feature articles, 433
Federal Communications Commission
    (FCC), 376
Federal Trade Commission Act, 58, 302
Federal Trade Commission (FTC),
    57–58, 207, 250, 327, 376
Federal Trademark Dilution Act of
    1995, 96
Feedback, 395, 400
Field order takers, 446
Field public warehouses, 352
Fishyback, 356
Fixed costs, 293
Fluctuating demand, 212, 291
F.O.B. destination price, 305
F.O.B. factory price, 305
Focus-group interviews, 136
Food and Drug Administration (FDA), 59
Foreign Corrupt Practices Act of 1977,
    108
Form utility, 337
Framing, 181

Franchises, 115–116, 345
Free merchandise, 460
Free samples, 458–459
Freight absorption pricing, 306
Freight forwarders, 356
Frequency, 422
Frequent-user incentives, 458
Full-service wholesalers, 380–381
Functional modifications, 257–258
Functions, organizing by, 42

Gender, 157
General Agreement on Tariffs and
    Trade (GATT), 111–112
General-merchandise retailers
    explanation of, 363
    types of, 363–368
General merchandise wholesalers, 381
Generation X, 36, 162
Generation Y, 34–35
Generic brands, 241
Geodemographic segmentation, 160
Geographic pricing, 305–306
Geography, as segmentation variable,
    159–160, 164
Germany, 86
Gifts, 460
Globalization, 118
Goods, 226
Government markets, 204–206
Green marketing, 70
Gross domestic product (GDP), 105
Groupware, 80
Growth stage of product life cycle,
    233–234

Heterogeneity, of services, 273–276, 279
Heterogeneous markets, 152
Hierarchy of needs (Maslow), 185
Hispanic subculture, 195–196
Husband-dominant decision making,
    190
Hypermarkets, 366
Hypothesis, 127–128

Idea generation, 260
Ideas, 226
Illustrations, 427
Immediate drop, 270
Importing, 106–107, 113–114
Import tariff, 106
Impulse buying, 179
Incentives, 89
Income
    discretionary, 55
    disposable, 55

explanation of, 55
    as segmentation variable, 157–158
India, 86
Individual branding, 243–244
Industrial buyers, 475–476
Industrial classification systems,
    216–218
Industrial distributors, 340–341
Industrial Revolution, 11
Inelastic demand, 210–211
Information technology, 42, 92. *See also*
    Technology
In-home interviews, 135, 145
Innovative packaging, 248
Innovators, 237
Inseparability, 273, 276
Inside order takers, 446
Insite transit advertising, 424–425
Inspection, 208
Installations, 229
Instant-messaging technology, 363
Institutional advertising, 416, 419
Institutional markets, 206
Intangibility, of services, 272, 276–277,
    279
Integrated marketing communications.
    See also Promotion
    criticisms and defenses of promotion
        and, 408–409
    explanation of, 391–392
    objectives of promotion and,
        395–399
    promotion and communication
        process and, 393–395
    promotion mix and, 399–404
    role of promotion in, 392–393
    selecting promotion mix elements
        and, 404–408
Intellectual property
    e-marketing and, 96
    global differences in view of, 107
Intensive distribution, 346
Interactivity, 81–82
Intermodal transportation, 355
Internal marketing, 40
Internal reference price, 300
Internal search, 180
International marketing
    brand protection and, 243
    contract manufacturing and, 116
    cultural and social forces in, 103–105
    customization vs. globalization of
        strategies for, 118–119
    digital revolution and, 35
    direct ownership and, 116–117
    economic forces in, 105–106

environmental forces in, 103–108
explanation of, 16–17, 102
importance of, 16–17
importing and exporting and, 113–114
Internet use and, 87
joint ventures and, 116
licensing and franchising and, 115–116
marketing research issues for, 143–145
new-product development and, 264
political, legal, and ethical forces in, 106–108
technological forces in, 102, 108
Internet. *See also* E-commerce; E-mail; E-marketing; World Wide Web
advertising on, 89
business-to-business auctions on, 209
consumer relationship management using, 90–93
distribution using, 87–88
global use of, 86
instant-messaging and, 363
interactive nature of, 88
legal and ethical issues related to, 93–97
marketing on, 18, 61, 79–90
pricing using, 90
promotion using, 88–90
real estate firms and, 28
sales training on, 450
surveys on, 133–135
viral marketing on, 404–405
Internet advertising, 422, 424–425
Interviews, 135–136. *See also* Surveys
Introduction stage of product life cycle, 233
Inventory management, 278, 350–351
Israel, 86

Japan, 86, 107
Job interviews, 470–471
Job searches, 466–473. *See also* Marketing careers
Joint demand, 211–212
Joint ventures, 116
Just-in-time (JIT), 351

Keyword ads, 89
Kinesic communication, 400

Laggards, 238
Lanham Act of 1946, 243
Late majority, 238

Layout, 427
Learning, 186
Legal issues
in e-marketing, 93–97, 107–108
in pricing decisions, 302
privacy and, 93–96
related to telemarketing, 376
social responsibility and, 65–66
Legislation
affecting marketing environment, 57
consumer protection, 58
procompetitive, 58
trademark and copyright protection, 59
Level of involvement, 177–178
Licensing, 115
Lifestyle analysis, 162
Lifestyles, 188
Lifestyle segmentation, 161–162
Limited-line wholesalers, 381
Limited problem solving, 178
Limited-service wholesalers, 381
Line extensions, 256–257
Logistics. *See* Physical distribution

Magazine advertising, 422, 424–425
Magnuson-Moss Warranty Act, 58
Mail-order wholesalers, 382
Mail surveys, 133, 134
Manufacturer brands, 241
Manufacturers' agents, 340–341, 382–383
Manufacturing
careers in, 475
contract, 116
Maquiladoras, 109
Marginal analysis, 293–295
Marginal costs (MC), 293
Marginal revenue (MR), 294
Marital status, 158
Market-based cost, 306
Market density, 160
Market-growth/market-share matrix, 33
Marketing. *See also* International marketing
buzz, 404
careers in, 465–466
cause-related, 69, 392
cultural differences and, 103–105
customers as focus of, 3–4
direct, 374–377
exchange relationships built by, 8
explanation of, 3
in global economy, 16–17

globalization of, 118
green, 70
internal, 40
relationship, 12–13
socially responsible, 18–19, 64–72
stakeholder orientation in, 64
value-driven, 13–15
viral, 404–405
Marketing careers
in advertising, 478–479
in direct marketing, 480
in distribution management, 477
in e-marketing and customer relationship management, 480–481
in industrial buying, 475–476
in marketing research, 473–474
overview of, 19–20
in product management, 477–478
in public relations, 476–477
in retail management, 479–480
in sales, 474–476
Marketing channels
for business products, 340–341
for consumer products, 339–340
explanation of, 335
importance of, 337–338
integration in, 344–345
leadership in, 342–344
market coverage and, 345–347
multiple, 341–342
Marketing citizenship, 64
Marketing concept
evolution of, 11–12
explanation of, 10–11
implementation of, 12
marketing unit and, 42
Marketing control process
explanation of, 15–16, 43
problems encountered in, 45
steps in, 43–45
Marketing decision support system (MDSS), 142
Marketing departments, organization of, 42–43
Marketing environment
analysis of, 28
competitive forces in, 53–54
economic forces in, 54–57
explanation of, 8–9, 52
legal and regulatory forces in, 57–60
overview of, 52–53
political forces in, 57
responding to, 53
sociocultural forces in, 62–63
technological forces in, 60–62

Marketing ethics. *See also* Ethical issues
 environment and, 19
 explanation of, 67, 68
Marketing implementation
 approaches to, 39–41
 controlling marketing activities for,
  43–45
 explanation of, 38–39
 organizing marketing activities for,
  41–43
Marketing information system (MIS),
 139–140
Marketing intermediary, 335
Marketing management, 15–16
Marketing mix
 development of, 36–38, 166–167
 distribution and, 7
 explanation of, 4–5, 9
 price and, 6–7, 298–299
 products and, 5–6, 225
 promotion and, 7
Marketing objectives, 31, 39
Marketing orientation
 explanation of, 11–12
 strategic planning and, 26
Marketing plan
 components of, 39
 creation of, 38
 explanation of, 27
 implementation of, 15
Marketing planning, 38
Marketing research
 benefits of using, 125–126
 careers in, 473–474
 data collection for, 129–138
 data interpretation for, 138
 ethical, 143
 explanation of, 125–126
 international issues in, 143–145
 reliability and validity of, 128
 reporting research findings for, 139
 steps in process of, 126–129
 types of, 128
 using technology for, 139–143
Marketing strategies. *See also* Strategic
  planning
 development of, 34–38
 explanation of, 27, 39
 implementation of, 38–45
 packaging and, 247
Marketing unit, structure of, 41
Market managers, 280
Market opportunities
 explanation of, 28
 identification of, 53
 et potential, 165

Markets. *See* Business markets;
  Consumer markets; Target markets
 business, 151
 consumer, 150
 explanation of, 33, 150–151
 heterogeneous, 152
Market segmentation
 concentrated strategy through, 152,
  154
 differentiated strategy through, 155
 explanation of, 152–153
Market segmentation variables
 behavioristic, 162–163
 for business markets, 164
 for consumer markets, 156–159
 demographic, 156–159
 explanation of, 155–156
 geographic, 159–160
 psychographic, 160–162
Market segments
 developing profiles of, 164–165
 evaluation of relevant, 165–167
 explanation of, 154
Market share
 explanation of, 33–34
 pricing objectives and, 314
Market test, 170
Markup pricing, 317
Maslow's hierarchy of needs, 185
Materials handling, 351
Maturity stage of product life cycle,
 234–235
M-commerce, 91
Media
 advertising expenditures by, 422
 characteristics of major, 424–425
 choice of advertising, 426
 number of exposures to, 434
Media plan
 decisions for, 422–423
 explanation of, 421–422
Medium of transmission, 394
Megacarriers, 356
Memory, 82
Merchandise allowance, 460
Merchant wholesalers, 380–382
Mexico
 economic conditions in, 109
 Internet use in, 86
 NAFTA and, 109
 recession in, 56
Micromarketing, 160
Missionary salesperson, 446
Mission statement, 30–31
Modified rebuy purchase, 210
Money refunds, 457

Monopolies, competition and, 302
Motives, 185–186
MRO supplies, 230
Multinational enterprise, 117
Multiple-choice questions, 137
Multiple packaging, 248–249
Multiple sourcing, 214
Multiple-unit pricing, 324

NAFTA. *See* North American Free Trade
  Agreement (NAFTA)
Natural environment, 70
Negotiated contracts, 209–210
Negotiated pricing, 320
Negotiation, 208
Neighborhood shopping centers, 371
Networking, 467
New-product development
 business analysis in, 261–262
 commercialization in, 263–265
 concept testing in, 261
 explanation of, 258–260
 idea generation for, 260
 product development in, 262
 screening in, 260–261
 test marketing in, 262–263
New products
 explanation of, 259–260
 pricing of, 320–322
Newspaper advertising, 422, 424–425
News release, 432–433
New-task purchases, 209–210, 213
Noise, 394–395
Noncumulative discounts, 305
Nonprice competition, 289–290
Nonprobability sampling, 132
Nonprofit organizations, marketing in,
 16
North American Free Trade Agreement
  (NAFTA)
 explanation of, 109
 industrial classification systems and,
  217
North American Industry Classification
  System (NAICS), 216–217
Nutrition Labeling and Education Act,
 58

Objective-and-task approach, 420
Observation method, 137–138
Odd-even pricing, 325
Off-price retailers, 369
Oligopolies, 302
Online retailing, 377
Online sales training, 450
Online surveys, 133–135

Open-ended questions, 137
Opinion leaders, 191–192
Opportunities, in SWOT analysis, 29–30
Order getters, 446
Order lead time, 350
Order processing, 349–350
Order takers, 446
Organizations. *See also* Nonprofit
    organizations
    assessing resources and opportuni-
        ties of, 27–29
    centralized, 42
    decentralized, 42
    importance of marketing for, 16–17
    mission as goals of, 30–31
    segmentation by type of, 164
    socially responsible, 64
Outdoor advertising, 422, 424–425
Outside order takers, 446
Outside transit advertising, 424–425
Outsourcing, 347

Packaging
    category-consistent, 248
    color preferences in, 247
    considerations for, 246–247
    family, 246
    function of, 245–246
    innovative, 248
    marketing strategy and, 247–248
    multiple, 248–249
    second-use, 248
Partnerships, 207
Patent and Trademark Office, U.S., 242
Patronage motives, 186
Peak demand, 277
Penetration pricing, 322
Percent-of-sales approach, 420–422
Perception, 183–185
Perceptual maps, 267, 269
Performance
    evaluation of, 44
    setting standards for, 43–44
Periodic discounting, 320–321
Perishability, 273–274, 276
Personal interview surveys, 133, 135
Personality, 160–161, 188
Personal selling. *See also* Selling
    communication in, 395
    explanation of, 442–443
    managing sales force for, 447–455
    process of, 443–446
    sales force for, 446–447
Phase-out, 270
Philanthropy, 69–70
Photographs, 433

Physical distribution
    explanation of, 347–348
    Internet use for, 87–88
    inventory management in, 350–351
    materials handling in, 351
    order processing and, 349–350
    transportation in, 353–356
    warehousing in, 351–353
Piggyback, 356
Pioneer advertising, 416–417
Pioneer promotion, 396
Place utility, 337
Point-of-purchase (P-O-P) materials,
    458
Political action, 53
Political forces
    in international marketing, 106–107
    in marketing environment, 57
Population, 132
Population trends, 62–63
Pop-under ads, 89
Pop-up ads, 89
Portable hand-held devices (PDAs),
    91
Portals, 83
Positioning. *See* Product positioning
Possession utility, 337
Postpurchase evaluation, 182
Posttest, 429
Premium money, 460–461
Premium pricing, 322
Premiums, 459
Press conferences, 433
Press releases, 432–433
Prestige pricing, 325–326
Prestige products, 290
Prestige-sensitive customers, 301
Pretest, 428, 429
Price competition, 288–289
Price-conscious customers, 300–301
Price discounting, 303–305
Price discrimination, 302
Price elasticity of demand, 291–292
Price leaders, 326
Price lining, 323
Price skimming, 321–322
Prices/pricing
    assessment of target market's evalua-
        tion of, 315–316
    breakeven analysis and, 296
    in business markets, 303–306
    channel member expectations and,
        299
    competition-based, 288–289,
        301–302, 318
    cost-based, 317

costs and, 298
customer interpretation and
    response and, 299–301
customer perception of, 299–301
demand-based, 318
demand curve and, 290–291
demand fluctuations and, 291
differential, 319–321
elasticity of demand and, 291–292
evaluation of competitor's, 316
explanation of, 6–7, 287
external reference, 300
factors affecting decisions about,
    297–302
geographic, 305–306
as indicator of quality, 314–315
internal reference, 300
legal and regulatory issues affecting,
    302
marginal analysis and, 293–295
marketing mix variables and, 6–7,
    298–299
multiple-channel, 90
new-product, 321–322
objectives of, 297
product-line, 322–323
professional, 326
promotional, 326–327
psychological, 323–326
role of, 287–288
selection of basis for, 316–318
of services, 277–278
strategies for, 318–327
transfer, 306
Pricing objectives
    explanation of, 312
    function of, 328
    profit as, 13, 287
    types of, 312–315
Primary data
    explanation of, 129
    international marketing and, 144,
        145
Primary data collection
    experimentation for, 138
    explanation of, 130
    observation methods for, 137–138
    questionnaires for, 136–137
    sampling for, 132
    surveys for, 133–136
Primary demand, 396
Privacy, 93–96
Privacy Act of 1974, 94
Private distributor brands, 241
Private warehouses, 352
Probability sampling, 132

Process materials, 230
Producer markets, 203–204
Product adoption process, 236–238
Product advertising, 416, 419
Product deletion, 270–271
Product design, 266–267
Product development, 262. *See also* New-product development
Product differentiation
  design and features as, 266–267
  explanation of, 265
  quality as, 265–266
  support services as, 267
Product features, 266–267
Product items, 230
Product life cycle
  decline stage of, 235–236
  explanation of, 232
  growth stage of, 233–234
  introduction stage of, 233
  maturity stage of, 234–235
Product line, 230–231
Product-line pricing, 320, 322–323
Product management careers, 477–478
Product managers, 279–280
Product mix
  depth of, 231, 232
  explanation of, 231
  width of, 231, 232
Product positioning
  bases for, 268–269
  explanation of, 267
  perceptual mapping and, 267
  repositioning and, 269–270
Products
  business, 227–230, 340–341
  consumer, 227–228, 339–340
  convenience, 227, 407
  creating awareness of, 17–18, 395–396
  developing new, 258–265
  e-marketing and, 85–87
  explanation of, 226–227
  for government markets, 205
  high-involvement, 177
  intensity of coverage for, 345–346
  line extentions to, 256–257
  low-involvement, 177
  managing existing, 256–258
  managing services as, 272–279
  marketing mix and, 5–6, 225
  modification of, 257–258
  organizing by, 43
  organizing to develop and manage, 279–280
  ~tion mix for, 406–407

  segmentation by use of, 164
  shopping, 228
  specialty, 228
  unsought, 228
Product trials, 397
Professional pricing, 320, 326
Profit
  analysis of, 292–293
  pricing objectives and, 13, 287
Promotion. *See also* Sales promotion
  budget for, 405–406
  communication process and, 393–395
  costs of, 407–408
  criticisms and defenses of, 408, 409
  explanation of, 7
  on Internet, 88–90
  as marketing mix variable, 7
  objectives of, 395–399
  role of, 392–393
  of services, 279
Promotional pricing, 320, 326–327
Promotion mix
  advertising and, 399–400
  explanation of, 399
  personal selling and, 400–401
  public relations and, 401–402
  sales promotion and, 402–404
  selecting elements in, 404–408
Prospect identification, 397–398
Prospecting, 443–444
Prosperity, 56
Proxemic communication, 400–401
Psychographic variables, 160–161
Psychological influences
  attitudes as, 187–188
  on buying decision process, 183–189
  explanation of, 183
  learning as, 186
  lifestyles as, 189
  motives as, 185–186
  perception as, 183–185
  personality and self-concept as, 188
Psychological needs, 185
Psychological pricing
  explanation of, 323
  types of, 323–326
Publicity, 432–433
Public relations
  careers in, 476–477
  dealing with unfavorable, 434–435
  evaluating effectiveness of, 434
  explanation of, 401, 431–432
  tools for, 401–402, 432–434
Public relations audit, 434
Public warehouses, 352
Pull medium, 83

Pull policy, 408
Purchase stage, 181
Pure Food and Drug Act, 58
Push medium, 83
Push money, 460–461
Push policy, 408

Quality
  consistency of, 266
  price as indicator of, 314–315
  product, 265–266
Quality modifications, 257
Quantity discounts, 304–305
Questionnaires
  construction of, 136–137
  methods for introducing, 144
Quotas, 106–107, 447
Quota sampling, 132

Race
  population projects by, 63
  as segmentation variable, 157
Rack jobbers, 381
Radio advertising, 422, 424–425
Random discounting, 321
Random factor analysis, 169–170
Random sampling, 132
Raw materials, 230
Reach, 422
Rebates, 457
Receiver, 393–394
Recession, 56
Reciprocity, 206
Recognition test, 429
Recovery, economic, 56
Reference groups, 191
Reference pricing, 323–324
Referrals, 443
Refunds, 457
Regional issues, 426
Regional shopping centers, 371–372
Regions, organizing by, 43
Regression analysis, 170
Regulatory agencies, 57, 59
Regulatory issues, in pricing decisions, 302
Reinforcement advertising, 417
Relationship marketing, 12–13. *See also* Customer relationship management (CRM)
Reliability, 128
Reminder advertising, 417
Repositioning, 269–270. *See also* Product positioning
Research. *See also* Marketing research
  causal, 128
  descriptive, 128

explanation of, 125
exploratory, 128
interpretation of, 138
reliability and validity of, 128
reporting on, 139
Research design, 127–128. *See also*
    Marketing research
Reseller markets, 204
Reseller support, 398
Résumés, 370, 469
Retailers
    explanation of, 204, 362–363
    general-merchandise, 363–368
    image projected by, 372–373
    location of, 370–372
    positioning by, 372
    specialty, 368–369
    types of, 363–368
Retailing
    careers in, 479–480
    explanation of, 362–363
    online, 376
    scrambled merchandise, 373
    strategic issues in, 370–374
    wheel of, 373–374
Return on investment (ROI), 313
Right to Financial Privacy Act of 1978,
    94
Robinson-Patman Act, 58, 302
Roles, 189–190
Roll-out, 264
Routinized response behavior, 178
Run-out, 270
Russia, 86

Safety needs, 185
Safety stock, 351
Sales
    careers in, 474–476
    estimating potential, 165–166
    orientation toward, 11
    reducing fluctuations in, 399
Sales branches, 384
Sales contests, 461
Sales force. *See also* Personal selling
    compensation for, 450–452
    controlling and evaluating perform-
        ance of, 454–455
    determining size of, 448–449
    establishing objectives for, 447–448
    functions of individuals on,
        446–447
    managing territories for, 453—454
    motivation of, 451, 453
    recruiting and selecting individuals
        for, 449
    training of, 449–450

Sales force forecasting survey, 168–169
Sales forecasts
    executive judgment for, 168
    explanation of, 167–168
    market tests for, 170
    multiple methods for, 170–171
    regression analysis for, 170
    surveys for, 168–169
    time series analysis for, 169–170
Sales offices, 384
Sales potential, 165–166
Sales promotion
    consumer, 456–459
    explanation of, 402–404, 455
    trade, 459–461
    use of, 455–456
Sales territories, 453–454
Samples, 132
Sampling
    as business purchase method, 208
    explanation of, 132
    types of, 132
Scan-back allowance, 460
Scrambled merchandising, 373
Screening, 260–261
Seasonal analysis, 170
Seasonal discounts, 304–305
Secondary data
    explanation of, 129
    international marketing and, 144
    sources of, 129–131
Secondary-market pricing, 320
Second-use packaging, 248
Selective demand, 396–397
Selective distortion, 184
Selective distribution, 346–347
Selective retention, 184
Self-actualization needs, 185
Self-concept, 188
Self-image, 188
Self-regulation
    of e-marketing, 96
    explanation of, 59–60
Selling. *See also* Personal selling
    creative, 446
    direct, 378
    responsible, 448
Selling agents, 383
Services
    business, 230
    characteristics of, 272–275
    creating marketing mixes for,
        275–279
    development of, 275, 277
    distribution of, 278
    explanation of, 226, 272
    nature and importance of, 272

pricing of, 277–278
    promotion of, 279
Sherman Antitrust Act, 58, 302
Shopping centers, 370–372
Shopping mall intercept interviews,
    136
Shopping products, 228
Single-source data, 141, 430
Situational influences, 182–183
Situational involvement, 177
Social audit, 434
Social class, 192–194
Social influences
    explanation of, 189
    family as, 190–191
    opinion leaders as, 191–192
    reference groups as, 191
    roles as, 189–190
    social class as, 192–194
Social needs, 185
Social responsibility
    consumerism and, 70–71
    economic dimension of, 64–65
    ethical dimension of, 67–68
    explanation of, 18–19, 64
    legal dimension of, 65–66
    philanthropic dimension of, 69–70
    pyramid of, 65
    strategic planning and, 71–72
Sociocultural forces
    explanation of, 62–63
    in international marketing, 103–105
Software
    marketing channels for, 343–344
    marketing system support system,
        142
    sales automation, 92
Sole sourcing, 214–215
Source, 393
South Africa, 86
Spam, 95–96
Special-event pricing, 326–327
Specialty-line wholesalers, 381
Specialty products, 228
Specialty retailers, 368–369
Specifications, 207
Sponsorship ads, 89
Stakeholder orientation, 64
Stakeholders
    explanation of, 3, 431
    socially responsible marketing and,
        18–19
Standard full cost, 306
Standard Industrial Classification (SIC)
    System, 216–217
State employment offices, 467–468
Statistical interpretation, 138

Status quo, 314
Stockouts, 350
Storyboard, 426
Straight commission compensation plan, 450, 452
Straight rebuy purchase, 210
Straight salary compensation plan, 450, 452
Strategic alliances, 116
Strategic business unit (SBU), 32–33
Strategic channel alliance, 342
Strategic philanthropy, 69
Strategic planning. *See also* Marketing strategies
  assessing organizational resources and opportunities for, 27–29
  components of, 26–27
  creating marketing plan for, 38
  developing business-unit strategy for, 32–34
  developing corporate strategy for, 32
  developing marketing strategy for, 34–38
  establishing organizational mission and goals for, 30–31
  explanation of, 26–27
  implementing marketing strategies for, 38–45
  for international marketing, 119
  SWOT analysis for, 29–30
Strategic windows, 28
Stratified sampling, 132
Strengths, in SWOT analysis, 29–30
Styling, 266
Subculture
  African American, 194–195
  Asian American, 196–197
  explanation of, 194
  Hispanic, 195–196
Supermarkets, 365
Superstores, 365–366
Supply-chain management
  channel partnerships and, 342–343
  explanation of, 335–336
  inventory management in, 350–351
  materials handling in, 351
  order processing in, 349–350
  physical distribution in, 347–349
  tasks in, 336
  transportation in, 353–356
  warehousing in, 351–353
  wholesalers and, 378–379
Support personnel, 446
Surveys
  comparison of, 133
  explanation of, 133–134

mail, 133, 134
online, 133–135
personal interview, 133, 135, 136
sales forecasting based on, 168–170
shopping mall intercept interview, 136
telephone, 133, 134
telephone depth interview, 136
Sweepstakes, 459
Switzerland, 105, 106
SWOT analysis, 29–30, 39
Syncratic decision making, 190

Tactile communication, 401
Target audience, 417–418
Targeting strategies
  concentrated, 152–154
  differentiated, 153, 155
  undifferentiated, 152–153
Target markets
  customizing global, 118–119
  explanation of, 4, 84–85
  price evaluation and, 315–316
  promotion mix and, 406
Target market selection
  explanation of, 34–36
  final phase of, 167
  market segment profile development and, 164–165
  relevant market segment evaluation and, 165–167
  segmentation variable selection and, 164
  strategy identification and, 152–155
Tariffs, 106
Technical salespeople, 447
Technology. *See also* Internet; Software; World Wide Web
  advertising and, 428
  customer relationship management and, 42, 91–92
  effects of, 60–62
  explanation of, 59
  information gathering and analysis using, 139–143
  international marketing and, 102, 108
  marketing and, 60–62
  in retail environment, 363
  supply-chain management and, 336–337, 347–348
  telecommunications, 18, 80
  wholesalers and, 379–380
Technology assessment, 62
Telecommunications technology, 18, 80

Telemarketing, 375–376
Telephone Consumer Protection Act, 58
Telephone depth interviews, 136
Telephone surveys, 133–134, 136
Television, 495
Television advertising, 422, 424–425, 428
Television home shopping, 376
Test marketing, 262–263
Test markets, 263
Threats, in SWOT analysis, 29–30
Time series analysis, 169–170
Time utility, 337
Total costs, 293
Total quality management (TQM), 40–41
Trade deficits, 107
Trade discounts, 304
Trademark Law Revision Act, 243, 417
Trademarks, 96
Trade salespeople, 447
Trade sales promotion methods, 459–461
Trading companies, 114
Traditional specialty retailers, 369
Transfer pricing, 306
Transit advertising, 424–425
Transportation
  coordination of, 355–356
  explanation of, 353
  intermodal, 355
  modes of, 353–355
Trend analysis, 169
Truck wholesalers, 381
Turkey, 86

Unaided recall test, 429
Undifferentiated targeting strategy, 152–153
Uniform geographic pricing, 305
Uniform Resource Locator (URL), 96
United Kingdom, 86, 326–327
United States
  advertising in, 416, 420
  economic conditions in, 105–106
  Internet use in, 86
  NAFTA and, 109
  population trends in, 62–63
  social class in, 192
  top test markets in, 263
Unsought products, 228
Uruguay Round, 111–112
Usage rate, 350–351
Utility, 337

Validity, 128
Value, 13–15
Value analysis, 214
Value and Lifestyle Program (Stanford University), 162
Value-conscious customers, 301
Variable costs, 293
Vendor analysis, 214
Venture team, 280
Vertical marketing system (VMS), 344–345
Vietnam, 107
Viral marketing, 404–405

Warehouse clubs, 367–368

Warehousing, 351–353
Weaknesses, in SWOT analysis, 29–30
Wealth, 55
Wheeler-Lea Act, 58, 302
Wheel of retailing, 373–374
Wholesalers
  agents and brokers and, 382–384
  explanation of, 204, 378–379
  manufacturers', 384
  merchant, 380–382
  services provided by, 379–380
Wholesaling
  careers in, 474–475
  explanation of, 378–379
Wholly owned foreign subsidiaries, 117

Wife-dominant decision making, 190
Willingness to spend, 55
Work force, changes in, 465
World Trade Organization (WTO), 112
World Wide Web. *See also* E-commerce; E-marketing; Internet
  marketing research resources on, 142–143
  as pull medium, 83

Yellow pages advertising, 422

Zone pricing, 305